Manchester Medieval Sources Series

series advisers Rosemary Horrox and Janet L. Nelson

This series aims to meet a growing need amongst students and teachers of medieval history for translations of key sources that are directly usable in students' own work. It provides texts central to medieval studies courses and focuses upon the diverse cultural and social as well as political conditions that affected the functioning of all levels of medieval society. The basic premise of the series is that translations must be accompanied by sufficient introductory and explanatory material, and each volume, therefore, includes a comprehensive guide to the sources' interpretation, including discussion of critical linguistic problems and an assessment of the most recent research on the topics being covered.

already published in the series

Simon Barton and Richard Fletcher *The world of El Cid: Chronicles of the Spanish reconquest*

J. A. Boyle *Genghis Khan: history of the world conqueror*

Trevor Dean *The towns of Italy in the later Middle Ages*

John Edwards *The Jews in Western Europe 1400–1600*

Paul Fouracre and Richard A. Gerberding *Late Merovingian France*

P. J. P. Goldberg *Women in England* c. *1275–1525*

Janet Hamilton and Bernard Hamilton *Christian dualist heresies in the Byzantine world* c. *650–*c. *1450*

Rosemary Horrox *The Black Death*

Graham A. Loud and Thomas Wiedemann *The history of the tyrants of Sicily by 'Hugo Falcandus' 1153–69*

R. N. Swanson *Catholic England: faith, religion and observance before the Reformation*

Elizabeth van Houts *The Normans in Europe*

Jennifer Ward *Women of the English nobility and gentry 1066–1500*

OTTONIAN GERMANY

MANCHESTER
UNIVERSITY PRESS

D1599983

Medieval Sources*online*

Complementing the printed editions of the Medieval Sources series, Manchester University Press has developed a web-based learning resource which is now available on a yearly subscription basis.

Medieval Sources*online* brings quality history source material to the desktops of students and teachers and allows them open and unrestricted access throughout the entire college or university campus. Designed to be fully integrated with academic courses, this is a one-stop answer for many medieval history students, academics and researchers keeping thousands of pages of source material 'in print' over the Internet for research and teaching.

titles available now at Medieval Sources*online include*

John Edwards *The Jews in Western Europe 1400–1600*

Paul Fouracre and Richard A. Gerberding *Late Merovingian France: History and hagiography 640–720*

Chris Given-Wilson *Chronicles of the Revolution 1397–1400: The reign of Richard II*

P. J. P. Goldberg *Women in England c. 1275–1525*

Janet Hamilton and Bernard Hamilton *Christian dualist heresies in the Byzantine world c. 650–c. 1450*

Rosemary Horrox *The Black Death*

Graham A. Loud and Thomas Wiedemann *The history of the tyrants of Sicily by 'Hugo Falcandus' 1153–69*

Janet L. Nelson *The Annals of St-Bertin: Ninth-century histories, volume I*

Timothy Reuter *The Annals of Fulda: Ninth-century histories, volume II*

R. N. Swanson *Catholic England: faith, religion and observance before the Reformation*

Jennifer Ward *Women of the English nobility and gentry 1066–1500*

visit the site at *www.medievalsources.co.uk* for further information and subscription prices

OTTONIAN GERMANY

THE *CHRONICON*
OF THIETMAR OF MERSEBURG

translated and annotated by David A. Warner

Manchester University Press
Manchester and New York

distributed exclusively in the USA by Palgrave

Published by Manchester University Press
Oxford Road, Manchester M13 9NR, UK
and Room 400, 175 Fifth Avenue, New York, NY 10010, USA
http://www.manchesteruniversitypress.co.uk

Distributed exclusively in the USA by
Palgrave, 175 Fifth Avenue, New York, NY 10010, USA

Distributed exclusively in Canada by
UBC Press, University of British Columbia, 2029 West Mall,
Vancouver, BC, Canada V6T 1Z2

British Library Cataloguing-in-Publication Data
A catalogue record for this book is available from the British Library

Library of Congress Cataloging-in-Publication Data applied for

ISBN 0 7190 4925 3 *hardback*
     0 7190 4926 1 *paperback*

First published 2001

07 06 05 04 03 02 01   10 9 8 7 6 5 4 3 2 1

Typeset in Monotype Bell
by Koinonia Ltd, Manchester
Printed in Great Britain
by Bell and Bain Ltd, Glasgow

CONTENTS

SERIES EDITOR'S FOREWORD

Shortage of suitably rich and reflective material often makes it difficult to access the mentalities of an earlier medieval society. But in the case of Ottonian Germany, Thietmar of Merseburg, an idiosyncratic yet wide-ranging and highly conscientious chronicler, offers a wealth of entrées and insights into his world but also – belying the notion that introspection comes only with the long twelfth century – himself. David Warner's fine translation of Thietmar's stylish Latin now opens the entrées wide to new audiences. His substantial Introduction sets the work in social and cultural as well as political contexts, making sense of authorial concerns that blended the public with the private, the genuinely altruistic with the intensely self- and kin-centred. The Manchester Medieval Sources Series has never confused accessibility with dumbing down: readers need the whole text. The Press has been admirably undeterred by the scale of Thietmar's work, since in this case scale is of the essence. Thanks not only to Thietmar's literary talents and the range and variegated interest of his themes, but also to David Warner's expertise as translator and historian, this large book will surely get and keep readers' rapt attention. It reveals, like no other work of its place and period, the textures and contexts of the Ottonians' regime, as the activities of the German rulers and their contemporaries, and their dealings with Slav and Scandinavian neighbours, enable Thietmar, and his readers, to make their own analyses and comparisons. With this volume, Germany, hitherto insufficiently represented in the series' European panorama, takes its full place. Thietmar's perspective, personal as it is, also embraces, and is representative of, Europe's early eleventh-century culture.

Janet L. Nelson
King's College London

LIST OF ABBREVIATIONS

Adalbold	Waitz, G. (ed.) 1841
Adam	Schmeidler, B. (ed.) 1917
Ado	Dubois, J. and Renaud, G. (eds) 1984
AE	Pertz, G. (ed.) 1839a
AfD	*Archiv für Diplomatik*
AfKg	*Archiv für Kulturgeschichte*
AH	Waitz, G. (ed.) 1878
Alpert	Pertz, G. (ed.) 1841a
an.	anno
AQ	Pertz, G. (ed.) 1839
Arnold	Arnold of St Emmeram, *De miraculis et memoria beati Emmerammi libri duo*, Migne, J. P. (ed.), PL, vol. 141, cols 971–1090
Arnulf	Bethmann, L. C. and Wattenback, W. (eds) 1848
AS	Waitz, G. (ed.) 1844
Aug., *Civ. Dei*	Dombart, B. and Kalb, A. (eds) 1955
Aug., *Div. Quaest.*	Matzenbecher, A. (ed.) 1975
Aug., *Enn. Ps.* 63	Augustine, *Ennarratio in Psalmum*, vol. 63. Migne, J. P. (ed.), PL, vol. 36, cols 759–72
Aug., *Ep.*	Goldbacher, A. (ed.) 1904
BdLg	*Blätter für deutsche Landesgeschichte*
B Mt S	Zuchetti, G. (ed.) 1820
BG	Böhmer, J. F. 1971
BM	Böhmer, J. F. 1950
BO	Böhmer, J. F. 1967
BU	Böhmer, J. F. 1956
Bon., *Ep*	Tangle, M. (ed.) 1955
Brun, *Ep*	Karwasin'ska, J. (ed.) 1969
Brun, *VA*	Karwasin'ska, J. (ed.) 1973
Carm. Cant.	Strecker, K. (ed.) 1926
CCL	Corpus Christianorum, Series Latina
Const.	Weiland, L. (ed.) 1893
Cont. Reg.	Kurze, F. (ed.) 1890
CSEL	*Corpus scriptorum ecclesiasticorum Latinorum*
D, DD	Diploma, Diplomata
DA	*Deutsches Archiv*
DBI	*Dizionario biografico degli Italiani*
D H I	Sickel, T. (ed.) 1879–84
D H II	Bresslau, H. *et al.* (eds) 1957
DHP	Levillain, P. (ed.) 1994
DMA	*Dictionary of the Middle Ages*

D O I	Sickel, T. (ed.) 1879–84
D O II	Sickel, T. (ed.) 1888
D O III	Sickel, T. (ed.) 1926–31
Ecbasis Captivi	Trillitzsch, W. (ed. and trans.) 1964
EHHW	Boyd, K. (ed.) 1999
EHR	*English Historical Review*
EME	*Early Medieval Europe*
FB	Waitz, G. (ed.) 1883
FMSt	*Frühmittelalterliche Studien*
FS	Festschrift
FSI	*Fonti per la storia d'Italia*
Gallus	Maleczyn'ski, C. (ed.) 1952
Gerhard	Waitz, G. (ed.) 1841
GH	Weiland, L. (ed.) 1874
Greg., *Dial*	Moricca, U. (ed.) 1924
Greg., *Hom. Ev.*	*[Gregory I] XL homiliarum in Evangelia libri duo*, Migne, J. P, (ed.), PL, vol. 76, cols 1073–1314
Greg., *Hom. Ez.*	Adiaen, M. (ed.) 1971
HJb	*Historisches Jahrbuch.*
Is., *Etym.*	*Sancti Isidori Hispolensis episcopi etymologiarum libri xx*, Migne, J. P. (ed.), PL, vol. 82, cols 73–728
Jer., *Ep. 22*	Wright, F. A. (trans.) 1933.
JGMO	*Jahrbuch für die Geschichte Mittel- und Ostdeutschlands*
JMH	*Journal of Medieval History*
John, *CV*	Monticolo, G. (ed.) 1890
Jotsald	*[Jotsald] Sancti Odilonis Cluniacensis abbatis*, Migne, J. P. (ed), PL, vol. 142, cols 895–940
L. A.	Becker, J. (ed.) 1915
Leo	Hoffmann. H. (ed.) 1980
LMA	*Lexicon des Mittelalters*
LTK	*Lexikon für Theologie und Kirche*
Manaresi	Manaresi, C. (ed.) 1958
MdF	Mitteldeutsche Forschungen
MGH	Monumenta Germaniae Historica
Const	Constitutiones
SrG	Scriptores rerum Germanicarum
ss	Scriptores
MIÖG	*Mitteilungen des Instituts für Östereichische Geschichtsforschung*
MPH	Monumenta Poloniae Historica
NDB	*Neue Deutsche Biographie*
NMag.	Althoff, G. and Wollasch, J. (eds) 1983
NMer.	Althoff, G. and Wollasch, J. (eds) 1983
Notker	*Notker Balbulus, Martyrologium*, Migne, J. P. (ed.), PL, vol. 131, cols 1029–1164
Odilo	Paulhart, H. (ed.) 1962

ABBREVIATIONS

Odilo	Paulhart, H. (ed.) 1962
P&P	*Past and Present*
PL	Patrologia Latina
PW	*Pauly-Wissowa Real Encyclopädie der classischen Altertumswissenschaft*
QFIAB	*Quellen und Forschungen aus italienischen Archiven und Bibliotheken*
Radulf	Radulf of Cambrai, *Vita sancti Lietberti episcopi Cameracensis*, Acta Sanctorum, 4 June, Antwerp, 1707, pp. 585–606
Richer	Latouche, R. (ed. and trans.) 1930/1937
Ruotger	Ott, I. (ed.) 1951
RVjB	*Rheinische Vierteljahrsblätter*
SMGBZ	*Studien und Mitteilungen zur Geschichte des Benediktiner-Ordens und seiner Zweige*
Thangmar	Pertz, G. (ed.) 1841
UbM	Israäl, F. and Möllenberg, W. (eds) 1937
V. Burch	Waitz, G. (ed.) 1841c
V. M.	Tenckhoff, F. (ed.) 1921
V. Mat. Ant./Post	Schütte, B. (ed.) 1994a
V. Nili	Waitz, G. (ed.) 1841b
VF	*Vorträge und Forschungen*
Widukind	Lohmann, H.-E. and Hirsch, P. (eds) 1935
Wipo	Bresslau, H. (ed.) 1915
Wolfher I	Pertz, G. (ed.) 1854
ZBL	*Zeitschrift für bayerische Landesgeschichte*
ZKg	*Zeitschrift für Kirchengeschichte*
ZRG	*Zeitschrift der Savigny Stiftung für Rechtsgeschichte*
GA	*Germanistische Abteilung*
KA	*Kanonistische Abteilung*
ZSKg	*Zeitschrift für Schweizerische Kirchengeschichte*

1 Walbeck and Querfurt

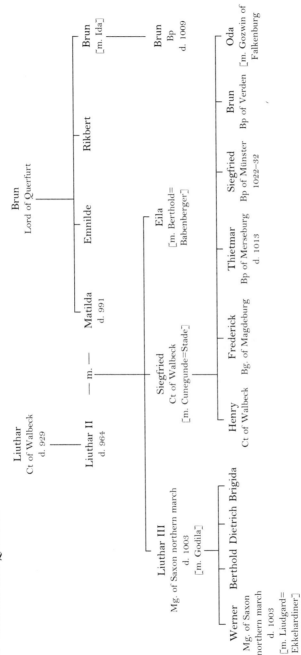

Source: adapted from W. Trillmich (ed/trans), *Thietmar von Merseburg. Chronik,* Ausgewählte Quellen zur deutschen Geschichte des Mittelalters, Freiherr vom Stein-Gedächtnisausgabe, vol. 9, Darmstadt, 1974.

2 Babenberger and Ekkehardiner

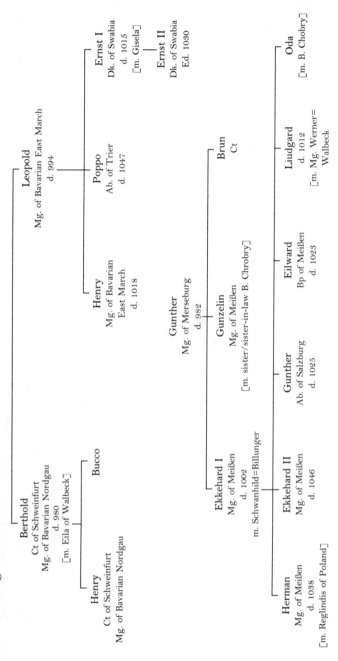

Source: adapted from W. Trillmich (ed/trans), *Thietmar von Merseburg. Chronik*, Ausgewählte Quellen zur deutschen Geschichte des Mittelalters, Freiherr vom Stein-Gedächtnisausgabe, vol. 9, Darmstadt, 1974.

3 Stade and Billunger

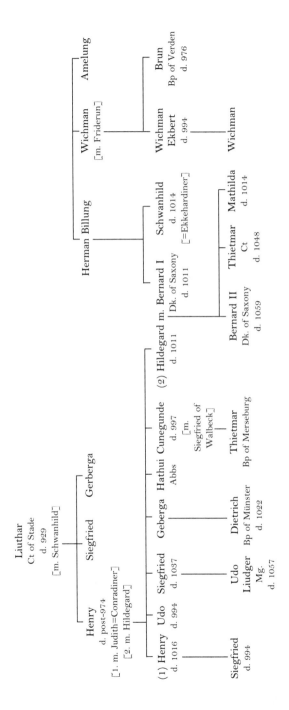

Source: adapted from W. Trillmich (ed/trans), *Thietmar von Merseburg. Chronik, Ausgewählte Quellen zur deutschen Geschichte des Mittelalters, Freiherr vom Stein-Gedächtnisausgabe*, vol. 9, Darmstadt, 1974.

4 Conradine

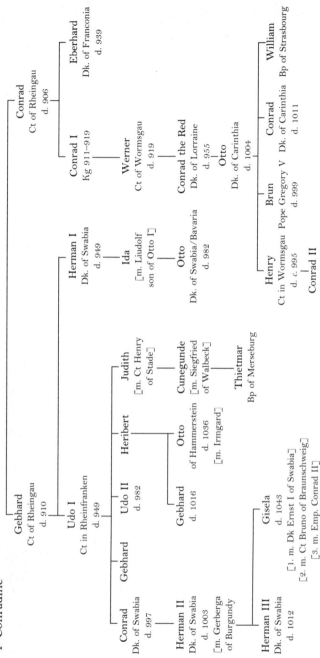

```
                                          Conrad
                                          Ct of Rheingau
                                          d. 906
                        ┌────────────────────┴────────────────────┐
                  Conrad I                                    Eberhard
                  Kg 911–919                                  Dk. of Franconia
                        │                                          d. 939
                  Werner
                  Ct of Wormsgau
                  d. 919
                        │
                  Conrad the Red
                  Dk. of Lorraine
                  d. 955
                        │
                  Otto
                  Dk. of Carinthia
                  d. 1004
        ┌─────────────┴──────────────┬──────────────────┬──────────────┐
      Henry                         Brun              Conrad          William
      Ct in Wormsgau     Pope Gregory V    Dk. of Carinthia    Bp of Strasbourg
      d. c. 995               d. 999             d. 1011
        │
      Conrad II
      Emp.
```

```
Gebhard
Ct of Rheingau
d. 910
      │
Udo I
Ct in Rheinfranken
d. 949
```

```
                              Herman I
                              Dk. of Swabia
                              d. 949
                                    │
                              Ida
                              [m. Liudolf
                              son of Otto I]
                                    │
                              Otto
                              Dk. of Swabia/Bavaria
                              d. 982
```

```
                    Judith
                    [m. Ct Henry
                    of Stade]

              Heribert

                    Cunegunde
                    [m. Siegfried
                    of Walbeck]

                              Thietmar
                              Bp of Merseburg
```

```
Conrad          Gebhard          Udo II
Dk. of Swabia                    d. 982
d. 997
```

```
              Otto
              of Hammerstein
              d. 1036
              [m. Irmgard]

        Gebhard
        d. 1016

  Herman II
  Dk. of Swabia
  d. 1003
  [m. Gerberga
  of Burgundy]
```

```
                    Gisela
                    d. 1043
                    [1. m. Dk Ernst I of Swabia]
                    [2. m. Ct Bruno of Braunschweig]
                    [3. m. Emp. Conrad II]

  Herman III
  Dk. of Swabia
  d. 1012
```

Source: adapted from W. Trillmich (ed/trans), *Thietmar von Merseburg. Chronik,* Ausgewählte Quellen zur deutschen Geschichte des Mittelalters, Freiherr vom Stein-Gedächtnisausgabe, vol. 9, Darmstadt, 1974.

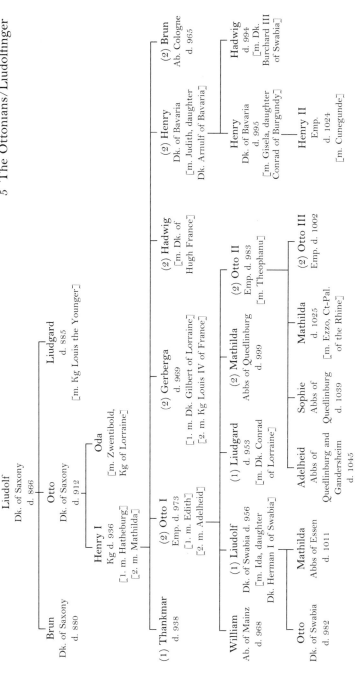

Liudolf
Dk. of Saxony
d. 866

Brun
Dk. of Saxony
d. 880

Otto
Dk. of Saxony
d. 912

Liudgard
d. 885
[m. Kg Louis the Younger]

Oda
[m. Zwentibold,
Kg of Lorraine]

Henry I
Kg d. 936
[1. m. Hatheburg]
[2. m. Mathilda]

(2) Brun
Ab. Cologne
d. 965

(2) Henry
Dk. of Bavaria
[m. Judith, daughter
Dk. Arnulf of Bavaria]

Hadwig
d. 994
[m. Dk.
Burchard III
of Swabia]

(2) Hadwig
[m. Dk. of
Hugh France]

(2) Gerberga
d. 969
[1. m. Dk. Gilbert of Lorraine]
[2. m. Kg Louis IV of France]

(1) Thankmar
d. 938

(2) Otto I
Emp. d. 973
[1. m. Edith]
[2. m. Adelheid]

Henry
Dk. of Bavaria
d. 995
[m. Gisela, daughter
Conrad of Burgundy]

Henry II
Emp.
d. 1024
[m. Cunegunde]

(2) Otto II
Emp. d. 983
[m. Theophanu]

(2) Mathilda
Abbs of Quedlinburg
d. 999

William
Ab. of Mainz
d. 968
[m. Ida, daughter
Dk. Herman I of Swabia]

(1) Liudolf
Dk. of Swabia d. 956

(1) Liudgard
d. 953
[m. Dk. Conrad
of Lorraine]

(2) Otto III
Emp. d. 1002

Mathilda
d. 1025
[m. Ezzo, Ct-Pal.
of the Rhine]

Sophie
Abbs of
Quedlinburg
d. 1039

Adelheid
Abbs of
Quedlinburg and
Gandersheim
d. 1045

Mathilda
Abbs of Essen
d. 1011

Otto
Dk. of Swabia
d. 982

Source: T. Reuter, *Germany in the Early Middle Ages, 800–1056,* London and New York, 1991, p. 337.

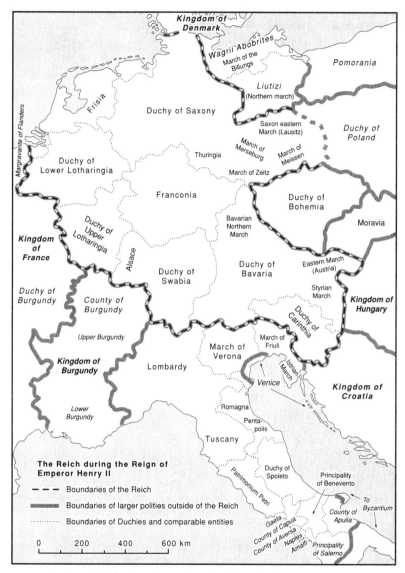

Map 1 The *Reich* during the reign of Henry II

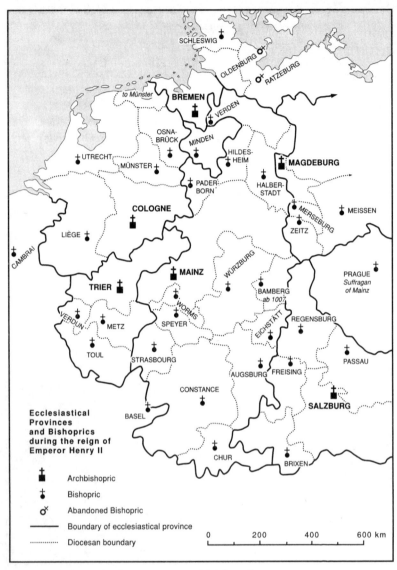

SCHLESWIG

OLDENBURG

RATZEBURG

to Münster

BREMEN

VERDEN

MAGDEBURG

OSNA-
BRÜCK

MINDEN

HILDES-
HEIM

MEISSEN

UTRECHT

MÜNSTER

PADER-
BORN

HALBER-
STADT

MERSEBURG

COLOGNE

ZEITZ

LIÈGE

CAMBRAI

MAINZ

WÜRZBURG

PRAGUE
Suffragan
of Mainz

TRIER

WORMS

BAMBERG
ab 1007

VERDUN

METZ

SPEYER

EICHSTÄTT

REGENSBURG

TOUL

STRASBOURG

AUGSBURG

FREISING

PASSAU

CONSTANCE

SALZBURG

BASEL

CHUR

BRIXEN

**Ecclesiastical
Provinces
and Bishoprics
during the reign of
Emperor Henry II**

■   Archbishopric

✝   Bishopric

⚥ˣ   Abandoned Bishopric

——   Boundary of ecclesiastical province

········   Diocesan boundary

0   200   400   600 km

Map 2 Ecclesiastical provinces and bishoprics

INTRODUCTION: THIETMAR, BISHOP AND CHRONICLER

With its 'heroic values and norms' and preoccupation with the marvellous, the era of the tenth and early eleventh centuries may strike the modern observer as both strange and, in the latter case at least, oddly familiar.[1] As such, it might be said to offer that combination of 'alterity' and attraction sometimes seen as typical of the Middle Ages as a whole.[2] It was an important era as well, one in which trends such as the decrease in Viking and Hungarian raids and growing productivity of agriculture laid the groundwork for a resurgence of the European economy. We may seek the spiritual ancestors of the merchant princes of the High Middle Ages and Renaissance among the hustling residents of tenth-century trading entrepots.[3] This era has also been characterized as an 'age of iron' in which widespread resort to the feud and an absence of authoritative courts contributed to extraordinary levels of violence and mayhem. And yet it also developed innovative mechanisms for resolving conflict and witnessed the first stirrings of a European peace movement, the *Peace of God*.[4] For women, unprecedented opportunities emerged in a wide variety of economic, social, and political venues although patriarchy was still the order of the day.[5] Persons whose status or rank permitted them to profit from the period's more progressive developments may well have contemplated the millennium with a sense of 'optimism and returning hope'.[6] Others, less well positioned, would likely have viewed it with a degree of ambiguity. In particular, for those least capable of self-defence, the 'multiplication of fighting men, of castles, and of harsh new lordships of command', trends equally characteristic of the tenth and eleventh centuries, may have offered a fearful prospect.[7]

---

1 Compare Leyser 1979: 1; Fichtenau 1991: xv.

2 Spiegel 1997a: 79–80.

3 E.g. Tiel on the river Waal (Alpert 2.20).

4 Geary 1994b: 124–28, and passim; and, in general, Head and Landes (eds) 1992.

5 Wemple 1992: 183–86.

6 Leyser 1982a: 8.

7 Bisson 1994: 12.

For medievalists concerned specifically with Germany and the Empire, the tenth and early eleventh centuries represent, above all, the era of the Ottonian kings. Ottonian rule commenced, in 919, when an assembly of East Frankish aristocrats gathered at Fritzlar to acknowledge the first representative of the dynasty, Henry I (919–36), as king, or rather to elect him. Henry's son, Otto I (936–73), succeeded him on the throne and subsequently designated his own son and eventual successor, Otto II (955–83), as co-ruler. Otto II's son, Otto III (980–1002), followed, succeeding at the age of five years old and ruling, initially, with the aid of a regency comprised of female relatives. Otto III died young, unmarried, and without an obvious successor. After a relatively brief but violent interregnum, he was succeeded by Henry II (1002–24), erstwhile duke of Bavaria and lineal descendant of Otto I's younger brother. There was a note of irony to Henry's succession in that his father and grandfather, each named Henry, had led uprisings against one or more of the three royal Ottos. No less worthy of note are the queens, empresses, and dowagers of the Ottonian line, formidable women whose stature approached and occasionally eclipsed that of their husbands, sons, and grandsons. Their ranks included Queen Mathilda (d. 968), wife of Henry I, and her daughters-in-law Edith (d. 946) and Adelheid (d. 999). Each acquired that aura of sanctity with which their contemporaries tended to endow spiritually or otherwise extraordinary individuals. Though apparently never a candidate for sainthood, Otto II's wife, Theophanu (d. 997), brought the lustre of Byzantium to the Ottonian court even if she was not the 'purple-born' princess the emperor's father had ordered.[8] She would subsequently join Adelheid and Abbess Mathilda of Quedlinburg in acting as regent for her son, Otto III. Queen Cunegunde (d. 1033), as Henry II's consort, played an active role in her husband's government and presided over the interim regime that ruled the *Reich* in the period between her husband's death and the succession of Conrad II (1024–39), the event which customarily marks the beginning of a new dynasty known as the Salians.[9]

Although there is sufficient evidence of continuity between the Ottonians and the early Salians to justify a long Ottonian period extending at least to 1056, it is the Ottonians alone who defined the mental landscape of Bishop Thietmar of Merseburg (b. 975, 1009–18). And it is with Thietmar, his world, and his *Chronicon* that the present

---

8 Thietmar 2.15.

9 Wipo c. 1, p. 9; Mommsen and Morrison (trans.) 1962: 58.

volume is chiefly concerned. Indeed, if the period of the tenth and
early eleventh centuries is worthy of closer examination, there could
scarcely be a better witness than Thietmar. He was nothing if not
well informed, at least in regard to matters of government and high
politics, and he belonged, both by birth and profession, to the elite
that dominated virtually every aspect of Ottonian society. No more
than a few degrees of separation stood between Thietmar and virtually
anyone who mattered in his world. As a Saxon, moreover, he dwelt in
a geographical area so dense with royal property and so frequently
visited by the kings themselves that modern scholars treat it as the
political centre of the realm. He was an eyewitness to many of what
historians traditionally identify as the major events of Ottonian
history, and actively participated in more than a few. For reasons such
as these, the eight books of the *Chronicon*, compiled between 1013 and
Thietmar's death in 1018, figure among the era's most important
narrative sources. Indeed, their striking combination of regal, episcopal,
and family history has inspired at least one modern commentator to
characterize the *Chronicon* as a 'work unlike that of almost any other
historian of the early and high Middle Ages'.[10] Another, noting its
extraordinary value as a 'repository of popular beliefs', suggests comparisons with the *Chronicle* of Gregory of Tours, one of the landmarks
of early medieval historiography.[11] It should come as no surprise,
then, that scholars concerned with Ottonian Germany have tended to
rely rather heavily on Thietmar. Among anglophone readers, in particular, Thietmar's reputation rests chiefly on the various studies of
Ottonian society and politics produced by the late Karl Leyser, one of
the most influential historians of his generation.[12]

Aside from its value as a witness to Ottonian history, Thietmar's
Chronicon also provides a personal testament, comparable to such
medieval expressions of individuality as the autobiography of Guibert
of Nogent. As it emerges from his text, Thietmar's personality might
best be described as complex and fraught with ambiguity. Thus, while
individual holy men and women might earn his admiration, he viewed
monastic reform as rank hypocrisy and took umbrage at criticism of
more accommodating forms of spirituality.[13] Thietmar's own devotions
focused on a methodical collecting and disbursement of prayers,

10 I.e. by Reuter in *EHHW*, vol. 2. pp. 1183–84.
11 Lerner in *DMA*, vol. 12, pp. 27–28.
12 A biography and appreciation in *EHHW*, vol. 1, pp. 721–22.
13 Thietmar 6.21; 7.25.

vigils, and masses. The siren call of missionary work and martyrdom seems never to have tempted him. He could be brutally honest in regard to his personal failings, lamenting that he had shown excessive favour to his kin, for example, and describing his physical appearance in terms that take objectivity to the level of masochism.[14] And yet, self-criticism does not appear to have made him more magnanimous, especially towards anyone he considered a threat or merely inferior.[15] He paints brutal portraits of the Ottonians' enemies and indulges in a particularly virulent brand of ethnic stereotyping.[16] The supernatural occupied a prominent place on Thietmar's mental landscape, as it did for most of his contemporaries. He shifts effortlessly from prosaic accounts of military campaigns to ghost stories and tales of the marvellous. The dead materialize with alarming frequency to admonish the living, while the Devil lies in wait for the morally suspect, and even stalks the dormitories of the clergy.[17] Still, Thietmar apparently felt no compunction about exploiting the supernatural as a means to promote his personal agendas. Regardless of their personal sanctity, individuals he admired tended to exhibit signs and wonders after their deaths, and he could hint broadly at a miscarriage of justice by asserting that the victim's corpse remained undefiled after a year in the grave.[18]

Despite its obvious importance, Thietmar's only extant work has never appeared in a complete English translation. It is this omission that the present volume seeks to address. The introduction that follows is intended to make the perusal of this translation less confusing. What it does not do and, in practical terms, could not do is provide a complete overview of Ottonian history. For master narratives, the reader is advised to turn to the works by Reuter (1991), Beumann (1991), and Holtzmann (1935), which are listed in the bibliography. What the introduction will attempt to do more specifically is facilitate the critical reading of Thietmar's text by accounting for key events and personages. In this sense, the criteria for inclusion or exclusion will essentially reflect Thietmar's own judgements. Since Thietmar had a compelling interest in 'the lives and *mores*' of the Ottonian kings, for example, the latter will

14 Thietmar 8.13; 4.75.
15 See below pp. 19, 40.
16 See below pp. 40–41.
17 Thietmar 4.66–67.
18 Thietmar 3.9.

inevitably assume a prominent place in our discussion.[19] Indeed, royal *gesta* provide the basic backbone of the entire *Chronicon*. In his first book, Thietmar recounts the career of Henry I, beginning with his youth and progressing through his accomplishments as duke and, later, as king. Books Two to Four consider the reigns, respectively, of Otto I, Otto II, and Otto III. The remainder of the *Chronicon*, books Five to Eight, centres on the reign of Thietmar's contemporary, Henry II.

Although Thietmar placed great importance on kings and royal politics, he was scarcely reticent when it came to expressing his opinions on other matters. Indeed, he cluttered his mental landscape with a variety of prejudices, antipathies, and cherished agendas, ranging from professional and family loyalties to a pronounced dissatisfaction with contemporary women's fashion. The introduction will discuss a selection of his ruminations on these and other topics as well. It will also consider a few of the more pertinent historiographical issues. Thietmar provides crucial testimony for the evolution of relations between Poland and the *Reich*, for example, and for events surrounding the difficult succession of King Henry II. Here, in the choice of issues discussed, my own interests as an historian will be readily apparent. A folklorist, slavicist, or, for that matter, a historian with a different scholarly focus would clearly have produced a very different text. I can only ask of my readers, as Thietmar did of his, that they forgive any mistakes (and omissions!) born of ignorance.[20]

Ottonian government and society

Royal elections, such as Henry I's, were neither representative nor democratic and they figured as only one of a series of public acts that effectively 'made' a king.[21] From a modern perspective, however, they represent one of the most characteristic features of a polity which seems always to have pursued its own historical path.[22] Whatever it may have owed to Carolingian precedent, there seems little doubt that this German *Sonderweg* acquired direction and solidity during the

19 Thietmar 1, prologue. On the following: Schneider 1962: 47–60.
20 Thietmar 1, prologue.
21 For a useful overview in English consult J. B. Freed's article in *DMA*, vol. 4, pp. 425–29.
22 Reuter 1993: 180–81.

tenth and early eleventh centuries, and that the election of Henry I had a lot to do with it. Indeed, modern scholars have sometimes identified Henry's election as the real beginning of German history. As descendants of Duke Liudolf of Saxony (d. 866), the Ottonians (or Liudolfinger) clearly were not Franks nor, despite a few marital alliances, could they be considered Carolingians. Hence, so the argument goes, their advent represents the point of demarcation between what should properly be called an East Frankish or late Carolingian realm and a true kingdom or realm of the Germans. Debate on this point is quite vigorous, however, and strong arguments have been raised for a number of other dates or historical milestones.[23] Be that as it may, there is little doubt that the events of 919 represented an important turning point. Among its more noteworthy effects, the fact that a Saxon dynasty occupied the throne encouraged an eastward shift of the *Reich*'s political focus, reflecting the close and continuing association between the ruling house and its homeland, that 'flowery hall of Paradise' as Henry II reportedly called it.[24] It was in eastern Saxony or Ostphalia, under the leadership of Duke Liudolf, Duke Otto 'the Illustrious' (d. 912), and Henry himself that the Liudolfinger-Ottonians began the upward climb that ended at Fritzlar, an altogether typical story of shrewd marriage alliances, military success, and opportunistic use of the resources of the church. It was a climb marked by shifts in fortune, such as the unexpected death in battle of Liudolf's eldest son, Brun (d. 880), which changed the family's dynamics by elevating a younger brother, Otto 'the Illustrious' (i.e. Henry I's father) to a position of leadership.[25] It was also marked by conflict. Thietmar had dim memories of a feud involving Duke Henry and King Conrad I (911–19) that included, among other things, a murder plot (with Henry as victim) hatched by the notorious Archbishop Hatto I of Mainz (891–913).[26]

It was in Ostphalia, as well, that the clan's landed wealth had its greatest density, and there, at Gandersheim and Quedlinburg, that they established their most important religious foundations. The Ottonians also founded bishoprics, some (Magdeburg, Merseburg) within the boundaries of Saxony, others in adjacent marches (Brandenburg, Havelberg, Zeitz, Meißen, Oldenburg). Henry II, reflecting his

23 A useful historiographical treatment is provided by Fleckenstein 1987: esp. 9–11.
24 Thietmar 6.10.
25 Thietmar 2.23.
26 Thietmar 1.7.

southern connections, founded a bishopric at Bamberg (1007), in an area of eastern Franconia bordering on the Duchy of Bavaria. In matters of diplomacy and foreign relations, the new importance of Ostphalia also meant that issues affecting the *Reich's* eastern frontier became more prominent. It was here, along the frontier with the East Elbian Slavs, that Ostphalian aristocrats gained honour on the battlefield and acquired the tribute of defeated foes. Thietmar knew that Henry I had tested his mettle on those battlefields prior to becoming king.[27] More tests would follow, as Henry and his successors initiated the first period of German expansion in the East, a trend of profound significance for the subsequent history of Europe as well as for modern European historiography.[28] The Ottonian period of expansion came to an abrupt and traumatic end in 983 with a massive Slavic uprising.[29] The moving force behind this revolt was a confederation of tribes, known as the Liutizi, which resided between the Elbe and the Oder and had its focal point at the cult centre of Rethra, in the territory of the Redarii.[30] For the *Reich*, a period of territorial and political consolidation followed.[31] Active expansion would not be taken up again until the twelfth century, and then chiefly under the sponsorship of great lords rather than the monarchy. On a less violent but equally important note, the era of the Ottonian kings marked the permanent incorporation of Poland, Bohemia, and Hungary within the community of Latin Christendom.

On a more general level, the election of Henry I and advent of the Ottonians figured within a larger historical trend that saw rulers emerge from among the aristocracies of the Frankish Empire to replace or at least rival the traditional ruling house of the Carolingians. For the most part, these new rulers were men of proven ability with substantial followings and families that had long ranked among the dominant elite of their regions. In West Francia (the future kingdom of France), Duke Hugh of Francia and his descendants struggled with the last royal descendants of the Carolingian house, Louis IV (936–54) and Lothar V (954–86), finally supplanting them in 987 with the

27 Thietmar 1.3.

28 A substantial body of literature, much of it in German, has now brought the highly partisan historiography of this issue into much clearer focus. In English, one may consult Burleigh's studies on the subject of German *Ostforschung* during the era of National Socialism (Burleigh 1988, 1988a).

29 Thietmar 3.17–19.

30 Beumann 1991: 123–24, Reuter 1991: 178–79.

31 Reuter 1991: 179–80.

election of Hugh Capet (987–96), founder of the long-lived dynasty of the Capetians. The areas of modern day Switzerland and the Rhone region of France were incorporated into a realm generally known as the Kingdom of Burgundy by Rudolf I (888–937) and his successors, Rudolf II (912–37), Conrad (937–93), and Rudolf III (993–1032). In northern Italy, the former kingdom of the Lombards, no one family succeeded in establishing a permanent claim to the throne. Instead, a number of magnates, both indigenous and imported, competed for dominance. The most important of these for Thietmar were Hugh 'of Provence' (926–47) and his son Lothar (947–50), Berengar II 'of Friuli' (950–66), and Arduin I 'of Ivrea' (1002–14). Among these upstart kings, the Ottonians found allies, enemies, and the occasional son-in-law.

Although generally the dominant party in their relations with neighbouring rulers, the Ottonians had much in common with them, not the least being the need to seek consensus with occasionally unruly aristocracies. In contrast to their high medieval counterparts, the aristocracies of the Ottonian era may seem to have an amorphous, ill-defined character. This was due, in part, to inheritance practices, but also reflected a willingness to define kinship itself in particularly expansive terms, according comparable weight to maternal and paternal lines, and including collateral branches. A sense of corporate identity was retained through the use of leading-names over multiple generations, a practice exemplified by the royal dynasty which reserved the name Otto for the oldest male heir to its main branch, while using names such as Henry for secondary kin. Many families were also becoming more closely associated with a permanent family seat, often a fortified residence (i.e. a burg) with a nearby ecclesiastical establishment in which they could bury their dead. That an aged widow, the mother of Margrave Henry of Schweinfurt, would risk her life to prevent the king's representatives from burning down her family's chief residence testifies to the deep affinity between lineage and burg which would later result in the incorporation of the latter into personal names.[32] In Thietmar's time the two forms of identification existed more or less side by side. Hence, though modern historical practice refers to Thietmar's lineage as the house of Walbeck, from its residence and ecclesiastical foundation at Walbeck on the river Aller, it might also be referred to as the house of Liuthar,

32 Thietmar 5.38.

from the name borne by several prominent representatives of its senior branch.[33]

Men of substance, like Margrave Henry and the counts of Walbeck, figured prominently in that hard, relentless struggle for lands, high office, and military commands which, for lack of a better term, we may call politics. The dominant figures in that struggle were individuals known to Thietmar as *principes*. These were the most important or leading men (as we shall call them) among the aristocracy. Their opinions carried weight in deliberations; foreign rulers sought their services as sponsors, persons of lesser stature turned to them as protectors or benefactors. During constitutional crises or disputes involving the monarchy, they could function like a high court or, alternatively, a board of mediation.[34] They might disagree with the ruler or even presume to rebuke him.[35] In short, they were far too important to overlook or ignore in a decision of any importance and alienating them could lead to disaster.[36] In the aftermath of Henry I's election, the leading men of Ostphalia emerge as an important factor in the politics of the court and the realm. The families they represented included the comital house of Stade and the Billunger, as well as the earliest representatives of the house of Wettin, each destined to find a place among the first ranks of the Saxon aristocracy. The Saxon aristocracy also included kin-groups whose trajectories were less impressive or in decline. This group included, among others, the senior branch of the Billunger, under Wichman the Elder, and the comital house of Walbeck, Thietmar's lineage. Competition between aristocratic haves and have-nots would prove a continual source of tension as the latter persisted in their efforts to join the ranks of the former or, failing that, at least to wreak vengeance upon them.

To the extent that their ability to help or hinder a family's upward mobility made Ottonian kings party to this struggle, they too became objects of disaffection and violence. The succession of a new king, in particular, could mean rehabilitation and advancement for anyone who had failed to prosper under his predecessors, while less agile members of the 'old guard' fell by the wayside, providing fertile

---

33 See below pp. 49–52.

34 Thietmar 4.1; 7.9.

35 Thietmar 3.9; 7.12.

36 The consequences of profound alienation between a king and the 'leading men' of the realm became increasingly evident under the Salian kings, successors to the Ottonians, and especially under King Henry IV (Leyser 1983: 21).

ground for conspiracies, uprisings, and disturbances of various types. Unrest and discontent were 'part of the normal stuff of politics' in the Ottonian realm and did not threaten the stability of the system as a whole, indeed, they often coalesced around disaffected members of the royal house.[37] That the 'frailty of authority' was at issue rather than the political structure itself scarcely reduced the danger from the monarch's perspective, however.[38] Nor was the sacred authority derived from his anointment and crowning (at least after 936) much help. The Frankish tradition of royal anointment originated with the first of the Carolingian kings, Pippin III, whose precise reasons for employing the rite are still subject to debate.[39] It only became a prerequisite for the exercise of power in the East Frankish/German realm in 936, when Otto I became the first anointed king of his line and established a model for all his successors. Royal sacrality could enhance a monarch's personal stature and was particularly useful when it came to justifying the kind of intrusive ecclesiastical policies that the Ottonians, like all powerful rulers, saw as their right. Thietmar cited the king's anointment and crowning (after the model of Christ) to justify the rulership of kings over bishops although he may have meant this more as an obligation to protect them than a theoretical right to direct or appoint them.[40] If aristocratic conspirators and rebels took any note of it, they did so chiefly in the breach, when submitting to Christ's vicar instead of an ordinary mortal may have made defeat and surrender less humiliating.[41] If the 'breath of worldly men' would not suffice to 'depose the deputy elected by the Lord', Ottonian Germany had no lack of angry aristocrats and ambitious royal progeny willing to give it a try.[42]

The office of emperor and the imperial church

For the relatively brief period in which they occupied the royal throne, the Ottonians could claim a number of important accomplishments, but surely one of the more long-lived was the emperorship,

---

37 Reuter 1991: 207.
38 Gluckman 1958: 28; Leyser 1979: 102.
39 McKitterick 1983: 193; Nelson 1988: 214–15.
40 Thietmar 1.26; Reuter 1982: 371–72.
41 Leyser 1979: 95.
42 Shakespeare, *Richard II* 3.2.56–57.

acquired by Otto I in 962 and part of the titulature of German rulers until 1806.[43] Modern scholars have claimed much for this institution, both positive and negative, and even Otto's contemporaries were at odds regarding its significance and pondered, in particular, the degree to which it depended upon Rome and the papacy.[44] An Italian commentator simply declared Otto I's coronation a disaster, a virtual apocalypse for the 'eternal city'.[45] One can say, at the least, that the imperial office enhanced the prestige of its holders, no small advantage in a world that placed high value on external manifestations of worth. More concretely, it implied a duty-cum-right to guard and direct the papacy and a vested interest in southern Italy. Each of these supposed rewards brought the Ottonians as much difficulty as benefit. Protecting the papacy required a more or less active involvement in the politics of Rome, for example, which meant that they also had to deal with local power brokers, such as Crescenzio 'Nomentano' (d. 998).[46] Crescenzio presided over a loosely organized aristocratic faction (i.e. the Crescentii) which dominated the city of Rome and competed with the Ottonians for control of the papacy.[47] Although contemporary witnesses portray his relations with the Roman church in highly negative terms, one might argue that Crescenzio was no worse than other regional magnates who tried, in similar fashion, to influence the distribution of ecclesiastical resources within their territories. Indeed, the office of pope stood at the apex of the Roman aristocracy's network of patronage, and the power to choose its occupants was both eagerly sought and surrendered with great reluctance. Attempts by Ottonian emperors to secure the pope's independence, among other things, by imposing candidates of their own, met with resistance because they appeared to threaten both the network itself and the dominance of the noble houses which had hitherto been its chief beneficiaries.[48] In regard to the Italian south, the degree to which Ottonian policy remained consistent and the question of how deeply into the Italian peninsula the emperors wished to extend their influence remain subject to debate. It has been suggested, for example, that only Otto II saw his claims in the region as anything other than a

43 On the following Reuter 1991: 170–74.
44 Arnold 1997: 84–87.
45 Thietmar 4.32. n. 104.
46 The addition of 'Nomentano' to Crescenzio's name occurs only in later sources (e.g. *AQ*, an. 998, p. 74).
47 *DBI*, vol. 30. pp. 661–62.
48 Görich 1993: 250–63.

potential bargaining chip with Byzantium although both he and Otto
I were active in central and northern Italy.[49] Free from controversy,
however, is the fact that the Ottonians, by intervening south of Rome,
inserted themselves into a fierce and long-running struggle for control
involving Arabs, various south Italian states, and the Byzantine
Empire, a struggle in which the last of these had essentially come off
the worse.[50] Reports of the violence that accompanied Ottonian forays
into the area even reached eastern Saxony, where Thietmar duly
recorded them, along with his account of Otto II's disastrous defeat in
Calabria, an event that had a dramatic impact on German public
opinion and further destabilized south Italian political relations.[51]

As with most medieval emperors, the model for the Ottonians
generally derived from the Carolingian Empire rather than classical
Antiquity, but an association with the latter was an inherent possibility. During the reign of Otto III, this association briefly emerged in
a plan to create a revived Roman Empire with the city of Rome as its
capital, a *renovatio imperii Romanorum*. The plan generated a fair
amount of controversy among Otto's contemporaries, to whom, in
retrospect at least, it appeared utterly quixotic. Thietmar remarks
that the emperor's effort received a rather mixed reaction.[52] Others
were even less generous.[53] Modern scholars have been similarly at
odds on the subject, chiefly because neither Otto nor any of his
contemporaries explicitly defined what *renovatio* was all about,
therefore requiring that its content be deduced from a disparate body
of evidence consisting, *inter alia*, of new forms of titulature and court
ceremonial, isolated statements by court favourites, and visual images.
That these witnesses should be subsumed within the context of a
unified, imperial programme was the conclusion proposed by P. E.
Schramm more than fifty years ago.[54] More recent studies have
challenged various aspects of Schramm's argument, in some cases
denying its validity altogether, and have been met, in turn, with
equally vigorous counter-arguments.[55] Although the jury is still out
on this issue, there is little doubt that individuals close to the court

49 Houben 1989: 35–38.
50 Kreutz 1991: 119–25.
51 Thietmar 2.15; 3.20; Kreutz 1991: 119–25.
52 Thietmar 4.47.
53 Cf. Brun, *VA*, c. 7.43.
54 Schramm 1929: 118
55 Görich 1993: 187–274; Dormeier 1997: 17; and in general, Warner 1999.

were placing a new emphasis on Roman themes, both antique and Christian, even if *renovatio* may not have been a coherent programme in any modern sense.[56] Controversy also swirled (and continues to do so) around the Ottonian monarchy's remarkably close and mutually exploitative relationship with the German church. In part, this relationship was simply a matter of logistics. As with virtually all monarchs of the Middle Ages, the Ottonians dispensed with a capital city in the modern sense, but they had relatively firm places – religious communities, royal residences, and episcopal cities – that served as *ad hoc* centres of political life and venues for the assemblies, legal proceedings, and ceremonial occasions through which royal power had its most direct and visible impact upon the populace of their realm. The processions, ceremonial arrivals and departures, and other ritual moments that occur periodically in Thietmar's narrative are probably typical of what occurred when kings visited any royal church or monastery. The Ottonians did not visit every region of the realm, however, and even for those they did, the frequency and duration of their visits could vary widely. By charting the most and least visited stopping points modern scholars have arrived at a picture of the structure of the realm, distinguishing areas in which Ottonian rule was direct and personal from those in which it chiefly relied on surrogates of varying degrees of dependability.[57] Saxony, as we have mentioned, figured among the most visited regions. Wherever they travelled, however, Ottonian kings drew heavily on the resources of royal churches and religious communities which, among other things, contributed to their upkeep and maintenance. In return, such communities received rights of immunity and royal protection, and election privileges – which is to say that they were freed from any secular jurisdiction other than the king's, could call on the king to defend them, and (within certain limits) elect their community's head, each a benefit thought to enhance the residents' ability to pursue a truly religious life.[58]

Ottonian kings also drew heavily on the personal resources of the clergy, chiefly to provide the loyal, qualified agents that they, like all medieval rulers, found in such short supply.[59] In turn, these royal clerics reaped the benefits, in the form of royal patronage and

56 Reuter 1991: 281; Reuter 1991a: 23.
57 Bernhardt 1993: 45–70.
58 Schieffer 1991: 53–55.
59 Hollister and Baldwin 1978: 868.

promotion to high office, especially the episcopate.[60] To fuel that patronage, the Ottonians tried to ensure that a selection of the more important bishoprics were presided over by men they themselves had chosen, with particular preference being given to members of the royal chapel, the community of court clerics who ministered to the king's spiritual needs and performed various administrative tasks. Royal control over appointments, or over the episcopate itself, was never complete, however. The king's appointees never constituted a majority of the episcopate and he frequently had to take account of local interests or the ambitions of the leading men and their families. Furthermore, even prelates who did owe their advancement to the monarch could not be counted on absolutely, especially when royal policies had negative implications for their particular diocese. Nevertheless, the whole arrangement was sufficiently effective that later generations tended to recall it, alternatively, as a 'summer solstice of peace and tranquillity' or as a violation of the boundaries between sacred and worldly things.[61] Followers of the late twelfth-century abbot Joachim of Fiore, offended by Ottonian domination of the church, would go so far as to associate Emperor Henry II with the Dragon of the Apocalypse.[62] Among modern scholars, in contrast, debate has focused less on issues of morality than on the extent and consistency of royal control, and on the narrower question of whether or not the term 'imperial church system' might serve as an appropriate descriptor for whatever it was the Ottonians had.[63]

At least some portion of the Ottonian clergy also had concerns about relations between church and monarchy, although they were relatively restrained in terms of their rhetoric. The role of bishops, in particular, seems to have represented something of a flashpoint. And there were good reasons for this. The Ottonian episcopate encompassed men of all levels of enthusiasm – venality and modern-sounding social problems were not unknown – but each of its members possessed a similar combination of duties and responsibilities.[64] Every bishop exercised sacramental, jurisdictional, and pastoral authority within his own diocese. Most also fulfilled a number of secular duties relating

---

60 On the following, Schieffer 1989: 297–98; Reuter 1991: 195–96.

61 Radulf, c. 1, p. 588; Humbert, p. 217.

62 Patchovsky 1998: 294–95, 298–300.

63 See the fundamental assessment by Reuter 1982.

64 Thietmar 3.16; 7.56. On the following: Arnold 1989: 162–64; Parisse 1991: 497–501.

to their positions as great landholders, and many would have possessed a military retinue consisting, in part, of *ministeriales*, an unfree class with specialized skills that might include fighting.[65] Although not without interests of its own, a bishop's retinue provided a measure of security and status in a world that tended to equate each of those qualities with the capacity to dispose of military force. For anyone reluctant to assault the anointed of the Lord directly (and not everyone was!), a bishop's military retainers or *milites* also offered a handy target for the feuds and random acts of violence that occurred with some frequency in Ottonian society.[66] A few bishops could rightly be classed as major political figures. Such, clearly, was Archbishop Willigis of Mainz, a prelate whose advice and service were highly valued at court and who played a decisive role at certain key moments in the history of the realm.[67] Many others appear to have collaborated with the ruler on an as needed basis. Over all, then, we might say that the duties of German bishops 'demanded the combined talents of a politician, an administrator, and even sometimes … a soldier'.[68] Scriptural authority for the episcopate's involvement in secular activities was ready at hand in Matthew's injunction to 'render unto Caesar' (Matt. 22: 21) and it could also be defended on the basis of utility (i.e. that it benefited the people under a bishop's rule).[69] Such justifications did not ring true for everyone, however. For some churchmen, the secular persona of bishops occasioned real anxiety, especially when it involved contact with *milites*, and service at court was scarcely more assuring despite the advantages that might accrue to a courtier-bishop's clients and favoured communities.[70]

The emperorship and the 'imperial church', the papacy, relations with Slavs, Italians, and with their Saxon homeland, these figured among the chief reference points for Ottonian kings and have continued to do so for modern historians who study the Ottonian *Reich*. For our purposes, however, it is especially important that the reign of the Ottonians coincided with a cultural revival which, if not quite a 'renaissance', did produce such notable monuments as the Aachen Gospels, the plays of Hrothswitha of Gandersheim (d. *c*.975), and the

65 Reuter 1991: 231.

66 Thietmar 7.44; 8.24.

67 E.g. Thietmar 4.2

68 Benson 1968: 3.

69 E.g. Thangmar, c. 41, p. 776; Ruotger, c. 29, pp. 29–30.

70 Nightingale 1992: 61–62; Jaeger 1985: 58–66.

liturgical compilation known as the Romano-German Pontifical.[71] Although less prolific than their Carolingian predecessors, Ottonian literati made equally noteworthy contributions to the writing of history.[72] Hrothswitha of Gandersheim compiled a history of her convent and a poetic treatment of the reign of Emperor Otto I. Liudprand of Cremona, an Italian writing with Ottonian patrons in mind, skewered both popes and Italian dynasts in his *Antapodosis* and compiled a history of Otto I's reign. Widukind of Corvey and Adalbert of St Maximin/Magdeburg compiled chronicles. Biographers of bishops, queens, and martyrs flourished as well. It is among such illustrious company that one would place Thietmar and his *Chronicon.*

Thietmar on kingship and politics

Although the Ottonian episcopate seemed to require active involvement with the world, there were always some prelates, albeit a small minority, who impressed contemporaries with their extraordinary piety. Thietmar speaks admiringly of Archbishop Liawizo of Bremen whose appearance resembled that of a corpse, owing to the severity of his fasts and vigils, and of Bishop Eid of Meißen whose devotions were so severe they endangered his life.[73] Among his childhood friends, he included Brun of Querfurt, who left the king's service to pursue a life, successively, as hermit, missionary-bishop, and martyr.[74] It is not among either the saints or the power brokers that one should place Thietmar, however, but rather among that middling group of prelates whose piety never exceeded the mundane and whose influence largely remained rooted in their own dioceses. Although privileged to 'touch the hem' of great and powerful men, Thietmar never entered their ranks, and no one would have mistaken him for a saint. Piety and influence aside, however, he remained an imperial bishop and, as such, was intensely aware of the influence of kingship and politics on the church, his diocese, and his own career. Indeed, that awareness suffuses his entire narrative. When it came to matters of high politics, the presence of an anointed king on the throne opened a ready avenue for divine intervention. By Thietmar's account, God had granted

71 Reuter 1991: 246.
72 Hofmann 1991: 898–905, and passim.
73 Thietmar 6.88; 7.25.
74 Thietmar 6.94–95.

Ottonian kings all manner of benefits: victory in battle, advice on their choice of prelates, and timely revelations regarding important acts of state. Often, so he asserted, 'the grace of Heaven revealed to the emperor what it wished to occur on earth', and even a royal miracle was not out of the question.[75] Thietmar was equally clear regarding the punishments that rulers and the realm suffered when they strayed from the divinely ordained path. Military defeat, death, and destruction followed Otto II's suppression of the diocese of Merseburg, for example, and his predecessor's temerity in deposing a pope (Benedict V) stood condemned both by Thietmar's allusions to divine punishment and intimations of the victim's potential sanctity.[76] Still, he seems never to have forgotten the more prosaic issue of royal patronage.[77] It should not be far from the thoughts of Thietmar's modern readers either, since the prelate was no stranger to duplicity and obfuscation when the interests of his diocese were concerned. The history of those interests had a particularly convoluted character owing to the diocese's temporary suppression between 981 and 1004, an episode that wreaked havoc with property-holding and disrupted the east Saxon church for decades. That Thietmar continually emphasizes the ties between Merseburg and the royal house, and generally favours the latter's interests, at least in part reflects a desire to compensate for his bishopric's troubled history.

In organizing his work around the regnal periods of kings, Thietmar could draw on a well-established literary tradition of monarch-centred 'golden ages', of which he had an example ready at hand in the reign of Emperor Otto I, a monarch whose abilities as ruler and defender of the homeland bore comparison with Charlemagne, the traditional paragon of medieval rulership.[78] Others among Thietmar's contemporaries and near contemporaries shared his positive opinion of Otto I and it resonated in later tradition as well.[79] Thietmar knew, however, that ages of lesser worth inevitably followed an age of gold and he sensed the void that great Otto's death had left in the realm.[80] The already unbearable loss was compounded by the passing of Otto's generation and, with it, the withering away of the virtues it had

75 Thietmar 2.27; 6.9.
76 Thietmar 3, prologue (Otto II); 2.28, 35; 4.62 (Benedict V).
77 Thietmar 8.14.
78 Thietmar 2.13; Graus 1967: 14–17.
79 Thietmar 2.44, 45; Jank 1979: 85.
80 Thietmar 2.44, 45.

represented so well.[81] Although the theme of decline resurfaces in the
eighth book of the *Chronicon*, where the reader encounters a mournful
portrait of Henry II meditating on the sorry state of the realm and his
own inadequacies, it is hardly a leitmotiv.[82] In fact, Thietmar seems to
have had a sufficient amount of both praise and blame to distribute
among all the Ottonian kings.[83] Even Otto I did not escape criticism.[84]
For Thietmar, the virtues of rulership included qualities, such as
cunning, that were equally appropriate for members of the aristocracy. As far as Thietmar was concerned, if it was commendable for
his uncle to employ his cunning to escape from a boat full of pirates,
it was equally so for Otto II, who escaped a less hostile boatload of
Greeks.[85] Henry II, in particular, appears to have been a master of the
art.[86] Anger, a manly virtue, was also a royal one, especially when
directed at anyone presuming to usurp royal prerogatives.[87] When
Otto I heard that Duke Herman of Saxony had received a regal
reception at Magdeburg and had even presumed to sleep in the
monarch's bed, he was filled with anger and immediately set about
rectifying the situation.[88] Later, he expressed another royal virtue,
clemency, by restoring Duke Herman to favour.[89] Although Thietmar
could cite instances in which the Ottonians failed to exhibit sufficient
virtue, his bias in favour of the royal house generally ensured that he
turned to their enemies, rivals, and neighbours for models of truly bad
or ineffective kings. He paints a particularly venomous portrait of
Arduin of Ivrea, one of Emperor Henry II's major rivals in Italy,
characterizing him as a destroyer rather than a governor, dangerous
to his own people, and so disrespectful towards the episcopate that he
had seized one prelate by the hair and forced him to the ground like a
common cowherd.[90] He was also corrupt and, as Thietmar saw it, no
true king, notwithstanding that the Lombards might call him that.[91]

81 Thietmar 2.44.
82 Thietmar 8.34.
83 Lippelt 1973: 141–73.
84 See above p. 17.
85 Thietmar 3.22; 4.25; Althoff 1988: 303.
86 E.g. Thietmar 5.21.
87 Althoff 1998a: 59–65.
88 Thietmar 2.28.
89 Ibid.
90 Thietmar 4.54; 5.24.
91 Thietmar 6.7, 93; 7.24.

In his treatment of King Arduin, as elsewhere in the text, the reader must reckon with Thietmar's partisanship in favour of the Ottonians and his general dislike of Italians with their (in his eyes) predisposition towards conspiracy, treachery, and other forms of disreputable behaviour.[92] In point of fact, Arduin's rise to power scarcely differed from that of the Ottonian kings and his claim to the throne, arguably, was no less legitimate than that of Henry II. Like other Italian clans, the Arduini had exploited the opportunity offered by a weak central authority to extend their territory, eventually consolidated, under Arduin 'the Bald' (c.945–c.975) as the March of Turin.[93] That the 'Lombard' aristocracy elected Arduin's like-named grandson as king simply recognized the family's dominant position within the north Italian realm and this, however tyrannical he may or may not have been, made Arduin a king.[94] One might say much the same for another of Thietmar's iniquitous Italian kings, Berengar II. As margrave of Ivrea, this powerful magnate had surmounted the factional politics of the north Italian *regnum* and married the daughter of King Hugh. During the latter years of Hugh's reign, and under the latter's son, King Lothar, he exercised a dominant influence at court, perhaps being tacitly recognized as successor.[95] Thietmar ignores these more positive aspects of Berengar's persona and focuses instead on his abusive treatment of Lothar's widow, Adelheid (subsequently wife of Otto I), and on his defeats and eventual exile in Germany.[96]

For weak kings, Thietmar could cite the example of King Robert 'the Pious' of France (996–1031) who stood by, 'ready for peace and respectful to all', while three thousand of his countrymen were killed, or of Rudolf III, 'the mild and effeminate' king of Burgundy.[97] As with the 'wicked kings' of Italy, neither of these assessments can be taken at face value. In King Robert's case, Thietmar's views constrast with a generally positive (or at least energetic) image purveyed by West Frankish sources.[98] Thietmar's disdain for Rudolf derived from the fact that he had allowed the Burgundian magnates to dominate the episcopate and exhibited inconstancy in negotiations regarding the

92 E.g. Thietmar 7.2.
93 *DBI*, vol. 4, pp. 49–52; Sergi 1988: 16–17.
94 Wolf 1993: 19–22.
95 *DBI*, vol. 9, pp. 28–30.
96 Thietmar 2.5, 13.
97 Thietmar 7.46 (Robert); 7.27–30; 8.7 (Rudolf).
98 Hallam 1980: 69–72.

nomination of Henry II as heir to the Burgundian throne. Shorn of
their patronizing tone, Thietmar's comments refer to a tendency,
evident virtually everywhere in Europe, for bishoprics to fall into the
hands of local comital dynasties.[99] Although the Rudolfing kings did
not oppose this trend, they carefully retained several of the more
important bishoprics for their own use and, in that sense, their
ecclesiastical policies did not differ substantially from those of the
Ottonians.[100] Rudolf's vacillation regarding the succession, moreover,
merely suggests the difficulty of maintaining a consistent policy when
all decisions ultimately had to rest on a consensus among the leading
men of the realm.

King Vladimir I of Kiev (980–1015), whose sins ran to cruelty and
fornication, was more or less in a class by himself.[101] Venerated by the
Orthodox community as a saint and recognized as the first Christian
ruler of the Rus, the prince is generally credited not only with having
facilitated the Christianization of his still largely pagan subjects, but
also with having secured his people's historic orientation towards
Byzantium.[102] Ironically, Thietmar's characterization of Vladimir's
persona generally corresponds with Slavic sources which calculate
that, prior to his conversion, he possessed eight hundred concubines,
and describe him as a libertine, 'insatiable in vice', who 'seduced
married women and violated young girls'.[103] Thietmar knew, as well,
that the prince's guilt extended to abuse of his family and of a bishop,
Reinbern, sent to spread the Christian faith among Vladimir's
'extremely ignorant people'.[104] In a bit of partisan etymology, he added
that Vladimir's refusal to lay aside his passions and patiently direct
his attention to the Kingdom of Heaven meant that his name did not
correspond with its meaning, 'power of peace'.[105] Whatever truth may
be ascribed to Thietmar's characterization, it is worth noting that his
school chum, the missionary Brun of Querfurt expressed rather more
positive views regarding the prince, praising, in particular, his pious

99 Parisse 1991: 458–62.
100 Sergi 1991: 224–28.
101 Thietmar 8.72–74.
102 Martin 1995: 1–20.
103 Cross and Sherbowitz-Wetzor (trans.) 1953: 94; also cf. 3 Kings 11: 3 (RSV 1
    Kings 11: 3).
104 Thietmar 7.72.
105 Thietmar 7.73.

impulses and willingness not just to support, but even sacrifice for the sake of peace.[106] Among all the rulers that Thietmar despised, he reserved a special place for Boleslav Chrobry, offspring of Duke Miesco I of Poland and Dobrawa, duke of Poland in his own right, and perhaps even king.[107] Although Thietmar could not deny Boleslav credit for a particularly good deed, the ransoming of Adalbert of Prague's body after the Prussians had assisted the future saint in his quest for martyrdom, he nonetheless maintained that there was something innately wicked about the duke.[108] That wickedness manifested itself in a willingness to lay violent hands upon his own flesh and blood, and in a personal morality sufficiently off key to justify Thietmar's referring to him as 'the old fornicator'.[109] For the most part, however, Thietmar's antagonism focused on Boleslav's arrogance or, more specifically, his striving for a position vis-à-vis the *Reich* that exceeded what the prelate thought he deserved. At the instigation of Emperor Otto III, so Thietmar complained, a man whose father would scarcely have refused deference to a Saxon margrave had been transformed from a payer of tribute into a lord, and even dared to subjugate those who were rightly his superiors.[110] It is generally accepted that Thietmar's remarks constitute a negative reaction to a meeting between Otto III and Boleslav at Gniezno, Poland (in 1000). The meeting, for which Thietmar provides particularly detailed testimony, marked the elevation of Gniezno's church to the rank of archbishopric, an important milestone in the establishment of an independent Polish church. It also appears to have altered the character of Boleslav's relationship with the *Reich* in a way that enhanced his personal stature.

Both the establishment of Poland's first archbishopric and the honour bestowed upon its duke have been viewed as an aspect of Otto III's *renovatio*. During his progress to Gniezno, the emperor had issued

106 Brun, *Ep*, pp. 98–100.
107 Thietmar 4.55–56.
108 Thietmar 4.28.
109 Thietmar 4.57–58. Thietmar refers to the brutal but efficient manner in which the duke disposed of his father's second wife, her children, and their supporters, thereby resolving the problem of a disputed succession at one blow. While he enumerates, without comment, the various wives taken on and discarded by the duke (5.58), Thietmar's disgust is palpable when describing how the 'old fornicator' had seized another man's wife (8.33).
110 Thietmar 5.10.

diplomata in which he described himself as the 'Servant of Jesus Christ', and he had punctuated his return trip with a stop at Aachen where he unearthed and gazed upon the corpse of Emperor Charlemagne.[111] After his return to Italy, he had employed forms of titulature based on the epithet 'Servant of the Apostles'. The significance of these new titles remains subject to debate. It has been suggested, for example, that the first of the two was intended to place the emperor within the evangelical tradition of the Apostles, an appropriate image given his contribution to the establishment of a new church, and, for both titles, analogies have been drawn to the usage of the Byzantine and papal courts.[112] They may also have testified to the monarch's enthusiasm for a form of ecclesiastical *renovatio* based on collaboration between pope and emperor.[113] In any case, they certainly appear to emphasize both the Christian and Roman elements in Otto III's public persona and to associate them with the events at Gniezno. The same might be said of the opening of Charlemagne's tomb which might have suggested comparison with models from classical Antiquity, especially the opening of the tomb of Alexander 'the Great', but also with the cult of saints.[114] Indeed, it has been argued that Otto intended nothing less than the elevation of Charlemagne himself to the ranks of Christian saints.[115]

Among modern scholars, discussion regarding the events at Gniezno has chiefly focused on the question of whether or not they included the bestowal of a crown upon Boleslav and his recognition as king of Poland. In fact, a coronation is documented by a much later witness, a French monk (the so-called Gallus Anonymous) who compiled a chronicle while residing at the court of Duke Boleslav III of Poland (1102–38). Aspects of this testimony are highly suspect, however. In its earlier sections, up to the twelfth century, the work includes material that has clearly entered into the realm of legend.[116] Nor is there any doubt that the entire piece was intended to glorify both the current duke and his dynasty, the Piasts, for which the events at Gniezno had come to represent a kind of political coming of age.[117]

---

111 Thietmar 4.47.
112 Althoff 1996: 136; Ladner 1960: 463, 470; Reuter 1991a: 23–24.
113 Arnold 1997: 90.
114 Beumann 1984: 92.
115 Görich 1998: 406–9.
116 Bisson 1998: 276–77; Skibinski 1996: 94; Tymowski 1996: 243–49.
117 Michalowski 1992: 62.

The fact that Boleslav actually did have himself crowned, following the death of Emperor Henry II (1025), might suggest that Gallus was simply conflating these two events.[118] On the positive side, Otto seems to have bestowed crowns upon other monarchs, suggesting that the diplomatic climate would not have been inimical to a Polish coronation.[119] Finally, it is also possible that Thietmar was being less than honest in his assessment of Boleslav's status, surely the most novel aspect of a royal programme (renovatio) towards which he expressed, at the very least, ambivalence.[120] Although he never refers to Boleslav as king, it is suggestive that he compares him with Arduin of Ivrea who, whatever his faults, was a duly elected monarch.[121]

Given the murky state of the evidence regarding Boleslav's coronation, one should not be surprised to find that modern opinions have diverged radically. Johannes Fried, one of the more influential commentators on the issue, has argued forcefully for the validity of the anonymous chronicler's testimony, asserting that Boleslav's coronation had a secular character which would have allowed for a second ecclesiastical coronation in 1025.[122] Gerd Althoff, the major opponent of this view, has argued that what took place at Gniezno was a relatively conventional pact of friendship rather than a coronation.[123] Still others have suggested that the question may never be definitively answered.[124] In any case, Boleslav seems to have had little difficulty ruling within the confines of Poland and could exercise a certain influence beyond its frontier as well.[125] Indeed, if Thietmar found Boleslav's arrogance offensive, it was his skill in 'foreign affairs' that made him appear threatening. Boleslav played an active role in the politics of the Reich, appearing at assemblies, taking sides in internal conflicts, and forging alliances with members of the Saxon aristocracy. He married his daughter to the son of Margrave Ekkehard of Meißen and the latter's brother, Gunzelin of Kuchenburg, married

118 Boleslav's son, Miesco II, also assumed the title of king, but was forced to surrender his crown in 1032 (Reuter 1991: 261).
119 A crown had been conceded to Stephan of Hungary and some new status may also have been intended for the Doge of Venice (Thietmar 4.59; Giese 1993: 233–34).
120 Thietmar 4.47.
121 Thietmar 6.93.
122 Fried 1989: 69–76; also Bisson 1998: 278.
123 Althoff 1996: 143–47.
124 Warner 1999: 5–6.
125 Bardach 1982: 217.

Boleslav's sister, or perhaps his sister-in-law.[126] The alliance represented a particular prize for Boleslav since Ekkehard enjoyed Otto
III's favour to a remarkable degree.[127] With Otto's death and the
succession crisis that followed, relations between Boleslav and the
Ottonian house began to take on ominous overtones.[128] In his account
of the interregnum, Thietmar tends to give the impression that Henry
of Bavaria's success was a foregone conclusion, among other things,
by emphasizing his hereditary right as descendant of Henry I and
highlighting moments which reveal him as that monarch's rightful
heir and successor.[129] Some modern historians, following his lead,
have therefore interpreted the events of 1002 as a constitutional debate
between factions favouring, respectively, the principles of hereditary
succession or free election.[130] Others have argued that the political
issues were by no means so straightforward and that both Duke
Herman [II] of Swabia and Margrave Ekkehard [I] of Meißen, the
other major candidates for the throne, could have claimed descent
from the ruling house as well, albeit with varying degrees of closeness.[131] In any case, one can easily infer from Thietmar's narrative
that their support was far from negligible. Ekkehard enjoyed the
support of important Saxon churchmen and most of the Ostphalian
counts.[132] Archbishop Heribert of Cologne, a powerful and influential
churchman, masterminded Herman's candidacy and the duke also had
supporters among the aristocracy.

For all concerned, moreover, the path to the throne was neither easy
nor painless, and it was accompanied by acts of violence, mayhem, and
sacrilege. Herman had sacked the cathedral of Strasbourg, Margrave
Ekkehard of Meißen had been murdered, and only the 'cries of the
poor' had convinced Duke Henry to cease his ravaging of Duke
Herman's lands.[133] Resentment among both winners and losers tended
to linger, sometimes long afterwards. Archbishop Heribert of Cologne,

126 Thietmar 4.58; 5.18, 36.

127 See below p. 27.

128 In general see Görich 1997.

129 Thietmar 4.50–51; 5.3.

130 E.g. Faußner 1991: 9–14.

131 E.g. Wolf 1991; Hlawitschka 1987: 20–42, 43–79; cf. Reuter 1990: 189. The
   specific character and degree of these relations and the possibility of further
   candidates from other branches of the Ottonian line continue to be hotly debated
   (e.g. Hlawitschka 1993; Wolf 1995).

132 Thietmar 5.7.

133 Thietmar 5.5, 6, 12, 13.

the object of harsh treatment at Duke Henry's hands, seems to have recovered rather quickly from his fit of pique, for example, although he was certainly no slacker when it came to vendettas.[134] At least, after some hesitation, he was willing to accompany Henry to Aachen, site of the king's enthronement.[135] By 1004, Thietmar places him in Henry's entourage, suggesting that all had been forgiven, or simply that he was too important to dispense with.[136] In contrast, fifteen years passed before the murderers of Margrave Ekkehard could be reconciled with his kin.[137] It is against this background of anxiety and resentment that we should place Boleslav's emerging relationship with Henry II. Boleslav had been an ally of Margrave Ekkehard, but with the latter's death both he and the like-named duke of Bohemia went over to Henry's side.[138] He later appeared at Merseburg where he joined other notables in formally acknowledging Henry as king.[139] In the process of shifting his allegiance, the Polish duke had seized territory within the boundaries of the *Reich*, asserting that he was acting with Henry's consent. Later, at Merseburg, he made an unsuccessful bid for the burg of Meißen, but received other territories instead. He also succeeded in having Gunzelin of Kuckenburg appointed margrave. Thietmar suggests that he was still on good terms with Henry when he left Merseburg, but that an ambush, for which Boleslav held the monarch responsible (wrongly, according to Thietmar), caused a radical change in his attitude. In turn, personal animosity between Boleslav and Henry II set the stage for a war-cum-feud that would dominate relations between Poland and the *Reich* for more than fifteen years.

Although Thietmar represents our unique witness for the rapid and rather curious souring of relations between Henry II and Boleslav Chrobry, there is reason to suggest at least moderate scepticism. The strategy of winning friends and supporters with empty promises was one that Henry employed to good effect at other points in his career, and he was more than willing to hold a grudge. Thietmar's assertions to the contrary, Boleslav may well have had, or thought he had, Henry II's support for his efforts at territorial aggrandizement and

134 Cf. Thietmar 8.26.
135 Thietmar 5.20.
136 Thietmar 6.7.
137 Thietmar 5.20; 7.50.
138 Thietmar 5.7, 10–11.
139 Thietmar 5.18.

the territories received at Merseburg may have represented a compromise, willing or otherwise. That, by this point, Boleslav had found a firm ally and kindred spirit in Margrave Henry of Schweinfurt is more than a little suggestive. The margrave, one of Henry II's early supporters and, subsequently, one of his most determined enemies, appears to have been denied a promised duchy (i.e. Bavaria) largely because the king still recalled that their fathers had engaged in a feud.[140] As for the ambush, though Thietmar protests the king's innocence, his comments hint at 'an affair of honour' even if the perpetrators were not acting directly at the king's order. Boleslav's warriors had refused to disarm when entering the king's court and refused to leave when ordered to do so. In any case, there is likely to have been more to the story than Thietmar lets on, even if we can no longer recover the precise truth of the matter.

Disruptive effects of royal power

Notwithstanding his emphasis on the Divinity's role in directing Ottonian kings, Thietmar did not conceal the fact that the effect of royal government could be disruptive. This is nowhere more evident than in his ruminations on the effect of the king's favour (*gratia*). Beneficiaries of the king's favour could experience a dramatic rise in power, influence, and prestige. Those who lost it could suffer a whole range of negative results, finding themselves more vulnerable to their enemies perhaps or to the confiscation of their property. Rehabilitation might require difficult negotiations, payment of compensation, or a public act of humiliation.[141] The last of these was by no means the least offensive. To appear before the king and a potentially raucous crowd of one's peers, with bare feet, in the sackcloth and ashes of a penitent, was certainly preferable to capital punishment, but it could not have been a pleasant or otherwise desirable experience for anyone with honour or 'face' to lose. Overall, the bestowal or withholding of royal favour, along with its material rewards, produced a kind of 'carrot and stick' effect that drew the aristocracy to the king. It could also have the opposite effect, however. Honour had a palpable quality and implicitly political implications in the aristocratic society of the German *Reich*.[142] Men risked their lives to gain it and its loss drove

140 Thietmar 5.14.
141 E.g. Thietmar 6.2, 54.
142 Reuter 1993: 185–86.

them to acts of desperation. Indeed, much of what may seem irrational or inexplicable in Ottonian politics ultimately derives from these two factors: the desire for honour and fear of disgrace. To the extent that individual success or failure in gaining the king's favour upset established hierarchies of honour, the result could be not only an atmosphere of competition, but also one of anxiety and conflict. In Ekkehard of Meißen's case, for example, confidence in Emperor Otto III's support had encouraged a type of behaviour rational only in a man who believed himself beyond reprisal. The margrave had refused to offer satisfaction for an unjustified attack on dependants of the archbishop of Magdeburg, an act of profound disregard for legal custom that left Thietmar mystified, and had virtually dared the house of Walbeck to engage in a feud by reneging on a marriage agreement.[143] An excellent warrior named Bevo had been blinded by the margrave and he had used his influence with the emperor to have another nobleman flogged.[144] Finally, he had offered a calculated insult to the royal princesses, Adelheid and Sophia, by seizing a table set for their dinner and dining with a group of his supporters.[145] Ekkehard's assaults on the honour of his peers contributed first to the rejection of his candidacy as king and then to his murder.

Rulership provided other sources of disruption as well. In a society that tended, more often than not, to identify 'the state' with the person of the king, the latter's personal 'rites of passage' could assume the character of a constitutional crisis. This was nowhere more evident than in that crucial moment when a king allocated his inheritance. Here, we may recall that inheritance meant something rather different in Thietmar's era from what it did in later centuries, due to the practice of partible inheritance. This custom dictated that the heritable property and rights of Saxon families be divided among all surviving heirs, thereby multiplying the number of legitimate claimants and ensuring that even distant relations might benefit.[146] It also enhanced the potential for domestic strife and feud. Uncles, as Thietmar remarked, always raged against their nephews.[147] A wiser approach was to satisfy potential claimants by putting one's house in order well before the inevitable, thereby giving the intended

143 Thietmar 4.39–40.
144 Thietmar 4.67; 5.7.
145 Thietmar 5.4. See similar acts at Thietmar 7.9.
146 Leyser 1968: passim; Reuter 1991: 221–29.
147 Thietmar 6.53.

distribution at least a chance of success. Count Frederick of Eilenburg
employed this strategy when he wished to ensure that his brother's
family would respect the inheritance he had bestowed upon his
daughter.[148] What was good for members of the aristocracy was also
good for the king who faced similar decisions in distributing his
wealth and risked opposition from relatives who felt slighted or left
out. Since the wealth of the king generally encompassed a claim to the
throne, however, both the stakes and the danger were correspond-
ingly higher. Within the royal family, the potential for disputed rights
of inheritance to generate domestic strife was evident already during
the reign of the first Ottonian king. Like any person of substance, King
Henry I was concerned to effect an orderly division of his inheritance, a
process he initiated in 929 with his so-called *Hausordnung*, a series of
interlocking legal proceedings that, among other things, provided
Queen Mathilda with income and probably included the designation
of their eldest son, Otto, as king.[149] In the same year, and equally part
of this process, there occurred a marriage between Otto and Edith of
England, daughter of King Edward the Elder (900–24) and sister of
King Athelstan and King Edmund.[150] It was both a brilliant match,
from a diplomatic perspective, and a highly opportune one as young
Otto's budding sexuality was beginning to complicate the inheritance
situation – a captive Slavic woman had just presented him with a son,
William.[151] William would go on to a successful career as archbishop
of Mainz and an occasionally difficult relationship with his father.[152]

Thietmar thought well of Otto's bride and intimated (in retrospect)
that she might well be a saint.[153] He might have added that her arrival,
in conjunction with Henry's *Hausordnung*, presented a problem which
would trouble the realm and his successors for generations to come. A
division of property always had the potential to leave at least some
parties dissatisfied, but Henry's situation was complicated by the fact

148 Thietmar 7.50.
149 Thietmar 1.21. It is worth noting that Duke Hugh of Francia, Henry's con-
    temporary and father of King Hugh 'Capet', instituted a similar *Hausordnung* for
    his lineage (Lewis 1992: 47–48). There is admittedly some disagreement regard-
    ing Otto's designation. An earlier date (927) has been suggested, and doubts
    raised regarding the precise character of the act, but there seems little doubt that
    Otto was being prepared for the succession (Reuter 1991: 144–45; cf. Beumann
    1991: 42–43; Laudage 1992: 24; Wolf 1994: 84).
150 Glocker 1989: 18–27; *LMA*, vol. 3, p. 1571.
151 Thietmar 2.1.
152 See below p. 36.
153 Thietmar 1.3.

that Mathilda was not really his first wife and Otto was not his eldest
son, at least in biological terms. Henry had previously been married
to Hatheburg, daughter of 'Count' Erwin of Merseburg and heir to a
good part of her father's landed wealth.[154] That she was a widow and
had taken the veil was scarcely an obstacle in light of her obvious
assets, although Henry may have been sensitive to the sinfulness of
his marriage, or at least to the opposition it aroused among the local
clergy.[155] Along with incest, the problem of women who married after
taking the veil figured among the Ottonian clergy's chief complaints.[156]
Nor, to be fair, was the aristocracy altogether oblivious to the
problem of invalid marriages although their concern appears to have
focused on the issue of incest.[157] Thietmar raises and condemns the
practice at other points in his text.[158] In any case, the marriage to
Hatheburg brought Henry and his lineage a number of material
advantages, including a dramatic expansion of their landholdings in
the region of Thuringia, their traditional stronghold.[159] It also produced
a son, Thankmar (d. 938). Neither consideration was sufficient to hold
the marriage together, however.[160] In 909, Henry repudiated Hatheburg
and married Mathilda, a member of the Immeding clan. That the
process moved along so effortlessly suggests that a bargain of some
sort was struck with her kin who would otherwise have expressed their
resentment and sought vengeance.[161] Later witnesses were inclined to
pass over the existence of an earlier union in silence.[162]

Henry's second marriage strengthened the already substantial position
of the Liudolfinger in Ostphalia and brought them new influence and
possessions in Mathilda's homeland of Westphalia.[163] It also enhanced
their collective prestige since the bride was descended from Duke
Widukind, a celebrated hero and leader of Saxon resistance during the
wars with Emperor Charlemagne (i.e. in the eighth century).[164]

154 Thietmar 1. 5.
155 Thietmar 1.6, 9.
156 Corbet 1990: 199.
157 Bouchard 1981: 270–73.
158 Thietmar 4.57; 4.64.
159 Glocker 1989: 46–47; *LMA*, vol. 3, p. 2191.
160 Thietmar 1.9.
161 Leyser 1979: 12–13.
162 E.g. *V. Mat. Ant.*, c. 2, pp. 115–17.
163 Leyser 1979: 12; *LMA*, vol. 6, pp. 390–91; Beumann 1991: 26–27.
164 Schmid 1964: 11–15.

Nevertheless, the marriage was not without negative consequences. Even if Hatheburg's kin were satisfied, Henry's second marriage had placed his first-born son, Thankmar, at a distinct disadvantage in matters of inheritance.[165] Indeed, in the eyes of the clergy at least, the status of Henry's first-born son may now have been viewed as something less than legitimate.[166] Adalbert of Magdeburg goes so far as to identify him as 'the brother of the king [i.e. Otto I] by a concubine'.[167] Henry apparently made an effort to satisfy Thankmar in the context of his *Hausordnung*, but the latter's mounting resentment eventually provided an incentive for him to revolt against his half-brother, Otto I, after the latter's succession to the throne.[168] Thankmar's revolt was one of several, related uprisings that broke out in the first years of Otto I's reign.[169] The first of these involved Eberhard, son and heir of Duke Arnulf of Bavaria, who seems to have been reacting to the monarch's efforts to curtail Bavarian independence.[170] Thietmar knew that Thankmar's revolt had its origins in two major disappointments.[171] Thankmar apparently believed that he had been denied his maternal inheritance, especially Merseburg and its fortress, which were bestowed upon his half-brother, Henry. Then, he had been passed over for an important honour to which he also believed that he had a right. A border county (march) previously held by a distant relative, Margrave Siegfried, was given instead to Siegfried's brother Gero (937–65).[172] The revolt was soon joined by Duke Eberhard of Franconia and Count Wichman [I]. Wichman had been passed over, in favour of his younger brother Herman Billung, when Otto assigned control of yet another Saxon march. Herman Billung figured among the more prominent beneficiaries of Otto I's patronage, having been allotted important military commands in the East and being trusted to act as the king's representative in Saxony.[173] Duke Herman's success ensured that his descendants would figure

165 Thietmar 2.2.

166 Glocker 1989: 46; *LMA*, vol. 8. p. 610.

167 Cont. Reg. an. 939, p. 161;

168 Thietmar 2.2.

169 Leyser 1979: 12ff; Reuter 1991: 152; Bernhardt 1993: 16–17.

170 E.g. Thietmar 1.26.

171 Thietmar 2.2.

172 Like Thankmar and Siegfried, Gero had ties to the comital house of Merseburg and his father had been a close adviser and supporter of King Henry I (*LMA*, vol. 4, p. 1349).

173 Thankmar 2.28.

among the first ranks of the Saxon aristocracy, but it also engendered
a bitter and long-lived feud within the Billung clan.[174] The favour
bestowed upon Duke Herman left not only Wichman but also his
sons, Wichman II and Ekbert 'the One-eyed', with a sense of injustice
so profound that they were inclined to join 'every enemy of Hermann
Billung and Otto they could find'.[175] Duke Eberhard of Franconia's
motivation for joining Thankmar is less clear, but he may have felt
that his power or independence was being threatened. Although both
men made peace with Otto, following Thankmar's death, the revolt
broke out again as soon as another member of the royal house
emerged to lead it.[176]

The type of the disgruntled delegitimized son appears at other points
in Thietmar's narrative as well. Liudolf, eldest son of Otto I and
Edith, reacted in similarly violent fashion after his mother, Edith, died
and the king's second marriage (i.e. to Adelheid) began to negatively
affect his position at court. From Thietmar's account, it would appear
that Liudolf had started out with every advantage a son and heir
could want, and then some. He had impressed all the leading men and
an opportune marriage had brought him wealth and the duchy of
Swabia.[177] His father had gone so far as to publicly designate him as
his successor.[178] All this changed with Otto's marriage to Adelheid
and, presumably, the realization on Liudolf's part that he was likely to
be shunted aside and supplanted by the new queen and her future
offspring. Shortly afterwards, he appeared with other malcontents at
the centre of an uprising.[179] As with the preceding revolt of Thankmar,
Liudolf's revolt was caused by a combination of frustrated ambition
and a threatened loss of face.[180] Aside from qualms regarding his
status as heir, he had also been prevented from expanding his power
in Italy and had seen his influence at court supplanted by that of the
king's younger brother, Henry.[181] Given a leader from the royal
family, it was not long before other parties with grievances (Conrad

174 Leyser 1979: 11–12, 21–22; Althoff 1991a : 309–17.
175 Leyser 1979: 12.
176 Thietmar 2.5; cf. Widukind 2.11, pp. 76–78.
177 Thietmar 2.4.
178 Ibid.
179 Thietmar 2.5, 6, 7, 8.
180 Leyser 1979: 20–22; Reuter 1991:155–56, Beumann 1991:72–76, Bernhardt 1993:
    24–25.
181 Widukind 3.6, p. 108.

'the Red' and Archbishop Frederick of Mainz) joined the revolt. That men who participated in Thankmar's revolt (or whose fathers had) also appear among Liudolf's followers has suggested to some modern scholars that there may have been a more cohesive organization behind the revolt, something similar to a guild or prayer confraternity.[182] For Liudolf at least it all ended in ignominious defeat and surrender though without the loss of his duchy.

Younger sons might also have complaints about their inheritance. In particular, Henry I's decision to pass the realm in its entirety to Otto had profound implications for the royal heir's younger brother Henry, who harboured ambitions of his own and boasted a body of supporters that included Queen Mathilda.[183] Although, as Thietmar notes, the situation was resolved by a kind of settlement whereby Henry received a kinglike position within the Duchy of Bavaria, the fact that he had to be kept under guard during Otto's coronation (936), and his subsequent involvement in uprisings against his brother in 939 and 941, attest to the depth and seriousness of his resentment.[184] In fact, Henry's line continued to represent a source of tension within the royal house.[185] In 974, Henry's son, Duke Henry 'the Quarrelsome' initiated a rebellion against Otto II, apparently because he resented the king's intervention in the succession to the Duchy of Swabia, following the death of the childless Duke Burchard III.[186] By installing his nephew (i.e. Duke Liudolf's son) as duke rather than allowing the former duke's widow, Hadwig, to dispose of the office by remarrying, Otto had placed a major obstacle in Duke Henry's way. As Hadwig's brother, he would have expected to exercise a substantial influence within the duchy and over her choice of husbands.[187] Henry's rebellion came to an ignominious end with his capture and exile in 978. Later, in a more serious rebellion (984), Duke Henry came close to seizing the throne from Otto II's minor son, Otto III.[188] Initially, the duke seems to have given the impression that he merely wished to act as the young king's guardian, a right due him as the latter's nearest adult male relative. Gradually, however, it became

---

182 Althoff 1982: 130–33.

183 Thietmar 1.21.

184 Widukind 2.2, p. 67.

185 Beumann 1991: 127–30; Reuter 1991: 184–85; Althoff 1996: 39–48.

186 Thietmar 3.5, 7.

187 Beumann 1991: 114; Reuter 1991: 175–76; Glocker 1989: 174–75.

188 Thietmar 4.1–5, 7–8.

clear that he intended much more: to exercise power in his own right or perhaps to rule alongside Otto as a dominant co-ruler, on the Byzantine model.[189] The latter option may have appealed to the clergy, who tended to emphasize suitability and usefulness as prerequisites for the royal office and supported Henry in large numbers.[190] With defeat and forgiveness, Duke Henry returned to Bavaria, bestowed upon him once more as a reward for submission, and reportedly ruled with justice and beneficence, to the acclaim of all.[191]

On his death-bed, so Thietmar asserts, the once 'quarrelsome' Duke Henry expressed regret that he had ever opposed his king and advised his like-named son not to follow his example.[192] These sentiments, though altogether appropriate, probably reflect Thietmar's judgement more than the duke's, but they hint at the difficulty posed by the next episode in the multi-generational epic of the Henrician lineage: the ascent to the throne of Duke Henry the Quarrelsome's son, as King Henry II. This profoundly ironic moment presented Thietmar with something of a dilemma. After denying the Bavarian line any right to the throne, based on the hereditary claims of Otto I and his offspring, he now had to fervently support the succession of King Henry II and, no less, justify it on the basis of hereditary right. To excuse the discordant influence of Henry II's ancestors and remove any negative caste from his succession, Thietmar resorted to two of his favourite themes, illicit sexual relations and diabolical influence. The first Duke Henry, so he proposed, had been the product of a diabolically inspired coupling, on a forbidden day, between King Henry I and his wife, Mathilda.[193] The king was also inebriated. Through no specific fault of their own, therefore, Henry and his lineage had acquired a kind of hereditary stain that obliged them to make trouble for the Ottonian house. Henry II, assuming a kind of messianic role, had redeemed his lineage and inaugurated an age of peace (or at least Thietmar hoped that he had), through his now legitimate and divinely willed succession.

If royal government could have a disruptive effect on the royal house, the aristocracy, and the realm in general, its effect was not necessarily

189 Erkens 1993: 272–89.

190 Ibid.

191 Thietmar 4.20.

192 Ibid.

193 Thietmar 1.24. That his readers might have no doubts regarding the principle involved, Thietmar followed his account with a similar though more prosaic one involving a burgher from Magdeburg and his wife (Thietmar 1.25).

more positive on the church and clergy. Thietmar complained bitterly, among other things, of monasteries emptied of their inhabitants due to royally imposed reform and, as we have mentioned, he implied that divine penalties had followed Otto I's deposition of Pope Benedict V.[194] As a bishop himself, however, he was especially concerned with the impact of royal power on the episcopate. In general, Thietmar's views on the episcopal office can be characterized as worldly. That the prospect of bishops shedding blood (or at least directing those who did) did not faze him is evident from his admiring portraits of warrior bishops such as Arn of Würzburg, Ramward of Minden, and Michael of Regensburg.[195] Nor did he expect a bishop to forgo the obligation to pursue a feud.[196] Feud was, after all, one of the fundamental institutions of aristocratic society and, to the extent that bishops had been integrated into that society, there was no compelling reason for them to reject its values. Thietmar's attitude changed dramatically, however, when bishops were the victims of violence rather than perpetrators or abettors of it. A prelate pursued by hunting dogs, like some wild beast, or forced to stand by, powerless and disgraced, as dependants were killed or mutilated: such were the results of the (to his mind) unjustified fury of the laity.[197] Even worse, he knew of bishops who had themselves endured physical mutilation and death.[198] Violence is a cultural construct and the types and levels of it that Ottonian society found acceptable clearly differed from those of later centuries. For Thietmar it appears to have been not so much the violence itself that was offensive, but rather the fact that the manner in which it was perpetrated infringed the honour of the episcopate as a whole. A similar tone emerges in his views on the relationship between bishops and kings. Thus, far from seeing the royal court as a potential source of spiritual danger, he appears to have viewed the king's service and those who undertook it in a positive, even noble, light. He owed his career to Archbishop Tagino of Magdeburg, one of the most politically orientated prelates of his time, and his account of that prelate's final farewell to Emperor Henry II testifies to the mutual respect and empathy engendered by the collaborative effort of bishops and kings in governing the realm.[199]

194 Above p. 17.
195 Thietmar 1.4; 2.27; 4.29.
196 Thietmar 7.48, 49.
197 Thietmar 7.28; 8.24, 26.
198 E.g. Thietmar 2.40.
199 Thietmar 6.61.

Still, he expressed deep misgivings when the Ottonians moved from supporting and protecting bishops, something Thietmar felt was their obligation, to intervening in the methods through which they were chosen – that is, elections.

A bishop's election, like a king's, figured as a single element in a series of legal and ritual moments (consecration, enthronement, and investiture) that effectively endowed their beneficiary with his office. Because an episcopal election allowed for, and even required, the participation of an unusually large number of participants, however, it was an act uniquely subject to manipulation. In theory, bishops were to be elected by the clergy and people, but according to tenth-century practice the choice might be influenced by local factions among the nobility and clergy, by the king and court, and by the will of the candidate's predecessor.[200] Although it was considered uncanonical, bishops occasionally tried to appoint a successor prior to their own deaths, Bishop Ulrich of Augsburg's efforts to pass his see to his nephew being the most obvious example.[201] As was always the case in the distribution of ecclesiastical resources, aristocratic patronage and familial strategies for advancement played a central role.[202] There were also networks of patronage among the clergy. Throughout the *Chronicon*, Thietmar provides evidence of successful churchmen who, in turn, assisted other strivers in their upward climb.[203] As the counterpoise to clerical cooperation, there is also evidence of bitterness and animosity, and efforts to hinder career advancement.[204] German churchmen may have been 'bound together by ties of confraternity, as well as by links of *cognatio* and patronage', but they were also divided by feuds, rivalries, and the incessant competition for rights, honours, and property.[205] It is against this background and in conjunction with these conflicting interests and emotions that Ottonian kings brought their own influence to bear.

Thietmar had a personal interest in episcopal elections because, as a canon at Magdeburg and later, as suffragan of that see, he had witnessed the chapter's continuing efforts to elect a prelate in the face of continued obstruction by the monarch. In light of its substantial

200 Fichtenau 1991: 186–94; *DMA*, vol. 4, pp. 421–25.

201 Lotter 1973: 131.

202 Thietmar 7.26; Schreiner 1989:185–89.

203 Thietmar 2.37; 4.6.

204 Thietmar 3.2; 6.36.

205 Reuter 1982: 369

investment in the community, the attitude of the ruling house towards the ecclesiastical foundation at Magdeburg is perhaps under standable. In 937, King Otto I had founded a monastery there (St Maurice), in part, because of the location's already well-established military and economic importance.[206] Located strategically at a ford over the river Elbe, Magdeburg already functioned as a customs post and commercial entrepot during the reign of Charlemagne. Continuing prosperity would be assured by its proximity to the mining and new agricultural lands of the Harz region, and by its ready connections with ports on the North Sea. Otto later added an impressive palace, ensuring that, like its counterpart at Aachen, Magdeburg would juxtapose a place of rulership with a religious structure.[207] As the focus of politics and government continued to shift to the east, Magdeburg's importance increased as well, as did its wealth, which came to rival that of older communities with much longer histories of royal favour.[208] Otto I's patronage culminated in a plan, apparently conceived in 955, to transform Magdeburg into the seat of an ecclesiastical province. The plan was delayed because of opposition from his son, Archbishop William of Mainz, and Bishop Bernhard of Halberstadt, both of whom stood to lose from any redistribution of jurisdiction and ecclesiastical property in eastern Saxony.[209] To provide an endowment for the new archdiocese, in particular, it was foreseen that property and incomes would be separated from Bernhard's diocese, a prospect that prelate resisted to the bitter end. Archbishop William's anxiety about, among other things, the creation of a rival province in the east, appears to have been mollified by the bestowal of various rights and privileges, including primacy within the German church. By 961, he was no longer in opposition. Finally, in 968, the plan was brought to fruition and an archbishop and chapter took over St Maurice while most of the monks moved to a new establishment at Berge, a suburb several kilometres south of the cathedral.

In 979, Otto II granted the canons an election privilege, an event that Thietmar describes in great detail, suggesting the importance he attached to it.[210] Issued at the intercession of Empress Theophanu and the request of Archbishop Adalbert, Otto's diploma proposes that the

206 Mayr-Harting 1992: 129–50.
207 Zotz 1993: 93–94.
208 Bernhardt 1993: 162–69.
209 Thietmar 2.11, 20–21; 3.14; Claude 1972: 73–78, 81–84.
210 Thietmar 3.1.

right to elect their own pastor will make the clergy of St Maurice
equal to the clergy of other churches, especially Cologne which, as an
archbishopric, represented a logical benchmark for Magdeburg.
It adds that any king or emperor who might rescind this right would be
anathema, a clause that ultimately proved useless whenever Magdeburg's
royal benefactors chose to intervene in archepiscopal elections.
Indeed, as the canons discovered, it was one thing to possess a
privilege and quite another to have it recognized. Their first attempt
to use it came to naught because it conflicted with Otto II's plan to
suppress the diocese of Merseburg and transfer its prelate, Giselher,
to Magdeburg.[211] A delegation, sent to inform the emperor of the
chapter's choice, asked the then Bishop Giselher to intervene on its
behalf. Instead, he used his influence to obtain the archbishopric for
himself. The delegation then held a second election and confirmed the
monarch's will. Upon Giselher's death (1004), the canons once again
found their efforts to elect frustrated by the monarch, in this case
Henry II, who imposed a candidate of his own, namely Tagino,
presumably because his plan to reverse Otto II's policy regarding
Merseburg required an archbishop of unquestioned loyalty.[212] The
chapter had originally elected the popular and influential provost
Walthard, and it took some bargaining to convince everyone to go
along with Henry's II's choice.[213] Upon Tagino's death, the canons
finally succeeded in electing a prelate, Walthard again, but the success
was qualified since the new archbishop died soon afterwards.[214] In the
election that followed, the king's will prevailed once more, as the
canons dutifully elected a royal chaplain, Gero.[215] Although Thietmar
would not live to see it, the subsequent history of the chapter would
offer only a few, qualified successes in achieving this, one of its pre-
eminent goals.[216]

At a later point in the Middle Ages, during the twelfth and thirteenth
centuries, both the proper procedure for electing bishops and the
constitutional status of the *electus* at various points in the process
would be the subject of intense debate.[217] By this time, the revival of

211 Thietmar 3.13–14.
212 Thietmar 5.41–43.
213 Thietmar 5.41; Claude 1972: 215.
214 Thietmar 6.62, 66–67, 72.
215 Thietmar 6.74, 81.
216 Warner 1994: 147.
217 Benson 1968: 3.

legal studies had provided a new, more subtle vocabulary for discussing all questions relating to canonical practice and, of course, continuing tension between *sacerdotium* and *regnum* ensured that discussion would, in fact, occur. Thietmar lived in a different though no less concerned era and his intentions in the *Chronicon* clearly transcended issues of canon law. Still, one can deduce a more or less consistent position on episcopal elections from a selection of his mostly anecdotal comments on the subject. Thietmar basically accepted that the influence of king and court would be a factor in the allocation of bishoprics. There was, after all, a long tradition of permitting the ruler's involvement and the sacral status of the Ottonians may have made this appear self-evident.[218] Perhaps Thietmar was just being pragmatic. In any case, for a duly elected candidate to succeed without opposition, as Thietmar knew, it was wise to secure the 'favour and aid of powerful men' at court and for chapters to act in a spirit of unity so as to avoid the contested elections that virtually invited outside intervention.[219] His own elevation to the episcopate had almost been derailed when Henry II's attention began to turn towards another candidate. Only Archbishop Tagino's angry insistence impelled the monarch to stay the course.[220] Still, Thietmar knew that the prospect of a bishop imposed by royal fiat could provoke local power brokers to feud and that the candidate himself might prove divisive.[221] He presumably knew from one of the chief protagonists, Archbishop Tagino, about a thwarted election attempt at Regensburg. Bishop Gebhard I (994–1023), a former royal chaplain, had been appointed to the see by Otto III, thereby overriding the will of the cathedral chapter which had tried to elect a bishop from its own ranks. The local candidate, Tagino himself, had been a protégé of Bishop Wolfgang (972–94) and also enjoyed the support of Duke Henry 'the Quarrelsome'.[222] Otto III's interevention in the ecclesiastical politics of Tagino's erstwhile diocese was not just a disagreement about theories of election, however. Along with other Bavarian bishops, the saintly Wolfgang of Regensburg had supported Duke Henry the Quarrelsome's attempt to seize the throne from the infant

---

218 See above p. 10.
219 Thietmar 1.22; 4.26.
220 Thietmar 6.39.
221 Thietmar 5.43.
222 Thietmar 5.42–43.

Otto III.[223] Coming so soon after the settlement of the duke's attempted *coup d'état*, the king's intrusion into the local power structure clearly represented a hostile move, and was perceived as such by Henry and his son, Duke Henry IV (the future Henry II). That Otto and Duke Henry (IV) managed to resolve their differences, and relatively quickly, is suggested by the latter's appearance as intercessor in a royal diploma issued for the Bavarian bishopric of Freising on 16 August 995.[224] Elsewhere, however, the election continued to generate tension. Tagino subsequently joined the ducal service where he remained until his elevation to the archbishopric of Magdeburg. Gebhard also managed to antagonize the monks of St Emmeram (Regensburg) and his own archbishop.[225]

Thietmar's ideal seems to have been a procedure that allotted an appropriate degree of influence to both royal and local interests. As he often did, when he needed to bolster one of his personal agendas, Thietmar turned to the supernatural. Thus when political concerns prompted Emperor Otto I to deny the archbishopric of Cologne to a certain candidate, though he had been duly elected by 'clergy and people', an angel appeared and threatened the monarch with death.[226] In another anecdote, a vision advised Otto that he should bestow the bishopric of Regensburg on the first person he met, presumably rather than doing so on the basis of political calculations.[227] The emperor announced the eventual candidate's name to an assembly of the clergy and people, and they elected him. In his account of the career of Bishop Ansfrid of Utrecht, a relatively rare example of a *conversus* (i.e. an adult layman who entered religious life) and apparently a pristine example of both courtly and spiritual virtue, Thietmar also found a model of the proper procedure for episcopal elections. Ansfrid was called to his bishopric at the instigation of Emperor Otto II, but Bishop Notger of Liège did the calling.[228] The candidate also insisted that the whole procedure be according to the canons. And so it was! The Archbishop of Cologne solicited the consent of his suffragans and consulted with the emperor. Then he presided over a proper election by 'the clergy and people'.

223 See above p. 32.
224 D O III 170.
225 Thietmar 6.41, 60.
226 Thietmar 2.24.
227 Thietmar 2.25.
228 Thietmar 4.35.

Social distinctions and the political role of women

Thietmar's was a world profoundly sensitive to the distinctions and
categories separating one human being from another, and upward
social mobility, though scarcely the norm, occurred with sufficient
frequency as to attract the attention of clerical literati and represent a
matter of concern at the imperial court.[229] His own viewpoint was that
of a cleric and an aristocrat, which meant that he observed his social
inferiors with a sense of arrogance tinged with ambiguity. Hence,
even moderately low birth in a fellow bishop was sufficient cause for
embarrassment, requiring the manufacture of an account of miraculous
birth to set things right.[230] It is indicative of Thietmar's acute
perception of status that the prelate in question was Archbishop
Willigis of Mainz, one of the most powerful churchmen of his day and
a man who, surely, had no need to apologize for his parentage. One
can draw much the same conclusion from Thietmar's admiration for
Archbishop Tagino's ability to keep the riffraff at bay without
appearing ungracious. He did not so much disdain persons of less
noble lineage and manner as keep his distance from them.[231] Thietmar's
opinions sharpened as he lowered his gaze. Peasants, in his view, were
untrustworthy, deserving of rough treatment.[232] Although it has
already been discussed above, as evidence of his views on kings and
kingship, Thietmar's anger at King Arduin for having treated a
bishop like a common cowherd, grabbing his hair and forcing him to
the ground, says as much about his opinions on the treatment of
cowherds as it does about his attitude towards wicked kings.[233] And
yet, perhaps because of their very lowliness, Thietmar accepted that
the poor and powerless might act as messengers of the divine and that
their cries rightly merited the attention of God's ministers.[234] That he
himself had failed to give them that attention figured among his
greatest regrets.

Distinctions of ethnicity also weighed heavily with Thietmar. His
mental landscape was populated, *inter alia*, with treacherous Italians,
feckless Greeks, capricious Lotharingians, and stubborn Poles who

229 Leyser 1979: 163; Fichtenau 1991: 373–78.
230 Thietmar 3.5.
231 Thietmar 6.65.
232 Thietmar 5.33; 7.4, 20.
233 Thietmar 5.24.
234 Thietmar 7.15.

were useless unless punished as one would an ass.[235] Bavarians were
fine, but travelled poorly.[236] More serious, virtually insurmountable
boundaries separated Christians from pagans. Thietmar was a militant
Christian with a visceral hatred of pagans and the 'cults of demonic
heresy' which they preferred to the worship of 'Christ and his
fisherman, the venerable Peter', here referring to the revolt of the
Liutizi (981) which effectively wiped out a generation or more of
missionary activity in the east.[237] Seemingly despite himself, however,
he provided such uniquely detailed accounts of the religious customs
of the pagan Slavs and Scandinavians that he has been characterized
as an 'ethnological expert'.[238] Methods of divination, types and pro-
cedures for human and animal sacrifices, each is described in detail
though with a mixture of horrified fascination and disgust.[239] The
temple at Rethra, religious centre of the confederation of the Liutizi,
merits three detailed chapters.[240] Not surprisingly, the prospect of an
emperor actually allying with pagans, and against Christians, did not
sit well with him. This of course was the situation that ensued when
Emperor Henry II allied with the pagan Liutizi against his nemesis,
Boleslav Chrobry.[241] The terms of the alliance are not entirely clear,
but they certainly involved an obligation to provide military support.
More important, the pact preserved the independence of the Liutizi
and did not require conversion to Christianity.[242] Indeed, at one point
Henry II had to pay compensation to the confederation after one of
his warriors damaged a pagan cult object, a rather surprising action
for the anointed of the Lord.[243] Such alliances were not altogether
unheard of, and this one lasted for a generation.[244] Thietmar seems to
have been particularly sensitive on the subject, however, and he may
not have been alone in this regard.[245] Ironically, despite his antagonism towards paganism, the assertion that even the pagan Slavs

235 Thietmar 7.2, 72; 6.48; 8.2.
236 Thietmar 5.19.
237 Thietmar 3.17.
238 Leyser 1986: 21.
239 Thietmar 1.3, 5, 17.
240 Thietmar 6.23–25.
241 Thietmar 6.26.
242 Brüske 1955: 57–62; Reuter 1991: 213.
243 Thietmar 7.64.
244 Reuter 1991: 262–63; Tellenbach 1993: 4–5.
245 See note at Thietmar 6.26.

recognized a particular Christian wonder appeared to enhance its credibility in his eyes.[246]

Further representatives of the non-Christian Other were of less interest to Thietmar. There is evidence, for example, that the small, but economically significant Jewish population of Ottonian Germany was a subject of concern and even sporadic persecution.[247] The *Annals of Quedlinburg*, a work familiar to Thietmar, report that Emperor Henry II expelled the Jews from Mainz in 1012.[248] It was also during Henry's reign that a cleric named Wecilin became a *cause célèbre* by converting to Judaism and openly condemning his former faith.[249] Still, Thietmar displays little interest in Jews or Judaism, much less overt hostility. He noted that Otto II had placed the Jews of Merseburg under the authority of the then bishop, Giselher, along with other royal property, and that the Jewish community of Magdeburg turned out *en masse* to mourn Archbishop Walthard who had been like a father to them.[250] The Jew Calonmius played a noteworthy though subsidiary role in Thietmar's account of Emperor Otto II's defeat in Italy, and he noted complaints that Margrave Gunzelin of Meißen had been selling the dependants of other lords to the Jews.[251]

Thietmar's interest heightened substantially, however, when he turned to perhaps the most important Other of all: women. And he had good reason to be interested. High-born women played a prominent and active role in Ottonian society. They could both accumulate and transmit property.[252] They also figured among the benefactors of religious communities and as both patrons and producers of art and literature.[253] Women's religious communities played a key role since, like their male conterparts, they were often centres of learning. Among such communities the Saxon convent of Quedlinburg deserves particular attention, both because of its stature and because it had particular significance for Thietmar. It will be useful to say something

---

246 Thietmar 1.4.

247 Lotter 1993: 226, 228–29; Fichtenau 1991: 401; Blumenkranz 1960: 102–3, 206–7.

248 'At Mainz, the king undertook the expulsion of the Jews; but also the insanity of certain heretics was refuted' (*AQ* an. 1012, p. 81).

249 Abulafia 1981: 154–55.

250 Thietmar 7.73.

251 Thietmar 3.21; 6.54.

252 Leyser 1979: 49–73.

253 McKitterick 1990: 90–93.

about that community and the character of its inhabitants before proceeding to discuss Thietmar's views on women.

Quedlinburg had been established in 936 as a memorial foundation for King Henry I whose body, along with that of Queen Mathilda, lay entombed in its crypt. It possessed the usual benefits and obligations associated with royal status and enjoyed an unusually close relationship with the royal family.[254] Indeed, to some extent the community's connection with the Ottonian lineage outweighed its association with the monarchy itself.[255]

Quedlinburg had an active scriptorium, presumably staffed by its female residents, and probably a school as well. Widukind of Corvey dedicated one version of his history to its first known abbess, the royal princess Mathilda (b. 955, 966–99).[256] He thought that she would benefit from reading it and use her influence at court to benefit the monks of his community. Mathilda had been sent to Quedlinburg at an early age and presumably acquired her primary education there as well. Although one can only speculate as to her influence at the age of thirteen, when Widukind penned his dedication, her stature at court in later years was substantial indeed.[257] It is likely that the *Annals of Quedlinburg*, a work to which we have already referred, was also initiated by one of the sisters at Quedlinburg.[258] Although dependent upon other sources in its earlier sections, the *Annals* do provide an independent and, in some cases, eyewitness account of the reigns of Otto III and Henry II. Again, there is little reason to doubt that the author was a canoness and a woman of remarkable intellectual attainments who deserves to be placed in the company of Hrothswitha of Gandersheim as evidence of women's contribution to Ottonian literate culture. Indeed, the weight that both Hrothswitha and the Quedlinburg annalist place on reports concerning prominent Ottonian women has inspired at least one historian to argue that they represent a specifically female view of history.[259] Finally, the compiler(s)

254 Thietmar 1.21.

255 Thietmar 1.21, n. 64.

256 Widukind 1, prologue; Fuhrmann 1991: 16.

257 Glocker 1989: 201–3.

258 The text appears to have been produced by a single author, who began working *c.*1000 and concluded in 1030 (Holtzmann 1925: 114–25). In recent years, an ever-growing consensus has emerged in support of the idea that the annalist was a woman. See, for example, Houts 1992: 58.

259 Sonnleitner 1988: 236–38; Sonnleitner 1987: 118.

of two biographies of Queen Mathilda may also have resided at Quedlinburg, and most likely would have been a member of the community.[260]

The canonesses of Quedlinburg inhabited a world in which women exercised a remarkable degree of political influence. Female members of the royal house, for example, figured among a small circle of well-connected individuals who had direct access to the king. They were therefore in a position to act as brokers or patrons for less-privileged petitioners and to accumulate the debts of gratitude and obligation that counted for so much in a world that revolved around patronage.[261] Queens and empresses shared in their husband's authority, and women of royal lineage fulfilled a variety of supporting roles in government.[262] Empress Adelheid is said to have participated 'in the highest matters of government'.[263] Indeed, she convoked councils of bishops, installed abbots, and established peace among the unruly vassals of her nephew, King Rudolf III of Burgundy.[264] Abbess Mathilda served in the regency government during Otto III's minority and later acted as the monarch's viceroy in Saxony, a position previously held by no less a figure than Duke Herman Billung.[265] The Quedlinburg annalist paints a glowing portrait of Mathilda's tenure, praising her for having made the 'stubborn heads of the barbarians' submissive and for establishing peace, not through any instruments of war (though capable enough of this), but rather through prayers and vigils.[266] Women could also be fierce competitors at court. Thus, although some witnesses assert that Queen Mathilda's support for her son Henry rested on a matter of principle, she may actually have used his candidacy to gain leverage within the royal house, where a newly anointed queen with a prestigious lineage, namely Edith, appeared to threaten her influence.[267]

---

260 McKitterick 1993: 67. The question of whether the two extant biographies of Queen Mathilda were composed at Quedlinburg or Nordhausen has yet to be resolved. Each opinion can readily be supported with evidence from the text. The issue is discussed in detail by Schütte (1994: 22–23) who takes issue with Althoff's arguments (1988: 125) in favour of Nordhausen.

261 Althoff 1997: 189–97.

262 Erkens 1991: 245–59.

263 Odilo, c. 11, p. 38; Warner (trans.) 2000: 266.

264 Odilo, c. 10, p. 37; c. 12, pp. 38–39; Warner (trans.) 2000: 266, 267.

265 Beuman 1991: 145; Reuter 1991: 279; *LMA*, vol. 6, pp. 391–92.

266 *AQ*, an. 999, p. 75.

267 Nelson 1999: 194. In addition to Thietmar's testimony, Mathilda's support for Henry's succession is noted by the later of her two biographers, who asserts that

The infighting between Empress Adelheid and her daughter-in-law Theophanu got so vicious that the younger woman reportedly threatened that her mother-in-law would soon 'reign nowhere in the entire world, [and] her dominion [would] not even fill the palm of one's hand'.[268] Surely, such fighting words belie any image of feminine reserve. Equally lacking in that quality was the redoubtable Abbess Sophia of Gandersheim (1002–39), an accomplished courtier and major player in the ferocious world of ecclesiastical politics, who initiated a particularly aggressive legal dispute with the bishops of Hildesheim.[269] Contemporary sources suggest that Sophia was richly endowed with those characteristics of self-confidence, assertiveness and cunning that her society generally found admirable, albeit in men only.[270] Although we rarely encounter them as individuals, Quedlinburg's royal connections would have assured its canonesses an insider's view of Ottonian politics and, given their aristocratic status, there is no reason to believe that they would have been substantially less engaged or assertive than the princesses of the Ottonian house. For part of his life at least, their view would have been Thietmar's.

During his early childhood Thietmar had been sent to Quedlinburg to study under the supervision of a maternal aunt, Emnilde (d. 991).[271] He remained there until he was twelve years old. Although probably not in residence while the *Annals of Quedlinburg* were being compiled, he may well have known the annalist and he certainly knew and relied upon her work in compiling the later books of his *Chronicon*. If it is among the sisters at Quedlinburg that one should place the author of the earliest *vita* of Queen Mathilda (composed *c*.973/974), Thietmar may have known her as well. In any case, whether from reading Matilda's biography or from oral traditions associated with her cult and tomb, Thietmar was familiar with accounts of the queen's good deeds and shared in her veneration.[272] Although Thietmar was young while he resided at Quedlinburg, his time there would have opened his

---

the queen's opinion was shared by others and implies that she helped reconcile the two brothers (*V. Mat. Post*, c. 6, p. 157; c. 9, p. 161). Both Mathilda's biographer and Liudprand of Cremona assert that Henry's claim to the throne derived from his status as the first son born after his father had become king (ibid; *L. A.*, c. 18; Wright (trans.) 1930: 110–11).

268 Odilo, c. 7, p. 35; Warner (trans.) 2000: 265.

269 Goetting 1973: 89–93.

270 E.g. Thangmar, c. 14, c. 16; Althoff 1991: 131–32.

271 Thietmar 4.16.

272 Thietmar 1.21.

eyes to a much larger world than he had known previously. Ottonian kings customarily celebrated Easter at Quedlinburg.[273] It was also the site of major acts of state. As a young student, for example, Thietmar would have witnessed both the provocative moment when Duke Henry 'the Quarrelsome' came to the convent and celebrated Easter, in regal fashion, and Otto III's triumph as he celebrated the duke's defeat by replicating the occasion while Henry looked on![274]

Overall one might argue that Thietmar had spent his most formative years in the midst of a vibrant intellectual community dominated by politically savvy and well-connected women. It would seem logical, then, to ask what if any effect this had on his viewpoint. In fact, Thietmar's views regarding women are mostly what one would expect from a fundamentally conservative man in a fundamentally patriarchal society, though not entirely so. The reader will have little difficulty discovering negative, occasionally ironic stereotypes. Hence, while a man who showed too much anxiety was like a woman, a woman who exhibited patience in the face of adversity was *ipso facto* manly.[275] Concerning the wife of a Hungarian king who drank immoderately, rode a horse like a warrior, and killed a man in a fit of anger, Thietmar's judgement was firm: her polluted hands would have been better employed at the spindle.[276] And yet, he seemed to approve when the women of Meißen assisted in the defence of their burg by throwing rocks from the walls and putting out fires.[277] Women were equally adept at defending men's souls. That man was eternally blessed, so Thietmar declared, whose wife prayed for him when he was absent and saw to his spiritual welfare when he was present.[278] Indeed, throughout the *Chronicon*, women appear engaged in the work of praying, caring for the dead and dying, and inciting their male relations to acts of piety.[279] Several female recluses receive moving tributes.[280] Although the association of women with spiritual tasks was stereotypical, such tasks were by no means negligible in a society that sincerely believed in and placed great emphasis on

273 Althoff 1991: 127–29; Beyreuter 1991: 248–50; Claude 1972: 59.

274 Thietmar 4.1, 9.

275 Thietmar 2.23, 29.

276 Thietmar 8.4.

277 Thietmar 7.23.

278 Thietmar 1.25.

279 E.g. Thietmar 2.3, 40; 3.1, 10.

280 Thietmar 7.55; 8.8.

relations with the supernatural. Indeed, Thietmar assures the reader that it was Queen Mathilda's service to God that ensured her son, Otto I's prosperity.[281]

Among the pagan kings of central and eastern Europe Christian wives served as a vehicle for conversion and, subsequently, as models of proper Christian behaviour. Thietmar credits Dobrawa, wife of Miesco [I] of Poland, with having facilitated the latter's acceptance of Christianity.[282] He even forgave her for eating meat during Lent (thereby breaking a vow) as this promised to make her husband more amenable to the proverbial 'call to the altar'.[283] Otherwise, in regard to marriage, and sexuality in general, Thietmar's judgements could be quite harsh indeed. Wicked women incited men to dangerous or dishonourable acts and played the part of the temptress, clothing 'their bodies in unseemly fashion' and making a spectacle of themselves in public.[284] He offered a rare word of praise for the Poles who, prior to their conversion to Christianity, had inflicted horrific penalties upon prostitutes and adulterers, and he commended their former practice of having every wife follow her husband on to the funeral pyre.[285] Even within marriage, as we have already noted, Thietmar assumed that sexual relations at prohibited times would lead to disaster and also that violations of canonical practice cast doubt upon a union's legitimacy.[286] Thietmar's assertion that Henry I felt profoundly guilty for having married a nun, and Bishop Sigismund of Halberstadt's reportedly zealous opposition to the marriage, reflected very real concerns, however convenient they may have been as an excuse to dispense with an unwanted wife.[287] Even a hint of indiscretion, moreover, could make a noble matron vulnerable to gossip or blackmail.[288] On a more personal level, among his kin, there were women who made a deep emotional impression upon Thietmar. Among these, aside from Emnilde, one would include both his mother, Cunegunde, and Liudgard, the wife of his cousin Margrave Werner. As a young widow, Cunegunde earned Thietmar's admiration by helping to

281 Thietmar 2.4.
282 Thietmar 4.55.
283 Thietmar 4.56.
284 Thietmar 7.4; 4.63.
285 Thietmar 8.2.
286 Thietmr 8.1.
287 Thietmar 1.6, 9.
288 Thietmar 2.39, 41.

organize the ransoming of her brothers from their pirate captors and successfully resisting her brother-in-law's efforts to reduce her share in the Walbecker patrimony.[289] In Liudgard, Thietmar seems to have found a close friend and confidant.[290] He attended her on her death-bed and offered a moving tribute to her piety and concern for her husband's welfare.[291] He also seems to have had a close relationship with another cousin, Brigida, who advised him on one of his periodic encounters with the supernatural.[292]

In view of his fairly traditional outlook, it may be surprising to find that Thietmar had few if any reservations regarding the prospect of women in politics, even if he rarely employs the admiring tone of the Quedlinburg annalist. He describes Abbess Mathilda's activities as Otto III's viceroy in Saxony, including the tribunal she called (and presided over) to deal with Margrave Werner's attempt to kidnap his future wife, Liudgard, from Quedlinburg.[293] Empress Theophanu's service as regent for Otto III is presented in a positive light and he expresses pride in the fact that his father had served her faithfully.[294] Indeed, Thietmar praised the empress as one who 'was always benevolent to the just, but terrified and conquered rebels'.[295] Nor did he appear to blame her, in particular, for bestowing her favour on John Philagathos.[296] An ethnic Greek from Rossano (Calabria), John attracted the empress's attention while serving as her notary, and through her patronage subsequently acquired a number of important and influential offices, including that of tutor to her son Otto III. Later, after Otto reached his majority, John took on the delicate task of obtaining a Byzantine princess as a bride for the young ruler. That this trust was misplaced came to light when, through the machina-tions of Crescenzio 'Nomentano', and without the emperor's permis-sion, he ascended the papal throne as Pope John XVI (997–98, d. 1001). Thietmar also has much to say about Empress Cunegunde. He notes her efforts on behalf of candidates for high office, her vigorous

289 See p. 57.

290 Thietmar 1.13.

291 Thietmar 6.84–85.

292 Thietmar 1.12.

293 Thietmar 4.41.

294 Thietmar 4.10, 16.

295 Thietmar 4.10.

296 Thietmar 4.30. On the following, Zimmermann 1968: 105–6; Pauler 1982: 83–87; LMA, vol. 5, pp. 542–43.

support of her husband's ecclesiastical policies, and the fact that she had been given responsibility for organizing the defence of a threatened frontier.[297] Thietmar also notes the occasion on which Empress Cunegunde reinstated her brother Henry [V] as duke of Bavaria.[298]

Thietmar's mixed views regarding women suggest no ready explanation, and none will be offered here. Perhaps his negative comments were simply a parroting of the well-documented misogynist trends in patristic and medieval Christian literature. That he so readily accepted the notion of women exercising political power may indicate that issues of status and rank outweighed considerations of gender. Perhaps he never saw these powerful Ottonian women as anything other than representatives of more powerful men or, given his strong sense of family and lineage, interpreted their influence as a mere reflection of the ruling dynasty's power. Ultimately, however, it may simply be a matter of his being able to hold two mutually contradictory ideas in his mind at the same time.

Personal life and career

Thietmar's proximity to the events and people he described represents one of the more valuable aspects of his *Chronicon*. More often than not, he wrote about events that he himself had witnessed and could claim a personal acquaintance with many of the people involved in them. In part, this closeness to his material reflected Thietmar's professional status as bishop, but it also rested on a network of blood and marital relations encompassing most of the more prominent families of eastern Saxony.[299] In regard to his family, Thietmar's historical memory extended to approximately three generations. Thus he knew that both his paternal and maternal great grandfathers, Liuthar I of Walbeck and Liuthar of Stade, had died of wounds incurred during a battle with the Slavic Redarii (near Lenzen, 929).[300] Liuthar of Walbeck's like-named son, Thietmar's paternal grandfather, married Mathilda of the comital house of Querfurt which

297 Thietmar 6.35, 54, 74, 81; 7.29.

298 Thietmar 8.18.

299 Thietmar's family tree and life have been the subject of frequent and, in some cases, more detailed discussion by Holtzmann 1935: vii–xxvii; Lippelt 1973: 46–65; Trillmich 1974: ix–xvii; Goez 1983: 70–83; and, more briefly, Leyser 1994f: 27–28.

300 Thietmar 1.10.

included, among its members, the celebrated martyr Brun of Querfurt.[301]
Liuthar [II] had figured among a group of conspirators who plotted
unsuccessfully to assassinate King Otto I in 941 and lost all of his
property as a result.[302] Thietmar knew that he had regained the
monarch's favour by paying a heavy fine and that he had founded the
canonry at Walbeck as an act of atonement.[303] Following his submission, Liuthar had been placed in the custody of Margrave Berthold,
a powerful lord of the Bavarian Nordgau who enjoyed Otto I's
favour.[304] Subsequently, the count married Liuthar's daughter, Eila,
who gave birth to Margrave Henry of Schweinfurt (d. 1017), future
nemesis of Emperor Henry II. Thietmar's maternal grandfather,
Henry [I] of Stade, was married to Judith, from the lineage of the
Conradines, a dominant family in the Rhineland and Swabia. Their
marriage produced three sons and three daughters. Of the sons,
Liuthar-Udo fell in battle against the Vikings (i.e. in 994). His
brother, Count Henry [II] founded the monastery of Harsefeld. When
Count Henry died, in 1016, the third brother, Siegfried, took over the
countship. A sister, Gerberga, appears to have been the mother of
Bishop Dietrich of Münster, and yet another, Hathui, became abbess
of Heeslingen at the age of twelve, despite the reluctance of Archbishop Adaldag of Bremen.[305] The third sister, Cunegunde, married
Thietmar's father. After the death of his wife, Judith, Henry [I] of
Stade took a second wife, Hildegard, whose like-named daughter
married Duke Bernhard of Saxony, thereby cementing an alliance
with the powerful Saxon clan of the Billunger.

By the time Thietmar was born, his family had split into two branches.
The senior branch had its seat at Wolmirstedt on the river Ohre and
was presided over by Margrave Liuthar [III] whose territories
included the Saxon northern march, one of the large border counties
charged with securing the realm's eastern frontier against the Slavs.[306]
Liuthar was succeeded by his son Werner who married Liudgard,
daughter of Margrave Ekkehard I of Meißen. Although apparently long
agreed to by their parents, the marriage had begun inauspiciously when
the girl's father, as we have already noted, attempted to back out of

301 Thietmar 4.17; 6.43.
302 Thietmar 2.21.
303 Thietmar 6.43.
304 Thietmar 4.14; 5.38. See also Endres 1972: 7–8.
305 Thietmar 2.42.
306 Thietmar 6.46, 84.

the deal.[307] The jilted bridegroom responded by kidnapping his betrothed from the convent at Quedlinburg, where her father had placed her for safekeeping, but was forced to give her back although she reportedly desired to remain with him. Following Margrave Ekkehard's murder, Werner and Liudgard were permitted to reunite, presumably because a substantial portion of the leading men and clergy recognized the validity of Werner's claim. Werner's career marked something of a watershed for the Walbecker clan, seemingly a family on the rise. A series of disastrous encounters with Emperor Henry II, including yet another attempt at bridenapping, brought personal ruin upon Werner himself and apparently dealt a mortal blow to his family's ambitions.[308] After Werner's death, his brother and heirs tried to regain something of their position by bringing suit against Margrave Bernhard, the recipient of Werner's confiscated lands, but Henry II decided against them (1017).[309] Werner's younger brother, Berthold, subsequently involved himself in a disastrous feud in the Rhineland that ended with his surrender to the emperor.[310] Liuthar's third son, Dietrich, a canon at Magdeburg, failed to secure the monarch's confirmation of his election as archbishop of that see although he had enjoyed the patronage of Archbishop Tagino, his predecessor, and substantial support within the community.[311] He subsequently entered the royal chapel, however, which might have held out the prospect of a bishopric (had he lived long enough) and was entrusted with at least one important diplomatic mission.[312] Liuthar also had a daughter, Brigida, who was abbess of the convent of St Lawrence at Magdeburg.[313]

The junior line of the Walbecker clan, headed by Margrave Liuthar [III]'s younger brother, Count Siegfried (d. 991), occupied the original residence at Walbeck on the Aller. Siegfried's wife, Cunegunde, was the daughter of Count Henry [I] of Stade (d. c.974). That her relations figure prominently throughout Thietmar's narrative suggests how deeply aware he was of his relationship with them.[314] That

307 See above p. 27.
308 Thietmar 7.4–5.
309 Thietmar 7.50.
310 Thietmar 7.53; 8.17.
311 Thietmar 6.38, 66, 67.
312 Theitmar 6.74, 81; 7.10.
313 Thietmar 1.12.
314 See below p. 57.

Siegfried and Cunegunde named their eldest son after his maternal grandfather (i.e. Henry), moreover, suggests that they placed great value on their collateral relations, and implies a clear recognition of the division within the lineage of Liuthar. Among their legitimate offspring, Siegfried and Cunegunde produced a daughter and five sons, of which Thietmar was the third born. The daughter, Oda, married Gozwin of Falkenburg.[315] The eldest son, Henry (b. 973), inherited his father's countship.[316] Frederick (b. 974), the second born, would later become burgrave of Magdeburg, an office with responsibilities similar to those of an advocate.[317] In 998, both brothers helped their cousin Werner kidnap Liudgard from Quedlinburg.[318] Frederick also helped with the murder of Count Dedi of Wettin, an event which resulted in the confiscation of Werner's march. Later, Henry II would employ Count Henry's services as his intermediary with Werner, and Henry went on campaign with the emperor in 1004.[319] Thietmar's two younger brothers pursued clerical careers. Siegfried, to whom Thietmar dedicated his chronicle, became a monk and later abbot at Berge, and still later was appointed bishop of Münster (1009–22).[320] During Thietmar's lifetime, the youngest brother, Brun, was a monk at Corvey, but was subsequently elected abbot at Berge and Nienburg (1025), and ended his career as bishop of Verden (1034–49).[321] He was presumably Thietmar's source for events and marvels at Corvey. Willigis, a son fathered by Siegfried prior to his marriage, was installed as provost of the family's house of canons at Walbeck in 1009, following Thietmar's installation as bishop of Merseburg.[322]

Very little is known of Thietmar's childhood other than what he himself recorded. He notes his birth on 25 July 975 and that he was baptized and confirmed by Bishop Hildeward of Halberstadt whose spiritual jurisdiction included the comital residence at Walbeck.[323] We have already noted his period of residence at Quedlinburg. In 987, his father removed him from the community and sent him to the

315 *AS*, an. 1049, p. 688.
316 Thietmar 6.15; 7.6.
317 Claude 1975: 248–52.
318 Thietmar 4.41.
319 Thietmar 6.15; 7.6.
320 Thietmar 1, prologue.
321 Thietmar 4.70.
322 Thietmar 6.47.
323 Thietmar 3.6; 4.18.

monastery of Berge for further educating.[324] After three years (i.e. in 990), when it became apparent that he could not be given a permanent place among the brothers, his father had him accepted into the cathedral chapter at Magdeburg. The occasion was celebrated with a two-day feast on St Andrew's Day (30 November). At Magdeburg, Thietmar continued his studies under particularly auspicious circumstances. The cathedral school figured in a wave of significant educational centres, chiefly associated with bishoprics, that arose during the reign of Emperor Otto I. It appears to have reached a highpoint, just prior to Thietmar's entry, under the leadership of Master Ochtrich (d. 981), a scholar whose greatest claim to fame may well have been his public debate with Gerbert of Reims, later to become Pope Sylvester II, one of the foremost intellects of the day.[325] Ochtrich subsequently left Magdeburg, because of a conflict with Archbishop Adalbert, and joined the royal chapel.[326] Thietmar, generally a believer in clerical *stabilitas*, felt strongly that he ought to have remained at Magdeburg, whatever the cost.[327] Still, it is a mark of the esteem that Ochtrich continued to enjoy among the canons that he was their, admittedly unsuccessful, candidate to succeed Adalbert.[328] Despite a bad showing against Gerbert of Reims, Ochtrich left a deep impression on his students.[329] Brun of Querfurt, who studied under one of the master's successors, Geddo, offered high praise for his intellectual and pedagogical skills.[330] He added that Ochtrich and his pupils were accustomed to read together, that instruction took place exclusively in Latin, and that the rod was applied liberally when necessary. Thietmar also studied with Ekkehard, who appears to have kept the school on more or less the same level as his predecessor. As with other cathedral schools, but in contrast to their monastic counterparts, the educational programme at Magdeburg appears to have been heavily weighted towards the classics, especially Virgil.[331] It has been argued that such

324 Thietmar 4.16.

325 Fleckenstein 1956: 40, 50–51; Claude 1972: 126–28. The debate, which Ohtrich lost, is related by the historian Richer (Richer bk. 3. c. 55, vol. 2, pp. 64–66).

326 Thietmar 3.12.

327 Thietmar 3.15.

328 Thietmar 3.12.

329 Claude 1972: 126–28.

330 '… an exceedingly eloquent man, a veritable Cicero of that age whose memory still shines bright through all of Saxony. His greatness is declared, without speaking, by the faces of his pupils and, like a pointing finger, is revealed by the wisdom diffused among neighbouring burgs' Brun, *VA*, c. 5, pp. 5–6.

331 Lippelt 1973: 71–76.

programmes aimed at forming the character as well as the intellect and that, insofar as they had the practical goal of providing candidates for the king's service, they may well have been the seedbed for the later ideals of courtliness.[332] It is at least arguable therefore that Thietmar's admiration for 'courtier bishops' has its roots in a viewpoint acquired during his school years.

The prelates with whom Thietmar consorted as student, canon, and suffragan of Magdeburg were a diverse and especially talented lot. The multifaceted career of the first archbishop, Adalbert (968–81), for example, has inspired a recent biographer to characterize him as 'one of the most brilliant princes of the tenth century' and, indeed, prior to his appointment to the see of Magdeburg, he had been a monk, court notary, and chronicler.[333] He had already been consecrated bishop in preparation for a mission to the Kievan Rus (961) who, however, preferred the glories of Constantinople to the comparatively threadbare ceremonial of the German church.[334] Thietmar credits the archbishop with having actively demonstrated his concern for the discipline of monks and canons under his authority, but also notes his vindictiveness towards enemies and the fact that he was not immune to political mistakes.[335] He paid dearly for having allowed Duke Herman of Saxony to sleep in Otto I's bed at Magdeburg and assume other privileges normally reserved to the emperor.[336] Adalbert's successor, Giselher (981–1004), was perhaps the most controversial of Magdeburg's prelates owing to his involvement with the suppression of Merseburg, the diocese to which he had received his first vocation (971–81). As the scion of a Saxon aristocratic house and erstwhile monk at St Maurice (Magdeburg), Giselher's roots in the region ran deep.[337] He had also been a royal chaplain and continued to be active

332 Jaeger 1994: 36–52; and Jaeger 1985: passim, in which the association with
    medieval courtliness is developed in greater detail.

333 Rader 1995: 77.

334 According to Russian sources, emissaries sent to Germany by Vladimir I (980–
    1015) found no glory in the liturgy of its churches, thereby convincing the prince
    to ally with the Byzantine church instead (Cross and Sherbowitz-Wetzor [eds]
    1953: 111). Admittedly, the true story of the prince's conversion is likely to have
    been rather more prosaic (Martin 1995: 7–8).

335 Thietmar 3.9, 11–12.

336 Thietmar 2.28.

337 It is generally assumed that Giselher entered the monastery of St Maurice (i.e.
    Magdeburg) under Abbot Anno, since the latter, as bishop of Worms,
    subsequently pushed for Giselher's promotion to bishop of Merseburg (Thietmar
    2.37).

in the emperor's service throughout his career in the episcopate, a factor that may have caused him to neglect his pastoral duties.[338] Later, when Otto II decided to suppress the diocese of Merseburg, Giselher was translated to the see of Magdeburg.[339] Although there were undoubtedly good reasons for the monarch's decision and, clearly, Giselher was not solely responsible for it, Thietmar laid much of the blame at the prelate's feet, ensuring that the persona presented to the reader is strongly coloured with negative attributes such as naked ambition, duplicity, and corruption.[340]

Thietmar knew a great deal more about the past of Giselher's successor, Tagino (1002–12), presumably because he had spent time as a member of the archbishop's entourage. He knew, for example, of that prelate's earlier career at Regensburg and of the overturned election which denied him his apparently preordained succession as bishop of that see.[341] Tagino's long association with the Bavarian ducal house may have weighed heavily in Henry II's decision to appoint him archbishop of Magdeburg.[342] His subsequent career, as Thietmar's narrative reveals, saw him active in the high politics of the court, leading diplomatic missions and military campaigns, advising the ruler on matters of statecraft, and facilitating royal projects.[343] Along with the king and other prelates, he attended the Synod of Dortmund (1005), an assembly which imposed upon participants a kind of 'spiritual death tax' consisting of masses and other devotions.[344] He also played an intrumental role at the Council of Frankfurt (1007) which established the new diocese of Bamberg.[345] Although he may have relied heavily on his provost, Walthard, to take care of the diocese's internal affairs, he had an impact here as well. In a manner appropriate to the community's proprietary status, but to Thietmar's utter dismay, he took a firm hand with the monastery of Berge, going so far as to depose its abbot and transform the community into a

338 Thietmar 3.1, 11.

339 Thietmar 3.16.

340 Thietmar cites some of the archbishop's less attractive qualities at 3.13–14. It should be noted, however, that Thietmar's views were not universal and other, somewhat later witnesses present a more positive interpretation of Giselher's career (Warner 1994: 164).

341 See above p. 38.

342 See below, p. 56.

343 Thietmar 6.27, 33, 54.

344 Thietmar 6.18.

345 Thietmar 6. 31.

house of canons.[346] Thietmar seems, nonetheless, to have held him in high regard for his piety, concern for the clergy subject to him, and general demeanour.[347] Tagino had an impact on his career as well, having elevated him to the priesthood (1004) and later insisted on his appointment as bishop of Merseburg.[348]

Walthard, Tagino's short-lived successor, had been provost of the cathedral and enjoyed substantial support within the chapter. As provost, he defended Archbishop Giselher before a council that seemed likely to send him back to Merseburg and, following that prelate's death, he had served as the canons' spokesman and leader in their effort to exercise their election privilege.[349] When his own election was suppressed in favour of the king's candidate (Tagino), Walthard was compensated by being allowed to act as the prelate's representative within the diocese.[350] The king had already entrusted him while he was provost with an important diplomatic mission, and he continued to perform such services following his own election as archbishop, a success he owed, in part, to Thietmar's timely intervention.[351] Petitioners sought him out in the apparent belief that he had the monarch's ear.[352] Thietmar's personal relationship with Walthard can be characterized as respectful but distant prior to the latter's elevation to the episcopate, and strained afterwards, presumably due to the archbishop's less than cooperative attitude towards efforts to restore property taken from Merseburg during the period of its suppression.[353] He alludes to rumours regarding Walthard's loyalty to the emperor and suspicions that he may have committed suicide, but praised him nonetheless for his piety, generosity, and concern for his church.[354] Indeed, he reports a vision in which Walthard, Tagino, and Eid of Meißen, each having earned his heavenly reward, granted absolution to a particularly holy recluse.[355]

346 Thietmar 6.20.
347 Thietmar 6.66.
348 Thietmar 6. 38, 46.
349 Thietmar 4.46; 5.40–41.
350 Thietmar 5.44.
351 Thietmar 6.56, 69.
352 Thietmar 6.71.
353 Thietmar 6.72, 79.
354 Thietmar 6.72, 75.
355 Thietmar 7.55.

The years at Magdeburg also saw a number important changes in Thietmar's personal life. In 991, his father, Count Siegfried, had died and the death of his paternal grandmother, Mathilda, followed soon afterwards.[356] The departure of these two influential figures left Thietmar's mother, Cunegunde, in a perilous situation which Margrave Liuthar, her brother-in-law, used to his advantage. As Thietmar noted, Liuthar could legitimately claim a portion of Siegfried's property, but he attempted to deprive Cunegunde of her share as well though his own mother (Mathilda) had committed her to his protection. In what might be viewed as an initial milestone in the decline of Liuthar's lineage, Otto III intervened to secure the widow's rights and thereby prevent the margrave from consolidating more of the Walbecker patrimony under his control. Liuthar had not given up, however. Cunegunde's death was followed by the customary division of her property among various heirs. Along with other properties, Thietmar acquired one half-share in the family's religious foundation at Walbeck.[357] Several years later (1002), when Thietmar wanted to add Liuthar's half-share in the house of canons at Walbeck to the half he had inherited from his mother, the margrave drove a hard bargain which probably involved at least some of what he had failed to acquire earlier.[358] Thietmar was troubled both by the high price he had paid and the subsequent realization that he had committed simony, but neither concern prevented him from assuming control of the foundation after he had compensated its former provost.[359] Another significant personal crisis occurred in 994 when his maternal uncles, Henry and Siegfried, were captured by Vikings who demanded both a large ransom for their release and hostages.[360] Thietmar, summoned directly from the cloister, figured among the latter, having been drafted for that purpose because Siegfried had no sons. With his clerical garb concealed under his secular garments, and seemingly without a trace of resentment, he set out on this dangerous task, but was relieved, at the last minute, when his uncle managed to escape.

The undoubted highpoint of Thietmar's career came with his appointment as bishop of Merseburg. In that capacity, Thietmar had

356 Thietmar 4.17.

357 Thietmar alludes to property held by him at a number of different locations (Thietmar 1.13; 6.39, 42, 47; 8.15).

358 Thietmar 6.44.

359 Following his elevation to the episcopate, Thietmar turned the provostship over to his half-brother, Willigis (Thietmar 6.43, 47).

360 Thietmar 4.24.

many of the same concerns as other prelates, but they acquired a distinctive cast because of the diocese's convoluted history and close association with the Ottonian house. Meditations on the possible involvement of the ancient Romans aside, Thietmar knew that it was chiefly to the Ottonians (or rather, the Liudolfinger) that his bishopric owed its foundation.[361] Henry I had acquired a dominant influence in Merseburg through his first wife, Hatheburg, and Thietmar gave him credit for establishing its first church.[362] Under Otto I, a decision was made to elevate the church to the level of a bishopric, according to Thietmar, in conjunction with the king's victory over the Hungarians at the Lechfeld (955).[363] Given Thietmar's highly partisan approach to matters touching on the history and welfare of his diocese, his interpretation of that event has been and should rightly be viewed with a degree of scepticism. That the Battle of the Lechfeld consti-tuted a decisive moment in the history of the Ottonian dynasty and of the *Reich* as a whole has long been recognized. It was significant for the Hungarians too, in that it marked the end of their 'heroic period' of wandering and raiding, and the beginning of their integration into the political and cultural community of western Europe.[364] Thietmar's account of this event, and especially his assertion that Otto swore to found a bishopric in honour of St Lawrence, Merseburg's patron saint, is not implausible. St Lawrence enjoyed universal veneration in the Latin West and the German church observed his feast with particular solemnity.[365] Furthermore, there is no shortage of precedents for a king promising to establish a church in return for a military victory.[366] Still, other sources provide somewhat different accounts of Otto's great victory. According to Widukind, Otto simply ordered his army to observe a fast on the eve of the battle.[367] Ruotger's biography of Archbishop Brun of Cologne confirms the holding of a fast and adds that Otto also invoked the intercession of St Lawrence.[368] Assuming an inclination to trust Thietmar, there is still no ready explanation for the fact that Otto seemingly fulfilled his oath not by founding a

361 Thietmar 1.2.

362 Thietmar 1.3, 18.

363 Thietmar 2.10.

364 Leyser 1965: 65–67; Bowlus 1995/96: 8.

365 Weinrich 1972: 47–56; Amiet 1976: 37–46.

366 Schaller 1974: 16–17.

367 Widukind 3.44, p. 124.

368 Ruotger, c. 35, p. 36.

bishopric at Merseburg, but rather by initiating plans to establish an archbishopric at Magdeburg.[369] Attempts at resolving the issue, for example, by assuming that the king swore two oaths, have not been entirely convincing.[370]

Whatever the truth of Thietmar's account of Otto's oath at the Lechfeld, the fact is that a diocese of Merseburg was not actually established until 968, in conjunction with the elevation of Magdeburg to the rank of archbishopric. Boso, the first bishop, received his office as a reward for distinguished service in the royal chapel and success as a missionary among the Sorbs.[371] In 981, Otto II decided to suppress the diocese, for reasons that remain subject to debate. A document generated by the synod that empowered the king's decision, cites a number of apparently crucial issues: (1) that the bishop of Halberstadt had not given formal consent to the dismemberment of his diocese and, moreover, that the latter had been diminished to such an extent that it could no longer fulfil its pastoral responsibilities; (2) that disputes between the two prelates had led to bloodshed; and (3) that the suppression of Merseburg would benefit neighbouring dioceses (i.e. Meißen, Zeitz, Halberstadt).[372] Each of the issues cited by the synod, and others, such as Merseburg's diminutive size, have attracted both support and scepticism.[373] According to Thietmar, most of the blame fell on Giselher and his unbridled ambitions, an overly simplistic explanation, perhaps, but one consistent with the dynamics of personal patronage.[374] In any case, the results of this decision are clear. Parts of the diocese located to the left of the river Saale were granted to Halberstadt, those on the right side were to be divided between Zeitz and Meißen. The former cathedral of Merseburg was turned into a proprietary monastery of the archbishops of Magdeburg.[375] Efforts to restore the diocese and reinstall Giselher as bishop were evident as early as 997, but he managed to fend them off till his death in 1004, the knowledge that he would be buried as an archbishop presumably giving him some measure of satisfaction.[376] A few days after the

369 Thietmar 2.11.
370 Hehl 1997: 109–12.
371 Thietmar 2.36.
372 Thietmar 3.14; *UbM*, no. 92.
373 Cf. Holtzmann 1926: 50–53; Claude 1972: 195–98.
374 Reuter 1991: 195–98.
375 Thietmar 3.16.
376 Thietmar 4.10.

prelate's demise, King Henry II came to Merseburg, restored the bishopric,
and bestowed it upon Wigbert (1004–09), a royal chaplain with deep
connections to the area.[377] Thietmar gives Wigbert high marks for his
personal virtue and effectiveness as a pastor, even while noting that
ill-health seriously hindered his performance during his latter years.[378]

Merseburg was the location of a royal residence favoured by Emperor
Henry II and, during that monarch's reign, rivalled Quedlinburg as
the site of royal celebrations of Easter.[379] It seems always to have
provided an appropriate place to hold assemblies, negotiate with
enemies, and preside over judicial proceedings.[380] Thietmar could
scarcely avoid some level of involvement in such matters, if only
because he would have assumed ultimate responsibility for logistics and
other practical issues.[381] He also took part in the military campaigns and
garrison duty that figured among his responsibilities as a frontier
bishop.[382] As with most prelates, pastoral care occupied a major part
of those responsibilities as well. In the diocese of Merseburg, this task
was made all the more difficult by the shaky condition of the population's faith, a challenge even to the formidable skills of Thietmar's
predecessors. Despite linguistic abilities that permitted him to translate basic catechetical texts into Slavic, Bishop Boso had experienced
profound difficulty in appealing to the sceptical and apparently rather
impertinent Slav population of his diocese.[383] Bishop Wigbert seems
to have had more success with his 'enthusiastic preaching', reinforced
by the destruction of pagan holy sites.[384] At best, one can assume that
Thietmar's flock, like many medieval converts, were poised some-
where between adherence and true conversion, but the situation may
not even have been that good.[385] Thietmar complained that his people
rarely came to church, showed little interest in pastoral visits, and
continued to practise pagan rituals which (typically) he described in
some detail.[386] As a suffragan of Magdeburg and former canon,

377 Thietmar 6.36.
378 Thietmar 6.37, 42.
379 Beyreuter 1991: 250.
380 Thietmar 6.54, 59, 81, 83.
381 On the following see Lippelt 1973: 115–18.
382 Leyser 1994e: 38.
383 Thietmar 2.37.
384 Thietmar 6.37.
385 Muldoon 1997a: 3.
386 Thietmar 7.69.

Thietmar also continued to take an interest in and express personal empathy for the cathedral chapter of that diocese. Following the death of Archbishop Tagino, for example, it had been Thietmar who stiffened the brothers' collective spine, so that they held an actual election rather than simply recommending a candidate to the emperor, as the latter had requested.[387] A cousin, Dietrich, who belonged to the chapter, and a brother, Siegfried, monk and abbot at Berge, surely kept him informed of current events and ensured his continued personal interest. Thietmar also had another, more pragmatic reason to concern himself with his colleagues at Magdeburg, for they retained property that Thietmar viewed as rightly belonging to his own diocese. As bishop, Thietmar could not help but see its recovery as one of his most important tasks. To that end, he took advantage of opportune moments, such as elections, to oblige both archbishops and the emperor to support his cause.[388] The archbishops and the other prelates who had benefited from Merseburg's suppression were at best reluctant collaborators, but the monarch, Henry II, was himself by no means unequivocal in his support. An effort to regain property from the bishop of Meißen, for example, went awry when the emperor's anticipated support failed to materialize.[389] Although forced to accept an unattractive compromise, Thietmar declared that he had by no means surrendered the claim. Indeed, it was a task he expected to hand on to his successor.

Finally, it was at Merseburg that Thietmar started working on the text of his *Chronicon.*[390] He may have begun planning the work while still at Magdeburg where, according to later sources, he began keeping a weekly diary. He actually started writing in 1012, and by the summer of 1013 the first three books were essentially finished. At this point, he acquired a copy of the *Quedlinburg Annals* which he used, in conjunction with other sources, to make additions to the first three books. He continued to draw on the *Annals* for the remainder of his text. Books Four and Five appear to have been compiled in the second half of 1013. Book Six may belong to the first half of 1014 with Seven and Eight having been written between that year and 1018. By Book Seven, Thietmar appears to have been writing not long after the events he recorded and by the eighth book he seems to have been exactly contemporaneous. Thietmar's own copy of the

387 Thietmar 6.62.
388 Thietmar 6.62, 67, 81.
389 Thietmar 7.52.
390 The following discussion draws heavily on Holtzmann 1935: xxviii–xxxi.

Chronicon resided in the collection of the state library at Dresden (Msc. Dresden, R 147) until the end of the Second World War, when it was so severely damaged as to be completely unusable. Fortunately, a facsimile edition of the manuscript was published in 1905. A second copy of Thietmar's text is preserved in a late medieval manuscript in the collection of the Royal Library at Brussels (Mss 7503–7518). This copy is actually more of a second edition since it includes interpolations and stylistic improvements generally believed to have been added at the monastery of Corvey though it is possible that Thietmar himself was responsible for at least some of them.[391] Although Thietmar claims to have had few written sources, he drew extensively on Widukind's *Saxon History* in the first three books and seems to have known Gerhard's biography of Bishop Ulrich of Augsburg and Ruotger's life of Archbishop Brun of Cologne.[392] He may also have known the more recent of the two biographies of Queen Mathilda.[393] For Books One to Four, he used the *Quedlinburg Annals*, as noted above. His other sources included the necrologies of Merseburg and Magdeburg, from which he seems to have taken numerous dates, and documents from Merseburg, Magdeburg, and Walbeck. He also had oral sources, including his relatives, Emperor Henry II, Archbishop Tagino, and various friends or aquaintances.[394] His work was appreciated by others too. A few years after Thietmar's death, Bishop Adalbold of Utrecht employed the *Chronicon* as the foundation for his biography of Emperor Henry II, and it was later used by a number of twelfth-century chronicles associated with Magdeburg and its environs.[395]

On this translation

This translation is based on the edition by Robert Holtzmann which, in turn, relies upon the two surviving manuscripts of the *Chronicon* preserved at Dresden (now available only in a facsimile edition) and Brussels. Of these, the former is by the far the most important, as I have already mentioned, since it was produced under Thietmar's personal direction. I have also noted and, occasionally, incorporated

391 Cf. Hoffmann 1993: 151–76.
392 Thietmar 1, prologue; 1.8; 2.23.
393 Thietmar 1.21.
394 Thietmar 5.43; 7.32.
395 Warner 1994: 148.

emendations suggested by Fickermann and other more recent critics of Holtzmann's edition. In spite of the limited number of manuscripts, Thietmar's *Chronicon* is a rather complex text. Aside from Thietmar, the efforts of at least eight other hands have been detected in the Dresden manuscript, presumably scribes taking dictation from or working under the bishop's direction. Moreover, Thietmar went through the text making corrections in his own hand and adding additional material in the margins, between the lines, or on leaves added to the manuscript. The presumed contributions of the various scribes are noted in Holtzmann's apparatus, as are Thietmar's subsequent additions. Since this information is likely to be of interest only to specialists, and is readily available elsewhere, I have not noted it in this text. What has been noted, however, are those instances in which major lacunae in the text have been resolved with material taken from the Brussels manuscript, a solution already employed in the German-language translation published by Trillmich. These lacunae are the result of folia (at least fifteen) destroyed or lost from the Dresden manuscript prior to the sixteenth century. Drawing text from the Brussels manuscript is a less than happy solution because of the interpolations and stylistic changes introduced by the scribes at Corvey where the codex presumably originated. In the absence of any viable alternative to an empty space, however, I have followed Trillmich's lead and indicated that a given passage derives from the Corvey version by placing it in italics.

Aside from problems derived from the state of the manuscripts, Thietmar's text presents a typical array of difficulties for the translator. Thietmar's Latin has rightly been described as 'wilful, crotchety and jarring'; I have attempted to retain some semblance of those qualities while still producing a translation that is both accurate and readable.[396] Personal and place names have been standardized and given in their modern German form or an anglophone equivalent where such exists. Exceptions have been made when a modern English or German name seemed out of place in a medieval context. Thus Emperor Heinrich II and Bishop Thiedric of Metz are referred to as Henry and Dietrich, respectively, while the fourth archbishop of Magdeburg remains Walthard, rather than Walter. Following a common medieval practice, Thietmar calls the Hungarians, relatively new arrivals in the Carpathian Basin, by the name of their predecessors, the Avars.[397] Here they are given their correct modern name (i.e. Hungarians). I have also tried to

396 Leyser 1979: 40.
397 Bowlus 1995/96: 6.

observe contemporary political geography. Hence the reader will encounter Strasbourg rather than Strassburg, and Gniezno rather than Gnesen, but Aachen rather than Aix-la-Chapelle. As with other early medieval authors, Thietmar faced the challenge of trying to describe the institutions and practices of his own day with a language (Latin) developed in the far different circumstances of classical and late Antiquity.[398] At times, this language was clearly inadequate. So, for example, Thietmar uses the terms *urbs* or *civitas* to describe everything from a bustling commercial or ecclesiastical centre to a fortress occupied by nothing more than a temporary garrison. Except where a locale can clearly be identified as an urban settlement (e.g. Magdeburg), I have employed the relatively neutral term 'burg'. For the Latin *amicus* I have employed such terms as 'ally' or 'supporter', in order better to capture the rich variety of interpersonal relationships barely hinted at by the term 'friend'. A somewhat different problem is posed by Thietmar's use of social terminology. Following the lead of Timothy Reuter, whose translation of the *Annals of Fulda* appears in this same series, I have tried to avoid the feudal vocabulary of the High Middle Ages and favoured neutral terminology wherever possible. Hence, *principes* or *primates* have been translated as 'leading men' rather than 'princes' or 'nobles'. A similar strategy has been followed in regard to *miles* (or *milites*). Although generally employed for vassals, eleventh-century usage could also endow these terms with a variety of less restrictive, non-feudal meanings.[399] Given the uncertainty, it has seemed advisable to leave them untranslated.

To supply annotations for a text as important and dense as Thietmar's *Chronicon* is a surprisingly difficult task. There is no lack of material to comment on. Rather, one must decide when and where to stop. The present annotations reflect my interests and background as an historian. My chief goals have been to help the reader by explaining potentially confusing or misleading passages, and to note where Thietmar's text is relevant to some larger issue in Ottonian historiography. Thietmar's allusions to classical authors and to the Bible are cited in the footnotes, but since the relevant texts are available in standard editions, they have not been included in the bibliography. In any case, the reader will generally have to compare the texts in Latin before Thietmar's borrowings are apparent. Medieval and patristic texts are cited in the footnotes and also in the bibliography.

398 In general, Stach 1952
399 Johrendt 1976: 427–29.

THE *CHRONICON* OF
THIETMAR OF MERSEBURG

BOOK ONE

Here begins the prologue to the deeds of the Saxons of the venerable lord,
Bishop Thietmar of Merseburg

Siegfried, rightly joined by the love of sweet fraternity and dear to me,
I, Thietmar, now humbly ask that you gaze benignly on my writings,
adding what may please and removing whatever may be superfluous.[1]
They do not glitter with any ornament of rhetoric, but merely relate,
  plainly and in order,
the lives and mores of the pious kings of Saxony,
In their times, our land rose up, as the towering cedar,[2]
and inspired fear far and wide.
My writings also speak of the establishment and destruction of our church,
of those happy years in which it was repaired,
and at the same time, of all of its pastors.
If anything in this book is wrong or omitted,
do not blame me, but rather the paucity of the sources.
Accept mistakes born of ignorance, my dear,
knowing that I should never have begun to write anything,
if not for what I have already told you above. Therefore, kindly
pour forth prayers with me from a sorrowful heart:
Christ, glory of kings and moderator of governments,
Grant to your kingdom and those subject to it,
that the glory of praise may be to you and not to us,[3]
and that your flock may never fall under foreign rule.
O you Christians, pray now with the voice of your hearts.
May the majesty of the Lord mercifully grant
that evil not bind and distress us, as we much deserve.

1 Thietmar addresses his younger brother who was abbot of the monastery of St
John the Baptist (1009–22) and subsequently, bishop of Münster (1022–32).

2 *Regnum*, a term with multiple meanings in early medieval Latin (Goez 1987: 139–
61) has been translated, somewhat vaguely, as land rather than kingdom because it
is unclear from the context whether Thietmar refers to the duchy of Saxony or the
Reich as a whole.

3 Ps. 113: 9 (RSV 115: 1).

Certain things to come, which a prescient voice predicted in our times,
having been revealed to a great and unfortunate extent,
will be revealed more completely.
You who must care for my throne,
read this weak writing carefully, with love.
However summarily, it reveals much that you will want to know.
What now is dispersed here and there, collect gradually.
Strive not for the gifts of servile fame but rather for eternal life
and be vigilant that you may deserve it.
Think also on me, I say, guilty of many sins and inferior to any of my
*   predecessors.*
I commit myself to you and request your intercession.
Thietmar's chronicle requires affection, dear reader,
and with constant use it will banish sorrowful thoughts.
Place it above games and other vain things:
May you be found praising the just and praying for sinners.

Here ends the prologue.

Here begins the first book, concerning Henry the first emperor.[4]

CHAPTER ONE

It is the intention of anyone who ties himself to some useful work to profit
himself in the present and future, and also, as opportunity and skill permit,
not only to propagate the matters committed to him, but also to preserve their
memory for ever. For this reason, though unworthy of the dignity and even
the name of bishop, I, Thietmar, am eager to reveal the history of the city of
Merseburg, once famous far and wide but now shrouded in the gloom of
oblivion. I fear that my ignorance will produce smoke from brilliance and,
like the lowest workman, I may succumb to failure from the character of the
work.[5] *But fortified with good intentions, and as St Gregory says, with*
Christ inspiring me, I will begin and humbly commit to his unknowable
clemency both the conclusion of this writing and the entire fate of the city of
Merseburg.[6]

4 See note at 1.15.

5 Horace, *Ars Poetica* 143.34.

6 Greg., *Hom. Ez.* 1.1, p. 5.

CHAPTER TWO

Dear reader, know that the initial foundation and building up of the city and its territory were undertaken by the people of Romulus who were formerly led here by Julius Caesar, the all powerful son-in-law of Pompey who was illustrious in both capabilities.[7] *Because they were then proficient in military matters and always triumphant, they followed the ancient custom of naming it after Mars. Later, it was called 'Mese' which means 'middle of the region' or perhaps refers to a certain young girl.*[8] *Neither from the memory of ancient sages nor in books have I been able to uncover the identity and character of its princes, either before the Incarnation of Christ or afterwards. Hence, I will omit them rather than appear a liar.*

CHAPTER THREE

Merseburg had its beginning with Henry who unified the city's holdings, legally belonging to many at the time, and greatly added to them through his virtue and industry.[9] Born of the noble lineage of Otto and Hadwig, he grew from boyhood like a tree in secret.[10] Like a flower in early spring, moreover, he gradually revealed himself to be a warrior of good character. His father sent him with a large army to that province which we Germans call Daleminzia but the Slavs call Lommatzsch.[11] After much destruction and burning, he returned

7 Illustrious both in body and mind. Julius Caesar was actually the father-in-law of Pompey as the latter had married his daughter Julia. Thietmar's assertion that Merseburg owed its foundation to the Romans is a bald-faced lie probably intended to give his see a history comparable to those of the much older dioceses of the Rhineland (Lippelt 1973: 142).

8 According to Holtzmann (1935: 4, n. 7), the name has its roots in Old Sorbian.

9 The future King Henry I (919–36). At least one of the 'owners' was the Count Erwin whose daughter became Henry's first wife (1.5).

10 Horace, *Odes* bk 1, ode 12, verse 45. Thietmar refers to Henry's parents, Duke Otto 'the Illustrious' of Saxony (d. 912) and his wife, Hadwig (or Hathui, d. 903). The anniversary of Hadwig's death is noted in the necrology at Merseburg (*NMer.*, 24 December, fo. 84, p. 17). The glowing account of Henry's youth and his campaign against the Daleminzi is based on Widukind (1.17, p. 27), but the observations regarding Slavic religious practices are Thietmar's own.

11 Here, as throughout the translation, I have chosen to supply the appropriate modern place name rather than use the archaic form employed by Thietmar (i.e. Glomaci). Widukind (1.17, p. 29) notes that the defeated Daleminzi subsequently called on the Hungarians for aid. As the first known raid by the Hungarians occurred in 906, it has been assumed that Henry's campaign occurred in the same year (BO 1b). As king, Henry continued and even intensified his aggressive posture towards the Slavs and, by 929, had sufficiently dominated them that they could be forced to pay tribute (Brüske 1955: 16–19).

victorious. But I should now relate how that region acquired its name. Lommatzsch is a spring located not more than two miles from the Elbe. It is the source of a pool which often produces marvels, so the local populace claims, and many others have verified this with their own eyes, If a good peace is to be expected, and the earth does not falsely promise its fruits, it is covered with wheat, oats, and acorns. This brings joy to the hearts of the populace which frequently gathers there. When the savage storms of war threaten, it gives a clear indication of the outcome with blood and ash. The entire population venerates and fears this pool more than the churches, albeit with dubious expectations, and this region, which extends from the Elbe up to the Chemnitz, derives its name from it.[12]

CHAPTER FOUR

While returning from an expedition against the Bohemians, Bishop Arn of Würzburg set up his tent near this river, in the region of Schkeuditz, on a hill by the road leading to the north.[13] As he chanted the mass, he was surrounded by a hostile army. After all his companions had been martyred, he too was offered to God, along with the host which had been consecrated to the sacrifice of praise. This occurred in the year 892 of the Incarnation and in the times of Emperor Arnulf.[14] Nowadays, burning lights are often seen there and not even the Slavs doubt that these are the holy martyrs of God. During his period of office, the aforementioned priest built a temple to God in the city of Würzburg and, in ten years, built nine churches on the same model within his bishopric.[15] When he consecrated the greatest of these, relics of Christ's martyr Kilian were carried around

12 Holtzmann (1935: 7, n. 6) maintains that Thietmar has confused the Chemnitz with the Zschopau.
13 Bishop Arn of Würzburg (855–92). A former cathedral canon at Würzburg, Arn was installed as bishop of that see by King Louis the German and subsequently played an active role in the governance of church and realm. As this chapter suggests, he was not averse to involvement in military matters (*NDB*, vol. 1, p. 356; Arnold 1997: 34). In its combination of spiritual and political tasks, Arn's career corresponded with a recurring model in the chronicle and he also figured in the so-called Babenberger feud referred to at 1.7. Either association might explain why Thietmar included this incident.
14 Emperor Arnulf *of Carinthia* (887–99).
15 Here, Thietmar refers to the new cathedral, dedicated to St Killian, that replaced an earlier structure damaged by fire (Oswald 1966: 382).

it. Kilian was an Irishman who, after coming here, at first preached the word of Christ to Duke Gozbert, his wife Geilan, and their countrymen.[16] Then, at the prompting of a second Herod, he was martyred with his companions Coloman and Totman. Through him the Lord has worked seventy miracles. When the master of the cooks learned of this, he exhorted his assistants, saying: 'Do not delay, but rather perform your allotted tasks diligently and without delay, just as our lord Kilian himself is now performing miracles without any delay.' Although I cannot describe the extent of Bishop Arn's virtues with a pen, I believe in my heart that he enjoys great merit with God.

CHAPTER FIVE

Meanwhile, Henry had learned of a certain woman called Hatheburg and, burning with youthful love, desired to unite with her in marriage. She was the daughter of lord Erwin who held the largest part of the previously mentioned city, which we call the old city.[17] When he died, he left this to his two daughters, as he had no son. Though Henry knew that Hatheburg was widowed and had taken the veil, her beauty and the usefulness of her inherited wealth inspired him to send representatives with an offer of marriage, so that he could accomplish what he desired. After being convinced by the entreaties and advice of many, she agreed. Thereafter, she was honourably received and treated with affection by Henry, as was proper. After the marriage had been performed, according to custom, the husband came with his wife to Merseburg and convened all of their neighbours. As he was an ambitious man, moreover, he treated them with such familiarity that they loved him as a friend and honoured him as a lord.[18]

16 St Kilian d. *c*.689; feast day 8 July.

17 The so-called *Altenburg*, the original fortified settlement, located to the north of the cathedral and possibly including a monastic foundation (Herzog 1964: 47). Whether or not Erwin (d. before 909) was really a count is unclear, as are the names of Hatheburg's first husband and her sister. As Thietmar's practical assessment of the bride's attractiveness indicates ('her beauty and the usefulness of her inherited wealth'), Henry's pursuit of Hatheburg represented a typical example of medieval matrimonial politics (Fichtenau 1991: 90–94). See also p. 29.

18 Here, I follow Fickermann's suggestion (1957: 55) in retaining the adjective 'industris', as in the original text, rather than correcting it to 'illustris'. The decision to translate this as 'ambitious' (rather than industrious or energetic) is mine, and reflects what I perceive as the gist of Thietmar's comments.

CHAPTER SIX

At that time, Conrad, formerly duke of the Franks, held the throne as successor to Louis the Child.[19] All the leading men of the realm had initially elected Otto but he, as if unworthy of this, had instead supported Conrad's candidacy and commended himself and his sons to his faith and power.[20] The spiritual father and pastor of the East was Sigismund, bishop of the church of Halberstadt, an ingenious man who exceeded all his contemporaries in his multifaceted knowledge of matters both spiritual and mundane.[21] As soon as he heard of the outrage perpetrated through this marriage, this man, fervent with the greatest piety and with that zeal of Christ which is the pinnacle of perfection, groaned at the guilt of his sheep. By messenger and letter, and by the ban of his apostolic authority, he forbade the couple to engage in further sexual relations. Then, he summoned the two to a synod. Disturbed by such talk, Henry approached the emperor, explained the situation to him, and asked for his help. In this he succeeded because he was close to him and because of the faithful service rendered by his father. A representative was quickly sent to the bishop to request the release of those who had been bound and to indicate the emperor's desire to have the issue deferred until he could be present.

CHAPTER SEVEN

After Otto went the way of all flesh, on 30 November, he was succeeded by the often-mentioned young man who received his inheritance by right and the greatest part of his benefices by free grant of the king. He and his supporters still resented what was lacking, however. Hence, like a weed in the wheat, the plant of secret hatred grew from that resentment.[22] The king considered this carefully but pretended ignorance. Because he did not dare to use force against Henry, he tried to trick him through the famous cunning of

19 King Louis 'the Child' (900–11); King Conrad I (911–19).

20 '... the entire folk of the Franks and the Saxons sought to impose the crown of the realm upon Otto. He refused the burden of rulership, however, because of his advanced age. On his recommendation, Conrad, the former Duke of the Franconians, was anointed king. Still, at all times and places, Otto was treated as though he possessed the highest power' (Widukind 1.16, pp. 26–27).

21 Bishop Sigismund of Halberstadt (894–924).

22 Matt. 13: 24–30.

Archbishop Hatto, just as his predecessor had defeated that Count Adalbert who was decapitated at Theres.[23] The wisdom of God confounded this plot, however. For the artisan who, at the bishop's order, was skilfully making the gold torque in which Henry was supposed to be killed, learned of the plot from the disturbing conversation of his lord. Hence, when the work was completed to standard and presented, he secretly escaped, met with the duke, and told him everything. As he was returning home, Henry sent a representative to inform the bishop that he had been found out and should quickly see to his own safety. He then appropriated whatever pertained to the bishopric in Saxony or Thuringia, even as he plundered and expelled all the king's supporters from these lands. The archbishop died soon afterwards, rather suddenly, and the good fortune with which the king had previously been blessed quickly shifted to Henry. It would be tedious for me to relate how many times each was victorious in battle or defeated and how, at last, the initiative of good men brought about a reconciliation. So, I will move on to more pressing matters.

CHAPTER EIGHT

Meanwhile, Conrad had long been restrained by illness. Because only evil men remember the anger of a past hatred,[24] he forgot all the hostility that Henry had directed at him and gave the following advice to his brother Eberhard and an assembly of the leading men:

---

23 Archbishop Hatto I of Mainz (891–913). Hatto, scion of a Swabian noble house, figured prominently among the supporters of Emperor Arnulf and Louis 'the Child'. His support for the election of Conrad I, and for the latter's struggle with the Saxon duke, reflects the archbishopric's general policy of maintaining good relations with the Conradine house (*LMA*, vol. 4, pp. 1957–58) . Count Adalbert (d. 906) belonged to the house of the Babenberger/Popponen, whose possessions included the eponymous Babenburg, located on the site of the present cathedral of Bamberg (*NDB*, vol. 1, p. 42; Arnold 1997: 35). Adalbert's 'defeat', to which Thietmar merely alludes, occurred within the context of a deadly feud between the Babenberger and the Conradines, their rivals for control of the duchy of Franconia (Reuter 1991: 131–32). In brief, Hatto promised Adalbert safe passage to the court of Louis 'the Child' (viz., that the count would return to his residence unharmed). The archbishop got round this by tricking Adalbert into briefly returning to his castle for a meal (thereby fulfilling the promise!), and setting out again after they had eaten. Adalbert was subsequently put to death. Hatto's treacherous character and deeds were widely reported in contemporary sources (see esp. Widukind 1. 21–22, pp. 31–35; Althoff 1994: 440–42). The attempt on Henry's life reflects King Conrad I's generally confrontational relations with the German dukes (Reuter 1991: 135–36).

24 Cato, *Disticha*, 2.15, p. 117.

when the time came for him to pay his debt to their common nature, they should elect Henry to the government of the realm, as he was most suitable to the task. They should also commend Conrad's soul and the multitude of his surviving blood relations and dependants to Henry's protection. And, they should give their consent to this without delay. They received the king's last request with great sorrow and promised to implement it if life permitted. Soon afterwards, alas, they were also present at his death, in the eighth year after his consecration, on 19 October. After the funeral obsequies had been completed at Weilburg, they hurriedly assembled at Fritzlar where, before Christ and the witness of the entire church, they crowned Henry and tearfully commended to him what he was due as their lord and king.[25] As was proper, he humbly accepted the gift of divine grace and only then acknowledged the general outpouring of affection, giving thanks to God and promising that he would agree to these and all other demands which they put forward in common. He neither desired nor wished to receive the unction of an episcopal blessing, a custom of his predecessors which was offered by Archbishop Heriger [of Mainz], but rather affirmed that he was thoroughly unworthy of this.[26] But in truth I fear that he sinned by doing this. In the biography of the holy father Ulrich, whom the king later promoted to the priestly order, one can read that the holy martyr of Christ, St Afra,[27] showed many things to her beloved bishop in a vision. Among these things were two swords, one with a hilt, the other without. The second sword represented King Henry who lacked a consecration.[28] But, leaving this to the secret judgement of God, I will go on.

25 Other sources for this much-noted event are listed in BO 1p.

26 Archbishop Heriger of Mainz (913–27). Although Heriger, following his predecessor, Archbishop Hatto's lead, had strongly supported Conrad I and the Conradines, he apparently had no trouble making his peace with the new king and subsequently served as his archchancellor (*LMA*, vol. 4, pp. 2156–57). Thietmar's source, Widukind of Corvey (1.25–27, pp. 38–39), describes Henry I's designation, election, and investiture in greater detail. Thietmar comments on this situation at 1.26.

27 *Circa* 304; feast day 7 August.

28 Bishop Ulrich of Augsburg (923–73). Ulrich is commonly identified as the first saint to be solemnly canonized by a pope and, moreover, was the object of widespread veneration (Pötzl 1973: 82–115; cf. Wolf 1994: 85–104). Thietmar refers to him as a 'jewel among the clergy' (3.8). The specific passage referred to here (Gerhard, c. 3, pp. 388–89) is actually more pointed than Thietmar lets on. St Afra leads Ulrich to the Lechfeld where the Apostle Peter presides over a synod attended by a multitude of bishops and saints. As the meeting proceeds, many complaints are raised in regard to Duke Arnulf of Bavaria (907–37) who is in the

CHAPTER NINE

The fame of the new king spread everywhere, bringing joy to the hearts of supporters while saddening those of opponents. Indeed, both recognized him as a man who knew how to treat his supporters wisely and to conquer his enemies by cunning and with force. In the meantime, Tammo was born.[29] But the king's love for his wife was waning because he secretly burned for the beauty and wealth of a certain maiden by the name of Mathilda. By and by the fervour of his inner soul burst out and, after declaring that he had hitherto sinned greatly through an illegal marriage, he had relatives and his representatives ask the daughter of Dietrich and Reinhild, a descendant of the lineage of King Widukind, if she would agree to his desire.[30] Because the mind of a woman is flexible and she knew him to be judicious in all things, she consented and, as his wife, was useful to him in both divine and

---

habit of bestowing churches and monasteries upon laymen. Here, already, we encounter the beginnings of a process which, by the twelfth century, would transform Henry from a 'glorious duke' into a 'tyrant' (cf. 1.26; and Geary 1994: 155). At one point, St Peter shows Ulrich the two swords and admonishes him to 'tell King Henry that the one sword signifies a king who possesses his kingdom without the pontifical blessing [i.e. of a bishop], the other, with the hilt, the king who governs with God's blessing'. Though it was a growing trend, anointment was not an absolute prerequisite for kingship (Henry obviously got by without it). Indeed, it has been argued that the term *capulus*, in *Gerhard's text*, should be translated as pommel rather than hilt in that a sword which lacked the former was not altogether useless but less than fully effective (Giese 1993: 160). For later generations of Ottonian clergy, exposed to the full force of the Ottonian ruler cult, the absence of an ecclesiastical sacring would have seemed inexplicable. In fact, Henry probably wished, among other things, to signal his willingness to cooperate with the German dukes rather than follow his predecessor's (i.e. King Conrad I's) example in attempting to dominate them (Reuter 1991: 140; cf. Arnold 1997: 136). Although the message may have been intended chiefly for Henry's rival for the throne, Arnulf of Bavaria, Thietmar knew that Conrad had attempted to intervene in Saxony as well, withholding part of what Henry viewed as his inheritance and even conspiring to have him killed (Thietmar 1.7). In the biography of Ulrich, St Afra also predicts King Otto I's victory over the Hungarians (955) which took place on the Lechfeld and plays an important role in Thietmar's historical scheme (2.10).

29 Thankmar/Tammo (d. 938), the son of Henry I and Hatheburg.

30 Mathilda (c.896–968). In his more detailed description of Mathilda's background Widukind observes: 'The queen herself was the daughter of Dietrich whose brothers were Widukind, Immed, and Reginbern. This Reginbern was the one who fought against the Danes who had been ravaging Saxony for a long time. He conquered them, freeing the homeland from their attacks up to the present day. Furthermore, they [Mathilda and her brothers] were of the line of the great duke, Widukind, who had vigorously waged war against the great Charles for almost thirty years' (Widukind 1.32, p. 44).

human matters. She bore him three sons in suitable time: Otto, Henry, and Brun. She raised them successfully, thereby conquering the pain of birth with the sweetness of such a great lineage.

CHAPTER TEN

As I will be speaking of Otto, I think it unnecessary to discuss each of his father's accomplishments. The extent of King Henry's dignity can be perceived in his son and, in any case, the brilliance of his life shines sufficiently in the writings of many others.[31] But I will add certain things which I find particularly noteworthy. He made the following regions pay tribute: Bohemia, Daleminzia, and the lands of the Abodrites, Wilzi, Hevelli, and Redarii. They immediately rebelled and, inciting others to join them, attacked, destroyed, and burned the burg Walsleben. To avenge this, our army convened and besieged the burg Lenzen.[32] Meanwhile, they beat back and utterly defeated a counter-attack by the burg's defenders, allowing only a few to escape. The burg was also taken. Among our people, two of my great-grand-fathers, both named Liuthar, fell with many others on 5 September.[33] They were distinguished men, the best of warriors, of illustrious lineage, and the honour and solace of the homeland.[34]

CHAPTER ELEVEN

That no one faithful to Christ may doubt the future resurrection of the dead, but rather proceed to the joy of blessed immortality, zealously, and through holy desire, I will intimate certain things which are believed to have occurred at Walsleben, the burg having been rebuilt after its destruction. In the darkness of early morning, the priest of the church there was accustomed to sing matins. When he came to the cemetery, however, he saw a great multitude bringing offerings to a priest who was standing before the doors of the church. At first, he stood stock still. But after fortifying himself with the sign

---

31 Presumably a reference to Widukind whose chronicle (Widukind 1.36, pp. 51–53) forms the basis for this chapter.

32 A Slavic burg located approximately fifty km north-west of Havelberg, at a strategic crossing over the river Elbe. The Saxons occupied it in 929, and in 948 it was assigned to the bishops of Havelberg. After the Slavic uprising of 983, it was occupied by the Abodrites (*LMA*, vol. 5, p. 1875).

33 *NMer.*, fo. 5r, p. 11.

34 Virgil, *Aeneid* 10. 858–59.

of the cross, he passed through all of them and approached the oratory, trembling, and without acknowledging even one. A woman, recently departed from this world and well known to him, asked what he wanted. After being informed why he had come, she replied that they had already taken care of all these things but also that he would not live much longer. He later reported this to his neighbours, and it proved to be true.

CHAPTER TWELVE

In my time in Magdeburg – I was living there continuously, so I have this from reliable witnesses – guards who were keeping watch in the church of the merchants by night, seeing and hearing things similar to what I have just described, brought the best citizens here to observe.[35] These citizens, while they were standing far from the cemetery, saw candles burning in candleholders and heard two men singing the invitatory and all of the morning praises in order.[36] Coming closer, they perceived nothing at all. On the next day, I recounted this event to my niece Brigida who exercised pastoral care over the monastery of St Lawrence and was then suffering an infirmity of the body.[37] She was not at all astonished and I immediately received the following response from her: 'Bishop Baldric who occupied the see of Utrecht for more than eighty years renewed and consecrated a church in Deventer which had been destroyed by old age.[38] He then commended it to one of his priests. One day, at dawn, as the priest was proceeding there, he saw dead people making offerings in the cemetery and

35 Thietmar resided in Magdeburg from 987 to 1002 (4.16; 6.44). The 'market church' in Magdeburg was consecrated to the Apostle John.

36 Ps. 94 (RSV 95), i.e. the 'invitatory'.

37 It is now generally agreed that this convent was located in Magdeburg (rather than Calbe on the Saale). Claude (1975: 317–20) argues that it must have been established by 975 and that it had ceased to exist by 1017/1018. Thietmar seems to refer to the community again at 4.64.

38 Bishop Baldric of Utrecht (918–75). Baldric presided over his diocese for close to sixty years and numbered among the Ottonian monarchy's more reliable supporters in that region. Indeed, Henry I entrusted him with the education of his youngest son, Brun, the later archbishop of Cologne (Ruotger, c. 4, p. 5; *NDB*, vol. 2, p. 550). Deventer, a commercial centre and port on the river Ijssel, was especially prosperous at the end of the tenth century (*LMA*, vol. 3, pp. 919–22). In 952, Otto I had granted his property there to the monastery of St Maurice at Magdeburg, a fact which may have heightened Thietmar's interest in this, for him, rather distant locale (D O I 159; 30 December 952).

church, and heard them singing. As soon as he reported this to the
bishop, he was ordered by him to sleep in the church. But on the
following night, both he and the bed he was resting on were thrown
out by the dead. Terrified by this, he again complained to the bishop.
But after being blessed with the relics of saints and sprinkled with
holy water, he was still ordered to continue guarding his church.
Following his lord's order, he again tried to sleep in the church but
the stimulus of fear kept him awake. And behold, coming at the
accustomed hour, the dead lifted him up, placed him before the altar,
and burned his body to fine ash. Hearing this, the bishop was moved
to penance and ordered a three-day fast that he might aid both himself
and the souls of the departed. I could relate much concerning
these matters, my son, if my infirmity did not prevent me. As the day
to the living, so the night is conceded to the dead.' As St Paul warns,
it is not proper for a mortal to know more than is conducive to
sobriety.[39]

CHAPTER THIRTEEN

Because the testimony of two or three suffices,[40] moreover, I have
written these things which happened in our most recent times so that
the incredulous may learn that the words of the prophets are true.
One of the latter testifies as follows: Lord, your dead will live!
Another states: the dead in their graves will rise, hear the voice of the
Lord and rejoice.[41] Whenever the living hear of or see this, it foretells
a change, as an appropriate example very much indicates. Concerning
this incident, I know a good part personally, but for the greater part,
of which I am ignorant, I will trust in reliable witnesses. When I was
at my estate, Rottmersleben, on Friday, 18 December, a great light
streamed from the church at the first cock-crow, filling the whole
cemetery, and a loud grunting was heard. My brother Frederick
observed this along with my retinue and others who gathered there
and the chaplain who was sleeping next to me heard it. The next
morning, when I learned of this and asked if such a thing had ever
happened there before, certain old people recalled that something
similar had once occurred. And sadly, I saw this event fulfilled, and in
the very same year, with the death of that illustrious lady Liudgard.

39 Rom. 12: 3.
40 Deut. 19: 15; Matt. 18: 16.
41 Isa. 26: 19; John. 5: 28.

On the one side, Liudgard was my niece, and on the other, my cousin's wife. As is most important among friends, moreover, she was also close to me.[42] I will speak in greater detail about her later.[43] It often happened that in the night I would hear wood falling and once, while everyone else was asleep, my companion and I clearly heard the dead conversing. From these two signs I concluded that a death would occur on the following day.

CHAPTER FOURTEEN

Though I may act as the whetstone which sharpens the iron but not itself, I would not be marked by the shame of a mute dog.[44] Thus I direct the following to the ignorant and especially to the Slavs who believe that everything ends with temporal death, firmly indicating to all the faithful the certainty of future resurrection and of reward according to merit. There are three types of souls which begin and end in different ways.[45] The first is that of the incorporeal angels which is without beginning or end. The second is of men which begins with their birth but does not share in their death. It is immortal and, as certain heathens think, does not have the same task in the future as it has now. The third type of soul is of livestock and fowl which begins and ends together with the body. Hence, just as it is taught in the law given by the Lord to Moses, true Christians are forbidden by canonical authority to pollute themselves with their blood.[46] There are many poor people who are accustomed to eat this without being conscious of any sin and are resistant to all who suggest otherwise. Therefore you, O man, crowned with glory and great honour by God and placed by him over all of his works, above all give thanks to the most high, repaying what he did for you in his compassion to the best of your ability. And now, I will return to the theme from which I have long digressed.

---

42 As the daughter of Swanhild, sister-in-law of his aunt Hildegard, daughter of Henry of Stade by his second marriage, Liudgard (d. 13 November 1012) was Thietmar's niece. She was also the wife of Margrave Werner, the son of Thietmar's uncle Liuthar.

43 Thietmar 4.39–42; 6.84–86.

44 Horace, *Ars. Poet.* 304–5.

45 Greg., *Dial.* 4.3, p. 231.

46 Lev. 6: 26; 17: 13.

CHAPTER FIFTEEN

The king repeatedly expelled the invading Hungarians.[47] But one day, when the king tried to attack them with insufficient forces, he was defeated and fled to a burg called Püchen. Because he had escaped the danger of death there, he honoured the occupants with glory greater than they had hitherto held and their neighbours hold today, and bestowed upon them worthy gifts. Throughout his life, as often as he raised himself up in pride against God and his Lord, with his power humbled, he would submit to a worthy penance. I have heard that when he went to Rome for the sake of prayer, he travelled more on foot than by horse. When many asked why he did this, he revealed his guilt.[48] In the year 931 of the Incarnation he was made emperor.[49]

CHAPTER SIXTEEN

He established a settlement on a then densely forested mountain next to the Elbe and built a burg there which he called Meißen from a certain brook which flowed from it in a northerly direction [928/929].[50] As is the custom today, he strengthened it with a garrison and

47 The Hungarians appeared in the Carpathian Basin in the second half of the ninth century and subsequently launched innumerable raids on the Empire as well as other territories in the West. Far from unsophisticated when it came to matters of strategy, and well informed regarding local conditions, the Hungarian leadership launched their raids at times and in places that appeared to favour their success (Bowlus 1995/96: 6–8). Indeed, contrary to Thietmar's report, the Hungarians were quite successful during most of Henry's reign, and it was only in 933 (at the Battle of Riade) that the king clearly demonstrated his ability to expel them (Widukind 1.38, p. 56–57).

48 Widukind gives a rather more prosaic version of this controversial report: 'Having subjugated all the peoples of the surrounding areas, he [King Henry] then decided to go to Rome, but abandoned the journey when he was beset by illness' (Widukind 1.39, p. 59). What precisely Henry (and Widukind!) had in mind is difficult to say. The passage may allude to a nascent Italian 'policy', similar to that subsequently undertaken by Otto I, but a pilgrimage would be just as likely and more in tune with contemporary piety, especially if Henry already sensed that his life was coming to an end (Beumann 1991: 50–51; Reuter 1991: 146–47; Wolf 1992: 37). Thietmar's reading of the passage would tend to support the second interpretation although he clearly is wrong in asserting that Henry actually went to Rome.

49 Although Henry I was never crowned emperor, Thietmar could read, in Widukind's chronicle (1.39, p. 58), that the army had greeted the king as 'father of the fatherland, powerful lord, and emperor', following his victory over the Hungarians at Riade (in 931).

50 The Meisabach. Seat of both a margrave and a bishop by 968, Meißen figured among a chain of burgs that formed the chief support of German rulership in the east (LMA, vol. 6, pp. 475–80).

certain other measures. From here, he compelled the Milzeni, already subject to his will, to pay tribute. Furthermore, after long besieging the burg Lebusa, of which I will speak more extensively later, he forced the residents to flee to a small inner fortress and then to surrender. From that day, on which he justly destroyed it by fire, to the present, the burg has been uninhabited.[51] If, as many say, Henry enriched himself unjustly during his reign, may merciful God forgive him.[52]

CHAPTER SEVENTEEN

He also made the Northmen and Danes submissive through force of arms. After they had been recalled from their ancient error, along with Cnut, their king, he taught them to bear the yoke of Christ.[53] Because I have heard marvellous things about their ancient sacrifices, I will not allow these to pass by unmentioned.[54] In those parts, the centre of the kingdom is a place called Leire, in the region of Seeland. Every nine years, in the month of January, after the day on which we celebrate the appearance of the Lord [6 January], they all convene here and offer their gods a burnt offering of ninety-nine human beings and as many horses, along with dogs and cocks – the latter being used in place of hawks. As I have said, they were convinced that these would do service for them with those who dwell beneath the earth and ensure their forgiveness for any misdeeds. Our king did well when he forbade them to practise such an execrable rite. The only sacrifice acceptable to God the Father is that which refrains from spilling human blood. Indeed, the Lord declared: you should not kill the innocent and pious.[55]

CHAPTER EIGHTEEN

The previously mentioned king improved the work of the ancient Romans in Merseburg with a stone wall inside of which he had the church, now the mother of others, constructed out of stone and

---

51 Rebuilt by King Henry II in 1012 (see 6.59).

52 Lippelt (1973: 148) suggests that Thietmar may be reflecting the complaints of the clergy in this passage, namely that Henry had used church property to pay tribute to the Hungarians.

53 Cf. Widukind 1.41, p. 59.

54 Cf. Adam 4.27, pp. 259; Tschan (trans.) 1959: 208.

55 Exod. 23: 7.

dedicated on 19 May.⁵⁶ With a devout spirit, he also built other burgs for the protection of the kingdom and, for his own salvation, temples to God. After innumerable signs of virtue, with the course of his life completed, in the sixteenth year of his reign and the sixtieth of his life, he died on 2 July at Memleben.⁵⁷ Rightly mourned by all the leading men, he was buried at Quedlinburg which he himself had constructed from the ground up.⁵⁸

CHAPTER NINETEEN

Henry's death and burial occurred in the year of the Lord 936. Meanwhile, the excellent character of his remaining posterity brought joy to the sorrowful hearts of the princes and made them certain of an election, according to their will. Woe to a people for whom there is no hope of rule through the succession of their lords' offspring and to whom, with dissension and long conflict engendered among them, neither advice nor solace is quickly offered. If someone worthy of such an office should not be found within the royal lineage, with all hatred put away, a suitable candidate should be accepted from a different one because rule by foreigners is the greatest punishment. From thence come oppression and great danger to liberty. Beginning with this Henry and continuing with his successors, down to the present day, the Saxons have been raised up and honoured in every way. Whatever is praiseworthy among these kings has been diligently continued by the present King Henry [II] of whom I shall write from personal experience. But after him, I fear, it will all come to an end.⁵⁹

CHAPTER TWENTY

Whatever matters relating to these men I now omit or, if life fails me, are left undiscussed, you dearest successor should complete, preserving the character of the times through the memory of writing. Until

---

56 The later cathedral of St John the Baptist and St Lawrence (2.36; 6.16). The structure's precise location is unclear, but presumably it was subsumed within the new church constructed during the reign of Henry II and dedicated by Thietmar (7.13). The necrology at Merseburg notes the older church's dedication on 23 May (*NMer.*, fo. 2v, p. 6).

57 Other sources add details regarding the time of Henry's death, presence at the death-bed of his sons, etc. (see BO 55a). On Memleben see note at 3.1.

58 Cf. 2.4 = Mathilda.

59 That is, because Henry II's marriage to Cunegunde had produced no children.

now, I have been a sinner negligent in all things, devoid of goodness and zealous in evil things. I have come very late to distinguish such things from what is better. In no way have I exercised a healthy concern for my soul. After I was made pastor, I only taught my charges with words and not with examples. Externally, I appeared good but I violated my inner being with the worst thoughts. Born of an impure seed, I wallowed in filth like a stinking sow. Someone may say: 'You have praised yourself badly.' To that one I respond: this is true, and I do not know anyone worse than myself. I accuse myself in this manner so that, with my wounds revealed, you may comfort me with the necessary medicines and, as a colleague, so to speak, you may help me in every way just as you yourself would wish to be helped.

CHAPTER TWENTY-ONE

As a good model for all the faithful, I will now devote a few words to the illustrious deeds performed by the venerable Mathilda after the death of her lord. Scripture teaches that the intent to pray for the dead and seek their absolution with alms is both holy and salutary.[60] We read of a captive whose wife, thinking him dead, cared for him with continual masses for the dead.[61] Every time she offered these acceptable sacrifices, on his behalf, to God the Father, he was released from his chains. He related this to her afterwards, when he returned home a free man. Following this example, Mathilda aided her husband, oppressed by the chains of temporary death, by giving sustenance not only to paupers but even to the birds.[62] She also established a convent of nuns on the thirtieth day, in the burg mentioned above.[63] With her sons' agreement, she endowed it out of her own property with whatever was necessary for sustenance and clothing.[64] This was

---

60 2. Macc. 12: 46 (RSV 12: 45).

61 Greg., *Dial.* 4.59, p. 320; also his *Hom. Ev.* 2. 37. 8, p. 1279. For the *Dialogues*, Holtzmann (1935: 27. n. 3) erroneously cites c. 57, an error repeated by Trillmich (1958: 24, n. 64) and subsequently misunderstood by Lippelt (1973: 146, n. 23).

62 Cf. 4.36. Prayer and the distribution of alms on behalf of a dead spouse were viewed as special obligations of widows (Platelle 1990: 174; Corbet: 1993: 242–46).

63 Quedlinburg.

64 Quedlinburg, or at least some portion of the dynasty's property there, was bestowed upon Mathilda as part of her dower, on 16 September 929 (D H I 20). The economic basis and legal status of the community were laid out in a diploma issued by Otto I soon after his succession (D O I 1, 13 September 936). That distinctions between royal and dynastic (or family) foundations should not be drawn too sharply is suggested by one clause in particular, which seems to place

conceded and confirmed by her in writing. Some say that she strove
vigorously and long to secure the paternal seat for her younger son,
Henry. But God did not want this, always preordaining those chosen
by him for anything, nor did the greater part of the leading men
assent. But through prudent and therefore readily persuasive reason-
ing they deflected the mind of the sorrowful queen somewhat from
this proposition, advising that it would be better to assign the
Bavarians to his protection and give precedence to his older brother.[65]

CHAPTER TWENTY-TWO

In the year of the Incarnation of the Lord 923, in the eleventh
indiction, in the fifth year of the reign of the first King Henry, the
venerable Sigismund, sixth bishop of the church of Halberstadt,
whom King Arnulf had installed in the seventh year of his reign, died
on 14 January. As this holy man had previously predicted, he was
succeeded by his chaplain, Bernhard.[66] For during a long illness,
Sigismund had a dream in which Bernhard, who was following him,
picked up the pastoral staff, which had fallen from his hands, and
carried it openly. Upon awakening, the bishop summoned Bernhard
and said: 'Go to the king's court, taking with you anything of mine
which might be necessary for this. And there, you should acquire the
favour and aid of powerful men so that you will be allowed to succeed

Quedlinburg under the perpetual dominion and protection of the king while
reserving advocacy rights for the Liudolfinger, regardless of who might occupy the
throne (Bernhardt 1993: 138–39; Thiele 1995: 8–11): 'If anyone of our lineage
should occupy the royal throne in Franconia and Saxony, may both the aforesaid
convent and the nuns gathered there in the service of God, be in his power and
under his protection. If someone else should be elected king, from among the
people, may he exercise his royal power over these [i.e. the convent and its
occupants], as he would over other congregations gathered, in similar fashion, in
the service of the Holy Trinity. Nevertheless, whoever may be the most powerful
of our lineage should have the advocacy both of the aforesaid place and its
occupants.'

65 Henry, duke of Bavaria from 947 to 955. Prior to his death (937), Duke Arnulf of
Bavaria had agreed to the marriage of his daughter Judith with Henry. Arnulf was
succeeded by his son, Eberhard, who offended the king in some way and was
subsequently forced into exile. In place of Eberhard, Otto installed Duke Arnulf's
brother, Berthold, who essentially maintained his loyalty until his death in 947. At
this point, rather than allowing the duke's minor son, Henry the Younger, to
succeed to the duchy, Otto instead gave it to his own brother (i.e. Henry; Reuter
1991: 151–2; Beumann 1991: 58, 62).

66 Bishop Bernhard of Halberstadt (923/24–68).

me without opposition. God will provide you with all of these things, dearest son!' In humble obedience, Bernhard immediately fulfilled his beloved lord's command. While returning from King Henry, however, he learned that his lord and father had migrated from this light to Christ, in the thirtieth year of his ordination. Immediately retracing his steps, he acquired that which he sought by grant of the aforementioned king. As the bishop had previously requested, his body was interred to the right of the altar of Christ's protomartyr, at the front step, and seated on his throne rather than lying down, as he had previously indicated. He thereby hoped to be eternally protected by the holy intercession and benediction of his own patron.

CHAPTER TWENTY-THREE

Though I have never drunk from the spring of the muse,[67] I shall nonetheless reveal to all the faithful how, throughout his life, the king benefited from the mercy of God. In the West, there was a certain king whom the people jokingly called Charles Sot, that is, 'the Simple'.[68] He was captured by one of his own dukes and held in a dark prison.[69] Imploring the aid of our King Henry, his cousin, Charles swore that, in return for being freed by him, he would surrender the right hand of Denis the martyr of Christ and the entire kingdom of the Lotharingians.[70] Without delay, the illustrious warrior girded himself with unconquerable arms and went to his distressed relative's assistance. As a worthy helper in securing the king's freedom and restitution, Henry earned his reward and thereby increased for himself and his successors the honour which he had initially received.

---

67 Statius, *Silvae* 1.2.1.6.

68 King Charles 'the Simple' (893–929).

69 By Count Heribert II of Vermandois (*c.*905–43).

70 Here again, Thietmar draws on the testimony of Widukind of Corvey (1.33–34, pp. 45–47). The differences between the two accounts are worth noting, however, as they suggest how Thietmar edited his material to fit his own agenda. Although Widukind describes Henry's acquisition of the relics of St Denis in some detail, the incident merely serves as an introduction to his actual theme, the translation and subsequent influence of the relics of St Vitus (836), patron saint at Corvey. In brief, Widukind maintains that the arrival of Vitus had led to a dramatic reversal in the respective fortunes of the Franks and Saxons, causing the former to decline while the latter were elevated to the height of empire. Since this was more or less the role that Thietmar wished to attribute to St Lawrence, patron saint at Merseburg, it is not surprising that he chose to use Widukind's relatively brief comments on St Denis, but pass over the more substantial material relating to Vitus.

CHAPTER TWENTY-FOUR

Because human nature is more inclined to surrender than stand fast, and also as a terrifying admonishment to the pious, I will not keep silent regarding the wretched sin that the king once committed. He got very drunk on Maundy Thursday and, in the following night, driven by the Devil, he illicitly coupled with his much-protesting wife.[71] The author of this great outrage, Satan, the destroyer of human salvation, revealed this deed to a certain venerable matron, saying: 'At my instigation, Queen Mathilda has just consented to marital desire and conceived a son who is undoubtedly mine. You must carefully conceal this secret.' As the matron was much troubled because of this, she quickly revealed everything to the queen, warning that she should always have bishops and priests with her and that, at the boy's birth, whatever had happened to him as the evil demon had his pleasure should be washed away in the water of baptism. Thus she gave thanks to God. When the Devil, who knows all,[72] saw that he had been thoroughly duped, he reproached the matron in the following manner: 'Even if my will has now been frustrated by your blasphemy, I have still gained because my companion, Discord, will never leave that one and all who spring from his loins.[73] Nor will they ever enjoy a secure peace.' I hope that the liar and enemy of truth was wishing for these things rather than predicting them. As the following account indicates, many affirm that during his and his son's lifetime disruption was frequent and tranquillity uncertain. In these days when Henry began to rule, the third of that name in the ducal succession and second in the order of sceptre bearers, the weed of iniquity dried up and the vigorous bloom of a good peace burst out. If he should endure something similar to that which struck his predecessors, this would not be his fault but rather that of the instigator of impiety.

CHAPTER TWENTY-FIVE

We have read that all ages have their duration, but not all things.[74] Indeed, at the beginning, no place was allotted by God for moral

71 According to early medieval penitentials, sexual relations were prohibited on a large and quite specific number of fast and feast days, including Maundy Thursday (Brundage 1987: 157–58).
72 Is., *Etym.* 8.11.15, col. 315.
73 Duke Henry I of Bavaria, and his son, Duke Henry the Quarrelsome.
74 Eccles. 3: 1.

failings. Because our frail flesh cannot exist without some contagion, however, one should at least abstain from mortal sins and remain chaste on all feast days. Scripture teaches that in a legitimate marriage nothing is forbidden,[75] but only when the feasts are properly honoured and no storm of imminent danger threatens. To further prove this I will offer one example. A certain man, named Uffo, a citizen of Magdeburg, urged on by drunkenness, forced his wife Gelusa to consent to him on the feast of the Holy Innocents and impregnated her on the same night [28 December]. When she gave birth prematurely to an infant with crippled toes, she was horrified and, immediately summoning her husband, showed him the marvel. Complaining that this had happened because of their mutual guilt she said: 'Did I not previously warn you against such behaviour? Behold, the anger of God reveals itself to us and with cruelty demands that we never do this again. It was your great sin to command me and mine was in not obeying you.'[76] After the infant was baptized, it was led from this exile and placed among the host of the innocents. Eternally blessed is the man whose wife tirelessly prays for him in his absence and, heedless of her sex, beseeches him to guard his soul when he is present.

CHAPTER TWENTY-SIX

In that time in which the king was most powerful, there was a certain duke in Bavaria named Arnulf who was outstanding both in mind and body. He had the unique power to distribute all the bishoprics in his territories on his own initiative.[77] But when he concluded his life, after giving various indications of his virtue, he did not leave this great honour to his successors. Rather, this right pertains to our kings and emperors alone, who have been placed in this world as representatives of the highest ruler. Only they rightly take precedence over all their pastors. Indeed, it would be most incongruous for the latter, whom

---

75 1. Cor. 7: 28.

76 According to Holtzmann's edition this sentence should read: 'and mine was obeying you'. I have followed Fickermann's suggestion (1957: 76, n. 186) and restored a *non* which Holtzmann suppressed. Fickermann makes the plausible argument that the sin was mutual because, whatever the consequences, Gelusa should have willingly performed her marital obligations.

77 Both Arnulf and Duke Burchard II of Swabia retained wide-reaching powers within their territories and substantial control of the church though, like the king, they had to take account of local sentiment when exercising it (Reuter 1991: 140; Beumann 1991: 33–4, Bührer-Thierry 1997: 47–48, 160). See also Thietmar 1.8.

Christ instituted for his sake as the first men of this world, to be
subject to any dominion other than that exercised by rulers who, after
the model of the Lord, exceed all other mortals through the glory of
the benediction and crown. Nevertheless, I have heard that some of
them endure great slander under the power of dukes and, even worse,
under counts. They cannot do anything unless these lovers of the
world permit it. Moreover, the impious power which God permits to
oppress those who rightly dominate will soon rage with even more
cruelty.

CHAPTER TWENTY-SEVEN

In the king's palace a miraculous event occurred. In the view of
everyone present, a certain dog, recognizing his enemy sitting among
them, approached and unexpectedly took off his right hand with a
quick bite. Then, as if having done something very good, he quickly
went away with his tail wagging. While everyone was still dazed and
astonished, they asked the object of the attack what he had done. He
answered that what had just happened to him was a matter of divine
retribution which he then explained: 'I discovered an exhausted man,
the master of this dog, asleep and, like a miserable wretch, killed him.
After enduring many attacks by the persecutor who has just now
wounded me, I barely escaped. Now, after hoping that all was
forgotten, but still guilty, I have met him again. Now, I know that no
criminal can hide from judgement without penalty, whether in this
world or the next.

CHAPTER TWENTY-EIGHT

Dear reader, many deeds of our king and emperor are worthy enough
to be remembered for ever but because I cannot describe them as they
occurred, sadly, I must omit them. As I have already said, he justly
obtained his title from our kings and acquired his preeminence
through an abundance of virtue. I have written a small book concerning his great deeds but hope that his memory will be inscribed in the
book of life. He was a faithful servant of the precursor of Christ,
greatest among those born of women, as Christ our Lord and God
affirms.[78] In our city, he first established the foundations for future
worship and hence, whatever was subsequently added to this should

78 Matt. 11: 11, Luke 7: 28.

redound to his praise. For a correct beginning and a good end, wherever possible, accord best with one another. And if this cannot be implemented in all things, let us praise the Lord in what he has done. The faithful, and especially you illustrious Merseburg, with your spiritual offspring, having been exalted above your neighbours like a cypress in the time of your beloved king, should humbly beseech God's beneficence and majesty that he may deign to bring this work to completion. Give thanks continually to God, ever zealous and constant in the fear of the Lord, so that good things may so much more readily be accomplished in you through divine guidance, for it is the custom of evil people to be unmindful of the good and to change for the worse that which the Omnipotent has created for the better. If I should ever wish to add something to this work, I will in no way hesitate. Meanwhile, may he who listens to all creation be favourable to one who thinks kindly on this great ruler of ours.

May this first book conclude with the death of the first Henry.

BOOK TWO

Otto, glory of the kingdom, born of the lordly lineage
of his father Henry, and shining everywhere with brilliant deeds,
thus ascended the paternal throne.
At first, many evil men opposed him, from jealousy,
but he conquered all their pride, with divine aid,
which he sought always from on high.
Since the death of Charles, there had been no greater patron,[1]
and I believe that the realm will not see a similar pastor again.
He established six bishoprics.
Conquering Berengar's pride,
he forced the Lombards to bend their necks
Rome made this powerful man her emperor,
and the distant maritime regions paid tribute.[2]
He was a friend of peace and greatly suppressed warfare.
He pacified the western folk and the ferocious Danes.
Now, no enemy appeared from the East.[3]
As the highest bearer of the sceptre,
he ruled the kingdom for thirty-eight years.[4]
Then, also Otto the invincible departed,
but he left a son, born of his loyal wife,
as surety for the future and source of joy to his supporters

CHAPTER ONE

All the leading men of the realm, desiring to alleviate Queen
Mathilda's great sorrow, unanimously elected her son, Otto, as their
king and lord, this having been the order and request of his father.[5]

1 Since Charlemagne. A similar reference appears at 2.45.

2 Reference to southern Italy (cf. Thietmar 2.13, 31).

3 Horace, *Odes* bk 1, ode 35, verse 31.

4 Actually, thirty-seven years, from 7 August 936 to 7 May 973.

5 The description of Otto I's elevation to the throne relies on Widukind 2.1, pp. 63–66.
  Other sources relevant to Otto's succession are noted and discussed by BO 55g–h.

With their right hands raised, they acclaimed him: 'May the king live and be victorious for ever!' Then, they went with him to Aachen. As they approached, they were met by all the nobles who swore fidelity and obedience. Afterwards, they led Otto to the imperial throne where they installed him in the place of his predecessors, acclaimed him as their king, and gave thanks to God. In the year of the Incarnation 936, with permission from Archbishop Wigfried of Cologne, in whose diocese they were, and with the aid of the archbishop of Trier, Hildebert, who had custody of the cathedral of Mainz, consecrated Otto in the church of the blessed Virgin Mary which Charles the Great had constructed with all diligence.[6] Then, strengthened both by God and within the kingdom, Otto, greatest of the sceptre bearers, ordered the consecration of his wife, Edith, the God-fearing daughter of King Edmund of England whom he had married during his father's lifetime.[7]

CHAPTER TWO

Many adversities disturbed his fortunes. For the wicked Boleslav [I], having killed his brother Wenceslaus, Duke of the Bohemians and faithful to God and the king, remained full of pride for a long time.[8] But afterwards, the king conquered him by force and placed him in the custody of his brother Henry, the duke of the Bavarians [i.e. in 950]. The Hungarians, once enemies of his father but long pacified,

6 Archbishop Wigfried of Cologne (923–53), Archbishop Robert of Trier (931–56), Archbishop Hildebert (927–37).

7 The mistaken reference to Queen Edith's descent from King Edmund derives from the more detailed account provided by Widukind (1.37, p. 54). Thietmar's allusion to Edith's consecration represents a significant departure from Widukind and, moreover, so closely resembles the consecration attributed to Queen Cunegunde in 1002 (5.19) as to suggest that the earlier event merely echoes the later one (Wolf 1990: 62–88, cf. Leyser 1994c: 87).

8 Widukind 2.3, pp. 68–70. According to Widukind, Boleslav I, 'the Cruel', murdered Duke Wenceslaus I in 935 although modern scholarly opinion seems to favour 929 (*LMA*, vol. 2, pp. 357–58). Wenceslaus had adopted a conciliatory policy towards the Empire (indeed, he had done homage to King Henry I in 929). His death ushered in a period of hostile relations lasting for some fourteen years, until Otto I forced Boleslav I to pay tribute (Beumann 1991: 44, 78). The murdered duke's relics were translated to the cathedral of St Vitus in Prague (4 March), thereafter the centre of an indigenous cult which sprouted almost immediately. The common depiction of the murdered duke as a warrior, and his reputation as a saint whose patronage encompassed the welfare of the Bohemian realm, suggest comparisons with St Maurice, who developed a similar reputation under the Ottonians (Graus 1980: 207–10, 221–23).

again invaded but quickly retreated [February 937].[9] No small
amount of discord arose among our fellow countrymen and colleagues
who incited Tammo, son of the king and Liudgard.[10] All of this
because the office formerly possessed by Count Siegfried of Merseburg,
which he claimed for himself, had been given to Margrave Gero and,
so it appeared, Tammo's maternal inheritance was to be entirely taken
away from him.[11] The king besieged his son in the Eresburg and tried
to move him from his evil presumption both with threats and
promises.[12] But then the army entered the captured city and drove the
youth, exhausted by the fighting, to retreat to the church of St Peter
where previously the ancient Irminsul had been worshipped.[13] At last,
pierced from behind through a window by Maginzo's lance, he died
before the altar [28 July].[14] Later, in the second year of his reign, the
king punished Maginzo with a cruel death.[15]

CHAPTER THREE

Through the grace of divine mercy and through the continual intercession of his most holy wife, Edith, Otto escaped whatever open or
secret dangers confronted him. It was at Edith's urging that he began
to establish the city of Magdeburg, to which he brought the relics of
Innocent, the martyr of Christ, with great honour.[16] Then he acquired
and constructed this city for the sake of his eternal salvation and the

9 Widukind 2.5, p. 71; BO 63b.

10 In fact, son of Henry I and Hatheburg (1.5, 9).

11 'Thankmar claimed Siegfried's legation [i.e. the territories and responsibilities of a
margrave] because he was his relative – for the mother by whom King Henry
produced Thankmar was the daughter of Siegfried's aunt. When, by royal
bestowal, the legation was ceded to Count Gero, Thankmar was afflicted by great
sadness' (Widukind 2.9, p. 73).

12 Saxon burg dating to the pre-conquest era (i.e. prior to Charlemagne) now
incorporated in the modern city of Ober Marsberg. The church mentioned in the
following sentence belonged to the monastery of Corvey. See LMA, vol. 3, pp.
2129–30.

13 Pagan cult object in the form of a column or tree-trunk which was destroyed
during Charlemagne's conquest of Saxony (LMA, vol. 5, p. 663).

14 NMer., fo. 4r, p. 9. Other sources note that any of Thankmar's supporters who
survived were hanged, according to Frankish law (BO 76c).

15 According to Widukind, he died in battle somewhat later (Widukind 2.17, p. 83).

16 Otto did not found the 'city' (though he certainly boosted its prospects!), but rather
a monastery which he later transformed into an archbishopric. The acquisition of
the relics of St Innocent, one of Maurice's companions in the Theban Legion, are
also mentioned by Widukind (2.7, p. 72).

general welfare of the homeland.[17] Edith, of blessed memory, assisted him in this project as much as she could. Endowed with innumerable virtues, she lived the span of years conceded to her in a manner acceptable both to God and humanity, as signs revealed after her death.[18] She was with her husband for nineteen years and died in the eleventh year of his reign on 26 January, leaving behind her only son, Liudolf, then in his full vigour.[19] She was buried in the main church of the aforementioned city, in the north chapel.[20]

CHAPTER FOUR

The king received the painful news of Edith's death while he was out hunting, in the hope of refreshing himself a little. His unspeakable sorrow was only relieved by the arrival of his beloved son. As a boy, Liudolf had followed the branched letter of Pythagoras of Samos, signifying the course of human life, in praiseworthy simplicity. At the parting of the ways, he chose the right branch, the shorter but better path. Thereafter, he increased as the flourishing ivy and, imitating his father in all ways, so adorned his innate nobility with deeds that he was pleasing to all the leading men, which is no small compliment.[21] The father favoured Liudolf to such an extent that he decided, with the common election of the entire nobility, to share his dignity and labour with him and designate him as successor.[22] He also arranged a marriage for him with Ida, a daughter of Duke Herman who was noted for her surpassing beauty and womanly

17 Thietmar may be echoing the language of Otto's foundation diploma (D O I 14; 21 September 937), with which, as a former member of the cathedral's chapter, he would most certainly have been familiar.

18 Although never the object of a formal cult, Edith's piety and her illustrious lineage, which included St Oswald of Northumbria (d. 642; feast day 9 August), attracted the admiration of Ottonian literati. Thietmar's comments, in particular, have been interpreted as evidence that rumours of her sanctity persisted in some popular, largely oral tradition (Corbet 1986: 46–50). Leyser (1994c: 93) has argued that the death was not only deeply disturbing, but also that efforts were made to find Otto another wife from the same lineage of Wessex.

19 *NMag.*, fo. 2r, p. 37.

20 In Magdeburg.

21 Ivy: Horace, *Odes*, bk 1, ode 25, verse 17, No small praise: Horace, *Epistles*, bk 1, no. 17, l. 35.

22 'After Queen Edith died, the king transferred to his only son, Liudolf, all the love he had previously given to the mother and, in his last will, ensured that he would succeed him as king. He was still a tender youth, however, no more than seventeen years of age' (Widukind 3.1, p. 104).

virtue.²³ Shortly afterwards the two were joined by the bond of matrimony. Otto also granted Liudolf the duchy and heritable property of his deceased father-in-law.²⁴ One can scarcely measure how much the realm flourished in the days of such a great father and son. After establishing a church at Quedlinburg with a congregation of nuns, as I have mentioned, the venerable Queen Mathilda insured her son's prosperity through her faithful service to God.²⁵

CHAPTER FIVE

Meanwhile, Berengar invaded the kingdom of Louis and, after capturing his widow at Como on 20 April, robbed and afflicted her with imprisonment and hunger.²⁶ Our king, hearing of her beauty and laudable reputation, pretended that he was going to Rome, but as he

23 Duke Herman I of Swabia (926–49). Scion of the Conradine lineage and loyal supporter of both Henry I and Otto I, Herman had acquired the duchy of Swabia by marrying the widow of Duke Burchard I. He also numbered Alsace among his possessions. See *LMA*, vol. 4, p. 2161.

24 'Observing that his son Liudolf had become a man, the king gave him a wife, namely, Duke Herman's daughter, Ida, who was noted for her wealth and nobility. Shortly after Liudolf received her, his father-in-law died, leaving him the duchy and all of his possesions. After acquiring this power, he shed the peaceful demeanour he had assumed as a boy and led an armed expedition to Italy. He captured a few cities, placed garrisons in them, and returned to Franconia' (Widukind 3.6, p. 108).

25 See 1.21.

26 'At that time, by virtue of the authority he had usurped, Berengar ruled in Lombardy, a wild and greedy man who sold every form of justice for money. Fearing the virtue of the singularly prudent queen that King Louis had left behind, he afflicted her in many ways, to the end that he might extinguish or at least darken the luster of such exceptional splendour' (Widukind 3. 7, p. 108).

Adelheid's capture was noted in the necrology at Merseburg: 'On the same day, Empress Adelheid was captured at Como by King Berengar' (*NMer.*, 20 May, fo. 2r, p. 5). Other sources are noted in BO 196a. The opponent of King Berengar II (950–63, d. 966), former margrave of Friuli, was not Louis, but Lothar (931–50), son of King Hugh 'of Provence' (926–47). Hugh, a Burgundian magnate, had been invited to Italy by an aristocratic faction which included Berengar and members of his family. Presumably, the betrothal and subsequent marriage of Hugh's son to Adelheid was part of a plan to extend the king's power to Burgundy where the death of King Rudolf II, and his heir's youth (Conrad), had created a political vacuum. Otto I's swift intervention blocked these plans (Beumann 1991: 66–70). In Italy, Hugh eventually faced opposition from powerful and independent magnates, including Berengar himself. With Lothar's death, Adelheid became the focus of opposition to Berengar and, hence, his hostility towards her is understandable. The lurid stories of her ill-treatment (e.g. Odilo, c. 2, pp. 30–31; Warner (trans.) 2000: 262–63) are probably much exaggerated since, somewhat later, she seemed perfectly willing to forgive him. On Berengar see above p. 19.

was travelling through Lombardy, sent representatives to the lady who by then had escaped from her imprisonment.[27] After winning her favour with gifts, he convinced her to agree to his request and, together with her, laid claim to the city of Pavia.[28] His son Dudo was very disturbed by this turn of events and hurried back to our land, holding up at a place near Saalfeld which was well suited for secret things and treachery.[29] Meanwhile, the king had strengthened Pavia with a garrison and, after taking care of other matters, could now depart. Berengar followed, in the company of Duke Conrad.[30] He regained the king's favour at Augsburg, after he and his son had offered their submission.[31] He also placated the queen's anger with his humility and so returned to his homeland in peace.[32]

27 BO 196b. Adelheid's escape from captivity is also noted in the necrology at Merseburg: 'On the same day, the Lord freed Queen Adelheid from her chains' (*NMer.*, 20 August, fo. 5r, p. 11)'.

28 'The virtue of the previously mentioned queen did not remain hidden from him, moreover, and so he decided to go [to her], on the pretext of making a trip to Rome. After he arrived in Lombardy, he attempted to test the queen's love for him with a gift of gold coins. When that had been reliably ascertained, he took her as his wife and, with her, obtained the city of Pavia, the seat of the kingdom. When his son Liudolf had seen this, he sadly parted from the king, travelled to Saxony, and lingered for some time in Saalfeld, a place of evil council' (Widukind 3.9, p. 109). For other sources relative to the marriage, see, BO 201a.

29 See above p. 31.

30 Duke Conrad 'the Red' of Lotharingia (944–53, d. 955). Through his participation in the rebellion of Liudolf, son of Otto I (below 2.6–8), Conrad would subsequently lose both his dukedom in Lotharingia and any hope of reconstructing his family's (i.e. the Conradines') duchy in the area of Worms (*LMA*, vol. 5, p. 1344). He died at the battle of the Lechfeld (2.10).

31 At a *Reichstag* and synod (BO 217a). After offering their submission, Berengar and Adalbert received the kingdom of Italy as a benefice, with the exception of the marches of Trent, Verona, Aquileia, and Istria which were commended to Otto's brother, Duke Henry of Bavaria.

32 Here, Thietmar compresses events reported by Widukind and neglects to note that a loss of face associated with this incident provoked the duke into joining Liudolf's revolt. Berengar actually caught up with Otto I at Magdeburg where: 'he was met at a distance of one mile by the dukes, counts, and leading men of the palace, who received him in a regal manner. After being led into the city, however, he was ordered to remain in a hospice which had been prepared for him, and not allowed to see the king's face for three days. Conrad, who had brought him there, took offence at this and the king's son, Liudolf, shared these sentiments. Both men now distanced themselves from the king's brother, Henry, suspecting that he had provoked the incident, perhaps because of some old grudge. Henry, moreover, knowing Liudolf to be deprived of maternal support, began to treat the young man with disdain and showed no hesitation in insulting him. In the meantime, the king [Berengar] spoke with the king. The king [Otto] and queen bestowed their favour upon him, and he promised submission, setting a day and place, in Augsburg, when he would willingly fulfil his agreement' (Widukind 3.10, p. 109).

CHAPTER SIX

While the king was travelling through Franconia, fufilling his office
as ruler, he learned of the secret plans prepared by his son and
brother-in-law, Hugh.[33] Furious, he sent representatives who demanded
that they surrender the authors of such a shameful deed.[34] Otherwise,
they should know for certain that they would be treated as the king's
enemies. As they did not wish to agree to this demand, the king
collected an army and pursued them as far as Mainz, taking by siege
or surrender every town his son possessed.[35] Surrounding Mainz with
a powerful army, he inflicted much suffering on the rebels through
continuous attacks. After both sides had offered selected hostages, the
father spoke with the son and promised to return him to favour if he
would reveal the conspirators who were plotting such things and
hand them over for punishment. The young man had neither the
desire nor the capacity to do this because he did not wish to violate an
oath he had sworn to his supporters. After being reviled by his uncle
Henry, he returned to the city and to his rebellion, having won over
Count Ekbert and many of his uncle's warriors.[36] Secretly, in the

33 'Indeed, while the king was making the rounds of the lands and burgs of the
   Franks, he heard that ambushes were being prepared for him by his son and son-
   in-law. Thereafter, the archbishop was summoned from the place where, in
   preparation for Easter, he had been living an austere life in the company of hermits
   and recluses. He received the king at Mainz and, for a while, ministered to him
   there. When the son and son-in-law realized that their detestable plans had been
   revealed, they followed the archbishop's advice in seeking and obtaining an
   opportunity to exonerate themselves. Although they now stood openly accused of
   the crime, the king yielded to their arguments in every respect because of the
   danger of the place and the circumstances' (Widukind 3.13, p. 111). Thietmar has
   interpreted 'gener' in Widukind's text as referring to Otto's brother-in-law (i.e
   Hugh of Francia, husband of his sister Hathui), when it is more probably his son-
   in-law, Conrad 'the Red', husband of the king's daughter, Liudgard, who is meant.

34 'Now, encouraged by the presence of his friends and his own people, he repudiated
   the agreement, confessing that he had agreed to it only under duress. He then
   decreed that his son and son-in-law should surrender the authors of the crime, for
   punishment, or know that they would henceforth be considered enemies of the
   realm. As if counselling peace and concord, the archbishop spoke in favour of the
   earlier pact, thereby arousing the king's suspicions and causing the royal friends
   and advisers to utterly reject him' (Widukind 3.15, p. 111). The demand that
   Liudolf surrender his co-conspirators signified the repudiation both of this
   agreement and of Archbishop Frederick of Mainz, who had negotiated it. The
   resulting loss of face apparently caused the prelate to temporarily align himself
   with Otto's opposition.

35 Widukind 3.18, pp. 113–14.

36 Count Ekbert 'the One-eyed', was the son of Wichman *the Elder* (d. 944) and
   nephew of Queen Mathilda (*LMA*, vol. 3, p. 1762). Widukind notes that he had

silence of night, he and his supporters escaped and captured the
centre of the Bavarian duchy, Ratisbon, which is called Regensburg,
along with the most securely fortified cities.[37] The duchess Judith was
forced to leave, accompanied only by her children.[38] As his father
pursued him, Liudolf tried to regain the city of Mainz by bribing
Duke Dietrich and Count Wichman who were continuing the siege.[39]
Of the two, Dietrich stood firm, but Wichman was quickly corrupted
by his enticing promises.[40] Meanwhile, after his warriors had prepared
themselves for a campaign, the king went to Bavaria. Finding the
doors of every city closed to him, he went away again, but left the
countryside depopulated and ravaged by fire.[41]

CHAPTER SEVEN

Realizing that resistance to his father and king was hopeless, Dudo
took on the Hungarian bowmen as allies, a development which did
not escape the king's notice [954].[42] With his battle standards flying,
he went out to meet the invading enemy but, alas, things did not turn
out as expected. Led by certain wicked men, the invaders followed a
different road and invaded Franconia, which they utterly wasted. But
if anyone may wonder, either secretly or aloud, where this alien folk
acquired such audacity that they presumed to invade a region that
was both distant and heavily populated, let him hear this response,

---

been placed in the city as a hostage in order to facilitate negotiations (Widukind
3.18, p. 114). His and Wichman II's participation in Liudolf's revolt are probably a
manifestation of their continuing antagonism towards Herman Billung, their uncle
(Leyser 1979: 21). In Ekbert's case, Widukind cites a personal affront as the more
immediate cause (namely, he was angry at the king because he had 'blamed him for
the reckless battle in which he lost an eye' (Widukind 3.19). Given the importance
placed upon honour and 'face' in Ottonian society, Widukind's explanation should
not be discounted. Ekbert later turns up among the supporters of Duke Henry 'the
Quarrelsome' (Thietmar 4.1).

37 Widukind (3.20, p. 115) adds that Duke Henry's Bavarian entourage abandoned
him and went over to Liudolf, this at the instigation of members of the Liutpolding
clan, the former ducal house, who viewed the king's brother as a usurper
(Widukind 3.21, p. 115).

38 Daughter of Duke Arnulf, married to Henry since 937/938.

39 Widukind 3.23, pp. 115–16. Dietrich (965–85) took over Margrave Gero [I]'s
march, following the latter's death. The Wichman refered to here is Count Wichman II 'the Younger' (d. 967).

40 Widukind adds that Wichman 'now began to accuse his uncle, calling him the
robber of his paternal inheritance and plunderer of his treasures' (3.24, p. 116).

41 Widukind 3.26, 28, pp. 116, 117.

42 Widukind 3.30, pp. 117–18.

based on my personal knowledge and what I have learned from books. With divine consent, they were aroused as God's vengeance for our sins and we fled like cowards, terror-stricken because of our injustice. So it happened that we, who rejected the fear of the lord in prosperous times, rightly endured the lash of the lord. Having made no attempt to placate the anger of heaven, we were not heard when we cried out to God. Germany, standing firm as a wall against their arrows, suffered more from these invaders than its neighbours.

CHAPTER EIGHT

Finally, moved by the merits of the just and the cries of the wretched, God drove away the treacherous horde. The king, once again following them in an unexpected direction, had to invade Bavaria a second time. Soon they began negotiating for peace, asking for and obtaining a truce.[43] Those who were always untrustworthy and unfaithful to their lord, as they could not justify themselves before the king, wandered about with their leader, Liudolf, and sought the noted defences of Regensburg.[44] The king followed them and placed that city under siege. Although they fought for a long time, it was the threat of starvation that ultimately forced the son and his supporters to sue for peace.[45] After this, Dudo was moved to penance and, along with Hugh, threw himself at his father's feet, humbly asking forgiveness for the past and present, and promising caution for the future.[46] Won over by the advice of his leading men, the king received him, forgave his offences, and firmly assured him of his favour. Thereafter, he restored his brother's long-lost duchy and returned to Saxony victorious, hoping that all his enemies had been pacified.[47]

CHAPTER NINE

But again, as if they had forgotten their recent outrage, the Hungarians moved against us under arms.[48] Duke Henry notified the king of their arrival, recalling him from a journey he had just begun.

43 The Bavarians (Widukind 3.31–32, pp. 118–19).
44 Widukind 3.34, p. 120.
45 Widukind 3.36–37, pp. 120–21.
46 Widukind 3.40–41, p. 122.
47 Widukind 3.4, p. 123.
48 In 955; Widukind 3.44, pp. 123–25.

Then, the king ordered all of his dependants to meet him at the city of Augsburg, declaring that he would rather die than permit such evil to continue.[49] He promised rewards and favour to those who complied, and punishment to those who fled. From everywhere, he collected only eight warbands. When they had been organized for battle, he encouraged them, noting that those who died would be rewarded in eternity and referring to the earthly benefits conferred by victory. Without being noticed, the shrewd enemy was able to surround and overwhelm the king's rearguard, near the fast-flowing Lech. Many were killed and plundered. As soon as the king learned of this, he sent Duke Conrad and his warriors to the rear, where they seized the captives and all the booty from the throats of the ravaging wolves and returned victorious to the camp.

CHAPTER TEN

The next day, that is on the feast of the martyr of Christ, Lawrence, the king alone prostrated himself before the others and confessed his sin to God, tearfully swearing the following oath: if on that day, through the intercession of such a great advocate, Christ would deign to grant him victory and life, he would establish a bishopric in the city of Merseburg in honour of the victor over the fire and turn his newly begun palace there into a church [10 August].[50] After raising himself from the ground and after his confessor, Ulrich, had celebrated the mass and holy communion, the king took up his shield and the holy lance and led his warriors against the enemy forces, annihilating and pursuing them till evening when they fled.[51] After the slaughter, the king camped with his victorious band in the verdant meadows and diligently inquired if anyone of his warriors had been killed. Then, he learned of the death of Duke Conrad, his son-in-law and an illustrious man of arms.[52] He sent his body to Worms, duly mourned and carefully prepared for burial. Messengers were also sent ahead, to alleviate the concerns of his sainted mother with a complete report of what had happened, and also to arouse the souls of the faithful in praise of Christ. All of Christendom, but especially that part

49 Possible allusion to Terence, *Eunuchus* 1.1, 21, 3, 7.
50 See above p. 58.
51 Widukind 3.46, pp. 126–28. Bishop Ulrich's biography (Gerhard c. 12, p. 401) places him in Augsburg, directing the city's defence, rather than in Otto's camp.
52 Widukind 3.47, p. 128.

committed to the king, received such a great gift of divine piety with ineffable joy, offering praise and thanks to God in the highest with one voice.[53] In this year, Henry, duke and brother of the king, died.

CHAPTER ELEVEN

Meanwhile the king happily saw his Saxon homeland again and was received with great enthusiasm by all the leading men who came from far and wide to meet him. Amid tears of joy, he was embraced by his venerable mother who had long awaited his arrival. Immediately, he revealed his promise to them and asked insistently for their advice and help so that he might fulfil it. After they praised his plan and agreed with his pious requests, the king established an abbey in the city of Magdeburg, beginning a church of a marvellous sort at the gravesite of the holy Edith, by whose side he himself wished to rest when he died.[54] His intention of founding a bishopric there could not be fulfilled during the lifetime of Bernhard, seventh bishop of the church of Halberstadt, in whose diocese the city was located.[55] Whatever lands and other possessions he had acquired in the time permitted to him, he gave in their entirety to God and his warrior Maurice.

CHAPTER TWELVE

As these events were transpiring, the Slavs started a horrible war at the instigation of Counts Wichman and Ekbert under the leadership of Nacco and his brother Stoignew.[56] Lacking confidence in his own ability to defeat them, the commander, Herman, asked the king for

---

53 Widukind 3.49, pp. 128–29.

54 Very little is known about the appearance of this church which was destroyed by fire in 1207 and rebuilt in the Gothic style, on new foundations, with a reoriented axis. Otto's church appears to have been a basilica with a double choir and atrium in the west although even this remains highly speculative. Part of Thietmar's amazement may have derived from the architectural elements which the monarch imported from Italy (e.g. 2.17) and incorporated into the structure of his new foundation. These *spolia* included the marble columns that currently support the Gothic choir and probably supported the nave of the Ottonian church; and possibly the marble slab which eventually served as the cover of the king's tomb (Oswald 1966: 190–91; Heidenreich 1967: 265–68, Götz 1988: 101–2; Jacobsen et al. 1991: 260–61). That all of this represented a kind of 'imperial programme' has been argued, most recently, by Schubert (1998: 16).

55 See above p. 36.

56 Widukind 3.50, p. 129.

help.[57] Energetic as he was, the latter took a strong force and invaded those northern regions which, as scripture teaches, so often produce evil.[58] There, the king had Stoignew beheaded, after capturing him in a wood in which he had hidden as his supporters fled. He pursued the authors of this outrage, the brothers Wichman and Ekbert, sons of his maternal aunt. Liudolf, the king's son, misled by the advice of evil men, once again rebelled. Leaving the homeland, he went to Italy where, after scarcely a year, he died on 6 September, alas.[59] His supporters brought his body to Mainz where, with great sadness, it was buried in the church of the martyr of Christ, Alban. The king received the unhappy news while leading an expedition against the Redarii and, highly distraught, mourned for his son as David did for Absalon. Bishop Diethard of Hildesheim died, and was succeeded by Abbot Otwin of the church of Magdeburg.[60]

CHAPTER THIRTEEN

Once the violence of the wars had been put to rest, Otto again pretended to be travelling to Rome, but instead invaded Lombardy with a powerful army and besieged Berengar on Monte San Leo.[61]

57 Duke Herman Billung (936–73) had received a permanent military command along the lower Elbe from Otto I and occasionally acted as viceroy in Saxony during the king's absence (cf. 2.28; *LMA*, vol. 4, pp. 2160–61). Widukind makes no mention of an appeal to the king and presents a much less attractive picture of the duke's behaviour. He apparently ordered the occupants of a burg: 'to seek peace on whatever terms possible. The troops disagreed vehemently with this plan, however, especially Siegfried who was particularly zealous on the battlefield. Nevertheless, the Cocaresceni [i.e. the occupants of the burg] followed the duke's instructions and obtained peace on the following terms. The freemen were to ascend the wall, unarmed and accompanied by their wives and children. Persons of servile status were to be left for the enemy, in the middle of the burg, along with all the occupants' household possessions. As the barbarians stormed into the burg, one of them recognized the wife of a certain freed man as his serving woman. When he tried to snatch the woman from her husband's arms, he received a blow of the fist, and promptly declared that the Saxons had broken the agreement. Thus it transpired that all turned to slaughter, and none were spared since everyone of mature age was killed and mothers with children were led away as captives' (Widukind 3.52, p. 131).

58 Jer. 1: 14.

59 Widukind 3.57, p. 135. Liudolf's death is noted in the necrology at Merseburg (*NMer.*, fo. 5r, p. 11).

60 Bishop Diethard of Hildesheim (928–54), Bishop Otwin (954–84). The latter was previously abbot of St Maurice, at Magdeburg (950–54).

61 Widukind 3.63, pp. 137–39. Mt S. Leo: region of Montefeltro, 10 km south-west of San Marino.

After two years, he captured him, along with his wife, Willa, and his sons and daughters. Berengar was sent into exile at Bamberg where he died. Then, the king took his army and went to Rome where, after inflicting two defeats on the stubborn populace he celebrated a glorious entry into the city in the year of the Incarnation 961. Along with his wife, he also received the imperial benediction from Pope John, at whose request he had come.[62] As patron of the Roman church, he also laid claim to Benevento, Calabria, and Apulia, having conquered their dukes. All of this occurred in the twenty-ninth year of his reign.[63] In his lifetime, an age of gold came forth.[64] Among us, for the first time, a vein of silver was discovered.[65] Also, Wichman was conquered.[66]

CHAPTER FOURTEEN

The priest Poppo renewed the Christian faith among the Danes who were then ruled by Harald.[67] Admonishing both king and people for abandoning the religion of their predecessors and turning to other gods and demons, he affirmed that there was one God in three persons. The king asked if he wished to prove what he said with burning iron and he responded that he would be happy to do this. On the following day, he carried a very heavy piece of iron, which had been blessed, to a place determined by the king. Without fear, he held up his uninjured hand. The king was made very happy by this miracle and, along with all of his people, humbly submitted himself to the

62 Pope John XII (955–64), debauched son and heir of Alberich II of Rome, combined both spiritual and political authority in the city, but needed Otto's protection against King Berengar (see above p. 19). After a brief period of cooperation which resulted *inter alia* in Otto and Adelheid's coronation, the pope took up with the king's Italian enemies, a decision that ultimately led to his deposition in favour of Leo VIII (*LMA*, vol. 5, pp. 541–42; *DHP*: 936–37).

63 This should read, 'twenty-fifth year'.

64 Cf. 2.45.

65 Commonly taken as an allusion to the silver mines on the Ramelsberge near Goslar (e.g. Trillmich 1974: 48, n. 63), but strong objections, based on archaeological excavations, appear to have completely undermined this assumption (Ehlers 1997: 47).

66 Widukind 3.64.

67 King Harald 'Bluetooth' (936–986). A more detailed version of this anecdote is provided by Widukind (2.65, pp. 140–41). Demidoff (1973: 46) considers the history of the Poppo legend in detail and suggests that Widukind may well be the source for Thietmar's version (miscited as 1.14) even though he does not mention Poppo's elevation to the episcopate. On King Harald see also 3.6.

yoke of Christ. Until the end of his life, in the manner of the faithful, Harald remained obedient to the divine precepts. When the emperor heard this, he summoned the venerable man Poppo, asked if he was a fighter for Christ, and made him a bishop. Gero, margrave of the eastern march, subjugated Lausitz, Selpuli, and even obligated Miesco and his subjects to pay tribute to the emperor.[68] Duke Herman also made Selibur, Mistui, and their followers pay tribute to the emperor.[69]

CHAPTER FIFTEEN

On the feast of the birth of the Lord, the emperor's like-named son, Otto, offspring of the venerable Adelheid, was made emperor at Rome [25 December 967].[70] This was done at the order of his father, who then delayed at Capua in Campania. Wishing to acquire a wife for his son from the emperor at Constantinople, in good faith, he commended leading men as bearers of this request to an imperial embassy which had been sent for a different reason. But during the trip, the Greeks, with their customary slyness, unexpectedly attacked and killed some of them.[71] Others, having been taken captive, were presented to their august lord. The few who managed to escape related the whole incident to their emperor. Taking the loss of his envoys very seriously, the emperor quickly sent his best warriors, Gunther and Siegfried, to Calabria to take revenge for this outrage.[72] They killed the Danae who, made arrogant by their previous victory, attacked them. They seized others as they fled, and cut their noses off.[73] Then, after forcing the Greeks in Calabria and Apulia to pay tribute, they returned happy

68 Widukind 3.66–67, pp. 141–42. Duke Miesco I of Poland (d. 922).

69 Selibur ruled the Wagrii, Mistui the Abodrites (Widukind 3.68, p. 142).

70 Widukind 3.70, pp. 146–48.

71 Widukind 3.71, p. 148.

72 Widukind 3.72, pp. 148–49. Count Gunther of Merseburg (965–76, 979–82), who was temporarily deprived of his office (4.39), and Count Siegfried of Hassegau.

73 Mutilation of this type was common in late Antique and Byzantine political culture, but relatively rare in Ottonian Germany, the notion of saving 'face' being taken on both a figurative and literal level among the aristocracy (Nitschke 1983: 40–53). In this respect, one might note Thietmar's ironic comments on Bishop Michael's missing ear (2.27). Without denying their value as an act of terror, the mutilation of the Byzantine emperor's ostensible subjects may, therefore, have been intended to send a more specific message regarding his authority in Italy. Punishment by blinding was also relatively rare in the West though the Carolingians seem to have employed it (Bührer-Thierry 1998: 88–91). Thietmar notes two instances of blinding, as an act of revenge, which seem to have elicited strongly disapproving reactions (2.40; 4.21).

and loaded down with spoils. At Constantinople, people grieved over
their dead and captured countrymen. Conspiring against their lord,
they followed the advice of the treacherous empress in having him
killed by a certain warrior whom they then designated in his place as
ruler of the entire empire.[74] Immediately, this ruler sent across the sea
to our emperor, not the desired maiden, but rather his niece, Theophanu,
accompanied by a splendid entourage and magnificent gifts. He
thereby absolved his people's guilt and obtained the desired friendship
of Caesar Augustus. There were some who tried to dissuade the
emperor from this alliance and recommended sending the bride home.
He did not listen to them, however, and gave her to his son, in
marriage, with the approval of all the leading men of Italy and
Germany.

CHAPTER SIXTEEN

The emperor had many bodies of saints brought from Italy to
Magdeburg by his chaplain, Dodo.[75] Here, I cannot omit something
noteworthy that I heard from his priest Poppo, the brother of Count
William.[76] After serving the emperor long and faithfully, he became
very ill and had a vision in which he was led to a high mountain
where he saw a great city with beautiful buildings. Then he came to a
high tower which he ascended with great difficulty. On its large top
level, he was favoured with the sight of Christ sitting with all the

---

74 Widukind 3.73, pp. 149–50. The murdered 'lord', Emperor Nikephoros Phokas
(963–69), had succeeded Romanos II, by acclamation of the army, and married his
predecessor's widow. He was overthrown and replaced by John Tzimiskes (969–
76) who then sent his niece, Theophanu, to Otto. The circumstances are discussed
by Beumann 1991: 108–9; *LMA*, vol. 5, pp. 532; vol. 6, p. 1156.

75 The Ottonians possessed sufficient influence that they could avoid professional
relic merchants/thieves and rely on their own ministers and friends to acquire
these valuable commodities for them (Geary 1990: 44). Holtzmann (1935: 57, n. 8)
identifies Dodo with Liudolf, Otto's chancellor (953–67) and later bishop of
Osnabrück (967–78). Apparently, the ouflow of relics was so substantial that the
abbot of San Miniato, in Florence, had to undertake an active campaign (e.g.
composing a new *vita*) to convince the local populace that the church's patron saint
had *not* gone north with Otto's entourage (Dameron 1987: 134–35)

76 Count William of Weimar (963–1003). Although they figured among the more
important representatives of the Thuringian aristocracy, the origins of the counts
of Weimar are not entirely clear (Patze 1962: 101–6). Widukind thought that they
were native Thuringians (Widukind 3.16, p. 112). The earliest references to the
counts, a diploma issued by Otto I in 949 (D O I 109), simply mentions William I
as count in Thuringia. Weimar first appears among the family's possessions under
William II who succeeded to the countship upon his father's death.

saints. There, Archbishop Brun of Cologne stood accused by the highest judge because of his useless devotion to philosophy. But he was defended and again enthroned by St Paul. Then, after he was himself summoned, accused of a similar offence, but supported by the humble intercession of the saints, he heard a voice say the following: 'After three days you will come to me and possess the throne which I now show to you.' When he awoke, the priest summoned the emperor and revealed all of these things to him, confirming that this was not a dream but a true vision.[77] After thanking the monarch for all the good things he had ever done for him, he confessed his sins, was granted remission by all present, and abandoned this foreign place to seek the peace of his true homeland, having consoled his weeping lord with such a blessed death.

CHAPTER SEVENTEEN

The emperor had precious marble, gold, and gems brought to Magdeburg.[78] And he ordered that relics of saints should be enclosed in all of the columns.[79] He had the body of Count Christian, as well as those of others among his familiars, interred next to the same church in which, while he still lived, he wished to have a burial place prepared for himself.[80] In the year 961 of the Incarnation and in the twenty-fifth year of his reign, in the presence of all the nobility, on the vigil of Christmas, the body of St Maurice was conveyed to him at Regensburg along with the bodies of some of the saint's companions and portions of other saints. Having been sent to Magdeburg, these relics were received with great honour by a gathering of the entire populace of the city and of their fellow countrymen. They are still venerated there, to the salvation of the homeland.[81]

77 Cf. St Jerome's account of a dream in which he was accused of being 'a Ciceronian rather than a Christian' (Jer., *Ep.* 22, pp. 127–28).

78 Cf. 2.11.

79 The practice of embedding relics in columns and other architectural elements, thereby transforming the church itself into an oversized reliquary, was not uncommon though Magdeburg appears to be the earliest documented example (Keller 1975:105–7).

80 Christian is documented in 937 as count in north Thuringia and Schwabengau and, in 945, as margrave in Serimunt (D O I 64). His wife was Hidda (2.24–25), sister of Margrave Gero I, and his sons were Margrave Thietmar (d. 979) and Archbishop Gero of Cologne (969–76). See, *LMA*, vol. 4, p. 1350.

81 D O I 222b, issued in 961, would seem to indicate that the relics were placed in a new crypt.

CHAPTER EIGHTEEN

Meanwhile the venerable and aged Bishop Bernhard went to sleep in the Lord, in the forty-eighth year and on the very day of his ordination, that is 3 February.[82] Archbishop William of holy Mainz also died, at Rottleberode, on 2 March, as he awaited news of the death of the ailing Queen Mathilda.[83] The emperor, his lord and parent, had committed to him the founding of Magdeburg and other matters necessary to the governance of the realm. The queen, very much oppressed by infirmities of the body, announced his death in this manner to all present though no messenger had confirmed it: 'Alas, my son William is now dying and requires our remembrance for his salvation.'[84] On the very night in which he died, Abbot Liudolf of Corvey saw him in the body, advancing to meet him.[85] Horrified, he announced the archbishop's death to the brethren. After this, holy Mathilda migrated from this exile on 14 March, committing and returning her spirit to God her creator. She was buried in front of the altar of the bishop of Christ, Servatius, next to her lord.[86] As long as she lived, it had been her desire to be joined in death to the one she had so loved while living.

CHAPTER NINETEEN

Also Gero, the defender of the fatherland, was deeply saddened by the death of his only son, the noble Siegfried. Going to Rome, the aged veteran laid his victorious arms before the altar of the Prince of the Apostles, Peter, and received the arm of St Cyriacus from the lord pope. Then, he commended himself and all his property to God. After returning to his fatherland, he established a convent in a forest bearing his name.[87] His son's widow, Hathui, who had already taken

82 In 968, therefore the forty-sixth or forty-seventh year.

83 Widukind 3.74, p. 150.

84 Cf. *V. Mat. Post*, c. 25, pp. 198–99.

85 Abbot Liudolf of Corvey (965–83).

86 At Quedlinburg.

87 Gernrode. Though Gernrode fits the model of a typical dynastic foundation, it also shared certain qualities of a royal convent. Otto I and Otto II confirmed Gero's foundation with diplomata (D O I 229, D O II 3, both issued in 961), which granted the canonesses the characteristically royal privileges of immunity, protection, and the right to elect their abbess (though only after Hathui had died). Both kings were mentioned among the individuals whose souls were to benefit from the community's prayers. The community also appears to have enjoyed the protection

the veil, was installed as abbess and consecrated by Bernhard [88] After
settling all of these matters, he happily preceded both of them in
death, on 20 May [965].

CHAPTER TWENTY

After receiving the sad news of the deaths of his mother, son, and
various leading men, Otto complained mournfully about the irreparable loss to the whole realm.[89] Inspired by the fear of approaching
death, he dedicated himself to the task of completing, at an opportune
moment, that which he had promised to God in a time of distress.[90]
Then, he ordered Hildeward, the provost of the church of Halberstadt, to come to Rome. Hildeward had been elected bishop by all the
clergy and people, and designated as successor by his lord Bernhard.[91]
With him, the emperor discussed the plan he had long concealed in
his heart, namely, that in the hope of eternal reward and for the defence
of their common fatherland, he had always wanted to establish an
archbishopric in the city of Magdeburg. He promised that he was
ready to grant whatever Hildeward might ask if he would agree to the
fulfilment of this oath. Being a wise man, he went along with this
pious request and conceded to God, St Maurice, and the emperor that
part of his diocese situated between the rivers Ohre, Elbe, and Bode,
and also the road known as Friedrichsweg. Furthermore, at the
emperor's affectionate request, he gave to God and St Lawrence the

---

of the pope, a not uncommon privilege which, at this time, offered no threat to the
king's influence. Gradually, the distinction between Gernrode and a typical royal
convent tended to blur, though without completely disappearing (Schulze 1965: 3–
14; Bernhardt 1993: 175–76). The lingering ambiguity may, however, explain some
of the tensions evident in the canonesses' relations with their diocesan bishop and
with King Henry II (6.96–98, 7.3). Although not the first Saxon religious
community dedicated to the fourth-century Roman martyr Cyriacus, Gernrode
quickly became the regional centre for his cult (Schauerte 1964: 70–71).

88 Subsequent efforts by bishops of Halberstadt to exercise jurisdiction at Gernrode
were not always welcome (cf. 6.96).

89 Widukind 3.75, p. 151. Only the first sentence is taken from Widukind who, in
contrast to Thietmar, uses it to introduce his discussion of Otto I's death at
Memleben.

90 The moment was opportune, among other things, because the death of Bishop
Bernhard of Halberstadt (2.18) had removed a major opponent of his plans for
Magdeburg (Beumann 1991: 82–83, 103).

91 Bishop Hildiward of Halberstadt (968–96).

parish located between the flow of the Wilderbach, the salt lake, the
Saale, Unstrut, Helme and the ditch near Wallhausen.[92]

CHAPTER TWENTY-ONE

Joyful at this gift, the emperor took him by the hand and, with the
staff, commended to him the pastoral office with the following words:
'Receive this compensation for your father!' The father, Erich, had
been beheaded along with Bacco, Herman, Reinward, Wirin, Eserich,
and others for having attempted to kill the emperor while he was
celebrating the feast of Easter at Quedlinburg. He would gladly have
ordered the execution of my grandfather Liuthar, a participant in this
plot, but was convinced by his most trusted advisers to send him to
Bavaria, to be held in captivity by Count Berthold.[93] Moreover, all of
his property was seized and distributed widely. After a full year, he
won back the king's favour and all of his property by offering a large
sum of money and property located in Santersleben and Gutenswegen.[94]
But now I return to the subject.

CHAPTER TWENTY-TWO

The emperor summoned Richer, the third abbot of the church of
Magdeburg – for Anno and Otwin, then bishops, had preceded him –
and wanted to decorate him with the episcopal dignity.[95] But after

---

92 This would appear a fairly straightforward exchange in which Hildiward's
cooperation in the foundation of Magdeburg and Merseburg was the price for the
king's agreement to his election (e.g. Claude 1972: 84–85; Reuter 1991: 164, 197).
The grim comments regarding the bishop's father (2.21) would have added a futher,
ironic nuance to the occasion (Leyser 1979: 33). According to another view, however,
Hildiward offered only a limited agreement, without surrendering his church's rights
or the possibility of future negotiation (3.14; Beumann 1991a: 384–89). Hildeward's
agreement to the new foundations apparently left a residue of ill-will and
disatisfaction among the clerical community at Halberstadt (Althoff 1998: 272–75).

93 Count Liuthar of Walbeck (d. 964). See also 6.43. Berthold (d. 980) was margrave
of the Bavarian Nordgau and, after 973, count of Schweinfurt. His career was
marked by continual loyalty to the Ottonian house, which explains why he was
also entrusted with the task of guarding Berengar II and his wife, Willa (Endres
1972: 7–11). Liuthar's confinement was not entirely a loss to his family, since
Berthold subsequently married Liuthar's daughter, Eila (d. 1015).

94 On 28 March 942? (BO 104a). Whether Liuthar was giving these properties or
receiving them is not entirely clear from the Latin. My translation reflects the
views of Leyser (1979: 113–23) who has argued at length and persuasively for the
former.

95 Anno, abbot (937–50), bishop of Worms (950–78). Otwin, abbot 950–54, bishop of
Hildesheim (954–84). Richer, abbot (954–68).

examining a letter which had been secretly given to him, he changed
his mind. Instead, he chose the monk Adalbert of Trier who had been
previously ordained bishop for Russia but expelled by the heathen.
Otto promoted that illustrious and much-tested father to the archepiscopal dignity on 18 October, in the year 970 of the Incarnation,
and with papal authority.[96] Then, he sent him to his see with great
honour, ordering all the leading men of Saxony to be with him at the
next celebration of Christmas. The archbishop was received with
magnificence by the clergy and the whole populace. During these
feast days, he consecrated Boso as first pastor of the church of
Merseburg, Burchard as first overseer of the church of Meißen, and
Hugh as first bishop of Zeitz.[97] Also present was Dudo, the first
guardian of Havelberg who had been previously consecrated.[98] All of
these promised obedience to him and to his successors and to each
was conveyed his specific diocese. Thietmar, first pastor of the church
of Brandenburg who had been previously consecrated and Jordan first
bishop of Poznań joined these brethren.[99]

CHAPTER TWENTY-THREE

Although I may rightly be blamed for disturbing the order of events,
it will be useful to add here an account of how, after the death of
Wigfried who occupied the see of Cologne, the emperor gave both
this bishopric and the office of duke over Lotharingia to his brother,
lord Brun. The latter was named after his great-uncle, Duke Brun,
who had been sent on an expedition against the Danes by King Louis
and was drowned in a flooded river on 2 February, along with two
bishops, Dietrich and Markward, and many other warriors.[100]
Although the wisest of men, Archbishop Brun was later misled by evil
counsel and plotted to return evil for good to his king and brother. He

---

96 Archbishop Adalbert of Magdeburg (968–81).

97 Bishop Boso of Merseburg (968–70), Bishop Burchard of Meißen (968–69), Bishop
   Hugh I of Zeitz (968–79).

98 Bishop Dudo of Havelberg (948–81/92).

99 Bishop Thietmar of Brandenburg (948–68), Bishop Jordan of Poznań (968–84).
   Bishop Jordan had arrived in Poland as part of the entourage of Dobrawa, wife of
   Miesco I, and probably acted as a mission bishop until his appointment to the see
   of Poznań (*LMA*, vol. 5, p. 627).

100 The death of Duke Brun (d. 880), elder brother of Duke Otto (880–912), uncle of
    Henry I, is noted by Widukind (1.16, pp. 25–26). The king Louis in question is the
    Carolingian, Louis 'the Younger' (876–82). The two bishops are Bishop Dietrich
    of Minden (853–80) and Bishop Markward of Hildesheim (876–80).

held a feast to which he invited his brother-in-law Hugh, a man very unfaithful to the king, as we have already said.[101] He then offered him the kingdom with a gem-encrusted crown, unmindful of the bonds of blood and his oath.

On the holy day of Easter, all the royal regalia was ready and he was preparing to crown his brother-in-law who awaited the fulfilment of the promise like an anxious woman. But with his hatred somewhat relieved through the effect of God's mercy and all moving wisdom, Brun grew ashamed of what he had undertaken and repented. Secretly summoning his secretary, Folkmar, whom we have already mentioned, he revealed the wound concealed in his heart and asked insistently for advice on how it might be cured. God, who is always ready to help those who repent, gave him a heavenly cure by which he responded to and alleviated his lord's concerns, saying: 'My dearest lord, the Holy Spirit has advised that the hateful author of this outrage shall no longer prevail against us and I think that he can be confounded without endangering your honour. Tomorrow, I will present the crown which you promised to give to your brother-in-law, thereby revealing your good faith in the view of all. Then, suddenly letting it fall, I will break it apart, thereby permitting the now cold fraternal love to grow warm again in the future.' This plan pleased the archbishop who humbly implored God with constant prayers for success. In the morning, the deed was accomplished as planned. The archbishop pretended to be deeply troubled. Hugh and his supporters, their hopes frustrated, were inconsolable. When the day's festivities were finished, he was honoured with gifts other than those he had expected and went home.

The brothers, king and bishop, were later reconciled and, henceforth, took care to banish any trace of hostility as they persevered in the zeal of mutual love. With Christ always protecting him, Otto safely escaped these and many other plots of his enemies. But the archbishop, after distinguishing himself in all matters divine and human, slept the sleep of peace on 11 October, in the thirteenth year after his ordination, leaving his brother sorrowful. I have spoken of only a few of this great man's innumerable deeds – there were greater ones than this – because his noble lifestyle is fully described in another book, to which I can add nothing.[102]

101 Thietmar, 2.6.
102 Here, Thietmar refers to Brun's *vita* (i.e. Ruotger).

CHAPTER TWENTY-FOUR

Saddened by his brother's death and inspired by love, the emperor commended his bishopric and the care of his soul to Folkmar, Brun's trusted chaplain.[103] During the time that God permitted him to occupy his see, Folkmar acted admirably in all things, departing from our midst on 18 July. Then, all the clergy and people elected Gero, the brother of Margrave Thietmar.[104] The emperor was immediately informed of this but did not wish to give him the bishopric because he was angry at his brother for various reasons. Meanwhile, Gero was still a chaplain. One day, as he fulfilled his office by celebrating mass in the city of Pavia, he alone saw St Peter and St Ambrose blessing him with holy oil. He said nothing of this to anyone, however, preferring to receive the gift of divine love with equanimity. Moreover, on the feast of the Resurrection of the Lord, an angel with an unsheathed sword appeared before the emperor as he prepared to enter the church while wearing the crown [27 March 970].[105] The angel declared: 'Unless you fulfil Gero's election today, you will not leave this place in safety.' Frightened by this, the emperor said: 'Call lord Gero!' He came immediately and the emperor conveyed the pastoral office to him with the staff and humbly begged his indulgence. Afterwards, he was consecrated by his suffragans and, as long as he lived, carried both his name and office with sincere humility and in a manner acceptable to God and men, as is proven today by miraculous signs.

CHAPTER TWENTY-FIVE

Gero's holy mother, Hidda, went on pilgrimage to Jerusalem and took ill there. She commended this message to her companions: 'When my soul is freed from the dwelling place of its long exile, quickly give over my body to mother earth and immediately take news of this to my son Gero, so that he may not deny such honour to his pilgrim mother on earth as a loving God in heaven has deigned to grant her. He should also establish an altar for me in the church of St Cecilia.' Obedient to these orders, Hidda's devoted companions buried their mistress, following her blessed death, and immediately departed.

103 Archbishop Folkmar (965–69).

104 Archbishop Gero (969–76).

105 Here, referring to the common royal practice of wearing the crown on high holy days (i.e. *Festkrönung*; Warner 1994: 137).

Without realizing it, they thereby escaped the misery which followed.
For the Saracens invaded Jerusalem, leaving nothing to the conquered,
as the holy matron had secretly predicted to them when she ordered
that they immediately bury her corpse and depart. After arriving at
Cologne, they related the whole story to the archbishop. He received
them kindly, gave thanks to God, and fulfilled their just requests.
Because I have said little about the as yet unknown accomplishments
of this great prelate, I will say more about him later so that his virtue
will appear more evident.[106]

CHAPTER TWENTY-SIX

When the emperor heard of the death of the bishop of Regensburg, he
went there and was warned in a dream that he should give the
bishopric to the first person he met, and no other.[107] The next morning,
at dawn, and with no warning to the monks, Caesar went with a few
companions to the monastery of the martyr of Christ, Emmeram.[108]
Knocking gently on the door, he was admitted by a certain Gunther,
the church's vigilant custodian and a father venerable in all things.
Gazing at him, the king approached in humble veneration and spoke
the following words: 'What will you give me, brother, if you are
granted the office of bishop?' The old man laughing at this, answered:
'My shoes!' But when he and his brethren came to St Peter for the
episcopal election, Caesar revealed both his dream and the events
which followed, and with the advice of the clergy and all of the people
made him bishop.[109] After his consecration, Gunther had only occupied
his see for six months when, during a severe illness, he gathered his
strength sufficiently to rise up, take ashes in his hand, and indicate by
making the sign of the cross where he wished to migrate from this
world. Then, lying on the ground and being blessed himself, he sang

106 Thietmar, 3.2–4.
107 Refers to the death of Bishop Isingrim (930–40).
108 Otto's decision to go to St Emmeram was scarcely a coincidence. St Emmeram
was a proprietary monastery of the bishops of Regensburg, and at least one
witness suggests candidates for the episcopate were chosen, alternately, from the
ranks of the monastery and chapter (Rädlinger-Promper 1987: 92). In particular,
Provost Arnold of St Emmeram (d. 1050) observes that: 'From the time that St
Boniface established bishops in Bavaria, acting as vicar of the Apostolic See and in
accordance with the canonical decrees, monks and canons succeeded to this
bishopric [i.e. Regensburg] in alternation. If a bishop's predecessor was a canon,
a monk would be his successor and, likewise, a canon would succeed him. This has
remained the custom down to our own time' (Arnold, bk 2, col. 1027).
109 Bishop Gunther of Regensburg (d. October 940).

the song of the blessed Job: 'I heard of you, Lord, by the hearing of
my ear, now however my eye sees you. Therefore I rebuke myself and
do penance in dust and ashes.'¹¹⁰ He had barely finished his tearful
confession when he gave up the spirit. So was fulfilled what his predecessor, a man similar to him, had predicted when he said: 'Brother,
you will rule this church after me but live only a short time and only
God in his mercy will crown you.' But as long he pursued his earthly
pilgrimage, he desired that God's will would be done.

CHAPTER TWENTY-SEVEN

I have related the stories of these two bishops so that you, the reader,
may know that the grace of heaven often revealed to the emperor
what it wished to occur on earth. When Otto heard of the death of
this great father, he had Michael succeed him.¹¹¹ When the bishop had
ruled the see committed to him long and well, he and other Bavarian
leaders went to rescue the eastern regions where the Hungarians
were again causing trouble. But the battle between them had barely
begun when, alas, our forces were beaten and utterly demolished by
the enemy. The bishop lost an ear, was also wounded in his other
limbs, and lay among the fallen as if he were dead. Lying next to him
was an enemy warrior. When he realized that the bishop alone was
alive, and feeling safe from the snares of the enemy, he took a lance
and tried to kill him. Strengthened by the Lord, the bishop emerged
victorious from the long, difficult struggle and killed his enemy.
Finally, travelling by various rough paths, he arrived safely in
familiar territory, to the great joy of his flock and all Christians. He
was held to be a brave warrior by all the clergy and the best of
pastors by the people, and his mutilation brought him no shame, but
rather greater honour. But now I must return to narrating the course
of events.

CHAPTER TWENTY-EIGHT

The powerful and august emperor of the Romans consented to the
deposition of the lord Pope Benedict, his superior in Christ, who may
be judged by no one but God. I hope that the accusations were unjust.
He ordered him to be exiled to Hamburg, as I reveal more fully

110 Job 42: 5–6.
111 Bishop Michael of Regensburg (941–72).

later.[112] Would that he had not done it! Meanwhile, Duke Herman was ruling Saxony and had called for an assembly at Magdeburg.[113] With burning tapers and with all the bells ringing, he was received by the archbishop and led by the hand to the church.[114] There, my grandfather, Henry, resisting such arrogance, tried in vain to capture the duke by deception but the latter was surrounded by a large crowd of warriors. Nevertheless, the duke ordered him to go to the emperor in Rome. Doing this willingly, he crossed the Alps. As soon as he saw the emperor, having spotted him at a distance, he prostrated himself on the ground. When asked the purpose of this, he responded tearfully that he stood accused before him and feared to lose his favour and love. The emperor immediately raised him up, kissed him, and, inquiring carefully, learned of the duke's reception and how he had taken the emperor's place at dinner, among the bishops, and slept in his bed. The august Caesar was filled with manly anger because of this and sent letters to Bishop Adalbert ordering that he should send him horses in numbers equal to those of the bells that had been rung and chandeliers that had been lit. In carrying out the imperial edict, the archbishop tried as best he could to excuse himself, through representatives. But the aforementioned count was so clever that he placated the emperor's anger more easily than the other leading men and, because he was related by blood, he faithfully preserved the imperial favour as long as he lived. After giving him a gold torque, Caesar allowed him to depart, to the joy of his supporters and sorrow of his enemies.

112 Elected by the Romans in 964, Benedict V's deposition took place at a synod held in Rome (June 964) and rested on the charge that he had violated the oath that obliged him, and all other Romans, to refrain from electing a pope without permission from the emperor and his son (BO 355e; Beumann 1991: 97). See also 2.35; 4.18, 62; 6.88.

113 See note at 2.2.

114 The precise significance of this passage remains subject to debate. Althoff (1982: 141–53; 1991a: 312) has argued that Herman's behaviour at Magdeburg represented a usurpation of the king's ceremonial prerogatives, but with the aim of warning Otto about the dangers of his long absence from the realm rather than actually seizing the throne. Similar usurpations are documented at other points in Thietmar's chronicle (e.g. 5.4). Although Althoff's interpretation has enjoyed widespread support, it has also attracted criticism. More recent studies (Reuter 1991: 160; Becher 1996: 291–98) argue that Herman was not usurping anything (dukes were also entitled to a ceremonial reception!), but rather attempting to demonstrate that he possessed the same degree of independence as the 'king-like' dukes of Swabia and Bavaria, a point which Otto was by no means willing to concede. Of course, given the multivalent character of ritual, it may well have conveyed both meanings at the same time (Leyser 1994d: 199–201). Despite the use of the term 'count' the context suggests it was Herman who retained Otto's favour.

CHAPTER TWENTY-NINE

Meanwhile, the illustrious Margrave Hodo collected an army and attacked Miesco though the latter was faithful to the emperor and paid tribute for territory extending to the river Warthe.[115] Only my father, Count Siegfried, then a young man and unmarried, came to his aid with warriors of his own.[116] When the battle began at Zehden, on the feast of John the Baptist, they were initially successful [24 June 972]. But then Miesco's brother, Cidibur, attacked and killed all the best warriors, with the exception of the two counts. The emperor was very disturbed when he heard this miserable news and sent representatives from Italy who ordered Hodo and Miesco to leave off their fighting and preserve the peace until he returned, or risk losing his favour.

CHAPTER THIRTY

After subduing all of his enemies, the emperor made the arduous trip over the Alps and visited Bavaria.[117] After wisely disposing of various matters there, he went directly to Magdeburg where he celebrated Palm Sunday with great solemnity [16 March 973].[118] Indeed, it was his custom on all feast days to be led to the church for vespers, matins, and the mass by a procession composed of bishops and other orders of clerics carrying crosses, relics of saints, and censers. With that great fear of God which is the beginning of all wisdom, he would stand and sit, uttering nothing but prayers until the liturgy ended.[119] Afterwards, an entourage of priests, dukes, and counts accompanied him to his quarters with many candles. The next morning, for the salvation of his soul, he gave many gifts of land, books, and other royal paraphernalia to God and his unconquered duke, Maurice, and confirmed all the rights of the advocates. Written documents were issued in the presence and with the agreement of the empress and his son, and with all the faithful of Christ as witnesses.

115 Margrave Hodo of the Saxon eastern march (d. 993) was successor to Margrave Gero I and also belonged to his lineage (*LMA*, vol. 5, p. 63).

116 Count Siegfried of Walbeck (d. 991).

117 The emperor's departure from Italy and events at Quedlinburg are noted by Widukind (3.75, p. 151).

118 It has been suggested, on occasion, that the emperor's visit was commemorated in the so-called 'Magdeburg Reiter', one of the most important pieces of late medieval German art (thirteenth century), although Frederick II appears the more likely subject (Kaufmann 1989: 208).

119 Prov. 1: 7.

CHAPTER THIRTY-ONE

From thence, he went to Quedlinburg to celebrate the upcoming feast
of Easter with divine praise and earthly joy [23 March 973]. Here
also, at the emperor's order, Dukes Miesco and Boleslau, and legates
of the Greeks, Beneventans, Hungarians, Bulgarians, Danes, and Slavs
gathered along with all the leading men of the kingdom.[120] When all
matters had been settled peacefully and gifts had been distributed,
they went home satisfied. But the emperor's joy was disturbed when
Duke Herman died there on 1 April.[121] While his son Bernhard was
preparing to transport Herman's body to Lüneburg, he encountered
Bishop Bruno of Verden, who was near by.[122] Because the bishop had
placed the duke under the bann during his lifetime, the son tearfully
asked that he might immediately grant absolution and permit burial
in the church. But his request was not granted.

CHAPTER THIRTY-TWO

Because I have mentioned this bishop, it would please me to speak of
him more fully. He was a blood relative of the duke and had been a
monk at Corvey. The emperor held him in high regard and designated him as successor to Bishop Amolong who had presided wisely
over the church of Verden.[123] Because stone was not available,
Amolong had erected and consecrated a magnificent wooden church
which surpassed others in its size and quality.[124] He died at a *good old
age* on 5 May and was the duke's brother.[125] When Bruno, weighed
down by old age and severe illness, began to slow down, the emperor
asked that he treat his chaplain Herman, a brother of Archbishop
Folkmar, as a son and designate him as his assistant and heir. He

120 Duke Boleslav II of Bohemia (972–99). Thietmar apparently added the reference
to legates sent by various peoples after consulting the Quedlinburg annals (*AQ,*
an. 973, p. 62).

121 Mistaken date. Duke Herman III of Saxony's death (1002–12) is confused with
that of Duke Herman of Swabia (d. 27 March 973). See Holtzmann 1934: 77, n. 6.

122 In excommunicating and refusing burial to Duke Herman, Bishop Bruno of
Verden (962–76), one of Wichman the Elder's sons, may have been pursuing, by
other means, his family's vendetta against its senior branch (Leyser 1979: 12; and
general comments by Geary 1994a: 149).

123 Bishop Amolong of Verden (933–62).

124 Archaeological evidence tentatively suggests that this structure, the second
wooden church on this site, was a 'hall church' with a small, attached structure in
the west (Oswald 1966: 360; Jacobsen 1991: 435).

125 Gen. 25: 8; *NMer.,* fo. 2r, p. 5.

received this request sorrowfully and responded: 'Though unworthy, up to now I have carefully administered the office which my lord deigned to grant me. And as long as I must remain here, I wish to live without such words, if possible. There can be no equal concourse between humility and pride. Power accepts no consort.[126] Whatever else my lord requests, I will devotedly fulfil. The hope of a young man should not rest on the death of a decrepit old man, for that is a sin. It should be recalled that the calf's hide is often hung on the wall.' After having said such things, he had himself carried to the church of Cecilia, the virgin of Christ, where he lay prostrate on the floor and tearfully admitted that he had hitherto served her unworthily, saying: 'I know that my wretched self has been abandoned by God and by you, now that an outsider is placed ahead of me and is held to be more worthy in your service. Hence I now wish to depart from here and, in this, merely await the grace of Christ and your holy intercession. Even as I seek a foreign place, not unjustly, so should no one ever presume to rejoice over my misfortune. Now I ask from God whatever may please him and be useful to my church.'

CHAPTER THIRTY-THREE

When he had finished this prayer, he rose up and departed, remaining in his diocese until he knew for certain that the aforementioned youth was dead and then, with his supporters gathered together, declared: 'You have no new lord, rather bring me to my monastery and there, with great concern and without diversion, I shall await the day of judgement.[127] And you mortals must learn that all the things which will profit you are not to be had by running or hurrying but rather through the mercy of God.[128] May we be an example to you that no one trusting in God is abandoned and also that he who trusts in his own powers obtains nothing useful. Place your hopes in God the Father, my sons, and conquer harmful fear with the aid of his only Son and of the consubstantial Paraclete. Pray to God that, in his grace, he may emend our mutual failings to the better – whatever

---

126 Lucan, *Bellum civile* 1.92–93.

127 At Oldenstadt. Bishop Bruno established this community of nuns on his allodial property in 973 and apparently dedicated its first church (D O II 33; D H II 107; Leyser 1979: 65, 67; cf. Jacobson 1991: 317). Though essentially an *Eigenkloster* of the bishops of Verden, it enjoyed benefits, such as immunity, that were typical of communities with royal status (see D H II 107).

128 Rom. 9: 16.

through human frailty I have done to you or you to me – and that, after I am gone, you will be dear to God and have a lord useful to you and a time of prosperity. After these words, he went to the place he had chosen. Although many misfortunes accompanied his old age, he was nonetheless a man of affable and praiseworthy character.

CHAPTER THIRTY-FOUR

Having briefly related this emperor's deeds, I am moved to say[129] something about those who died in his time and in his and the church's service, and also to recall other contemporary events, before moving on to describe his death. Archbishop Hildebert, who anointed Otto, went to sleep in Christ in the second year of his reign on 31 May [937].[130] Frederick who succeeded him pleased both God and the world. At the end of his life, he gave thanks to God that he had never acquired anything unjustly for his church or lost anything. In that year the Hungarians devastated Thuringia and Saxony but perished in the more strongly fortified areas and only a few of them, flying on wings of fear, managed to return to their fatherland. Duke Eberhard of Franconia, long unfaithful to the king, was deposed and Count Wichman was reconciled as a humble supplicant [938].[131] In the following year, the king's brother Henry was captured by Count Eberhard and held in chains. In the third year of the king's reign, his brother Henry, Duke Eberhard, Duke Giselbert of Lotharingia, and other supporters of their iniquity pillaged this side of the Rhine [939].[132] One of the king's allies, Udo, learning of this, killed Eberhard.[133] Giselbert and his companions drowned in the Rhine and Henry was compelled to seek the king's favour. After this, legates from the Greeks twice brought gifts from their emperor to our king, both rulers being in a state of concord.[134]

---

129 Ovid, *Metamorphoses* 1.1.

130 Archbishop Hildebert of Mainz; *NMer.*, fo. 3r, p. 7. Most of the material in this chapter is also reported by the annals of Quedlinburg (*AQ*, an. 937, p. 56).

131 Count Wichman I 'the Elder' (d. 944).

132 Duke Giselbert of Lotharingia (915–39), son of Reginar I and brother-in-law of Otto I.

133 Count Udo I of Rheingau and Wetterau (d. 949).

134 Emperor Constantine VII Porphyrogennetos (911–59).

CHAPTER THIRTY-FIVE

Archbishop Frederick, a very abstemious man, died in the seventeenth year after his consecration and was succeeded in the year 954 of the Incarnation by William, who was the offspring of a captured Slavic noblewoman and the king.[135] Four years later, the salutary sign of the cross miraculously appeared on the clothing of human beings, helping those who received it worthily but injuring those who were sceptical. In the year of the Incarnation 963, because of the deposition and exile of Pope Benedict, which I have already mentioned, during which he died, savage death pursued the emperor's army, taking Archbishop Henry of Trier, Duke Gottfried, and innumerable others.[136] In the third year, on 31 March, the church of Halberstadt collapsed [965]. Also, the emperor travelled from Italy to Frankfurt where, during a lengthy stay, he established peace and concord among this people. In the following year, the emperor again visited the land of the Romans.[137] In the fourth year, the emperor's like-named son came to Rome, along with Archbishop William of Mainz, and was elevated to his father's dignity by Pope John [967].[138] In the seventh year, the temple of the Lord in Dornburg burned down [971].

CHAPTER THIRTY-SIX

Here, I would like to mention that Boso, instituted as my predecessor by the emperor, ruled the office entrusted to him for one year, ten months, and three days. He died in his Bavarian fatherland on 1 November and was buried in Merseburg before the high altar of the church of St John the Baptist. He was educated in the monastic life at the monastery of the martyr St Emmeram which is located outside

---

135 *AQ*, an. 954, p. 58. Archbishop Frederick of Mainz (937–54), Archbishop William of Mainz (954–68).

136 Thietmar, 2.28. Archbishop Henry of Trier (956–64). Duke Gottfried of Lower Lotharingia, (953–64). Benedict V's deposition actually occurred in 964, but Thietmar is following the Quedlinburg annalist (*AQ*, an. 963, p. 60) who dates it to the preceding year and, moreover, does not see a direct causal relationship between that event and the deaths.

137 Roman campaign 966–72.

138 Pope John XIII (965–72). A Roman, former papal bureaucrat, and bishop of Narni, John's election as successor to Leo VIII represented a compromise between Roman and imperial interests. Though generally supporting the latter, he also fostered the local aristocratic house of the Crescentii, from whose ranks would come one of the Ottonian dynasty's most persistent enemies, Crescenzio 'Nomentano' (*LMA*, vol. 5, 542; *DHP* 937–38).

the city of Regensburg, to the south. From there, he was taken into the king's service and, as due compensation for his great labours, received the church at Zeitz as a benefice. Next to this city, in a certain forest which he himself had cleared and named after himself, he built a temple to the Lord, in stone, and had it consecrated.[139] Moreover, prior to his ordination, he also received all the benefices pertaining to the churches located in Merseburg and Memleben, and also at Dornburg and Kirchberg. Because his ceaseless preaching and baptizing had won numerous people for Christ in the East, the emperor was pleased and offered him a choice of three proposed bishoprics: Meißen, Zeitz, or Merseburg.[140] Out of all these, he asked for the church of Merseburg because it was peaceful and, as long as he lived, he ruled it zealously.

CHAPTER THIRTY-SEVEN

Boso wrote his instructions for the faith in Slavic to make them more accessible to those who had been committed to him. He also demanded the singing of the *kyrie eleison*, after explaining what it meant. The fools mockingly changed this to *ukrivolsa* which, translated into our language, means 'the alder stands in the bush'. As often as he tried to correct them, they replied, 'so has Boso spoken'. The emperor granted him a few villages which belonged to the previously mentioned city [Merseburg] and also a certain burg in the district of Schkeuditz, called Magdeborn, which means 'protect the honey'. The emperor's like-named son also gave him a church in Helfta.[141] The church had been established in honour of St Radegund by his father and consecrated in his presence by Bishop Bernhard. When the first father of our church died, as I have mentioned, Bishop Anno of Worms interceded with the emperor who thereupon gave the bishopric to Giselher, a man noble in birth and customs.[142] Archbishop Adalbert consecrated him at Magdeburg in the month of June.

139 My translation differs from Trillmich and Holtzmann who suggest that Boso named the *church* after himself. The church and mission station were located at Buosenrod on the former site of a sacred grove (*NDB*, vol. 2, p. 482).

140 Only a choice between Zeitz and Merseburg, according to D O I 366: 'And because that venerable man, Boso, laboured much to convert the same people of the Slavs to God, he may have a choice between Merseburg and Zeitz, as he wishes. In accordance with our agreement, he should cede the other to the disposition of our archbishop'.

141 Near Eisleben. See D O I 373a, issued on 6 June 969.

142 Bishop Giselher of Merseburg (971–81), Archbishop of Magdeburg (981–1004).

CHAPTER THIRTY-EIGHT

Because I have already spoken briefly about Duke Conrad, the emperor's son-in-law who was killed at the river Lech, I believe that it would be appropriate for me to reveal certain things which were not discussed at that time. Much later, during a stay at Merseburg, the emperor learned from an informant that the Slavs at Zwenkau under lord Kuchawiz, whom he much esteemed, had possession of the duke's armour. With Kuchawiz's aid, a judicial duel was held and the losers were hanged at the emperor's order. Most of the booty was restored. I do not know whether they took these things as murderers or, without guilt, discovered the duke's death by chance. In any case, they rightly paid with their lives for having presumed to keep this secret.[143]

CHAPTER THIRTY-NINE

Because she refused to offer him compensation, a certain Cono publicly defamed the emperor's daughter, Conrad's wife, and claimed that she had secretly become his wife.[144] Taking this very seriously, the emperor cleared her name in the following way. After all the leading men of the realm had assembled, he first asked them in private whether she was guilty of this thing. Afterwards, when he saw that she had absolved herself by invoking the witness of Christ and by swearing oaths, he announced to all present that anyone of his *familiares* who wished to defend her in a duel would find in him a firm friend on that day and for ever. Hearing this, Count Burchard stepped forward and openly declared that Cono had lied about everything. After swearing that his accusations were true, Cono engaged with Burchard, but lost his false right hand at the first approach. His injustice was revealed by his defeat. Thus the merciful Lord rescued this woman, whose innocence of life pleased him, from a false accusation. During her husband's lifetime, she was often despised and burdened with troubles but suffered these with manly patience and tried to preserve her innate honour. Moreover, after finishing this life, she was tearfully

---

143 Lippelt (1973: 152) suggests that Thietmar, by emphasizing the factor of secrecy, is expressing doubt in the justice of Otto I's actions.

144 In other words '*quod sibi satisfacere noluisset*'. Liudgard (d. 953), the daughter of Otto and Edith, had the misfortune to be both the wife and sister of men who participated in uprisings against the king (*LMA*, vol. 5, p. 2040). A much less detailed account in Adalbert of Magdeburg's continuation of Regino's chronicle says the incident involved Otto's niece and identifies her accuser as Conrad, the son of Count Gebhard (*Cont. Reg.*, an. 950, p. 164).

buried in the church of the martyr of Christ, Alban, at Mainz. Her
silver spindle hangs there in her memory.

CHAPTER FORTY

I will say something about the impious deeds that Duke Henry
committed during his reign, as they also show that no opposition was
permitted to all that we have mentioned above.[145] He ordered the
patriarch of Aquileia to be castrated and the archbishop of Salzburg to
be blinded.[146] I do not want to mention the grounds for these actions,
but I know that they were not sufficient to justify them. At his death,
the duke was admonished for these misdeeds by Bishop Michael of
Regensburg, but admitted his guilt only in the first and not in regard
to the archbishop, being ignorant that there are few things in which
blame is absent. Hence, David humbly said: 'Purify me from my secret
sins, Lord!'[147] The duke's wife, Judith, was present and heard his
confession. After his death, she had his body interred with great
mourning in the church which he himself had built in honour of the
blessed and ever virgin Mary.[148] With tears and an abundance of alms,
she sought forgiveness for anything in which his soul had lapsed,
whether she knew of it herself or learned of it from others.

---

145 Thietmar, 2.34.

146 Archbishop Herold of Salzburg (938–58, d. c.970). The archbishop belonged to the
Bavarian family of the Liutpoldinger, formerly the ducal house of Bavaria (i.e. the
lineage of Duke Arnulf), which Otto I had effectively disenfranchised by installing
his younger brother, Henry, as duke. The clan remained powerful and apparently
irreconcilable. Hence one should not be surprised to find that its members readily
supported the similarly disenfranchised Duke Liudolf, Otto's son by Queen Edith,
in his uprising against his father and uncle (i.e. Duke Henry), in 953–55. After
some initial hesitancy, Archbishop Herold joined his kinsmen in revolt. His
blinding, an apparently spontaneous act with no semblance of due process, was
the duke's revenge. Later, presumably under compulsion, the archbishop abdicated
his office amid accusations that he had despoiled churches, distributed their
treasures among the heathen, and been unfaithful to his lord, the emperor. Similar
motives determined Henry's treatment of the patriarch of Aquileia, who seems to
have supported the rebels as well (Beumann 1991: 74–76; Bührer-Thierry 1997:
199–205).

147 Ps. 18: 13 (RSV 19: 13).

148 Niedermünster, Regensburg. Duke Henry's church was constructed, during his
lifetime, on the foundations of a smaller building dating from the mid-eighth
century. In addition to the duke himself, it subsequently provided a place of burial
for Judith (Oswald 1966: 276–77; Jacobsen 1991: 339–40).

CHAPTER FORTY-ONE

Thereafter, Judith lived chastely in widowhood but because she esteemed Bishop Abraham of Freising above all others, and despite her innocence, she was ripped by the malevolent teeth of public opinion.[149] After migrating from this light, she was exonerated in the following way, by the same bishop, who was singing the mass on the day of her burial. Before communion, he turned towards the people and described her merits to bystanders, saying: 'If she ever committed the offence for which she has been defamed, may the omnipotent Father bring me to judgement and due condemnation by the remedy of the body and blood of his Son, but may her soul enjoy perpetual salvation.' Then, with innocence of mind and body, he took the unique remedy of all faithful people. The people believed, albeit too late, and with their unjust criticism had actually helped her even though they wanted to cause harm.

CHAPTER FORTY-TWO

In the days of the previously mentioned emperor, there was a certain count, named Hed, who built a church in Heeslingen in honour of the athlete of Christ Vitus. Because he had no heir, he endowed it with the greatest part of his property and, after establishing a congregation of nuns there, placed the same abbey under the protection of Archbishop Adaldag of Bremen.[150] But alas, the two venerable matrons who were placed over this foundation – each named Wendelgard – died quickly. My grandfather had given his daughter to the convent and she had been educated there, but he had no success when he asked the archbishop to let her succeed the two departed matrons.[151] Afterwards, at the request of the emperor, her godfather, the archbishop gave her the veil on Sunday, 30 April, though she was but twelve years old, and on the next day ordained her as abbess in her father's presence.[152] Later, he regretted this. For within five days, as I will relate, Italy's glory and Saxony's salvation, namely Otto I, died. My grandmother Judith rests in a church which her daughter had constructed, with great effort, out of stone, a rare material in this

149 Bishop Abraham of Freising (957–93). On the relationship between Judith and Abraham see also note at 3.5.

150 Archbishop Adaldag of Hamburg-Bremen (937–88).

151 Here referring to Henry of Stade.

152 30 April = Wednesday.

region.[153] She departed from this world on 26 October.[154] The church
of Fulda, which had burned down, was restored under this emperor.[155]

CHAPTER FORTY-THREE

The emperor celebrated the Ascension of the Lord at Merseburg
where, in the spirit of devotion, he was eager to fulfil the remainder of
his oath [1 May].[156] On the Tuesday before Pentecost he went to
Memleben and, on the following day, happily sat at the dinner table
[6 May]. When the meal was finished, as vespers was being sung, he
suddenly became ill and weak. Those who were standing near by took
him and laid him down. He was quickly fortified with the last rites
and, as everyone prayed for him, he absolved his debt to nature on 7
May, in the thirty-eighth year after his consecration [973].[157] On the
following night, his viscera were removed and buried in the church of
St Mary. But his body, having been prepared with aromatic spices,
was transferred to Magdeburg where it was honourably and tearfully
received and placed in a marble sarcophagus.[158] The burial was
undertaken by the archbishops Gero and Adalbert with help from
other bishops and from all the clergy.

CHAPTER FORTY-FOUR

The emperor's like-named son, namely Otto the younger, had been
elected and anointed during his father's lifetime, but was once more

---

153 Judith was the wife of Henry of Stade.

154 16 October according to the necrology at Merseburg (*NMer.*, fo. 6v, p. 14).
Holtzmann (1935: 91, n. 8), suggests that Thietmar somehow dropped the X from
the necrology's entry (XVII Kal. Nov.).

155 Widukind 2.38, p. 98.

156 Widukind 3.75, pp. 151–53.

157 'Thus he died, on 7 May, the Wednesday before Pentecost, the emperor of the
Romans and king of the people, leaving to posterity many glorious monuments,
both spiritual and worldly' (Widukind 3.76, p. 154).

158 'The people, moreover, having praised him exceedingly and rendered thanks,
recalled how he had ruled his subjects with fatherly beneficence, freed them from
enemies, conquered the arrogant foe – Avars, Saracens, Danes and Slavs – by
force of arms, subjugated Italy, destroyed the sanctuaries of pagan gods among
neighbouring peoples, and established churchs and communities of clerics
(*ministrorumque ordines*). They also said many other good things about him as,
conversing among themselves, they attended the king's funeral' (Widukind 3.75,
p. 153). See also note at 2.11.

acclaimed by all as lord and king.[159] The great concern that Empress Adelheid exhibited for her husband's salvation, until her own death, can scarcely be comprehended in words or equalled in deeds. Whatever secular honour or success came to her she ascribed not to her own merits but rather to Christ, saying in the words of the praises of David: 'Not to us, Lord, but to your name give glory.'[160] Even if I were to combine eloquence, knowledge, and memory, they would still not suffice to express Caesar's praise. And just as the lord was, so also were his leading men. A superfluous variety of foods and other things did not delight them, but rather the golden mean in all things.[161] All the virtues, of which we read, flourished while they lived but withered with their deaths. Even if their bodies are dead, their immortal souls live on, rejoicing through blessed eternity in their good works.

CHAPTER FORTY-FIVE

But so will I conclude the book, not since Charlemagne has so great a ruler and defender of the homeland possessed the royal throne. Many of the best men had preceded him in death, as I mentioned, but all those who survived remembered that pleasant time and did not like or follow the new manner which now arose. Rather, they willingly held to the right path of ancient truth and justice to the end of their lives. For then they witnessed the fulfilment of that prophecy which a certain wise man had written down: 'First is the golden age, then follows silver and afterwards iron.'[162] May all the faithful hear the truthful admonition of the blessed Gregory: 'When gifts are increased, the motivation of the donors also grows.'[163] And, may they also tremble if they have offended in things committed to them, and with a humble spirit beseech God for the sake of the emperor's soul, that he may clemently forgive a sinful servant for the numerous shameful acts which could not be guarded against in so many of the tasks committed to him, and may the dominator of all kingdoms assist the people in the present and future as a vigilant and pious guardian. And you who may succeed me, being mindful of such great benefit,

---

159 Widukind 3.76. Otto II had been elected king during a *Reichstag* held at Worms early in May and was crowned at Aachen on 26 May (BO 297a, 299a).

160 Ps. 115: 1.

161 Horace, *Odes*, bk 2, ode 10, verse 5.

162 Horace, *Epode* 16.64–66. Thietmar also refers to an age of gold at 2.13. Similar language is employed by Brun of Querfurt (Brun, *VA* c. 9, p. 8).

163 Greg, *Hom. Ev.* 1.9.1, p. 1106.

preserve the memory of his soul in the custody of a faithful heart. Remember him, in particular, on the feast day of Lawrence [10 August], the athlete of Christ. Vigorously entreat Lawrence to intercede with God, moreover, so that, having granted Otto victory over mortal enemies on that day, through the saint's merits, he might bestow the absolution which the emperor always sought, and thereby permit him to evade the snares of invisible enemies as well. And so, on the Day of Judgement, may he be separated from those on the left and be found at the right hand of God the Father.

BOOK THREE

Otto, the second bearer of this name, but third in the number of kings,[1]
will now be described. He was installed on the throne of his great
    father
With worthy praise, he who helped all in need,
Living for another generation through his successor.
His youth was happy and fortunate, but sorrow arrived in his latter
    years
Through the heavy burden of our sins.
Then, this evil world did penance for rejecting the truth.
Many in the realm perished through the vengeful sword. We know
    of no certain cause,
Yet it is clear to all: since Merseburg tearfully suffered loss
Holy peace has departed from our lands, and the enemy reigns far
    and wide.
Who can describe how he raged, bringing cruel death,
And not even sparing the temples of Christ, the giver of life.
Many of our people died in battle and warfare, overcome by the
    Saracens.
Truly happy are they who, constant in the love of Christ,
Persist in the desirable tranquillity of peace,
Completely ignorant of that fear which strikes the hearts of the evil.
For more than thirty years that fear disturbed our predecessors
And, alas, armed our enemy who could even invade our own lands.
Now, may each of the faithful beseech the one who joins heaven and
    earth,
That he may grant an end to these afflictions.

CHAPTER ONE

May the subject of this book be Otto II who was the third to govern
our realm. As a young man he was noted for his outstanding physical

---

1 *Ecbasis Captivi* 1148.

strength and, as such, initially tended towards recklessness. Generous and unrestrained in his many works of piety, he rejected more mature counsel, but after enduring much criticism, learned to restrain himself with praiseworthy virtue. Thereafter, he comported himself more nobly, as I will explain below. At the instigation of that pious mother who directed his growth to manhood, he acquired Memleben, the place of his father's death, as well as tithes belonging to Hersfeld. This acquisition was accomplished through a lawful exchange.[2] He subsequently assembled a community of monks at Memleben and established a free abbey which he provided with every necessity and had confirmed through a papal privilege.[3] Furthermore, by imperial decree, and in the presence of Archbishop Adalbert, he granted the brothers serving God at Magdeburg the right to elect their archbishop.[4] He confirmed this gift with a book which included splendid portraits, in gold, of himself and the Empress Theophanu. It can still be seen there today. With the emperor's permission and in his presence, the archbishop, who was vested for mass, read aloud the imperial diploma containing the election privilege and displayed it.[5] This occurred after the gospel had been read and Adalbert, as usual, had delivered a pertinent sermon. Afterwards, he threatened anyone who might dare to infringe this privilege with a terrible excommunication and confirmed this as everyone shouted, 'Amen, so be it, so be it!' The emperor looked upon the still impoverished bishopric of Merseburg with generous concern, giving to Bishop Giselher, whom he loved greatly, first the abbey in Pöhlde and then the burg Zwenkau with all its appertinences, this for the service of St John the Baptist.[6]

2 D O II 191 (20 May 979). Memleben was already a place of some significance prior to Otto II's intervention. It was the site of a royal residence and at least one church, the latter having been established by Otto I in honour of the Virgin Mary and in memory of Henry I (2.43). In 968, this church was given to the bishop of Zeitz, an act rescinded by Otto II when he decided to establish a monastery there (Leopold and Schubert 1991: 376–79). Although Thietmar emphasizes both the piety and legality of the monarch's actions, there is no question that the exchange worked to the detriment of Hersfeld which lost some of its most valuable property and was effectively cut off from the Slavic frontier with its opportunities for misssionary work and colonization (Bernhardt 1993: 248–49). Under Henry II, Otto's arrangements were largely undone and Memleben itself became a proprietary monastery of Hersfeld (7.31).

3 The papal privilege is not extant.

4 D O II 207 (19 November 979).

5 Textual emendations suggested by Holtzmann make it appear that the book rather than the privilege is displayed. A convincing argument to the contrary is offered by Fickermann (1957: 33–38).

6 On the bestowal of Zwenkau see D O II 86 (28 June 974).

He also granted to him whatever lay within the walls of Merseburg, including the Jews, the merchants, and the mint; also the forest between the rivers Saale and the Mulde or rather between the districts of Siusuli and Pleißnerland; as well as Kohren, Nerchau, Pausitz, Taucha, Portitz, and Gundorf.[7] All of this was conveyed through a diploma which he confirmed with his own hand.

CHAPTER TWO

Meanwhile, Archbishop Gero of the see of Cologne died. As I have only spoken briefly about him, I will now relate a few things which I previously held back. At his command, the crucifix which now stands above his grave, in the middle of the church, was artfully fabricated from wood. When he noted a split in its head, he did not presume to heal it himself but rather relied upon the healthy remedy of the highest artisan. He took a portion of the body of the Lord, our unique comfort in every necessity, and part of the health-bringing cross, and placed them together in the crack. Then, prostrating himself, he tearfully invoked the name of the Lord. When he arose, he found that the damage had been healed through his humble benediction. On another occasion, he entered his chapel in full daylight and, as he afterwards told his confidants, saw St Victor in victorious battle with the Devil.

CHAPTER THREE

Being envious of all good things, the Devil took it upon himself to predict Gero's death, as he had previously done for other mortals. The recipient of this prediction was a certain Abbess Gerberga whose chastity of mind and body had endeared her to the archbishop and caused him to detain her frequently in his company. The Devil said: 'I

---

7 Archbishop Giselher exchanged the property at Nerchau with Count Becilin for Pausitz (D O III 74). In 997, the entire forest district of Nerchau was given to Magdeburg (D O III 247). This same forest 'between the Saale and the Mulde' is noted in D O II 90 (30 August 974) which conveys its possession to Giselher, then bishop of Merseburg. Though perhaps based on an authentic diploma, D. 90 is essentially a forgery concocted by Thietmar himself. In light of the bishop's subsequent problems with the clan of the Ekkehardiner (8.20 ff), the document's apparent grant of exclusive hunting rights (*Wildbann*) is noteworthy. In 997 (i.e. after the dissolution of Merseburg), Otto III gave a forest at Sömmering to the now Archbishop Giselher in return for a forest at Zwenkau (D O III 252). When Merseburg was restored, Henry II gave back both the burg and forest of Zwenkau (D H II 64).

would reveal my secret to you, if I did not know that, up to now, you have not preserved any secret that has been committed to you. If you promise that you will faithfully preserve my secret, I will share it with you, but know that if you ever reveal it to anyone, I will surely take your life. This year, for a period of three days, your friend Gero will be so ill that he will appear to be dead. During this period, if he is protected by someone, he will escape the danger unharmed.' Astonished by such words, the maid of Christ promised that she would faithfully conceal from everyone that which she had just heard. When she saw that the Devil had vanished, however, she immediately went to the archbishop and told him everything. When the Devil noted this, he struck her down, so that after a few days she traded this fragile life for life eternal. On the day of her burial, as the archbishop was singing the mass, he noted her accomplishments to all in attendance and asked that they grant her absolution. He also granted it to her himself.

CHAPTER FOUR

After this, he actually was struck by the infirmity that we have already mentioned and commended himself to the protection of Everger.[8] At Everger's orders, the archbishop, so exhausted by the excruciating pain that he appeared dead, was washed, brought to the church on a catafalque, and buried a day later. People say that, on the third night, he awoke as if from a deep sleep, heard the sound of a bell ringing and demanded three times with a loud call that they quickly release him. Horrified, one who had heard this accosted Everger, the previously mentioned custodian of the church, and demanded that he help the desperate archbishop. But Everger, judging this to be complete nonsense, hit him with a big stick. Thus the archbishop, of blessed memory, found rest on 29 June.[9] He appeared soon afterwards to Abbot Liudolf and, after saying, 'Sing the requiem for me,' disappeared right before his eyes. *By election and by the emperor's grant, Warin was quickly anointed in his place.*[10]

8 Everger held a number of offices at Cologne, including that of custodian (as Thietmar notes) and would later be elected archbishop of that see (i.e. 985–99), a promotion he owed to the influence of Empress Theophanu (*LMA*, vol. 4, pp. 141–42).

9 *NMer.*, fo. 3v, p. 8.

10 Prior to his election as archbishop (976–85), Warin had been the cathedral's provost. Whatever gratitude he may have felt towards Otto II (namely, for approving his election) did not prevent him from assisting Duke Henry 'the Quarrelsome' in his effort to unseat the emperor's son and heir (3.26; *LMA*, vol. 8, p. 204)

CHAPTER FIVE

In Otto II's second year, Duke Henry of the Bavarians was captured and brought to Ingelheim where he was carefully guarded.[11] *975: In this year the winter was harsh, long, and dry, and there was much snow.*[12] After Archbishop Robert of Mainz died, the emperor placed his chancellor, Willigis, over this church although many objected to his low birth.[13] As Peter attests, he knew that God does not look at the person, but rather loves all who cherish him in their hearts above all others; and he rewards them with unimaginable honour.[14] We may not fail to mention how divine mercy marked out this future pastor. Though poor, his mother was good, as the following account will reveal. While she was carrying him in her womb, she saw, in a dream, that the sun shone forth from her bosom and filled the whole earth with flaming rays. And, during the night in which she gave birth to this child, all the animals in her household responded in kind, as if to congratulate the lady. This infant resembled the sun because, through the rays of his holy preaching, he enlightened the hearts of many who were longing for the love of Christ. His own birth coincided with the births of a miraculous number of male offspring, clearly because a man of God had appeared whom the Divine Will had predestined to rule, for the salvation of the homeland. Blessed mother, whom the Lord so greatly favoured above all of her contemporaries in that she

11 *AQ*, an. 974, p. 62; BM 667b. The duke's supporters included Bishop Abraham of Freising and presumably his mother, Duchess Judith, since each was also placed in custody following the duke's capture and initial imprisonment. As punishment, the bishop was sent to Corvey while Duchess Judith had to enter the convent of Niedermünster, Regensburg. Duke Henry also enjoyed the support of Duke Boleslav II of Bohemia and Duke Miesco of Poland. After Henry escaped imprisonment and continued his rebellion, Otto II confiscated every office both the duke and Gunther of Merseburg held from him and added Henry's Duchy of Bavaria to Duke Otto of Swabia's territory. After being detached from Bavaria, Carinthia was bestowed upon Henry, the son of the former Bavarian Duke Berthold (d. 947) who nonetheless joined the rebellion shortly afterwards. A further rebel was added with Bishop Henry of Augsburg (973–82). Through his mother, the bishop was a descendant of Duke Arnulf (d. 937) and hence a member of the Liutpolding clan as well (Zoepfl 1955: 77–78).

12 *AQ*, an. 975, p. 62.

13 Archbishop Robert of Mainz (970–75). Willigis, chancellor (971–75), archbishop (975–1011). How 'low' Willigis's birth really was is difficult to determine from Thietmar's reference. It has been argued that he merely wished to indicate that the archbishop descended from the lesser nobility and not that he was ignoble or unfree (e.g. Heinemeyer 1976: 42).

14 Acts 10: 34.

bore a child equal to those more noble, and indeed, superior to some of them; and who learned both through her eyes and experience that the hope revealed in her vision was true. But I will say more about this later.

CHAPTER SIX

On his first campaign, the emperor captured the burg Boussu.[15] On a second campaign, he hurried to Schleswig to attack the rebellious Danes. There, he saw that his enemy had taken up arms and occupied a ditch built for the defence of their homeland as well as the portal called Wieglesdor. On the advice of Duke Bernhard and my grandfather, Count Henry, he forcefully overpowered all of these defences [August 974].[16] During this campaign, for the first time, exclamations of evil mockery were directed at the clergy. And they are still repeated by evil men today. It is abominable that when anything of worth is discovered by righteous people it is little used and immediately rejected by the greatest number as utterly detestable. That which displeases God and moves men to earn the penalty for their guilt, one learns and confirms by ruminating on it. Although many do not intend their jests to be taken seriously, nevertheless they can in no way proffer them without incurring the stain of sin.

The emperor established a burg on this border and secured it with a garrison. Bishop Bruno, whom we have already mentioned, died on 9 March and, at Archbishop Adaldag's suggestion, was succeeded by Erp, provost at Bremen.[17] In those days, on 25 July, I was born.

15 This campaign was directed at the brothers, Reginar IV and Lambert of Louvain (7.46).

16 Duke Bernhard I of Saxony (973–1011), son of Herman Billung, played an important role in defeating Henry the Quarrelsome's conspiracy to seize the throne (4.6) but later, ironically, represented the Saxon *gens* in approving the succession of the duke's son as King Henry II (5.16; *LMA*, vol. 1, p. 1986). In addition to pillaging Schleswig, the Danish king, Harald 'Bluetooth', attacked the border region beyond the Elbe (BM 667c, 671a). Harald, known for his great runic monument at Jelling, contributed to the revival of royal power in Denmark and may have extended his influence to Norway as well (Sawyer and Sawyer 1993: 55). Thitmar notes Harald's conversion to Christianity at 2.14. Harald was subsequently overthrown and replaced by his son, Sven, whose exploits Thietmar discusses at 7.36–37.

17 According to Holtzmann (1935: 104, n. 3), Bishop Bruno of Verden died on 14 February or 27 April. Bishop Erp of Verden (976–94).

CHAPTER SEVEN

In the year 976 of the Incarnation of the Lord, Henry, duke of the Bavarians, fled to Bohemia after being deprived of both his office and the communion of the church.[18] While he was residing there, with Duke Boleslav, the emperor attacked with a strong army, but gained nothing at all against these two. Moreover, through the treachery of one of Boleslav's warriors, he lost a great troop of Bavarians who were coming to his aid and had just set up camp next to the burg Pilsen.[19] In the evening, the Bavarians were washing themselves without having set a guard for security. Suddenly, the mailed enemy arrived and cut them down as they ran naked to their tents and through the meadow. The enemy returned with all of their booty, happy and unharmed. Hearing of the loss of so many men, and knowing that no other route of return was accessible to him, the emperor went directly to his burg at Cham.[20] In the following year, he brought the duke to submission as the latter sought refuge at Passau.[21] *In the next year, Duke Henry, Count Ekbert, and Bishop Henry were accused before the emperor at Magdeburg.[22] Afterwards, they were captured and sent into a long exile.*

18 And also after Otto had mounted two military expeditions in Bavaria (Beumann 1991: 115).

19 The location of the early medieval burg (Starý Plzenec) differed from that of the modern city founded in *c.*1295 (*LMA*, vol. 6, p. 2159).

20 Royal burg and mint (*c.*1000), located north-east of Regensburg, Bavaria (*LMA*, vol. 2, p. 1670).

21 BM 749a–b. Henry 'the Quarrelsome' had returned to Bavaria and, together with Duke Henry of Carinthia, had driven Bishop Pilgrim from his city of Passau. In turn, they were besieged there by Otto II. For his part, Bishop Henry of Augsburg had seized Neuburg on the Danube and several other burgs.

22 The king appears to have celebrated Easter (31 March 978) at Quedlinburg, so the court day must have occurred somewhat later (BM 763b). In any case, the assembly decided that Duke Henry and his allies would all be imprisoned. Subsequently, Duke Henry 'the Quarrelsome' and Count Ekbert were placed in the custody of Bishop Folkmar of Utrecht, Bishop Henry of Augsburg in that of Abbot Liudolf of Werden, and Duchess Gisela was exiled to Merseburg (4.7). Duke Henry of Carinthia's place of imprisonment is unknown although Thietmar later notes that he was released from it (3.24). Henry's duchy was given to Count Otto, son of Conrad 'the Red' and Liudgard, the daughter of Otto I (BM 763c; Beumann 1991: 115).

CHAPTER EIGHT

After this, the emperor zealously prepared for an expedition against the Carolingian king, Lothar.[23] At the head of a strong army, Lothar had presumed to invade the palace and royal seat at Aachen which had always belonged to our realm; and he had turned the eagle in his direction. This eagle stood on the east side of the palace and it was the custom of all who took possession of this place to turn it in the direction of their own kingdom.[24] As Lothar quickly departed, the emperor pursued him as far as his seat at Paris, wasting and burning everything in his path.[25] During this campaign, many were seized by severe illness, and Count Brun of Arneburg, a warrior laudable in all things, died on 30 November.[26] The emperor returned in triumph, having struck the enemy with such terror that they never again dared such a thing. Whatever insult had previously been inflicted upon us was repaid by this. Meanwhile, Ulrich, pastor of the church of Augsburg and a gem of the priesthood, departed from this world in the fiftieth year after his ordination, repaying to Christ the fruit of his devout labour on 4 July.[27] Henry succeeded him, but only ruled for a short time, as I will relate.

CHAPTER NINE

Count Gero was accused before the emperor by Waldo and captured at a place called Sömmering, at the instigation of Archbishop Adalbert and Margrave Dietrich.[28] He was then placed in the secure custody of

---

23 BM 771a. Thietmar refers to Lothar as *rex Karelingorum.* The military expedition in question was announced at a *Reichstag* held at Dortmund in the middle of July 978. On the same occasion, Bishop Henry was released from confinement at the request of a delegation of clergy from Augsburg and on the recommendation of Duke Otto.

24 Cf. Richer 3.71.

25 BM 771d–e. The king besieged Paris (September 978) while Duke Charles of Lotharingia and Bishop Dietrich of Metz attacked Laon. The effort was hardly as successful as Thietmar suggests. Paris was successfully defended by Duke Hugh of France and Otto ultimately had to order a retreat (November). On the return trip, his army suffered casualities from hostile troops and flooded rivers.

26 On 29 November according to the necrology at Merseburg (*NMer.*, fo. 7v. p. 16). Thietmar apparently dropped an I from the date (i.e. II Kal. Dec. instead of III Kal. Dec).

27 *NMer.*, fo. 3v, p. 8.

28 Gero, count in northern Thuringia and Morzani (*LMA*, vol. 4, pp. 1349–50).

my father and uncle.[29] Then, after all the leading men of the realm had convened at Magdeburg, the two men met on a certain island for a judicial duel. Waldo was twice wounded on the neck, but pursued his enemy all the more vigorously, striking him in the head with a strong blow and laying him out. When asked if he could continue fighting, Count Gero was forced to concede that he could not. Waldo then left the place of battle, laid aside his weapons, refreshed himself with water, and fell backwards dead. Then, by the decree of the judges and the emperor's instruction, it was ordered that Gero be beheaded by an executioner on 11 August.[30] This battle pleased no one except Archbishop Adalbert and Margrave Dietrich. Duke Otto of Bavaria, the son of Liudolf, who arrived on the same day, and Count Berthold, rebuked the emperor for allowing such a great man to be condemned on such a petty charge.[31] Here, I may briefly relate the admirable service of Abbot Liudolf of Corvey, to whom God has deigned to reveal much while the venerable father was labouring at his many vigils and fasts. At dawn, on the day of the duel, as he was celebrating the mass according to his custom, with humility and the fear of God, he saw Count Gero's head floating above the altar. After he had finished the first mass, he sang a mass for the dead and, after removing his vestments, silently left the church. Then, summoning the brothers, he told them of Gero's death and humbly asked that they offer prayers for him in common. The beheading took place on the same day, at sunset.

CHAPTER TEN

Gero's sister Tetta and his wife Adela established a monastery at Alsleben for the sake of his remembrance and to provide him with a final resting place. They conveyed a [lacuna][32] part of their hereditary property to God and his beloved predecessor [John the Baptist], and confirmed, through a privilege and by imperial decree, that the abbey should be free and subject only to the power and protection of the

29 Count Siegfried of Walbeck and Margrave Liuther.

30 Deaths of Gero and Waldo are noted in the necrology at Magdeburg (*NMag.*, fo. 11r, p. 55).

31 Count Berthold of Schweinfurt. The execution of Count Gero of Alsleben (11 August 979) represents an instance in which Thietmar (and many others) clearly believed that the king had made a serious error (Leyser 1979: 99). His report of the uncorrupted state of the count's body (3.10), a quality commonly attributed to saints, was intended to reinforce this opinion.

32 The Corvey edition says a 'tenth part'.

emperor and his successors.[33] After three years, when his wife was interred by his side, the count's body, and even his clothing were found to be uncorrupted. In the sixth year of Otto's reign, King Lothar and his son came to him with magnificent gifts and, after making amends, acquired his secure friendship. In the same year, our emperor went to Italy [November 980].[34] Alas, he would never see our homeland again.

CHAPTER ELEVEN

While the emperor was still in Rome, Archbishop Adalbert, in the thirteenth year after his consecration, was travelling around Bishop Giselher's diocese, teaching and confirming his flock – this because Giselher himself was then with the emperor. He celebrated mass at Merseburg on 19 June and happily spent the following night in Corbetha with Hemuzo, an honourable layman. The next morning, after arising, he complained bitterly of a severe headache. He departed nonetheless. When he had passed through the village of Zscherben, on the way to Freckleben, he began gradually to sink down on his horse and would have fallen to the ground had he not been supported by his companions. He was placed on a carpet and, after everything that priests are supposed to say had been said, he faithfully migrated to Christ on 20 June.[35] His corpse was transported to Giebichenstein and clothed in his episcopal vestments.[36] Then, it was carried by boat

33 D O II 190 20 May 979. This diploma attributes the initiative for the foundation to Gero although his wife's participation is emphasized throughout. As in the case of Gernrode (2.19), the founders of Alsleben surrendered their community to the king so that it could benefit from the protection and privileges that were the chief benefit of royal status (Bernhardt 1993: 174–75). Indeed, it is specifically noted that the new community's status was to be equivalent to that of Quedlinburg and Gandersheim. At the same time, the founders retained a significant avenue of influence by reserving the offices of abbess and advocate for members of their respective families, assuming the candidates' suitability and the approval of the canonesses. What the canonesses needed protection from is evident in clauses prohibiting bishops from interfering in their community's governance (i.e. by imposing an abbess or advocate), and counts or judges from demanding payments or services from members of their *familia*. That Gero is noted as having specifically requested the latter clause would suggest that, as a count himself, he was personally familiar with the problem it sought to address.

34 BM 831a.

35 *NMer.*, fo. 3r, p. 7; *NMag.*, fo. 8v, p. 50.

36 Giebichenstein, a burg located on the river Saale, somewhat downstream from the medieval settlement of Halle (the modern city has absorbed it). Under Henry I, the burg was a royal possession. In 962, Otto I bestowed both the burg and the nearby salt springs on the monastery of St Maurice at Magdeburg (D O I 232). Later, it figured among the possessions of the archbishops of Magdeburg who received the

to Magdeburg where it was tearfully received by the brothers, and especially by the monks. With the assistance of Abbot Harding, the illustrious Bishop Hildeward of Halberstadt committed Adalbert's body to the grave, in the middle of the church, before the altar of the Apostles Philip and James.[37] O reader, observe with how much care he guarded his flock! Often, in the silence of night and with only two companions, he would come to St John the Baptist and St Maurice so that, without warning, he might observe how the brothers convened for matins and note who remained in the dormitory. If all went well, he gave thanks to God. If otherwise, he would confront the guilty party and reprimand him appropriately.

CHAPTER TWELVE

Deeply troubled by the death of such a father, the clergy and people elected one of his brethren, Ochtrich, as their lord and archbishop. At the time, Ochtrich was faithfully serving the emperor. His election, however, violated the stated desires of Archbishop Adalbert who, while he lived and was in good health, had openly announced to many that such a turn of events would never occur. Ochtrich had been master of the school and expertly enlightened a large number both of the brethren and of outsiders, but because he and the bishop had never got along, he chose to leave rather than remain within the community. Only with great difficulty did the emperor obtain the archbishop's permission to take Ochtrich into his service. Hence, on the day of the Resurrection, as the subdeacon followed the usual practice of presenting the holy cross to the bishop, just prior to the beginning of the mass, Adalbert instead grasped the cross with both hands and tearfully begged that Ochtrich and Ico might never possess his see. After the divine ministry had been completed, and he was seated at the table, he indicated to all present that those two would never succeed him. He did not reveal the means by which he had learned this, nor did anyone else ever reveal it to me. After his death, he came to his beloved Walthard – he is also known as Dodico – in a dream, and assured him that everything would come about as he had

---

right to mint coins there, collect tolls, and probably hold a market (Herzog 1964: 63; Claude 1972: 48). Aside from serving as a kind of treasury (as in this chapter), the Giebichenstein provided the archbishops with a place to rest and recuperate – they seem to end up there when on the point of death (6.61, 6.70; 3.11) – and to guard political prisoners (6.3; 7.1). On the last point see Leyser 1981: 93.

37 Abbot Harding of Berge (968–*c*.990).

predicted while he lived.[38] Dodico himself related the following account to me. While lying in bed, with his spirit deeply troubled, he saw the archbishop standing in the south portal of the church, the one leading to the cemetery. He also saw himself, holding a staff, as if ready to set out for Rome. The archbishop then addressed him, in an irritated tone, saying: 'My Dodico, how is it that you would give my office to another?' He responded: 'Dearest lord, can you not see that, in my sorry condition, there is no will but only obedience?' To this, the archbishop replied, saying: 'You should know, for certain, that Ochtrich will never possess my see.'

CHAPTER THIRTEEN

When the election was finished, the clergy and people together sent Ekkehard, known as 'the Red', in the company of other brothers and warriors, to announce the result to the emperor and to remind him of his promise.[39] When they reached that region of Italy where the emperor was residing, they asked Giselher to intercede for them and revealed to him their secret mission. At that time, Giselher was very much in the emperor's favour and promised that he would faithfully intercede for them. And yet, among all who were involved in this matter, he showed the greatest concern for himself. For after insinuating what he had heard into the emperor's ears, he humbly threw himself at his feet and begged for the promised and long-awaited reward for his many years of service.[40] With God consenting, he immediately obtained it. After departing from the emperor's presence, Giselher was asked by the messengers, and especially by Ochtrich who had put his entire trust in him, if he had succeeded in the task with which they had entrusted him. He responded that he was unable to help them in the matter. After distributing bribes among all the leading men, and especially among the Roman judges to whom all

---

38 Provost (984–1012), archbishop (1012).

39 I.e. the election privilege he had granted them (3.1). Ekkehard 'the Red' was master of the cathedral school and custodian at Magdeburg.

40 That the Magdeburgers turned to Giselher for help probably had less to do with their naivety than with the norms of Ottonian political culture which restricted access to the king (Althoff 1997a: 193). That same culture would also have influenced Otto and Giselher's behaviour. The sense of obligation inherent in the monarch's relationship with loyal supporters and servants was mutual and governed by a powerful set of social conventions or norms. Otto could not have resisted Giselher's demands without sending a very clear message and potentially causing one or the other of them to lose face.

things are venal,[41] he secretly began to consider how he might acquire the archbishopric. At last, he earnestly and quite openly requested the aid of Pope Benedict VII, so called from the number of like-named popes who preceded him.[42] For his part, the pope promised that he would go along if all could be accomplished with the agreement of the senate.

CHAPTER FOURTEEN

A general council was held in Rome.[43] The wisest men gathered and the prophecy of Jeremiah was fulfilled: 'How has the gold darkened, its best colour changed, etc.'[44] For the pope asked the judges if it would be licit to promote Giselher to the archbishopric, noting that he was presently free of any constraint since he had no secure see, the one he possessed having been illegally taken from Bishop Hildeward, as the latter had constantly complained.[45] Both by words and examples, the judges affirmed that the authority of the canons permitted him to

---

41 Sallust, *Jugurtha* 35.

42 Benedict VII (974–83), former bishop of Sutri, was elected in the presence of an imperial *missus* (Margrave Sicco of Spoleto) after the previous occupant of the office (Boniface VII) had been expelled from the city. As Thietmar implies, Benedict showed a willingness to cooperate in Otto II's ecclesiastical projects and the emperor, in turn, provided him with a measure of security (*DHP* 202, *LMA*, vol. 1, p. 1859).

43 BM 856b, 9–10, September 981. Charges of venality aside, a document issued by the synod suggests other reasons for the decision to permit Giselher's translation to Magdeburg: 'because Giselher, a venerable and zealous man, had not acquired the rulership of the now suppressed church through impious desire, but rather through public election; and also, that his title might not appear to have been assumed in vain; it was decided by all the orders of the Roman church, mother of all churches, that he, being agreeable with these decrees of the apostolic judgement, might be called to rule as pastor of the church of Magdeburg which, by divine judgement, then lacked the care and oversight of a bishop. Indeed, sons of that church, standing and speaking in our presence, professed both that he was a son of their church and that they had truly elected him. This procedure appeared proper enough to us and in accord with the teachings of the holy fathers. [Several *exempla* follow.] Hence, after due deliberation, a decision was reached in regard to our dear brother. Because he has obtained this office through the election and petition of its sons, as we have already noted, and is not moved by desire; and also at the urging and with the assent of the bishops of his province and of the entire order of the Roman church, we declare the aforesaid Bishop Giselher to be appointed archbishop of the holy church of Magdeburg and grant him the pallium so that, as long as he lives, he may preside over that church in the capacity of bishop and administer whatever godly matters must be undertaken' (*UbM*, no. 92).

44 Lam. 4: 1.

45 See 2.11, 20–21.

justly and properly acquire that dignity. They thereby transgressed
the admonition of David: 'Judge rightly the sons of men!'[46] They also
confirmed that: 'A corrupt judge may never find the truth.'[47] O reader,
know that it causes me both disgust and embarrassment to put down
in words what was unhesitatingly enacted by these men who, though
far superior to me, were heedless of present or future shame.
Merseburg, whose lord had previously been independent, ceased to be
the seat of a bishopric and was subjected to the church of Halberstadt.
And Giselher, *not its pastor but rather a mercenary* who strove ever
upwards, attained his goal on 10 September, although without thinking on that famous proverb: *the higher the step, the deeper the fall.*[48]
Certainly, had he wished to remain in the office originally granted to
him, he could have overcome any obstacle that stood in his way, with
the emperor's help, and established both a secure position and a rich
endowment for himself and his successors. But the judgements of God
are a mystery to men though never unjust. Thus I do not cast the
blame on Giselher alone, but rather attribute it to our own common
sinfulness, the same quality to which any adversity that touches us
should justly be ascribed.

CHAPTER FIFTEEN

Afterwards, Ochtrich went to Benevento and took sick. According to
one of my brethren, Husward, he saw Adalleich, our deceased former
provost, at a distance, offering him the prebend of St Maurice.[49]
Terrified at such a vision, he asked, 'Brother, do you see anything?'
Then, after telling him everything, he exclaimed: 'Woe is me, wretch
and sinner, that I ever left my own church and obedience for the sake
of ambition! And if, through God's generosity, I should regain my
health, I will humbly go there and never leave.' Following these
words, his illness worsened and, after a few days, on 7 October, he
died and was buried in the same city.[50] He left no one behind who
could equal him in wisdom and eloquence.

46 Ps. 57: 2/RSV 58: 1.
47 Horace, *Satires* 2. 2.8–9.
48 John 10: 12; Prov. 16: 18.
49 Provost Adalleich/Adaldag (d. 968).
50 *NMer.*, fo. 6r, p. 13.

CHAPTER SIXTEEN

After receiving the emperor's permission, Giselher came to Magdeburg, on 30 November, in the company of Bishop Dietrich of Metz.[51] Dietrich was a friend of the emperor and very dear to him. He also belonged to that group of corrupt men who, in return for obscuring the truth, had accepted one thousand pounds of gold and silver from the archbishop. One morning, at the emperor's order, someone jokingly blessed Dietrich in the following manner: 'May God satisfy you with gold in the hereafter, since we here can by no means do so!' Then everything previously belonging to our church was wretchedly divided, as if in accord with the custom of the Slavs by which, after a family has been accused, its property is dispersed by being put up for sale.[52] Bishop Frederick of Zeitz received that part of our diocese which lay between the Saale, Elster, and Mulde rivers; and between the districts of Pleiße, Wethau and Teuchern; and including the villages of Possen and Pissen.[53] Bishop Folkold of Meißen was given a piece which included the villages of Wechselburg and Lastau and pertained to eastern Schkeuditz, being bordered by the rivers Chemnitz and Elbe.[54] For himself, Giselher kept nine burgs, namely: Schkeuditz, Taucha, Wurzen, Püchen, Eilenburg, Düben, Pouch, Löbnitz and Zöcheritz. Documents which conveyed royal or imperial gifts he either burned or, by altering the name of the recipient, made them refer to his own church.[55] Payers of tribute, and everything that was supposed to belong to Merseburg, he intentionally scattered so that they might never be gathered together again. He established an abbey at Merseburg itself and set over it Ohtrad, a venerable monk of the monastery of St John.[56] Later, he gave it to Heimo who came from the same monastery. But note, O reader, what came of this destruction!

51 As the cousin of Otto I, among other things, Bishop Dietrich I of Metz (965–84) had the sort of family connections that led to influence at the royal court. He was entrusted with important diplomatic missions, appears frequently as intercessor in royal diplomata, and served as one of Otto II's chief advisers (*LMA*, vol. 3, p. 1030). As Thietmar suggests, such connections also provided opportunities to acquire wealth.

52 See above p. 59.

53 Bishop Frederik of Zeitz (*c*.980–*c*.990).

54 Given the distance of these two locations from the Elbe, Thietmar may well be thinking of a different river, perhaps the Zchopau (Holtzmann 1935: 117, n. 12). Lippelt (1973: 96, n. 36) suggests that this passage should be translated as '[a piece of the diocese]...which extended from the Chemnitz towards the Elbe'.

55 Unlikely, given the number of surviving documents from Merseburg (but cf. Claude 1972: 151).

56 Berge.

CHAPTER SEVENTEEN

Margrave Dietrich's arrogance so irritated peoples who had already accepted both Christianity and the status of tribute payer in regard to our kings and emperors, that their members unanimously decided to take up arms.[57] This turn of events was predicted to my father, Count Siegfried, in the following way. In a dream, he saw a sky filled with dense clouds. Astonished, he asked what it meant and a voice replied: 'Now that prophecy must be fulfilled: "God allows the rain to fall both on the just and the unjust."'[58] The outrage began on 29 July, with the murder of the garrison and destruction of the cathedral at Havelberg. Three days later, at the sounding of prime, the entire band of Slavs attacked the bishopric of Brandenburg, a see established beyond Magdeburg some thirty years previously.[59] Folkmar, the third bishop of that see, had already fled, and his defender, Dietrich, barely escaped with his warriors on the same day as the attack.[60] The clergy who remained were captured. The second bishop, Dodilo, was dragged from his tomb. He had been strangled by his own people and, though three years in the grave, his body and priestly vestments were as yet uncorrupted.[61] The greedy dogs then plundered him and carelessly threw him back again. They also stole all of the church's treasures and brutally spilled the blood of many. Thus various cults of demonic heresy were venerated instead of Christ and his fisherman, the

---

57 Margrave Dietrich of the northern march. Thietmar refers to the great Slavic uprising of 983. As Thietmar suggests (3.18), the revolt initiated by the Liutizi expanded to include the Abodrites, under their leader, Mistui. Among the more likely causes of the revolt, one might cite the heavy burden of tribute and tithes imposed upon the Slavic population as a result of their dual subjection to the *Reich* and the church (Reuter 1991: 178). Nor can Thietmar's more personal explanation be discounted. Although the nature of Dietrich's 'arrogance' is difficult to determine from his comments, it presumably included behaviour that the population subject to him found provocative. For Magdeburg, the revolt meant not only a loss of property and income, but also the effective loss of two suffragans, Brandenburg and Havelberg, though both continued to exist in law and have bishops appointed who were, in theory, responsible for their care (Claude 1972: 157). Weinrich (1988: 79) has suggested that the term 'peoples' (*gentes*) in the first line should be replaced by 'heathen', a plausible translation which would better reflect the hostile tone of this passage. In my opinion, however, such a translation would not accord with the last line in which Thietmar emphasizes that Christians numbered among those who supported or at least sympathized with the uprising.
58 Matt. 5: 45.
59 Twenty years previously, in 948.
60 Bishop Folkmar (980–83, d. 1003).
61 Bishop Dodilo (965/68–80).

venerable Peter. And not only the heathen praised this sorrowful change, but also Christians!

CHAPTER EIGHTEEN

In those times, the church of Zeitz was captured and wasted by an army of Bohemians under the leadership of Dedi.[62] Its first bishop, Hugh, had already fled.[63] Afterwards, the Slavs devastated the monastery of St Lawrence at Calbe and pursued our people as if they were so many fleeing deer. Our spirits were fearful because of our sins, but their spirits were strong. Duke Mistui of the Abodrites burned and ravaged Hamburg which was formerly the residence of the bishop. Yet all of Christendom should piously note the miracle that Christ performed there from heaven. A golden hand came down from the highest regions and, with outstretched fingers, reached into the middle of the fire. This occurred in full view of all. The army looked on in astonishment, and Mistui was both terrified and dumbfounded. This incident was related to me by Avico who was then Mistui's chaplain, but later became my spiritual brother.[64] We both came to the conclusion that God had, in this way, taken the relics up to heaven and, at the same time, terrified and put the enemy to flight. *Later, Mistui lost his mind and was held in chains. After being immersed in water that had been blessed, he shouted: 'St Lawrence is burning me!' But before he could be freed, he died wretchedly.*

CHAPTER NINETEEN

By the time the Slavs had burned and pillaged all the burgs and villages as far as the river Tanger, there were more than thirty bands of warriors on foot and horseback. Without sustaining any losses and aided by their gods, they did not hesitate to ravage the rest of the region, as their blaring trumpets preceded them. We did not remain unaware of these events. Bishops Giselher and Hildeward joined with Margrave Dietrich and with the other counts: Rikdag, Hodo, Benizo,

---

62 The incident should be placed within the context of the count's feud with Otto II (Fleckenstein 1991: 89). Thietmar gives a more extensive account of Dedi's origins and career at 6.49–50.

63 The reference to Bishop Hugh (968–79) would place this incident somewhat earlier.

64 His death is noted in the necrology at Merseburg on 7 October, the same day as Ochtrich's death (*NMer.*, fo. 6r, p. 13).

Frederick, Dudo, my father Siegfried,[65] and many others. At dawn, on Saturday, they heard mass together. Then, after fortifying body and spirit with the sacrament of heaven, they confidently fell upon the approaching enemy and, except for a few who found refuge on a hill, completely annihilated them. The victors praised God, marvellous in all his works, and the truthful word of the teacher, Paul, was confirmed: 'There is neither prudence nor strength nor counsel against the Lord.'[66] Utterly abandoned were those who had once dared to reject God and stupidly chose to worship meaningless idols, which they themselves had made, rather than their own creator. Unfortunately, as night approached and our forces made camp some distance away, the Slavs of whom I have spoken above furtively escaped. The next day, our people happily returned to their homeland, after sustaining only three casualties. While on their way, or once they were at home, they were congratulated by everyone they encountered.

CHAPTER TWENTY

Meanwhile, the emperor of the Roman Empire ruled in such a way that he retained every possession that had previously belonged to his father. When his lands were attacked by the Saracens, he mounted a vigorous defence and compelled them keep their distance from his borders.[67] On the report that Calabria was suffering severely from the frequent attacks of the Greeks and the ravages of the Saracens, the emperor called upon the Bavarians and battle-ready Swabians to supplement his army. He himself hurried to the city of Taranto, in the company of Duke Otto, the son of his brother Liudolf. Taranto had fallen into the hands of the Greeks who had secured it with a garrison. The emperor managed to conquer the city, after a brief but forceful attack. Because he also wanted to deal with the Saracens, whose powerful army was ravaging his lands, skilful spies were sent to find out more about them. He first surrounded the Saracens in a certain city and then, after defeating them, forced them to flee. Catching up with them in an open field where they had assembled in battle order, he proceeded to kill a large number of them and believed that their

---

65 Margrave Rikdag of Meißen (979–85), Margrave Hodo of the Saxon eastern march, Count Binizo of Merseburg, count palatine of Saxony Frederick (995–1002). The identity of Dudo is unclear.

66 In fact, Prov. 21: 30.

67 Otto II is generally assumed to have taken a more active, interventionist approach to relations in southern Italy (Beumann 1991: 119–20; Arnold 1991: 88).

total defeat was imminent.[68] Yet, quite unexpectedly, they managed to gather themselves together and launch an attack on our forces, cutting them down with little resistance, alas. All of this occurred on 13 July [982].[69] [*The numbers of the fallen*] included: Richer the lance-bearer, Count Udo who was my mother's uncle, Counts Thietmar, Bezelin, Gebhard, Gunther, Ezelin and his brother Bezelin; as well as Burkhard, Dedi, Conrad, and innumerable others whose names are known only to God.[70]

CHAPTER TWENTY-ONE

Along with Duke Otto and several others, the emperor fled to the sea where, in the distance, he spotted a ship of the type known as a salandria. He hurried out to it on a horse belonging to the Jew Calonimus but the ship's crew refused to take him in and continued on their way. Returning to the safety of the shore, he found the Jew still standing there, anxiously awaiting the fate of his beloved lord. When the emperor saw that his enemies had also arrived on the scene, he sorrowfully asked this man: 'What now will become of me?'[71] Suddenly, he noticed that a second salandria was following the first one, and realized that among the ship's occupants was a friend who might be expected to help him. Once again, he urged his horse into the water and hurried out to the ship where he was recognized only by his warrior Henry, whose Slavic name is Zolunta. He was taken on board and placed in the bed of the ship's commander. Eventually, the commander also recognized him and asked if he was the emperor. After denying it for some time, Otto finally conceded and declared: 'Yes, it is I, reduced to this miserable state because of my sins. But listen carefully to what we may now do together. I have just lost the best men of my empire and, tormented by this sorrow, can never again set foot in this land and have no further desire to see those who have befriended it. Only, let us go to the city of Rossano where my wife awaits my arrival. We will take her and all the treasure, of which

---

68 Although scholarly opinion has tended to favour either Capo Colonne or Cotrone as the site of Otto II's defeat, other sites have been proposed and the issue is by no means closed (Alvermann 1995: esp. 124–30; Turano 1997: 63).

69 BM 874b.

70 I have supplied a possible reading for a lacuna at the beginning of this sentence. Among the casualties mentioned by Thietmar are: Count Udo II of Rheinfranken, Margrave Gunther of Merseburg, Count Burchard and Dedi of Hassegau. An important casualty not mentioned by Thietmar was Bishop Henry of Augsburg.

71 Incorporating an emendation suggested by Fickermann (1957: 76).

I have an unspeakable amount, and go to your emperor, my brother. As I hope, he will be a loyal friend to me in my time of need.' Delighted at this pleasant conversation, the ship's commander hurried day and night to reach this place. As they approached their destination, the warrior with the two names was sent ahead to summon the empress and Bishop Dietrich, who accompanied her, and also to fetch the many treasure-laden pack animals.

CHAPTER TWENTY-TWO

As soon as the Greeks saw the empress leaving the city with so many gifts, they dropped anchor and allowed Bishop Dietrich to come aboard with a few companions. At the bishop's request, the emperor laid aside his vile clothing and put on something better. But then, as he was standing at the bow of the ship, he suddenly leaped into the water, trusting in his own strength and skill at swimming. One of the Greeks who were standing near by tried to stop him by grabbing his clothing, but that celebrated warrior Liuppo ran him through with his sword and he fell backwards, dead. While the Greeks fled to the other side of the ship, our people followed the emperor in the boats which had brought them there, escaping without any injury. The emperor, safely ashore, was waiting for them and fully expected to fulfil his promises to the Greeks by bestowing rich gifts. The Greeks themselves, however, being both terrified and sceptical regarding the emperor's intentions, departed and sought the borders of their homeland. May all who are accustomed to conquer other nations through craft observe how these Greeks were fooled by similar means. I can scarcely describe the joy with which the emperor was received, both by those already present and by those who arrived later.

CHAPTER TWENTY-THREE

Dear reader, that you may be better informed regarding such matters, I shall briefly explain both what a salandria is and how it happened to be on these shores. It is, as I have already mentioned, a ship of marvellous length and speed, having two banks of oars on each side with space for one hundred and fifty sailors. Two ships of this type were sent to Calabria, at the order of Basileus Nikephoros, to collect tribute. Although that land is rightly subject to the Roman Empire, its residents voluntarily send an annual payment in gold to Constantinople to avoid any harassment from the Greeks. The two ships carried fire which was only extinguishable with vinegar and, as soon as they arrived, the emperor took them into his service, ordering that they head out to sea and burn the Saracen fleet. One of these ships, as I have already mentioned, refused to take the defeated emperor on board, perhaps because its occupants failed to recognize him or feared the enemies that pursued him. The other ship, which took him in at Henry's insistence, as I have already noted, was unwilling to let him go.

CHAPTER TWENTY-FOUR

After this short digression, I will now bring my theme to a conclusion. After all our leading men had heard the miserable news, they sadly gathered and, together, sent a messenger to the emperor with a letter that conveyed their humble desire to see him again [983].[72] As soon as he had heard their message, the emperor agreed to this demand. All the leading men were summoned to Verona for an assembly at which many pressing matters would be discussed. Only Duke Bernhard, though already under way, had to retrace his steps, because one of his burgs [lacuna] which the emperor had secured against the Danes with a wall and garrison, had been recaptured by them through treachery and burned to the ground following the murder of all its defenders. In the year 983 of the Incarnation of the Lord, the emperor held court at Verona and Henry the Younger, having been released from exile, was made duke of the Bavarians.[73] And in this same year, the Slavs united in resistance to the emperor and Margrave Dietrich.[74] Also, the emperor's son was unanimously elected lord.[75]

---

72 Saxony; BM 890d.

73 Pentecost, 27 May 983; BM 891b. The following noted also by *AQ*, an. 983, p. 64. Thietmar refers to Henry, duke of Carinthia (976–78, 983–89), duke of Bavaria (983–85). Henry's exile resulted from his participation in the uprising reported by Thietmar at 3.7. At the same time, the Duchy of Swabia was conferred upon Conrad, count in the Rhineland.

74 Thietmar has incorporated a passage from the annals of Quedlinburg without realizing that it refers to the uprising of 983, which he had already discussed at 3.177–19 (Weinrich 1988: 78).

75 This was the first German royal election to take place south of the Alps. The choice of location may simply have reflected the pressure of time and events, but it could also have represented an attempt to demonstrate Italy's place within the political context of the *Reich*. That the archbishop of Ravenna participated as co-consecrator during Otto III's consecration (i.e. at Aachen, 3.26) would tend to support the second conclusion (Althoff 1996: 38).

CHAPTER TWENTY-FIVE

After a few days, they said their final farewells to the emperor and departed. Indeed, after leaving his venerable mother at Pavia, the emperor came to Rome where he immediately became very ill. Sensing that his end was near, he divided his entire treasure into four parts, giving the first to the churches, the second to the poor, the third to his beloved sister, Mathilda, a devoted servant of Christ who presided over the abbey at Quedlinburg, and the fourth to his mournful servants and warriors.[76] After making his confession, in Latin, before the pope and the other bishops and priests, he obtained the absolution he desired and departed from this light on 7 December.[77] He was commended to the earth at that place where the entry to the paradise of St Peter's is open to all believers; and where a portrait portrays the lord standing and offering the blessing to all who enter. Being mindful of the fate of mortals and very much in need of forgiveness myself, I beseech the God and Lord of heaven and earth to mercifully absolve him of the sins he committed against my church. For his good works, however, may he be rewarded a hundredfold. By the power undeservedly bestowed upon me, I myself forgive him and strongly urge you, my successor, to for ever grant from your heart that favour which, at the end, can be denied to no one.

CHAPTER TWENTY-SIX

During the next celebration of the Lord's birth, Otto's noble son, born to him in the forest of Kessel, was consecrated king, at Aachen, by Archbishop John of Ravenna and Willigis of Mainz.[78] At the conclusion of this office, a messenger suddenly arrived with the sad news, bringing the joyous occasion to an end. The hearts of many were moved to unspeakable pain and all bemoaned the diminution of our strength, which remained intact despite the all too frequent assaults of human weakness and caprice.[79] After the death of his father, Otto ruled twice five in terms of solar years. He was the protector of the kingdom and empire, a terror to all his enemies, but an impregnable wall for the flock committed to his care. Although public opinion wavered anxiously in such important matters, it was quickly brought

76 Abbess Mathilda of Quedlinburg (966–99).

77 *NMer.*, fo. 7v, p. 16.

78 Archbishop John XII of Ravenna (983–98).

79 Horace, *Odes* bk 3, ode 24, verses 31–32.

to order through the mercy of the divine majesty. Duke Henry was released from custody in Utrecht and the young king was turned over to him for educating (or rather degrading!) by Archbishop Warin of Cologne, to whose reliable faith he had been commended by the emperor.[80] I shall now close the narration of this third book with the harsh bolt of our third emperor's lamentable death. Henceforth, through my pen, I will try to reveal the certainty of that gracious love which excludes all ambiguity.

80 End of December (BU 956y).

BOOK FOUR

In the year of the Incarnation of the Lord 984, the empress, Lady Theophanu, mother of the third and, unfortunately, last in the order of Ottos, oppressed by her horrible and recent loss and by the absence of her only son, came to the Empress Adelheid in the city of Pavia. Adelheid received her with deep emotion and soothed her with affectionate comfort. As I have already mentioned, the aforementioned duke came to Cologne in the company of Poppo, the venerable bishop in whose power he had long been held, and Count Ekbert 'the One-eyed'.[1] There, in his capacity as lawful guardian, he received the king from Archbishop Warin, the latter's support being firmly secured along with that of any others who could be won to his cause.[2] When all had been disposed according to his will, the duke and his supporters went to Corvey, where he refused to grant his favour to Counts Dietrich and Sicco who approached him with bare feet [early February 984].[3] Displeased at this treatment, they left and thereafter made every effort to withdraw their relatives and friends from the duke's service. When the duke decided to celebrate the feast of Palm Sunday at Magdeburg, he asked all the leading men of that region to assemble

---

1 Duke Henry 'the Quarrelsome' of Bavaria had been placed in the custody of Bishop Folkmar (or Poppo) of Utrecht after his rebellion against Otto II (3.7).

2 Cf. 3.26.

3 BU 956g1. Dietrich, count palatine of Saxony (982–995), and Sigbert (i.e. Sicco), count in Liesgau, were Bernward of Hildesheim's father and uncle, respectively (Goetting 1984: 172). They subsequently appeared with him among those opponents of the duke who met at the Asselburg to plot their strategy (4.2). Thietmar had good reason to emphasize this incident. In accordance with widely recognized social conventions, the two counts had performed a formal act of submission which Henry was virtually bound to accept, even if conditionally (see note at 6.2). By refusing to do so, Henry not only made enemies, he also proved that he lacked one of the virtues (clemency) that Thietmar and his contemporaries expected from their kings (Althoff 1997: 42–43; Warner 1995: 57–58, 69). Against the background of Henry's efforts to act like a king, his unwillingness to bestow his favour upon the two counts was particularly damning. Thietmar employed a similar technique to denigrate the character of Margrave Ekkehard of Meißen, a claimant to the throne in 1002 (4.52), and seems to express a similar viewpoint elsewhere in the chronicle (7.8).

there and, in the course of negotiations, demanded that they submit to his power and raise him to the kingship [16 March 984].[4] Most of them were able to agree to his demand by means of the following ruse, namely by saying that they would first seek permission from their lord king, to whom they had sworn an oath. When that permission had been secured, they would then serve their new king. Because of his indignation, however, some withdrew and secretly conspired to prevent his plan from ever being carried out.

CHAPTER TWO

After leaving Magdeburg, Henry went to Quedlinburg to celebrate the joyful feast of Easter.[5] The great men of the duchy also gathered there, and some who did not wish to come in person sent a representative who was to scrutinize everything carefully. During the celebration, the duke's supporters openly greeted him as king and he was honoured with divine *laudes*. Dukes Miesco, Mistui, and Boleslav converged here along with innumerable others and swore oaths confirming their support for him as king and lord. Many others, not daring to violate their oath to the king, for fear of God, withdrew somewhat and hurried to the Asselburg where their allies, now openly plotting against the duke, were meeting. These are their names: from the East, along with Duke Bernhard and Margrave Dietrich, there were the Counts Ekkehard, Binizo, Esiko, the count and priest Bernward, Siegfried and his son, the brothers Frederich and Ziazo; from that region also were the brothers Dietrich and Sigbert, Hoiko, the brothers Ekkehard and Bezeko, Brunig and his brother; and, at the order of Archbishop Willigis, the *milites* of St Martin, joined by a great multitude from the West.[6]

4 That Henry chose to announce his intentions at Magdeburg and Quedlinburg (4.2) is scarcely a coincidence given their importance for Ottonian political culture (above p. 13). Henry had already attracted the support of Archbishop Giselher who joined him at Quedlinburg and later served as his representative during negotiations with supporters of the king (4.7). In spite of this political misstep, Giselher easily reconciled himself with Otto's regents following the collapse of Henry's revolt (Claude 1972: 159–61). On 14 February 985, he was issued a confirmation of his rights and possessions as archbishop (D O III 10).

5 That Thietmar himself was present during these events is suggested by his comments at 4.16.

6 BU 956u1. Among the persons to whom Thietmar refers are: Duke Bernhard of Saxony, Margrave Dietrich of the northern march, Ekkehard, the later margrave of Meißen, Bio (i.e. Binizo) and Esiko, counts at Merseburg; Bernward, the later teacher of Otto III (987–93) and Bishop of Hildesheim (993–1022); Count Siegfried

CHAPTER THREE [984]

When the duke learned of this, he sent his supporters away with his favour and richly endowed with gifts. Then, intent on disrupting or pacifying this conspiracy, he hastened to Werla with a strong force. Bishop Poppo was sent ahead in an effort to divide or reconcile the opposition. While under way, he discovered the enemy assembled and prepared to attack the duke, and barely managed to arrange a mutual safe-conduct to a place called Seesen, on an agreed-upon day. At once, the duke set off for Bavaria, either not wanting to come to this meeting or unable to because of Duke Henry, to whom the previously mentioned emperor had granted control of Bavaria and Carinthia [*c.*10 April].[7] Then the hostile force besieged Count Ekbert's fortress, called Ala [mid-April].[8] After destroying the walls, they forced their way in and seized both the emperor's daughter, Adelheid, who had been raised there, and much treasure which had also been kept there. Rejoicing, they went on their way.[9]

CHAPTER FOUR [984]

The duke won over all the Bavarian bishops and some of the counts; and relying on these allies, approached the boundaries of Franconia where, on the meadow near Bürstadt, he sat down with the leading men of the region for negotiations [10–15 May].[10] Then, Archbishop Willigis of the church of Mainz came there, along with Duke Conrad

of Northeim and his like-named son, Count Frederick of Eilenburg and his brother Dedi (i.e. Ziazo) of the house of Wettin. Among the second group named are Bernward's father and uncle, the count palatine Dietrich and Count Sigbert of Liesgau, to whom Duke Henry had previously refused his favour; Hoiko, count in the Hedergau and later 'educator' of Otto III (4.8); Ekkhard was the founder of Helmarshausen; and Brunig may have been one of the counts of Braunschweig. The warriors of St Martin would be *ministeriales* dependent on the church of Mainz and its patron saint.

7 BU 956z1. Henry 'the Younger' had participated in Henry the Quarrelsome's previous uprising and had lost his duchy as a result. The younger Henry subsequently made his peace with the emperor and was granted the Duchy of Bavaria in 983. The current rebellion, as he undoubtedly recognized, threatened his possession of the duchy.

8 BU b2. The hostile force, namely supporters of Otto III.

9 Adelheid, the eldest child of Otto II, abbess of Quedlinburg (999–1045), Gernrode and Verden (from 1014) and Gandersheim (from 1039). It has been suggested that Adelheid and the treasure were being held as pawns for Duke Henry (Leyser 1979: 12).

10 BU 956e2.

and other great men.[11] The duke tried, in whatever way he could, to win these men to his side. But when he perceived from their unanimous response that, as long as they lived, they would never retreat from the promise of faith which they had sworn to their king, fear of the impending battle forced him to swear that, on 29 June, he would come to the place called Rohr and return the boy to his mother and her supporters.[12] Thereafter, they all returned to their homes though in diverse moods, some being joyful, others downcast.

CHAPTER FIVE

In the company of his supporters, Henry then sought out Boleslav [II], duke of the Bohemians, who had always been willing to help him, whatever the circumstances. The duke received him honourably and had his army conduct him from the boundaries of his territory through those of the territories of Nisan and Daleminzia as far as Mügeln. Then, with our people coming to meet him, he proceeded to Magdeborn. Meanwhile, one of Duke Boleslav of Bohemia's *milites*, Wagio, who had been among the troops which accompanied Henry, stopped at Meißen while making his way home. After conversing with the inhabitants of the place, he had an intermediary invite Frederich, ally and warrior of that Margrave Rikdag who then resided at Merseburg, to meet with him for a discussion at a certain church outside of the city.[13] As he went out, however, the door closed after him. Rikdag, guardian of that city and a celebrated warrior, was ambushed and killed by them, at a stream called Triebischbach.[14] The city was soon furnished with a garrison by Boleslav and it quickly accepted him both as lord and resident.

CHAPTER SIX

At the instigation of the ever capricious people, Boleslav drove out Bishop Folkold, who then went to Archbishop Willigis and was accorded a friendly reception.[15] The bishop had nourished him as if he were his own son and, when sent to those eastern regions, had

11 Duke Conrad I of Swabia (983–97).
12 Cf. 4.8.
13 Referring to Frederick of Eilenburg as Rikdag's *amicus et satelles.*
14 Namely, not Margrave Rikdag, but probably a burgrave with the same name.
15 Bishop Folkold of Meißen (969–92).

warmly recommended to Otto II that Willigis succeed him as the king's teacher. Willigis never forgot this favour and acknowledged it with all gratitude, especially now, when Folkold was in greatest need. He ordered that Folkold be cared for and given every consideration, at Erfurt, a location the bishop himself had chosen. After residing there for a long time, he was able to return to his own see after Margrave Rikdag died and was succeeded by the illustrious Ekkehard, and when Boleslav returned to his own lands [October/November 985].[16] Afterwards, he became Boleslav's close friend. When he was in Prague, where he had celebrated Maundy Thursday and, on the following day, which is Good Friday, he was rightly proceeding with the memory of the divine passion, he was paralysed by stroke and had to be carried away. Although he improved with time, his infirmity remained with him to the end of his days. He presided over his see for twenty-three years and escaped from the prison of this life on 23 August [992].[17] At the urging of Archbishop Giselher, Eid, a brother of our community and a man of justice and great simplicity, was ordained in his place. If there is time, I will relate many things about his admirable way of life which may be useful for our spiritual improvement. Now, however, I will persist with what I have begun.

CHAPTER SEVEN

Meanwhile, the king's supporters were besieging Count William, a close friend of the duke Henry's, at Weimar.[18] Upon learning that the duke himself had arrived, however, they rushed off to intercept him. They caught up with him near a village called Eythra and made camp, with the idea that they would attack on the following day. This did not escape the duke who sent Archbishop Giselher to inquire about their intentions and, if at all possible, arrange a truce.[19] When Giselher revealed his message to the assembled lords, they replied: if

16 BU 978a; Margrave Rikdag of Meißen (d. 985); allusion to Virgil, *Aeneid* 1.415.

17 *NMer.*, fo. 5r, p. 11.

18 Count William II of Weimar. During William II's lifetime, a feud seems to have broken out between the comital houses of Weimar and Meißen, the latter under Margrave Ekkehard I's leadership (5.8). This state of hostility may have had something to do with the count's decision to support Duke Henry the Quarrelsome's attempt to seize the throne from Otto III (Ekkehard supported the king), and it would certainly explain why he was not among Ekkehard's supporters during the interregnum of 1002.

19 Though acting as an intermediary, Giselher figured among the duke's clerical supporters (note at 4.1. and Althoff 1996: 45).

he would return their lord and king; and, until the day mentioned above, retain only his properties at Merseburg, Walbeck, and Frohse; and if he confirmed this with a credible oath they would permit him to leave this well-secured land in safety.[20] Otherwise, while he lived, he would find no way open to him, either for going forward or retreating. What more is there to say? On the following day, they received all that they had demanded. As they dispersed, they permitted him to go to Merseburg where Duchess Gisela was waiting, saddened by his long absence [20 June].[21] The duke, however, discussing the matter in detail with his supporters and indicating that, for the love of God and the welfare of their homeland, he wished to give up his plan, thanked them appropriately for their help and good will and cordially requested that they join him at the upcoming meeting.

CHAPTER EIGHT

The empresses, hitherto awaiting divine consolation at Pavia, came to Rohr along with all the leading men of the empire and kingdom [29 June].[22] The duke's promise was faithfully carried out as he bestowed his favour and bade farewell to every member of the royal party. The star of the ruler predestined by God was seen by all, shining brightly in the middle of the day.[23] Laymen and clerics joined together in

---

20 The Walbeck referred to here is not Thietmar's familial burg, but rather a royal estate near Mansfeld (Lippelt 1973: 49, n. 22).

21 BU 956, p. 2; Gisela's internment is noted at 3.7.

22 Other sources emphasize that the leading men of both Germany and Italy attended this meeting and that King Conrad of Burgundy played a key role by intervening on his son-in-law Henry's behalf (BU 956q2, *LMA*, vol. 7, p. 949).

23 'At Aachen, on the day of the birth of the Lord, the emperor's little son, Otto III, was anointed king by Archbishop John of Ravenna. Afterwards, when it was learned that the emperor had died, Henry, formerly a duke, returned from exile and also went to Aachen, accompanied by his supporters. Once there, he took custody of the king, by right of kinship. Initially, he pretended that he would faithfully protect the infant king's interests, but then, stimulated by the goad of increasing greed, and enticed by the wicked words of certain men, he tyrannically seized the throne. In that act of pride, it was revealed that he desired both to be called king and to be consecrated king. Although he managed to be called king by a few, he did not succeed in being consecrated king because he was prevented by God and by the decision of the faithful, who did not give their consent to him, but rather supported the lawfully elected and anointed king. Meanwhile, trustworthy messengers were sent to the king's grandmother in Lombardy, namely the august Empress Adelheid. These messengers, firmly bound by the chain of an oath to persist in aiding the king's interests, recounted these disturbing events in order and urgently requested that, if she cared for the kingdom and her grandson, she might quickly come to them with the strength of her presence and advice. Indeed,

offering acclamation of praise to Christ, former enemies offered supplication, and the dissonant multitude came together under a single ruler. The king's mother and grandmother received him affectionately and entrusted him to Count Hoiko for educating. A truce, extending until the above-mentioned meeting on the plain of Bürstadt, was arranged between the king and duke, and both returned to their homes. When they met [c.20 October], the promptings of evil men ensured that they went away angry, and so there was a long post-ponement.[24] Moreover, a great discord arose between Henry and Henry known as 'the Younger'.[25] After this was ended, through the mediation of Count Herman, Henry came to Frankfurt as a supplicant and acquired both the king's favour and his own duchy of Bavaria.[26]

---

once the help of God had been granted to her, the speed of her journey was increased. Accompanied by her daughter-in-law; the king's mother, Empress Theophanu; by her daughter, the celebrated Abbess Mathilda, aunt of the infant king; by her brother, King Conrad of Burgundy; and by the like-named Duke of the Franks [sic Swabia], she met, at Rohr, with all the leading men of Italy, Gaul, Swabia, Franconia, and Lotharingia. The Saxons, Thuringians, and Slavs also arrived. The minds of all were in agreement, that they would either die faithfully for the king or gain that which only the grace of God can grant, victory. After the highest deliberations had been held there, a marvellous and memorable sign appeared, to the astonishment of all who were present and saw it. During the conflict between the two parties, a brilliant star shone forth in the midst of the heavens and, in uncustomary fashion, in the middle of the day. It was as if divine aid were being proffered to the captured king. Seeing this, those on the unlawful side were terrified and quickly yielded. The aforesaid Henry, rightly deprived of the name and kingdom he had usurped, was compelled to surrender the king to his grandmother, mother, and aunt. After being pardoned, through the intervention of King Conrad, his father-in-law, and the favour of the leading men, he sadly departed for his homeland. When they had received that unique surety, the previously mentioned imperial ladies went to Saxony. They arrived, first of all, at the frequently mentioned burg, Quedlinburg, prominent on the top of a small mountain. They were received most courteously with the sweet melody of praise by a great crowd of clergy and people, and also by the virgins serving Christ there who piously offered thanks, joyful at the long-awaited arrival of their spiritual mother and at the king's triumph. They traversed the remainder of the way with the highest honour' (AQ an. 984, pp. 65–66).

24 BU 958b.

25 This 'great discord' is understandable, given the fact that Henry the Quarrelsome's reward for coming to terms was his reinstatement as duke of Bavaria. This office had been bestowed upon the younger Henry during the former duke's imprisonment (3.24). The 'younger' Henry received only the region of Carinthia.

26 'Meanwhile, with God inspiring him, the aforesaid Henry had returned to himself and, hence, began to act with greater fairness and honesty. In regard to his defeat, after anxiously considering his situation more than once, he realized that his pride had been humbled in accordance with the truthful witness of the gospel and he was both struck by a sense of disgrace and tortured by guilt. When the infant King, Otto III, came to Frankfurt, Henry also went there and rightly humbled himself,

CHAPTER NINE

The king celebrated the next feast of Easter at Quedlinburg where he was ministered to by four dukes: Henry at his table, Conrad as chamberlain, Henry 'the Younger' as cellarer, Bernhard as marshal [4 April 986].[27] Boleslav and Miesco also came here with their followers and, after everything was taken care of, departed again, richly endowed with gifts. In those days, Miesco commended himself to the king and, along with other gifts, presented him with a camel. He also joined the king on two expeditions.[28]

In the first year of his reign, on 1 December, Bishop Otwin of Hildesheim died and Osdag, provost of the same church, succeeded him.[29] When he died, after presiding over his see for five years, the cellarer, Gerdag, was consecrated.[30] Gerdag died in the third year after

---

thereby escaping the penalty of his unjust pride. Abject both in deportment and behaviour, he appeared before the imperial ladies in whose power was the care of the kingdom – clearly the infant King's grandmother, mother, and aunt – and in view of the entire people. Although Henry had captured the boy-king, bereft of his father, and had tyrannically usurped his throne, he was not ashamed to become his man, joining his hands together and promising to fight for him with true loyalty. He bargained for nothing but his life, and prayed only for the royal favour. The ladies who, as we have said, were caring for the realm and guiding the king in his infancy, rejoiced that such a great man had offered his submission. Moreover, because devout Christians not only refuse to return evil for good, but even return good for evil, Henry was received with appropriate honour, endowed with true favour, and, in similar fashion, elevated to the office of duke. Thereafter, the ladies esteemed him not only among their friends, but among their closest friends, as is appropriate for a kinsman. The illustrious margraves, Thiedrich and Rikdag died' (*AQ*, an. 985, pp. 66–67).

27 A similar event figured among the ceremonies associated with the coronation of Otto I in 936: 'After the praises of God had been sung and the sacrifice solemnly celebrated, the king descended [i.e. from the throne] and went to the palace. Here, he found a marble table, adorned with trappings fit for a king, where he sat with the bishops and the entire people. The dukes ministered to him, moreover. The duke of the Lotharingians, Giselbert, in whose power the place stood, procured everything for the feast. Eberhard presided over the table, while Herman the Frank saw to the drinks. Arnulf took care of all the mounted warriors, both locating and setting up a camp. Meanwhile, Siegfried, the best of the Saxons and second after the king, son-in-law of the former king and related by marriage to the new one, was watching over Saxony lest an enemy attack occur in the meantime. In his capacity as guardian, he also had the younger Henry with him' (Widukind 2.2, pp. 66–67).

28 *AQ*, an. 985, p. 66; *AQ*, an. 986, pp. 66–67. The second passage notes that 'Miesco came to meet [Otto] with a great multitude, and bestowed upon him a camel and many other gifts', and that he 'also made himself subject to Otto's power'.

29 Otwin (954–84), Osdag (985–89).

30 Gerdag (990–92).

his consecration, on 7 December, while returning from a pilgrimage to Rome. His body, divided into individual parts, was placed in two shrines by his grieving companions and brought to his church. Archbishop Giselher, arriving on the scene by chance, commended both bishops to the earth. *Then, Bernward, the king's teacher, was elected and consecrated.*[31] The king did not cease to assail the Slavs with many harsh campaigns [June–July 986].[32] He also conquered certain peoples in the East, who presumed to rise up against him. In the West, he contended by force and guile to conquer an enemy which repeatedly took up arms and plundered far and wide. It is unnecessary to describe Otto's childhood, and it would take too long to recount what he accomplished with the advice of prudent counsellors.

CHAPTER TEN

The appearance of a comet announced the imminent arrival of a pestilence, with great loss of life. The emperor, now grown to manhood, put aside childish things, as the Apostle says. Constantly lamenting the destruction of the church of Merseburg, he diligently planned for its restoration and, urged on by his pious mother, remained eager to fulfil this vow as long as he lived. The following things were seen by her in a dream and later reported to me, just as she had related them, by Meinswind. During the silence of midnight,[33] Christ's athlete, St Lawrence, appeared before her with his right arm mangled and said: 'Why do you not ask who I am?' And she said: 'I do not dare, my lord!' He answered, 'I am …' and gave his name, and said: 'That which you are now contemplating in me was done by your lord, who was seduced by the words of a man whose guilt causes discord among the great multitude of Christ's elect.'[34] Afterwards, she obliged her

31 Bernward (993–84).

32 BU 983e.

33 Virgil, *Aeneid* 12.846; *Georgics* 1.247.

34 Referring to Otto II and, presumably, Archbishop Giselher (3.13). A similar critique offered by Thietmar's relative and former schoolmate, Brun of Querfurt: 'Before [Otto II] died, God, who alone is always merciful, revealed the following vision to a certain wise man so that humankind might be moved to penance. We would not think it foolish to relate this vision below, recalling it just as we heard it. In the middle of the night, when humanity is usually embraced by the deepest slumber [Job 4:13], he saw the one of whom we have spoken, King Otto, sitting on a gold throne with a silver footstool under his feet. Standing around [the monarch], he saw a long line of bishops and nobles. A young man entered, handsome of face and burning like fire. He was dressed in white, and a purple stole encircled his chest. Instead of standing with the others, he continued his progress

faithful son to care for the eternal salvation of his father's soul by restoring the bishopric, and this was to be done whether Giselher was living or dead. Although of the fragile sex, her modesty, conviction, and manner of life were outstanding, which is rare in Greece. Preserving her son's rulership with manly watchfulness, she was always benevolent to the just, but terrified and conquered rebels. From the fruit of her womb, she offered daughters to God as a tithe, the first, called Adelheid, at Quedlinburg, the second, called Sophia, at Gandersheim.[35]

CHAPTER ELEVEN

At that time, Miesco and Boleslav [II] had a falling out and did much damage to one another. Boleslav called on the aid of the Liutizi who had always been loyal to him and to his forefathers. But Miesco sought help from Empress Theophanu. She was then in Magdeburg and sent Giselher, archbishop of that place, and the counts, Ekkehard, Esiko, and Binizo, along with my father and another of the same name, and with Bruno, Udo, and several others.[36] With barely four weak bands, they set off for the region called Selpuli. While under way, they stopped by a swamp, over which a long bridge extended. On the previous day, one of Willo's companions had been captured by the Bohemians as he was going ahead of the group to inspect his land. Now, in the silence of night, he escaped and gave Count Binizo the first news of an imminent attack. At his warning, our forces quickly roused themselves and prepared for battle. They heard mass in the

towards the emperor. Then, after indignantly pulling the silver footstool from beneath the monarch's feet, he headed for the door with his face averted. Being highly disturbed at this turn of events, he who had been found worthy of such a vision ran after the youth and said: "I ask you, my lord, return the footstool to me, that you might not be guilty of a shameful act! Whoever you may be, you who dare such an outrage, I beg you not to disgrace the king in the presence of the people!" As God subsequently permitted that bishop to recognize, this was the great, golden personage of powerful Lawrence. The saint responded: "On the contrary, if he does not make amends for my disgrace, I shall do even more! After I have taken away his footstool, I shall depose him from the throne itself!" The royal youth recognized both the terrors of this vision and the deadly threats. Nevertheless, be it that he himself was moved by human affection, or that God's anger had so decreed, the outrage was not corrected' (*Brun VA*, c. 12, pp. 13–15).

35 Abbess Sophia of Gandersheim (1002–39), and Essen (1011–39).

36 The persons mentioned include Margrave Ekkehard I of Meißen, counts Esiko and Binizo (Bio) of Merseburg, Count Siegfried of Walbeck (Thietmar's father), Count Siegfried of Northeim, Count Bruno of Braunschweig (?), and perhaps Thietmar's uncle, Count Udo of Stade (4.23).

grey dawn, some standing, others on horseback; and, anxious about the outcome of the coming battle, left their encampment as the sun rose.

CHAPTER TWELVE

Then, on 13 July, Boleslav came with troops and both sides sent out scouts. From Boleslav's side, a certain *miles* named Slopan approached to inspect our forces. After returning, his lord asked for his opinion regarding this army and whether or not he would be able do battle with it. Indeed, his *milites* had demanded that none of our people be permitted to depart alive. Slopan offered him the following assessment: 'This army is small in number, but of the best quality and armed entirely in iron. It is possible for you to do battle with it, but should the victory fall to you, you will be so weakened that you will have to flee your enemy Miesco and will only escape his constant harassment with great effort, or perhaps not at all. Moreover, you will acquire the Saxons as your enemy in perpetuity. If you are defeated, it will mean your end and that of your entire kingdom. There will remain no hope of resistance for you, surrounded everywhere by the enemy.'[37] Boleslav's fury was calmed by these words and, after peace had been concluded, he asked our leading men, who had come to attack him, if they would go with him to Miesco and, in the matter of restoring his property, put in a good word with that prince. Our people agreed to this and Archbishop Giselher, Ekkehard, Esiko and Benizo went with him. All the rest departed for their homes in peace. Now, with the day turning to evening, all were relieved of their arms until an oath was sworn, after which they were returned. Boleslav came with our people as far as the Oder. There, a messenger was sent to tell Miesco that his allies were in Boleslav's power. If he were to return the lands he had seized, he would permit these men to depart unharmed, if not, all would die. But Miesco responded to him in these words: 'If the king wishes to rescue his people or avenge their deaths, he may do so. In any case, he would not give up anything for their sake.' When Boleslav heard this, he plundered and burned the surrounding areas as much as he could but left all of our people unharmed.

37 A similar speech at 6.58.

CHAPTER THIRTEEN

Returning from there, he besieged a fortress called [....] and, with no opposition from the occupants, he conquered it along with its lord, whom he gave to the Liutizi for decapitation. Without delay, this sacrificial victim was offered to their supportive gods in front of the city and all departed for home. Boleslav knew that, without his help, our forces could not reach home without being attacked by the Liutizi. Thus he dismissed our people at dawn on the following day and warned them to move quickly. As soon as their enemies learned of this, they were eager to go after them with a large band of chosen warriors. Boleslav was barely able to restrain them with words such as these: 'You who came to help me, see that you complete what you have undertaken. Know that I took those men under my protection and dismissed them in peace; and, as long as I live, I will not suffer even one of them to be harmed today. It would be neither honourable nor wise for us to turn close friends into open enemies. I know of the hatred between you, but you will find much more suitable occasions for satisfying it.' After calming the Liutizi with words such as these, he managed to detain them for two more days. Then, after taking leave of one another and renewing their ancient alliance, they departed. Now, those infidels chose two hundred warriors who followed our forces which were few in number.[38] Our forces were soon informed of this by one of Margrave Hodo's milites. Immediately quickening their pace, they arrived in Magdeburg unharmed (thank God!), while their enemies laboured in vain.

CHAPTER FOURTEEN

When the empress heard this, she was pleased at their good fortune. Because too little has come to my notice regarding her admirable manner of life, I have only briefly described her great nobility. She was then residing in the regions of the setting sun, rightly referred to as such because there not only the sun but all justice, obedience, and mutual love decline towards extinction.[39] Night is nothing more than the earth's shadows and every act of the inhabitants is sinful. Holy preachers labour here in vain, kings and other great men have little power, thieves and law breakers rule. Many bodies of the saints reside in these regions but, as I see it, the fickle inhabitants spurn

---

38 As an indication of how loosely Thietmar employed the terms *miles* and *milites* (and similar terms), it should be noted that they are here applied to the forces of the Liutizi.

39 'occidentales regiones'. Western regions, in fact, but translated as it is, to preserve the pun.

them. But I shall be silent regarding such things that I might not be judged a disciple of bleary-eyed Crispinus.[40] *Indeed, I have no doubt that their destruction is imminent because of their illicit marriages and other unspeakable deceptions. They have disdained the innumerable excommunications of the bishops and hence, cannot long exist. I ask only this one thing, faithful Christians, pray that they may be changed for the better and that such practices may never appear among us.*

CHAPTER FIFTEEN

Now I must speak of the end of the aforementioned empress and relate the signs which preceded it. In the year 989 of the Incarnation, on 21 October, at the fifth hour of the day, there was a solar eclipse.[41] *But I urge all Christians to truly believe that this does not occur because of the incantations of evil women, or through being devoured, or that it can be assisted by any earthly means, but rather that it has to do with the moon, as Macrobius testifies and other wise men assert.*[42] In the following year, after a life filled with good works, the empress fell ill at Nijmegen and departed from this life on 15 June.[43] Everger, archbishop of the holy church of Cologne, buried her in the monastery of St Pantaleon which Archbishop Brun,

---

40 Horace, *Satires* I.1.120.

41 The correct date is 990, *AQ,* an. 990, p. 68.

42 *Comment in Ciceronis Somnium Scipionis* 1.15.

43 *NMer.,* fo. 3r, p. 7; The empress's death is described in greater detail in the Quedlinburg annals: 'Accompanied by her son, Emperor Otto III, Empress Theophanu celebrated the Pascal feast at Quedlinburg, with imperial glory. Margrave Hugh of the Tuscans and the Slavic Duke, Miesco, were present and other leading men of Europe also gathered there. For the service of the imperial honour, each offered, as a gift, whatever precious thing he possessed. Of their number, Miesco and many others returned to their homelands, after being honoured with gifts. Hugh followed and rendered service to the empress and her son as they travelled throughout the realm, ruling and governing. Finally, they arrived at Nijmegen. There, while she was bringing the entire empire under her authority, as if with a shackle – alas it is most wretched to say – Empress Theophanu, having filled her life with good deeds, was released by a premature death. From there, in the company of the sorrowful emperor, namely her son, and others faithful to her, she was brought to Cologne where she was interred tearfully and with the highest honour in the church of the martyr, St Pantaleon, as she herself had decreed. Crowds of bishops, an assembly of monks and virgins, and all the clergy and people looked on. In the same year, Bishops Erkanbald and Pilgrim, and Archbishop Frederick of Salzburg died, as did Emnilde, daughter of Bruno. Also, Manegold, the by no means inferior son of a Swabian mother, died in Saxony. Because of the faithful service he had shown to Empress Adelheid, she accompanied his body to Quedlinburg where it was interred honourably' (*AQ,* an. 991, p. 68).

who rested there, had built with his own funds.[44] Her son was present and gave generously to the brothers for his mother's salvation. When the illustrious Empress Adelheid learned of this, she was saddened, and immediately went to the king, who had then been reigning for seven years, and offered consolation.[45] She took his mother's place, residing with him until such time as he, being misled by the advice of impudent young men, sent her away in sadness.

CHAPTER SIXTEEN

In both military and domestic matters, my father, Count Siegfried, faithfully served this woman who was both high-born and adorned with virtues. On his last campaign, in Brandenburg, he fell from his horse and thereafter was afflicted by severe bodily pain. In addition to this, he thought that the eighth year had arrived, as had been revealed to him in a dream. Namely, while he was in Cologne, he was awakened from his sleep with the words: 'Siegfried, be watchful, and know for certain that your present life will end, on this day, after eight years have passed.' In his heart, he always looked forward vigilantly to this predetermined day, and did not cease to prepare for it with whatever fruits of virtue he possessed. He took me from Quedlinburg where I had been well instructed in my first letters by my maternal aunt, Emnilde, who had long suffered from paralysis, and commended me to Abbot Rikdag, the second abbot of St John in Magdeburg.[46] Three years later, because he could not give me to this altar, he had me accepted into the community of St Maurice on the feast day of All Saints [1 November 990]. On the feast of St Andrew [30 November], he provided a two-day feast which was highly acceptable to all.

CHAPTER SEVENTEEN

After departing from there, he became ill at the fortress of Walbeck, around the beginning of Lent. On 15 March, this defender of his

---

44 Archbishop Everger of Cologne (985–99). Although the empress's grave was frequently moved over the centuries, the church's *Westwerk* appears to have been its original location (Fußbroich 1991: 233).

45 Adelheid's sadness may have been mitigated somewhat by the knowledge that, with Theophanu's death, she had lost a bitter and dangerous rival (Odilo, c. 7, p. 35; Warner (trans.) 2000: c. 7, pp. 264–65).

46 Emnilde's death appears to have been noted in the necrology at Merseburg (*NMer.*, 2 December, fo. 7v, p. 16); Abbot Rikdag of Berge (*c.*990–1005).

homeland and truthful man paid the debt of our double nature [15 March 992].[47] He was mourned by his wife, Cunegunde, but also by his venerable mother, Mathilda, a truly upright woman who would quickly follow him. For, deprived of all solace, she awaited her last day in great sorrow and went to Christ on 3 December of the same year.[48] My uncle Liuthar, who shared this inheritance equally with us, renewed his old resentment[49] towards my mother and caused her much pain. Although his mother had firmly committed her to his protection, he attempted to deprive her of all Siegfried's possessions. But why dwell on this? With the emperor's help, all was restored to her.[50]

CHAPTER EIGHTEEN

Meanwhile Archbishop Adaldag of Bremen died and was succeeded by Liawizo who, from his homeland between the Alps and Swabia, had followed the exiled Pope Benedict here and so had put forward a claim to this office before God and the king [29 April 988].[51] After the fortresses on the Elbe were restored, the Slavs were attacked and made subject to the king. In the winter, a flood and a great wind did much damage.[52] Excessive heat did great damage to the crops and many people died from a savage pestilence.[53]

In the year of the Incarnation of the Lord 991, on 21 October, Hildeward, the venerable bishop of the holy church of Halberstadt, who baptized and confirmed me, dedicated a temple of the Lord which he himself had built from the ground up and completed down to the last detail.[54] The king was there along with his grandmother the

---

47 BU 1054a; *NMag.*, fo. 4r, p. 41.

48 No, in 991 (Holtzmann 1935: 151, n. 6); *NMer.*, fo. 7v, p. 16.

49 Virgil, *Aeneid* 2.3.

50 Thietmar subsequently had his own problems with his uncle Liuthar (6.44). See also his comments at 7.50.

51 BU 10001e; *NMer.*, 29 April, fo. 1v, p. 4; Liawizo accompanied Pope Benedict V.

52 *AQ*, an. 987, p. 67.

53 *AQ*, an. 988, p. 67.

54 The preceding church collapsed in 965 and construction appears to have started almost immediately on a new one, namely a basilica with a single choir and transept in the east and a *Westwerk* (Jacobsen et al. 1991: 162–63). Among the details that Hildeward saw to was the acquisition of new relics of St Stephan the protomartyr, the church's patron saint (*GH*, p. 86). According to Holtzmann (1935: 153, n. 7) Thietmar drew on a report from the Quedlinburg annals (an. 992, p. 69), but dated it one year earlier and gave the wrong day of the month (i.e. 21 rather than 16 October), the latter presumably having been taken from an account of a

Empress Adelheid, Abbess Mathilda, and these archbishops: Willigis, Giselher, and Liawizo along with sixteen of their colleagues. It was also the feast of Gall, the confessor of Christ, in whose monastery the bishop had been educated.[55] For this reason, he had worked consistently to fulfil his goal on this particular festival. It was also the twenty-fourth year of his consecration. He was aided in all things by his faithful chaplain, Hildo, who arranged everything with the greatest care. All the leading men of Saxony assembled there and were received with affection. As truthful men affirm, never before or after this were the praises of God and worldly matters fulfilled more completely and pleasingly in every respect.[56]

CHAPTER NINETEEN

In the following year, at the rooster's first crow, a light as bright as day shone from the north and remained for one hour but vanished as the rest of the sky grew red.[57] Some people claim that, in the same year, they saw three suns, three moons, and the stars doing battle with one another. After this, Archbishop Ekbert of Trier died and was succeeded by Liudolf; likewise Dodo of Münster after whom Swidger was consecrated; and Erp of Verden who was succeeded by the provost of the cathedral, Bernhar.[58] A great famine also oppressed our regions.[59]

In the third year after the aforementioned consecration, my uncles were captured by pirates, as will be related in what follows.

In the fourth year, a great pestilence broke out in the eastern regions

---

marvel that follows the annalist's description of the dedication. More recently, it has been argued that Thietmar was drawing on a contemporary source emmanating directly from Halberstadt (Althoff 1998: 270).

55 The monastery of St Gall.

56 The presence of the royal family and the large number of ecclesiastical and secular dignitaries certainly redounded to the prestige of Hildeward's diocese, but it also provided an opportunity to celebrate the divine basis of Otto III's kingship. The latter was demonstrated with particular effect when the young king, wearing his crown and other regalia, placed a golden sceptre on the high altar (Benz 1975: 49–54).

57 *AQ*, an. 993, p. 69.

58 Archbishop Ekbert of Trier (977–93), Liudolf (994–1008), Bishop Dodo of Münster (969–93), Swidger (993/94–1011), Bishop Erp of Verden (976–94), Bernhar (994–1014).

59 *AQ*, an. 994, p. 72.

along with famine and war [995].[60] Also, the king attacked the Abodrites and ravaged the lands of the Wiltzi.[61]

CHAPTER TWENTY

After this, the king held a meeting with his leading men, at Magdeburg. It was attended by Henry, the celebrated duke of the Bavarians [mid-August 995].[62] Through good counsel, a long-running dispute between the Henry and Gebhard of Regensburg was settled.[63] Afterwards, that pious duke who cleansed his every sin by constantly distributing alms, went on to Gandersheim where the lady Gerberga, his sister, was abbess.[64] There, after being struck by a sudden illness, he summoned his like-named son and gave him the following instructions: 'Go quickly to your homeland, put your government in order, and never oppose your king and lord. I much regret ever having done so myself. May you always remember your father whom you will never see again in this world.' The son immediately departed. Meanwhile, in his weakness, the illustrious duke continuously sang the *Kyrie eleison*

---

60 BU 1162e.

61 'For the Saxons, a year worse than previous ones began. Indeed, such a great pestilence raged among the people known as Ostphalians that not only their homes, but even many villages were empty because of the deaths of their inhabitants. Moreover, they were both pressed by great hunger and harassed by the constant attacks of the Slavs, having earned such troubles by their sins, so that the prophetic dictum might seem to apply to them: I will bring down upon you the three worst judgements; pestilence, the sword, and famine. Also, King Otto III attacked the Abodrites and certain lands of the Wiltzi, wasting them with fire and much pillaging, but in no way succeeded in suppressing their unrest. When he returned from that expedition, his aunt, Abbess Mathilda, whose memory we recall now and should recall for ever, accorded him a worthy reception at Quedlinburg, with the singing of royal laudes [i.e. the *laudes regiae*]. There, too, his sister Adelheid, bearing the same name as her grandmother, Empress Adelheid, spurned royal suitors and their emissaries, rejected not only the promise of treasure, but even mountains and cities of gold, exceeding one's capacity to imagine them, all this for the love of God and with the intention of living under the yoke of the rule of a canoness. In the presence of her brother, Emperor Otto III, and with the entire senate and people watching, she dedicated herself to the service of SS Dionysius and Servatius, for the sake of the homeland. At the same hour, through the contract of the holy veil, she was consigned to her heavenly spouse by Bishop Hildeward of that same church, with archbishops and bishops standing by' (*AQ*, an. 995, p. 72).

62 BU 1142a.

63 See introduction p. 38.

64 Abbess Gerberga (957–1001).

from his heart and migrated to Christ on 28 August.[65] He was buried at Gandersheim, in the middle of the church, before the altar of the Holy Cross. As soon as the son learned of this, he obtained his father's property through the election and with the support of the Bavarians, in the king's presence.[66] In the same year, the count palatine, Dietrich, and his brother Siegbert passed from this world.

CHAPTER TWENTY-ONE

At that time, my cousin, Margrave Henry, seized one of Bishop Bernward of Würzburg's men, an accomplished but overly proud *miles* named Eberger, and blinded him, at a place called Lindenloh, in return for injuries suffered at his hands.[67] The king was informed of this through the angry protests of the bishop's messengers and, taking the matter seriously, sent the margrave into exile. Later, he restored him to favour and reconciled him to the bishop with an appropriate indemnity. After this, the bishop invited Leopold, margrave of the East, and Henry, his nephew, to attend the mass of St Kilian which is on 8 July.[68] He treated them with great affection. But on that holy night, following matins, while the margrave was disporting himself with his warriors, he was wounded by an arrow shot through an opening by a friend of the man who had been blinded. In regard both to the carrying out and planning of that deed, he had been entirely innocent, but after making his confession, he died on 10 July.[69] A day

---

65 'In this year, moreover, Duke Henry II of Bavaria died prematurely. At the death of Emperor Otto II, he had been tempted, through an alien will rather than his own, to seize the government and, with the emperor's son his captive, aimed at having himself elected king. Prior to his consecration, however, he was seized by remorse and released his grasp on the kingdom. After making his submission to the king, the Bavarian duchy was bestowed upon him, in an honourable fashion. There, in negotiating peace, he flourished more than ever before, and so the inhabitants of that duchy called him Henry "the Peaceful" and "father of the fatherland". When he died, his son Henry, the future king, received the Bavarian duchy by bestowal of King Otto' (*AQ*, an. 995, p. 73). Henry's death is listed by the editors of the necrology of Merseburg (Althoff and Wollasch 1983: 26) as an 'uncertain reading' at *NMer.*, 28 August, fo. 5r, p. 11.

66 The right of the Bavarian nobility to elect their duke is also noted at 5.14 and 6.3.

67 Margrave Henry of Schweinfurt (i.e. of the Bavarian Nordgau) took over the countships of his father, Berthold, upon the latter's death on 15 January 980 (BM 802a). Bishop Bernward of Würzburg (990–95).

68 Margrave Leopold I of Austria (976–94).

69 *NMer.*, fo. 3v, p. 8. A different date is given by the Quedlinburg annals (VII Non. Junii: *AQ*, an. 994. p. 72).

later, he was buried there and rightly mourned, as there was no one more prudent and better in all his actions than he.

The preceding winter had been harsh, unhealthy, cold, windy, and unusually dry. At this time, the Slavs were defeated.[70]

CHAPTER TWENTY-TWO

But because I have spoken above about the destruction of the church of Brandenburg, now I will briefly explain how it was subjected to the king for a time. In our vicinity, there was a celebrated *miles*, named Kizo, who was treated by Margrave Dietrich in a manner that did not please him.[71] Because of this and because no other means were available to him, he went over to our enemies. The latter, recognizing him to be entirely faithful to them in all things, commended the above-mentioned burg to him in order to harm us that much more. But after being mollified by our flattery, he surrendered it and himself into the king's power. Thereafter, the Liutizi, burning with anger, attacked him there with every available warrior [October 995].[72] Meanwhile, the king was in Magdeburg. When informed of the situation, he quickly sent all the forces he had with him: Margrave Ekkehard, my three maternal uncles,[73] Frederick the count palatine, and my paternal uncle.[74] As they were arriving there together, along with their forces, they were dispersed by a ferocious enemy attack. After a number of *milites* had been killed, one part of our force managed to reach the fortress, the remainder had to retreat. Then, after assembling supporters from all sides, the king himself quickly went there. The enemy was severely pressing the burg's defenders, but when they saw our forces in the distance, they quickly abandoned their camp and fled. Rejoicing in their liberation, the defenders sang *Kyrie eleison*, and those who were approaching responded with one voice. The king provided the burg with a garrison and, after his departure, held it for a long time. Later, when Kizo came to Quedlinburg, he was deprived not only of his burg, but his wife and *milites* as well. Afterwards, he received everything back, except for the burg. The burg was placed in the power of one of his warriors called

70 *AQ*, an. 994, p. 72.
71 Margrave Dietrich of the Saxon northern march.
72 BU 1149b.
73 Henry, Udo, Siegfried, counts at Stade
74 Margrave Liuthar.

Boliliut, on whose advice all of this had been done though he was not then present. But Kizo, the best of warriors, secretly tried to exact revenge in those regions and was killed, along with his supporters.

CHAPTER TWENTY-THREE

As I have already mentioned, my three maternal uncles, Henry, Udo, and Siegfried, together with Adalgar and many others, went out in ships, on 23 June, to do battle with the pirates who were ravaging their territories.[75] Udo was killed in battle, but Henry was defeated and captured by those wretched men, and led away, along with his brother Siegfried and Count Adalgar [23 June 994].[76] News of this misfortune quickly spread among Christ's faithful. Duke Bernhard, who was near by, immediately sent messengers who were to promise the pirates payment in return for the captives' freedom and ask for an opportunity to meet and negotiate peacefully. They were prepared to agree but demanded a firm peace and an unheard-of ransom. How much the king initially contributed to this, how much then all the Christians of our region, in generous fulfilment of the due service of humanity, I can scarcely relate. My mother's pain was so great that she was willing to give whatever she had or could acquire in any way to secure her brothers' freedom.

CHAPTER TWENTY-FOUR

When the cursed band of pirates had received the greatest part of the ransom, an immense sum, they allowed Henry to be replaced by his only son, and by Gerward and Wolfram. For Adalgar, they accepted his uncle Dietrich, and Olaf, his aunt's son. They then permitted their captives to depart, so that the remainder of the promised treasure might be collected more quickly. Only Siegfried remained. Because he had no sons, he asked my mother to help him with one of hers. Desiring to fulfil this urgent request, she quickly sent a messenger to Abbot Rikdag, so that, with his permission, he might fetch my brother, Siegfried, who was residing there as a monk.[77] After giving the matter careful consideration, this exceedingly prudent man rejected

---

75 4.19. The following events are also reported by Adam of Bremen (Adam 2.31–32, pp. 92–93; Tschan (trans.) 1959: 75–77).

76 BU 1114a; Udo's death noted at *NMer.*, 23 June, fo. 3v, p. 8.

77 At the monastery of Berge.

the unlawful request, observing that the office bestowed upon him by God would not allow him to grant it. As he had been instructed, the messenger now went to Ekkehard, custodian of the church of St Maurice and master of its school, and asked if, given the urgency of the situation, he would send me back to my mother. I came and set forth, on a Friday, wearing the secular clothing in which I was to be given to the pirates as a hostage, but with my customary clothing underneath [28 June].

CHAPTER TWENTY-FIVE

On the same day, with God's help and in spite of his serious wounds, Siegfried escaped the attentive custody of his enemy. Placed in strict confinement, he constantly plotted his escape with Notbald and Ediko. Finally, he ordered them to take a fast boat and bring him as much wine and other things as would be sufficient to provision those who detained him. His order was carried out without delay and the ravenous dogs were sated. When morning came, the priest set about preparing for mass. The guards were absent, being heavy with the preceding day's wine. The count [i.e. Siegfried] chose this moment to go alone to the prow of the ship, as if to wash, and then leaped into the boat which had been prepared for him. A clamour was raised, the priest was seized as a presumed accomplice, the anchor was raised, and the oarsmen quickly set off in pursuit of the fugitives. The count barely avoided them. Reaching the security of the shore, he found horses prepared, as he himself had previously ordered, and hurried to his fortress called Harsefeld. Unaware of this joyous event, his brother, Henry, and wife, Adela, waited there. The enemy, in hot pursuit, forced their way into a burg called Stade, which lay near the shore. They carefully searched for him there. When they could not find him, they robbed the women of their ear-rings and went away deeply disappointed. The next day, aroused by a common anger, they cut off the noses, ears, and hands of the priest, my cousin,[78] and all the other hostages who were then thrown into the water. Though it caused us unspeakable sadness, we rescued each of them after the pirates left. After visiting my uncle, I returned safely, through the grace of Christ, and was received with affection by my close friends.

78 Henry's son, Siegfried.

CHAPTER TWENTY-SIX

At that time, on 25 July, the venerable bishop of Augsburg, Liudolf, died and Abbot Gebhard of Ellwangen was ordained in his place.[79] Meanwhile, in a certain village called Hordorf, an infant was born who was only half human; from behind he was similar to a goose, his right ear and eye were smaller than the left, his teeth were yellow as saffron; he lacked four fingers on his left hand with only the thumb being normal; before his baptism he had a rather dazed expression but afterwards nothing at all. He died on the fourth day.[80] Because of our misdeeds, this monster brought a great pestilence.[81] The aforementioned Bishop Hildeward, *a true Israelite,*[82] after he had ruled the church and flock committed to him for twenty-nine years, died and was buried outside the church, in the cloister, where he had previously prepared his resting place [25 November].[83] As the brothers were unable to agree on a successor, a royal chaplain, *Arnulf, was proposed and consecrated on 13 December.*[84] *During his own lifetime, his predecessor, that holy man had predicted this to all then present, saying: 'Honour this guest, and minister to him however you can, for he must provide for you when I am gone.'* As he lay in the agony of death, he saw the glory of God and, having summoned his chaplain Wulfher, asked: 'Do you see anything, brother?' When the chaplain responded that he had seen nothing, Hildeward answered that the room where he lay, in which two of his predecessors had died, was filled with the divine majesty. Having said this, he travelled from this prison to eternal light.

CHAPTER TWENTY-SEVEN

The king spent the birthday of the Lord in Cologne [995].[85] Then, after peace had been established in these regions, he set out for Italy where his presence had long been desired. He celebrated Easter in the city of Pavia [12 April 996].[86] From thence, he went gloriously to

---

79 *AQ*, an. 996, p. 73; *NMag.*, 25 July. fo. 10v, p. 54.; *NMer.*, 27 July (!), fo. 4r, p. 9. Bishop Liudolf of Augsburg (989–96), Gebhard (996–1000).

80 *AQ*, an. 995, p. 73.

81 Ibid.

82 John 1: 47.

83 *AQ*, an. 996, p. 73; *NMag.*, fo. 16r, p. 65; *NMer.*, fo. 7v, p. 16.

84 Bishop Arnulf of Halberstadt (996–1023).

85 BU 1162a.

86 BU 1166a.

Rome where, with the agreement of all present, he installed his cousin Bruno, the son of Duke Otto, in place of the recently deceased Pope John.[87] *On the feast of Christ's Ascension, then 21 May, in his fifteenth year, the thirteenth of his reign, in the eighth indiction, he received the imperial anointment from him and was made advocate of the church of St Peter. After this, he governed that empire in the manner of his predecessors, surpassing his years in character and industry.*

CHAPTER TWENTY-EIGHT

In the beginning of the summer, Adalbert, bishop of the Bohemians, arrived. He had received the name Woyciech at his baptism, the other name, at his confirmation, from the archbishop of Magdeburg. He was educated in letters, in that same city, by Ochtrich about whom we have already spoken.[88] As he was unable to separate his flock from the ancient error of wickedness through godly teaching, he excommunicated them all and came to Rome to justify himself before the pope. For a long time, with the pope's permission, he lived an exemplary life according to the strict rule of Abbot Boniface.[89] With the same pope's permission, he later tried to subdue the Prussians, their thoughts still estranged from Christ, with the bridle of holy preaching. On 23 April, pierced by a spear and beheaded, he alone received the best martyrdom, without a groan.[90] This occurred just as he himself had seen it in a dream and had predicted to all the brothers, saying: 'I thought I saw myself celebrating mass and communicating alone.' Seeing that he had now died,

---

87 Bruno's father, Duke Otto of Carinthia, was the son of Otto I's daughter, Liudgard; as pope he took the name Gregory V (996–99). These events are reported in greater detail in the annals of Quedlinburg: 'In the springtime of this year, after a peace had been negotiated between the Saxons and the Slavs, the king went to Italy and celebrated the Resurrection of the Lord at Pavia, according to paschal custom. From there, after forcefully taking possession of the whole Italian kingdom, he came to Rome where he discovered that Pope John, of blessed memory, had died. His cousin, Bruno, a most illustrious man, piously agreed to succeed him, after being elected pope not only by the will of the clergy, but also by the entire citizenry of the Romans. Putting aside the name Bruno, the Romans called him Gregory. He was enthroned at the seat of the Apostles. Thereafter, on 21 May, the venerable feast of the Ascension of Christ, in the ninth indiction, he consecrated Otto august emperor, to the acclamation not only of the Romans, but of all the people of Europe. Following his consecration, and after matters in the Italian kingdom had been properly disposed of, he returned to Francia where he celebrated the birth of the Lord, at Cologne, with honour appropriate to the highest emperor' (*AQ*, an. 996, p. 73).

88 Thietmar, 2.12, 13, 15.

89 In the monastery of St Bonifatius and St Alessio, on the Aventine.

90 *AQ*, an. 996, p. 73; *NMer.*, fo. 1v, p. 4; *NMag.*, fo. 6r, p. 45.

the authors of this wicked crime increased both their wickedness and the vengeance of God by throwing the blessed body in the water. His head, however, they scornfully transfixed with a stake. They returned home in great joy. After learning of this, Boleslav, Miesco's son, immediately purchased both the martyr's celebrated body and his head.[91] In Rome, after the emperor had been informed, he humbly offered praises to God because, during his lifetime, he had taken such a servant for himself through the palm of martyrdom.

At that time, the emperor ordered Bernward, of the holy church of Würzburg, to go to Greece.[92] He died in Achaia along with a large number of his companions. Many affirm that God has performed many miracles through him.

CHAPTER TWENTY-NINE

After departing from Romania, the emperor visited our regions and, having learned of a rebellion of the Slavs, advanced with an armed force on Stoderania which is also called the land of the Hevelli [latter half of May 997].[93] After wasting these lands with fire and great plundering, he returned victorious to Magdeburg [post-20 August].[94] Because of this, a great multitude of our enemies attacked Bardengau, but were conquered by our forces. Bishop Ramward of Minden took part in that battle.[95] Followed by the standard-bearers, he had taken up his cross in his hands and ridden out ahead of his companions, thereby greatly encouraging them for battle. On that day, Count Gardulf died along with a few others, but among the enemy, a great number were killed.[96] The remainder fled after abandoning their booty.

CHAPTER THIRTY

While the pope was absent from Rome – he was called Gregory after his benediction – Crescenzio put in his place John of Calabria, a count favoured by Empress Theophanu and who later became bishop of Piacenza [6–20 February 997].[97] Through such presumption, he usurped power, unmindful

---

91 Boleslav Chrobry (992–1025).

92 In the company of John Philagathos (the later anti-pope John XVI), Bernward was supposed to find a bride for Otto (Beumann 1991: 137).

93 BU 1226a; *AQ,* an. 997, p. 73.

94 BU 1234b.

95 Bishop Ramward of Minden (996–1002).

96 *NMer.,* 6 November fo. 7r, p. 15.

97 BU 1218b. See above p. 11.

of his oath and of the favour shown to him by august Otto. Furthermore, the usurper seized the emperor's messengers and held them in strict custody.[98] *As soon as he heard of this, the emperor went immediately to Rome and demanded through messengers that the lord pope meet with him.*[99] *John the usurper fled as they approached but later was captured by men faithful to Christ and the emperor and thereupon lost his tongue, eyes, and nose.*[100]

98 'In this year, a certain Crescenzio, deceived by diabolical fraud, seized Rome while Pope Gregory was absent, and installed a certain John of Calabria as pope, or rather as apostate. He also held the emperor's legates there in custody. The lord Emperor Otto had sent this John, along with Bishop Bernward, to arrange this marriage to the daughter of the Greek emperor. After returning with the Greek legates, he had grasped that honour of which he was unworthy. He was Greek by birth, of servile condition, and exceedingly adroit. In the manner of a pauper, he approached emperor Otto II Augustus, of pious memory, and through the intervention of the latter's beloved wife, Empress Theophanu Augusta, was first bound to the royal service. As time passed, like the fox from whom he had learned much, he used his cunning to deceive the aforementioned Augusta to such an extent that, at appropriate places and times, she most clemently bestowed her favour upon him. Indeed, he held an honoured place among the leading men until her death. After the death of Otto II Augustus, during the reign of his son, Otto III, who, from his mother's womb, and aided by God's compassion, had been elevated to rulership over the Roman Empire, the power of the aforementioned John, with his inborn cunning, was even more secure since the infancy and carelessness of the king allowed him to assume the first place. Thus, when the bishop of Piacenza died, and a man of good quality was chosen to succeed him, the latter was ejected undeservedly and the church was given to the aforementioned John, a wolf rather than a shepherd, who did not so much govern as plunder it. After he had held this church for several years, being drunk with the venom of diabolical avarice, he was so elevated above himself that, as we have mentioned, rather than occupy the seat of the blessed Apostle Peter, at Rome, with veneration, he instead soiled it with fornication' (*AQ*, an. 997, p. 74).

99 'When he heard of these events, the lord emperor prepared for a second expedition to Italy. The venerable Pope Gregory came to meet him at Pavia where he related to him the worst deeds of John and Crescenzio. Aroused by a divine zeal, he went to Rome as quickly as possible, accompanied by the Pope. When the aforementioned ministers of Satan heard this news, John took flight and Crescenzio took refuge, with his followers, in the fortress that joins the old Roman and the Leonine walls. Then, not only the friends of the emperor, but also those of Christ were pursuing John. They captured him and, fearing that if they sent him to the emperor, he might depart unpunished, they cut off his tongue and his nose, and completely pulled out his eyes. After this man had been punished by God, the lord Pope Gregory received the Apostolic See, with honour, and occupied it without hindrance until his death. The august emperor, coming to Rome, celebrated the holy Resurrection of Christ there. Then, immediately after White Sunday (see below n. 101), using ladders and siege machinery, he stormed the fortress occupied by Crescenzio which had hitherto been impregnable. Crescenzio was captured and beheaded, and it was ordered that he be hanged by the feet, from a gibbet, on the highest precipice of the fortress' (*AQ*, an. 998, p. 74).

100 In addition to the mutilations, the now 'anti-pope' had to endure an act of ceremonial humiliation: 'John the Greek entered an impregnable tower some distance from Rome, but with the arrival of the emperor, was not permitted to

Crescenzio had entered the Leonine precincts and vainly tried to offer resistance to the emperor. In Rome, the emperor celebrated the Resurrection of the Lord [17 April]. After the feast days, siege machinery was prepared. After White Sunday [24 April],¹⁰¹ he ordered Margrave Ekkehard to assault the fortress of Thiedric where that perverse man had taken refuge. He assailed it continuously, throughout the night, but finally ascended its heights by means of a previously constructed apparatus. Then, at the emperor's order, Crescenzio was beheaded and hanged with a rope by his feet, which inspired unimaginable fear among all present [27–28 April 998].¹⁰² Pope Gregory was enthroned with great honour and Caesar then ruled without opposition.

CHAPTER THIRTY-ONE

I would like to recall certain events of this time which seemed childish and marvellous to some, but are acknowledged to have been predestined by God in terms of their worth. Count Ansfrid, a man of happy memory whom I would call conspicuous in all goodness, while still a youth, sprung from the high lineage of his ancestors, was instructed in all earthly law and then especially in divine law by his paternal uncle, Robert, Archbishop of Trier.¹⁰³ Then, his like-named paternal uncle, a count holding fifteen countships, commended

---

remain there for long. After being captured by the emperor's warriors, his eyes were put out, ears cropped, nose and tongue cut off, and he was forced to wear a shameful head covering. But even this revenge did not suffice for such an outrage. After a council decreed his deposition and he had been degraded, the horrible Romans placed him on the back of a donkey, facing towards the tail, and a public crier led him through the various parts of the city' (John, *CV*, p. 31). Other accounts of John's punishment are listed at BU 1262a. Both mutilation and ritual humiliation seem to have been entirely consistent with contemporary Roman legal practice (note at 2.15. and Zimmermann 1968: 112–14). The punishment of riding backwards, moreover, has a long history as a symbolic form of humiliation (Mellinkoff 1973: 153–76).

101 The first Sunday after Easter which originally took its name from the white clothing of the newly baptized, also named after its introit, *Quasi modo geniti* (*LTK*, vol. 10, cols 1012–13.

102 BU 1272a. A reference to the execution was included in the date of an imperial diploma (D O III 285) issued, at Rome, for the monastery of Einsiedeln (i.e. it was issued 'when Crescenzio was beheaded and hanged'). Attached to the diploma is a lead seal bearing the phrase '*Renovatio imperii Romanorum*', a reference to Otto's plan to create a revived Roman Empire with the city of Rome at its centre. The punishments inflicted on Crescenzio and his pope appear to have had a dramatic impact on public opinion (Tellenbach 1973: 9–10). For the mutilation of John Philagathos, in particular, Otto and Pope Gregory were reproached and threatened with eternal damnation by St Nilo of Grottaferrata (*V. Nili*, c. 91, p. 617).

103 Ansfrid's father was a brother of Queen Mathilda (Holtzmann 1935: 168, n. 3).

him to the vigorous lord Brun, archbishop of Cologne, to be educated in
military matters. And so, this young man of good character progressed daily
until he was taken into the service of the great emperor, Otto, who was about
to win Rome with his army. At the very beginning of his service, he was
ordered to place his beautiful tent opposite the emperor's own, every day, and to
carry the ruler's sword. This was done so that Otto could judge how quickly
Ansfrid adapted to the routine of the court. Ansfrid was especially grateful for
this duty because, as the emperor's companion when he sought entertainment, by
hunting birds in remote regions, he could secretly and without embarrassment
attend the sweet psalms which issued from his mouth.

CHAPTER THIRTY-TWO

When the aforementioned Caesar entered Rome, he made this trustworthy
youth his sword-bearer, with the following words: 'Today, while I am
praying at the threshold of the Apostles, you must continually hold the sword
above my head. For I am well aware that the Romans' loyalty to our pre-
decessors was often suspect.[104] *It is wise to foresee adversity while it is still*
distant. and thus avoid being found unprepared for it. When you return to
Monte Mario, pray as much as you wish!' After he returned from there,
Ansfrid established an abbey called Thorn on his hereditary property. With
the bishop's agreement,[105] *he installed his daughter as abbess and mother to*
the many who devoted themselves to God in that place; and surrendered it
completely to St Lambert,[106] *for the salvation of his soul.*

104 Like many of his countrymen, Thietmar had little respect for the political
    steadfastness of contemporary Romans. It is useful to consider the contrasting
    and near contemporary opinions of Benedict, an Italian monk of the monastery of
    Mt. Soratte: 'Alas, O Rome! You have been oppressed and trampled by so many
    people; and now, captured by a Saxon king! Your armed men and strength have
    been reduced to nothing! They take away your gold and silver in their pockets.
    You were once a mother, but now have been made a daughter. What you had you
    have lost. You have been dispoiled of your first virtue; in the time of Pope Leo it
    was first trampled by Julius. At your height, you triumphed over the nations,
    trampled upon the world, and slaughtered the kings of the earth. You who held
    the sceptre and the highest power have been despoiled and violently ravaged by
    the Saxon king. Just as certain wise men have said, and as can be found written in
    your histories, when you fought against foreign peoples, you conquered the entire
    world, from north to south. Seized by the peoples of Gaul, you were all too
    attractive. Of all your walls with towers and ramparts, just as they are now, you
    had 381 towers, 46 castles, 6,800 ramparts, and 15 doors. Alas Leonine city! Now
    you have been captured, now through the Saxon king truly [lacuna]' (*B. Mt. S,*
    p. 186).
105 Bishop Everger of Liège (959–71); the daughter of Ansfrid was Benedicta (BU
    1159a).
106 Died *c.*705; feast day 17 September, patron of Liège.

CHAPTER THIRTY-THREE

Because we have made mention of this servant of Almighty God, we will not pass by in silence what the Lord has done through her in our own times. Ever hospitable, she was so generous towards paupers and pilgrims that, on one occasion, there was no wine left over for her or for sharing benevolently among the sisters. When the cellarer announced this to her, she said: 'Stay calm and be strong, my dear! Through the grace of God, we will be given enough!' Then, in her accustomed fashion, prostrate before the cross in the oratory of St Mary, she began to pray. The wine receptacles, which had been emptied completely the day before, began to fill with wine until they overflowed. Not only did the nuns drink from them for a long time, but also many neighbours and guests, in praise of the Lord.

CHAPTER THIRTY-FOUR

Meanwhile it happened that the Countess Hereswind, Ansfrid's revered wife, took sick at her estate, called Gilze. As soon as she perceived that death was imminent, she hastened to make her way to Thorn. So great was her pain, however, that she could not travel the entire distance and had to stop along the way, at the house of a certain steward. The steward, as he related to us, had extremely ferocious dogs whose barking greatly disturbed the sick woman. When the host learned of this, he expressed his willingness, at her request, to restrain or even kill them, if he could. He could accomplish neither of these, but, miraculously, it happened that thereafter none of the dogs tried to bark until the holy servant of God slept in peace. The companion of her labour and holy simplicity had her buried in the sacristy next to the church. Her chambermaid suffered for many years from dropsy. On the vigil of the birth of the Lord, it was revealed to her in a dream that she should place candles on the sepulchre of her mistress, which she did. She left while the morning offices were being celebrated, received absolution, and was revealed, before the entire populace, to be healthy once more.

CHAPTER THIRTY-FIVE

After the lady Hereswind's departure, her blessed companion, not despairing of the usefulness of earthly works but rather consciously choosing the path of virtue, determined that he would pursue the monastic life wherever he might find the strictest observance. While he was still wrestling with this decision, Emperor Otto III had him called to the bishopric of Utrecht, with all urgency, by Bishop Notger of Liège.[107] *When he heard that, he went to the chapel at Aachen and entreated the mistress of the world that, if this was God's will, all should proceed according to the canons, but if not, that it should be mercifully annulled. But after Archbishop Everger of Cologne had obtained the consent of his suffragans and consulted with the emperor, and with the candidate himself, Ansfrid was acclaimed bishop whether he wished it or not.*[108] *Soon afterwards, he gave five curtes of his own property to St Martin, guarantees to the faithful, so to speak, of their compensation.*

CHAPTER THIRTY-SIX

In old age, after losing his eyesight, he became a monk. Every day, he fed seventy-two paupers with his own hand. At night and accompanied only by his chamberlain, the blind man carried water from the valley to the top of the mountain and prepared a bath for those who were sick; and also provided a change of clothing and other goods necessary for the body, thereafter ordering them to go in peace to keep his good deed secret. On the same mountain, he had established a community of monks whose leaders often punished him with the rod when he was disobedient to their orders. At the end, he gave whatever he had been able to acquire into the hands of the poor. In winter, his piety inspired him to hang bundles of food in the trees to feed the birds on his mountain.[109] *Concealed under his mantle he always wore a hair shirt. From the birth of the Lord until the feast of the Discovery of the Holy Cross he was ill, and during that time ate not more than three pieces of bread. As the dissolution of his mortal flesh approached, he saw a cross in the window which had been placed there after he lost his vision; and revealed to all present that he saw it, praising God and saying: 'In your presence, Lord, is a light which is never extinguished.' He fortified himself by receiving the viaticum and, as he had learned to love his judge while constantly expecting him, one might say that he had conquered the fear of eternity by fearing in the present. Trusting much in the intercession of the holy mother of God, to whom he had dedicated himself and his people, he signed himself with the sign of the cross until, going to sleep in peace, he rested both in hand and mind.*[110]

107 Bishop Notker of Liège (972–1008).

108 Bishop Ansfrid of Utrecht (995–1010).

109 Cf. 1.21.

110 Listed by the editors of the Merseburg necrology as an uncertain reading at 3 May (*NMer.*, fo. 2r, p. 5).

CHAPTER THIRTY-SEVEN

After his death, the residents of Utrecht arrived, tearful and barefoot but with weapons in their hands, and humbly spoke to the local people as follows: 'In the name of God, give us our pastor, that he may be transported to the seat of his own bishopric for burial!' The reverend abbess who was also his most sacred daughter, and was accompanied by her chaplains and warriors, countered this by saying: 'He ought to be buried in the same place where God permitted him to depart from this present existence!' Matters went so far that armed men from both sides confronted each other threateningly. Many would have lost their lives if the abbess had not prostrated herself in their midst and asked God to establish peace among them, at least for the moment. Meanwhile, the warriors wanted to carry his sarcophagus from the outbuildings of the brothers on the Eembach to the mountain above. But while they were engaged in this, the body was seized by the people from Utrecht and, as they still swear, easily transported across the water. So, with the Lord's agreement, the stronger party of the warriors was tricked. After the translation of the holy body, the fragrance of a miraculous odour was perceived along the way and, according to the testimony of very reliable men, filled both nostrils and hearts at a distance of more than three miles.

CHAPTER THIRTY-EIGHT

Let us recall to memory what wretched damage occurred to Archbishop Giselher because of his carelessness. For the protection of our homeland, the emperor had the Arneburg reinforced with necessary defensive works and placed it in Giselher's custody for a period of four weeks [early to mid-June 997].[111] Through some as yet unknown ruse, he was invited to a meeting with the Slavs and went out, accompanied only by a small entourage. Some went ahead, while others remained in the fortress. Suddenly, one of his companions announced that their enemies were bursting out of the woods. After *milites* from both sides were joined in combat, the archbishop, who had been travelling in a cart, fled on a fast horse. Only a few of his companions escaped death. Thus, the victorious Slavs plundered the belongings of the dead in complete security – it was 2 July – and complained only that the archbishop had escaped.[112] In spite of the fact that his forces had been so severely cut up, Giselher guarded the fortress up to the agreed-

111 BU 1226c.

112 In its entry for 2 July, the necrology at Magdeburg notes the 'death of the warriors of St Maurice who were killed at the Arnaburg' (*NMag.*, fo. 9v, p. 52).

upon day. While he was returning home, in great sadness, he encountered my paternal uncle, Margrave Liuthar, in whose care the aforementioned burg was now to reside. Without hesitation, he commended it to him and departed. When the margrave arrived, he saw smoke and fire coming from the fortress. A messenger was sent to request that the archbishop return, but without success and Liuthar himself tried to put out the fire, now raging in two different places. When nothing came of this, he surrendered the portal, open to the enemy, and sadly returned home. Afterwards, when complaints about him were brought before the emperor, he purged himself of any guilt by swearing an oath. *Nine days after the aforementioned slaughter, on 13 July, my mother, Cunegunde, died at burg Germersleben.*[113]

CHAPTER THIRTY-NINE

Ekkehard, scion of the most noble lineage of eastern Thuringia, as he grew to manhood, honoured his entire family with his character and celebrated deeds, but as we read: 'misdeeds dishonour good birth'.[114] After enduring the cruelty of many wars, along with his father, Gunther, long deposed from his dignity, he regained the favour of Emperor Otto III and returned to his homeland in honour. Thereafter, he joined himself in marriage to Swanhild, widow of Count Thietmar and Duke Bernhard's sister. As their first-born child, she presented him with a daughter, named Liudgard.

Liuthar sprang from an illustrious lineage of northern Thuringia and, when he had become a man, was virtuous beyond his years and highly valued by Otto II. With the emperor's help, Liuthar was betrothed to and acquired a certain nobly born woman from the West, named Godila. This occurred with the permission of her cousin, Bishop Wigfried of Verdun.[115] In her thirteenth year, she bore him his first son, Werner, who was named after her father.

CHAPTER FORTY

Almost as soon as these two offspring, the boy and the girl, emerged from the branch of such a noble vine, they began to strive towards the

---

113 Actually, eleven days; *NMer.*, fo. 4r, p. 9.

114 Margrave Ekkehard I of Meißen (985–1002). The citation refers to Horace, *Odes* bk 4, ode 4, verses 35–36.

115 Bishop Wigfried of Verdun (959–84).

maturity of the fruit through the celebrated stairs of virtue. As soon as Margrave Liuthar became aware of the girl's beauty and good character, he began secretly to ponder how he might bind her to his son. No longer able to restrain himself, he revealed his long-concealed desire to Margrave Ekkehard through reliable intermediaries; and it was quickly granted. Then, after the kin of each had assembled together, Ekkehard gave Liuthar a binding promise that he would give his daughter in marriage to his son, affirming this according to custom and right in the presence of all the leading men. But later, as Otto III was very pleased with him and valued him more than the other leading men, and misled by some cause of which I am ignorant, he tried as much as he could to break that agreement which had been so firmly established. None of this remained hidden from Liuthar who anxiously considered how he might prevent it from happening.

CHAPTER FORTY-ONE

While the emperor and Ekkehard were both in Romania, the care of the kingdom had been committed to the venerable abbesss, Mathilda, of whom I have already spoken.[116] It was in her fortress of Quedlinburg that the girl was being educated. The abbess held an assembly at Derenburg where all the nobility convened as one. Meanwhile, without the advice of his father, but rather from love of the girl and fear of public dishonour, Werner, accompanied by my brothers Henry and Frederick, and other excellent warriors, scaled the aforementioned fortress. After seizing his betrothed by force, despite her resistance and complaints, he and his companions arrived at Walbeck, happy and unharmed. When the abbess learned of this through a certain messenger, she was greatly disturbed and tearfully complained to all the leading men, asking and demanding that all arm themselves and quickly pursue these law breakers; and having captured or killed them, try to return the girl to her.[117] Without delay, the warriors hurried to

116 See above p. 164.

117 The church and secular authorities generally condemned the practice of marriage 'by capture' (Brundage 1987: 128–29; Corbet 1990: 193–96). The fact that Liutgard was under the protection of a member of the ruling house who also happened to be acting as regent ensured that resolution of the matter would not be left to the mechanisms of private justice (i.e feud). One of the rare capitularies issued by an Ottonian king (Otto I in 951) prohibits such abductions and threatens perpetrators with the permanent loss of their right to a legitimate marriage (*Const.* 6) although there is no evidence that it came into play on this occasion. According to custom, if the capture of a bride took place with her consent, it was treated more tolerantly, as a kind of elopement. Hence, the concern

carry out this order. They intended to intercept those men by taking a short cut, and capture them by force, kill them, or drive them away before they could reach their secure fortress. But they were informed by travellers that the ones they pursued were now rejoicing in their fortress, with the doors shut, and that they were numerous. They would permit no one to enter and would either die or defend themselves there; and would never return the bride. When the pursuers heard this, they became discouraged and turned back.

CHAPTER FORTY-TWO

Then Liuthar, along with lord Alfrik and Thietmar, a *miles* of Margrave Ekkehard, went off to find out what the bride wished to do. After being sufficiently convinced that she preferred to remain there rather than return, they related her response to the abbess and the others. The abbess consulted with the leading men concerning this matter and was told that it would be best if an assembly were held in Magdeburg; that the betrothed and his bride should come there; and that all of his helpers should either present themselves there as equally blameworthy or be forced into exile. And so it was done! After a great multitude had assembled, Werner appeared barefoot along with his helpers [January 999].[118] He returned the woman and, with the help of the leading men, offered compensation and obtained forgiveness for himself and his companions. But when the meeting was concluded, the most venerable Mathilda took Liudgard with her, not to guard her, but rather to strengthen her in the fear of God.

CHAPTER FORTY-THREE

Mathilda's good intention was interrupted by the sudden arrival of death. For, a few days after she had arrived at the place which God had prepared for her, she suddenly became ill. After summoning Bernward, then Bishop of the holy church of Hildesheim, who granted her the absolution she requested, she departed from this human shell on 6 February.[119] She was buried in the church, at the head of King

to ascertain Liutgard's wishes (4.42). The issue was further complicated by the fact that a legally binding contract was involved (namely between Liuthar and Ekkehard). A similar incident in 1014 led to Werner's death (7.4–5).

118 BU 1299h. On Werner's pose of humility see the discussion at 6.2.

119 Suggested dates for Mathilda's death vary within a few days (Holtzmann 1935: 181, n. 2).

Henry, her grandfather. The death greatly disturbed the Empress
Adelheid, her mother, who sent a messenger to inform the emperor
and ask that Mathilda's sister, also named Adelheid, be permitted to
succeed her as abbess. The emperor mourned the death of his aunt
and gave his assent to the pious request. From afar, he committed the
abbey to his beloved sister with a golden staff *delivered by Bezelin* and
ordered that she be consecrated by Bishop Arnulf.[120] Meanwhile,
Empress Adelheid built up the fortress called Selz and after monks
had been gathered there and everything was completed, she happily
sought her heavenly homeland on 17 December of the same year.[121]
Compensating her faithful service with a just reward, God now works
many miracles at her tomb. *After fulfilling his duties virtuously, Pope
Gregory died in Rome on 4 February. He was succeeded by Gerbert.*[122]

CHAPTER FORTY-FOUR

Afterwards, the emperor went before the Roman synod and accused
Archbishop Giselher of holding two dioceses, ordering through a
legal judgement that he be suspended from office and summoned
there by the pope's envoys.[123] Giselher had suffered a stroke and, as he
was prevented from coming there, sent the cleric Rotman who was to
justify him by oath should he not be believed. At this point, discussion
of the issue was postponed until the emperor could meet with the
bishops of Giselher's province. Afterwards, the emperor heard of the
miracles which God was performing through his beloved martyr

120 Bishop of Halberstadt.

121 Namely, at Selz; *NMer.*, fo. 8r, p. 17. Otto I granted Adelheid property at Selz,
Alsace, in 968 (D O I 368). Odilo of Cluny, author of Adelheid's biography, notes
that the monastery she established there was placed under the protection of the
pope and that Otto III attended the consecration on 18 November 996 (Odilo c.10,
p. 37). Papal protection in no way removed the community from the authority of
the emperor, however. In 992, Otto III granted the community royal protection,
immunity, and the right to elect its own abbot (D O III 79). Later (993), he added
the right to hold a market and to mint coins after the model of those issued at
Strasbourg and Speyer (D O III 130).

122 Pape Silvester II (999–1003); consecration and installation on Easter Sunday, 9
April 999 (BU 1305). Followed by the synod described in 4.44.

123 Thietmar partially confuses the results of the Roman synod with an earlier synod
at Pavia (BU 1299e). This synod was also the occasion for a judgement against
Margrave Arduin of Ivrea who admitted to the assembly that he led an armed
band which had killed Bishop Peter of Vercelli and that he had done nothing to
prevent the burning of the prelate's corpse. The emperor declared Arduin a 'public
enemy' (BU 1305e). Arduin and his supporters were punished by having their
lands confiscated and granted to the bishopric of Vercelli (D O III 323, 383).

Adalbert and made haste to go there for the sake of prayer.[124] When
he arrived at Regensburg, the emperor was received with great honour
by Gebhard, bishop of that church [c.20 January 1000].[125] The imperial
entourage included the patrician Ziazo, the oblationarius Robert, and
the cardinals. Indeed, no emperor ever exited from Rome or returned
there with greater glory.[126] Giselher went to meet him and obtained his
grace, though not permanently, and also accompanied him.

CHAPTER FORTY-FIVE

When he arrived at Zeitz, the emperor was received in a manner
appropriate to an emperor by Hugh II, third pastor of that see [c.10
February].[127] Then he went by a direct route to Meißen where he was
honourably received by Eid, the venerable bishop of this church, and
by Margrave Ekkehard whom he regarded highly.[128] Then, having
traversed the territories of the Milzeni, he was met as he arrived at
the district of Diadesi by Boleslav whose name is interpreted as
'greater praise' not by merit but by old custom. With great rejoicing,
Boleslav offered the emperor hospitality at a place called Eulau. It
would be impossible to believe or describe how the emperor was then
received by him and conducted to Gniezno. Seeing the desired city
from afar, he humbly approached barefoot. After being received with
veneration by Bishop Unger, he was led into the church where, weeping profusely, he was moved to ask the grace of Christ for himself
through the intercession of Christ's martyr.[129] Without delay, he
established an archbishopric there, as I hope legitimately, but without
the consent of the aforementioned bishop to whose diocese this whole
region is subject.[130] He committed the new foundation to Radim, the
martyr's brother, and made subject to him Bishop Reinbern of

124 I.e. to Gniezno.
125 BU 1341a.
126 See pp. 21–23
127 BU 1349b; Bishop Hugh II of Zeitz (c.990–1003).
128 4.40.
129 Bishop Unger of Poznań (c.983–1012).
130 The establishment of the archbishopric of Gniezno diminished the lands and
    rights of the archbishopric of Magdeburg and therefore aroused the opposition of
    Archbishop Giselher and others who identified their interests with those of the
    archdiocese. It was apparently due to Giselher's opposition that the bishop of
    Poznań remained subject to Magdeburg rather than Gniezno. Bishop Unger
    opposed the emperor's plans because they involved a loss of territory for his diocese
    (Claude 1972: 188–92).

Kolberg, Bishop Poppo of Kraków, and Bishop John of Wrocław, but not Unger of Poznań . And with great solemnity, he also placed holy relics in an altar which had been established there.

CHAPTER FORTY-SIX

After all issues had been settled, the duke honoured Otto with rich presents and, what was even more pleasing, three hundred armoured warriors.[131] When the emperor departed, Boleslav and an illustrious

---

131 'Emperor Otto the Red came to St Adalbert to pray and seek reconciliation, and also to recognize the fame of Boleslav, as one can readily read in the book of the martyr's passion. Boleslav received him with such honour and magnificence as a king, a Roman Emperor, and an illustrious guest was worthy to receive. For at the emperor's arrival, Boleslav revealed an amazing sight; he had many columns of warriors first, and then of nobles, arranged in a spacious plain as if in choirs. The clothing of each individual column varied in regard to its colour. And, no type of ornament was common, but rather what would have been found most precious anywhere. Indeed, in Boleslav's time, both warriors and ladies of the court wore fine cloth instead of linen or woollen clothing. Nor were furs at all precious, even if they were new. At his court, they were worn without a cloak and with gold embroidery. Moreover, in Boleslav's time, everyone thought gold as ordinary as silver, and valued silver as cheaply as straw. After observing Boleslav's glory and wealth, the Roman Emperor declared, in admiration: "By the crown of my empire, that which I see far exceeds what rumour had reported". Then, with the advice of his great men, he added: "It is not worthy for such a great man to be named duke or count like one of our leading men, but rather to be encircled with the diadem and elevated to the royal throne". Then, taking the imperial diadem from his head, he placed it on Boleslav's head in a bond of friendship and, as a symbol of triumph, gave him a nail from the cross of the Lord, along with the lance of St Maurice. In return, Boleslav gave him the arm of St Adalbert. On that day, they were joined together with such great affection that the emperor made Boleslav brother and cooperator of the Empire, and named him friend and ally of the Roman people. Moreover, he conceded to Boleslav and his successors whatever ecclesiastical rights pertained to the Empire in the Kingdom of the Poles, or in other regions of the barbarians subjugated by him, or in regions which were to be subjugated. Pope Sylvester [II] confirmed the pact with a privilege of the holy Roman church. After Boleslav had been so gloriously made king by the emperor, he displayed his generosity to him. For the three days following his consecration, he celebrated a feast in a manner both royal and imperial. Each day, he had all the vessels and utensils changed, replacing them with others which were different and even more precious. For when the feast was finished, he ordered the butlers and stewards to gather the gold and silver vessels – nothing there was made of wood! – that had been used for three days at each of the tables; namely goblets and bowls, platters, dishes, and drinking horns, and presented these to the emperor as a mark of honour and not as his principal gift. Similarly, he ordered his chamberlains to collect and carry into the emperor's chamber the large cloths and curtains, carpets, bedding, towels, napkins, and whatever had been presented for his use. Moreover, he gave him many other vases, diverse in form and of gold and silver, and clothes of diverse colours, ornaments of unique type, and precious stones. He presented such an abundance of

entourage conducted him to Magdeburg where they celebrated Palm
Sunday with great festivity [24–25 March].[132] On Monday, the
archbishop of that church was enjoined, by imperial edict, to resume
his previous see but barely managed to have the issue postponed until
the assembly at Quedlinburg by offering a great deal of money to
certain intermediaries. At Quedlinburg, a great assembly of the nobility
convened in conjunction with the joyful celebration of Easter [31
March]. On Monday, Giselher was again summoned before the synod.
His absence, due to a still serious illness, was again excused by
Rotman, and Walthard, then provost of the cathedral, presented many
arguments on his behalf. A council was arranged for him at Aachen,
to which he himself came with his supporters and where once again he
was addressed by an archdeacon of the Roman see [19 May].[133]
Following wise council, he demanded to present his case before a
general council and all of these matters were therefore postponed,
without discussion, until God deigned to bring them to a favourable
resolution in our time.

CHAPTER FORTY-SEVEN [1000]

Because the emperor wished to renew the ancient custom of the
Romans, now mostly obliterated, he did many things which received a
rather mixed reaction.[134] He dined alone at a semicircular table which,
moreover, was elevated above the others. As he had doubts regarding
the location of the bones of Emperor Charles, he secretly had the
pavement over their supposed resting place ripped up and excavations
carried out until they were discovered, on the royal throne. After
taking a gold cross which hung around the emperor's neck and part of
his clothing, which remained uncorrupted, he replaced everything
with great veneration.[135] But how should I recall each of his comings

---

such things that the emperor thought it a miracle. Moreover, he individually
rewarded each of the princes so magnificently that he transformed them from
friends into the best of friends. But who would be able to measure the quality and
number of the gifts he gave to the nobility, when out of such a multitude, not one
guest left without a gift. While the emperor went home, happy with these great
gifts, Boleslav, truly governing, renewed his ancient anger against the enemy'
(Gallus, c. 6, pp. 16–21).

132 BU 1351a.
133 BU 1370a.
134 See p. 12.
135 BU 1370b, and above p. 22.

and goings through all of his bishoprics and counties? With every-thing well disposed north of the Alps, Otto betook himself to the Roman Empire and, arriving at the Romulan citadel, was received with great honour by the pope and his fellow bishops [14 August].[136]

CHAPTER FORTY-EIGHT [1001]

Later, a man very dear to the emperor, Gregory, tried to capture him through deceit and by means of a secret ambush.[137] The conspirators gathered and began their uprising without any warning. But the emperor escaped through a door with a few companions, leaving the majority of his followers inside. Hence this people which has never been content with its rulers repaid the ineffable kindness of this ruler with evil. Then, through a messenger, the emperor requested and ordered that all of his familiars assemble there, demanding from each that they come quickly with armed men, if ever they cared for his honour and safety, in order both to avenge and defend him. The Romans, however, were shamed by the guilt of their now obvious crime and accused one another bitterly. They let all of their prisoners go free and humbly requested the emperor's grace and peace in every way. But Otto distrusted their deceptive words and did not hesitate to do injury to them or to their property wherever possible. All of the regions pertaining to the Romans and Lombards remained faithfully subject to his dominion, the only exception was Rome which he had loved above all others and always honoured. The emperor rejoiced when Archbishop Heribert of Cologne arrived with a large retinue [c.11 January 1002].[138] But though he outwardly assumed a cheerful expression, his inner conscience groaned under the weight of many misdeeds from which, in the silence of night, he continually sought to cleanse himself through vigils, earnest prayers, and rivers of tears. Often he spent the whole week in fasts, except for Thursdays, and he was very generous with alms.

---

136 BU 1390c.

137 This Gregory is usually identified with the like-named Count of Tusculum but may also have belonged to the de Imiza clan, among Otto III's strongest Roman supporters (Görich 1994: 37–38).

138 BU 1437b; Archbishop Heribert of Cologne (999–1021).

CHAPTER FORTY-NINE [1002]

His death was preceded by many troubling events. Indeed, our dukes and counts conspired against him in many ways, not without the knowledge of the bishops. The conspirators sought the support of Duke Henry, who later succeeded the emperor, but he refused to become involved, having been loyal up to then in all things and preserving in his heart the final admonition of his like-named father who died and rests at Gandersheim.[139] The emperor, learning of this immediately and bearing it with a patient soul, took sick at the fortress of Paterno, having been afflicted by internal sores which gradually burst. Thus the crown of the empire exited from this world on 24 January, with a bright expression and extraordinary faith, but leaving an insurmountable sorrow to his people because in that time there was no one more generous and compassionate in all things than he. May He who is both alpha and omega be merciful unto him[140] and, bestowing great things in return for lesser ones, grant him eternity in return for his temporal existence.

CHAPTER FIFTY [1002]

Those who were present at the time kept his death a secret until the army, then widely dispersed, could be assembled by messengers. Then, the sorrowful band accompanied the body of their beloved lord, continuously enduring vicious attacks by enemies which did not cease until they reached Verona. From there they went on to Polling, an estate belonging to Bishop Siegfried of Augsburg, where Duke Henry received them and revived their sorrow with his tears.[141] Henry urged each of them, individually, to choose him as their lord and king, and made many promises. He took custody of the emperor's corpse, and also of the imperial insignia, except for the holy lance which Archbishop Heribert had secretly sent ahead. The archbishop was briefly taken into custody but released, after his brother was left there as a surety, and soon sent back the holy lance.[142] Along with all the others who followed the emperor's corpse, with the exception of Bishop Siegfried, Heribert did not then favour the duke and made no effort to

---

139 4.20.

140 Apocal./Rev. 1: 8.

141 Bishop Siegfried of Augsburg (1000–1006).

142 Bishop Henry of Würzburg (995/96–1018).

conceal it, but rather declared that he would freely give his assent to whomever the better and greater part of the entire folk inclined.[143]

CHAPTER FIFTY-ONE

With them, the duke reached the city of Augsburg where he gave the beloved emperor's intestines, carefully preserved in two small vessels, an honourable burial in the oratory of the holy Bishop Ulrich.[144] The oratory had been constructed in his honour, in the southern part of the church of St Afra, by Bishop Liudolf of Augsburg.[145] For the salvation of his own soul, Duke Henry also donated one hundred manses of his hereditary property. Then, after dismissing the multitude in peace, he followed Caesar's corpse to Neuburg, one of his possessions. At the urging of Henry, whose name he shared and whose sister he had married during the emperor's lifetime,[146] the duke allowed the corpse to proceed to its intended destination, after taking his leave individually from each member of the party escorting it.

CHAPTER FIFTY-TWO

Meanwhile, having learned of their lord's premature death, the leading men of the Saxons sadly convened at the royal estate of Frohse, held as a benefice from the emperor by the then Count Gunzelin.[147] Giselher, archbishop of Magdeburg, along with his suffragan bishops, Duke Bernhard, the margraves Liuthar, Ekkehard, and Gero, and the

---

143 Above p. 24.

144 By openly demonstrating his concern for the emperor's mortal remains, Henry was effectively representing himself as his legitimate heir (Warner 1995: 72). Adalbold of Utrecht, who based his biography of the king on Thietmar's text, observed that Henry had treated Otto's corpse in a manner befitting a lord and a relative (Adalbold, c. 3, p. 684). Thietmar may have also wished to compensate for the fact that Henry had not been in attendence at Otto's funeral in Aachen. From Thietmar's comments at 4.54, it would appear that Duke Herman was.

145 The precise location of the structure is unclear though presumably it was in the area of Ulrich's underground grave-chamber which is, indeed, located on the south side of the nave (Jacobsen et al. 1991: 38–39).

146 Referring to Henry of Luxembourg, brother of Cunegunde.

147 Presumably this is the Count Gunzelin who intervened on Archbishop Giselher's behalf in a diploma issued by Otto II in 979 (D O II 186) and also the man identified by Thietmar as the father of Albi whose countship had been received by Giselher (4.69). Henry II would later give Frohse to the church at Magdeburg as a reward for Archbishop Tagino's vigorous and loyal service (D H II 242; Claude 1972: 266).

great men of the region pondered the condition of the realm.[148] When
Margrave Liuthar realized that Ekkehard wanted to exalt himself
over them, he called the archbishop and the worthier part of the
magnates outside for a secret discussion. During this discussion, he
proposed that they swear an oath to refrain from electing a lord and
king, either as a group or individually, until a meeting could be held
at Werla. This was agreed and consented to by all, with the exception
of Ekkehard. Angry at being held back somewhat from the royal
dignity, he shouted: 'O, Count Liuthar, what do you have against me?'
Liuthar responded, saying: 'Indeed, have you not noticed that your
cart lacks its fourth wheel?'[149] Thus the election was interrupted, and
the saying of the ancients was confirmed: to delay for one night is to
postpone for a year, *and that means to defer for a lifetime. In the time of
the aforementioned Caesar, the convent Hillersleben was burned down and
its nuns were carried off; and on the same day many of our people were killed*
[summer 999].[150]

CHAPTER FIFTY-THREE

After this long digression, I will finally return to my theme by briefly
describing the emperor's funeral procession. When his corpse arrived
in Cologne, it was first received by Heribert, archbishop of that city.[151]
On the Monday following the feast of Palms [30 March], it was
carried to the church of St Severinus, on Tuesday to St Pantaleon [31
March], and on Wednesday to St Gereon [1 April]. On Maundy
Thursday, it was carried to St Peter where, according to ecclesiastical

---

148 Margrave Gero II of Serimunt (since 979) and of the Saxon eastern march (993–
1015).

149 Though clearly intended to deny Ekkehard's claim to the throne, the precise
significance of this pithy remark has been much debated. According to one
argument (Hlawitschka 1978: 297–99), Ekkehard's missing wheel refers to the
absence of one of the four cardinal virtues (of Stoic philosophy), namely, humility.
It is, in fact, an absence of humility that Thietmar identifies as the margrave's
major fault (5.7). But in any case, it is scarcely a coincidence that the remark was
delivered by Margrave Liuthar, who had a personal grudge against Ekkehard
because of the latter's refusal to honour the marriage contract between his
daughter and Liuthar's son, Werner (above 4.40).

150 BU 1322f.

151 In the events that follow, Archbishop Heribert essentially integrates the
emperor's funeral obsequies into the stational liturgy of Easter. From Thietmar's
comments regarding the support voiced for Duke Herman by those in attendance,
one would suspect that the entire occasion was intended to bolster his candidacy
for the throne (Warner 1995: 70).

custom, penitents are admitted and receive absolution [2 April]. With the body present, the archbishop granted absolution, assisting priests called everyone to remembrance, and the people responded tearfully and in all humility. On Friday morning, the body was raised again and, on Holy Saturday, taken to Aachen [3, 4 April]. On Sunday, it was buried in the church of the holy, ever virgin Mary, in the middle of the choir [5 April]. The generosity he had shown to all brought forth constant prayers and loud weeping. The congregation could not accord due honour to the feast of the Resurrection of the Lord, which both angels and humanity should celebrate with common rejoicing, because, in their fragility, they recognized that this was also God's well-deserved punishment for their sins. May any faithful person who confesses to God tearfully ask forgiveness for the soul of that one, who strove with every effort to restore our church. May he who always strove to comfort the wretched join, in the land of the living, the ever desired communion of the pious with the blessed immortals of the Lord.

CHAPTER FIFTY-FOUR

The majority of the nobles who attended the funeral procession promised Duke Herman their support in acquiring and securing the royal dignity and falsely declared that Henry was not suitable for this for a variety of reasons.[152] When they heard of the emperor's death, being unconcerned with the future and having no desire for the worthy fruits of penance, the Lombards elected Arduin as their king [15 February 1002 at Pavia].[153] He was a man more familiar with the arts of destruction than those of government and, by the judgement of God, those who had elected him subsequently learned this for themselves.[154] But leaving this for a later discussion,[155] I shall instead write about one who, by divine favour and his own virtue, defeated all who ever dared to rise up against him and forced them to do homage to him with their heads bowed. This one, the fifth in order, the second in name, will be the subject of my fifth book.

152 Duke Herman II of Swabia (997–1003). Cf. 5.3.
153 BU 1483ee.
154 BU 1450f.
155 Thietmar, 5.24.

CHAPTER FIFTY-FIVE

I cannot place in its correct order everything that ought to be treated within the context of this book. In what follows, therefore, I will not be embarrassed to add a few recollections. Indeed, I rejoice in the change of pace much as the traveller who, because of its difficulty or perhaps from ignorance, leaves the course of the more direct road and sets out on some winding secondary path. Hence, I will relate the remaining deeds of Miesco, the celebrated duke of the Poles, who has already been treated in some detail in the previous books. He took a noble wife from the region of Bohemia, the sister of Boleslav the Elder. Her life corresponded to her name – she was called Dobrawa in Slavic which, in German, means 'the good'.[156] For this one, faithful to Christ, and realizing that her husband was mired in various heathen errors, turned her humble spirit to the task of binding him to the faith as well. She tried in every way to conciliate him, not because of the threefold appetite of this evil world but rather for the sake of the admirable and, to all the faithful, desirable fruit of future salvation.[157]

CHAPTER FIFTY-SIX

She sinned willingly for a while, that she might later be good for a long time. For during Lent, which closely followed her marriage, though she intended to offer an acceptable tithe to God by abstaining from meat and through the affliction of her body, her husband asked and tried to coax her into giving up her plan. She consented, thinking that he might therefore be more willing to listen to her on some other occasion. Some say that she only ate meat during a single Lenten period, others say three. Now, O reader, you have heard her sin, now also consider the attractive fruit of her pious will. She laboured for the sake of her husband's conversion and was heard by the Creator in his kindness; and through his infinite goodness that most zealous persecutor came to his senses. After being admonished frequently by his beloved wife, he vomited out the poison of his unbelief and, in holy baptism, wiped away the stain of his birth. Immediately, members of his hitherto reluctant people followed their beloved head and lord and, after accepting the marriage garments, were numbered among

---

156 Dobrawa was the daughter of Boleslav I of Bohemia (d. 977) and sister of Boleslav II (d. 999). Her marriage, negotiated by Margrave Gero in 963/64 established a closer relationship between Bohemia and Poland and established ties between the *Reich* and the Polish dynasty of the Piasts (*LMA*, vol. 3, p. 1149).

157 1 John 2: 16.

the wards of Christ. Jordan, their first bishop, laboured much with them, while he diligently invited them by word and deed to the cultivation of the heavenly vineyard. Then the couple rightly rejoiced, namely the man and the noble woman, and all who were subject to them rejoiced at their marriage in Christ. After this, the good mother gave birth to a son who was very different from her and the misfortune of many mothers. She named him Boleslav, after her brother. He first revealed his innate evil to her and then raged against his own flesh and blood, as I will reveal in the following.

CHAPTER FIFTY-SEVEN [977]

But when his mother died, his father married Margrave Dietrich's daughter, a nun at the convent called Calbe, without the approval of the church.[158] Oda was her name and great was her presumption. She rejected her celestial spouse in favour of a man of war, which displeased all the pastors of the church but most of all her own bishop, the venerable Hildeward. But the welfare of the land, and the need to strengthen the peace, kept this from leading to a break; rather it provided a healthy and continuous incentive for reconciliation. For she increased the service of Christ in every way: many captives were returned to their homeland, prisoners were released from their chains, and the prisons of those who had been accused were opened. I hope that God will forgive her the magnitude of her sin, since such love of pious deeds was revealed in her. We read, however, that he who does not entirely abandon the evil he has begun, will try in vain to placate the Lord. She bore her husband three sons: Miesco, Swentepulk and [...]. She passed her life there, highly honoured, until her husband's death. She was beloved among those with whom she lived and useful to those from whom she had come.

CHAPTER FIFTY-EIGHT

But on 25 May, in the year of the Incarnation 992, in the tenth year of Otto III's kingship, the aforementioned duke, now old and feverish, went from this place of exile to his homeland, leaving his kingdom to be divided among many claimants. Yet, with fox-like cunning, his son Boleslav unified it once more in the hands of one ruler, after he had

---

158 Oda, a nun at the convent of St Lawrence in Calbe, was the daughter of Margrave Dietrich of the Saxon northern march (Engelbert 1954: 2–3).

expelled his stepmother and brothers, and had their familiars Odilien and Przibiwoj blinded. That he might be able to rule alone, he ignored both human and divine law. He married the daughter of Margrave Rikdag, but later sent her away and took a Hungarian woman as his wife. She bore him a son, named Bezprym, but he also sent her away. His third wife was Emnilde, a daughter of the venerable lord, Dobromir.[159] Faithful to Christ, she formed her husband's unstable character completely for the better and strove unceasingly to wash away both of her sins through the generous dispersal of alms and abstinence. She bore two sons, Miesco and another one whom the father named after his beloved lord.[160] She also produced three daughters of whom one was an abbess, the second married Count Herman,[161] and the third the son of King Vladimir.[162] I will say more about them later.

CHAPTER FIFTY-NINE

With the favour and urging of the aforementioned emperor, Waik, brother-in-law of Duke Henry of the Bavarians, established bishoprics in his kingdom and received the crown and consecration.[163] Nor shall I keep silent regarding a certain miracle which appeared in the sky, in Rome, during that same emperor's lifetime. For the warriors of Duke Herman forcibly seized a meadow belonging to the monks of St Paul and refused to give it up, even after the brothers had humbly and repeatedly asked them to do so.[164] Immediately, dark clouds appeared and lightning flashed, thereby revealing the anger of the Lord. At once, terrible thunder followed, killing four of the best of those and causing the rest to flee. This proved that, even in this world, the paupers of Christ should not be held in contempt. Merciful God is their protector. He rewards those who honour them and render assistance in time of need; and punishes their persecutors, either here, which is lighter, or for eternity, which is worse.

159 Dobromir's origins are unknown, though it has been suggested that he may have been ruler of Lausitz and the lands of the Milseni (*LMA*, vol. 3, pp. 1150–51).

160 Duke Miesco II of Poland (1025–34); the second son may have been named Otto after Otto III (Mitterauer 1988: 297).

161 The eldest son of Margrave Ekkehard I of Meißen married Boleslav's daughter, Reglindis (Beumann 1991: 160)

162 Sventipolk (8.32).

163 King Stephen of Hungary (1001–38).

164 Otto III issued a diploma at St Paul's on 4 June 1001 (D O III 405).

CHAPTER SIXTY

Mathilda, the emperor's sister, married Ezzo who was the son of Herman, the count palatine. This displeased many. Because the decision could not legally be changed, her only brother endured it patiently though he endowed her richly enough that the inborn honour she possessed by virtue of her celebrated ancestors would not be degraded.[165] Alas, in his time there died Conrad, illustrious leader of the Swabians [August 997], and Count Herbert, his brother,[166] and the celebrated Margrave Hodo [13 March 993]. Siegfried, the margrave's son, who had lived as a monk among the monks at Nienburg, where his father lay buried, threw off the cowl and put on secular clothing. After being summoned by his abbot, Ekkehard, and by Archbishop Giselher, he came to a synod at Magdeburg which judged that he must again be clothed in his former habit though he himself was unwilling.[167] Yet, he freed himself by swearing a twelve-fold oath, following the precedent of one who had purged himself of a similar sentence before the emperor in Rome. Their spiritual fathers had ample evidence against them, but because the judges had been corrupted, as I fear, they escaped any blame.

CHAPTER SIXTY-ONE

May I now recall the brief life of Bishop Franko of Worms. The august Caesar was pleased with this youth, who was distinguished for his high integrity. After including him among his intimates, the emperor recognized that he was also sincere and spiritually gifted.

165 Contrary to Thietmar's comments, the marriage with Ezzo would scarcely appear to have been degrading. Holders of a large number of countships in the Rhineland, the Ezzonen figured among the most important families in the Ottonian and Salian eras. Ezzo was heir to much of this property and also acquired the office of count palatine upon the death of his father (*LMA*, vol. 4, pp. 197–202, 6.392; Glocker 1989: 212–13; Lewald 1979: 120–26). A later source from Brauweiler, a monastery founded by Ezzo, asserts that the count palatine won the right to marry Mathilda by beating Otto III at dice or chess (*FB* c. 6, p. 128). More significant for any evaluation of the marriage are the source's assertion that the decision was approved by Theophanu, then acting as regent, and its characterization of Ezzo as one of the empress's supporters and 'second after the king' (*FB*, c. 10, p. 130). The marriage produced seven daughters who, with one exception (i.e. Richeza married Miesco II), became abbesses, and three sons. The sons would have been Otto III's closest male relatives, albeit through their mother, and there is some thought that they or their father may have been considered as candidates for the throne in 1002 (Lewald 1979: 130–38; Wolf 1995: 69–75).

166 Presumably the Count Heribert mentioned in D O II 128.

Thus, at the death of Hildebald, bishop of the aforementioned city, he had Franko succeed him.[168] He occupied his bishopric for no more than two years and died in Italy, where he was buried.[169]

If it were possible, I would that the work of my useless hands might cause the memory of the best of those to flourish anew, both in the present and future, so that, even if it brought them no pleasure, they might intercede for me with omnipotent God. *I myself acknowledge that I am less than I ought to be, and not confiding in the fragility of a rod of cane, I commit myself as a humble sinner to the just intercessors.*

CHAPTER SIXTY-TWO

The emperor also wanted to elevate his chaplains, Herpo of Halberstadt and Rako of Bremen, to the episcopacy and he gave them the pastoral staff as they lay in bed gravely ill.[170] But both died without being anointed as bishops. I do not know what more I may say of this as I have never read or heard anything about them. Omniscient God ordained this and he alone can know. Although they were pious, these two should not be reckoned among the bishops, as they could not be incorporated into their ranks though consecration. In obedience to his beloved lord's order, Razo transported Pope Benedict's bones from Hamburg to Rome, just as the pope himself had predicted.[171] For the venerable father, the lord pope, zealous in the service of Christ even as an exile, though this part of the north still rejoiced in a welcome peace, said: 'My fragile body must be loosed here. After this, the entire region will be left to the heathen to be devastated with the sword and to wild animals as a habitation. Prior to my translation, the inhabitants will not see a firm peace, but when I am at home, I hope to quiet the pagans through apostolic intercession.'

CHAPTER SIXTY-THREE

In the time of the aforementioned emperor, many pious people died, but I will not talk about them because their lives are unknown to me.

---

167 Abbot Ekkehard of Nienburg (995–1017), later bishop of Prague (1017–23).

168 Bishop Hildebald of Worms (979–98).

169 Bishop Franko of Worms (d. August 999). Bishop Franko was the brother of Bishop Burchard of Worms (1000–25).

170 The two men were Bishop Burchard of Worms's predecessors.

171 Pope Benedict V.

Among them was a certain Countess Christina who gave a large part of the property she held in the fortress of Stöben to St Maurice in Magdeburg. She travelled the brief course of this life while living in Christ and, on 8 March, came happily to the chamber of her long-awaited spouse. This was revealed to Giselher, then archbishop of Magdeburg, while he was visiting Quedlinburg. A man appeared to him and said: 'Do you not know that the entire army of heaven is preparing itself for the arrival of a soul faithful to Christ and for the worthy reception of such a spouse? Even now, she comes for her reward and for the blessed hope of an eternal abode.' When he awoke, he immediately notified Walthard who was then his provost. As soon as Walthard heard that the venerable matron had departed from this light during the same night on which the vision had been seen, he reported this to his lord and said that his vision had been fulfilled. Concealing her good deeds in her heart, she differed from other, modern women, most of whom clothe their bodies in an unseemly fashion and openly reveal to all their lovers whatever they have to offer. Although they are an abomination to God and the shame of our age, they shamelessly present themselves as a spectacle before the entire people. It is disgraceful and lamentable[172] that no sinner wishes to conceal himself but rather presumes to hold up the good for derision and the evil as an example.

CHAPTER SIXTY-FOUR

In those days, the nun Mathilda, a daughter of Margrave Dietrich, married a certain Slav named Przibislaw. Later, she was captured by Boliliut, the unlawful guardian of the fortress of Brandenburg,[173] and was held in such strict confinement that she could not observe the birth of the Lord, or any other feast day, with an appropriate fast, or celebrate it with festive joy. There, she gave birth to a son whom she raised in sadness. Afterwards, she was freed and received an abbey at Magdeburg, despite her unworthiness. Her husband had already been killed on 28 December, by the twin brothers Ugio and Uffiko. Liudolf, his brother, abandoned his clerical habit and took up arms, inflicting much damage on our people in his desire for revenge. He was captured by the emperor, however, and restored to his previous status.

172 Persius, *Satires* 1.3.
173 4.22.

CHAPTER SIXTY-FIVE

In the times of the aforementioned Caesar, there was a certain deacon named Hepo in the city of Magdeburg. He was a cheerful man and very useful in the monastery, especially in the choir. When he entered old age and was mature in all his actions, he was suddenly struck by paralysis and lost his voice. Nevertheless, with the aid of the highest physician, he was able to sing the psalms perfectly with the brothers though otherwise he could barely whisper. In this remarkable thing, we recognize the praiseworthy powers of Christ which, in many ways, serve to raise up men who faithfully serve him. The venerable father lamented during confession that he had greatly sinned by abandoning the monastic habit, and then, at the admonition of the brothers, wished to offer emendation by putting it on again. But not long after, on 5 January, he died and was buried at St John [in Berge], among the brothers with whom he ought to have lived if human fragility had permitted.[174]

CHAPTER SIXTY-SIX

Ekkehard, called 'the Red', was overseer of the aforementioned church and, being a grammarian by profession, head of the school. One day, he wanted to examine the great golden altar, which is encrusted with gems and amber, to see if anything was missing from it. Suddenly, it fell over on him. Following this incident, which left him crippled, he surrendered the wealth that he had long been gathering to the provost, Walthard, to be distributed generously. After a few days, on 4 September, he released his faithful spirit.[175] I do not wish to accuse him of anything, but I know this for certain; if anyone offends St Maurice he should be aware of the imminent danger. *On a particularly dark night, at the instigation of the Devil, a certain young man wanted to plunder his treasury. Already at the entrance, however, he was seized by fear and wanted to desist, as he himself subsequently recalled, but he heard a voice urging him to proceed with his audacious deed. The wretch had barely seized a crown when he was captured and placed upon the wheel, after having his bones broken.*

174 *NMag.*, fo. 1r, p. 35.
175 *NMer.*, fo. 5r, p. 11; *NMag.*, fo. 12r, p. 57.

CHAPTER SIXTY-SEVEN

Nor shall I conceal from you, dear reader, the constancy of a certain
brother of mine, Husward, who used to sleep next to me. The Devil,
our sly deceiver, repeatedly accosted him in the night and, in vain,
asked for room to lie next to him. At last, he humbly asked if Husward
would serve him in return for a reward. But that pious man did not
forget his oath to the Lord and asked to be shown the promised
reward before he gave his answer. Then the Devil said: 'If you agree,
I will reward you with a prize similar to that with which I recently
endowed my servant in the West.' When he heard these words, this
venerable priest, as he had done previously, drove him away with the
sign of the holy cross and with harsh reproaches. Moreover, when he
learned that a certain cleric had been hanged with a rope because of
the enormity of his crimes, he related to all of us what had preceded
and followed. It is astonishing that the evil one dared to try such a
thing, even though the true cross of Christ is carried into that dormitory every Sunday. In that same year, on 23 February, the aforementioned brother escaped the danger of this world, victorious, so I
hope, and having repented of his sins.[176] His now feeble mother, Bertha,
consoled him in his agony, patiently bearing her double pain. For it
was then the anniversary of the death of her son, Bevo, one of the best
milites, who had previously been blinded by Margrave Ekkehard.

CHAPTER SIXTY-EIGHT

Nor shall I keep silent regarding the vision of our brother Markward.
He was led to the common cemetery, as he himself complained to me,
where he saw a fiery grave. His guide said to him: 'You must soon be
thrown into this burning pit if you do not immediately stand as a
convert at Liudger's threshold; and Rudolf will follow you.' Both had
been monks in the monastery of that confessor who had established
this place out of his hereditary property at Helmstedt in the time of
Emperor Charles the Great.[177] He was the brother of Hildegrim,
Bishop of Châlons and first pastor of the holy church of Halberstadt
which he held for forty-seven years, departing from this world during
the reign of Emperor Louis the Pious in the year 827 of the Lord's
Incarnation.[178] Liudger was made the first pastor of the church of

176 *NMag.*, fo. 3r, p. 39.
177 *AQ*, an. 781, p. 38.
178 *AQ*, an. 827, p. 44.

Werden by Emperor Charles. After building up his diocese and church at Werden, which he constructed at his own expense, he received his heavenly reward in the year of the Lord's Incarnation 808. The aforementioned emperor survived him by only five years, giving up his spirit on 28 January, in the seventy-first year of his life, in the forty-seventh of his reign, and in the fourteenth of his emperor-ship. In the same year in which he had this vision, the previously mentioned priest resumed his former habit, vowed obedience, and, shortly after 14 April, died.[179] I have not said these things regarding my brethren in order to raise accusations but rather to encourage us to be cautious and follow the example of good men.

CHAPTER SIXTY-NINE

During the reign of Otto III, Albi, the son of Gunzelin, was killed by his retainer, in a certain forest, because of some minor grievance. Archbishop Giselher received his countship along with his benefice on the Mulde.[180] Giselher's chamberlain, my colleague Gunther, was dear to the emperor and served him faithfully. After the death of Dodo, bishop of the church of Osnabrück, he went to Italy.[181] He was received with kindness there and received an attentive hearing. During the following night, however, the martyrs of Christ, Crispin and Crispinian, appeared to come to him and ask if he wished to receive their bishopric. When he responded, 'If God wills it and it is pleasing to you,' they pierced him with two spears. Upon awakening, he was unable to rise unassisted. When, on the following day, the emperor learned of his illness, he faithfully fulfilled his promise. Following his convalescence, Gunther went home and, after being consecrated, lived for four years more, in great pain. On 24 November, he traded this temporal world for eternity.[182] I do not know if something in him was displeasing to God or his holy martyrs. I both saw and heard from others that he was a just and God-fearing man, mild and chaste. Those with whom he now rests assert that he is greatly valued by God, as many signs have confirmed. I know this to be true, God does not punish the same mistake twice.[183]

179 NMer., 15 April, fo. 1v, p. 4; NMag., 16 April, fo. 5v, p. 44.
180 The countship of Eilenburg; mid-September 991 (BU 1037).
181 Bishop Dodo II of Osnabrück (978–96).
182 NMer., fo. 7v, p. 16; NMag., fo. 16r, p. 65.
183 Nahum 1: 9.

CHAPTER SEVENTY

In order that you, O reader, may recognize through me that the reverence due the martyrs is sufficiently bright in old books, I will recount an event which occurred among the predecessors of my brother Brun who was brought up at Corvey and serves at its altar.[184] In the time of Abbot Liudolf, whose good qualities are especially to be recalled, there lived a certain young man, a brother and monk according to the rule. Once, as he performed the office assigned to him, he was carrying the relics of the aforementioned martyrs in the usual manner, but he treated them carelessly. He quickly recognized by the penalty which followed that he had sinned against the martyrs of Christ. For, one who neglects to serve God's saints in the spirit, must die in the flesh. That they might announce this to the abbot, the martyrs accosted him before the doors of the church, at night, as he was trying to leave. When he first saw them, he was struck by such fear that he could neither move nor speak. Immediately they said the following to him: 'Father, why do you not ask who we are or why we have come?' When the abbot answered that he did not dare, they quickly informed him of their names and their complaint, and told him that the latter would not remain unpunished. After they left, the abbot relayed this message to the brethren, saying: 'Because of his carelessness in regard to the saints that he carried with him, that young man who was subject to our rule is now dead. Alas that I ever permitted this.' Shortly afterwards, a messenger arrived and confirmed this to be true, and also noted that the corpse was being brought there.

CHAPTER SEVENTY-ONE

But the venerable man did not want to go to meet the corpse, nor did he let the brothers receive it in the usual manner. Rather, he addressed the dead man angrily, saying: 'How could you be so impudent as to treat carelessly those who are held in great honour by the only begotten son of the living God? And, how have you dared to come here, after such a deed, in the absence of any humble intercession?' The deacon defended the dead man as best he could but received this response from the abbot: 'My beloved brother, you know what this servant has done visibly in your presence, but you are

184 Brun, abbot of Nienburg and Berge (1025–34), bishop of Verden (1034–49).

ignorant of what he has done in your absence. I can judge best, knowing that he is presently in grave torment. And now, I will humbly invoke the intercession of our patrons, that through them I may be informed when God has freed this sinner, so that I may grant him absolution and communion with the Church. It is very serious to resist the good; and it is unseemly for mortals to grant indulgence if God is angry.' After these words, the pious abbot came, with bare feet, to that oratory which was his special refuge in difficult situations. He placated God and released the sinner. Then, amid many expressions of gratitude, he arose, remitted the dead man's sin through the power of heaven and before all the brethren; and granted his body communion with the church and burial.

CHAPTER SEVENTY-TWO

Since you have heard of the grievous penalty incurred by those who show contempt for the saints, now you shall learn about the healing medicine of constant love. In the time of Abbot Gottschalk,[185] there lived a certain monk named Alfrik who suffered severely from headaches, which can arise for two reasons: gout or worms. Just by chance, it happened that he was briefly left alone, becoming weaker and weaker from the pain, as each of the brothers who were caring for him had to leave. At this point, demons came out of the drain, each holding a book in his hands, and tried to fill the sick man with pointless terror by gravely reading out his deeds which had been inscribed there. But then, the celebrated martyr of Christ, Vitus, entered the room and sent them fleeing with a wave of his hand. Standing next to Alfrik, he consoled him, revealed his identity, and, after bestowing his blessing, ordered him to rise. He also commanded him to quickly deliver the following charge to the abbot: 'See that you no longer treat our many admonitions with such disregard, lest the future find you groaning in useless lamentation. Truly, I say that if you continue to disobey me, God will spurn you and, while you still live, you will see another ruling in your place.' Later, the still negligent abbot received ample proof of what the boy-saint had predicted through the sick monk. Hence, just as we do well to observe the continual admonitions of good men, so much more should we observe the admonitions of those who, by their merits, are numbered among the blessed sons of God and who know his will regarding future

185 Abbot Gottschalk of Corvey (890–900).

events. Whoever thoughtlessly ignores wise advice will have to see
what he can accomplish on his own. We know of many cases in which
they [i.e. the blessed sons of God] have led others who followed their
model to a well-deserved reward in eternity.

CHAPTER SEVENTY-THREE

Archbishop Giselher was held in high esteem by the emperor. This
annoyed Margrave Ekkehard, initially in secret, later quite openly, as
he painfully recognized that the archbishop was being placed ahead of
him in every respect. Meanwhile, persons subject to the margrave
committed a theft in the village of Görschen, an act which our people
immediately punished. In the presence of their countrymen, they
accused and hanged the perpetrators of this deed, not being aware
that they should rightly have notified Margrave Ekkehard. This
caused the margrave's still burning anger to flame up once again. He
ordered his warriors to arm themselves and exact vengeance.
Rambald, whom he particularly favoured, assembled a large number
of them and surrounded the aforementioned village. Seizing all the
menfolk, along with their belongings, he led them off to his fortress
and would release none of them unless they subsequently paid a heavy
fine. When our people complained to me, I asked how such an outrage
could be reconciled and was shocked to learn that no compensation
would follow. If divine law is to have any value in this province, the
secular power should not rage in this fashion. Moreover, I say that
this case can neither die down nor be legitimately concluded without
a judgement by the bishops. Whoever can keep silent may do so as
long as he wishes, but he can by no means diminish his successor's
right to pursue this unsettled claim. Wherever a similar case arises, it
is to be concluded according to the authority of the canons. The
stubborn audacity of wicked men would not be reinforced in this way
if the will of my episcopal colleagues was unified, as we read in the
Acts of the Apostles.[186] When any one of them is rightly accused, he is
defended by another in whatever way he can; and this is no
justification but rather a strengthening of injustice which will cause
much worse damage in the future. Therefore, may those who are
unified in the faith return to unanimity, that they may more forcefully
confound the venomous conspiracy of evil men. May these words
suffice.

186 Acts 1: 14; 15: 25.

CHAPTER SEVENTY-FOUR

Now, that I might not forget a man who loved his neighbour according to God's commandment, I shall say a few things about one of my brethren, named Conrad. He was the uncle of Archbishop Gero [of Magdeburg] and, insofar as this is possible in a mortal, he possessed both the desire and the capacity to bear the yoke of Christ's service.[187] For I have heard from a certain wise man that, after finishing with his part of the public singing or reading, he eagerly wanted to begin again. He was never disobedient to those who had been placed over him, but rather won them over, along with the other brothers, through his constant love. When the emperor got to know this exceedingly admirable person, he quickly granted him his trust and included him among his intimates. A premature death prevented him from receiving the desired dignity which the emperor had offered to him. He departed from this light on 28 August.[188] He was born in Saxony, rests in Italy, and illustrious Magdeburg mourns in him a spiritual son.

CHAPTER SEVENTY-FIVE

How excellent are the men I have seen in this city and yet, I have not imitated their praiseworthy lives as I ought to have, nor have I cultivated their memory following the dissolution of their flesh. Woe is me, a wretch joined in fraternity with so many, but with an existence so dissimilar to their worthy manner of life. Though almost dead in my sins, I hope to live again in the clear vision of God, revived by their merits. Even if I have done too little good in this world, I have always been mindful of the dead. Moreover, my intentions are good. But they have produced little because I have not troubled myself to devote sufficient force to them. I always accuse myself, but have not freed myself of guilt as I ought to have. Therefore, I require correction in all things because I have not directed myself to him who is praiseworthy above all. Acknowledge, O reader, the great Lord.[189] In me, however, you will see a tiny little man whose jaw and left side of the face are deformed by an ulcer which erupted there and continues to swell. The nose, broken in childhood, gives me a laughable appearance. Of all of that I would regret nothing, if only my

187 Archbishop Gero of Magdeburg (1012–23).

188 *NMag.*, fo. 12r, p. 57.

189 Juvenal, *Satires* 8.26.

inner character were bright. Now, I am a wretch, too prone to anger and resistant to virtue, envious, derisive towards others though myself worthy of derision, granting forgiveness to none though obligated to do so. I am a glutton and a hypocrite, greedy and disparaging.[190] And, to conclude these well-deserved reproaches, I can say that I am much worse than one can possibly say or estimate in any way. It would be permissible for anyone not only to mutter but to openly announce that I am a sinner, and it would be appropriate for me to humbly ask for fraternal correction. Many are praised by the people and very little prevents them from being included among the best. But because it is true that complete perfection is impossible for mortal men, what use is there in speaking of those who are even more inferior? The praise of each will be sung at the end and the lives of mortals will be tested in the fire.

---

190 Persius, *Satires* 5.112.

BOOK FIVE

After conquering infancy, Henry,
sprung from a lineage of kings, ascended the heights of valour.
Duke Henry was his father and his mother was Gisela
who added to her good qualities the imprint of a king,
namely her father, Conrad, who held the Burgundian realms.[1]
The brilliant pupil was nourished by Bishop Wolfgang[2]
who followed the Lord Christ with every effort.
After the death of his father, he succeeded him as duke and as his
    heir.[3]
At a distance, he also contemplated the government of the empire.
The greater part of the realm, wasted by the cruel Slav,
rejoiced exceedingly because, by his peace and justice,
he made himself master of the desired seats,[4]
with high-born bandits thoroughly repulsed and restrained by a
    harsh law.
He crushed every enemy who rose against him
while soothing all his allies with agreeable talk.
If he lacked moderation in anything, he immediately recovered
and saw to the wounds of the flesh with worthy fruits.
Helpful to the church, he was compassionate to all, everywhere.
Merseburg, if you knew his pious vows,
you would long for the arrival of such a great ruler,
praising the renowned gifts of Christ
and bestowing worthy rewards.

1 King Conrad of Burgundy (937–93), was the brother of Queen Adelheid, Otto I's
    second wife. Gisela, the wife of Duke Henry 'the Quarrelsome' and mother of
    Henry II, was Conrad's daughter by his first wife, Adelina.

2 Bishop Wolfgang of Regensburg (972–94). Educated at Reichenau and Würzburg,
    Wolfgang had been head of the school at Trier and Einsiedeln prior to his
    appointment as bishop. His pupils included various members of the Bavarian ducal
    house, including Henry II's brother Bruno and sister Gisela (*LMA*, vol. 9, pp. 307–
    8)

3 See 4.20.

4 Virgil, *Aeneid* 6.203.

CHAPTER ONE

The stream of divine grace, overflowing to human needs by the free
gift of God's compassion and not by our own merit, inspires the
hearts of the faithful to offer loving praise and thanks to him. It also
compels me, slow-witted by nature, clumsy in speech, and both
negligent and overly hasty in all things, to imitate good people in
this. God is great, as David testified, and very praiseworthy; no one
can discover the extent of his wisdom which created everything out of
nothing and also formed man.[5] Whoever, unmindful, does not reflect
on such things is justly called an animal rotting in its own waste.[6] But
whoever well retains the word *gnoti seaucton*, written in ancient times
on the lintels of the temple,[7] and troubles himself to fulfil all things
which in words or deeds are to be done in the name of the Lord, as St
Paul advises: he is the one who was chosen by God the Father for the
Son, receiving his payment for the day although he had arrived late.[8]
Considering these things, because I can scarcely respond to the Holy
Trinity and the indivisible unity with a worthy repayment, I, a
supplicant, implore the intercession of John the Baptist that in body
and heart I might be worthy to offer this.[9]

CHAPTER TWO

With a happier mind and a more expansive pen I will write about the
time in which God looked upon our church and deigned to remove its
shame and I will disclose the piety of Duke Henry who was elected
king according to the divine will. Concerning that, after the death of
Otto III, a certain venerable father had a revelation from heaven. A
voice said to him: 'Do you recall, brother, how the people sang, "Duke
Henry wants to rule, but God is unwilling"?[10] Now, however, Henry
must provide for the care of the kingdom by the divine will.' Everything pertaining to divine or human matters promoted him to the
kingdom before others contemporary with him, whether they were

---

5 Ps. 95: 4 (RSV 96: 4.), 2. Macc. 7: 28.

6 Possibly a vague allusion to 2. Pet. 2: 22.

7 I.e. 'gnotis eaucton' (Macrobius, *Saturnalia* 1.6.6). Thietmar has divided the two
   words in the wrong place (Fickermann 1951: 69).

8 Col. 3: 17; Matt. 20: 1–16.

9 John the Baptist was patron of the first church at Merseburg.

10 Reference to Henry the Quarrelsome's efforts to seized the throne from the infant
   Otto III (i.e. 4.1 ff).

willing or not. I will describe with a few words those who opposed him from our region. Then, I will relate the iniquitous presumption of the West which neither by council, nor prudence, nor strength could prevail against God.[11]

CHAPTER THREE [1002]

Herman, Duke of Swabia and Alsace, was a God-fearing and humble man. Seduced by many who were pleased by his mildness, he armed himself against Henry.[12] Duke Dietrich of Lotharingia, a wise man experienced in warfare, to whom the larger and better part of the people would incline, waited confidently.[13] Meanwhile my father's brother, whom I mentioned above, travelled secretly to Bamberg with his uncle Rikbert. Otto III had deposed Rikbert from his countship, which he then gave to Liudger, a *miles* of Bishop Arnulf.[14] With his nephew Henry's help, he received the duke's favour and the hope of retaining and increasing his benefice. Nevertheless, he preserved his oath by not doing homage.[15] On Liuthar's advice, the duke dispatched a certain *miles* to Werla where his nieces, the sisters Sophia and Adelheid, and all the great men of the realm had convened.[16] He revealed his commission to the whole assembly and promised many good things to those who helped his lord obtain the throne. The majority immediately responded with one voice: Henry should rule with the aid of Christ and

11 Prov. 21: 30.

12 See 4.54. As evident in this chapter, Thietmar consistently attributes greater legitimacy to Duke Henry, emphasizing his regal qualities, especially his lineage (4.54; 5, prologue), and noting the unkingly qualities of his rivals Ekkehard (5.7) and Herman (5.3).

13 Duke Dietrich of Upper Lotharingia (978–1026/27).

14 Thietmar's father's brother = Margrave Liuthar. Bishop Arnulf of Halberstadt (996–1023). A Count Liudger with lands in northern Thuringia and the Harz is mentioned in diplomata issued by King Henry II in 1021/22 (DH II 449, 452, 480). A falsified diploma also associates him with Derlingau (DH II 260). A royal diploma issued in 1003 (D H II 46) mentions a Count Rikbert in the Harz region, suggesting that the countship to which Thietmar refers was returned.

15 Thietmar refers to the oath which Liuthar and other Saxon lords had sworn at Frohse (4.52), namely that they would not give allegiance to any candidate for the throne prior to the assembly at Werla.

16 Thietmar refers to the daughters of Otto II. Adelheid (b. 977), became abbess at Quedlinburg (999–1045) and later at Gernrode and Vreden (1014), and Gandersheim (from 1039). Sophia (b. 978) was abbess at Gandersheim (1002–39) and Essen (from 1011). Thietmar mentions their oblation at 4.10. Sophia and her convent were at the centre of a bitter jurisdictional dispute between Mainz and Hildesheim (6.19).

by hereditary right, and they were prepared to be supportive in all that he asked of them. They affirmed this with their right hands raised.

CHAPTER FOUR [1002]

Along with his following, Ekkehard was not present but subsequently pretended to be in agreement because, as it is written, whatever sin is committed by many is unpunished.[17] Nevertheless, in the evening, when benches decorated with hangings and a table filled with various dishes had been prepared in the palace for the already-mentioned ladies, Ekkehard commandeered it and dined with Bishop Arnulf and Duke Bernhard.[18] Before the fall the heart will be exalted and before the glory it will be humiliated.[19] Ekkehard's actions greatly agitated the two sisters, who were already sorrowful, and many others who were present. Likewise, the long-concealed animosity towards the margrave was renewed and, alas, would quickly find an end.[20] For then, seeing that everything had turned out differently from what was expected, he thought it wiser to resort to the western regions where he could speak to Duke Herman and other leading men regarding the realm and its welfare. The next day, he bade farewell to his friends, carefully noted his enemies, and accompanied Bishop Bernward to Hildesheim where he was received as king and treated with honour.[21]

CHAPTER FIVE [1002]

Then, coming to Paderborn, he found the doors closed. After being admitted by order of Bishop Rethar, he first went to the church to

---

17 Aug. *Ep*. no. 137, para. 20, p. 124.

18 The absence of a male heir made the princesses the most visible representatives of the Liudolfing/Ottonian house. It has been suggested (Leyser 1994d: 203) that Ekkehard's provocative actions were intended to demonstrate that direct descent from the traditional ruling house was no longer a prerequisite for the throne.

19 Prov. 18: 12.

20 The reference to a 'long-concealed hatred' is somewhat opaque but probably should be associated with incidents such as his reneging on an agreement to marry his daughter to the son of Margrave Liuthar (4.40), and his feud with Archbishop Giselher of Magdeburg (4.73). Thus it is not surprising to find Liuthar among Ekkehard's opponents at Frohse (4.52) and Archbishop Giselher among the supporters of Duke Herman of Swabia (5.39). Thietmar hints at further outrages at 5.7. It may well have been Ekkehard's arrogant behaviour towards his peers (or towards those who believed that they were such) that prevented his being elected king in 1002 (see note at 4.52, and 5.7).

21 For a similar arrogation of a royal prerogative see 2.28.

pray, and then went to the episcopal residence where the bishop was dining, and was kindly received.²² There, he was informed that the meeting in Duisburg, which had been the reason for his coming, would not take place.²³ Moreover, he noticed that much of his unsuitable plan displeased the bishop. Leaving because of this, he journeyed to Northeim, a *curtis* belonging to Count Siegfried, where he was warmly received and invited to stay the night. The Countess Ethelind secretly informed him that Sigifrith and Benno, her husband's sons, were plotting with the brothers Henry and Udo and other conspirators to ambush and kill him.²⁴ She humbly beseeched him to remain there until the next day or else go in another direction. The margrave accepted this news in a kindly manner but responded that he neither could nor wished to interrupt the course of his journey. Setting out from there, he watched his companions the whole day through and, as he was the best of warriors, admonished them not to be frightened.²⁵ The enemy observed this at a distance, from their concealed ambushes. Because the circumstances appeared unfavourable, they decided to postpone their attack, confirming with raised hands that they would carry out the plot on the following night.

CHAPTER SIX [1002]

The count arrived at Pöhlde, his intended destination.²⁶ In the evening, he ate and bedded down with a few companions in a wooden sleeping chamber. Others, indeed just as many, slept near by in a loft. After the exhausted men fell asleep, the hostile band attacked, falling on the unwary. The excited clamour caused the count to quickly rise from his bed. With his own undergarments and whatever else he could find, he built up the fire and broke the windows. As he could not

---

22 Bishop Rethar of Paderborn (983–1009). Rethar was closely allied with Archbishop Willigis of Mainz, one of Henry II's strongest supporters. In limiting Ekkehard's reception essentially to what was due by general right of hospitality he made it plain that he opposed Ekkehard's plan (Bannasch 1972 126–33). The regal reception accorded him by Bernward of Hildesheim clearly sent the opposite message.

23 5.20.

24 The *Annalista Saxo* (an. 1002, p. 647) identifies the two brothers as Henry and Udo of Katlenburg. Thietmar suggests Henry's motivation at 5.7. The brothers' reconciliation with Ekkehard's heirs is noted at 7.50.

25 I.e. '... ut optimus erat miles'.

26 Location of a much visited royal residence and a monastic community in the region of the Harz mountains (*LMA*, vol. 7, p. 39).

foresee, this worked more to his injury than his defence, because he thereby revealed an entry to his enemies. At once, the *miles* Herman was killed in front of the door, as was Athulf, who was outside, as he ran to help his lord. Each was brave and faithful unto death. Also, Erminold, Otto III's chamberlain, was wounded.[27] Now Ekkehard, a man praiseworthy in both domestic and military matters, fought alone. With a strongly thrown javelin, Siegfried hit him in the neck and forced him to the ground. As soon as they realized that Ekkehard had fallen, all eagerly attacked, cutting off his head and, even more wretched, plundering his corpse. This was done on 30 April. Having carried out their savage crime, the attackers returned, happy and uninjured. Those cowards who were on the solarium neither helped their besieged lord nor attempted to avenge his death. Alfger, the abbot of the place, visited the corpse and commended Ekkehard's soul to God with the greatest devotion.[28]

CHAPTER SEVEN [1002]

I cannot truly explain what persuaded them to undertake such a shameful deed. Some say that Henry had been flogged by the emperor at the count's instigation and that he often thought about this. Others say, as I have already suggested, that they did this because of the insult inflicted on the sisters at Werla whom they were glad to serve. Thus the plot was undertaken in response to the meal and to threats publicly uttered by Ekkehard. I know only this, he was the glory of the realm, the solace of the fatherland, the hope of subjects, and the terror of enemies, indeed he would have been perfect in all things if only he had wished to remain humble. The course of Ekkehard's life was so worthy that his lord allowed him to hold the greater part of his benefice as personal property. He forced the free-born Milzeni under the yoke of servitude. With flattery and threats, he won Duke Boleslav [III] of Bohemia, called 'the Red', for his military service and turned the other Boleslav into a personal ally.[29] He acquired the office of duke over all of Thuringia by the election of the whole populace. With only a few exceptions, he reckoned on the support of

---

27 Otto III issued a diploma for Erminold in 993 (DO III 113); *NMer.*, 9 May, fo. 2r, p. 5.

28 Alfger later became abbot at Berge (1005–09: 6.20).

29 Boleslav III of Bohemia (999–1003, d. 1037) and 'the other Boleslav', Boleslav Chrobry of Poland.

the eastern counts and therefore of the duchy.[30] All of this came to such a miserable end.

The story of this event spread quickly, causing Swanhild to come to Pöhlde and disturbing the happiness of her son, Herman.[31] At his father's command, Herman and a powerful band of warriors had besieged the elderly and esteemed Count William at Weimar in order to avenge the murder of Widukind and Herman by the count's son.[32] Herman had compelled the old veteran to swear that he would come before his father, Ekkehard, and meet all of his demands. When he heard of his father's unexpected death, he quickly met with his mother and with great sadness received the body at Jena where he had it interred. After thirty days Swanhild and her son set out for Meißen.

Meanwhile, Boleslav, a son far inferior to his father Miesco, rejoiced over the death of Margrave Ekkehard. Shortly after this, he assembled an army and seized Margrave Gero's march as far as the river Elbe. Then, with siege troops sent ahead, he captured the burg Bautzen, with all its possessions, and immediately thereafter attacked Strehla. Secretly, he also tried to bribe the residents of Meißen who were always happy for something new. One day, when they realized that most of the garrison had left to find fodder for the horses, Duke Gunzelin of Kuchenburg led them in an assault on the east door, in that part of the city inhabited by *ministeriales* known in Slavic as Withasen. After killing Bezeko, one of Count Herman's *ministeriales*, they took up arms and met at the count's chamber where they threw large rocks at the window and loudly demanded that Ozer, the lord of the city, be handed over to them for execution. But the *miles* Thietmar, having no other protection than the room itself, asked them: 'Why are you doing this? What madness so seduced you that,

---

30 I.e. he reckoned on the Ostphalian counts' support in his bid for the throne. The term *regnum* may be translated either as kingdom or duchy (of Saxony), but the context appears to to suggest the latter.

31 Count Herman was married to Reglindis, daughter of Boleslav Chrobry from his marriage to Emnilde, daughter of Dobromir (4.58). Ekkehard's brother, Gunzelin, succeeded him as margrave (5.18) and, in turn, was succeeded by Count Herman (7.9).

32 See note at 2.16.

forgetful of the benefits bestowed by Margrave Ekkehard and your willing invitation, you rise up to destroy his son? If you wish to reveal the reason for such an outrage, either publicly or secretly to one of us, on behalf of my lords and all of us, I firmly promise you an agreeable settlement of the offence and security regarding your future concerns. As for the man you seek to have handed over, namely so that he can be killed, you will not receive him as long as we are living. We are few and you should know for certain that we will either die together or leave this city unharmed.' After they had heard this and consulted among themselves, the attackers granted the garrison freedom to leave. Then, they sent messengers to summon Duke Boleslav and received him with open doors. Hence, the words of the scriptures were fulfilled: 'They may rejoice when they act wickedly, and exult in evil things and again. Their beginnings are as honey and their end as absinthe.'[33]

CHAPTER TEN [1002]

Elated by this success, Boleslav occupied the entire region up to the Elster and secured it with a garrison. Then, when our people gathered together to resist him, that deceitful man sent a messenger who announced to them that these things had been done with the favour and permission of Duke Henry. He added that Boleslav would in no way injure the inhabitants and, if Henry came to power in the realm, he would assent to his will in all things, but if otherwise, he would willingly do whatever pleased them. Considering this, our people believed the beautiful words[34] and shamefully advanced to him as if to their lord, thereby exchanging their inborn honour for supplication and unjust servitude. How unequally are our ancestors and our contemporaries compared! In the days of the illustrious Hodo, this man's father, Miesco, would not have dared to wear furs when entering a house in which he knew him to be or to sit while he was standing.[35] May God forgive the emperor for making a lord out of a tributary and raising him to the point that, forgetful of his father's customs, he might dare to gradually drag his superiors into subjection and seize those caught with the shameful hook of temporal wealth to the detriment of both slaves and free.[36]

33 Prov. 2: 14; 5: 3–4.

34 Terence, *Phormio* 3.2.15.

35 On Hodo see 2.29; 4.60.

36 Here, Thietmar may well be referring to the controversial meeting, at Gniezno, between Otto III and Boleslav Chrobry (4.45).

CHAPTER ELEVEN [1002]

Also the other Boleslav [III], the Bohemian ruler nicknamed 'the Red' and generally a source of the worst impiety, departed from his usual custom and supported Duke Henry. At the beginning of June, Henry came to Worms with the leaders of the Bavarians and the eastern Franks with the intention of crossing the Rhine and proceeding to Mainz for his consecration. Duke Herman tried to prevent this and, with the Rhine favouring, offered him no entry. After consulting with his supporters, Henry went to Lorsch where St Nazarius rests, acting as if he had given up the idea of crossing the river and planned to return to Bavaria. And then, quickly going to Mainz, he crossed the Rhine in safety. At Mainz, on 6 June, Henry was unanimously elected king. Following his anointment, he was crowned by Willigis, archbishop of that see, with his suffragans assisting and all in attendance praising God.[37] Then, the great men of the Franks and the region of the Mosel commended themselves to the king and received his favour.

CHAPTER TWELVE [1002]

The king accepted all who came to him into his service. Then, the new king crossed the swollen Rhine again and invaded Swabia through eastern Franconia which was loyal to him. It was hoped that the pillaging of this territory, would cause Duke Herman to abandon his plan. But when the duke heard that his lands had been attacked by the king, he was not yet willing to be humbled, but instead rose up against his lord and king. With his son-in-law Conrad,[38] he launched an armed attack on Argentina, called Strasbourg, the main city of his duchy and see of Bishop Werner who had dared to oppose him.[39] After climbing the walls, they left nothing to the conquered. Without the duke's knowledge, a detestable horde of Swabians fearlessly entered the cathedral of the blessed mother of God for a bit of easy pillaging. They seized all the treasure and, most shameful of all, set the house of

37 Noted in entries for 7 June in the necrologies of Merseburg and Magdeburg (*NMer.*, fo. 3r, p. 7; *NMag.*, fo. 8r, p. 49). It is important to note that these acts chiefly affected the aristocracies of Franconia and Upper Lotharingia. Henry still had to secure the acceptance of their counterparts in Lower Lotharingia, Thuringia, and Saxony and, of course, the Swabians remained actively opposed to him (BG 1483yy).

38 Conrad, son of Duke Otto of Carinthia, was married to Herman's daughter, Mathilda. Later he too became duke of Carinthia (1004–11).

39 Bishop Werner of Strasbourg (1001–28). See also 5.13.

God on fire. If they had been fortunate, they would have been deterred by their cruelty as soon as they entered and would never have dared to go farther. At Reinward's instigation, the bishop's *ministeriales* were offering only half-hearted resistance. Meanwhile, the greater part of the enemy fell, stabbed by their own lances as they rushed in. Thus they ended their lives wretchedly through divine retribution. Although racked by guilt, Herman went away and left this crime unpunished because the number of perpetrators involved was too great.

CHAPTER THIRTEEN [1002]

On the feast of the birth of St John the Baptist (24 June), while the king was lingering on the island of Reichenau, a swift and, as so often, unreliable rumour reached him that Herman was coming to end the struggle by battle. This caused him to depart and await both the duke's arrival and the judgement of battle on a wide green meadow. There he celebrated the feast of the Apostles [29 June] and, after waiting for some time, learned for certain that the duke neither wished to nor was able to persist in his plan. Certain of his supporters, advising badly, suggested to Henry that Constance should suffer the same treatment as Strasbourg because Lambert, the bishop of that city, had joined Bishop Ulrich of Chur in supporting Herman.[40] The bishop's inclinations were not so much from conviction, however, as from consideration of the duke's proximity to his city.[41] But the king, as he was troubled by the fear of God and certain of winning, rejected the profane advice of these men and instead laid waste to the duke's lands. Finally, conquered by the cries of the poor, he decided to return to Franconia.

CHAPTER FOURTEEN [1002]

And behold, Margrave Henry, the son of Berthold and of my friend,[42] until now a faithful supporter of the king in his efforts to acquire the

---

40 Bishop Lambert of Constance (995–1018), Bishop Ulrich of Chur (*c.*1000–24).

41 The Swabian dukes exercised a substantial, virtually royal influence over the bishops resident within their area of rule (including Alsace and its chief city), and persistently attempted to obligate them to various court and military services. In attacking Strasbourg, Duke Herman was not just seeking revenge, but rather attempting to shore up a vital centre of his *regnum* (Maurer 1978: 153–58; Weinfurter 1986: 170–71). Proximity to the borders of Bavaria seems to have allowed the bishops of Augsburg to retain a somewhat greater degree of independence (e.g. 4.50).

42 Eila, daughter of Margrave Liuthar III.

throne, sensed that his lord was becoming somewhat distant from
him.[43] Hence, through prominent men in Henry's army, he asked to be
given the Duchy of Bavaria which had been firmly promised to him
for a long time. The king is said to have responded as follows: 'Do you
not know that such a thing cannot be accomplished on this campaign?
From the beginning the Bavarians have had the power to freely elect
their duke. One cannot so suddenly overthrow or take away an
anciently constituted right without their consent. If he wanted to wait
until I myself come to this region, with common counsel and by the
will of the great men, I would freely give satisfaction to him in this
matter.' When Henry heard this from his intermediaries, he despaired
even more of receiving the promised gift and began gradually to
distance himself from the king. Nevertheless, he accompanied the
king on the journey from Swabia to Franconia, and afterwards to
Thuringia. There Count William [II, of Weimar], then the most
powerful man in Thuringia,[44] came to meet his lord and, receiving
him with great joy, became the king's man. Then the king was
acclaimed as lord by the count and by the great men of that region
and, at the request of all, abolished the tax paid by them on swine.

CHAPTER FIFTEEN [1002]

From there, Henry went to Merseburg where he was received by
Abbot Heimo and by his faithful count Esiko [24 July].[45] Esiko had
manfully held this city along with Allstedt, Dornburg and all their
possessions until his lord arrived, though this had greatly angered

43 Margrave Henry of Schweinfurt. In amassing support for his claim to the throne,
   Henry II had clearly promised many things to many people (e.g. 5.3), and may
   never have intended to follow through on every promise he made. Indeed, the
   strategy of offering a reward which he subsequently refused to deliver served the
   king equally well on other occasions (see 6.30). Although the margrave initially
   enjoyed Henry II's favour (5.3), Thietmar suggests that the future king was
   nursing a grudge against him (5.33). This would help to explain the highly
   provocative manner with which he treated the margrave's request. The margrave,
   his ambitions frustrated and loss of face evident, now initiated an almost ritualistic
   progress towards open rebellion (Althoff 1989). Public opinion may well have seen
   the margrave's actions as fully justified (5.32). In any case, he was soon joined by
   other malcontents, among them the king's brother Bruno and the formidable Duke
   Boleslav Chrobry of Poland (5.18, 32–38). For Margrave Henry, the revolt's
   conclusion involved a ritual act of surrender and a period of imprisonment (6.2;
   6.13). In spite of this nearly total defeat, he continued to be held in high esteem, or
   so Thietmar implies (7.63).
44 Since the death of Margrave Ekkehard.
45 BG 1493b.

Ekkehard while he lived. Here also were Archbishop Liawizo of Bremen and Giselher of Magdeburg with other colleagues: Rethar of Paderborn, Bernward of Hildesheim, Arnulf of Halberstadt, Ramward of Minden, Eid of Meißen, Bernhar of Verden, Hugh [II] of Zeitz. Also present were dukes Bernhard and Boleslav with the margraves Liuthar and Gero and the count palatine Frederick. *Many others were also there, both bishops and counts, but it would take too long to give their names individually. All of these received the king with humble devotion.*

CHAPTER SIXTEEN [1002]

On the following day, that is, 25 July, and with the consent of all, Duke Bernhard stood before the king and revealed the will of the assembled people, expounding in particular the necessity and law of all, and diligently inquired what he wished from compassion to promise them orally or grant them by the deed. Such things he asked and, in return, the king responded: 'To God first and then to all of you I am unable to offer worthy thanks.[46] *Hence, I will reveal to you the secret intentions which, with the aid of Christ, I desire to carry out for all of you. I have noted how faithfully you strove always and everywhere to offer obedience and solace to your kings. Therefore it is our desire to honour you so much more in all things, to love and preserve you for the advantage of the kingdom and our salvation. And that you may be certain of these things, as it pleases you, I affirm, saving the honour of the kingdom, that it is not against your will or desire but rather with your agreement and at your invitation that I appear here honoured with the royal dignity. I have no desire to pervert your law in any way but rather, with life mercifully permitting, to observe it and in all circumstances to pay attention to your reasonable requests.'*

CHAPTER SEVENTEEN [1002]

Thus spoke the king, and immediately, with one voice, the crowd shouted praise and thanks to the king for such great benefits. Then, acting for all, Duke Bernhard grasped the lance and faithfully committed the care of the kingdom to him. Again voices were raised, and praises sung on all sides to you, O Christ, for such wonderful gifts. Indeed, virtuous hearts poured out tears of happiness. Illustrious Merseburg, rejoice, give thanks with the others. Give a worthy shout to Christ for that day. I say: solemnly venerate that sun, that day on which was chosen for you, when you were desolate, he who

46 Virgil, *Aeneid* 1.600.

afterwards thought constantly to foster and restore you to your prior state. May God be blessed who lifts up those who honour and love him from the heart, to the horror and disgrace of those who hate him. The end of your grief arrived, because a healthy southern wind blew a friendly climate to you. No longer will you labour in servitude, O Syon, because, once freed, you will once more rule. But let us proceed.

CHAPTER EIGHTEEN [1002]

Except for Liudger, everyone who had served the previous emperor offered his hand to the king and swore to aid him faithfully.[47] *Meanwhile, Boleslav schemed to acquire the burg Meißen at whatever cost. Because it was not advantageous to the realm, he got nowhere with the king and only barely succeeded in securing it for his brother-in-law Gunzelin.*[48] *He himself received the regions of Lausitz and the Milzeni. Margrave Henry, my cousin, held Boleslav in great esteem and aided him freely and amicably in whatever way he could. As he prepared to escort Boleslav, departing well rewarded and with the king's permission, he saw an armed multitude gathering and moving to attack them. May God be my witness, this was without the involvement or knowledge of the king! When he wanted to discover the cause of this great tumult, and resolve it so that more damage might not arise, he was barely able to get away and lead his companion out by breaking through the exterior door. Out of his entourage, some warriors were plundered by the surging mob while others though severely wounded escaped death with the help of Duke Bernhard. Because they had entered the royal court armed and refused to leave when ordered, the penalty they paid was justified by their own offence. Boleslav saw this as part of an evil plot and, deeply disturbed, blamed the king although unjustly.*[49] *After bidding farewell to Henry and firmly promising his aid, should it ever be required, he quickly returned to his own lands. When he arrived at the city of Strehla, he immediately set fire to it and abducted a large part of the local populace. At the same time, he sent back representatives through whom he tried to attract as many of the king's supporters as possible. Soon afterwards, when this came to the king's*

47 5.3.

48 It has been suggested (Görich 1997: 102–3) that Gunzelin had married a sister of Emnilde, daughter of Dobromir, who had married Boleslav Chrobry in 987. This would help to explain cooperative relations between Gunzelin and Boleslav Chrobry, and also Ekkhard's good relations with the duke. Thietmar's observation (5.7) that Ekkehard won Boleslav over with threats and flattery tends to strengthen this interpretation since marriages were a common method of ending rivalries and disputes.

49 See note at 5.14.

ears,[50] *he asked his dependants to inquire about the secret plots of the Slav and, if possible, to capture his spies.*

CHAPTER NINETEEN [1002]

After everything had been disposed as the current situation demanded, the king decided to go to the region of Lotharingia. His wife, the celebrated Cunegunde, came to meet him as he arrived at Corvey, a monastery which derives its name from that of Corbie of the Latin Franks and is also the place where the child and martyr St Vitus rests.[51] *The two were received with all honour by the venerable Abbot Thietmar.*[52] *After being celebrated in both ecclesiastical and secular fashion, they set off happily for Paderborn. On the following day, celebrated festively throughout the world because of the martyrdom of the blessed Lawrence, Cunegunde received the benediction and crown [10 August]. On the same occasion, the emperor's sister Sophia, who had been made abbess by the king, humbly received her consecration from Archbishop Willigis.*[53] *At that point, the assembly was filled with great joy though, unfortunately, it was seriously undermined by the insatiable avarice of the Bavarians. At home, these people are content with very little but when abroad they are nearly insatiable. When they forcibly seized the crops of the local population and beat those who tried to stop them, the result was a great battle. The king's own retainers came out; both local people and visitors anticipated this and followed them.*[54] *A great battle then broke out in which the Bavarians were defeated and fled to the royal curtis. It was on this*

50 Virgil, *Aeneid* 2.81.

51 Corvey = *Nova Corbeia.*

52 Clearly not Abbot Thietmar, who had died by 12 March 1001 and been succeeded by Abbot Hosed (Holtzmann 1935: 243, n. 3).

53 Sophia was the sister of Emperor Otto III. Henry II, still a king at this point, had made her abbess of Gandersheim. The significance of Sophia's consecration is clearer when placed against the background of the long-running jurisdictional dispute between Mainz and Hildesheim which was ignited when Sophia refused to take the veil from Bishop Osdag of Hildesheim (985–89), to whose diocese Gandersheim appeared to belong, and demanded instead to be consecrated by Archbishop Willigis. In treating the events at Paderborn, the historical tradition at Hildesheim emphasizes that Bishop Bernward gave permission, albeit unwillingly, for Willigis to consecrate Sophia (Thangmar, c. 39; Wolfher I, c. 24; *AH*, an. 1002, p. 28). Whatever the case may have been, Willigis's role in Sophia's consecration was clearly a setback for Bernward whose support for Henry's rival, Ekkehard of Meißen, had perhaps been too brazen for the monarch to forgive (5.4). Archbishop Heribert of Cologne, Duke Herman of Swabia's chief clerical advocate, suffered a similar setback (4.50; 5.11). Clearly, Henry was also rewarding Sophia and especially Willigis for their support.

54 I.e. 'Domestici regis'.

occasion that Henry, brother of the chancellor Eilbert and a constant attend-
ant at the king's table, was mortally wounded by a lance.[55] *Now, the Saxons,*
who had not participated in the battle up to this point, gathered together and
renewed the attack. If Duke Bernhard had not forcefully intervened, an
infinite number of milites *from both sides would have died. After this, all the*
authors of this shameful deed who could be discovered were reprimanded.
Later, the king eased the bishop's grief by giving him Böckenförde.[56]

CHAPTER TWENTY [1002]

The king went directly from here to Duisburg where he was much delayed by
the Lotharingians. For the bishops of Liège and Cambrai, arriving first,
awaited the long-hesitating archbishop of Cologne.[57] *The confinement in*
which he was detained for a short while, as I mentioned, secretly irritated
him more than anyone would believe.[58] *For this reason, he pretended that he*
had resorted so late to the king's grace because the king had wanted to favour
the archbishop of Mainz over him when receiving the benediction. Thus it
was these co-bishops who together elected the king, affirmed their loyalty by
oath, and accompanied him to Aachen. There, on the feast day of the Virgin
Mary [8 September], the leading men of the Lotharingians acclaimed him
king, raised him on the royal throne according to the custom of his ancestors,
and praised him. From thence he planned to go back to Franconia and spend
the upcoming winter there so that, with the coming of spring, he could use
force to compel the submission of Duke Herman, his only opponent on this
side of the Alps. But Herman, highly apprehensive because of the divine
vengeance suffered by Strasbourg and no longer withstanding the people's
suffering because of him, requested the king's grace for himself and his
supporters through faithful intercessors.

CHAPTER TWENTY-ONE [1002]

But before he resolved that matter, the Swabians did something which I
should not want to pass over. The king had given one of Duke Herman's
counties to Count Gerhard of Alsace who, on his way home, camped next to

55 Brother of Eilbert the Chancellor (1002–05) and later bishop of Freising (1005–39).
56 See DH II 121, issued on 24 October 1006 in memory of the queen's consecration.
57 Bishop Notker of Liège (972–1008), Bishop Erluin of Cambrai (995–1012).
58 4.50.

one of its burgs.[59] *After barely obtaining a truce for one night, the sly occupants came out as if for negotiations but really to spy. One of them who had frequently proved his cleverness and speed approached more closely. After looking around, he seized the banner lance used by the king in bestowing the duke's benefice on the count — it was standing upright in front of the latter's tent — and safely entered the burg with it as everyone vainly chased after him. There was great joy in the burg as the doors were closed and the count was mocked as if he had been robbed of his honour. The count initially tried to get the lance back with sweet promises but when the residents refused to hand it over, he left, saddened and deprived both of his benefice and his military standard. Another city which was heavily fortified, Breisach, was garrisoned by the bishops of Strasbourg and Basel.*[60] *Their* milites *customarily went out every day, under arms, to get fodder for their horses. The duke's allies watched carefully and at a time when the bishops' troops were absent, put on similar garments, loaded up their horses, and proceeded to the city, singing as they went. They were admitted as comrades by the guards. Once inside, they threw off their burdens and revealed themselves as enemies with a great shout, plundered everything. The bishops were barely able to get away.*

CHAPTER TWENTY-TWO [1002]

After this, Duke Herman, the son of my mother's uncle,[61] *with pious regret, as I mentioned, was humbly presented to the king at Bruchsal on 1 October. He mercifully obtained his grace and gave satisfaction for his benefice and all justifiable requests, only the damage in Strasbourg remained outstanding. By order and decision of the king, he made amends for this out of his own property and also repaired the abbey located in the city.*[62] *Hence, he became the king's faithful* miles *and ally. With this situation resolved, the king visited Bavaria, hoping to assure its people of his special love for them through his arrival and expressions of affection. Upon arriving at Regensburg, he was received by Bishop Gebhard, to the joy of the city's clergy and people, and was honoured in many ways as he celebrated the feast of St Martin there [11 November].*

---

59 Gerhard I, son of Count Eberhard of Alsace and husband of Eva, daughter of Siegfried of Luxembourg and sister of Queen Cunegunde.

60 Bishop Werner of Strasbourg (1001–28), Bishop Adalbero II of Basel (*c.*999–1025).

61 The son of Duke Conrad I of Swabia.

62 The convent of St Stephen.

CHAPTER TWENTY-THREE [1002]

Meanwhile, because the power of a consort and successor always inspires fear,[63] *the duke of the Bohemians, Boleslav [III], castrated his brother Jaromir and wanted to suffocate the younger brother in his bath. Then he sent both brothers and their mother into exile. Then, ruling alone like the noxious basilisk,*[64] *he oppressed the people unspeakably. When they could no longer bear the weight of this outrage, they secretly called Wlodowej from Poland, whose name means power of the army. He was a poisonous snake who treated his people without any respect for the law. After Boleslav the basilisk had been deposed, this one was unanimously elected in his place because of his consanguinity and because of the people's affection. I can say one thing about him that is incredible and not to be copied by any Christian, namely that he could not endure even one hour without drink. As this was the only path of escape open to him, Boleslav fled to Margrave Henry, then his neighbour, who seized him as an enemy because of past injuries. Afterwards, because he had arrived as a guest, he was set free and, being fond of his life, he went to the like-named son of his aunt who was his equal in shamefulness though unequal in ability. Inclined to better advice, the other one went to the king, then residing at Regensburg, and recognized him as his lord with humble subjection and the promise of loyalty. He received what he sought from him as a benefice and, after being treated warmly in all matters, returned in peace.*[65]

CHAPTER TWENTY-FOUR [1002]

While these events transpired, Arduin, of whom I spoke above, being very concerned about the king's success and about when he might arrive, secured all the entries to Lombardy with garrisons. These entries are called clusae *by the natives.*[66] *As I also mentioned, Arduin continued to accord those who had advised and supported his election the treatment they deserved. Thus he once seized the bishop of Brixen by the hair, as this prelate was saying things which displeased him, and revealed his unbridled rage to all by forcing him to the ground like a common cowherd. But why should I try to limit him to*

63 Lucan, *Bellum civile* 1.92.

64 Lucan, *Bellum civile* 9.726.

65 Here referring to Wlodowej, Duke of Bohemia 1002–03, in November 1002.

66 At least since late Antiquity, the natural defence provided by the Alps had been supplemented by a series of fortifications referred to as the *clusae*. Providing garrisons for the *clusae* represented the more or less standard response of Italian rulers to an imminent invasion (Settia 1989: 166–67)

individual instances when it is readily apparent in the realm and to the people what a multitude of iniquities prepared him for committing such things. Hence, some of the magnates who had submitted to him regretted what they had done and sent representatives and letters asking King Henry to come and defend them or, if he was detained by other matters, to send his leading men. In the expectation of receiving the abundant support promised by the Italians, the king sent Duke Otto of Carinthia and Verona, Otto the son of Count Heribert, Ernst the son of Margrave Leopold, and a few others to resolve the situation [December 1002 to beginning of January 1003].[67]

CHAPTER TWENTY-FIVE [1002]

Because I have not already mentioned it, I will briefly explain who that Duke Otto was. The offspring of Duke Conrad and Luidgard, the daughter of Otto the Great, he adorned his lineage with the gravity of his character and probity of his deeds. After the emperor's death, Henry, who was then duke, nominated him to be king by right of consanguinity, age, and maturity of virtue.[68] He humbly refused this great burden, however, and, initially through representatives and then personally, proposed that Henry himself was more suitable and faithfully aided him always. He came as representative of the king, and Archbishop Frederick of Ravenna hurried to aid him, along with Margrave Thedald and other faithful supporters of the king.[69] When Arduin discovered that, located as he was in the middle and scrutinizing everything with sharp eyes,[70] he came to Verona with a great multitude to separate them and seized the clusa *hitherto defended by the bishop of the same city.[71] Moreover, hearing that the Germans had stopped in the plain of Trent, he hastened there but, not finding them, quickly returned to the plain of Verona.*

---

67 Otto of Worms, duke of Carinthia (978–85 and 995–1004); Ernst, son of Margrave Leopold and later Duke Ernst I of Swabia (1012–15); and Count Otto of Hammerstein (BG 1524A).

68 As son of Duke Conrad 'the Red' and Otto I's daughter, Liutgard, Duke Otto was a generation closer to the throne than Duke Henry, albeit through the female line (Beumann 1991: 157; Wolf 1995: 75–77).

69 Archbishop Frederick of Ravenna (1001–4) and Margrave Thedald of Canossa (d. *c.*1015). The margrave's family figured among the Ottonian dynasty's strongest supporters and had benefited accordingly (Pauler 1982: 37, 58–60). On Thedald see also 6.6.

70 Horace, *Satires* 1.2.90.

71 Bishop Otbert of Verona (992–*c.*1010).

CHAPTER TWENTY-SIX [1002]

There, Arduin celebrated the feast of the birth of the Lord in a certain castle. As soon as Duke Otto understood all of his actions, he sent representatives to ask permission to cross the plain or for himself to be received. Arduin responded to these requests with profound craftiness: 'Stay the night here, so that, with the advice of my allies, I can send you back tomorrow well informed about all of these things.' Then, unbeknownst to our representatives, he spent the whole night visiting his troops in their encampments, admonishing them to strengthen their hearts for fighting the Germans in the morning and to prepare their arms. The next morning, at dawn, the duke's representatives were about to seek out the king for his response when they saw the Lombards, in battle formation, ready to settle the issue by force. When they asked him what this might mean, they were informed that the battle against the duke was decided and they were to depart. Arduin followed them with his army to the Hungarian mount where the duke awaited the representatives with his entourage, arriving at midday. He found the enemy prepared for battle although divided for purposes of gathering fodder and guarding the roads. Thus the powerful columns came together on both sides with violent force. If the flight of Otto, brother of Bishop Gebhard, had not disturbed and impeded the columns of the Germans, they would have proved their superiority to the Lombard opponent although unequal to it in numbers.[72] Instead, for the most part and most unfortunately, they were mutilated, surrendered, and the honour of victory was lost. Arduin also suffered great losses, however.

CHAPTER TWENTY-SEVEN [1002/1003]

Meanwhile, the king had left Bavaria and was celebrating the Incarnation of the Lord at Frankfurt [25 December 1002]. The many legations sent to him returned happily after a benevolent hearing and lavish gifts. There also Duke Herman was reconciled with the king and was treated by him with esteem, as befits such a person.[73] Departing from there, he visited the region of the Mosel and, coming to the vill of Theodonis, he held a general meeting there with the residents.[74] While the king wished benevolently to give the law

72 The reference is to Bishop Gebhard I of Regensburg.

73 Elaborating on Thietmar's account, Bishop Adalbold of Utrecht adds that Herman appeared barefoot, in the company of intercessors, and requested the king's favour on bended knee (Adalbold· c.13, p. 687).

74 A court-day and synod at Diedenhofen (BG 1524d). See, DH II 34f, 35; 15 January 1003. On this occasion, the king also complained about the marriage of Duke Conrad of Swabia and Mathilda, daughter of the Swabian duke, Herman II, which appeared to violate the church's definition of incest.

to all, whatever their need, Herman and Dietrich, dukes in name alone and not in reality, tried to obstruct him. All was in vain, however, as they soon saw themselves subjected deservedly to the author of justice. For the king, moved by the pressing need of the whole folk, firmly ordered that a certain castle belonging to the duke, called Morsberg, should be destroyed and never rebuilt.[75]

CHAPTER TWENTY-EIGHT [1003]

When these matters had been quickly settled, the king went to Aachen so that he could celebrate the anniversary of his lord and imperial predecessor, with the utmost solicitude, and meet with the Lotharingians as a whole [24 January]. Although his innate sickliness delayed him somewhat, the ineffable love of Christ infused him with the power to complete his justly desired goal. Then, out of love for Bishop Servatius, he came to Maastrict where he received news of the battle which our forces had fought so badly. As all things which cannot be changed are eased by patience, he received the bad news gravely but calmly.[76] *From thence he went to Liège to invoke the patronage of St Lambert and was struck by a severe colic. Nevertheless, the martyr's intercession freed him from it.*[77] *Then he returned to Aachen and solemnly observed the Purification of the Mother of God [2 February 1003]. From there he went to Nijmegen and remained there for several days during Lent, seeking above all the kingdom and justice of God and only afterwards to supply the needs of human fragility.*

CHAPTER TWENTY-NINE [1003]

Meanwhile Duke Wlodowej died and the brothers who had been expelled along with their mother were recalled by the repentant Bohemians.[78] *But Boleslav, the ruler of the Poles, collected an army and expelled them again. He then restored his exiled namesake to his previous dignity and went home, with his plots deeply concealed. He knew that his cousin would be too vindictive towards those who had supported his expulsion and hoped that at a more*

---

75 Morsberg = Marimont.

76 Horace, *Odes*, bk 1, ode 24, verses 19–20.

77 Henry is also reported to have experienced miraculous cures at Monte Cassino, through St Benedict (*Leo*, p. 248), and through St Adelheid at the monastery of Selz (Odilo, pp. 49–50). The cure at Monte Cassino, in particular, has been linked with a number of important cultural events and would later assume a prominent role in Henry's cult (Warner 1995: 62).

78 I.e. Jaromir, Ulrich, and their mother Emma (5.23).

auspicious moment he might himself intervene. And so it actually happened. When Boleslav [III] of Bohemia perceived that his people dedicated themselves to paganism in all security, his own impiety was fortified for breaking the peace treaty which he had confirmed by oath. Thus, when all the great men had been assembled before him in one house, he himself killed his brother-in-law by striking him in the head with a sword and then, with his evil supporters, this bloody and deceitful man who was unworthy of half the days conceded to him, killed the others although they were unarmed and it was the holy season of Lent.[79]

CHAPTER THIRTY [1003]

The rest of the people, in great fear because of this, secretly sent representatives to Boleslav of Poland who revealed the magnitude of the shameful deed and asked him to rescue them from fear of the future. He heard these things with pleasure and immediately asked the other Boleslav, through a faithful representative, to come to him at a certain citadel for a personal discussion regarding matters of mutual interest. The younger Boleslav agreed to this, came to the agreed-upon place, and was affectionately received by him. The following night he was blinded by the other's henchmen thereby ensuring that he would never treat his people in that manner again or even be able to rule there. He was also sent into a long exile. On the following day, the elder Boleslav travelled quickly to Prague where he was introduced and unanimously acclaimed as lord by the inhabitants who were always happy to have a new ruler. As his worldly power increased, his wilfulness became much greater than is normal in a restrained mind. Note this well, dear reader: he who becomes too proud in prosperity will often be brought lower in adversity. It is affirmed by scripture that a wise man does not do this.

CHAPTER THIRTY-ONE [1003]

The king learned all of these things from hearsay, and accepted them with the due seriousness of a patient mind. At least, he imputed to his sins whatever misfortune occurred in the kingdom in his time. Therefore, as seemed most opportune to him, he ignored everything that had happened to the Bohemians, and sent representatives to Boleslav with the following demand: if he wished to retain the land he had recently occupied,[80] *by the king's grace, as the ancient law requires, and serve him in all things faithfully, the king would*

79 Ps. 5: 7. 'Virum sanguinum et dolosum abominabitur Dominus'.
80 Bohemia.

agree to his requests. If otherwise, he would oppose him with arms. Boleslav received this legation unworthily, though it was just and well composed, and therefore deservedly brought revenge on himself in the future. When the Lenten fast was finished, as I have mentioned, the king followed the custom of his predecessors by celebrating Easter, in an appropriate manner, at Quedlinburg [28 March]. There, as befits such a great feast, he ignored both Boleslav's evil presumption and Henry's ambitions and enjoyed the company of his familiars. On the same occasion, the king bestowed royal gifts on Dukes Otto and Ernst, recently returned after their disastrous defeat, and consoled them with fatherly encouragement.[81] He also received representatives of the Redarii and the people known as the Liutizi and, calming these rebels with the sweetness of gifts and the joy of promises, turned them from enemies into friends.[82]

CHAPTER THIRTY-TWO [1003]

After this, the king celebrated the Rogation days, which should be observed by all the faithful of Christ, at Merseburg [3–5 May]. There he learned of the open rebellion of Duke Boleslav and Margrave Henry.[83] Then he celebrated the feast of Pentecost at Halberstadt [16 May]. After this, he travelled to Bavaria where he initially tried to defeat Henry, who was offering resistance with the help of Boleslav but afterwards concentrated on quashing conspiracies instigated elsewhere. In this regard, he learned that Ernst whom he had recently honoured and Bruno, his own brother, had also joined the conspiracy. They were heedless of what has been written: 'Virtue lacking council falls of its own weight.'[84] To restrain their arrogance, the king gathered his supporters from all sides and, at the beginning of August, wasted the lands of Margrave Henry, thereby forcing him to abandon his residence and hide wherever he could. Anyone aware of the cause of the margrave's stubbornness would say that his actions were necessary: the higher powers may not withdraw something firmly promised to a faithful servant without alienating the devotion of others. To those, I respond, every dominion in this world derives

---

81 5.24–26.

82 Here, referring to Henry II's controversial decision to form an alliance against Boleslav Chrobry with the pagan confederation of the Liutizi (see 7.26).

83 See note at 5.14.

84 Horace, *Odes*, bk 3, ode 4, verse 65. Bruno, Henry II's brother, was later bishop of Augsburg (1006–29).

from God and whoever rises against it offends the divine majesty.[85] One must weather the sudden burst of injustice with the rudder of patience and, with humble supplication, await a consolation which will be truly useful. I think it better to ascend the heights gradually rather than incur a sudden and insurmountable ruin. I admit that I would defend my cousin in some other way, if I did not fear to violate that truth which must be honoured by all faithful people.

CHAPTER THIRTY-THREE [1003]

In many ways, the proverbs of the ancients have been confirmed: the old crimes of humankind bring forth new acts of evil and shame. For Margrave Henry's father had often opposed the father of the king, as if an enemy rather than one of his *milites*, and himself admitted that he had supported the emperor's side because of a boon promised under oath.[86] In similar fashion, Margrave Henry had been faithful to Otto III until the latter's death and served King Henry strenuously up to this unhappy time. The king was still intensely aware of their fathers' rivalry,[87] but I believe that the love of Christ would have moved him to let it go entirely unpunished, if only he had not seen Margrave Henry in the company of his other enemies, opposing him so cruelly and openly. Although Margrave Henry alone might appear guilty in this crime, it was not undertaken without the advice of others from the very beginning. Because betrayal is deemed particularly shameful in this world, however, he preferred to pursue the matter, with his conscience groaning, rather than increase his own blame by endangering others. Thus, he who once zealously defended his realm from the enemy now opened it to pillaging. He secretly received aid from Boleslav though it did him no good.

CHAPTER THIRTY-FOUR [1003]

When the king was travelling to a place called Hersbruck, the royal treasure, having been sent ahead, was seized by the margrave's *miles* Maganus and his band. Dividing the booty among themselves, they returned happily to the burg at Ammerthal. The king followed and,

---

85 Rom. 13: 1.2.

86 Here referring to Margrave Berthold, Henry of Schweinfurt's father, who had sided with Otto II and Otto III, respectively, during Henry the Quarrelsome's rebellions against those two monarchs (Endres 1972: 10–11). On chs 32–38, see note at 5.14.

87 Virgil, *Aeneid* 1.26.

after preparing for a siege, forced them to ask only for their lives, through intercessors, and to return both the burg and booty. Then, after the burg had been virtually destroyed and the many Poles divided among his men, he set forth for the castle of Creußen where Margrave Henry's brother, Bukko, was supposed to be guarding the margrave's wife, Gerberga, and his children. From outside, Margrave Henry and his supporters fought the army which had surrounded the burg on all sides. He wounded some and killed others who were too careless while gathering fodder for their horses. By posting four hundred warriors for this purpose, the king prevented his enemy from continuing this strategy and also forced him to retire to the more secluded part of a certain valley. Through the loose tongue of a peasant, the guards discovered where he was laying out his camp. Secretly proceeding there in the heat of midday, they called their companions together by shouting *Kyrie eleison* as soon as they saw the tents and recognized the camp. The enemy fled, leaving everything behind, but only Ernst was captured. The guards returned in a sorrowful mood because of this, but made everyone else very happy. After the captive was presented to the king, the judges sentenced him to death. Nevertheless, through the persistent intercession of Archbishop Willigis of Mainz, this sentence was changed to a payment to be decided by the king.

CHAPTER THIRTY-FIVE [1003]

When he had heard of the flight of his lord, Count Bucco was very upset and consulted with his supporters regarding what he should do next. Their responses varied. Some said that because of the loyalty they had promised to their lord and the perpetual dishonour they would otherwise incur, they preferred to die rather than surrender the burg and such a surety to the king.[88] As long as their lord survived, it would be better to hope for aid. Others who were wiser said that it was difficult to resist a raging torrent or a powerful man and that defeated foes were rarely or never offered grace. They also maintained that now, while their numbers were undiminished and they were not slowed by injuries, they could negotiate with the king for freedom to leave and take with them not only their mistress but also other goods and dependants. On their advice, so I think, Bucco, acting as guardian

88 The reference is to Henry's wife and children who presumably would have provided the king with valuable hostages.

of that burg, spoke with Otto, brother of its mistress, and with his agreement surrendered it into the king's power. He himself departed in safety along with everyone who had been committed to his care. The king immediately ordered that the burg be destroyed but the forbearance of those charged with this task ensured that it survived, for the most part, along with all of its outbuildings.

CHAPTER THIRTY-SIX [1003]

Meanwhile, as the king was besieging Margrave Henry's burg at Creußen, Boleslav was straining with every effort to injure him in some way. Secretly collecting an army, he sent representatives to demand that his brother-in-law, Gunzelin, surrender the burg of Meißen into his power and renew their old alliance as he had promised. Gunzelin knew, however, that with Boleslav's entry he would virtually be excluded from the king's favour and from his own domain. Thus, he offered the following response: 'Everything you ask from me other than this, dear brother-in-law, I will freely provide and, if ever the opportunity arises for doing what you ask, I will not refuse. But my lord's retainers are with me and they would not suffer such things.[89] And, if this were revealed, my life and all that I possess would be endangered.' When Boleslav heard this message, he put the messengers under guard and ordered his army to hasten to the Elbe. He followed them, the next morning, after the character of the fords had been determined. At the burg Strehla, because it was his daughter's morning gift,[90] he declared that the occupants had nothing to fear from him but that they should not try to warn their neighbours by crying out. Without delay, the duke ordered the army to divide into four parts and reconvene in the evening at the burg Zehren. Two detachments were sent ahead to ensure that they would not be troubled by the margrave. In one day, the whole fertile region of Lommatzsch was ravaged with fire and sword and had its inhabitants abducted.

89 I.e. 'senioris mei satellites'.

90 Reglindis who married Herman, son of Ekkehard I. In general a morning gift was bestowed upon a wife in the early days of her marriage (though it could occur later as well) with the intent of providing her with an independent income (*LMA*, vol. 6, pp. 837–38).

CHAPTER THIRTY-SEVEN [1003]

Here, it might be recalled how Boleslav Chrobry who was so often accustomed to deceive others was himself fooled by the garrison of the citadel of Mügeln. When they were besieged by the detachment sent against them they asked: 'Why are you doing this? We know your lord to be the best and hold him above us. Just go on, and have no doubt that we will follow with our families and possessions.' After they said these things, their enemies ceased to harass them and reported to their lord that the garrison would arrive shortly. Nevertheless, when Duke Boleslav saw that his retainers arrived late at the agreed-upon spot, and that the garrison stayed at home, he was very angry and threatened to punish his false allies.[91] The next morning, at sun-up, a huge amount of booty was sent ahead. A large part of the enemy drowned in the Elbe, but the rest returned home uninjured and divided the booty, assigning the best parts to God and their lord. There were at least three thousand captives and eye witnesses have said that the actual number was still larger.

CHAPTER THIRTY-EIGHT [1003]

Margrave Henry, now perceiving that he had failed, hurried to the burg Kronach where he found Siegfried, the young son of Count Siegfried, who awaited him with aid.[92] Siegfried saw no hope of a rebellion in those parts, whether at his own or Henry's instigation. At last, after they had talked for a long time, Henry set the burg on fire and, together with lord Bruno and his remaining supporters, went to Boleslav the invader of Bohemia. Siegfried, his hope of open resistance frustrated, did not go with them, but instead returned, intent on making amends for what he had done. The king had followed his enemy to Kronach and was pleased to see that he had taken the trouble to destroy everything.[93] Then, he sent Bishop Henry of Würzburg and Erkanbald, abbot of Fulda, to burn and destroy the burg Schweinfurt.[94] When they arrived, Margrave Henry's illustrious mother, Eila, received and greeted them, as was proper for such persons. As soon as she understood the nature of the king's orders, she became agitated and hurried to the church, declaring that she would rather die in the

91 I.e. 'commilitones'.
92 August (BG 1547e).
93 Because it saved him the trouble of doing it himself.
94 Abbot Erkanbald of Fulda (997–1011).

flames than cooperate in the burning of this building by departing alive. Hence, the previously mentioned lords, putting aside secular concerns in favour of the love of Christ, modified the punishment and merely pulled down the walls and outbuildings. They also mollified the sorrowful woman with the promise that they would themselves restore everything, whenever the king's favour permitted.

After he had devastated all the count's property and distributed it along with his benefice, the king went to Bamberg where he dismissed his army and celebrated the birth of the Mother of God with joyful festivities [8 September]. From thence he went to the forest of Spessart and relaxed from the labour of the expedition with the pleasure of the hunt. Having passed a pleasant autumn there, he travelled through Franconia to Saxony where he announced that he would undertake an expedition against the Milzeni during the upcoming winter. After this, he celebrated the birth of the Lord at Pöhlde with spiritual and secular *splendour*, according to the custom of his predecessors.

CHAPTER THIRTY-NINE [1004]

After going to Dornburg, the king sent Archbishop Willigis of Mainz and certain other *familiares* to visit Archbishop Giselher, then very ill. It was hoped that the prelate, mindful of the Lord, might finally atone for the sin he had incurred in the destruction of the bishopric of Merseburg, namely, by returning to it and abandoning the see he held illegally [i.e. Magdeburg]. At first, the king had hated Giselher because of his tireless efforts to have Herman elevated to the throne instead of him, but the prelate was subsequently forgiven and came to number among the closest of the king's *familiares*. The king turned over all of his Saxon property to the prelate and found him a loyal administrator who accomplished much that pleased him. But he could no longer restrain his zeal for God and, pursuing him with perfect hatred, he sent the representatives of whom I have already spoken. Giselher barely managed to respond to them in the following way: 'Give me three or four days of respite, permit me to leave, and afterwards I will give you a definite answer.' The king granted this and the prelate, travelling in a wagon as was his custom, went to his estate at Trebra where he departed from this world after two days, on 25 January.[95]

CHAPTER FORTY [1004]

After receiving the news of Giselher's death, the king accompanied
the archbishop's corpse on the trip to Magdeburg. His chaplain,
Wigbert, was sent ahead to secure the canon's unanimous agreement
to the election of Tagino. Meanwhile, the provost of this church,
Walthard, assembled the brothers and, after announcing both the
death of their lord and the imminent arrival of the king, begged them
to find a successor so that they might retain their ancient right of
electing. Everyone responded that they wanted him to be their lord,
with God willing. Accepting this with great humility, as is proper, he
prostrated himself while requesting their favour. The archbishop's
body was taken to the monastery of St John and accorded due honour
during the following night [28 January, at Berge]. The next day,
when the body was taken to the church of St Maurice, the king came
along so that he could receive it along with the clergy and people and
join them in a vigil for the second night [29 January].[96]

CHAPTER FORTY-ONE [1004]

The next morning, the king sent Bishop Arnulf to the exceedingly
sorrowful canons and to the prelate's warriors in order to secure the
election of Tagino [30 January].[97] After he had given a clear explanation of his mission, Walthard responded for the community, saying:
'We know what your lord intends. If possible, we want to have the
power of electing and, though I am unworthy, everyone here wants
me to succeed to the empty place, as you yourself can discover. We
fear that our church will suffer much damage and, that this might not
happen, we ask the king's favour and your intervention. We are not
unmindful of the proverb of a certain wise man: whatever liberty
remains to a people under a king dies with the liberty of the ruler, but
its shadow is preserved if one follows all its commands.'[98] After this,
the bishop left and reported everything to the king. The king then
summoned the provost and, after promising many things, got both his
and the chapter's agreement to the election of Tagino. After everyone
had quickly gathered in the cathedral, the king committed the eternal
salvation of clergy and people to Tagino's care with the staff of Bishop
Arnulf, and set him on the episcopal throne as the entire assembly

96 BG 1553c.
97 BG 1553d.
98 Lucan, *Bellum civile* 3.145–47.

watched and sang praises to God. After a funeral mass had been celebrated, the body of the archbishop was buried before the southern altar.

CHAPTER FORTY-TWO [1004]

But before coming to the restoration of our see, I should say some-thing about the man who then was to be ordained. He was a cleric of the illustrious Wolfgang, the pious pastor who ruled the church of Regensburg though a monk in dress and manner of life. Tagino was so dear to him that he nourished him as a son from boyhood and, when he reached adulthood, put him in charge of all of his property. Moreover, he acquired for him the favour of duke and emperor to such a degree that he had no doubt that Tagino would succeed him when at God's will he was removed from this light.[99] When the venerable priest had finished the course of this exile in admirable sanctity ... [lacuna]... When he now understood that death was near, he had his beloved Tagino come to him and said: 'Place your mouth over mine, my son, and so receive from God the breath of my spirit so that if the ardour of youth should arouse you to the point that you grow cold towards the twofold love, you will be restrained by the highest power and my benevolence. And if perhaps you are denied my dignity, after ten years you will certainly rejoice in a greater one, while I do penance for my sins before God.' After this, understanding that his end was imminent, he had himself carried into the church. When he had finished his prayers and his other obligations had been seen to by the brothers, he commended to God both himself and those entrusted to him, and surrendered his holy spirit in peace on 30 September.[100]

CHAPTER FORTY-THREE [1004]

After being elected by all, Tagino went to the emperor, but did not receive what had been promised. Instead the emperor gave the bishopric to his chaplain, Gebhard. Tagino was faithfully commended to the bishop and held in high esteem but, as good and evil do not go together, this disparity in character *ensured* that he did not remain with him for a long time. For he attached himself to Henry who was

99 See above p. 38.
100 *NMer.*, 31 October, fo. 6v, p. 14.

then duke and pleased him with the chastity of his mind and body. He served him day and night up to this time, as I mentioned, to the annoyance of the bad, to the joy of the good, and troubling himself especially to give both God and humanity their due. Because of this, as lord Tagino himself often told me, the king fulfilled the prophecy of the holy man whom he especially loved, after ten years. He duly honoured his beloved lord, the queen, and all their many companions with rich gifts which, even so, were not equal to his generosity.

CHAPTER FORTY-FOUR [1004]

Then, the king went with Tagino to the archiepiscopal burg of Giebichenstein, carefully inspected everything that had been collected there by Giselher, and judged it to be excessive [1 February].[101] He then proceeded to Merseburg, long widowed of its pastor, and tried to restore its former status, as much as possible. There, on 2 February, that is, the feast of the Hypapante or meeting of the Lord with Simeon the Just, with permission from Hilderich who was first of those in the confraternal order,[102] Tagino was consecrated by Archbishop Willigis of Mainz.[103] This occurred in the presence of the king and the Roman legate, and with the favour of all his co-bishops. Pressing matters prevented Tagino from going to the pope, by whom, as his document attests, he was alone to be ordained. Thus it was also at Merseburg that he was anointed with holy chrism, as the third archbishop of his see. Tagino designated Walthard as his representative in the bishopric. The king, always full of hunger and thirst, then wanted to satisfy himself with a meal of justice.[104] So, he redeemed the episcopal ban over the burgward of Merseburg against a payment of one hundred manses, this because he knew that otherwise Bishop Arnulf would not have agreed. Whatever he demanded from his most beloved Tagino, he received as a gift from his abundant good will. Concerning the bishoprics of Meißen and Zeitz, he ordered a complete restoration, by royal power, because in this instance the earlier situation could justify the removal. Therefore, I will compose a preface and sing songs of Christ with these verses.

101 BG 1553e.
102 Bishop Hilderich of Havelberg (981/92–1008).
103 Meeting with Simeon the Just: Luke 2: 25.
104 Matt. 5: 6.

BOOK SIX

PROLOGUE

O Christ, son of justice shining brightly over the whole earth!
You redeemed the world at your first coming.
At your second, as creator, along with the Father, you will bring
    about its end.
As sole judge, dispensing punishment for various misdeeds to
    humankind
which has languished in sin since the Fall.
True light of the world, may you bless that day,
the one on which you lovingly visited our despoiled church.
May Merseburg praise you, rejoicing at your gift!
Now may its children and their pastors, restored and faithful, offer
    you heartfelt thanks.
Celebrated King of Kings, may you now receive the prayers of your
    people.
Look down from heaven upon your servant Henry,
And defend his faithful wife,
Bestowing upon them your great gifts in return for their small ones.[1]
May Tagino's soul live in the heavenly palace,
May Walthard and Gero be rewarded for a blessed end.
O Merseburg, may Christ save and place in the land of Elysium,[2]
all those whom love inspired to raise you up with kindly hands.
May you, God, the first and supreme king of all,
So rule this place that it willingly responds to your rudder.
May its guardians always follow your commands,
And its enemies be as nothing, having turned again to righteousness.
Look with kindness, I beseech you, upon the one who destroyed our
    church,
And also upon all those whose evil intentions supported him,

---

1 I.e. Emperor Henry II and Empress Cunegunde.
2 Lucan, *Bellum civile* 3.12. Here, referring to the archbishops of Magdeburg.

Grant them forgiveness, that they may enjoy eternal bliss[3]
So too, may the city of Worms rejoice in its liberty.
Until this time, it remained in darkness, and subject to the authority
    of its dukes.[4]
Among the noble lords, Bishop Burchard also rejoiced in his heart,
freed from any fear of enemies close at hand, having been moved far
    away by that one.[5]
The hall of the duke is now the splendid house of the Lord Christ.
And, the clergy may now suppress those fickle judges.
Inspired by love, our magnificent King Henry did this,
Ransoming the church with his own property and returning it to
    Christ.
The pious and kind Duke Otto agreed, fully confirming the royal gift.
May faithful Christians be ever joyful because of this.

CHAPTER ONE [1004]

After the unstained maiden had given birth, for the sake of the world's
salvation, in the numerical series of the millennium, in the fourth place

3 Aside from Emperor Otto II and Archbishop Giselher, to whom Thietmar assigned
  high levels of responsibility, the number of those who might have been blamed for
  supporting the suppression of the diocese of Merseburg (981) was potentially
  rather large and may have included not only members of the royal house (Empress
  Adelheid) and parties, such as the bishops of Halberstadt, whose interests were
  directly involved, but also the churchmen who signified their acquiescence by
  participating in the relevant synods and other public *acta* (Hehl 1997: 99, 105).
4 Here, Thietmar refers to the lineage of Conrad 'the Red', sometime duke of
  Lotharingia and progenitor of the future royal house of the Salians. The Salians
  had built up a quasi-ducal position on the middle Rhine based on their extensive
  alodial holdings, an accumulation of countships, and by taking advantage of the
  vacuum left when Otto I declined to appoint a successor to Duke Eberhard of
  Franconia. That the clerical community at Worms found the presence of the
  Salians oppressive is suggested by the biography of Bishop Burchard of Worms.
  Here, it is related that Duke Otto (d. 1004), the son of Conrad 'the Red', had
  constructed defensive positions within the city and given protection to bandits and
  to the bishop's enemies. In response to the resulting murder and mayhem,
  Burchard constructed defensive works of his own from which he resisted his
  enemies, terrorizing them with 'his words and deeds' (*V. Burch*, c. 7, p. 835; Glocker
  1989: 220–25). The 'freedom' mentioned by Thietmar can be explained by
  reference to a diploma issued by Henry II at Bruchsal, on 3 October 1002 (D H II
  20). In this diploma, the emperor conveys to the church of Worms all the property
  within the city that he had received from Duke Otto, the latter being identified as
  a relative. The *Vita Burchardi* explains that this was part of a deal in which the
  duke was compensated with property at Bruchsal and asserts that this represented
  the price for Burchard's support during the interregnum (*V. Burch*, c. 9. 836).
5 Henry II.

according to the series of ordinal numbers, and in the beginning of the fifth week of the month of February which is called the Purification, a bright morning illuminated the world.[6] For Henry, king by the grace of God, wished to erase the stain that marked his predecessors and to secure his own salvation. After setting out a detailed plan, he went to a residence at which he usually sought to refresh his body, but now also sought to refresh his spirit somewhat with the nourishment that he had long desired. Summoning all the leading men of the realm, he gave the bishopric of the holy church of Merseburg to Wigbert, one of his chaplains [6 February].[7] In doing so, he employed the staff of Archbishop Tagino who thereby returned whatever his predecessor had unjustly presumed to remove from this church and agreed to its restoration. Consent was also given by the bishops, Arnulf, Eid, and Hildeward, among whose dioceses the bishopric had been divided.[8] And all the people applauded. Thereafter, Wigbert was immediately conducted to his see with pious jubilation. On the same day, he was consecrated by his archbishop, Tagino, and by his fellow bishops, Hilleric and Wigo, who were joined by the bishops mentioned above.[9]

CHAPTER TWO [1004]

Meanwhile, because of his own madness and also at the instigation of Margrave Henry, Boleslav attacked the Bavarians and all of his countrymen with a large force.[10] In response, the king assembled an army and attacked the lands of the Milzini.[11] Had he not been impeded

6 Persius, *Satires* 3.1.

7 BG 1553g, 1554. It is likely that Henry II's decision to entrust Wigbert with the task of influencing local opinion at Magdeburg in Tagino's favour (5.40) and, subsequently, to appoint him as bishop reflects not only his loyal service as royal chaplain, but also his connections with the regional aristocracy (4.36) and the cathedral chapter at Magdeburg (6.36). He was familiar with the local situation and hence could negotiate with those likely to be harmed by the king's actions (Finckenstein 1989: 123; Warner 1994: 160). That Wigbert continued to enjoy Henry's support is suggested by the fact that the monarch resided there on six different occasions, most notably on the important feast of Easter (Beyreuter 1991: 250).

8 Bishop Hildeward of Zeitz (1002–32). Bishop Arnulf of Halberstadt, who stood to lose most by the restoration of Merseburg, was compensated with grants of property (*GH*, p. 90).

9 Bishop Wigo of Brandenburg (983/1003–17/19), Bishop Hillerick of Havelberg (981/90–1008).

10 See 5.36.

11 BG 1555.a. Here, supporting Thietmar's dating of this event versus that of the annals of Quedlinburg which place it in 1003.

by heavy snow which was followed by a quick thaw, the whole region would have been wasted and depopulated. He returned disappointed, but was aided by Margrave Gunzelin and other loyal supporters who supplied garrisons. When he arrived at Merseburg, trustworthy intercessors sent by Margrave Henry informed him that his brother had fled to the king of the Hungarians and desired forgiveness.[12] The margrave had also repented greatly for what he had undertaken. Accepting their petition, though unwillingly, and being influenced even more by the entreaties of his dear Tagino and Duke Bernhard, the king offered to forgive Margrave Henry, on the condition that all property and people be returned to him and to his supporters, and that the margrave himself be retained in custody as long as the king wished. In tears, Margrave Henry confessed that he was guilty in all things and, in the manner and clothing of a penitent, surrendered himself to the king.[13] At the king's order, the archbishop of Magdeburg led him off to the burg at Giebichenstein and had his warriors guard him carefully, both day and night. *Among his various good works there, the margrave sang the psalter with one hundred and fifty genuflections, all in a single day.*

CHAPTER THREE [1004]

Meanwhile, the king was mindful of the injuries he had suffered in Italy and exhorted all who were faithful to him to avenge them. Moreover, with Lent imminent, he decided to lead an army there himself. After leaving Merseburg, he went to Magdeburg to seek the heavenly intercession of St Maurice and good luck for his journey.[14] Then, travelling through Thuringia and the boundaries of eastern Franconia, he came to Regensburg where he held a royal assembly.[15]

12 The king's brother, Bruno, had taken refuge with King Stephen.

13 See 5.14.

14 BG 1556, 1556.a. While in residence, on 24 or 25 February, the monarch issued a diploma in which he compensated Magdeburg for its losses through grants of property and by a donation of relics of St Maurice (DH II 63). Local sources, of somewhat later date, relate that Henry carried relics of St Maurice (one of the cathedral's patron saints) from the monastery of Berge, through the snow-covered streets of Magdeburg, to the cathedral. He then decreed that the day should henceforth be celebrated as a local feast day. This spectacular demonstration of piety occurred in conjunction with a variety of royal *acta* intended to compensate the community for losses incurred as a result of the restoration of the diocese of Merseburg (Warner 1994: 141–42, 161–66).

15 On 4 and 5 March, Henry issued diplomata at Wallhausen in Thuringia, site of a royal residence. The diplomata relate to the recently completed restoration of

On 21 March, with the approval of all present, he gave a banner-
lance, which signified the Duchy of Bavaria, to Henry, his vassal and
brother-in-law.[16] Then, he sought out the city of Augsburg where he
was received and treated with great honour by Bishop Siegfried. After
remaining there for only two nights, he lovingly took his leave of the
queen, granted permission for her return to Saxony, and commended
her to the care of Tagino. Accompanied by his army, the king himself
moved on to a place called Thingau where lord Bruno, his brother,
was presented to him by Hungarian intercessors. The king bestowed
his forgiveness and received him with compassion.[17] At Archbishop
Tagino's request, I also came to the aforementioned city, and I
accompanied him on his return. We came to Gernrode where we
joined the venerable Abbess Hathui in the solemn observance of Palm
Sunday [9 April]. On Wednesday, the queen arrived in Magdeburg
where she observed Maundy Thursday and the subsequent feast of
the Resurrection of the Lord [13, 16 April].

CHAPTER FOUR [1004]

After a journey marked by many difficulties, the king came to the city
of Trent where he celebrated Palm Sunday and allowed his soldiers,
who were exhausted from their labours, to enjoy a brief respite on this
celebrated feast [9 April].[18] King Arduin, having learned of his arrival

Merseburg and are noteworthy in that they appear to confirm both Thietmar's
assertion that Otto I founded the bishopric to fulfil a vow (i.e. *ex voti debito*, D H II
64) and his belief that Giselher, the 'destroyer of the church' (D H II 65), was
primarily responsible for its temporary suppression. On 5 March, Henry issued
another diploma at Gebesee, also in Thuringia (D H II 66), in which he
compensated the diocese of Zeitz for losses incurred through Merseburg's
restoration. Located just north of Erfurt, at a convenient ford over the river Gera,
Gebesee would have represented a logical stopping point for the king, especially
since the royal monastery of Hersfeld possessed extensive land holdings there. It
was presumably on Hersfeld's central manor that the king and his entourage found
accommodation (Bernhardt 1993: 263–64).

16 Duke Henry V of Bavaria (1004–9, 1017–26). Henry was the brother of Cunegunde
and son of Count Siegfried of Luxembourg. He had figured among Henry II's supporters during the interregnum (4.51). A similar use of a banner lance is mentioned
at 5.21.

17 Aside from the Hungarian intercessors, the king's and Bruno's mother, Gisela,
seems to have been instrumental in achieving this reconciliation (*AH*, an. 1004, p.
29).

18 Henry issued a diploma at Trent, on 10 April, for the bishop of Brixen (D H II 67).
It was certainly appropriate, and probably no coincidence, that the diploma
invoked the memory of Otto III whose reign had been so closely associated with
Italy.

and being greatly frightened, sent experienced messengers to the aforementioned fortifications.[19] After gathering his troops, he himself took up position on the plain of Verona and was hoping that things would turn out as well as they had in the past.[20] Henry learned that this blockade could only be forced with difficulty or perhaps not at all. Turning in a different direction, he asked his advisers if it would be at all possible to seize the mountain passes, located some distance from there, with the help of the Carinthians. After careful consideration, this plan was carried out although it seemed arduous to many. Immediately obeying the royal commands, the Carinthians divided into two detachments. Before daybreak, one secretly seized a high point above the passes with foot soldiers. At dawn, the other detachment followed, in order to storm the passes. The soldiers who had been sent ahead gave them such a loud signal that their enemies would have heard it in their hidden ambushes. Thinking that their rear was secure, the enemy took up arms and rushed to meet the attackers. But then our forces attacked their flank, forcing some to flee and others to die by falling from the precipices or into the rising waters of the Brenta. The victors carefully protected the passes until the king arrived.

CHAPTER FIVE [1004]

After messengers informed the king of this, he left all his baggage behind and, with great difficulty, led only his best warriors through the passes and set up camp on the bank of the aforementioned river on a certain pleasant plain so that he could observe Maundy Thursday, the consecration of the chrism, the Lord's Passion, and his holy Resurrection with appropriate solemnity [13–17 April]. By the authority of the king, the count palatine forbade anyone to flee and promised that those who fought vigorously would be rewarded in the future.[21] On Tuesday, the king crossed the river, set up his tents once more, and rested [18 April]. He was anxiously awaiting the scouts who had been sent to discover the hiding place of his enemy, Arduin.

---

19 5.24.

20 5.26.

21 Here referring to Count Otto of Lomello, appointed count palatine and count of Pavia by Otto III (BU 1321d; DD O III 221, 398). Count Otto's brother (or uncle), Bishop Peter of Como, the former archchancellor of Otto III, was now acting in that same capacity for King Arduin (Pauler 1982: 46, 159–60).

CHAPTER SIX [1004]

At the prompting of divine piety, the Lombards who had previously
been united in evil, were now divided and alienated from that unjust
usurper.[22] Their retreat allowed Henry, crowned king by God, to
make a safe entry. Verona, the first to receive him, rejoiced in the
Lord that the homeland's defender had arrived and that the author of
all misery had departed. Together with his previously mentioned
supporters, Margrave Thedald hurried to meet the one who had long
been expected, rejoicing that the time had come when they could
openly reveal their good will towards him.[23] Proceeding to Brescia
with such an entourage, the king was received by the archbishop of
Ravenna and by the occupier of that see, Adalbero, along with his
countrymen.[24] From there, he travelled to Bergamo, a city once
conquered by Emperor Arnulf, and received the archbishop of Milan
who swore an oath of loyalty.[25] After this, he visited the city of Pavia
where he was received by the archbishop and leading men of the
region. Then, as the *laudes* were sung, in admirable fashion, he was
conducted to the church, elected by all in common, and installed on
the royal throne [14 May].[26]

CHAPTER SEVEN [1004]

But the same day also revealed that fickleness by which the unstable
course of this whole world is always impelled towards the depths. For
discord arose amid so much joy, namely the enemy of peace, as the
excessive consumption of wine allowed a minor incident to destroy
the union based on fidelity and an oath. The populace took up arms
against the newly elected king and hurried to the palace, especially
those who were displeased with Henry's justice and preferred Arduin's
laxness. When the king heard the clamour, he ordered that its cause
be quickly discovered. He was immediately informed that the commotion
had been initiated by the common people, inflamed by a sudden fury
and aroused by servile presumption, and that all the others had joined
in, to their detriment and shame. Attempting to calm the attackers,

22 Arduin.

23 On Margrave Thedald of Canossa see 5.25.

24 Archishop Frederick of Ravenna.

25 Archbishop Arnulf of Milan (998–1018).

26 Henry was anointed and crowned in the church of St Michael by Archbishop
   Arnulf of Milan (BG 1562g.).

the illustrious archbishop of Cologne, Heribert, went to a window and asked what the cause of such a great attack might be, but he was driven back by a shower of rocks and a rain of arrows. The palace, moreover, heavily besieged by the enemy, was bravely defended by members of the king's household whose numbers could easily have been counted.[27] While necessity had required that our forces be divided, the enemy's numbers steadily increased. When the rest of our forces finally heard the sound of the immense clamour, they flocked to the king and gradually expelled the still raging foe. As night began to fall, however, they were slowed by the onslaught of arrows and rocks. Looking to their safety, they then set fire to the city's buildings.

CHAPTER EIGHT [1004]

Those of our people who were outside the city bravely scaled the ramparts which had made it easier to resist them. In the process, a certain illustrious youth named Giselbert, the queen's brother, was wounded by the Lombards and died, greatly increasing his comrades' sorrow.[28] The warrior Wolfram avenged him, without injury to himself, by rushing into the midst of the enemy and slashing one of them open from the helmet down to the collarbone. In due course, they transformed the quiet beloved by all through the harshness of war. Our forces captured some of the enemy alive and presented them to the king. Suddenly, one of the houses that was protecting our exhausted people collapsed, having been set afire by the Lombards. But the absence of any certain protection only made them more eager to fight. Meanwhile, these evil things were finally made known to the Swabians, Franconians, and Lotharingians who then knocked down the wall, entered the city, and so harassed the residents that none dared leave the protection of their homes. Instead, they oppressed us by throwing missiles from the roofs until they were engulfed by the fire and died. It would be difficult to relate to anyone how much was destroyed there, in different ways. The king's warriors, now victorious, were unhindered in looting the possessions of the dead. Moved by this wretched prospect, the king firmly ordered that they should spare the rest. Then, seeking out the safety of the monastery of St Peter, he mercifully granted his favour to those of his enemies who humbly

---

27 I.e. there were not very many of them.

28 The cathedral canons at Merseburg noted his death in their necrology (*NMer.*, fo. 2v, p. 6).

requested it.[29] Those who were absent, after learning of the king's victory, either came to him so that they might avoid something similar or else sent hostages and promised loyalty, aid, and due submission to the king.

CHAPTER NINE [1004]

After the troubles in Pavia had been resolved, the king went to Pontelungo and received the homage of the remaining crowd of Lombards. He also held an assembly there and put everything in order with great prudence.[30] Then, for the love of holy Bishop Ambrose, he went to Milan. He soon returned to the plain of Pontelungo, however, where he calmed the populace, concerned about his sudden departure, with the promise that he would quickly return and with many other rewards.[31] He celebrated the upcoming feast of Pentecost at a place called Grumo [4 June].[32] As he was moving on from there, he encountered the Tuscans and received them into the community of his true servants.

Hastening to return to his homeland, he entered the boundaries of Swabia, both to rule and confirm, for it had recently been deprived of the solace of Duke Herman [II] and bestowed upon his like-named son, who was still a minor.[33] He then *travelled* to Strasbourg, which is located in Alsace, and there celebrated the birth of the venerable predecessor of Christ [24 June].[34] On the vigil of the feast, the Lord

29 S. Pietro in Ciel d'Oro, north of Pavia. A passage in Jotsald's biography of Abbot Odilo of Cluny may indicate that the saint interceded for the Pavese on this occasion: 'Italy would rejoice when Odilo arrived and Pavia was especially dear to him because, in the times of Emperors Henry and Conrad, his prayers and diligence had rescued it from destruction by the sword and from the danger of fire' (*Jotsald*, c. 6, col. 202).

30 BG 1562. The assembly apparently was supposed to take place in Pavia, in conjunction with the coronation, rather than at Pontelungo (12 km north of the city).

31 Henry was still in Pavia on 25 May, on which date he issued a diploma granting Abbot Winizo royal protection for and confirmation of the possessions of his monastery of S. Salvatore on Monte Amiata (D H II 68). At some point during his stay in Italy, Henry undertook to depose Bishop Peter of Asti (992–1005), a supporter of King Arduin, and replace him with Adelrich (1008–34), the brother of Margrave Odelrich-Manfred of Turin. The process was considerably delayed due to opposition from Archbishop Arnulf II of Milan (BG 1562.1; Pauler 1982: 14–18).

32 Near Cadempino, north of Lugano.

33 Duke Herman III (1003–12), the infant son of Duke Herman II (d. 1003).

34 Other sources assert that Henry held a court on the vigil of the feast (23 June), and this presumably was the occasion on which, as Thietmar notes, the king gave 'the justice of the law to the people' (BG 1572a).

performed a miracle through him which I must not pass over. May this be recounted for the edification of the pious and the terror of the damned. A house in which the king was giving the justice of the law to the populace suddenly collapsed, but only one priest was hurt. He had been living, unjustly and knowingly, with the wife of a man who had been excommunicated. Because of this crime, his guilt exceeded that of all the others and so, with his legs broken, his death served as punishment for the outrage he had committed. How sweet are the deeds of the pious, of which we ourselves have read or have discovered through the eyes and ears of others. And yet, with our wretched and stubborn heart, we are still ignorant. The certain punishment of the wicked does not move us from our inveterate depravity, nor are we enticed by the inestimable rewards of the just.

CHAPTER TEN [1004]

Departing from there, the king humbly sought the threshold of the church of St Martin at Mainz and celebrated the feast of the Apostles with due veneration [29 June]. After this, travelling through eastern Franconia, he visited Saxony which he often referred to as the flowery hall of paradise.[35] In the middle of August, he announced an upcoming military expedition to all who resided under his authority and were faithful to Christ. And, from his pious heart, he unleashed his secret and long-repressed desire to restrain the savagery of that arrogant Boleslav. At the stated time, an army was collected in Merseburg and finally moved against the enemy although by stealth. For the army gave the appearance of going to Poland, with ships having been reserved on the Boritz and Neußen, all this that its subsequent change in direction would not be revealed to the enemy by anyone whose support was only feigned. Meanwhile, a heavy rain greatly delayed the army's crossing of the river. Then, when one could have least expected it, the king suddenly headed towards Bohemia. The roaring lion, with his tail following, tried to prevent his arrival by setting archers on a certain height, located in a forest called Miriquidui, from which every approach could be blocked. Learning of this, the king secretly sent a small number of armoured warriors ahead to force a way through the unwilling enemy and prepare an easy path for those

35 The king was still in Mainz on 1 July (BG 1574, 1575). On 20 July, he was at Ohsen, near Hameln (BG 1576), and by 1 August was in Magdeburg (BG 1577, 1578). On 8 August, he attended the consecration of the monastic church at Nienburg (BG 1578a).

who followed. One day, as Boleslav was dining, one of our people, a
chaplain of Bishop Reinbern, remarked on the advent of our army.[36]
When Boleslav asked what he had said, he responded: 'If they could
leap like frogs, they could be here now.' But one thing is certain: had
divine love not inspired the king and inflamed the other's arrogance,
we would not have won this happy victory so readily.

CHAPTER ELEVEN [1004]

The king was aided by the presence of the exiled Jaromir – his name
means 'firm peace' – whose hoped-for arrival weakened the resistance
of the Bohemian warriors. Their advice and wish allowed the king to
proceed and, at the entry to that region, a castle was willingly
surrendered to him. The king's progress was delayed somewhat
because the Bavarians had not yet arrived. When he came to the city
called Saaz, the residents opened their doors to him, massacred their
Polish garrison, and were thereupon accepted as allies.[37] The king was
disturbed at the sight of so much bloodshed and ordered that the
survivors be hidden in a church. One of those present maintained that
Boleslav had been killed by his countrymen. While the king's supporters rejoiced in God, the corrupt supporters of the false duke were
saddened. The latter secretly murmured among themselves and spread
this falsehood from their unjust hearts: if the king were ever to feel
completely secure, they would be as nothing, and would have to suffer
much harm from him. Because of this, as fire hiding under the cinders,
on this campaign and quite often afterwards, they preferred the
enemy of all the faithful to their king. They were worse than brute
animals and did not know that God, the uncreated father who watches
from on high, would reach down from heaven to rescue his earthly
vicar from their wickedness.

CHAPTER TWELVE [1004]

Then, at the king's order, Jaromir was sent ahead with our best warriors
and with his local supporters to capture or kill the venomous serpent
at Prague. But among this group were informers who gave a detailed
account of the plan to Boleslav, already quite confident in the face of
such a danger. Warned by this message, he made secret preparations.

36 Bishop Reinbern of Kolberg.
37 Saaz on the Eger.

In the middle of the following night, as he heard bells summoning the
people to battle in the nearby burg Wyscherad, he went out with his
best warriors and fled to his homeland. Sobieslav, a brother of
Adalbert, bishop and martyr of Christ, pursued him and was wounded
on a bridge. This gave great joy to his enemies but caused his friends
unspeakable sadness. On the following day, Jaromir arrived. He
received petitioners before the door to the city, confirming rights and
granting forgiveness for past *offences.* After being allowed to enter, he
was joyfully installed in his former dignity and, removing his simple
clothing, put on more costly garments. His warriors presented him
with whatever booty had been seized as their enemies fled or were
killed. Delighted with the many gifts, he was then led to Wyscherad
where his rulership was acclaimed and he promised both the king's
favour and a long-desired reward to those who had persevered with
him until this point. From all sides, a huge crowd of both lesser and
greater men gathered both to seek the new duke's favour and to await
the glorious king's arrival. When the king finally arrived, he was
received by Bishop Thieddeg and Duke Jaromir and led to the church
of St George, amid the rejoicing of the clergy and people.[38] Then,
before an assembly of the entire populace, the king immediately
honoured Jaromir by bestowing upon him the rights held by his
father.

CHAPTER THIRTEEN [1004]

While in Prague, the king wished to celebrate the birth of the holy
Mother of God which the whole world celebrates [8 September].
Hence, he ordered Gottschalk, venerable pastor of the church of
Freising – true to his name! – to sing the mass and instruct the people,
permission for this having been given by the bishop of that place.[39]
When the gospel had been read, Gottschalk admonished all present to
fear God and preserve the bond of dual love, namely obedience to God
and respect for the higher powers.[40] At last, he sweetly admonished
the king to examine himself and recognize that, from childhood to the
present day, every honour and benefit he had obtained should be
ascribed to the mercy of God rather than his own merits. He also
mentioned that quality of mercy which is the unique source of salva-

---

38 Bishop Thieddeg of Prague (997–1017).

39 Bishop Gottschalk of Freising (993–1005). His name means 'servant of God'.

40 Holtzmann (1935: 291, n. 6) suggests that Gottschalk probably based his sermon
   on 1 Peter 2: 17 and Rom. 13: 1.

tion, a venerable ornament of the faith, and contributes to remission of sins. In pursuit of this, each faithful Christian should wish for three things: the ability, the desire, and the fulfilment. Although everyone should show mercy, it is particularly incumbent upon those who do injury to no one and wish to be similarly compensated by God. That their vow may be acceptable to God, their mercy ought to be granted from the heart and remitted to all debtors, lest they be bound by harsh torments like a wicked servant. Concluding these things, Gottschalk said: 'Dearest Lord, in the name and by the love of him who gave his debtor ten thousand talents, that is, forgave the circumcised Jews their transgression of his teachings, I ask you to forgive Henry, once margrave but now, I hope, truly penitent.[41] Release the chains and bestow your grace upon him so that, on this day, you may more freely say to God: forgive us our debts and so on.'[42] The king was pleased by this tearfully offered exhortation, firmly promising that he would comply, and actually did act mercifully when he returned home.[43]

CHAPTER FOURTEEN [1004]

After everything had been taken care of at Prague, the king sent the Bavarians home. In the company of the new duke of the Bohemians, he then invaded the nearby lands of the Milzeni, making his way by an unspeakably difficult march, and besieged the burg Bautzen. One day, while encouraging his faithful to attack, the king would have been injured by an arrow shot from the ramparts had divine providence not protected him. Instead, the arrow injured someone standing very close to him, thereby fulfilling the enemy's goal with another. The king humbly raised his heart and offered praise to God who had once again bestowed his love and protection upon him, despite his unworthiness. As for the aforementioned burg, fires had been set all around it and it would have gone up in flames if Margrave Gunzelin had not hindered this through a most unfortunate command.

CHAPTER FIFTEEN [1004]

Many were wounded on both sides and some were killed. On our side, Hemuzo, a warrior noble in lineage and vigorous in manner, had

41 Matt. 18: 23 ff.
42 Matt. 6: 12.
43 See note at 5.14.

repeatedly provoked the occupants to battle and pursued them almost to the walls, but he was killed when half of a millstone struck his helmeted head. The jeering enemy dragged his corpse into the burg. Count Henry, my brother, who was his vassal, ransomed his body and returned it to his homeland. Another warrior, called 'wild Tommo' because of his constant pursuit of wild game, was vigorously resisting the enemy on the river Spree when the wet rocks caused him to slip.[44] Alas, though protected for a long time by the best of armour, he finally died from a wound. While trying to prevent him from being dragged away, one of his retainers was stabbed from above by a spear and killed. Now, when the suffering of war was almost over, Boleslav sent a messenger who arranged for the burg to be surrendered to the king in return for the lives of the defenders. It was then secured with a new garrison. After this, the king returned home with his army which was exhausted by the journey and lack of food.[45] Wherever necessary, he supported the margraves with the usual reinforcements.

CHAPTER SIXTEEN [1004]

While in Merseburg, where he indulged in some long-sought rest, he learned that the venerable Count Esiko had died in Lübschtz after a long illness.[46] When the body arrived, he himself received it and had it buried honourably next to the church of St John the Baptist, on the north side.[47] For the sake of Esiko's soul, he donated to the holy altar, and to the brothers serving God there, a certain property of his called Obhausen and two silver candelabra.[48] Moreover, he restored to Bishop

---

44 Thankmar's death is mentioned by the Quedlinburg annals (*AQ* 1003, p. 78) and, if one follows Holtzmann (1935: 292, n.3), in the necrology at Merseburg which notes the anniversary of *Tanko laicus* on 25 October (*NMer.*, fo. 6v).

45 By 9 October, the king was at Magdeburg (BG 1582, 1583) and, by 15 October, at Frohse (1584). He apparently returned to Magdeburg and resided there between 13 and 23 November (BG 1586–88).

46 Esiko, Count at Merseburg, died on 22 November (*NMer.*, fo. 7r, p. 15).

47 Henry's concern for Esiko's corpse demonstrated that he considered himself to be the count's closest heir (compare similar situation at 4.50–51) although the now rather distant connection between their respective kin required a judgement prior to a transfer of lands (Leyser 1983: 39–41).

48 The property at Kuchenburg and Obhausen, 'which had been held by Esiko while he lived, but now pertained to [Henry's] royal power', was bestowed upon the canons by means of a diploma issued at Merseburg on 23 November 1004 (D H II 89). The monarch's efforts on behalf of Esiko's soul represented an altogether appropriate reward for the count's loyal support during the struggle with Ekkhard of Meißen (5.15; Borgolte 1993: 243).

Wigbert the merchants and Apaelline Jews previously acquired by Giselher, but long ago exchanged.[49] He conceded comital rights over Merseburg and the benefices pertaining to it to Burchard and the four burgs on the Mulde were given to Thiedbern as a benefice.[50] But according to a judgement, he retained all of the allodial property for himself. He had Margrave Henry released from custody and allowed him to depart with his favour.[51]

CHAPTER SEVENTEEN [1004]

Just as the prosperity of holy mother church should be proclaimed to her spiritual offspring in order to increase the glory of Christ, so should its losses be related in order to provoke repentance, so that these may thereby be conquered and accepted in unanimous joy in the one case and an equal degree of sadness in the other. In revenge for our wickedness, a fire consumed the church at Paderborn and all that belonged to it. The hearts of many of the faithful were moved by the church's fate, and the desire for a heavenly reward filled them with a common desire to restore it.

CHAPTER EIGHTEEN [1005]

Afterwards, a great synod was held in a place called Dortmund at which the king complained to the bishops and all others who were present about many abuses in the holy church and, after taking counsel with them, declared that these should then be prohibited. By the institution of this excellent new decree, the heavy burden of his own sin was also to be relieved. In the year 1005 of the Incarnation of the Lord, in the fourth year of Henry II's reign, the following decree was enacted on 7 July at Dortmund by the same most glorious king, his wife and queen, Cunegunde, Archbishops Heribert of Cologne and Liawizo of Bremen, Tagino, third archbishop of Magdeburg, and bishops Notger of Liège, Swidger of Münster, Ansfrid of Utrecht, Dietrich of Minden,[52] Thietmar of Osnabrück,[53] Bernhar of Verden, Bernward of Hildesheim, Burchard of Worms, Rether of Paderborn,

49 Horace, *Satires* 1.5.100. The gifts to Giselher are noted at 3.1.
50 Count palatine Burchard of Saxony (1002–17).
51 Margrave Henry of Schweinfurt.
52 Bishop Dietrich II of Minden (1002/3–22).
53 Bishop Thietmar of Osnabrück (1003–23).

Wigbert of Merseburg, Ekkehard of Schleswig,[54] and Odinkar: at the death of any one of the aforementioned persons, within thirty days, unless hindered by ill health, each of the bishops should celebrate a mass for the deceased person, and each priest in their church should do the same. Parish priests should celebrate three masses. Deacons and other members of the lower orders should sing ten psalms. Within thirty days, the king and queen should distribute 1,500 pennies for his soul's redemption and feed an equal number of paupers. Each of the bishops should feed 300 paupers, distribute 300 pennies, and light thirty candles. Duke Bernhard would feed 500 paupers and distribute fifteen gold coins. We decided to fast on bread, salt, and water on the vigils of the feasts of St John the Baptist, the Apostles Peter and Paul, St Lawrence, and of All Saints. Fasts on the vigil of the feast of the Assumption of Mary and the vigils of the feast days of the other Apostles were to be observed as in Lent. On Ember days the same observances were to be followed as in Lent, with the exception of the Friday before the birth of the Lord, on which it was decided that we would fast on bread, salt, and water.

CHAPTER NINETEEN [1005]

The king attacked the Frisians with a fleet, forcing them to cease their defiant behaviour and placate the fury of the queen's sister, Liudgard.[55] In the palace and in all the countships of his realm, and under the royal ban, he announced an expedition against Poland, naming Leitzkau as the place of assembly. The army assembled there at the proper time, that is 16 August. The king was celebrating the feast of the Assumption of the Mother of God, at Magdeburg [15 August]. Following the completion of his liturgical and charitable obligations, he crossed the Elbe on the same day as the army, with the queen accompanying him.

CHAPTER TWENTY [1005]

In these days, Bishop Tagino deposed Abbot Rikdag from his abbacy because of a certain misdeed and installed in the now vacant position

---

54 Bishop Ekkehard of Schleswig (995/1000–26).

55 Liudgard was the sister of Empress Cunegunde, daughter of Count Siegfried of Luxembourg, and was married to Count Arnulf of Holland (988–93). The latter was the son of Count Dietrich II of Holland and brother of Archbishop Ekbert of Trier. This campaign apparently took place in May or June and, hence, prior to the synod at Dortmund (BG 1595a).

Alfger, who presided over the monks at Pöhlde. Here, then, was the
first sign of future misery, that a pious way of life which had been
carefully preserved until then was wretchedly destroyed and changed
into a canonry. Would that the hand of God had changed that which
occurred in the course of time![56] Through the instigation of evil men,
I fear that what the founders of that holy institution zealously
constructed and, as it seemed to them, prudently brought to the
highest level of completion (men who utterly surpassed us in every
aspect of piety!) has not become better but rather worse. For our own
sake, I wish that this had not occurred.

CHAPTER TWENTY-ONE [1005]

In fact, those whose new fashion in clothing and manner of life is held
to be so admirable are not always what they appear. For scripture
says: feigned justice is not really justice at all, but rather double
injustice.[57] Of all the fruit of humankind, the most pleasing to God is
a good heart which, however, the just may sometimes conceal beneath
beautiful, golden clothing or moderation in food and drink. Indeed,
who really benefits from that which is taken from abstemious wearers
of cloaks? If it contributes to the increase of their churches, the profit
is doubled; if undertaken for the sake of God, the souls of the brothers
are benefited, but their domestic welfare also benefits from the alms
that are attracted. But how can this remain secure if all is displayed
outwardly; and if their gain means that many suffer privation?
Certainly, their exaltation will not last, but rather go sadly to ruin at
the end. Even if the teachings of Christ are silent on this matter, and
none of his preachers address it, is all of this free from any objection?
The trumpet of the gospel sounds: 'There is nothing covered that
shall not be revealed.'[58] After we have satisfied our desires in all things,
our hidden sins cause us to suffer unspeakable evil. We mortals are of a
fragile nature and know well that every weight is carried to earth by
its own inclination. In repenting, let us respect and not spurn those
who admonish us, so that, by observing the mandates of God, we may
acquire the reward promised to all faithful people. We should not
view ourselves as superior to our predecessors; we are very different
from them and equally deceived by the many faces of truth. No one

56 Ps. 76: 11 (RSV 77: 10).
57 Aug. *Enn. Ps. 63*, c. 11, p. 765.
58 Matt. 10: 26.

should become angry when another admonishes us privately in the name of God. Such love should be received by all in a kindly fashion, and the pure truth should be endured in return for divine compensation. May all the faithful humbly petition Christ that he may bestow the forgiveness necessary for these and other sins. Having long digressed, I will once again take up the thread of my narrative.

CHAPTER TWENTY-TWO [1005]

After putting the army in order, the king set forth. The queen quickly retraced her steps and anxiously awaited her beloved lord's return in Saxony. Our army arrived safely at a place called Dobrilugk, in the region of Lausitz, where it was strengthened by the forces of Dukes Henry and Jaromir. The dukes lifted the army's spirits and fortified it with their good council and bravery. Traitorous leaders, intent on preserving their own property, led the army through wastelands and swamps where it was much oppressed and, in their evil spitefulness, they prevented it from quickly attacking the enemy. After reaching the region called Neiß, a camp was set up next to the river Spree. There, the celebrated warrior Thiedbern learned that the enemy was preparing an ambush. Desiring to gain the highest praise for himself, he gathered the best of his comrades and tried to trap the enemy by stealth. But their enemies were very careful. That they might better hurt pursuers, they fled among the thickness of the fallen trees and, as usual, shot the arrows which were their best defensive weapon. Thus, on 6 September, they were able to kill and despoil any who were careless: chiefly Thiedbern, and then Bernhard, Isi, and Benno, illustrious retainers of Bishop Arnulf, as well as many other warriors.[59] The king and his entire entourage took the loss very hard and, so credible witnesses report, Boleslav also grieved. After this, the Liutizi joined us. They came, with images of their gods preceding them, on the day before we were to have arrived at the river Oder.[60]

CHAPTER TWENTY-THREE [1005]

Although I shudder to say anything about them, nevertheless, in order that you, dear reader, may better understand the vain superstition and

59 Bishop Arnulf of Halberstadt. The deaths of Bernhard, Isi, and Benno are noted in the necrology at Merseburg (*NMer.*, 7 September, fo. 5v, p. 12).
60 On the banners of the Liutizi see 7.64.

meaningless worship of this people, I will briefly explain who they are
and from whence they have come. In the region of the Redarii, there
is a burg called Riedegost which has three corners and three doors.[61]
It is surrounded everywhere by a great forest which the inhabitants
hold to be inviolable and holy. Two of its doors offer entry to all. The
third door faces east and is the smallest. It opens on to a path leading
to a lake that is located near by and is utterly dreadful in appearance.
In the burg, there is nothing other than a skilfully made wooden
shrine supported on a foundation composed of the horns of different
types of animals. Marvellous sculpted images of gods and goddesses
adorn its outer walls, so it seems to the observer. Inside, stand gods
made by human hands, each with a name inscribed and frightfully
clothed with helmets and armour. Among them, Swarozyc occupies
the first place and all the heathens honour and worship him above the
others. Their banners may never be removed from this place except in
time of war and then only by warriors on foot.

CHAPTER TWENTY-FOUR [1005]

To carefully protect this shrine, the inhabitants have instituted special
priests. When they convene there to offer sacrifices to the idols or
assuage their anger, these priests sit while everyone else stands.
Murmuring together in secret, they tremble and dig in the earth so
that, after casting lots, they may acquire certainty in regard to any
questionable matters. When this is finished, they cover the lots with
green grass and, after placing two spears crosswise on the ground,
humbly lead over them a horse which they believe to be the largest of
all and venerate as sacred. That which the casting of lots had already
revealed to them, should also be foretold by this almost divine beast.
If the same omen appears in both cases, it is carried out in fact.
Otherwise, the unhappy folk immediately reject it. An ancient but
equally false tradition also testifies that, if the harsh savagery of a
long period of internal warfare is imminent, a great boar whose teeth
are white and glistening with foam will emerge from that same lake
and appear to many witnesses while happily disporting itself in the
mire with a terrible shaking.

---

61 Adam of Bremen provides a somewhat different description of what appears to be
the same shrine (Adam 2.21, p. 78; Tschan (trans.) 1959: 66). Here the location is
called Rethra, the god worshipped, Redigast.

CHAPTER TWENTY-FIVE [1005]

Each region of this land has a temple and a special idol which is worshipped by these unbelievers, but the burg mentioned above has precedence over all. When going to war, they depart from here and, if they return victorious, they honour the place with appropriate gifts. Just as I have mentioned, they carefully inquire, by casting lots and consulting the horse, what their priests should offer to their gods. Their unspeakable fury is mitigated by the blood of human beings and animals. There is no individual lord who presides over all of these people who are collectively referred to as Liutizi. When important issues are discussed at an assembly, there must be unanimous agreement before any action can be undertaken. If one of their *countrymen* opposes such a decision during an assembly, he is beaten with rods. If outside the assembly, and openly, he must either lose everything through burning and immediate confiscation, or he must come before that body and, in accordance with his status, pay compensation for his sin. These unbelieving and fickle people nonetheless demand reliability and great loyalty from others. They make peace by offering hair cut from the top of their heads and grass, and by joining their right hands, but the desire for riches will easily move them to violate it. Such warriors, once our servants, now free because of our wickedness, came with their gods for the purpose of supporting the king. Dear reader, avoid both their society and their cult! Rather, hear and obey the mandates of divine scripture! If you learn and commit to memory the faith declared by Bishop Athanasius, the things that I have recounted above will rightly appear meaningless to you.

CHAPTER TWENTY-SIX [1005]

From there, under unequal leaders, the dissimilar bands advanced to the river Oder and set up their tents next to a stream called Bober in Slavic, but Castor in Latin.[62] Having fortified the banks of the river,

---

62 In light of his preceding comments, Thietmar's reference to *unequal leaders* and *dissimilar bands* should be understood as a veiled criticism of Henry II's alliance with this still pagan people. Similar antagonism was expressed by his relative and school chum, Brun of Querfurt, who sent the king a letter (in 1008) demanding that he break off relations with the infidel, make peace with the Polish duke, and return to a policy of active and forceful support for missionary work in the East. One of his more forceful arguments centred on a citation from Paul's second letter to the Corinthians (2. Cor. 6: 14–15) and on a saint, Maurice, who was closely associated with the see of Magdeburg, with the Holy Lance (a symbol of royal rulership), and with the Ottonian house in general: 'Is it good to persecute

Boleslav waited at Krossen with a large army, seeking at all costs to prevent a crossing. The king delayed there for seven days and had boats and bridges constructed, but then, divine providence revealed an excellent ford to the scouts he had sent out. At the king's order, six war bands entered the river there at dawn and came across safely. Boleslav's guards observed this from a distance and quickly sent the sad and incredible message to their lord. After three or more scouts had assured him that this was true, he quickly dismantled his camp and fled, along with his army, leaving much behind. After carefully observing this, at the head of his army, the king joined the clergy and people in chanting praises to God, and safely crossed the river. If we had not waited for the long-hesitating Liutizi, those who preceded could have surprised and overpowered their enemies while still in their tents. Although our forces pursued the enemy vigorously, they fled like deer and could not be caught. Hence, our warriors returned to their comrades.

CHAPTER TWENTY-SEVEN [1005]

From here, the king moved on to the abbey called Meseritz where he was able to celebrate the annual feast of the Theban legion with the greatest veneration [22 September]. He also took strong measures to prevent his forces from inflicting any damage on the church or the residences of the absent monks. The enemy did not dare to spend the night in any of their burgs as the king pursued them, wasting everything in his path and stopping barely two miles from the burg Poznań at the request of his leading men. Nevertheless, when the army scattered to gather food and other necessities, it suffered heavy losses from the enemy's ambushes. Meanwhile, Boleslav sought the king's favour through trustworthy intermediaries, and it was immediately granted. At Boleslav's request, Archbishop Tagino and others who were close to the king came to Poznań. After appropriate compensation and promises had been proffered, they concluded a peace agreement.

Christians and to ally with pagans? What alliance of Christ with Belial? What comparison of light with darkness? How do the demon Svarozic and the leader of the saints, your and my Maurice meet? By what consideration do the Holy Lance and the Devil's banner, which is nourished by human blood, come together' (Brun, *Ep.* pp. 101–2). Brun's apparent advocacy of the use of force to support conversion has been cited as a milestone in the development of the idea of crusade (Kahl 1955: 171–72; Erdmann 1977: 107–8), but however 'highminded' his arguments, Brun can scarcely be considered an impartial observer, given that he wrote the letter while residing at the Polish court.

Our forces, suffering grievously from the long journey, lack of food, and general savagery of war, were happy to return home.

After this campaign, the king sought to strengthen the wholesome security which our region had long desired by rooting out the authors of all iniquity [December 1005–April 1006].[63] He ordered that his celebrated retainer, Brunkio, be hanged with a rope, at Merseburg. Along with their followers, Boris and Vezemiskle, leading men among the Slavs, suffered the same fate at Fallersleben. At Werben on the Elbe, the king held frequent meetings with the Slavs during which, whether they wished to or not, he took up issues crucial to the realm and forcefully settled them. For the safety of the homeland, he restored the previously devastated Arneburg and returned property that had been wrongfully taken from it a long time ago.[64] Through the judgement of a synod, issued in his presence and by canonical and apostolic authority, he forbade both illegal marriages and the selling of Christians to the heathen, ordering that those who rejected the justice of God be destroyed with the spiritual sword.[65]

Meanwhile, a combination of immaturity, wealth, and wicked advisers persuaded Duke Baldwin of Flanders to take up arms against the king; and also to both seize and subject to his power the city of Valenciennes.[66] When the king learned of this, he led his battle standards against the city and made several attempts to take it [September 1006].[67] As he could accomplish nothing, he departed and

---

63 BG 1605b.

64 4.38.

65 In reference to the selling of Christians see also 6.54.

66 Duke Baldwin IV of Flanders (988–1035). Baldwin and Count Lambert of Hennegau had driven Count Arnulf from the city and ignored Henry's demands that he be reinstated. Although Henry had support from King Robert II of France, the initial attempt at reducing the city failed, as Thietmar notes. The strategy of granting the city and other territories to Baldwin as a benefice was similar to what had been employed in regard to the duke of Poland and Lausitz (Beumann 1991: 166–67). That Henry was not simply trusting in the bonds of loyalty, however, is suggested by other measures designed to counter the influence of his aristocratic rivals (note at 6.30).

67 BG 1621a.

informed his supporters in both the East and the West that an expedition would be mounted against Baldwin during the following summer [July 1007]. At the appointed time, a great army assembled and, with the king at its head, moved on to the river Scheldt. Although Baldwin appeared with his army, his plans to prevent the king from crossing were frustrated. According to a wise plan, our forces crossed secretly in boats at another location and confounded the duke's great presumption with a surprise attack. As Baldwin fled, the king rejoiced in the victory of Christ, crossed the river, and ravaged the surrounding countryside. When he arrived at the abbey of Ghent, the brothers received him, and he spared both the place itself and all of its property.[68] Compelled by necessity, Baldwin humbly sought forgiveness and, not long afterwards, the king granted him Walcheren and Valenciennes as a benefice.[69] *On 21 July, our king's venerable mother, the celebrated lady Gisela died and was buried in Regensburg.*[70]

CHAPTER THIRTY [1007]

After this region had been pacified, the king held a general council at Frankfurt that was attended by all of the bishops from lands north of the Alps [1 November]. But first, dear reader, you must hear of the dispute which preceded it! From childhood, the king had expressed particular affection for the city of Bamberg in eastern Franconia, favouring it above all others and bestowing it upon his wife as her dower. After divine providence had entrusted the realm to his care, he began to zealously pursue his secret plan to establish a bishopric there. Just as Horace declared that the beginning is half of the task, so the king began and completed a new church there, with two crypts.[71] As he was gradually accumulating everything necessary for the celebration of the divine mysteries, he constantly entreated Bishop Henry of Würzburg, one of his *familiares*, that he might agree to this

68 St Bavo, Ghent. The king entered the city on 19 August.
69 Count Baldwin offered his submission on October 1007, at Aachen, and, at some point, Count Lambert apparently did the same (BG 1644c). At or around the same time (22 October), Henry II granted the countship of Cambrai to the city's bishop, Erluin, who had fled to the German court to escape from Baldwin (BG 1645). Erluin and his successors received the right to: 'dispose of the countship in the interest of their church (*in usum ecclesiae supra dictae*): to choose a count, to exercise the bann, and to do [i.e. with the countship] whatever might please them in any way' (D H II 142).
70 *NMer.*, 21 July, fo. 4r, p. 9.
71 Horace, *Epistles* 1. 2. 40.

heartfelt plan and, in return for compensation, surrender parochial rights over that district which is named after the river Regnitz. The bishop took a favourable view of his beloved lord's request and gave his consent, with the understanding that he would receive the pallium for his church and that the pastor of Bamberg would be subject to him. He secretly confirmed this agreement by giving his pastoral staff to the king and accepting compensation in the form of a certain property. But when he realized that he absolutely would not receive the archiepiscopal dignity, he refused to fulfil his promise and rejected his summons to the council mentioned above.

CHAPTER THIRTY-ONE [1007]

When the archbishops and their suffragan bishops were all seated according to rank, the king threw himself prostrate on the ground.[72] He was raised up again by Bishop Willigis, in whose diocese the synod was being held, and spoke to the entire assembly as follows: 'For the sake of future compensation and because there remains to me no hope of acquiring offspring, I have made Christ my heir. For some time now, I have secretly offered my most valued possessions as a sacrifice to the Unborn Father, namely my own person and whatever I have acquired or am yet to acquire. With the agreement of my bishop, I have already conceived the desire to establish a bishopric in Bamberg and today I wish to bring this just plan to fruition.[73] Because of this, I beseech your most serene piety that my plan not be impeded by the absence of one who wished to obtain from me that which I had no right to concede. Indeed, it is clear from his staff, a sign of mutual agreement, that he has not fled for the sake of God but rather from resentment at the refusal of an office which he can never obtain. May the hearts of all present consider that he presumes to deny the increase of holy mother church with his deceptive message. In their kind generosity, my wife, who is present, and my only brother and co-heir, have favoured the establishment of this bishopric and both may be certain that I will give them satisfactory compensation. Moreover, the bishop will certainly find me prepared for all that seems right to you, if he deigns to come and fulfil his promise.'

72 BG 1645a–1678.
73 'Our prelate': Bishop Henry of Würzburg.

CHAPTER THIRTY-TWO [1007]

After this speech, Berengar, Bishop Henry's chaplain, arose and declared that his lord had not come because he feared the king and that he would never have agreed to anything that in any way damaged the church committed to him by God. For the love of Christ, he earnestly requested that the assembly not permit such a thing in the bishop's absence, as it might establish a precedent for them in the future. At this point, his privileges were read aloud. Throughout this procedure, the king would humbly prostrate himself on the ground whenever he foresaw that a detrimental judgement was about to be read. Finally, Archbishop Willigis asked for a judgement as to what should be done in regard to this matter. Tagino, speaking first, declared that the law would allow for the immediate enactment of everything that the king had requested in his speech. After the entire assembly had agreed to and signed this judgement, the king conveyed the pastoral office to his then chancellor, Eberhard, who was consecrated by the archbishop on the same day.[74] Later, Bishop Henry was restored to the king's favour, with the help of his brother, Heribert, and received satisfactory compensation.

CHAPTER THIRTY-THREE [1007]

It is rare for the heavens to shine brightly without the shadows of dark clouds following. Thus, while the king was celebrating Easter at Regensburg, representatives of the Liutizi and the large city of Wollin, and also Duke Jaromir, informed him that Boleslav was trying to instigate a great conspiracy against him and employing both his words and riches to lure them into it [6 April]. They also told the

---

74 Bishop Eberhard of Bamberg (1007–40), chancellor (1006–08/09), chancellor for Italy until 1012/13 and archchancellor for Italy until 1024. Henry's motivation in establishing a new bishopric at Bamberg is laid out in the council's protocol (namely 'that the paganism of the Slavs might be destroyed and the memory of Christ's name be celebrated there in perpetuity', D H II 143). It has also been suggested that the foundation, reflecting a policy of centralization, was intended to function as the centre of a new royal *Landschaft*, an area with a high concentration of royal lands and rights, and more specifically to limit the power of the Bavarian duke (Weinfurter 1986: 277–78; Arnold 1997: 140–41, Störmer 1997: 443). In any case, it is scarcely a coincidence that the first bishop was a man of proven loyalty who, in fact, may have figured among the king's relatives (Finckenstein 1989: 161–63). The protocol makes no mention of Henry's striking demonstration of humility, but such behaviour was quite in keeping with the public image of Ottonian kingship and, in this case, it served to intensify the pressure for an agreement (Warner 1995: 68; Hehl 1998: 296).

king that he could no longer rely on their loyal service if he continued to grant Boleslav his peace and favour. The king carefully considered the situation with his leading men. After receiving different opinions from them, and accepting their hostile viewpoint, he sent Boleslav's own son-in-law, Herman, to announce to the duke that their pact of mutual peace had ended.[75] Boleslav had learned of this embassy through intermediaries and, though he had previously invited the count to visit, did not accord him a friendly reception. When he received the king's message, he made a great effort to justify himself, saying: 'May Christ, who knows all, be my witness! That which I must do, I do unwillingly!' Afterwards, he assembled an army and ravaged the district of Möckern which is located near Magdeburg. Boleslav's hostility also destroyed the bonds of Christian fraternity which he had previously established with the Magdeburgers. Then, moving on to the burg called Zerbst, he conquered the occupants with dire threats and sweet encouragement, and led them away with him. Our forces learned of these events, but were slow to arrive and hesitant in their pursuit. Archbishop Tagino, their leader, knew about everything ahead of time, but had not made sufficient preparations. I was also with him. When we had all arrived at the place called Jüterbog, the wisest were of the opinion that pursuit of the enemy with such a small force would not be advisable and so, we returned.

CHAPTER THIRTY-FOUR [1007]

Nevertheless, Boleslav then occupied Lausitz, Sorau, and Selpuli. Not long afterwards, this wicked father-in-law also besieged the burg Bautzen which was defended by a garrison provided by Margrave Herman. Through messengers, he urged the occupants to surrender this burg to him without a fight, noting that they could hope for no rescue from their lord. A truce was arranged on the seventh day. While Boleslav prepared for an assault, the besieged sent a messenger to humbly ask for help from their lord and from the leading men of the realm, with the promise that they would resist the enemy for another seven days. Margrave Herman came to Magdeburg where he approached Walthard, who was then provost, and sent messengers to

75 Herman, son of Margrave Ekkehard I of Meißen, who was married to Boleslav's daughter Regelindis.

summon each of the leading men individually.[76] He complained bitterly about their sluggish response and sent messengers to reassure his own *milites*. The latter had suffered much from Boleslav's constant attacks which they had resisted both long and vigorously. When they saw that some of their comrades were wavering, however, and that their lord still had not freed them, they arranged with the duke to hand over the burg in return for permission to leave with all their possessions. In sorrow, they returned to their homeland.

CHAPTER THIRTY-FIVE [1008]

After Easter, Liudolf, the venerable archbishop of Trier, died [6 or 7 April].[77] His chaplain, Adalbero, who was the queen's brother and still an immature youth, was elected in his place although this occurred more from fear of the king than love of religion. When the king learned of these events, however, he recalled the earlier, unplanned installation of Adalbero's brother and decided to reject the pleas of his beloved wife and others close to him who wanted the bishopric to be granted to Adalbero. Instead, it was bestowed upon Archbishop Willigis's chamberlain, Meingaud, a man of noble lineage.[78] Because of this, the fury of this treacherous clan was inflamed. The residents of Trier secured the palace against the king, and this region, up to now peaceful, was repeatedly ravaged by fire. Whatever evil these harsh men may have done to their benevolent lord, they were now repaid in equal coinage. What can they all say, now, or at the Last Judgement? Their unspeakable guilt causes the uncorrupted, mother church to weep over the death and despoliation of her sons. Tears stream down her cheeks before the face of a vengeful God! Aroused by such presumption, the king immediately took an army to

76 It is not entirely clear why Thietmar suddenly refers to Herman as margrave and for this reason I have left it in the translation. Herman did not become margrave of Meißen until 1009 (6.54).

77 The necrology at Merseburg lists the archbishop's death on 6 April (*NMer.*, fo. 1v, p. 4), but cf. BG 1680b.

78 Achbishop Meingaud of Trier (1008–15). This incident marks the beginning of Henry II's feud with his in-laws who clearly thought they deserved to gain more from their sister's marriage to the king than the latter was willing to concede. The feud included various members of the house of Luxembourg: Duke Henry of Bavaria, Count Frederick of the Ardennes, and the clerics Dietrich and Adalbero. It also attracted Count Ezzo, the husband of Otto III's sister, Mathilda. Henry II had provoked the count by confiscating some of Mathilda's hereditary property (Beumann 1991: 168–69). Thietmar describes the surrender of the brothers at 7.9.

Trier and had the previously enthroned archbishop consecrated.[79] He also ordered that Adalbero be excommunicated. The defenders of the palace were so constrained by the long siege that, exhausted by hunger and the constant fighting, they had no choice but to perish inside, or come out and surrender unconditionally into the power of the king. This was avoided, however, because Duke Henry, with surprising shrewdness, managed to obtain free passage for them from the king. Afterwards, when the king learned of the true situation, he was very disturbed and sought revenge, as I will explain later.

CHAPTER THIRTY-SIX [1008]

Meanwhile, after a long illness, my predecessor anxiously awaited his last day.[80] Before concluding, however, I would like to relate certain things about him, so that they may not be forgotten. He was descended from one of the best families of eastern Thuringia and had undertaken his studies with Ochtrich at Magdeburg. Archbishop Giselher took this outstandingly educated man into his personal service, retaining him for a long time, and granted him both a special benefice and the office of archpriest. Finally, after suffering Giselher's constant, wicked murmuring, he became so alienated that he gave up everything and, as I have mentioned, took service with King Henry who was well pleased with him.[81] He was outstanding both in stature and appearance, an eloquent speaker with a beautiful voice, wise in counsel and extraordinarily generous. Hence, with divine aid and through his own virtue, he ascended to the dignity of bishop. In the days conceded to him by God, he acquired the following properties for his church: Sotterhausen, Burgwerben, nine manses in Niederröblingen, seven in Thaldorf, three in Nienstedt. From his own property, he gave seven manses and the hill known as Schönberg in Obhausen. He also collected many books and other objects pertaining to the celebration of the divine mysteries.

CHAPTER THIRTY-SEVEN [1008]

Because of a poisoned drink, he was frequently in pain, it being particularly severe in the month of March. He endured this condition for no less than ten

79 The campaign took place at some point between the end of July and November 1006. See BG 1693a, which also adds a few more details from other sources.

80 Bishop Wigbert.

81 5.40; 6.1.

years. If he was occasionally hostile to his own people or to outsiders, this was entirely due to his severe infirmity. Through enthusiastic preaching, he drew his flock away from their empty superstition. He completely destroyed the wood called Schkeitbar which was venerated as holy and, from time immemorial, had never been violated, constructing a church for the martyr St Romanus in its place.[82] *Along with many other churches, he dedicated a third and fourth church in Magdeburg. If capricious and often untruthful folk gossiped about him, I would urge good men to be very sceptical. In blaming others, many do not recognize that no one is without sin. This venerable man occupied his bishopric for five years, six weeks, and five days. At Merseburg, on Tuesday, 24 March, he migrated from this life (as I hope) to Christ after offering frequent,*[83] *tearful confessions and being absolved by Bishops Wigo and Erich who attended him on his deathbed.*[84] *He was buried at a place previously revealed to him in a dream by one of the elect of Christ, his leader and companion while he lived.*

CHAPTER THIRTY-EIGHT [1008/1009]

As his successor, the pious pastor Tagino, had decided on me, the one writing this, however unworthy. While the king was celebrating the birth of the Lord at Pöhlde, he and his trusted adviser, Tagino, considered how he might commend the church of Merseburg to a good rector, once Wigbert was dead. Tagino said to him: 'In my church there lives a certain brother named Thietmar, who is both well known to you and prudent. With God willing, I believe that he will be suitable for this office.' At this, the king responded: 'May he then accept it! And, he should have no doubt that I will be a most reliable supporter in all his endeavours.' My cousin Dietrich was sent to tell me what the king and archbishop had decided and, if possible, persuade me to cooperate.[85] *I was in Magdeburg when I received this proposal and responded*

---

82 A martyr under Valerian (c.258), who was converted and baptized by St Lawrence (feast day 9 August).

83 Not Tuesday but Thursday (Holtzmann 1935: 320, n. 5).

84 Bishops of Brandenburg and Havelburg, respectively.

85 Dietrich appears to be Margrave Werner's brother (6.66–67, 74, 81; 7.7) and may well be the Dietrich identified as Archbishop Tagino's chaplain by the necrology at Magdeburg (*NMag.*, 30 October, fo. 14v, p. 62; Holtzmann 1935: 321, n. 8; Lippelt 1973: 57). In any case, he appears to have enjoyed the prelate's favour and may have been his intended successor. That the provost, Walthard, following his election as archbishop, saw fit to pay Dietrich twenty pounds of silver (6.66) and the fact that Henry II 'commended' him (6.67), suggests that he was seen as deserving of compensation (i.e. his interests had been hurt by the election). Following Walthard's untimely death, moreover, the chapter elected Dietrich

as follows: 'May omnipotent God repay our pious lord and father for deigning to think well of me. I judge myself unworthy of this honour and hence, would never dare to agree to it. Indeed, God has the power to seize the still-living bishop from the hand of death. If I completely refuse, however, I fear that I will be separated from the customary favour of my lord. Aside from him, I have no other helper from whom I could either claim this honour or receive even more. After the bishop's death, if I still live, I will fulfil whatever pleases God and the powers established by him.

CHAPTER THIRTY-NINE [1009]

The king heard of the bishop's death while residing in Frankfurt and ordered that his due remembrance be celebrated. By then, however, certain people had already incited him to move his glance from me to one who was better. He wanted to bestow this honour on Adalger, who was quite deserving. When the king's intimate, Tagino, realized this, he disapproved vehemently. Through his vigorous intercession, he succeeded in having me summoned by the provost Geso, with the king's grace. Geso found me at my manor, Rottmersleben. During the night, I had seen a bishop's staff standing next to my bed and a voice had asked: 'Do you wish to receive the church of Merseburg?' I responded: 'If it is the will of God and of the archbishop who orders me to come.' The voice continued: 'Take care, because whoever arouses the anger of St Lawrence immediately loses his mind'. I responded: 'May Christ, the guardian of human kind, protect me that I may not in this, or in any other way, offend the majesty of God and forfeit the intercession of the saints.' When I awoke, I was dazed, but immediately got up and saw the bright light of day already streaming in the window.[86] Then, the man of whom I have spoken entered and, after showing me two letters, told me to come to the city of Augsburg on Holy Saturday.

CHAPTER FORTY [1009]

I came to Magdeburg and then departed on Palm Sunday [10, 19 April], with the permission of the provost and brothers. I arrived at my destination on the Tuesday following the Resurrection of the

archbishop, 'out of affection for Tagino' (6.74). As Thietmar notes (6.81), Henry overruled the election and gave him a place in the royal chapel where he undertook at least one important diplomatic mission (8.10).

86 Persius, *Satires* 3.1.

Lord, and was accorded a kindly reception by the archbishop though
he was annoyed at me for being late. On the following day, I was
summoned by him and, at the king's command, questioned as to my
willingness to aid my church with some part of my hereditary
property. I replied to him: 'I came here at your command and, concerning this, am neither able nor willing to say anything for certain. If
your intentions, always favourable to me, shall be realized here
through the will of God and the king's generosity, I will humbly do
whatever I can, in this or in other matters, for the salvation of my
soul and in repayment of the debt incurred.' Accepting and agreeing
with these words in a kindly fashion, the archbishop led me to Bishop
Bruno's chapel, where the king awaited him. After preparing for the
celebration of the mass, he commended me into the hands of the king.
I was elected by those who were present and the king committed the
pastoral office to me with the staff. Finally, as I prostrated myself and
sought indulgence, the cantor began the introit: *Come, you blessed of my
father.*[87] Immediately, all the bells in the cathedral church began to
ring. Even if this occurred by chance, no one had ordered it and it was
not occasioned by my dignity, so the king declared it an omen.
Afterwards, Bishop Bruno provided a great feast. On the following
Saturday we *travelled* to Neuburg [23 April]. There, in the king's
presence, on 24 April in the octave of the feast of the Lord, Archbishop Tagino anointed me to the episcopate with chrism. Our colleague,
Hildeward, supported him and no less than four other bishops assisted.
From there, we *travelled* down the Danube by boat, to Regensburg. *At
this time, there was a great famine in this region.*

CHAPTER FORTY-ONE [1009]

Meanwhile, Duke Henry had secretly attempted to come to Bavaria
for the purpose of fomenting rebellion, but as soon as he realized that
the way had been closed to him through the king's clever foresight, he
quickly retreated.[88] In response to this incident, the king ordered the
leading men of the Bavarians to convene at Regensburg. They had all
freely sworn to their duke that they would not elect another for three
years, but after being reproached for this, a combination of promises
and threats convinced them to abandon their support and aid for him

---

87 Introit to the mass for the Wednesday after Easter.

88 Duke Henry V of Bavaria, brother of Empress Cunegunde, who had joined the
uprising initiated by his brother, Adalbero of Trier (6.35).

and ally with the king. Then, all the brothers of the monastery of St Emmeram, the martyr of Christ – Emperor Arnulf had built it in the saint's honour and chose it as his final resting place – threw themselves at the king's feet. As I listened, they tearfully complained that they had suffered much at the hands of Gebhard, their bishop.[89] The laymen who were present followed with loud lamentations. It is difficult for me to relate, and for anyone to believe, all that the folk subject to this man said regarding his vain excess and harm to their souls. I know only this, I have never seen anyone similar to him in manner or as unique in his presentation, nor have I heard of such a man from the ancients. If his character agrees with his outer appearance, he is either better than the others or far worse. He destroyed the best old customs and devoted his greatest efforts to the new. He and his supporters abandoned the homeland and he cultivated foreign things, however different, with empty display. May God be my witness, I say these things not only to blame him. We should conceal the fragility of those close to us and only cast blame for the sake of improvement. Rather, truth has forcefully persuaded me to speak, and like many others, I am astonished. May God be favourable to him, so that, if he did these things with good intentions, he may travel the course of this pilgrimage justified before God and without complaint. If he did all of this because he was swollen with conceit rather than by the fire of spiritual love, and only for the sake of condemning the *mores* of his contemporaries, may he be converted from his wickedness and, by attracting the laity, pursue the edification of faithful souls and incur no damage to his own. Happy in Christ is he who obtains eternal remembrance through the cultivation of justice and, free from evil gossip, is called to the right hand of God.

---

89 The dispute between the monks and Bishop Gebhard had its roots in St Emmeram's uncertain status (on the following, Rädlinger-Prömper 1987: 91–213). From the time of its foundation until 975, the office of abbot had been held concurrently by the bishops of Regensburg. In 975, Bishop Wolfgang appointed an independent abbot to administer the community (i.e. Abbot Ramwold, formerly of St Maximin, Trier), a change which established a clearer separation between the monastery and the cathedral, but did not alter St Emmeram's essentially proprietary relationship with the bishops themselves. Hence, Gebhard I and his successors could treat the monks' endowment as their own and use it to defray their own expenses, especially the growing cost of providing hospitality for the king (see 4.44, 5.22). Arnold, Provost of St Emmeram (d. 1050), maintains that the bishops' depredations caused the monks undue hardship and led to a decline in discipline (Arnold, bk 2, col. 1027).

CHAPTER FORTY-TWO [1009]

While the king was dealing with the matters that I have just described at length, at his order, I went off to take possession of my bishopric. First, I went to my manor that is called Malacin in Slavic but Eisdorf in German. On the following day, the dependants of my church were assembled next to the river Elster, near the burg Eythra, and I spoke to them, comforting those who were present and summoning those who were absent. A large number of them had fled because of their own fickleness and because of my predecessor's serious illness. From thence, I proceeded to Merseburg where I was received with honour by the canons and enthroned by Bishop Erich. The next day was a Sunday [22 May]. Although a sinner, I sang the mass, enlightened those who were present with my admonitions – though deserving such admonitions myself – and, despite my own weakness, granted absolution, through the power of God, to those who confessed their sins. The Rogation days began on Monday and, at the archbishop's request, I *travelled* from here to Magdeburg. There, on Wednesday, my spiritual brothers received me in a manner reflecting the abundance and depth of their affection rather than my own worthiness. We celebrated the renowned and royal mystery of the Ascension, together, and with as much solemnity as possible [26 May].

CHAPTER FORTY-THREE [1009]

From thence, I went on to Walbeck [30 May]. As provost, I had governed the brothers there, who served God and the ever virgin Mary, for seven years, three weeks, and three days. Unfortunately, I had acquired this great burden in a simoniac manner, not in return for money, but rather by ceding property to my uncle. In spite of my abundant guilt, I hope for the forgiveness of my harsh judge because, in fact, I did this both to defend the flock of the lord and to preserve what my parents had established. Therefore, O reader, with God as my witness, I ask that you carefully examine my account, judge its merits, and anticipate the horrible countenance of that future judgement with tearful supplications. After his *offence* against his lord and king, my grandfather Liuthar, of whom I have spoken, diligently sought to erase the stain of his guilt by establishing a monastery in honour of the holy Mother of God, at Walbeck [941]. He installed Willigis as provost and ceded a tenth part of his hereditary goods to feed and clothe the brothers. After Liuthar's death, and with the agreement of his two sons, his wife, Mathilda, wished to complete the vow made by her lord [964]. When Willigis died, that illustrious father, she had the provostship bestowed upon Reinbert who stemmed from eastern Franconia. Many years later, when both my father and paternal grandmother had died, and with my uncle Liuthar's help, Reinbert was made bishop of Oldenburg by Otto III [993].[90]

CHAPTER FORTY-FOUR

At that time, a cleric of noble lineage, named Dietrich, lived in our vicinity. On the recommendation of the aforementioned count, he acquired the provostship in return for ten manses. After he had occupied it for more than ten years, my mother died [1002]. As the third son, I then inherited the abbey and received half of its property from my brothers. Thereafter, I frequently asked my uncle to let me assume the provostship and do so as a gift or at least for a modest price. After long and difficult negotiations, he asked me for a large payment, ignoring the obligations of both love and affinity. In the absence of support from my brothers, alas, I agreed to his demand, and was made protector of this church of which I was already a servant through my paternal inheritance, on 7 May of the year 1002. The cooperation of my predecessor was obtained in return for acceptable compensation.

CHAPTER FORTY-FIVE

As occupant of this office, I have inclined more towards wickedness than the justice of God and, in spite of this, have never tried to avail myself of the worthy fruits of penance. I do not complain about someone tied to me by the bonds of consanguinity, but rather wish them good in spite of all their evil deeds. When my brother's wife died, he asked me to prepare the place of burial that had already been requested. I initially refused because I knew that the venerable Willigis had been buried there. Afterwards, however, I ignored both justice and the shamefulness of his request and acted wretchedly. Would that I had not done it! In emptying the tomb and removing the bones of my brother, I, a Christian, committed an act that the heathen themselves would have regarded as sacrilege. I ordered that the silver chalice which I discovered there be set aside and used to support the distribution

90 BU 1078d.

of alms to the poor, but afterwards was unable to find it. From an illness that followed these events, I realized that I had greatly sinned against God. After recovering, with God's help, I went on pilgrimage to Cologne. One night, I heard a great clamour. Upon inquiring what it might be, I heard a voice saying, 'I am here, Willigis, forced by your sin to wander without rest.' In horror, I immediately awoke, and have continued to groan at my guilt in this matter up to the present day. I shall do so as long as I live.

CHAPTER FORTY-SIX

I was called by Lord Tagino to the burg Allstedt to receive the order of the priesthood. Along the way, I confessed my misdeed, but did not fulfil the penance I had promised, which was my obligation. Still, though unworthy, I received the priestly dignity, from the afore-mentioned archbishop, on 2 December. King Henry was present and gave me an excellent chasuble. Before I was consecrated bishop, in that week in which all the faithful, everywhere, celebrate the memory of the brothers, a voice made the following announcement to me in a dream: 'Within one year, Bishop Hilderich, Deacon Meinrich, and you, must fulfil your commission from God.' I responded: 'May it be as heaven wills it.' Not long afterwards, in that same month, on 30 October, the bishop died in Christ.[91] His end had already been revealed to him. Because God often deigns to visit and console us in our weakness, it is appropriate to transmit this incident to posterity, both praising it and committing it to writing. The name of the Lord may thereby be glorified and unstable humanity encouraged to look to the future. While the bishop was in Magdeburg, suffering from a serious physical ailment, he was admonished by an illustrious man who appeared to him in a dream and said: 'Do not be concerned with your death, now, as you must wait another four years and two or three weeks. You should, therefore, do as much good as you can.' After saying this, he vanished. Just as he predicted, the bishop survived, as I hope, with a vigilant spirit, until a sudden death concluded the course of his life on earth. *During the following night a great light appeared and was seen by many.*[92]

---

91 I.e. Hilderic *NMer.*, fo. 6v, p. 14; *NMag.*, fo. 14v, p. 62. The entry in the necrology from Magdeburg adds: 'On the same night as Archbishop Tagino was coming home, along with two of his chaplains, Dietrich the subdeacon and Eric the priest, a bright light shone for almost an hour, as if a door had opened in the sky.'

92 See preceding note.

CHAPTER FORTY-SEVEN

After the feast of All Saints [1 November], being very concerned about my welfare, I asked the deacon for permission to leave and admonished him to look to his own fate as well. Then, I went to my estate Rottmersleben. During the following night, I humbly prayed that God might deign to reveal something more certain regarding my future. As I was gradually falling asleep, in early hours of the following day, which was the vigil of St Martin [10 November], it seemed to me that Walthard, then our provost, appeared and said to me: 'Do you wish to know your fate?' Sensing my agreement, he carefully examined a martyrology upon which he had silently lowered a plumb, an instrument employed to ensure that a wall's measurement is true. After a long time, the plumb stood still. And I said to him: 'What now?' He responded: 'Five!' I clearly saw this number written in ink, but was uncertain whether it referred to days, weeks, months, or years. I immediately asked him whether the time previously indicated was meant, or a later one, but he left in silence. For my part, I noted the period of grace allotted to me with profound concern, but did not at all employ it for good works. When the fifth month arrived, I expected death rather then anything else. Instead, both dreams were fulfilled when I received my bishopric because, in so doing, I both obeyed the precepts of God and fulfilled the designated number. Now, it seemed to me that it would be inconvenient for that church, over which I myself had hitherto presided, to be left without its own rector. With the agreement of all the brothers, I installed, as servant of this altar, Willigis, who was my brother from my father. Thereafter, I proceeded to Merseburg where I celebrated the upcoming feast of Pentecost with my lord and king [5 June 1009].

CHAPTER FORTY-EIGHT [1009]

From there, we all *travelled* to Magdeburg where my cousin, Margrave Werner, accused of many things by the king, stood to lose both the king's favour and the benefices he held from him. This had occurred at the instigation of Count Dedi. Werner's sudden illness prevented the issue from being resolved, however, and the count palatine, Burchard, succeeded in having it postponed, through his prudent council. Moving on, the king concerned himself with the always fickle spirits of the people of the West, attempting to calm them and thereby preclude their usual tendency towards arousal. Some praise these people for their unwillingness to suffer any injustice from their lords, but we condemn them as cowards. There are many who serve only their bodily desires and disregard the bridle of equity which God has placed in the hands of the king. Such people, unmindful of the future, defend their ways with as much force and craft as possible, and persecute all who disagree with them with slander and insatiable hatred. I cannot agree with these people or their supporters. Rather, I align myself with those who humbly submit themselves to God and to the powers he has established, those who find it wiser to endure all for the sake of God than to offend the divine majesty through strife and detestable perjury. Our ancestors were ever faithful to their lords and, as the best of warriors, fought against foreign peoples rather than against each other. Future generations should learn this and avoid the alternative. When something must be changed, moreover, they should try to ensure that it is always for the better and not for the worse. Furthermore, they should willingly attend the eight beatitudes and aim to fulfil them while avoiding their opposite.[93] Nevertheless, why should I persist in condemning the one and praising the other? At the future harvest, the fruit obtained by each will surely correspond to the quality of their seed. We constantly labour to acquire corruptible things, why do we not hasten fearlessly after the crown of eternal honour, if only a little? During his travels and in other difficult situations, our king showed great concern with such matters, as I have already mentioned, and made enemies whom he justly hated into friends.

CHAPTER FORTY-NINE [1009]

Meanwhile, Count Dedi brought great shame upon my cousin through his words and deeds and, in so doing, reawakened an evil that he thought long forgotten. For with his advice and aid, the burg of Werner's father, our Wolmirstedt – it is called Ustiure in Slavic, because Ohre and Elbe flow together here – had been burned down and pillaged. All of this roused the spirit of the excellent young man's heart.[94] Thus, when he learned for certain that Dedi was riding out of the burg Tangermünde, so called because there the river Tanger flows into the Elbe, he went after him, taking only my brother Frederick and no more than twenty armed men. He caught up with Dedi near

93 Matt. 5: 3–10.
94 Virgil, *Georgics* 3.81.

the village of Mose, on a high plain that permitted one to see very far.
He attacked vigorously, and immediately more than forty of his
enemy's allies fled, leaving Dedi and his retainer, Egilard to die,
despite their valiant resistance.[95] After this, Werner justly lost that
which he had previously come close to losing unjustly through Dedi's
slander.

CHAPTER FIFTY [1009]

If you wish to hear of Dedi's origins you should know that he was of
the lineage of the Bukkonen and his father was Dietrich.[96] From childhood, he served Margrave Rikdag, who was a relative, and distinguished
himself through both his spiritual and physical excellence. As I have
mentioned, he also led the rebellious Bohemians against us at the
church of Zeitz.[97] Ranging far and wide with them, he brought
devastation to the land and went so far as to capture his own mother,
including her among the booty as if he were her enemy rather than
her son. After this, he made his peace with King Otto III and quickly
gained his favour and trust. Meanwhile, Count Bio of Merseburg died
during a military expedition.[98] Through Archbishop Giselher's
influence, Bio's county, which lay between the Wipper, Saale, Salza
and Wilderbach, was ceded to Dedi. For himself and his brother
Frederick, Dedi also obtained the fortress district of Zörbig that his
ancestors had possessed as a benefice. Finally, he married Margrave
Dietrich's daughter, Thiedburga. Because of all this, he became so
arrogant that he secretly began to foment evil against the king and
openly did so in regard to others.

The king celebrated the upcoming feast of the Lord's birth at Pöhlde
where, by right and on the advice of the queen and the leading men,
he gave Dedi's countship and all of his benefices to Dedi's son,

95 The death of a Count Dedi is noted by the necrology of Merseburg on 9 July.
(*NMer.*, fo. 3v, p. 8). But cf. Holtzmann 1935: 336, n. 7.

96 Here, Thietmar refers to the origins of a lineage that would later be known, from
one of its more important burgs, as the house of Wettin. Dietrich appears to have
been of *Edelfrei* status, that is, he was noble, but possessed neither offices nor
benefices from the king. With Dedi, count in Hassegau, and his brother Frederick,
count of Eilenburg, the family began a precipitous though not untroubled rise into
the first ranks of the Saxon aristocracy (Fleckenstein, 1991: 85–95).

97 3.18.

98 Giselher died in 1004 and Thietmar refers to Bio (i.e. Binizo) for the last time
c.990 (4.12), therefore the latter's death must have occurred at some time during
this period.

Dietrich. Werner's march and whatever he held from the king were
conceded in their entirety to Count Bernhard.[99]

In those days, Bishop Dietrich of Metz and his brother, Duke Henry,
along with other conspirators, were a source of great annoyance to
the king and his supporters [July–August].[100] Nevertheless, Dietrich
also brought irreparable harm upon himself and his successors. For
the Slavs, who have no fear of God, pillaged both a church located
outside the city of Metz and the congregation that served it.[101] The
king compensated for most of the damage through oaths and from his
own property, and ordered all of his warriors to take care that such an
incident did not occur again. They had destroyed vineyards, buildings,
grain, and other useful things.[102] Not long afterwards, I saw a letter
which stated that hunger and need had forced eight hundred dependants of St Stephen to flee their homeland, without the permission of
their superiors.[103] The letter did not mention those who had been
given permission to leave. It would have been better for this church if
that man had never been born.[104]

CHAPTER FIFTY-TWO

I will describe one of their outrageous deeds, an incident that occurred
at Odernheim.[105] The king had held an assembly in the city of Mainz
that the rebels also attended.[106] When the rest of the participants

99 Son of Margrave Dietrich (Thiedrich) of the Saxon northern march and therefore
  Thiedburga's brother.
100 Henry besieged Bishop Dietrich and his brother, the now deposed Duke Henry of
  Bavaria, at Metz and, in the process, systematically pillaged the surrounding areas
  (BG 1716a).
101 Here, referring to allied members of the Liutizi, which would explain why the
  king felt compelled to offer compensation (Brüske 1955: 66).
102 Although the verb is in the singular (*lesit*), the context suggests that it is to the
  depredations of Henry II's army or possibly of the Slavs alone that Thietmar refers.
103 St Stephen: the cathedral church of Metz.
104 Dietrich. Cf. Matt. 26: 24.
105 A later tradition, at the monastery of Brauweiler, asserts that Ezzo, count palatine
  of Lotharingia, played a major role in this battle (*FB*, c. 11, p. 132; Lewald 1979:
  130–31).
106 The assembly was held during the first half of July 1011, and attended by Duke
  Henry, Bishop Dietrich II of Metz and also by the king's Lotharingian allies,
  Duke Dietrich and Bishop Heimo (BG 1747a).

would not respond as they wished, however, they went home angry.
Still, a temporary truce had been established. Bishop Heimo of
Verdun and Duke Dietrich followed the rebels as they departed,
unaware of any evil doings, and were surprised by an ambush.[107]
Many men were killed and, apart from the bishop, few escaped. Duke
Dietrich was severely wounded, but because he numbered among
their friends, he was taken captive and held in custody for many days.
Later, he was released in return for hostages, and without losing the
king's favour. *In the year 1000 of the Incarnation of the Lord, Duke
Bernhard died at Corvey.*[108]

CHAPTER FIFTY-THREE [1009]

Meanwhile, Count Herman and Margrave Gunzelin were feuding, but
did battle with each other in a manner unusual for our region.[109] For
after vainly trying to conquer the burg Strehla, which was guarded by
Herman's *milites*, Gunzelin turned his attention to the burg Rochlitz,
located next to the river Mulde and not well guarded, and had it
burned to the ground. And indeed he did not hesitate to inflict
whatever damage he could upon the count, because uncles always
rage against the sons of their brothers.[110] Without warning, moreover, the brothers Herman and Ekkehard surrounded and attacked a
burg located near the Saale and particularly valued by Gunzelin. It
was here, protected by walls and a garrison, that the margrave had
deposited much of his treasure. After dividing all the treasure, the
brothers had the burg completely destroyed and set on fire.

CHAPTER FIFTY-FOUR [1009]

After this incident came to the king's attention, he immediately
hurried to Merseburg in order to study it more carefully. There, after

---

107 Bishop Heimo of Verdun (990–1025), Duke Dietrich of Upper Lotharingia.

108 Duke Bernhard I of Saxony (d. 9 February 1011).

109 After the murder of his brother, Margrave Ekkehard I, Gunzelin (d. post-1017)
     was installed as margrave of Meißen by Henry II. Presumably, the monarch
     intended to drive a wedge between the Ekkehardiner and Boleslav Chrobry. The
     feud to which Thietmar alludes had its origins in disputes between Gunzelin and
     his nephews (Herman and Ekkehard II) regarding Ekkehard I's inheritance. The
     issues in question were eventually decided in the nephews' favour. See below 6.54,
     and *LMA*, vol. 4, p. 1795.

110 Thietmar spoke from personal experience, see 6.44.

listening to the statements of the two counts, he assigned all the blame to Gunzelin. The latter, having disregarded the king on many occasions in the past, should not have expected him to avenge his present disgrace. The king added that he had received more than a few complaints from people that Gunzelin had sold their dependants to the Jews. Gunzelin had shown no inclination either to order their return or to restrain the banditry which he himself had instigated to the detriment of so many. It was also noted that he enjoyed more favour with his brother-in-law, Boleslav Chrobry, than was appropriate for him or acceptable to the king. Among those present were some who personally wished to accuse Gunzelin of treason. The king then asked the leading men to give their collective opinion regarding the many complaints and also to assess the justification suggested by Gunzelin and his supporters. After deliberating in private for a long time, they offered the following response: 'We recognize that this man's behaviour towards you is not inexcusable. It is our opinion that he should submit himself unconditionally to your mercy. You, however, following the admonitions of our most merciful God, should provide an example to all who might wish to turn to you, namely by displaying that mercy of which you possess an abundant supply and by rejecting the model of behaviour that he himself has followed.' Concurring with this opinion, the king received Gunzelin and placed him in the secure custody of Bishop Arnulf.[111] He provided for the continued protection of Meißen against enemy attacks and placed it temporarily in the care of Frederick.[112] The following autumn, on the recommendation of the queen and instigation of his dear Tagino, and also with the advice and agreement of the same leading men, he gave the march to Count Herman.

CHAPTER FIFTY-FIVE [1009]

Meanwhile, it was the turn of Count Brun, the brother of Gunzelin, to guard the previously mentioned burg Meißen. And behold, the day before Count Herman was to arrive at the burg that had been promised to him, a large band of Poles crossed the Elbe at dawn and silently approached its entrance. Because the warriors were in place, however, the invaders found no easy way to enter, and so they returned sadly though unfortunately without injury. As it turned out,

111 Bishop Arnulf of Halberstadt.
112 Frederick of Eilenburg. See 6.50.

the leaders of this incursion were two Withasen from the suburb.[113] They rightly paid for their presumption with their own blood. Boleslav awaited them at Bautzen, suspended between hope and fear.[114] When he saw his people arriving, he took the loss very seriously. After this, Count Herman was installed by a representative of the king and thereupon repaid his debtors whatever they had given him, affirming this with his right hand.

CHAPTER FIFTY-SIX [1009]

During this summer and the winter following, the king made peace with his enemies, thereby following both good advice and his own inclination. His thoughts turned constantly, moreover, to the shame and injury that Boleslav had inflicted upon him. Accordingly, after Easter, he issued a ferocious order indicating that an expedition was to be undertaken. The army was to assemble on Margrave Gero's lands at Belgern, which means 'beautiful mountain'.[115] Then, Duke Bernhard and Provost Walthard went ahead to see if they could bring Boleslav to his senses. Finding nothing there that pleased them, they returned. Among those who came to Belgern was Jaromir, the illustrious duke of the Bohemians and a faithful supporter of the king. I also cannot omit the great misfortune that befell the margrave. All of us – and I exclude no one – acted as though we were Gero's enemies rather than his friends. With the sole exception of his dependants, we destroyed everything, much of it by fire. The king did not seek revenge for this offence, nor did he offer protection.

CHAPTER FIFTY-SEVEN [1010]

From Belgern, we went to the district of Lausitz. The burg Gehren is located at the entrance of this district and takes its name from Margrave Gero. As Gero was a large man, he was called Gero 'the great'. At Gehren, two brothers from the burg Brandenburg, in the district of the Heveli, were captured. They had sought out Boleslav in order to provoke his animosity against the king. When they left, however, they were snared in the trap which they themselves had

113 See 5.9.
114 Virgil, *Aeneid* 1.218.
115 Alt-Belgern. The expedition took place between the middle of August and the end of September, 1010 (BG 1735a).

secretly prepared.[116] After being questioned about many things, and having indicated their unwillingness to provide any answers, both were killed by being hanged from the same height. At this point, both the king and his dear Tagino became ill. This caused the leading men anxiously to consider what should be done in regard to the expedition that had just begun.[117] Finally, they decided that the king should return, along with certain of the bishops and everyone else who had taken ill. Bishops Arnulf and Meinwerk,[118] Duke Jaromir, Margrave Gero, Herman, and several others were to pillage the districts of Silesia and Diadesi. And so it was done.

CHAPTER FIFTY-EIGHT [1010]

Together and fully armed, these lords passed by the burg Glogau where Boleslav himself was residing and could see them. This aroused the spirits of his warriors who were watching from the walls. Addressing their duke, they asked why he suffered such an outrage and requested permission to do battle. Boleslav answered them in the following way: 'The army you see may be small in numbers, but it is great in courage and its warriors have been specially selected. If I were to attack them, regardless of whether I won or lost, I would be weakened in the future. The king can always raise another army. It is much better for us to endure this now and find some other occasion to attack their arrogance, if possible, without much harm to ourselves.' Thus he calmed the insolent spirits of his warriors. During this campaign, his wish to do us harm remained unfulfilled. Although frequently delayed by rain, our forces inflicted much damage on the enemy. Finally, after pillaging far and wide, the Bohemians went back to their homeland and our forces happily returned to the Elbe, through the lands of the Milzeni. Messengers were sent ahead to inform the king of our success and imminent return. By the grace of God, the king was again healthy and happily received both the messengers and those who followed, at Merseburg. Archbishop Tagino had separated from the king at Strehla. He rejoined him after his own health returned, and after he had celebrated the feast of the Thebans at Magdeburg [22 September].

116 *Ecbasis Captivi* 1.767.

117 Literally, 'considered in an anxious breast' (*angusto versant in pectore*), apparently alluding to Virgil, *Georgics* 4.83.

118 Meinwerk of Paderborn (1009–36). Thietmar discusses the bishop's mother, Adela, at 7.47.

CHAPTER FIFTY-NINE [1011/1012]

After deliberating on many issues of pressing concern to our troubled homeland, the king again visited the western regions and subdued the fickle minds of the inhabitants with the bridle of wisdom. He happily celebrated the feast of the birth of the Lord at Pöhlde.[119] Afterwards, he again visited dear Merseburg where he established a mutual peace for five years. On the advice of a few, he ordered that the burg Lebusa be rebuilt and strengthened. Alas, in the same year, the outcome that many predicted would follow the king's order actually did occur.[120] We went to Lebusa at the end of January and celebrated the feast of the Purification of the holy Mother of God [2 February]. Our assigned task was accomplished in fourteen days and, after securing the place with a garrison, we departed. Near by and to the north was another burg which was separated from the first only by a single valley. This burg had twelve doors. I surveyed it with great diligence and decided, on the authority of Lucan, that it was a large Roman structure and the work of Julius Caesar.[121] It could have held more than ten thousand men. The smaller structure, which we had just restored, had been empty since the time of King Henry.[122] After I have recounted the events that occurred in the meantime, I will explain the tearful fate that quickly befell this place.

In the previous summer, on 10 August, the monastery at Walbeck was destroyed by fire, along with four churches, all of its bells, and with other structures belonging to it.[123] All of this happened because of my sins.

CHAPTER SIXTY [1012]

When the cathedral in the city of Bamberg had been completed, all the leading men of the realm gathered there on 6 May, the king's thirty-fifth birthday, to participate in its consecration.[124] Patriarch John of Aquileia and more than thirty other bishops undertook the consecration of this bride of Christ. Though a sinner, I was present as

119 Or possibly at Dornburg on the Saale (BG 1750c).

120 6.80.

121 Lucan, *Pharsalia* 6.29–65.

122 See 1.16.

123 1011.

124 As the king was born in 973, 1012 was the beginning of his fortieth, not his thirty-fifth, year. The structure appears to have been a basilica with two choirs and transept in the west (Oswald 1966: 32; Jacobsen et al. 1991: 42–43).

well and saw how the church had been decorated in a manner altogether worthy of the Highest King. After this, there was a great synod at which a complaint regarding Bishop Gebhard of Regensburg was submitted by his archbishop.[125] The king also rebuked Bishop Dietrich of Metz for having raised unjust accusations against him in a letter sent to the pope. Through prudent counsel, a resolution was found both for these matters and many others.

CHAPTER SIXTY-ONE [1012]

After matters in eastern Franconia had been settled, the king returned to Merseburg where he celebrated the holy feast of Pentecost [1 June]. On the morning of that Sunday on which the Holy Spirit filled the Apostles, Archbishop Tagino became ill and could not sing the mass. Though unworthy, I was ordered to undertake this task in his place. By the following day, the archbishop's health had improved somewhat, but he overly exerted himself by visiting the king [2 June]. Afterwards, he declined to such an extent that he was altogether incapable of doing anything for himself. Summoning Abbot Siegfried (my brother) and Bishop Erich, he made his confession in their presence. On Thursday, he decided to leave [5 June]. After being carried on his chair to the king's sleeping chamber, he raised his head from the pillow and addressed his sleeping lord: 'My dearest lord, may omnipotent God grant you a worthy reward for all the kindnesses with which you have hitherto consoled and comforted me in the course of my earthly pilgrimage.' Thereafter, he heard mass in the church and bestowed his blessing upon those who were present. He was then carried to a boat which took him to Giebichenstein where he spent Saturday resting [7 June]. On Sunday, he *travelled* by boat to his burg Rothenburg [8 June]. On Monday, while under way again, he realized that death was imminent and summoned Provost Walthard, to whose care he commended himself and his dependants. On 9 June, he did not die, but rather departed on his happy voyage to Christ whom he had always loved.[126] The brothers tearfully offered up a prayer and sent the warrior Bodo to convey the news to the king. On that very day, the archbishop's corpse was taken to Frohse where it was clothed in his episcopal vestments. Then, it was transferred to the seat of his bishopric and received by all with great sadness.

125 Archbishop Hartwig of Salzburg (991–1023).
126 *NMer.*, fo. 3r, p. 7.

CHAPTER SIXTY-TWO [1012]

I learned of all this too late, in Merseburg. By the time I arrived at
Magdeburg, it was already the day of the archbishop's burial [11
June]. After offering up a few words of prayer in the cathedral, I went
to the refectory, where the provost sat with all the brothers and
milites and deliberated on the matter of the election. Deeply sorrowful,
I poured out my tears as I stood there before them. After they had all
greeted me, I took my place among them and asked what had been
decided. Walthard responded: 'I sent a messenger to inform the king
regarding the misfortune that has befallen us, and to ask what we
should do about it. In turn, he sent Bishop Erich who has indicated
that we should not hold an election, but merely present him with our
unanimous recommendation. Now, inspired by love, everyone here
has turned to me, assuming that God consents and the king agrees,
and despite my unworthiness.' Immediately, I said: 'I am among those
who have a right to participate in this election and consecration. I
offer the following advice and as much help in realizing it as possible.
Let my lord order what he wishes. You, however, should see that
what has been bestowed by God and the king's predecessors is not
lost. As the first to elect, I choose you, my brother, as my archbishop.
And, I do this not as a matter of personal affection, but rather because
I recognize your suitability. Now, I wish to hear, individually, the
opinions of each of those here present.' Their response was unanimous:
'We elect Walthard as our lord and archbishop.' After this confirmation, Walthard arose, threw himself on the floor, and sought the
indulgence of God, praying that he might reward us and, for his part,
promising every kind of benevolence. Then, bowing my head, I
requested full restoration of the diocese that rightly pertained to my
currently despoiled church. I did this in the name of the Lord, for the
sake of true and fraternal affection, and on the assumption that he
would attain the office of archbishop. I also asked that he agree, under
oath, both to this proposal and to the return of other property taken
from my church. He firmly promised this to me, in the presence of all.

CHAPTER SIXTY-THREE [1012]

Meanwhile, Bishop Erich had gone to sleep, exhausted from his
journey, and Bishop Wigo had arrived, adding his voice to our election.
Reding, the cathedral's sacristan, was sent to the king so that the
latter, being mindful of the Lord and his own promise, might console

the sorrowful family of St Maurice which had so recently been deprived of its father. At the sounding of prime, Bishop Erich awoke and sang the mass for the dead. After the gospel had been read, he announced to all those who were present why the king had sent him. Along with us, he then granted absolution to the dead archbishop and prayed that all others might do so as well. It had been three days since this priest had died. The third, seventh, and thirtieth days following the departure of any believer should be dedicated to his remembrance, because these days embody the mystery of our faith in the Trinity and the sevenfold gifts of the Holy Spirit. After being blessed, the corpse was brought to the place of burial, to the accompaniment of mournful chants. It was placed in the western part of the choir, at the front of the crypt that the archbishop himself had built and consecrated. Tagino had frequently offered up his tearful prayers at the altar of this crypt, and it was there, while he still lived, that he had asked to be buried. For the salvation of his beloved lord's soul, Walthard devoted so much care to this hitherto unconsecrated place, in which his body now rested, that it was found noteworthy by all who entered.

CHAPTER SIXTY-FOUR [1012]

With Christ, the blessed live on through their virtues, but in this world they survive through writing. Hence, it would not be good to remain silent regarding the excellent lifestyle of such a father. Rather, it should be described in the light of truth, to the advantage of all. Tagino was righteous, moreover, and a man both fearful and great in his love of God. He was generous and loyal, chaste, mild, prudent, and steadfast. Although he wore the vestments of a canon, his manner of life was that of a monk, in every respect. He harshly judged the failings of others, for the sake of improvement, but also praised whatever he found virtuous. Among his contemporaries, no pastor was closer to his brothers. He both esteemed and praised them before the people. In the first year after his ordination, he undertook the construction of a temple to the Lord and he increased the clothing allowance of his priests and deacons by eight shekels, those of the subdeacons and boys by four. Unless hindered by illness, he sang the mass and the psalter daily. Since constant fatigue did not permit him to fast, he redeemed himself with an abundance of alms. He also laboured excessively at his vigils and, because bad teeth did not permit him to eat much, readily satisfied his hunger by drinking, albeit in moderation.

CHAPTER SIXTY-FIVE [1012]

Although nobility of lineage and manner attracted Tagino's admiration, he did not disdain persons of lesser character, but merely kept them at a distance. He loved those who worshipped Christ, but persecuted anyone who spurned him, with righteous anger. He carefully tended to everything that God had committed to him, and tried to increase it. Before celebrating the divine mysteries, he was very serious. Afterwards, however, he smiled and was friendly with everyone. He frequently sang the *Kyrie eleison* with his household. For my part, I can scarcely number the many gifts he lovingly bestowed upon me, though I was unworthy of them. I know only this, that I never responded to him with suitable repayment. By no means, did I render the obedient service which, during my examination, I had promised to him and to his successors. For his church, he acquired the burgs Arneburg, Frohse, and Prettin, as well as an estate formerly belonging to Count Esiko. The episcopal vestments he acquired were splendid and rich. As I have already mentioned, this column of the church stood for eight years, four months, and eight days before it fell, at least in terms of this world. Nevertheless, it will stand for ever in the invisible temple of the Lord, to which it has been removed. Unger, pastor of the monastery at Poznań, died on the same day, in the thirtieth year after his ordination [9 June]. What has been said here will suffice, and I can now return to my original theme.

CHAPTER SIXTY-SIX [1012]

In the presence of the king, Reding humbly delivered his message and achieved the desired result though not without difficulty. He then sent a messenger to summon Walthard, still busy with the funeral solemnities of his beloved lord. Walthard had supplemented my cousin Dietrich's prebend with a pious gift of twenty pounds of silver. I was also summoned, and *travelled* with Walthard. We arrived at Grona on Saturday and immediately sought out the king who granted us a very gracious reception [14 June]. The king spoke with us briefly and then permitted us to go to our lodgings. We had set up camp beyond the palace, by a grove in which the church of St Alexander is now located. The following day was a Sunday and the feast of St Vitus [15 June]. Early in the morning, I sang mass for my brothers. Then, after being summoned to the palace, we went to the king's sleeping chamber. Only Walthard entered, however, and remained there until the hour of terce, deep in conversation. When he emerged, Walthard was wearing the ring on his hand, which he displayed to us, saying: 'Behold, you have a surety for future grace!'

CHAPTER SIXTY-SEVEN [1012]

After we had all assembled in the presence of the king, we complied with the latter's request, and followed his example in electing Walthard, a decision with which each of the leading men then concurred. Walthard immediately received the pastoral staff from the king and swore to support him. Then, as everyone sang praises to the Lord, he was led into the church – it had been built by the king himself and consecrated by Walthard's own predecessor. At this point, I asked the king whether he might intercede with Walthard regarding the needs of my church. As I had requested, he placed me most securely under his protection. Following his own inclination, the king also commended my nephew Dietrich to the archbishop. Furthermore, since he wished to launch another attack on his brothers-in-law, he asked those of his leading men who were present how matters stood in their campaign against Boleslav. The king committed the entire issue to the care of the newly installed bishop, along with all of his property in Saxony. On the same day, we all departed for home [15 June].

CHAPTER SIXTY-EIGHT [1012]

The following Saturday, at the king's command, Bishop Arnulf enthroned Archbishop Walthard at Magdeburg, where both were received with honour and great joy [21 June]. The following day, Walthard was anointed by the venerable Eid, third bishop of the church of Meißen, with help from his fellow bishops, Wigo, Hildeward, and Erich [22 June]. I assisted as well, though most unworthy, and we were aided by Bishop Arnulf. On Monday, we all departed, richly rewarded with expressions of love and magnificent gifts [23 June]. It was now the vigil of St John the Baptist. On this day, Archbishop Walthard installed Reding as provost, following the latter's election by the brothers. On the day of the feast itself, according to custom, he made a solemn procession to the monastery of Berge, where my brother Siegfried and I received him [24 June]. While celebrating mass there, he instructed the people for the first time. Afterwards, the Abbot urged Walthard to join him in a feast, for the sake of fraternal love, but the archbishop refused because of the large crowd that had accompanied him. On the feast of the Apostles, once again at the seat of his bishopric, he addressed salutary admonitions to all who had been committed to his care [29 June].

CHAPTER SIXTY-NINE [1012]

Meanwhile, at the request of messengers sent by Boleslav, Walthard went to Zützen for the purpose of making peace. He was accorded a magnificent reception and remained there for two nights. He returned, having accomplished nothing, but richly rewarded with gifts. Soon it was 24 July, the day on which the proposed military campaign was supposed to begin. We assembled at the village of Schrenz, and from there moved up towards Belgern. Meanwhile, the leading men decided that it would be better to secure the march with troops rather than proceed any farther. During the following night, the archbishop suffered from severe headaches [2 August]. In the morning, I tried to visit him, and had to wait for a long time as he lingered in his tent. When he finally came out, he complained that he was in great pain, but noted his plans to visit the queen, then residing in Merseburg, and promised to speak with me there. After I departed, Walthard celebrated the mass, though previously disinclined to do so, because it was the feast of the first martyr of Christ as well as a Sunday [3 August]. Unfortunately, it was the last time he would perform this task.

CHAPTER SEVENTY [1012]

On Thursday, I arrived at Merseburg [7 August]. There, while my brethren and I were preparing for the archbishop's arrival, messengers informed me that he was ill and had been taken to Giebichenstein in a wagon. The following day, I rode down to see him and encountered Bishop Bernward of Hildesheim, who had been summoned to give his blessing, but also because of his skill in the art of healing [9 August]. Also present was Count Frederick whose brother was Count Dedi.[127] When I entered, the archbishop was seated on a chair and greeted me warmly. Gazing at his feet, he lamented the fact that they were not in their usual swollen state, because when his feet swelled his lower body felt lighter. He then indicated to me that, if he were to survive

127 I.e. Count Frederick of Eilenburg.

this illness, I would find no truer friend than he. I remained with him until evening and then departed, reluctantly, because the following day was the vigil of St Lawrence, Christ's champion, whose feast day would be celebrated on Sunday [9 August; feast day 10 August]. During that celebration, as I was preaching a brief sermon to the assembled congregation, I humbly asked that they offer a common prayer on behalf of the ailing Archbishop.

CHAPTER SEVENTY-ONE [1012]

On Tuesday, before prime, I visited Walthard again [12 August]. This time, Bishop Eid was present and continually offered prayers for him. When I had entered the chamber in which that pious man lay, I no longer heard him speaking and realized that he was no longer entirely conscious. While he still lived, bishops Arnulf, Hildeward, Meinwerk, and Erich arrived and, together, offered him their blessing and absolution. I, though a sinner, anointed the most painful spots with consecrated oil. Duke Jaromir was also present. On Holy Saturday prior to the most recent celebration of the Lord's Resurrection, his brother and retainer, Ulrich, completely unmindful of his debt, had expelled him from the kingdom of the Bohemians [12 April]. The duke then tried to flee to Boleslav who, though close in terms of blood relations, had hitherto treated him as an enemy.[128] Jaromir had hoped that Walthard's intercession would allow him to obtain the king's favour, knowing that he was helpful to all in need and expecting to find him healthy. When he saw how Walthard had declined, however, he tearfully sought to commend himself to his care, and thereby to ours as well. As for the archbishop, I do not know what he saw to his left, but as his end approached, he protected himself by vigorously making the sign of the cross with his right hand. Then, with body and face turned, his face contracted as though he was about to cry, but soon relaxed and seemed happy.

CHAPTER SEVENTY-TWO [1012]

Seeing this, I sadly left the room. Meanwhile, the others realized that his end was imminent and, immediately lifting him off his bed, placed him on a carpet. They then lit candles and summoned me. I now saw

---

128 Boleslav and Jaromir were cousins as the latter's father (Boleslav II of Bohemia) was the brother of Dobrawa, the Polish duke's mother (4.55–56).

him wearing his stole and engaged in his final struggle. As Bishop Eid had stipulated, a cross had been placed on his chest, he held ashes in his hands, and there was a hair-shirt beneath him. On the afternoon of 12 August, as the sun began to decline and the smell of incense enveloped him, Walthard's soul abandoned this meaningless existence and departed for his creator. Everyone offered up tearful prayers on his behalf, but I did not join them, as I ought to have, miserable wretch that I am. I can tell no one what was going through my mind at this time. I say only this: 'Faithful Christians, pray with me that the Lord, from whom nothing can be concealed, does not lay this either to my charge or to his.'

CHAPTER SEVENTY-THREE [1012]

After this, the viscera were removed from Walthard's body and buried between the church and his chamber. The body was prepared for burial and placed before the altar. After celebrating the office of the dead, we ate and, on the same day, transported the body as far as Könnern. Along the way, we were met by his mournful dependants. On the following day, as we arrived at a village near St John's Mount, we encountered the sorrowful community of the clergy [13 August]. There was also a large crowd of Jews, to whom Walthard had been like a father, and a multitude of orphans whose lamentations revealed their sadness.[129] When we entered the cathedral, our funeral procession was received with great sadness by the archbishop's friends and heirs who raised their hands in grief. Who would not have grieved at such a sight! And yet, all these lamentations were not equal to the loss we had suffered.

CHAPTER SEVENTY-FOUR [1012]

We brothers assembled as a chapter and, except for Benno, elected my cousin. Although we knew that the candidate's youth made approval unlikely, we elected him nonetheless, both to preserve our right to do so and especially out of affection for Archbishop Tagino. In the evening, Bishop Arnulf arrived and encouraged us as best he could. On the following day, after the election had been renewed, the archbishop's body was entombed, to the right of his predecessor, in

129 Other examples of Jews participating in the funerals of great churchmen are noted by Blumenkranz 1960: 42–43.

the south transept. It was the vigil of the feast of the Assumption of St Mary [14 August]. As soon as the queen learned of these events, she sent her cup-bearer, Geso, to communicate them to the king, who was camped with his army near the city of Metz. The king was astonished at the news and, after asking how things stood with us, quickly sent Geso to advise the queen that she should see to the welfare of the realm.

CHAPTER SEVENTY-FIVE [1012]

O reader, mark well the archbishop's Epitaph! It should not be inscribed on mere stone, but rather in attentive hearts! Although his name, Walthard, means 'harsh in power', only his exterior was severe. Within, he was exceedingly mild. He regarded God and his neighbour with constant fear and righteous love. He atoned for the weakness of the flesh with an abundance of bitter tears and an indescribable generosity in the distribution of alms. Virtuous in spirit and body, the king held him in high esteem and he was greatly honoured among the leading men of the realm. His lord surpassed him only by virtue of his consecration and office. He was forthright, compassionate, and a vigorous defender of his church. Without a hint of ostentation, he rendered much assistance to his neighbours, but proved to all that he could provide for himself. I frequently heard him swear that personal ambition had not moved him to seek his office, but rather the desire to help his oppressed and virtually exhausted church. He maintained that he was unworthy of this honour and, indeed, that there were two brethren whom he would willingly have elected, if there had been any hope of their being approved. A righteous man who pursued his goals with tenacity, he neither sought praise on his own account, nor denied it to others.[130] He descended from the highest nobility, and in no way diminished the honour he had inherited, but rather enhanced it through his excellent zeal. His father was lord Erp, a man of praiseworthy life and esteemed by all of his contemporaries. His mother, Amalred, surpassed other matrons by virtue of her pious chastity and noble deeds. As much as possible, she devoted herself entirely to her husband's salvation.

130 Horace, *Odes* bk 3, ode 3, verse 1.

CHAPTER SEVENTY-SIX ⌊1012⌋

It had previously been predicted to Walthard that he would receive the archbishopric of Magdeburg and possess it for a short time. In the very year that this prediction was supposed to be fulfilled, his mother, now already dead, appeared in a vision to a certain venerable matron. The matron greeted her and asked how she was. Walthard's mother responded: 'Good,' and added: 'Do you not know that our Archbishop Tagino must migrate from this world? Walthard will succeed him, though not to reign for any length of time, but rather that he may sit among the judges on the last day. In heaven, his deeds have been inscribed upon a silver tablet that is now almost complete. As soon as it is finished, he will be snatched from the eyes of men in order to receive his reward.' Walthard knew all of this in advance, so his lay sister informed me (his other sister was a nun). He summoned this sister, moreover, and said the following to her: 'Do you recall your earlier promise that, if ever you became my heir, you would contribute to my spiritual salvation by giving my property at Olvenstedt to St Maurice?' After she acknowledged and confirmed what he had requested with a raised finger,[131] he tearfully responded: 'My life must now come to an end and it is for you, my sister, to act in accordance with your word. Be assured, however, that I will not take any of the remaining property from you.' He knew that all of these things had to happen, but hoped for more time.

CHAPTER SEVENTY-SEVEN [1012]

He was provost for twenty-eight years and bore both the title and the office more honourably than all of his contemporaries. To hold the relics of saints, he had a large sarcophagus made out of silver. After a great fire in the city had destroyed the round church, he rebuilt it from the ground up.[132] He had intended to install a community of canons there and had wanted to bestow upon it the property we have already mentioned. Though a man of few words, he instinctively knew whatever needed to be said and at the appropriate time. His only real complaint was that he had not consecrated any churches or clergy. In regard to the pallium, he had no regrets.[133] He procured

---

131 I.e. using a customary gesture associated with the swearing of oaths (Schmidt-Wiegand 1982: 376).

132 The church is also mentioned at 7.55.

an indescribable number of books and liturgical utensils, as well as a variety of secular things. Following his sudden death, all of this was scattered by many unsuitable hands.[134]

CHAPTER SEVENTY-EIGHT [1012]

I have said all of this so that no one will wonder about his sudden death, either openly or in secret, or think that he was in any way responsible for it. Many before him occupied their sees for more than thirty years, but were no more deserving, whether in this world or the next. Alas, there are some who travel this earthly pilgrimage for a long time, but waste their efforts in evil deeds. More praiseworthy are those who, with care and solicitude, devote whatever time is conceded to them to the service of Christ. Evil deeds increase the penalties suffered by the doer. For those whose earthly lives are abbreviated, assuming they are guilty, a quick repayment of their misdeeds awaits. All good people, however, will share equally in the eternal joy of heaven, even if they were not equal in this world. Indeed, Walthard was not alone in possessing his office for only a short time. We read that Tertullian was made a priest by Pope Stephen and then, only four days later, was martyred by a tyrant for the love of Christ and the constancy of his faith.[135] He retained each of these dignities for eternity. Walthard paid for his sins and God quickly rewarded him for his righteous labours. This was revealed to many, in incidents too numerous to recount. Instead, I will describe my own experience. May God be my witness! I will not lie!

CHAPTER SEVENTY-NINE [1012]

I was on guard duty at Meißen when that venerable man appeared to me, on the feast day of the Apostles Simon and Jude, just after matins [28 October]. Since I knew the dead man well, I immediately asked how things were with him. He said: 'I have been punished, as I deserved,

---

133 The papal bull authorizing Walthard's use of the pallium was issued only after the archbishop had already died (27/28 August, *UBM* 131).

134 Perhaps a reference to the customary, though unsanctioned, practice of plundering dead churchmen. See Fichtenau 1991: 214–16; and more general comments by Elze 1978: 9–12; and Ginzburg et al. 1991: 20–41.

135 The martyrologies of Ado and Notker list a St Tertulinus who was martyred in this fashion under the emperor Valerian (Ado, 4 August, p. 248; Notker, 4 August, p. 1132).

but all of that is behind me now.' I immediately rejoiced at this, and said: 'May I ring the bells and urge the people to praise God?' He responded: 'Certainly, because it is true.' Then, continuing the conversation, I said: 'Did you know that the king has turned against you? Indeed, it is widely rumoured that, following your ordination, you intended to work against him in many different ways.' At that, he said repeatedly: 'Believe me, I pray you, believe that I am not guilty of this!' When I wished to ask him why he had died so suddenly, I awoke, and so was not permitted to learn this. Reliable witnesses have informed me that, on the feast of All Saints, he was found worthy to appear before the face of God. Whatever I have said about Walthard has nothing to do with personal affection. Prior to his consecration, he actually held me in only moderate esteem, and in defending his own church, created many obstacles for mine. Rather, I have said all of this for the sake of truth and to avoid any reproach in the future (and I have said less than I could have), since none of his successors was any better. Following Walthard's burial, we sent Bishop Erich to share the results of our election with the king. I also gave him a letter in which I described the damage to my church and asked the king for help.

CHAPTER EIGHTY [1012]

Upon learning of the archbishop's death, Boleslav [Chrobry] assembled an army and attacked Lebusa. He even set up camp there, knowing that the flood waters of the Elbe would prevent us from coming to its aid. His warriors approached, eager for battle, but encountered little resistance from the defenders. No more than one thousand men defended this burg although three times that number would barely have sufficed. While still sitting at his morning meal, Boleslav watched as his victorious followers joyfully entered the burg. The door was opened and the blood of many was spilled. Among the most prestigious captives were Gunzelin, Wiso, and Isich, the commander of the burg, who had also been wounded. For whatever reason, the burg had been entrusted to Isich's protection, but he had finally lost it, not through cowardice but rather through wretched misfortune. All of these men were brought before their proud conqueror who immediately ordered that they be taken away and carefully guarded. Among the duke's followers, no fewer than five hundred remained on the field of battle. This miserable slaughter took place on 20 August.[136]

136 The large number of casualties is noted in the necrology at Merseburg (*NMer.*, 20 August, fo. 5r, p. 11).

After the booty had been divided and the burg set afire, the victorious army departed for home, amid much rejoicing, and accompanied by its lord.

CHAPTER EIGHTY-ONE [1012]

Messengers hurried to Merseburg to inform the queen of these events. I first learned of them at Magdeburg where, at Provost Reding's request and despite my unworthiness, I consecrated two altars on 22 August. One of these altars was located at the archbishop's resting place, the other was on the north side of the church. Upon hearing the news, I hurried off to see the queen who ordered me and all my countrymen to take up position on the Mulde, and to have everything in readiness for the king's arrival. Meanwhile, the king had returned from his western campaign and was trying to appoint his chaplain, Gero, to the now vacant office of archbishop. Bishop Erich came to him, but got no hearing for the message he had brought. Then, my cousin Dietrich was summoned to Grone where the king accepted him into his service, in Gero's place. On the feast of St Matthew the Apostle, the king came to Seehausen [21 September]. I also went to Seehausen. At an appropriate moment, in the presence of all who had assembled there, I asked the king to discuss with his candidate the matter of my diocese and the various properties unjustly taken from me. I also requested that he do this before making him archbishop. He then took me under his protection so that these issues might be resolved through a legal proceeding or in some other beneficial way. On the following day, the king came to Magdeburg and ordered all of us to gather in the canons' refectory. There, at the king's request, and without prejudice to any future election, we elected Gero who thereupon commended himself to the altar and was accepted by the chapter in return for a gift of ten manses. The king granted him his pastoral staff and Bishop Eid immediately enthroned and anointed him with assistance from us, his brethren. The king remained in Magdeburg for the feast of the Theban martyrs [22 September]. Thereafter, both he and his entourage were honoured by the archbishop with splendid gifts. They then moved on to Merseburg, remaining there for some time so that the king could discuss the welfare of the realm with his leading men.

CHAPTER EIGHTY-TWO [1012]

In this year, Bishop Erluin of Cambrai died along with the illustrious Dukes, Conrad and Herman 'the Child'.[137] A certain monk who suffered from a severe illness had visions in which many things were revealed to him. While he related these matters to them, those who were present recorded them in writing. All of this was thought to be quite miraculous. In those days, as well, two brothers were born with teeth, and with faces similar to that of a goose.[138] One of them had only half of a right arm which, moreover, looked like the wing of a goose. Three days after their birth, as the populace debated their fate, both died with smiles on their faces. One day, a *miles* who had seized the property of St Clement and refused to offer satisfaction was attacked in his chamber by an indescribable number of mice. At first, he tried to fight them off with his fist, and then attacked them with his naked sword, but without success. Finally, at his request, he was enclosed in a chest that had been suspended in mid-air by a rope. When the plague outside subsided and it was time to free him, it was discovered that he had been gnawed to death by still other mice. Thus it was revealed both to his contemporaries and to future generations that the vengeful anger of God alone had consumed him as payment for his crime.

CHAPTER EIGHTY-THREE [1012]

Meanwhile, Jaromir, of whom I spoke, humbly sought the king's favour.[139] *Instead of mercy and restitution, however, he found exile and imprisonment with Bishop Adalbold, Bishop Ansfrid's successor.*[140] *Such punishment was due to Jaromir for having slaughtered the Bavarians as they were bringing gifts to Boleslav, and for having killed persons entrusted to his care, but not because of any disloyalty to the king. Our enemies made sport of us when they heard the news, but our countrymen feared that it would not be to their advantage. Those who gave such advice to our king should themselves experience the results of this deed. After this, at the king's invitation, Jaromir's brother, Ulrich, came to Merseburg.*[141] *There, the kingdom he had unlawfully seized was willingly conveyed to him as a gift. At the same time, alas, there*

137 Duke Conrad of Carinthia, and Herman III of Swabia.
138 Cf. *AQ,* an. 1012, p. 81.
139 6.71.
140 Bishop Adalbold of Utrecht (1010–26).
141 Duke Ulrich of Bohemia (1012–34).

was much destruction due to flooding, the result of frequent downpours, and an invasion of pirates. With the Danube flooding in Bavaria, and the waters of the Rhine covering the land, an unspeakable number of people, cattle, and houses were destroyed. Indeed, the force of the flood uprooted a large number of trees. The inhabitants of these regions asserted that neither they nor their ancestors had ever experienced such a thing. Lamenting that this had occurred because of their many sins, they feared that something worse was still to come. Yet, after this long digression, I should return to my theme.

CHAPTER EIGHTY-FOUR [1012]

After departing from Merseburg, the king went by boat to Arneburg. He discussed many things with the Slavs who had gathered there. When he had established peace, he returned and celebrated the feast of All Saints in Helmstedt [1 November]. He then hurried to visit the western regions.

Meanwhile, the lady Liudgard was very ill and sent a messenger to summon me. She was especially close to me and, as I have already mentioned, we were joined by bonds of consanguinity.[142] I arrived at her resting place, in Wolmirstedt, after sundown. When I entered her chamber, however, I saw that her suffering was great and that, because of this, she continually recited the psalms. Above all, she spoke and thought on these words: 'Your right hand receives me, O Lord, they that seek my soul do so in vain.'[143] To me she offered not a single word, but when I asked if she wished to be anointed with oil, she responded: 'Gladly, because afterwards I will quickly be subsumed in the will of Christ.' When she had been prepared with fresh clothing, she summoned me. Then, after everything relating to the anointment had been correctly performed, I said to her: 'How beautiful you are now!' She responded: 'I see a handsome youth to my right.' She indicated the direction with her eyes. After this, I withdrew and, being fatigued from my journey, slept for a long time. When I awakened, I heard her groaning heavily with pain and, quickly going to her, sang the psalter until it became clear to all of us that her end was at hand. After all of the appropriate prayers had been said, her blessed soul, invited by the saints themselves, made its transit to the chamber of her heavenly bridegroom. It was 13 November.[144]

142 1.13.
143 Ps. 62: 9–10 (RSV 63: 8–9).
144 *NMer.*, fo. 7r, p. 15.

CHAPTER EIGHTY-FIVE [1012]

While on his sick bed, a certain layman among the citizens of Magde-burg predicted her death, saying: 'Lady Liudgard will depart from this world, and whoever merits to follow her path will be truly blessed.' At dawn, we accompanied her body to Walbeck [14 November]. The following day, we buried her on the northern side of the monastery, at the final resting place of Father Liuthard who had been enclosed there for twenty-six years [15 November]. Her husband's grief at her death was indescribable. She had been the faithful guardian of his life and soul, devoting herself to the service of God more for his sake than her own. Above all, she protected him from the plots of the enemy by fasting in the cold, through her constant prayer, and by distributing alms. For my contemporaries' sake, as well as for future generations, I declare that God does not disdain any good deed performed by the faithful on someone else's behalf. If one performs the deed with devotion, moreover, it makes no difference that it is of no use to the intended beneficiary.

CHAPTER EIGHTY-SIX [1012]

In January, during the first year of Henry's reign, and following the death of her father, Liudgard returned to the husband from whom she had been separated unjustly for a long time.[145] Following the marriage, while residing in the West, Margrave Liuthar became ill after overindulging in the Pauline drink.[146] He died unexpectedly on 25 January [1003]. As he had requested, he was buried in Cologne, in the southern part of the church, at the place where penitents appear on Maundy Thursday. For the sake of his salvation, his widow, Godila, constantly performed as many good deeds as she could. For her son, she acquired his father's benefice and march with a payment of 200 talents. She remained unmarried for four years, but then married her relative, Herman, doing this without regard for the ban imposed by Bishop Arnulf and heedless of a promise to three bishops who forbade this in the name of God [1007].[147] Because of this, the bishop struck her with the sword of excommunication and, thereafter, she was denied any hope of future offspring.

---

145 4.42.

146 1 Tim. 5: 23.

147 Holtzmann (1935: 378, n. 1) identifies the Herman in question as Count Herman II of Werl.

CHAPTER EIGHTY-SEVEN [1012]

But I am wandering, and gradually deviating from my theme. I shall therefore return to the subject of King Henry's excellent manner of life. For the purpose of condemning Bishop Dietrich of Metz, he held a great synod at which all the bishops in attendance forbade the accused to celebrate the mass until he had justified himself [10 November].[148] After this, the king celebrated the joyful feast of the Lord's birth, at Pöhlde.[149] During that same visit, Walker, a servant of the church of Trier and loyal guardian of the royal chapel, became ill and had to remain when the rest of us moved on. Alas, he died on 11 January [1013].

CHAPTER EIGHTY-EIGHT [1013]

Meanwhile, after a long illness, Archbishop Liawizo of Bremen awaited the end of his life with pious solicitude. On the night preceding his last day, he addressed the following words to his companions, now exhausted from many vigils: 'O dearest brethren and sons, that you may not doubt the clemency of heaven, and that your labours may be somewhat relieved, I shall speak of my own life which, in turn, may provide you with a trustworthy model. When Pope Benedict was an exile in these parts, I wished to seek him out, but my intentions were repeatedly obstructed by others.[150] And yet, I did not at all agree with their friendly warnings. I devoted myself to him as long as he lived. Following his death, I became the trusted servant of my lord Adaldag and, in consideration of this, he entrusted me with the care of his paupers. Then, he made me his chamberlain. Finally, this pious man

148 A somewhat more detailed account is preserved in the annals of Quedlinburg: 'Travelling to Koblenz, King Henry held a great synod on the feast of St Martin, at which he planned to accomplish many things. In particular, it was his intent to condemn Bishop Dietrich of Metz, and others who had rebelled against him, if they refused to surrender. Being somewhat fearful of the king's judgement, the rebels sent representatives to ask for forgiveness. The king was still smarting from a recent attack, however, and would not comply with their request. Nevertheless, on the advice of his loyal followers, he granted them permission to meet with him at Mainz. Some neglected to come, others, as was proper, complied with the king's order. When they returned to their homes, they were unable to report the good news of a complete peace, but rather anticipated that those who had offered their oaths would be hanged nonetheless' (*AQ*, an. 1012, p. 81).

149 It was on this occasion that the 'anti-pope' Gregory appeared to complain that he had been unjustly expelled from Rome by Pope Benedict VIII (see 6.101).

150 See 4.18.

made his way to the heavenly homeland that he had always desired. I succeeded him, though unworthy, by virtue of your unanimous election and through the gift of the king. For the love of Christ, let us offer mutual and heartfelt forgiveness for all the misdeeds we have committed against each other. If we part from one another in perfect peace, we may well deserve to meet again on the last day. At the end of my life, I offer you this salutary advice: For the welfare of our homeland, you should unanimously choose Otto, a member of your chapter, as rector of our church.[151] And, you should beseech the grace of God, in whose hand is the heart of the king, that he may find this agreeable.' They all listened to his exhortations and unanimously promised him their support and devotion. On the following day, a Sunday, that blessed father raised his arms and commended both his flock and his soul to the highest shepherd. He died on 4 January and went to that place which had been his goal even while he lived. He was one of that number who, to the astonishment of the prophet, flew to their windows as if they were clouds and doves.[152] Even while he lived, strangers thought that he resembled nothing less than a corpse, due to his constant vigils and fasts. He never approached the altar without gifts. He also provided continual guidance to his people and gave cheerfully to all. God was so pleased with him, moreover, that his bishopric remained unharmed amid the constant incursions of savage pirates.

CHAPTER EIGHTY-NINE [1013]

Meanwhile, the king departed from Allstedt where he had celebrated the Lord's Epiphany [6 January] and had received messengers from Boleslav who asked for a truce and promised that Miesco, Boleslav's son, would confirm it. Then, the king came to Merseburg where he learned of Archbishop Liawizo's death. Although he lamented the loss to our own age, he expressed gratitude for his future intervention. He celebrated the archbishop's memory with great enthusiasm. After this, he left us and celebrated the Purification of the holy Mother of God at Magdeburg [2 February]. On the same day, that Otto of whom we have already spoken appeared with an entourage of clerics and laymen. With the help of trustworthy intercessors, as previously, he humbly sought the king's favour for the completion of the election.

151 Cf. Adam 2.29, pp. 89–90; Tschan (trans.) 1959: 74.
152 Isa. 60: 8.

But the king did not listen. Instead, he gave the bishopric to his chaplain, Unwan, a decision to which the legation gave its consent, even if not spontaneously.[153] The king took Otto into his service and tried to mollify him with the promise of his favour. Then, at the king's order and in his presence, and with the consent and assistance of Bishops Ekkehard and Thorgut, Archbishop Gero presided over Unwan's consecration as archbishop.[154]

CHAPTER NINETY [1013]

After a few days, Boleslav's son, Miesco [II], arrived bearing splendid gifts. He became the king's man and swore an oath of loyalty to him. Then, he was sent off with great honour and satisfaction so that he would come again. In those days, after sundown, a great storm raged and greatly disturbed all of us. Indeed, it destroyed a church, located outside the city, which had been constructed of red wood during the reign of the first Otto. A fire also destroyed much of the archbishop's property. Furthermore, it came to the king's attention that my cousin Werner, and Ekkehard, the brother of Margrave Herman, had visited Boleslav without permission and said many things contrary to the king's favour. Here, in our homeland, they had secretly received Boleslav's messengers. The king took all of this very seriously and ordered both men to appear before him. When they did not dare to comply, all their property was confiscated and they were declared guilty of resisting the king's power. Nevertheless, by offering land and gold, my cousin managed to regain both the king's favour and the right to remain within the realm. Ekkehard was only restored to grace much later, through faithful intercession. In that same year, on 18 March, the hermit Wonlef died. He was a true Israelite.[155]

CHAPTER NINETY-ONE [1013]

During the following Lent, the king came to Werla where he suffered from an extended attack of colic and had visions in which many things were revealed to him. Finally, through the tears and prayers of many, he recovered his health. There was no longer enough time for him to

---

153 Archbishop Unwan of Hamburg-Bremen (1013–29).

154 Bishops Ekkehard of Schleswig and Thorgaut of Skara in Sweden. On the latter see Adam 2.58, p. 119.

155 John 1: 47. Wonlef was founder of the hermitage Wonlefsrode.

reach his intended destination.[156] Hence, he celebrated the paschal feast at Paderborn, with appropriate solemnity, in the company of Meinwerk with whom he was very close [5 April]. He spent Pentecost with us [24 May]. Boleslav arrived on the vigil of this feast, having left hostages at home to guarantee his safety [23 May]. He was accorded the best reception. On the feast day itself, he commended himself into the king's hands and became his man. After swearing an oath, Boleslav acted as the king's arms-bearer as he processed to the church while wearing the crown. On Monday, he appeased the king by bestowing magnificent gifts that came not only from him, but also from his wife.[157] He received much better and more through the king's largesse, and also obtained the long-desired benefice. His hostages were thereupon released, with honour, and in a friendly manner. Afterwards, with our help, he attacked Russia and laid waste to a good part of its territory. When a fight broke out between his own people and the generally hospitable Petchenegs, he ordered all of the latter to be slaughtered, even though they had supported him.

In those days, Abbot Branthog of Fulda was deposed and succeeded by the *conversus*, Poppo, then pastor of Lorsch.[158] Thereafter, as the brethren scattered far and wide, the monastery's previous status was altered. In the same year, in Duke Bernhard's burg, Lüneburg, there was marvellous change and motion of the air and a great opening appeared in the earth. This astonished the residents, who swore that they had never seen anything like it before.

CHAPTER NINETY-TWO

While travelling in the regions to the west, the king made preparations for his trip to Lombardy and returned again to us. From thence, on 21 September, he set forth for the place called [lacuna], hastening through the lands of the Bavarians and Swabians. From all directions, the army converged on this place and duly expressed its desire to render assistance. Without a hint of anxiety, the king then went on to Rome. The queen accompanied him. Although his support

---

156 Aachen, according to *AQ* an. 1013, p. 81.

157 Emnilde (4.58).

158 Abbot Branthog of Fulda (1011–13) was later elevated to the episcopacy as bishop of Halberstadt (1023–36). Poppo was deemed a *conversus* because he had been a layman prior to becoming abbot of Lorsch, an office which he retained in conjunction with the abbacy of Fulda.

for this trip had already been requested, Boleslav did nothing and, as usual, was revealed as a liar despite his attractive promises. Moreover, in a letter to the pope, he had complained that the king's secret plots prevented him from paying the tax he had promised to St Peter, Prince of the Apostles. Then, he sent spies to find out how the king was held in these parts and, wherever possible, lure men away from his favour. Thus did he show his respect for God, and thus did he seek the intervention of pious men! So firm was the faith of the celebrated warrior and so did he observe his terrible oaths! Observe, dear reader, how the king acted in the course of so many shameful acts. If he either recognized that he had greatly sinned or knew of any justifiable complaint against him, he ordered the canons to be placed before him so that he could discover how this sin ought to be emended. Then, in accordance with those writings, he immediately set about correcting whatever crime had been committed. Nevertheless, he is still more inclined to sin recklessly than to remain in salutary penance.

CHAPTER NINETY-THREE

Arduin, Boleslav's equal and virtual colleague, falsely called king by the Lombards, was aggrieved at the arrival of the great king and at the power of his army. Having no confidence in the ability of his own forces to do battle with them, however, he immediately withdrew to the protection of a burg. He lamented merely this, that the king had been called and elevated to a greater dignity. After deliberating long and angrily, Arduin sent legates to the king to ask if a certain countship would be given to him in return for a promise to surrender not only his crown and but also his son. The king trusted his advisers and refused this offer, thereby causing his supporters to suffer grievously. Later, he himself recognized this. I will explain all of this below.

CHAPTER NINETY-FOUR

Before I take up these matters, however, I will add to my text a few things that were omitted owing to my forgetfulness. Among my contemporaries and fellow students there was a certain Brun, a scion of the most noble lineage, who nonetheless surpassed any of his relatives because, among all the children of God, he had been singled out by divine love. He was particularly loved by his venerable mother, Ida, who sent him to Master Geddo to be educated in philosophy.[159] Everything that he needed he received in abundance. His father was Brun, an illustrious and praiseworthy lord. He was my friend by virtue of our blood relationship, but was very friendly to everyone else as well. In the morning, before leaving the hospice to go to school, Brun's like-named son would ask for some time to himself so that, while we played, he could devote himself to prayer. He preferred work to leisure, and so bore fruit and grew to maturity. He was admired by Otto III who took him into his service. Not long afterwards, however, he left the king's service to pursue a life of solitude and lived by his own labours. Following the death of that most glorious emperor, when Henry II ruled by the grace of God, Brun came to Merseburg, with the pope's permission, to ask for the office of bishop. At the pope's command, he was consecrated by Archbishop Tagino and also received the pallium which he had brought with him.[160] Then, for the profit of his soul, he took upon himself the labour of a long and wide-ranging trip, while constantly chastising his body with fasts and torturing it with vigils. He received many gifts from Boleslav and other wealthy people, but quickly divided them among churches, his companions, and the poor, retaining nothing for himself.

CHAPTER NINETY-FIVE

In the twelfth year of his most excellent conversion, Brun *travelled* to Prussia. He hoped to make this sterile land bear fruit by sowing a divine seed, but could not easily soften that horrid place, bristling with thorns.[161] Later, while he was trying to preach near the border between this land and Russia, the residents first forbade him to do so, and then, when he continued evangelizing, seized him. For the love of Christ, the head of the church, Brun was himself beheaded on 14 February, meek as a lamb, and accompanied by his eighteen companions.[162] The bodies of so many martyrs remained unburied until Boleslav, being informed of this, ransomed them and thereby secured the solace of his house for the future. These events occurred in the

159 Geddo (d. 1016) succeeded Ekkehard the Red as master of the school at Magdeburg and later became the cathedral's custodian (7.35).

160 Probably in August or November 1004 (6, 10, or 16), when the king resided in Merseburg (Holtzmann 1935: 387, n. 9).

161 Matt. 13: 3–8.

162 The actual date of the martyrdom appears to have been 9 March. See, e.g., *AQ*, an. 1009, p. 80.

time of that most serene King Henry. Through the triumph of such a great bishop, omnipotent God had both honoured and, as I hope, saved him. Much later, the bishop's father became ill and, as he himself told me, was advised by his son to receive the habit of a monk. He slept in peace on 19 October.[163]

CHAPTER NINETY-SIX [1013]

The arrogance of Gero's retainers can scarcely be accepted. The faithful Christian should be astounded at it and avoid it for the sake of piety.[164] Let us first present the case, and then judge whether it is worthy of praise or should be detested by all. Bishop Arnulf came to Gernrode, having been invited by Abbess Hathui to dine with her on the feast day of the martyr Cyriacus [16 March]. On the holy day itself, as the mass ended and Arnulf was leaving the church, he spotted a priest holding a hawk on his hand. Indignant, he put his arm around the man and tried to lead him away, his intention being to offer some constructive criticism rather than inflict any punishment. As quickly as a rumour flies, however, the previously mentioned *milites* gathered together.[165] Their leader, Hugal, approached the bishop and asked why he wished to dishonour their lord. The bishop responded, saying: 'What have I done? I witnessed an offence against Christ and, as it occurred in my bishopric, could not ignore it.[166] Nothing bad has happened here. Only let us meet on a day acceptable to you and I will offer appropriate restitution, assuming that I am found guilty by friends known to both of us.' But Hugal continued, saying: 'It must not and will not be as you have said. You must immediately purify yourself with an oath, or promise that you will compensate both my lord and us.' At this, the bishop declared: 'On this holy feast, I am forbidden to swear an oath, and you are forbidden to accept one [16 March]. And I find it most deplorable that you would deny me alone the right to a judgement.'

163 *NMer.*, fo. 6v, p. 14.

164 Arrogance was never in short supply among the aristocracy, but lingering ambiguity regarding Gernrode's status may represent the more fundamental cause of this confrontation between the community's diocesan ordinary and a magnate who may have been its advocate and was undoubtedly the closest surviving relative of its founder (2.19; Schulze 1965: 18, 70; Lippelt 1973: 125–26).

165 Virgil, *Aeneid* 11.139.

166 Referring to the priest with the hawk.

CHAPTER NINETY-SEVEN [1018]

After this, Hugal went away angry and, unbeknownst to the margrave, assembled a band of armed men. The bishop saw them all coming as he was preparing to dine. The house in which he presently resided was then secured by his companions, and fortified in every way, so that his enemies could not enter without difficulty. As Hugal and his men prepared to storm the building, they were told, in all honesty, that the bishop had left and was nowhere to be found. They then sought him in the cloister and even in the church. By the grace of God, however, he stayed hidden – with no dishonour to himself – and observed all of this without being discovered. Finally, the uproar subsided. The bishop's enemies returned to their hospice and then departed for their homes, greatly disappointed. On the following day, Arnulf summoned his *milites*, returned to the seat of his bishopric, and comforted the weeping abbess [17 March].

CHAPTER NINETY-EIGHT [1013]

When the king learned of these events, he ordered the perpetrators to appear before him. The margrave, realizing that the king was very angry, tried to placate him through trustworthy intercessors. The king agreed to listen, but with the provision that three hundred pounds of silver would first have to be paid to the bishop's tribunal. Furthermore, anyone found culpable in the dispute would have to purge himself by means of an oath, with the support of twelve oath-helpers, or else render satisfaction in accordance with the canons. After a mutual peace had been established, it was agreed that the judgement would be carried out after Easter [5 April]. Our supporters and theirs assembled at Halberstadt, I along with them. To accept the stipulated payment, the bishop went to the western part of the cathedral where he sat on a throne placed at the top of a flight of stairs. There too the margrave, alone, purged himself of guilt with a most credible oath. In turn, the bishop imposed the penance of a fast on each of the margrave's retainers, this with the provision that the burden would be assumed at such time as he might demand it.

CHAPTER NINETY-NINE [1014]

Here, I must add that Duke Ulrich of the Bohemians, whose name means 'mammon of iniquity', ordered that his celebrated warrior,

Boso, be put to death along with many others.[167] He did this because he had heard false rumours that they were giving aid to his exiled brother. From these murders, all should carefully learn how to protect themselves in the future. Because of blind ambition, that which the Lord strongly orders to be observed, in both testaments, cannot be fulfilled in those regions. Ulrich feared his brother, though he should have loved him above all, and was always concerned to keep him at a distance. At one time, during the reign of Duke Swentepolk, the Bohemians were our rulers.[168] Indeed, our ancestors paid an annual tribute to the duke and he had bishops in his land, which is called Moravia. He and his successors lost all of this because of their excessive pride since, as the gospel testifies, humility always increases while the height of arrogance declines.[169] Without the greatest fear, no one can rule in those lands. Falsehood reigns there, in alliance with deceit, and pure love laments an outcast.

CHAPTER ONE HUNDRED

I have already spoken of our universal pope, Bruno, but only mentioned his successor, Gerbert. It would be appropriate for me to say something more about the latter. He was born in the western regions and, finally, but illegally, promoted to rulership over the city of Reims.[170] He was particularly skilled in discerning the movements of the stars and surpassed his contemporaries in his knowledge of various arts. When he was driven from his diocese, he sought out Emperor Otto. He resided with him at Magdeburg for some time and there built an oralogium, positioning it correctly, after he had observed through a tube the star that sailors use for guidance [14 June–1 July].[171] After Pope Gregory died, he was made pope, by the grace of the emperor. He reigned, under the name Sylvester, up to the time of King Henry.[172] John Fasan, that is, 'the rooster', followed him

---

167 Luke 16: 9.
168 Duke of Great Moravia (870–94).
169 Matt. 23: 12.
170 Gerbert was abbot of Bobbio (982–99) and Archbishop of Reims (991–98). The validity of his election was disputed by supporters of Archbishop Arnulf (989–1021).
171 BU 1229a.
172 After briefly serving as archbishop of Ravenna (998–999), Gerbert was elected pope as Sylvester II (2 April 999–12 May 1003).

on the apostolic throne and ruled during the days allotted to him.[173] During his reign, the authority of his privileges restored and strengthened the church of Merseburg. He was succeeded by Sergius, known as the 'Hog's snout', and Benedict, two significant supporters of our church.[174]

CHAPTER ONE HUNDRED AND ONE

All of these popes greatly desired the king's advent, but the hostility of various enemies long delayed it. May Omnipotent God be blessed in all his works! He who has deigned to send such a pastor to console and pacify Rome, oppressed constantly and for so many years! Indeed, Benedict had prevailed over a certain Gregory in the papal election. Because of this, Gregory came to the king in Pöhlde wearing full papal regalia, and sadly complained to everyone about his expulsion from the city. After taking custody of his cross and ordering him to abstain from all official duties, the king promised that, upon his arrival in the city, he would carefully decide the issue according to Roman custom. The long-desired day quickly arrived. Pope Benedict now ruled more forcefully than any of his predecessors. In February, he received King Henry in the Romulan city, with indescribable honour [1014]. And the king was made advocate of St Peter.

CHAPTER ONE HUNDRED AND TWO

Before speaking of King Henry's second ordination, it would first be appropriate for me to praise the one through whose grace this gift has been bestowed. *As Paul, the teacher of the gentiles, instructs us: Brethren, give thanks to God the Father above all and in all! For this is his will in our Lord, Jesus Christ'.*[175] *It is also right that we praise King Henry who*

173 Pope John XVIII (1003–9), a Roman and erstwhile cardinal priest of St Peter, was elevated to the papal throne during the period of John II Crescenzio's dominance of the city. To the extent that it was feasible, he pursued a policy of cooperation with Henry II that included confirmation of the restoration of Merseburg and of the foundation of Bamberg (*LMA*, vol. 5, p. 543; *DHP* 940–41).

174 Pope Sergius IV 'Boccaporco' (1009–12), former bishop of Albano, was elected pope at the instigation of John II Crescenzio, but also pursued a policy of cooperation with the Ottonians. In particular, he confirmed the possessions of the restored bishopric of Merseburg and Benedict VIII's (1012–24) privileges for Bamberg (*LMA*, vol. 7, pp. 1787–88; *DHP* 1567–68). On Benedict VIII see also note at 7.1.

175 Eph. 4: 20; 1. Thes. 5: 18.

has done so much for us, by the gift and grace of the eternal king. King Henry endowed our church with many useful things, liturgical objects above all. From each of his estates in Thuringia and Saxony, moreover, he gave us two families.[176] *He also gave us a gospel book decorated with gold and an ivory tablet, a gold chalice decorated with gems, with a paten and fistula, two silver crosses and lamps, a large chalice also made of silver, and yet another paten and fistula. Whatever property had been neglected by my predecessors was restored at his order.*

---

176 D H II 221 (Merseburg 28 July 1010). This diploma also conveys a certain royal serf named Ezeka, along with her sons and daughters.

BOOK SEVEN

Whomever heaven praises, we servants should also venerate,
Singing worthy odes from our hearts.
For God is triune but of one nature,
And no one may rule without him,
That beneficent God, the highest good, who dispels all wickedness;[1]
And, from heaven, provides all of our needs.
His truth now confounds the lying testimony of those
Who say that King Henry will not acquire the imperial dignity,
or rule for any length of time, but much more, suffer a most cruel
    death.
He has now presided over the kingdom for two times six years,
An excellent ruler, ascending the imperial throne,
In the very month in which he freed my throne.
That bright day should be distinguished with an equally bright
    marker,[2]
since it was then that Rome bowed before our most generous king.
He himself, anointed with holy oil, rejoiced
And rendered heartfelt thanks to that God who, from on high,
had visited both him and his dear wife, Cunegunde.
Our highest pastor rejoices, and his choir sings,
because they will enjoy safety under such a ruler.
Merseburg, you too should sing, along with all the others.

CHAPTER ONE [1014]

Since the Incarnation of the Lord *a full millennium* and thirteen years
had passed and from the following year two months and three weeks.
In the thirteenth year of his reign, on Sunday, the fourteenth day of
February, Henry, by the grace of God a most celebrated king, and his
esteemed wife, Cunegunde, came to the church of St Peter where the

---

1 *Ecbasis Captivi* 749.
2 Martial, *Epigrammata* 9.52.4.

pope awaited them.[3] The king was accompanied by twelve senators, *of whom six were shaved, according to some mysterious custom, while the rest had full beards and walked with staffs.*[4] Before entering the church, he was asked by the pope if he wished to be the patron and defender of the Roman church, faithful in all respects to him and to all of his successors. After responding with a pious oath, he and his wife were anointed and crowned by the pope. He ordered that his previous crown be suspended over the altar. On the same day, the pope hosted a banquet to celebrate the coronation. On the eighth day, a great commotion arose between the Romans and our people on the bridge over the Tiber. Many on both sides fell and only night brought an end to the fighting. The authors of this affair were three brothers, *Hugo, Azzo, and Adalbert*, who afterwards were captured and detained in custody.[5] Of these, one escaped, the second was taken to *Fulda*, and the third was confined at the fortress of Giebichenstein for a long time.

CHAPTER TWO [1014]

Caesar again ordered that his brother, Arnulf, whom he had previously installed in the church of Ravenna, be consecrated and enthroned by the pope.[6] At first, he wanted to degrade the usurper

3 Actually the twelfth year, but Thietmar apparently reckoned the entire year, 1002, as the first of Henry's reign rather than beginning with 7 June, the day of his coronation (5.11; Holtzmann 1935: 396, n. 3). The change in Henry's status was quickly noted in his public *acta*. On 15 February, a diploma issued for the monarch's foundation at Bamberg, a church dedicated to the quintessentially Roman saints Peter and Paul(!), refers to him as *August Emperor of the Romans* (D H II 283). Pope Benedict VIII (1012–24), second son of the count of Tusculum, successfully asserted his claim to the throne against that of Pope Gregory VI, albeit with imperial help (*LMA*, vol. 1, p. 1859, *DHP* 202–3; *DBI*, vol. 8, pp. 350–54). Benedict owed his position to Henry II (6.101) and, as Thietmar suggests, went out of his way to reciprocate. Other sources note, for example, that the pope hosted a banquet at the Lateran and that an epidemic broke out among the German troops (BG 1800b.)

4 Various explanations have been offered for this custom which is mentioned only by Thietmar. The twelve 'senators' may represent the various urban districts or perhaps refer to the lictors who customarily accompanied the emperors of classical Antiquity (see Eichmann 1942: 1, 187).

5 I.e. 'Hug, Hecil, ac Ecilin'. The correct names of the rebels are supplied by Arnulf of Milan whose chronicle of the deeds of his city's archbishops dates from *c.*1072 (Arnulf 1.18, p. 11; *LMA*, vol. 1, p. 1019).

6 Henry's brother was the illegitimate son of Duke Henry 'the Quarrelsome'. The clergy and aristocracy of Ravenna had elected Arnulf's rival, Adalbert, during the confusion following Otto III's death, presumably with the intention of reasserting

Adalbert who had long occupied that see unjustly but he was moved by the constant entreaties of pious men and so installed him in an another church, *called Arezzo. In Ravenna, through the judgement of a synod, the pope deposed two bishops who had been consecrated by Archbishop Leo, now dead, and at Rome the same number. He renewed the institutions of the fathers in regard to sacred orders, long neglected there and unfortunately among us as well, and he restored the threat of excommunication. Namely, the canons prohibit a deacon from being ordained before his twenty-fifth year, a priest or bishop before his thirtieth.*[7] *Because we have not maintained this, we are wretched sinners and fall into excommunication.*

The emperor celebrated Easter in the city of Pavia and won the fickle support of the Lombards by showing affection for all [25 April].[8] After peace had been established everywhere, he returned from Italy. Rejoicing at this, Arduin then attacked the city of Vercelli, from which Bishop Leo barely managed to escape. Seizing this whole city, he again assumed his arrogant character.[9] *I shall explain later how the divine majesty humbled and forced him to recognize his guilt. In these parts, the emperor established a bishopric as the third adornment of his pious labour.*[10] *With the advice of all and with the permission of the other bishops of the province, Caesar established a bishopric at Bobbio, where rest the bodies of the Christian saints and illustrious confessors, Columba and Attala.*[11] *He was instigated to do this by the highest necessity and, what is more*

---

their traditional dominance of the archepiscopal office (Fasoli 1979: 131). That dominance included access to the archbishopric's revenues. At a *placitum* held in front of the imperial palace on 22 January 1014, a group of nobles subsequently returned various income-producing rights which presumably had been bestowed upon them by Arnulf's deposed rival (Manaresi 1958, vol. 2.2, no. 279).

7 Aside from regulating the ages of ordination, respectively, to the priesthood and diaconate, the synodal decrees prohibited the acceptance of payment in return for consecrating churches, and forbade the misappropriation of ecclesiastical paraphernalia (*Const.*, vol. 1, no. 30, pp. 61–62). Though the edition in the MGH (ibid.) places this synod in Ravenna, prior to Henry II's imperial coronation, it seems equally likely to have taken place in Rome, immediately following that event (Fornasari 1964: 51–54; Hoffmann 1993: 56).

8 Henry's 'affection' involved the issuing of judgements in favour of various Italian religious communities and the bestowal of diplomata confirming their rights and possessions (BG 1819–22; 1823–29?).

9 Aside from Vercelli, Arduin's uprising included attacks on Como as well as Novara; and the latter's bishop (Bishop Peter of Novara) felt constrained to seek refuge in Germany (BG 1839a, 1846).

10 I.e. along with Merseburg and Bamberg.

11 The same synod also attempted to resolve the dispute between the prelates of Aquileia and Grado regarding rights to the office of patriarch though without success (BG 1831a).

important, by the love of Christ. The qualities of the atmosphere and inhabitants of that region differ from ours, hence it was with the greatest prosperity and glory that he crossed the difficult Alps and approached the serenities of our region. Alas, there are many conspiracies in the regions of Rome and Lombardy. For all visitors there is scant affection and everything that a guest requires must be bought, treachery being part of the deal. Many here also die from poisoning.

CHAPTER THREE [1014]

On 28 April of the same year, Count Charles, the son of Margrave Rikdag, died.[12] The unjust accusations of his enemies had previously caused him to lose his entire benefice, and this without any guilt on his part. He endured this outrage with equanimity. My cousin Mathilda departed from this flesh on the same day.[13] She had long resided at Gernrode with Abbess Hathui, to whom she was related by blood. Indeed, the venerable mother was disconsolate when she died, having always desired that Mathilda succeed her. Not long afterwards, on 4 July, she followed her.[14]

I will briefly discuss Hathui's admirable life. The illustrious niece of Queen Mathilda, she was married to Siegfried, the son of Margrave Gero, in the thirteenth year of her life. But she was only joined with him for seven years. After his death, for the love of God and the salvation of her poor husband, she received the veil from Bishop Bernhard and was immediately consecrated, as I have already mentioned.[15] She fulfilled the duties of her office for fifty-five years; as constant as Anna in her devotion to Christ, as generous as the widow of Sarepta, and similar in her abstinence to Judith.[16] She adorned the church committed to her with all manner of decoration. Her death

---

12 A diploma issued by Otto III identifies Charles as count in the southern part of the Harz region, near Walbeck (D O III 81).

13 *NMer.*, 28 April, fo. 2r, p. 5. Daughter of Duke Bernhard I of Saxony and Hildegard, a sister of Thietmar's mother.

14 After Hathui's death, Henry II disregarded the canonesses' right to elect their own abbess – a right Hathui herself had apparently planned to circumvent! – and granted the community to Abbess Adelheid of Quedlinburg (1 November 1014; *AQ*, an. 1014, p. 82), an arrangement which only lasted until the latter's death (Schulze 1965: 7–8, 23). The monarch also made Adelheid abbess of Vreden, an act apparently signifying its transformation into a specifically royal convent (2 November 1014; *AQ* ibid.; Bernhardt 1993: 205).

15 2.19.

16 Luke 2: 36–37 (Anna); 1 Kings 17: 9–16 (widow of Sarepta); Judith 8: 4–8.

was predicted by the following signs: a fishpond in the eastern part of that locale appeared red as blood, until midday, when it became tinged with green.[17] It was due to her virtue, so it seemed to many, that my cousin was able to take precedence in regard to the palm of virginity. This bride of Christ was buried by Bishop Bernhard of Oldenburg, though not in the location desired, but rather in one requested by her sorrowful congregation; in the middle of the church in front of the altar of the Holy Cross. There, through her noble virtue, God granted the ability to walk easily to a man who had long been ill and previously relied upon crutches.

CHAPTER FOUR [1014]

After crossing the Alps, the emperor travelled through neighbouring regions, exercising his royal prerogatives. He celebrated the birth of the Lord at Pöhlde.[18] Afterwards, he went to Merseburg, where he revealed to his supporters how things stood with Boleslav's loyalty and support [6 April 1015]. He asked them to recommend unanimously either that he seek justification or redress. Meanwhile, my cousin Margrave Werner, inspired by the recklessness of youth and the machinations of evil women, went with a few companions to the burg called Beichlingen [November 1014]. After tricking the guards, he abducted the mistress of that place, Reinhild, whom he had previously desired and who was not at all agreeable to the idea.[19] Indeed, she had already given the emperor her solemn promise that she would be joined in marriage to no one without his knowledge and advice. For this reason, she cried and wailed as she was led away. Hearing this, her retainers and servants hurried to arms, and one of them, Vulrad, was seriously wounded. Meanwhile, one of the serving-women asked to go along with her mistress, but as the noble Alwin was preparing to take her, as his lord had commanded, he was surrounded. He called for my cousin, who had already left, to come back and help him. Alas! Before help could arrive he died. When his lord finally arrived, he was surrounded inside the fortress. He was wounded by one of the servants, but immediately fixed him to the wall with a lance, thereby terrifying the others so much that they did not dare to come any closer. Seeing that his companions had long since left with the lady,

17 My translation reflects emendations suggested by Fickermann 1957: 57.
18 See also 7.8.
19 Cf. 4.41.

and finding no way of escape, he abandoned his horse and leaped over the wall. He barely reached his anxious companions amid a hail of stones. His companions carried him as far as Wiehe where they left him in the house of an imperial steward. While a few remained with him, the rest quickly carried off the lady, concealing her first here and then there, as they anxiously waited for their lord to catch up with them.

CHAPTER FIVE [1014]

But the *wicked steward* immediately betrayed his ailing guest to the emperor, who was very happy indeed at this turn of events.[20] He had hoped to make an example of Werner, once he had him in his power, by putting him to death or demanding an unspeakably high price for his freedom. It was night when Counts Bernhard, Gunzelin, and William, who had been sent by the emperor, arrived at the invalid's resting place.[21] After his companions informed him of the counts' presence, Werner greeted only his friend, indicating to the other two that they would never have taken him alive if he had been able to lift his sword. William bound up Werner's wounds and realized that they would prevent his coming to Merseburg. Instead, he had him carried to the neighbouring village of Allerstedt where he placed him under guard in a sturdy house made of stone. He himself returned to the emperor.

CHAPTER SIX [1014]

On the same day, we were summoned to the emperor's presence and listened as he tearfully complained about my cousin's audacity in violating his oath. Indeed, when Brun had been murdered in his own house (where all should be safe!), by his enemy Milo, the residents of the area had sadly reported the incident to the emperor.[22] In turn, he had been strongly urged to follow the custom of his predecessors, namely, by denying wicked men such as this the rights of property and habitation. For his part, the emperor had ordered that this

---

20 Luke 16: 8.

21 Margrave Bernhard of the Saxon northern march (6.50). The Gunzelin referred to here is not the former margrave of Meißen, then in custody (6.54; 7.66), but perhaps the Count Gunzelin mentioned at 7.18. The third member of the party (i.e. Werner's friend) is Count William III of Weimar.

22 Possibly refers to Brun of Braunschweig (Wolf 1995: 100).

judgement be confirmed by an oath At that time, Werner had raised his right hand and promised to God and the entire assembly that he would uphold that oath as long as he lived. Knowing that it is far better to refrain from promising God a good thing than to break the promise afterwards, and assuming that the oath was broken through human weakness or evil counsel, [the emperor declared] that we should beseech the one to whom the oath was sworn that Werner might repent and offer appropriate redress. At the conclusion of the emperor's complaint, the leading men advised that all Werner's property should be confiscated; that the surrender of the lady should be demanded; and that the authors of the deed should be captured and brought to justice, or, if they had fled, be pursued to their deaths.[23] The count himself, after regaining his health, ought to be decapitated if found guilty, but if everything occurred with the lady's consent, it would be best for him to marry her. My brother, Count Henry, was sent to carry out this decision and the various parties involved were commanded to appear before a public assembly at Allstedt. He was already under way when the counts arrived and announced to the emperor what had happened.

CHAPTER SEVEN [1014]

Werner died on the following day, that is on the feast of St Martin, having patiently endured whatever misfortunes had hitherto come his way.[24] Though his enemies gained nothing from his death, the loss to his supporters was insurmountable. The king was deeply troubled by this turn of events, and Werner's enemy Dietrich burst into tears.[25] After hearing what had happened, I asked my cousin Dietrich for permission to leave and had my retainers at Memleben – at the time, there was an abbey there whose rector, Reinhold, presided over it with appropriate humanity – transport my friend's body to Helfta where I awaited it. As the body had now begun to stink, I immediately had the viscera removed and ordered that they be buried next to my church. Then, I accompanied the body to Walbeck where it was buried to the left of Werner's beloved wife.[26] *Fourteen days later, on 26 November, Werner's mother-in-law, the lady Swanhild, died suddenly.*

23 See 4.41.
24 *NMer.*, 11 November, fo. 7r, p. 15.
25 Werner had murdered Dietrich's father, Dedi (6.49–50).
26 Liudgard.

CHAPTER EIGHT [1014]

Meanwhile, at Allstedt, the emperor *gave the law to the people*, but denied it to my friends, as those who were present affirm.[27] With the help of biased judges, he ordered that the island called Parey be conceded to Count Bernhard, because the latter had previously wanted to kill Werner. Count Wichman forbade this and declared it to be unjust.[28] All the people murmured, moreover, and secretly complained that the anointed of the Lord was sinning. At that time, a star appeared in the middle of the day and was seen by many. *On the octave of St Andrew, the priest Rigman died in Christ, having presided over his church for eighty-five years.*[29] Departing from Allstedt, the emperor spent the birth of the Lord at Pöhlde. On the Wednesday before Easter, he came to Merseburg [6 April]. On Maundy Thursday, though unworthy, I consecrated the chrism in his presence. Abbot Redbald of Werden died on the vigil of the holy Resurrection, which fell on 9 April, and Heidenreich, the monastery's provost, was elected in his place.[30] On the holy day itself, Archbishop Gero sang the mass. In the meantime, Ulrich, duke of the Bohemians, had arrived, and we spent these solemn days in good spirits.

CHAPTER NINE [1014]

Meanwhile, Margrave Herman celebrated the feast of Easter with his father-in-law, Boleslav Chrobry. Immediately thereafter, he went to see the emperor, in the company of Stoignev, one of Boleslav's emissaries. His coming had long been awaited by the emperor who was then residing in the West. This emissary was well acquainted with the art of lying and had been sent by his fickle lord to make trouble, rather than peace, as he pretended. The emperor commended him to his familiars. At the same time, he mercifully bestowed his grace upon his brothers-in-law who had asked for it with bare feet.[31] To ensure that the big windbag would see this and accurately inform his lord, he ordered him to appear ahead of time. Upon his return, however, he reported things quite differently from how the emperor

27 Virgil, *Aeneid* 1.507.
28 Wichman III, grandson of Wichman I, son of Ekbert 'the one-eyed'.
29 *NMer.*, 7 December, fo. 7v, p. 16.
30 Abbot Redbald (1001–15), Abbot Heidenreich (1015–30).
31 Henry, Adalbero, and Dietrich of Luxembourg. Cf. 6.2.

had ordered, and so the wretched duke sent him back, along with the margrave, who still wished to make peace. In the presence of the emperor and his leading men, Boleslav's emissary was denounced as a liar and sower of discord. Then, the emperor again invited Boleslav to justify himself and offer compensation for his disobedience, but the latter refused to come into his presence, and instead asked that the matter be resolved before the leading men.

CHAPTER TEN [1014]

O reader, observe how much kindness the emperor showed to this man on a previous occasion. The wily duke of Poland was skilled in a thousand stratagems. He sent his son Miesco to Ulrich, ruler of the Bohemians, to propose that they make peace, on the basis of their mutual kinship, and thereby offer a unified resistance to all of their enemies, especially the emperor. After trustworthy informants told Ulrich that this plan was intended to work to his detriment, he had Miesco seized and ordered that the most prominent members of his entourage be murdered. The rest of Miesco's companions were taken back to Bohemia, along with their captive lord, and imprisoned. After being informed of these events, the emperor sent my cousin, Dietrich, to demand the return of his retainer and to warn that he should not be harmed, assuming that Ulrich placed any value whatsoever on the emperor's favour. Dietrich received the following response: 'My highest obligation is to obey my lord's orders in all things, and to do so to the best of my ability and willingly. Despite my unworthiness, Omnipotent God has just seized me from the lion's mouth and delivered into my hands the lion's cub, sent with the intention of destroying me. If I should permit this one to go free, there is no question that both father and son will be my enemies for ever. If I hold on to him, however, there is a chance that I may obtain some advantage. Let my lord determine what pleases him in this matter, and what might work to my benefit, and I will obediently carry out his every request.'

CHAPTER ELEVEN [1014]

When Dietrich returned with this message, however, another messenger was quickly sent back to demand and sternly order Miesco's release. In return, he offered the emperor's promise that all of Ulrich's concerns would be resolved and a fair peace concluded. At this, Ulrich

had to surrender his captive, whether he wished to or not, and
thereby greatly pleased the emperor. Boleslav was overjoyed at his
son's release and sent messengers who duly expressed his gratitude to
the emperor. These messengers also asked the emperor to send Miesco
home, an act which would do honour to their lord and confound his
enemies. In return for this boon, they promised appropriate compensation in the future. The emperor responded that this could not then
be done, but promised that the request would be granted, upon the
recommendation of his leading men, if Boleslav would come to
Merseburg, The duke received this message and did not take it very
well. Discreetly, through emissaries, he repeatedly sought to have his
son returned.

CHAPTER TWELVE [1014]

When the emperor came to the agreed upon place, he asked the
leading men what he should do in this matter. Among them,
Archbishop Gero spoke first: 'When there was time, and when it
would have redounded to your honour, you did not listen to what I
had to say. Now, however, Boleslav is exceedingly hostile towards
you because of your long custody and imprisonment of his son. I fear
that if you send Miesco back to his father, without hostages or some
other surety, neither of them will be inclined to render loyal service in
the future.' The majority of those present agreed with this opinion,
but the part which had been bribed complained that no great honour
could be gained through such a strategy. Gold won out over sound
advice. That all of this might be more pleasing to Boleslav, his
supporters took over custody of Miesco from the emperor and delivered
both the son and all of the captives' possessions to his father. After
receiving their promised reward, they admonished Boleslav and his
son that, being mindful of Christ and their oath to God, they should
neither cause the emperor any further harm nor attempt to deceive his
supporters. The two immediately responded to this friendly warning in
flattering, flute-like tones which in no way corresponded with their
future behaviour. Despite the fact that they themselves had displayed
little or no loyalty, they blamed the emperor and us for having
delayed so long before sending Miesco back, though he numbered
among our *milites*.

CHAPTER THIRTEEN [1015]

They had always had this in mind and so maintained that they would not appear before the emperor. And truly, it is confirmed by the gospels that whoever wishes to desert a friend, first asks him for an excuse.[32] Recognizing this, the emperor left us. He spent the upcoming Rogation days at Kaufungen, to which he also conveyed a manor located in Kassel. There too, on the advice of his archbishop, Heribert, he commended to Heidenreich the office which has already been mentioned.[33] *Meanwhile, in the presence of Archbishop Gero, the construction of our church was begun. On 18 May, I myself placed its foundation stones in the form of a cross.* After having considered the most important issues at Kaufungen, the emperor arrived at Imbshausen on the vigil of Pentecost and observed that holy solemnity with Bishop Meinwerk. There too, Abbot Wal of Corvey was deposed, having already been suspended from his office. Without the brothers' consent, Druthmer, a monk of the monastery of Lorsch, was installed in his place. During that same week, he went to his new seat. Except for nine brothers, the entire congregation departed in tears. Just as Abbot Liudolf predicted, they had been forced to abandon this virtually empty place.[34]

CHAPTER FOURTEEN [1015]

During these festive days, the illustrious Duke Ernst of Swabia, successor to Herman the Child, was wounded by one of his *milites* while hunting illicitly in a certain forest.[35] This happened, more from ignorance than intention, as the *miles* was trying to shoot a doe with his arrow. Seeing that death was imminent, the duke summoned his companions and asked them to forgive him for his misdeeds. Then, because no priest was available to absolve his sins, he instead ordered one of his *milites* to undertake this task. When he realized that this *miles* was present, he said to him: 'Come, and listen with the ears of your heart to the deeds of your fellow mortal and sinner; and join

32 Luke 14: 18–20.
33 The abbey of Werden (7.8).
34 The deposition of Abbot Wal was associated with the monarch's support of monastic reform along the lines practised by the community at Gorze. Henry also appears to have secularized some of the monastery's property, thereby making it available for his own use, but also reducing the amount of income available for the monks. This last aspect, as much as the violation of the community's right to elect, may have incited their apparently mass exodus (Bernhardt 1993: 123–24).
35 Duke Ernst I, brother-in-law of Herman III, first husband of his sister Gisela.

with me in deciding how I might atone for them. I ask that you commend my sinful soul to those of the faithful who are absent, and admonish my wife to preserve her own honour and be mindful of mine as well.' After saying these things, he revealed to everyone present any occasion he could recall in which he had somehow been guilty of a sin. Immediately afterwards, he departed from this world – it was 31 May – and, according to his wish, was buried in Würzburg next to his father, Margrave Leopold. I hope that this young man's soul was saved. As he himself attested while he lived, he preferred to suffer embarrassment before many rather than conceal anything in the presence of Almighty God. Follow this example, brothers in Christ, and reveal your secret illness to the heavenly physician, and do not in any way reject his healing antidotes. Whoever one's confessor may be in the end, no sinner should delay in making his mournful confession, he will thereby find a more gracious pardon in heaven.

CHAPTER FIFTEEN [1015]

At the celebration mentioned above and at the place already mentioned, a certain peasant arrived from the West, bringing a new mandate for the emperor which he would reveal only to him.[36] *He still carried the goad that he was using to drive the oxen before his plough* when a dove from heaven ordered him to undertake this legation. He was so tall that all who saw him were astonished. *Upon his return, he said to all who questioned him that, at the conclusion of the emperor's upcoming military campaign, he was to go to Aachen and would then receive a response to his message. The emperor had to accept the penalty for ignoring this warning, and many others as well.*

CHAPTER SIXTEEN [1015]

The emperor went to Goslar for the feast of the birth of St John the Baptist which was fast approaching. While there, he gave Duke Ernst's duchy to the duke's cousin and her son.[37] Then, he moved on to Magdeburg where he humbly asked St Maurice, Christ's *miles*, to help him conquer his obstinate enemy, Boleslav. After an army had been assembled, the emperor proceeded to a place called Schlenzfurt

---

36 At Imbshausen.

37 Gisela, the daughter of Duke Herman II of Swabia and widow of Ernst I, and her son, Duke Ernst II of Swabia (1015–30).

where he inflicted much damage on the populace and their margrave, Gero. We assembled on 8 July, but instead of giving the inhabitants the protection that was their due, we plundered them. Afterwards, our forces crossed the Elbe. Meanwhile, I accompanied the empress and her entourage to Merseburg where we awaited the emperor's return. When our forces came to the district called Lausitz, they were confronted by troops issuing forth from the burg of Zützen. Accepting the challenge, they killed a great number. They also captured Erich 'the Proud', who had fled our region because of a homicide, and presented him, in chains, to the emperor.

CHAPTER SEVENTEEN [1015]

The emperor went to a place called Krossen, on the Oder, where Miesco was sitting with his forces. He then sent a delegation, composed of the leading men of his army, who reminded Miesco of his oath to the emperor and unanimously asked that they might not lose their property on his account, this having been anticipated by his surrender. He responded to them with the following words: 'I concede that the emperor rescued me from the power of my enemies and that I promised you my loyalty. I would willingly fulfil that promise, if I were free. At present, however, as you yourselves know, I am subject to my father's dominion and he has forbidden this. Nor would it be permitted by his *milites*, who are here with me. Hence, I must reluctantly decline. To the best of my ability, I will defend this land which belongs to me, but is desired by you. When my father arrives, I will try to win him over to the emperor's favour and to friendship with you.' After hearing this, our representatives returned and relayed Miesco's response to the emperor. Meanwhile, Duke Bernhard and his supporters, with bishops, counts, and a band of the heathen Liutizi, moved against Boleslav from the north, and encountered him on the Oder which was defended on all sides.

CHAPTER EIGHTEEN [1015]

On the feast of the discovery of Christ's protomartyr, the emperor crossed the Oder and crushed the resistance of the Polish multitude [3 August]. We had no losses, except for that famous youth, Hodo, along with Eckerich and another dependant of Count Gunzelin.[38] The

---

38 Deaths of Hodo and Eckerich noted by *NMer.*, 3 August, fo. 4v, p. 10.

emperor had accused this Hodo and Siegfried, the son of Margrave Hodo, of having been too familiar with Boleslav, but on this day each vindicated himself completely. While Hodo was pursuing the enemy and quite alone, having outdistanced his companions, he took an arrow in the head. Initially, he lost only his eye, but then lost his life as well. Miesco's tears flowed freely when he recognized the corpse of the man who had been his guardian and companion during his period of captivity. After showing every concern for the body, he returned it to our army. The enemy's dead numbered no fewer than six hundred, which left us with a great deal of booty.

CHAPTER NINETEEN [1015]

Messengers quickly brought news of these events to the place where Boleslav then resided. Although the duke would willingly have hurried to the field of battle, he did not wish to leave an entry for his enemies, who were so close at hand. Indeed, wherever our forces tried to land their boats, Boleslav and his warriors followed on horseback, At last, our people quickly raised their sails and travelled for a whole day. Since the enemy could not follow, our people reached their destination and safely came ashore. They set fire to the surrounding areas. Some distance away, Duke Boleslav was made aware of what had happened and fled, as usual, thereby leaving us – albeit unwillingly – with both the confidence and an opportunity for destruction. Duke Bernhard, who had been unable to support the emperor with his own forces, as previously arranged, sent messengers who secretly revealed all that had occurred and indicated the reason for his disobedience. The duke then returned home, after pillaging and burning everything in the vicinity. Ulrich, who should have come to the emperor's aid, along with his Bavarians, also gave up, for many and varied reasons. Even though these men did not accompany the emperor, they rendered faithful service while in the area. In particular, Ulrich attacked a very large burg, called Biesnitz. Aside from the women and children, he took no fewer than one thousand men prisoners. After setting the burg afire, he returned victorious. Henry, count of the eastern march, learned that Boleslav's *milites* were in the area and had captured much booty. Accompanied by the Bavarians, he immediately fell upon them. Although the enemy resisted vigorously, eight hundred of them were killed and all of their booty was taken.

Meanwhile, Reding, provost at Magdeburg, died on 5 August.[39] On the nineteenth day of the same month, the venerable Countess Eila died and was buried, by Bishop Eberhard, in the monastery which she had constructed.[40]

CHAPTER TWENTY [1015]

The emperor, still unaware of what had occurred, acted with great care because of the smaller number of his forces. Nevertheless, as long as he wished to, he maintained a powerful presence in this region. Thereafter, he returned to a district called Diadesi. Unfortunately, the army had set up camp in a very narrow location where only a bee-keeper resided – he was immediately put to death. Boleslav, hearing that the emperor planned to leave by a route other than the one by which he had entered, secured the banks of the Oder in every way possible. When he learned that the emperor had already departed, however, he sent a large force of foot soldiers to the place where our army was camped, ordering that they try to inflict injury on at least some part of it, should the opportunity present itself. He also sent his Abbot Tuni to the emperor with a sham offer of peace. The abbot was immediately recognized as a spy and detained. In the meantime, virtually the entire army crossed the swamp that lay before it, using bridges constructed during the preceding night.

CHAPTER TWENTY-ONE [1015]

Only then was Abbot Tuni permitted to leave, a fox in a monk's habit, whose craftiness was highly esteemed by his lord. The emperor commended the remainder of his forces to Archbishop Gero, the illustrious margrave Gero, and the count palatine Burchard, advising them that they should be even more watchful than usual. After this, in fact, a great clamour and three shouts went forth from the enemy, concealed in a nearby forest. Immediately, they attacked our troops and shot arrows at them. Archbishop Gero and Count Burchard, who was wounded, barely managed to escape and tell the emperor what had happened. The young Count Liudolf was captured, along with a

---

39 *NMER.*, fo. 4v, p. 10.

40 Thietmar's aunt, widow of Count Berthold of Schweinfurt, mother of Margrave Henry of Schweinfurt (see 5.38), was buried by Bishop Eberhard of Bamberg in the monastery located at Schweinfurt (the family's burg). The community also provided a burial place for other members of the family (7.63).

few others. Count Gero, Count Folkmar, and two hundred of our best *milites* were killed and plundered.[41] May Omnipotent God look upon their names and their souls with mercy! May all of us who caused their deaths, through our sins, be reconciled to him through Christ! And, may God mercifully protect us so that we never need to endure such a thing again!

CHAPTER TWENTY-TWO [1015]

When the emperor received this unhappy news, he wished to go back and fetch the bodies of the dead. Many advised him to wait, however, and he reluctantly complied. Instead, he sent Bishop Eid of Meißen, who was to press the cursed Boleslav for permission to bury the dead and beg for the body of Margrave Gero. The venerable father willingly agreed to the emperor's request, and quickly proceeded to his destination. Gazing upon the scene of such wretched slaughter, he began to groan and weep as he offered up prayers for the dead. The victors, still intent on plundering, noticed Bishop Eid when he was still some distance away. Believing that he was accompanied by others, they initially fled in fear. As he came closer, however, they greeted him and allowed him to proceed unmolested. Boleslav, overjoyed at our destruction, readily granted Eid's requests, and the bishop quickly returned to the battlefield where, with great effort and the enemy's indulgence, he buried our dead comrades. He had the corpses of Margrave Gero and Widred, his companion-in-arms, transported to Meißen. At Meißen, a tearful Count Herman took custody of the bodies and, in the company of his brothers Gunther and Ekkehard, transported them to Nienburg.[42] During the reign of Otto II, Archbishop Gero of Cologne and his brother, Margrave Thietmar, had founded an abbey there in honour of the Mother of God and St Cyprian.[43] Thietmar was Herman's stepfather and the father of the dead margrave.[44] Archbishop Gero

41 Deaths noted at *NMer.*, 1 September, fo. 5r, p. 11.

42 Gunther, chancellor for Germany (1009–23), archbishop of Salzburg (1024–25). See also 8.22.

43 Orginally established at Thankmarsfeld in 970, the community was moved to Nienburg in 970. It acquired the status of a royal monastery at some point between 971 and 975. Whatever the motivation, the change in location seems to have enhanced both the monastery's contribution to royally sponsored missionary efforts among the Slavs and its capacity to assist with the king's upkeep and maintenance (Bernhardt 1993: 170–74).

44 Margrave Herman's mother, Schwanhild, had previously been married to Margrave Thietmar I (d. 987; 4.39).

commended the bodies to the earth and offered consolation to Gero's lady, Adelheid, to his son, Thietmar, and also to his sorrowing friends and *milites*.[45]

CHAPTER TWENTY-THREE [1015]

Meanwhile, the emperor and his entourage moved on to Strehla. But knowing that Miesco was following with his army, he had also sent Margrave Herman to defend the burg at Meißen. The emperor himself went directly to Merseburg. Miesco, instructed by his wicked father, knew that our forces had divided prior to their departure and had not left any guard behind them. At dawn, on 13 September, he brought seven war bands across the Elbe near Meißen, ordering some to lay waste the surrounding areas, others to lay siege to the burg itself. When the Withasen saw this, they had no confidence in the safety of their suburb and instead sought the protection of the upper burg, leaving virtually every possession behind.[46] Full of joy at this turn of events, the enemy entered the abandoned suburb and set fire to it, after removing all the booty they could find. They also launched repeated attacks on the upper burg which had caught fire in two places. Seeing his few exhausted helpers, Margrave Herman threw himself prostrate on the ground and invoked both the mercy of Christ and the intercession of Donatus, his illustrious martyr. He also called on the women to help. They hurried to the walls and helped the men by throwing rocks. They also put out the fires, using mead because they had no water. Thanks be to God! The enemy's fury and audacity abated. Miesco watched all of this from a nearby hill where he awaited the arrival of his companions who were busy ravaging and, wherever possible, setting fire to everything up to the river Jahna. They returned late in the evening, with their horses exhausted, and spent the night with their lord. They were to attack the burg on the following day. The fact that the Elbe was rising escaped their notice, however. Because of this, the army went home, extremely tired, but in unexpected safety. This good fortune eased the anxious heart of their leader. The emperor, as soon as he learned of these events, sent whatever forces he could assemble to help the margrave. Shortly afterwards, he restored the suburb. To support this undertaking and provide security, Archbishop Gero and Bishop Arnulf met with the

45 Reference to Margrave Thietmar of the Saxon eastern march (1015–30).
46 Cf. 5.9.

counts and many others on 8 October. I was by far the least of these. Within fourteen days the task was completed and we could leave. Count Frederick was to assume custody of the burg for four weeks.

CHAPTER TWENTY-FOUR [1015]

Archbishop Gero and I, his companion, came to the place called Mockrehna. There, after I reminded him of his sweet promises, he conveyed to me, with his staff which I still possess today, parochial rights over four fortresses: Schkeuditz, Taucha, Püchen, and Wurzen as well as the village of Raßnitz. He postponed any decision concerning the remaining five: namely, Eilenburg, Pouch, Düben, Löbnitz, and Zöchritz, saying that he would return them later. All of this occurred on 25 October in the presence of the following witnesses: Heribald, Hepo, Ibo, Cristin, and Siegbert. On the same day we came to the fortress of Zörbig where, after the archbishop's *milites* had assembled, I revealed how mercifully their lord had treated me. We also learned of the illness of the venerable Friderun whose guests we were. Alas, after a few days, on 27 October, she abandoned this human flesh.[47] From thence, the archbishop moved on to Magdeburg where he celebrated the feast of All Saints [1 November]. I did the same in Walbeck.

Meanwhile, Arduin, king only in name, having lost the city of Vercelli which he long possessed unjustly after Bishop Leo's expulsion, sickened and became a monk after shaving his beard.[48] He died on 30 October and was buried in the monastery.[49] The emperor, moreover, went to the regions of the West where he corrected everything there that needed to be corrected.

CHAPTER TWENTY-FIVE [1015]

After this, having just returned from Poland with many impressive gifts, Bishop Eid became ill and surrendered his faithful soul to Christ, at Leipzig, on 20 December.[50] Bishop Hildeward of Zeitz was asked to attend to him and arrived quickly, but upon entering the house in which the holy man had died, discovered that it was filled with a

47 *NMer.*, 28 October, fo. 6v, p. 14.
48 At the abbey of St Benedict at Fruttuaria, on 14 December rather than 30 October (BG 1870a).
49 The correct date is 14 December (Holtzmann 1935: 427, n. 8).
50 *NMer.*, 20 December, fo. 8r, p. 17.

wonderful odour. He accompanied the body to Meißen and buried it in front of the altar, with the aid of Count William whose turn it was to guard the burg. Because I promised that I would say something about his life, in what follows I would like to relate a few of his greater accomplishments. He was of noble lineage and richly endowed with material goods, but held these as nothing because he was poor in spirit. Prior to his consecration, he had lived according to the rule, and most admirably, along with the other brothers at Magdeburg. Even after his spiritual flock grew and he himself rose higher, he imitated the apostolic life as much as he could. He only wore a shirt and hose when singing the mass, a task he often avoided because he judged himself unworthy. Many were astonished that he could survive the harshness of winter. Often, after his people had all but given him up for dead, he could just barely be revived in the warm room. He greatly afflicted his body with fasts and went about with bare feet more often than was wise. If he and his companions were on a long trip and he noted they lacked food, or if any other misfortune occurred, he gave thanks to God and had the others do the same. Through baptizing, constant preaching, and confirmation, he was useful not only to his own church, but also to many others. By separating the income from which he and his household were to live, he acquired almost two hundred manses for his church. He consecrated chrism or clergy rarely, temples of the Lord frequently, but often without a mass. *His vision had already become blurred from the too constant outflow of tears.* Because of our sins, his way of life displeased us, just as ours displeased him. He spent more than twenty-three years in indescribable labour.[51] Foreseeing his end, however, he often asked that he might never be buried in Meißen. Indeed, from fear of future destruction, he had always hoped instead that he would be found worthy of burial at Colditz, resting place of the body of Magnus, the martyr of Christ. But Margrave Herman, hoping that the church would benefit from his prayers, still had him entombed at Meißen, as I have already mentioned.

CHAPTER TWENTY-SIX [1016]

On the vigil of the birth of the Lord, Meingaud, Archbishop of Trier, died at his residence in Coblenz, having occupied his office for eight years and seven months.[52] From thence, his body was taken to his

51 I.e. as bishop.
52 *NMer.*, 24 December, fo. 84, p. 17.

own see and honourably interred among his predecessors. The
emperor was disturbed at the news that so many bishops had died,
and discussed with his closest advisers how he might best fill the
empty positions. He celebrated the birth of the Lord at Paderborn
with joy and festivity.[53] Afterwards, he conveyed the archbishopric of
Trier to Poppo who was the son of Margrave Leopold and provost of
the church of Bamberg.[54] At the emperor's order, and with the permission of the bishop of Verdun, who took precedence among his
episcopal colleagues,[55] Poppo was to be consecrated by Archbishop
Erkanbald of Mainz. In vain, Bishop Dietrich of Metz tried to prohibit
this, maintaining, in his constant protests and humble requests, that
he himself had the better right to perform the ordination. But the
emperor did not listen as Dietrich presented his documents and raised
the threat of excommunication; rather he ordered that the consecration
be completed. In those days, the emperor installed Eilward, Margrave
Thietmar's chaplain, in place of Bishop Eid. This was done on the
recommendation of the candidate's brother, Herman. On the Sunday
before the feast of palms, the new bishop was consecrated by
Archbishop Gero, at Merseburg, with our assistance [18 March].

CHAPTER TWENTY-SEVEN [1016]

The emperor spent the following Palm Sunday with the venerable
Bishop Henry of Würzburg [25 March]. On Wednesday, he moved
on to Bamberg where he celebrated Maundy Thursday, the Passion of
the Lord, and the joyous feast of Easter with appropriate solemnity
[28–30 March; 1 April]. King Rudolf of Burgundy, the emperor's
uncle, was unable to attend these festivities, to which he had been
invited, and instead asked his beloved nephew to come to him. Their
meeting took place in the city of Strasbourg where the bountiful

53 That Henry and Bishop Meinwerk discussed the condition of the latter's diocese is
   suggested by a royal diploma, issued shortly after the monarch's stay (10 January),
   which granted all the bishop's hereditary possessions to the church of Paderborn
   (D H II 341, BG 1874). The diploma reflects a pattern in Henry's relations with
   Meinwerk and with the occupants of at least a few other episcopal sees. Indeed, the
   monarch had impressed upon this 'well-placed and wealthy aristocrat' that a
   virtual prerequisite for accepting the see of Paderborn was a willingness to support
   it with donations from his own rather substantial resources (Reuter 1995: 165–66).
   A similar understanding preceded Thietmar's elevation to the see of Merseburg
   (6.40).
54 Archbishop Poppo of Trier (1016–47).
55 Bishop Heimo of Verdun.

kindness of mutual love also smiled upon each king's entourage. King Rudolf's wife[56] was also present and contributed to their friendship by commending to the emperor her two sons, the stepsons of her husband. From his uncle, the emperor received properties previously held by William of Poitou as a royal gift.[57] He granted these to his beloved *milites* in the form of benefices.[58]

CHAPTER TWENTY-EIGHT [1016]

Benefiting from wise counsel, the emperor hoped that these measures would more firmly secure that which King Rudolf had long ago promised to him, under oath, in the event of his death.[59] Through his uncle, he had accepted the oaths of all the leading men of the Burgundian region and received firm assurances that important matters would not be decided without his advice.[60] He granted a bishopric in this region to a certain noble man who, afterwards, was barely able to escape from it in safety.[61] For as soon as the appointment was reported to William, the most powerful man in those parts,

56 Irmgard.

57 Count Otto-William of Burgundy (d. 1026), son of King Adalbert of Italy and Gerberga of Burgundy, and founder of the comital lineage of Franche-Comté. Thietmar has confused him with his later son-in-law, William V, duke of Aquitaine and count of Poitou. See Holtzmann 1935: 432, n. 5.

58 To be more precise, the emperor has taken lands confiscated from Count Otto-William and granted them to his new vassals, Rudolf III's stepsons. The count's antagonism towards King Rudolf and Henry II would therefore have a more concrete basis than Thietmar lets on.

59 The Burgundian king had acknowledged Henry II as his heir, an action understandable in light of the Rudolfing monarchy's history of dependence on the Ottonians and one that could also be justified by the German king's status as Rudolf's nephew (5, prologue). The agreement to which Thietmar alludes may have been reached as early as 1006, in which year the city of Basel, ceded to the Rudolfinger by Henry I, passed once more into the power of the Empire (BG 1616a). As an anonymous annalist at the monastery of Einsiedeln observed, '[after] coming to the kingdom of Burgundy, King Henry added the city of Basel to his realm' (*AE*, an. 1006, p. 144). Presumably the transfer of possession occurred in July, since Henry issued diplomata in the city on the fourteenth and fifteenth of that month (D H II 117, 118). As Thietmar appears to suggest, the relationship between the two rulers may have assumed a more overtly hierarchical cast with Rudolf ceding his kingdom to Henry and receiving it back as a benefice. In any case, the events described in this chapter ultimately led to the full incorporation of Burgundy into the Empire although the fact that Henry predeceased Rudolf ensured that this could only occur during the reign of Conrad II (Beumann 1991: 174–76; Reuter 1991: 266–68).

60 I.e. 'per manus ab avinculo suimet accepit'.

61 Archbishop Berthald of Besançon.

he ordered that the bishop be hunted down, and went so far as to set
his dogs on the lonely fugitive. As he heard their baying, the
exhausted bishop availed himself of his only defence. After making the
sign of the cross over his tracks, he lay upon the ground as if dead and
ready to be plundered. But behold! When the scent of that blessed
spot reached the furious dogs, still some distance away, they turned
back as if propelled by a great whirlwind. And so, by travelling
through the trackless forest, the true servant of God was able to reach
more friendly lands.

CHAPTER TWENTY-NINE [1016]

The emperor gave a large sum of money to the king, his wife, and all
of his leading men; and permitted them to depart, after their earlier
agreement had been confirmed. After collecting an army, the emperor
himself proceeded to the city of Basel, where he heard that William
was planning to offer resistance from within certain strongly defended
burgs; and that he wished to deny him entry. Lacking confidence in
his much smaller force, the emperor summoned warriors friendly to
him, from every direction. With fire and sword, but with no danger to
himself, he laid waste the regions that had presumed to rebel against
him. He was certain that he could not conquer any of the burgs, and
so his return was marked by sadness. Indeed, neither here nor in the
East had he inflicted serious damage on his enemies. In the meantime,
the empress resided in our region and, along with our leading men,
made plans for the defence of the homeland. During this time, our
enemy Boleslav did not attack the region, but rather saw to his own
defence. He was quite happy and rejoiced when informed of the result
of the emperor's campaign. Many people familiar with the situation
assert, however, that if the emperor had chosen this moment to attack
Boleslav, the latter would have regained his respect for us and
returned whatever property of ours he possessed. He would also have
been most ready and willing to assume his previous state of
subservience, and with nothing more than peace as compensation.

CHAPTER THIRTY [1016]

Yet now, at the instigation of people who found it pleasing to relax
the bridle of justice and run free like some foolish calf,[62] the mild and

62 *Ecbasis Captivi* 66ff, 248–49.

effeminate king of the Burgundians wished to withhold the property
he had promised to his nephew. Later, when he tried to return to his
original plan, he was prevented from doing so by their plotting and
furious opposition. From what I have heard, there is no other ruler
like him. He has only a title and crown, and grants bishoprics to
whomever the leading men propose. He retains a few for his own use,
thereby living from the incomes of the episcopate, but he can in no
way prevent either these or others from being seized by outsiders.
Hence, with their hands tied, the bishops serve each magnate as if he
were the king himself. Only in this way are they left in peace. Such a
king rules among them only so that, in turn, the madness of wicked
men may continue without restraint; and that some other king might
not appear and create a new law which would uproot the practices to
which they had become so accustomed. Count William, of whom I
have already spoken, is a *miles* of the king in name, but a lord in fact.
In those regions, moreover, there is no count who does not possess
the position of a duke. That the king's power might not be even more
diminished, the count struggled against the emperor's majesty with
both advice and deeds, as I have also mentioned.

CHAPTER THIRTY-ONE

During the preceding summer, Bernhar, the pious father and bishop
of the church of Verden, realized that he was nearing the end of this
life.[63] In a friendly manner, therefore, he summoned all his debtors
and reminded them of their mortal failings, in regard to God and the
church over which he himself had presided. To all who acknowledged
their guilt, he offered forgiveness. Those who denied their guilt, he
reproached in the following way: 'My sons, do not behave in this way!
Neither I nor my successors have any interest in deceiving you. I
merely wish for you to be freed from such things, that I might depart
from you in sincere peace.' He increased the wealth of his church by
lawfully acquiring three hundred manses; and he regarded both his
emperor and all faithful Christians with heartfelt affection. Following
the example of the highest pastor, however, he loved his own flock
most of all. That venerable man occupied his see for twenty-four
years.[64] Next to the church at Verden, he began construction of a

---

63 Thietmar places Bernhar's death during the summer of 1015 though it actually
took place on 25 July 1014 (Holtzmann 1935: 435, n. 6).

64 In fact, only twenty years, but Thietmar apparently reckoned that Bernhar took up
his office in 992 (Holtzmann 1935: 436, n. 2).

tower, in stone, a material quite rare in these regions.[65] On 25 July, our eyes were denied the sight of his bright light.[66] When the emperor was informed of this, he lamented the death of such a great lord as a son mourns an absent father. On 24 August, he installed Wigger as Bernhar's successor though the former had long resisted the offer.[67] Wigger had been provost at Cologne but was deposed by Archbishop Heribert. The emperor had Archbishop Erkanbald consecrate him and, with great honour, sent him off to his own see.

It is with great sadness that we must also note and describe how the monastery at Memleben was deprived of its liberty, so often confirmed in the past, and reduced to servitude. For after Abbot Reinhold had been deposed, and the brothers scattered far and wide, the monastery itself was made subject to the church of Hersfeld and its abbot, Arnold.[68]

CHAPTER THIRTY-TWO

In a certain region of Swabia, in the county of Count Bezelin, there occurred a marvellous and most frightening event. A married woman died, having been seized in the grasp of an unexpected death. After her body was washed and duly attended to, she was carried into the church by her sorrowful friends and relatives. Suddenly, she raised herself from the bier, causing all present to flee. She then summoned her husband and others to whom she had been close, and gave each a special charge along with the comfort of her sweet words. After this, she found rest and peace. My story is marvellous, to be sure, but I see it only as the work of our miraculous God. So that no one may refuse to believe it, I will provide an unimpeachable witness: the count, whom we have already mentioned, gave a truthful account of these

65 It has been suggested this may have been a secular building of some sort, but certainly does not pertain to the first stone church at Verden which dates no earlier than 1015 (Jacobsen et al. 1991: 434–35).

66 *NMer.*, fo. 4r, p. 9.

67 Bishop Wigger of Verden (1014–31)

68 These actions should be seen against the backdrop of Henry II's efforts to revise Ottonian policies along the Slavic frontier, efforts which, among other things, included several striking changes in the area's ecclesiastical structure (Bernhardt 1993: 250–51). In particular, the emperor acted to reverse the property exchange with Hersfeld (see 3.1) which had helped to place Memleben on a more solid financial basis (D H II 330, 26 January 1015). Shortly thereafter, he subjected the community itself to Hersfeld, along with all of its remaining property (D H II 331: 5 February 1015).

events to the emperor, who then recounted them to me, in the presence of many of my brethren. It often happens that the cunning enemy of mortals appears in the image of dead people, and tries to delude us in various ways. Fools accept his deceit as truth. Nevertheless, I would truthfully proclaim to all faithful Christians that, following the commendation of the soul and completion of the solemn office of burial, no corpse will rise from the dead until that resurrection of all flesh which must undoubtedly occur in the future. Exceptions only occur on special occasions, in instances of particular merit, and especially if the glorious life of the departed has caused the world to blossom. I believe that the woman of whom we have spoken was very highly valued because, after tasting death, she was permitted to fulfil her just desire and then, without lament, fall once more into the sleep of peace.

CHAPTER THIRTY-THREE

Blessed is he who devotes himself to the completion of a good work, with continuous zeal, and without permitting himself to be interrupted by any hesitation. On the other hand, whoever spurns or postpones righteous tasks, that they might not be completed, should be assigned a place among the most miserable wretches. I have often been guilty of both failings, but will mention only two instances in which my behaviour was especially blameworthy. Following the agreement at Dortmund, Richer, a priest at Magdeburg and my spiritual brother, became ill.[69] I was not present and, hence, was unable to visit him. When I did arrive, on the day prior to his death, I did not seek him out. Instead, I put this off until the following day, which meant that Richer died in the absence of any comforting from me. His body was carried to the church by our brethren and watched over by my vicar, since I could not endure the nightly vigil. Shortly after his burial, the dead man appeared to me, in a dream, and said: 'Why did you not visit me and sing the psalter? And why have you not offered prayers for my soul, as we agreed at Dortmund?' When I tried to excuse myself, he said: 'You have badly neglected these matters!' Then, when I asked how he was doing, he said: 'I went to sleep on one Saturday and, on another, entered into the joy of sweet repose.' As I inquired how things stood with my father and mother, he replied that they were 'good' and, continuing, said: 'Through me, your mother

69 6.18.

wished to inform you that you will follow her on a Monday or Thursday.' I awoke, groaning, because I was well aware that a friendly message from the just is both holy and healthy, if obeyed. Otherwise, it represents a great danger. Although I accuse only myself, I fear that most people have violated both this and other agreements. The more we spurn the mandates of our superiors, the more guilty we will appear in their judgement.

CHAPTER THIRTY-FOUR

I am also guilty of another offence, for which I feel a deep and abiding regret. When I arrived in the city of Magdeburg, Reding, the provost of the cathedral chapter, accorded me a most kindly reception and asked to speak with me in private.[70] It was Lent, the season which he had foreseen as the time of his death. He began to weep as he spoke, saying: 'I must reveal to you certain signs which have led me to fear that I shall die suddenly. Once, in the Arneburg, and on two occasions here, I suddenly found myself unable to see or hear anything. With Christ's help, I quickly recovered. Since then, however, I have become extremely anxious and, so I believe, have revealed to my brethren a wound appropriate to my iniquity. Since I know that you have always been faithful to me, I humbly ask that you bear witness to my confession. Indeed, I judge that I will not live much longer.' I accepted this petition, with great reverence, and promised to satisfy him in every way. Later, he reminded me of this promise, but since the moment was inappropriate, I did not fulfil his altogether laudable request. To be sure, because of the constant stench of my own sinful conscience, I would not willingly inspect the wounds of a convert, and would despair of healing them. Still, I would freely have shouldered my brother's burden, if I could have found a more opportune time to do so.

CHAPTER THIRTY-FIVE

On the following Good Friday, Rotman, a priest and provost of Archbishop Gero, died suddenly, in the middle of the night [8 April]. He was found in his bed, dead. This event seemed both astonishing and frightening to all who heard of it. But, thanks be to God! On the preceding day, he had distributed alms and tearfully offered a public

---

70 Redding succeeded Walthard as provost in 1012 (6.68).

confession of his sins. I arrived on Holy Saturday and joined my archbishop in a festive celebration of this holy solemnity. On this occasion, Reding, a man both prudent and cautious in all things, divided his wealth between his brother and beloved sister, saying: 'Take this for yourselves and, if my mortal self should soon be lost to you, see in this gift a sign of my loyalty to you.' I observed the birth of St John the Baptist with my brother, Abbot Siegfried [24 June, at Berge]. Here too, I took my final leave of Provost Reding. Alas, I showed no concern to grant him absolution. Nor did I sense that he still desired this from me. When informed of his death, as I have mentioned, I expressed belated regret for that promise which I had previously neglected to fulfil. This pious, wise, and exceedingly faithful man presided over his brethren for three years and six weeks. He was buried in the south portico, next to the church. In the following year, on the feast of the Apostles Peter and Paul, Reding was succeeded by the venerable father, Geddo, who had been master of the school and was later made custodian of the church [29 June]. On the day preceding this feast, Esiko died.[71] He was a recluse who, for the love of Christ, had frequently changed his place of residence.

CHAPTER THIRTY-SIX

Sometimes, though rarely, I am consumed by zeal for the house of the Lord which, in Christ, is our spiritual mother. Indeed, such zeal has compelled me to add to my work that which I have just related.

I have often heard that the Angles, so called because of their beautiful angelic faces or because they are located in an angle of this earth,[72] endured unspeakable suffering at the hands of Sven the son of Harald;[73] and were compelled to pay an annual census imposed upon them by this filthy dog although they were previously tributaries of the prince of the Apostles, St Peter, and spiritual sons of their holy father,

71 *NMer.*, fo. 3v, p. 8.
72 '... because that island is situated in a certain angle of the sea, they have been called Anglo-Saxons up to the present day' (Widukind 1.8, p. 10). On Thietmar's veracity regarding events in England in 1012 and 1016 (7. 36–42) see Whitelock (ed.) 1955: 127, who notes the abundant errors and confusion over names, but also the valuable feature that his account cannot have been written long after the events themselves occurred.
73 Sven 'Forked Beard' (986–1014). After extending Danish power in Scandinavia, Sven launched several large-scale attacks on England, culminating with its conquest in 1013. Sven's empire did not survive his death in 1014 although his son Cnut would later reunite it (Sawyer and Sawyer 1993: 56–57).

Gregory.[74] Then, they reluctantly handed over the greatest part of their kingdom to the enemy, as a permanent place of residence, its inhabitants having been captured or killed. The Lord agreed to this and compelled the enemy to do it in order to punish the sins of certain non-believers. So much did the persecutor rage who did not even know to spare his own people. Sven, whom I have mentioned above, not a ruler but a destroyer, was captured by invading Northmen and redeemed by the people subject to him, at great cost.[75] He then learned that, because of this, rumours spread by the worst of people were secretly referring to him as a slave. The revenge which could profitably have been exacted from a few, he rashly inflicted on all. Had he wished to consider this, he might have realized that he inflicted the greatest damage on himself. For by giving over his power to foreign enemies, he traded security for constant wandering, peace for war, a kingdom for exile, the God of heaven and earth for the Devil. He wasted a populous land and often boasted that he was not a lord who could be bought or influenced by his people, but rather one who, according to his whim, could rule far and wide as an enemy.

CHAPTER THIRTY-SEVEN

Sven lived for a long time, a burden on his own people and his contemporaries, an impious man among the pious. Though he himself was the cause of many deaths, death came to him very late. He was buried in the place where he had died, as his companions fled.[76] When Aethelred, the long-exiled king of the Angles, was informed of this, he gave thanks to God and happily returned to his homeland.[77] After gathering all of his *milites* together, he then made plans to disinter his enemy's corpse. A certain woman, warned of Aethelred's intentions by close friends, and intent on obstructing them, had the corpse raised from the earth. Although she herself was a native Angle, she returned Sven's body to his Arctic homeland – that is, to the north.[78] The name Arctic derives from the two Arctic stars, namely the small and the large bear, which are surrounded and divided by a snake, so astrologers

74 Pope Gregory I 'the Great' (590–604) who first sent missionaries to the Anglo-Saxons.

75 Adam 2.29, pp. 90–91; 2.34, pp. 94–95; Tschan (trans.) 1959: 75, 77–78.

76 In 1014, at Gainsborough.

77 King Aethelred II (978–1016).

78 Other sources assert that he was initially interred at York and then, ten years later, transferred to Norway for burial at St Olaf (Whitelock [ed.] 1955: 319, n. 4).

assert. One part of that region is extremely cold because it is far from the warmth of the sun. Both kinds of love are unfamiliar to its population. There, too, reside the Scythians who carry their houses around with them and are nurtured by the milk of wild animals and horses.[79]

CHAPTER THIRTY-EIGHT

In this region lives King Göttrik, who was educated as a cleric in the monastery of Verden, under Erp, the bishop of that place. Though unworthy, he had attained the rank of deacon. After the bishop died, however, he slipped away and, like a second Julian [the Apostate], abandoned both his name and order. He had only pretended to be a Christian and, in many ways, was found to be something quite different. As soon as he was recognized by his people, he was immediately taken up and raised to his hereditary honour. That which displeases God should be praised or imitated by no one; and fear of the future should cause us to reject the fruits of the present. That king, the servant of sin and son of death, did not rule, as he expected, but instead took on new burdens every day. Of him the Lord said, through Isaiah: 'Sons have I nourished and exalted, but they themselves have rejected me.'[80] All Christians should pray for his and his companions' conversion, with appropriate compensation and constancy, and should implore God that they should never have to suffer such a thing again. I have said this of him alone, but there are others, unfortunately, to whom the same judgement might be applied since they do not observe the word of St Paul: 'it is better not to have recognized the way of truth than to decline from it after having found it.'[81]

CHAPTER THIRTY-NINE

No one can comprehend the variety of the northern regions, and what marvellous things nature creates there. Nor can one believe the cruel deeds of its people. Hence, I will omit all of this, and merely say a few things concerning that brood of vipers, namely, the sons of Sven the Persecutor. These sons were born to him by the daughter of Duke Miesco, sister of the latter's successor and son, Boleslav.[82] Long exiled

79 Horace, *Odes* bk 3, ode 24, verse 9; Virgil, *Georgics* 3.483.
80 Isa. 1: 2.
81 The reference is to 2 Peter 2: 21.
82 Adam 2.35/*Schol.* 24, pp. 95–96; Tschan (trans.) 1959: 78.

by her husband, along with others, this woman suffered no small amount of controversy.[83] Her sons, who resembled their beloved parent in every way, tearfully accepted their father's corpse and placed it within a burial mound. Afterwards, they prepared ships and made plans to avenge whatever shame had been inflicted upon their father by the Angles. The many outrages they committed against this folk are not familiar to me and so I shall pass them by. I will briefly describe with my pen only that which has been related to me by a reliable witness.[84]

CHAPTER FORTY [1016]

In the year of the Incarnation, 1016, King Aethelred of the Angles died. In July of that year, the brothers Harald and Cnut arrived, along with their Duke Thurgut and 340 ships, and laid siege to a certain burg called London.[85] In this burg resided the queen, still mourning the death of her husband and protector,[86] as well as her sons, Aethelstan and Edmund,[87] two bishops, and other leading men of the realm. After bringing their ships up the Thames, each of them holding eighty men, they besieged the place for six months. Finally, the queen was exhausted by the constant fighting and sent messengers to seek peace and to carefully inquire what they wanted from her. The insatiable enemy immediately responded that, if the queen were willing to have her two sons killed, redeem herself for fifteen thousand silver pounds, redeem the bishops for twelve thousand, and all of her armed men for the unbelievable sum of twenty-four thousand pounds, and if she would give three hundred hostages as surety for this agreement, only then would she obtain peace and life for herself and her companions. Otherwise, so they shouted three times aloud, they would put all of them to the sword. The venerable queen and her advisers were greatly disturbed by this message. After long and tumultuous deliberations, however, she agreed to the demands and confirmed this through the *milites* whom we have already mentioned.

83 On the identity of this 'husband' see Whitelock (ed.) 1955: 319, n. 6.
84 Presumably Sewald (7.42).
85 King Harald of Denmark (1014–18), King Cnut of England (1016–35) and Denmark (1018–35). On the identity of Thurgut (Thorkel?) see Whitelock (ed.) 1955: 319, n. 7.
86 King Aethelred.
87 The product of Aethelred's first marriage and hence, Emma's stepsons. See Whitelock (ed.) 1955: 320, n. 1.

CHAPTER FORTY-ONE [1016]

Meanwhile, in the middle of the night, the two brothers took a small boat and escaped the danger. They then gathered together whatever forces they could find, to the end that they might defend the homeland and rescue their mother. They did all of this without attracting the enemy's attention. But one day, when Thurgut, the leader of the pirates, set forth with a multitude of warriors to pillage the surrounding areas, he had an expected encounter with the enemy. Observing the latter's approach, from a distance, he roused his companions' spirits and launched a vigorous attack. Both Edmund and Thurgut were killed, along with many of their companions.[88] Since the bloodshed had been heavy and neither side had any prospect of victory, they parted voluntarily, lamenting only that fortune had permitted them to meet. Scripture forbids us, however, from believing that anything occurs through fate or accident.[89] Though weakened, the Danes managed to return to their own ships. When they realized that Aethelstan, who had survived the recent battle, and the Britons, who had just arrived, had each brought aid to London, the Danes put their hostages to the sword and fled. May God, protector of all who place their trust in him, destroy and utterly ruin these men, so that they may never again inflict such suffering on these, or any other faithful Christians. Let us rejoice at the rescue of the city, but grieve over the rest.

CHAPTER FORTY-TWO

I have also received a report from Sewald, whom I have already mentioned, of a lamentable and therefore memorable event. Led by Thurkil, a band of heathen Northmen captured, among others, the illustrious Archbishop Dunstan of Canterbury whom they kept in chains, hungry and in unspeakable pain, as is their wicked custom.[90] Overwhelmed by human weakness, Dunstan promised them a ransom and arranged a truce so that he could obtain it. In the meantime, he planned to purify himself with frequent lamentations, as a living sacrifice to God, in the event that he could not avoid the moment of death

88 Whitelock ed. 1955: 320. n. 2, notes that Edmund was not killed in battle and that if Thurgut is really Thorkel, the reference to his death is also an error.

89 Aug., *Civ. Dei* 5.9, pp. 136–40; *De div. quaest.* 24, pp. 29 ff.

90 Archbishop Dunstan of Canterbury (959–88). In fact, this report concerns Dunstan's successor, Archbishop Aelfheah (1005–12; Holtzmann 1935: 449, n. 3).

through an acceptable ransom. When the designated time had passed, the voracious Charybdis of these magpies summoned the servant of God and, in a threatening manner, demanded that he quickly hand over the promised ransom. As meekly as a lamb, Dunstan responded: 'I am ready and prepared for whatever you may now wish to do with me. Through the love of Christ, I no longer fear the possibility that I might be made a worthy model for his servants. If I appear to have lied to you, this was not my intention, but rather the result of my harsh poverty. I offer to you this guilt-ridden body of mine, having loved it excessively during my period of exile, and realizing that you have the power to do with it as you wish. My sinful soul, over which you have no power, I humbly commend to the Creator of all things.'

CHAPTER FORTY-THREE

As he said these things, he was surrounded by a crowd of the heathen who took up various weapons with the intention of killing him. Seeing this at a distance, their leader, Thurkil, rushed over to them and said: 'Do not do this, I beg you! I will gladly give you gold and silver. Indeed, with the exception of the ship, I will give you everything I possess or can in any way acquire. Only refrain from harming this one who has been chosen by the Lord.' Such sweet words could not mollify the unbridled anger of his companions, more unyielding than iron or stone. Indeed, their anger could only be satisfied by the innocent blood, which they caused to flow freely by hitting Dunstan with the skulls of cattle, showering him with stones, and striking him with sticks. After being struck down, amid such a great clamour, he obtained the joy of heaven. This was immediately confirmed through a most efficacious sign. For one of the leaders was suddenly crippled, thereby revealing through his own body that he had harmed the chosen one of Christ. So it is written: 'Revenge is mine, and I will exact retribution, says the Lord.'[91] In this triumph of the athlete of Christ, his wretched and defeated persecutors lost not only the grace of God and the riches offered by their leader, but also their souls, unless they recovered them by offering compensation. Dunstan was pleasing in the eyes of God, with his stole, formerly white from the innocence of his mind and body, but now tinted red with blood. We sinners should seek his intercession, through constant prayer, and believe that the divine majesty values him most highly.

91 Rom. 12: 19.

CHAPTER FORTY-FOUR [1016]

Not without deep sorrow can I describe the evil which the avenger of sin imposed upon Christians during the leap year noted above. In the middle of the night, Margrave Bernhard fell upon the city of Magdeburg with a great multitude.[92] This attack led to the capture of one of the archbishop's dependants, though he was completely guiltless, and left another wounded. On the morning of 10 February, a Friday, thunder, lightning, and heavy storms caused terrible damage in various locations, and appeared to signal future misery.[93] Some people were killed when their houses collapsed under the onslaught, others were injured and barely escaped with their lives. Great destruction also occurred in the forests, from falling trees and branches. The count palatine, Burchard, suffered a stroke.

In the region called Hassegau, the four brothers, Aelli, Burchard, Dietrich, and Poppo gathered a war band and attacked Bern, a free man and good *miles*, who had often treated them with contempt. They managed to kill him although he was accompanied by no fewer than one hundred armed men.[94] There were casualties on both sides, however.

CHAPTER FORTY-FIVE [1016]

Travelling by ship, the Saracens came to Lombardy and seized the city of Luna whose bishop was barely able to escape. Then, without opposition and in complete security, they occupied the whole region and abused the occupants' womenfolk. When news of these events reached Pope Benedict, he summoned all the rectors and defenders of holy mother church, and both asked and commanded them to join him in an attack on these presumptuous enemies of Christ. With God's help, they could annihilate them. Furthermore, he secretly sent a powerful fleet to eliminate any possibility that the enemy might retreat. When informed of these developments, the Saracen king was initially disdainful, but then, with a few members of his entourage, chose to escape the approaching danger on a ship. Yet his forces rallied and, attacking first, quickly put the approaching enemy to flight. Sad to say, the slaughter continued for three days and nights. At last, placated by the groans of the pious, God relented and put

92 Margrave of the Saxon northern march.
93 Not a Friday but a Saturday (Holtzmann 1935: 452, n. 1).
94 *NMer.*, 26 July, fo. 4r, p. 9.

those who hated him to flight. Indeed, so thoroughly were they defeated, that not one of the murderers remained alive and the victors could scarcely count their abundant booty. Their captured queen was decapitated as payment for her husband's audacity and the pope, choosing before the others, took her gold, gem-encrusted crown. Later, he sent it to the emperor, as his share. It was judged to be worth one thousand pounds. When all the booty had been divided, the victorious warriors happily returned to their homeland, as they sang worthy odes to the triumphant Christ. The king, whom we have mentioned, was very disturbed by the death of his wife and companions. He sent a sack full of chestnuts to the pope and had the bearer intimate that, during the following summer, the king would return with an equal number of *milites*. After receiving this message, the pope had the sack filled with purses and returned it to the messenger, saying: 'If he has not done sufficient damage to the lands of the Apostle, let him come again, but he should be certain that he will encounter so many or even more armed men.' Man thinks and speaks, but God judges.[95] Thus, every Christian should humbly beseech him that, in his mercy, such plagues may be turned away and we may thereby obtain the security necessary for that peace which we so greatly desire.

CHAPTER FORTY-SIX

Near the island of Reichenau, on 16 October, a boat filled with people of both sexes sank. In the West, Lambert, the much hated son of Reginar, and his companions, were attacked by his enemy Gottfried.[96] Lambert himself was killed. In that land, he was then the worst of men. Indeed, he had strangled many people, in churches, with bell ropes. No one can count the number of men he disinherited or killed. Nor did he ever care to do penance for his shameful deeds. Together, he and his brother, Reginar, also killed Werner and his brother Reginald. Lambert's father had been exiled to Bohemia by Otto, and

---

95 Perhaps Prov. 16: 9.

96 Lambert of Louvain was the son of Count Reginar III of Hennegau and grandson of Duke Giselbert I of Lotharingia. The Reginareds had suffered a severe setback in 958 when Otto I sent Reginar III into exile and confiscated his lands (the family partially regained them in 977). The violence perpetrated by Lambert and his brother, Reginar IV of Hennegau, probably reflects an effort to solidify their position in the region (Beumann 1991: 116; Reuter 1991: 159). It was presumably in the interest of creating a counterweight to this powerful and dangerous family that Henry II installed Count Gottfried of Verdun as duke of Lower Lotharingia (1012–23; Beumann 1991: 167).

died there. While these men lived, their homeland mourned, but it rejoiced when they died. This alone should we regret, that on that day, the misdeeds of one man caused the deaths of so many, and on both sides. Unfortunately, those regions then saw even more destruction. For in the realm of King Robert, a man always ready for peace and respectful to all, the populace battled among themselves.[97] More than three thousand were killed. Nor can I omit the irreparable loss that occurred after this. For on 2 October, my uncle, Count Henry, a man of great stature in this world and in the eyes of Christ, paid the debt of our dual nature.[98] He is to be congratulated for his long and righteous life, and for his admirable end.

CHAPTER FORTY-SEVEN [1016]

Count Wichman [IV], a man very valuable for our homeland, was killed by a presumptuous serf and at the instigation of a second Herod.[99] Through my sad report, I shall reveal how this occurred. There had been a long-running feud between Count Wichman and Count Balderich, in which the latter had often suffered defeat.[100] Indeed, Balderich had brought such humiliation upon himself that the other leading men treated him with great disdain. Wichman accepted his good fortune with equanimity, however, ascribing it to the mercy of God, and planned to settle the long-raging feud through a truce. In a most friendly manner, he invited his enemy to his home and attempted to mollify him with food and gifts. To confirm these new bonds of affection, he was similarly invited to the home of his former enemy. And yet, the ancient serpent, hissing at Balderich through his wife, argued that since he had been unable to take Wichman by force, he might at least capture him in the net of his cunning.[101] Thus, the

---

97 King Robert *the Pious* of France. See above p. 19.

98 Count Henry II of Stade whose entry in the necrology at Merseburg characterizes him as 'Count and Servant of Christ' (*NMer.*, 1 October, fo. 6r, p. 13).

99 Count Wichman III. A more detailed account of the feud is given by Alpert of Metz (*De diversitate temporum*, bk 2, pp. 709ff; and in general, Leyser 1994e: 40). A comparison with Herod is also made at 1.4. Here the reference is to Count Balderich.

100 Count Balderich of Drenthegau.

101 Adela, daughter of Count Wichman of Hamaland. Balderich was her second husband. Bishop Meinwerk of Paderborn was the product of her first marriage, with Immad. Aside from Wichman [IV], Adela's machinations encompassed Abbess Liutgard of Elten (her sister) and her own children. Property, a typical incentive for aristocratic violence, was the heart of the matter in each case (Beumann 1991: 172; Platelle 1990: 181–83).

praiseworthy simplicity of a noble spirit agreed to the seemingly amicable demands of a false friend. Wichman was initially accorded the best of receptions, but evil followed in the form of a drink laced with poison. After this, he experienced severe and steadily increasing pain, and could scarcely remain in Balderich's home for another day. When Wichman departed, endowed with abundant gifts and the apparent affection of his hosts, his *milites* were delayed through some kind of ruse, so that a servant could kill him without being observed.[102] Although this occurred in the presence of the servant's lord, Balderich, the latter made no effort to avenge the deed. Indeed, when one of his companions killed the author of this outrage, he himself was killed.

CHAPTER FORTY-EIGHT [1016]

After Balderich fled, thereby revealing his guilty conscience, rumour spread the wretched story even farther. Bishop Dietrich of the holy church of Münster, the son of my mother's sister, happened to be in the area and was the first to arrive.[103] Inconsolable in his sorrow, he bemoaned the death of his beloved friend and, after accompanying the body to the burg Vreden, took great care to see that he was placed among his ancestors. Afterwards, he dispatched his messengers throughout the region for the purpose of inciting countrymen and relatives to take vengeance. He also directed a substantial force against the enemy's burg, Uflach, devastating nearby areas and setting them afire. Finally, my cousin, Duke Bernhard, arrived. He was the rightful guardian of the count's son, still a minor, and also of his entire inheritance.[104] He now stepped forward as avenger of this heinous crime. As much as he could, Bernhard consoled the count's unhappy *milites*. He also joined other supporters in continuously assailing the occupants of the burg.

CHAPTER FORTY-NINE [1016]

Meanwhile, the emperor left Burgundy where he had spent a good part of the summer. As soon as he learned of the events surrounding Wichman's murder, however, he boarded a ship and quickly travelled to

102 *NMer.*, 5 October, fo. 6r, p. 13. But different dates of death are reported by other sources (cf. Holtzmann 1935: 457, n. 7).
103 Bishop Dietrich of Münster (1011–22).
104 Count Wichman IV.

the scene of the crime. During this trip, Gebhard died. He was my cousin, and Count Herbert's son, a man well regarded by the emperor and distinguished by his exceptional probity.[105] His death left both the emperor and his own countrymen in great sorrow. Archbishop Heribert of Cologne, being very concerned about the situation of his *miles*, Balderich, frequently urged the emperor to give him possession of the latter's long-besieged burg. The emperor finally conceded, overcome by Heribert's constant petitions. When the emperor's enemy left, however, the burg Uflach was completely destroyed. Alas! Though the unhappy countess remained there somewhat longer, she still managed to escape with all her possessions intact. May all the afflictions that Job called down upon himself, also strike this woman who so clearly deserves them. May she endure so much suffering in this life that she may at least hope for forgiveness in the future. Whoever aided her in this matter should turn to God, fervently confess his sin, and make worthy restitution. Indeed, through the hissing of this poisonous adder, the church lost a great defender. In this same year, Bishop Dietrich[106] and Count Herman, the son of Gerberga,[107] wasted each other's lands because of some insignificant dispute.[108] Finally, they were persuaded by friends, and especially by an order from the emperor, to cease their attacks and postpone the matter until the emperor returned.

CHAPTER FIFTY [1017]

On 1 January, in the year of the Incarnation 1017, and at the emperor's order, Archbishop Gero received Margrave Bernhard, who approached him barefoot and promised compensation. The margrave was then released from all the banns which had been imposed upon him and presented in the church. After celebrating the birth of the Lord at Pöhlde, the emperor moved on to Allstedt where he solemnly observed the feast of Epiphany [6 January]. On that same holy night, Count Frederick, a man faithful to Christ and his lord, died in his burg Eilenburg. This wise man, recognizing that the end of his life was fast approaching, had conveyed the burg to his brother's son, Dietrich.[109] It

---

105 Count Herbert was an uncle of Thietmar's mother (4.60). Gebhard's death is noted on 8 November in the necrology at Merseburg (*NMer.*, fo. 7.r, p. 15).

106 Bishop Dietrich of Münster.

107 Count Herman II of Werl.

108 Cf. 8.26.

109 Frederick's brother was Dedi (6.49–50).

was agreed, however, that the remainder of the count's land would pass to his three daughters. Such arrangements were necessary because Dietrich was an heir, and to have done otherwise would not have been legitimate.[110] Later, Dietrich received from the emperor both Frederick's countship and control over the district of Siusuli.

A general assembly of the leading men took place at Allstedt. Here, a dispute between Margrave Bernhard and my paternal cousins was settled with an offer of compensation acceptable to the margrave, and through the swearing of oaths.[111] By 29 September, the emperor had also resolved the long-standing hatred between Bishop Dietrich and Count Herman,[112] and the mutual loathing that existed between Ekkehard and his brethren, the sons of lord Udo.[113] There too, Margrave Bernhard promised Archbishop Gero compensation, amounting to five hundred silver pounds, for any damage he had suffered. During his extended stay at Allstedt, the emperor did many other good things. Peace was made between Counts Gebhard and William.[114] Messengers from Italy arrived, offered their good wishes, and returned. The emperor's plans for a trip to the West had to be postponed because the roads were in such poor condition. The emperor also agreed to what Boleslav had requested: the leading men would be assembled in the duke's presence. Should the emperor wish to propose something to his profit, it could then be enacted on their advice. Messengers were sent back and forth and a truce was arranged.

CHAPTER FIFTY-ONE [1017]

Meanwhile, the emperor came to Merseburg where he awaited the outcome of this matter. While he was there, many highwaymen were put to death by hanging, after champions had defeated them in single combat. The two archbishops, Erkanbald and Gero, Bishop Arnulf, Counts Siegfried and Bernhard, and other leading men, camped for

110 Thietmar was well aware of the difficulties that could ensue when the ambitions of a kinsman were not satisfied ahead of time (cf. 4.17; Leyser 1979: 59).
111 This represents the nadir of the Walbecker clan which clearly had been attempting to regain the property lost at Margrave Werner's death (Lippelt 1973: 56).
112 Count Herman II of Werl.
113 Henry and Udo of Katlinburg, murderers of Margrave Ekkehard I (5.5; Hucke 1956: 78).
114 Counts Gerhard and William of Querfurt.

fourteen days on the river Mulde.[115] Through intermediaries, they asked Boleslav to come to the Elbe for the meeting which he had so long desired. The duke was then residing at Zützen. As soon as he had heard this message, he responded that he would not dare to go there, for fear of his enemy. The messengers asked: 'What would you do, if our lords come to the Elster?' But he said: 'I do not wish to cross that bridge.' After hearing this, the messengers returned and related everything to their lords. The emperor was with us, celebrating the Purification of the blessed Mother of God [2 February]. Somewhat later, the bishops and counts arrived, outraged that Boleslav had so contemptuously tried to deceive them. In turn, they sought to arouse the emperor's ire by describing how things had gone during their legation. At this point, they began to discuss a future campaign, and everyone loyal to the emperor was advised to prepare for it. The emperor firmly prohibited any exchange of messengers between us and Boleslav, that enemy of the realm, and every effort was made to identify persons who might have presumed to do so in the past.

CHAPTER FIFTY-TWO [1017]

After his parting from us, the emperor went to Magdeburg, where he was received with great honour. Because the next morning, a Sunday, marked the beginning of Septuagesima, he stopped eating meat.[116] On Monday, the archbishop consecrated the north chapel in the emperor's presence. On the following day, a quarrel arose between the archbishop's people and Margrave Bernhard's, but the matter was settled without violence and in the bishop's favour. At the emperor's order, thieves who had been defeated in duels assembled there, and were put to the rope. It was at Magdeburg as well that many questions relating to the welfare of the realm were decided and, from thence, that the convert Gunther set out to preach to the Liutizi.[117] In the

---

115 Count Siegfried was the son of Margrave Hodo (4.60), and the Margarve Bernhard referred to here is the same one referred to in 7.50.

116 The third Sunday before Easter (17 February) which concluded the pre-fast period of the Lenten season.

117 Feast day 9 October. A scion of the Thuringian comital house of Käfernburg-Schwarzburg and a classic example of a noble *conversus* who abandoned the warrior's life for that of a monk (Hersfeld, Niederaltaich) and hermit (Rinchnach, Bavarian forest). His status as a monk and hermit did not prevent Gunther from leading an active life, however. Aside from preaching to the Czechs and Liutizi, he was a guest at the Hungarian royal court and sometime diplomat/adviser at the German court (*LTK*, vol. 4, pp. 1275–76; Lang 1942: 45–54; Fichtenau 1991: 248).

emperor's presence, I raised many complaints regarding a part of my
diocese which had been unjustly appropriated by the church of
Meißen. The restitution of this property had been promised, in
writing, but just when it seemed that I might profit from that, I had
to recognize that things had gone rather differently from how I had
planned. On the feast of St Peter's throne, 22 February, the emperor
held a court. It was attended by Bishops Gero, Meinwerk, Wigo, Erich,
and Eilward. On this occasion, I arose and presented my complaint,
expecting help from the emperor and the bishops. Instead, they
ordered me – God knows, I was unwilling, but dared not resist – to
concede to Eilward a parish on the east bank of the river Mulda, in
the burgward of Püchen and Wurzen. In return, he was to give me a
parish that he held on the west bank, though I never desired it. The
transaction was confirmed with an exchange of episcopal staffs. I give
witness before God and all his saints: in no way did I surrender the
rest of my claim! The emperor also ordered Margrave Herman to
prove by oath that he was the rightful possessor of three villages
which he held from the church of Meißen, or surrender them to me.

CHAPTER FIFTY-THREE [1017]

On the same day, Archbishop Gero honoured the emperor and his
wife with splendid gifts [22 February]. They left Magdeburg on the
following day. Three days later, on a Sunday, they arrived in
Halberstadt, where Bishop Arnulf accorded them a magnificent
reception [24 February]. They remained with the bishop for two
days. On Tuesday, they travelled to Quedlinburg, where they were
received with no less honour by the venerable Abbess Adelheid [26
February]. On 27 February, a Wednesday, Bishop Arnulf dedicated
the convent on the western hill.[118] This was a place where consecrated
women served their heavenly bridegroom while clothed as nuns.
Archbishop Gero assisted Arnulf at the consecration, as did other
brethren. Thereafter, the emperor donated a pound of gold for the
altar. Having received ample proof of his cousin's love, the emperor
then travelled to his estate at Goslar and resided there for four weeks.
Through his efforts, it had been much improved.[119] Because the season
of Lent had arrived, he sought both to fulfil his obligations to Christ

118 The convent of St Mary on the Münzenburg.
119 Henry's 'efforts' mark the beginning of Goslar's development as a palace complex
(Ehlers 1997: 56–57).

and tend to the urgent needs of mortals. Somewhat later, Berthold, Liuthar's son, bribed the guard at the burg Monreberg and forced his way in, along with his supporters. Once inside, he killed Balderich, a most excellent vassal of Count Wichman who, along with his companions, had offered fierce resistance. Thus Berthold established himself as the victor. On the previous day, I had come to Meißen for garrison duty [31 March].

CHAPTER FIFTY-FOUR [1017]

During this week, at the emperor's order, our leading men gathered at Goslar. On this occasion, my uncle Siegfried received his brother Henry's countship, a campaign in our region was announced, and there was discussion of other useful and urgent matters pertaining to our endangered homeland. The emperor first heard of the evil doings at Monreberg after he was again under way, and he was greatly concerned at the prospect of further trouble. During the spring, in Margrave Bernhard's territory, a lamb was born with five legs. On 8 April, though the moon was supposed to be full, it appeared to many as a new moon; and for a long time, at the third hour of the day, it appeared to be red. The king celebrated Palm Sunday at Mainz and Easter at Ingelheim [14, 21 April]. Greater splendour and magnificence had never been seen in these lands. Because the high solemnity of the occasion prevented the most important matters from being concluded, another assembly was held at Aachen. There, on the advice of Archbishop Heribert, the emperor was reconciled with Bishop Dietrich of Metz and his brother, Henry. The queen had parted from the emperor at Frankfurt. Arriving at a place called Kaufungen, she became ill, and promised God that she would honour him by establishing a monastery there.[120]

CHAPTER FIFTY-FIVE

At this point, it would not be inappropriate for me to note certain events that occurred in the meantime. In the city of Magdeburg, there were two sisters, of which the elder was named Alfrad, the younger Irmgard.[121] Both devoted their admirable lives completely to the

---

120 See 8.18.

121 A possible reference to Alfrad can be found in the 'Cambridge Songs' which cite a 'place called Homburg where Alfrad pastured a donkey' (*Carm. Cant.* 20. 1. 60).

service of Christ and his beloved mother, but not in association with
other nuns, rather alone, in a church referred to as the Rotunda.[122]
After losing the exterior vision of her eyes, the younger sister rejoiced
in the eternal splendour of her inner vision, and not long afterwards,
on 8 February, migrated to that most desirable homeland. The elder
sister was then supported by her niece, Friderun, but enduring sorrow
at the loss of her sister and constant illness caused her to decline. She
lived only fourteen weeks and three days longer.[123] On the day before
she was to pay her mortal debt, she was spiritually transported into
the presence of the holy Mother of God. There, her worthiness was
such that she was granted absolution by Archbishops Tagino and
Walthard, and the venerable Bishop Eid, each of them gleaming with
great honour. She also saw Archbishop Gero's maternal aunts, Mires-
wind, Emnild, and Eddila. For the love of Christ, one of them had left
her abbey and been enclosed next to the monastery of the teacher of
the heathen, Paul, at Rome. She also saw Odda. Together, they were
all singing the words of the psalmist: 'I will please the Lord in the
land of the living.'[124] Meanwhile, she appeared dead to all those who
attended her. But then, after she awoke and opened her eyes, she
revealed what she had seen, saying: 'Up to now, I have happily resided
among you, but now, having seen much better things, I can no longer
bear to remain in this filthy house. I say to you in truth that tomorrow I shall leave you and assume the place preordained for me
through the gift of God.' And so it happened. Her soul happily
migrated to Christ on 22 May.[125] This is all true, O brothers in Christ,
believe me, and know for certain that such helpers of our church are
most valuable. They have included me, a sinner, in their holy prayers
although, alas, they have never received anything good from me in
return.

CHAPTER FIFTY-SIX [1017]

The emperor, hearing that his wife had recovered and had made a
vow to the Lord, rendered heartfelt thanks to Christ. He devoutly
celebrated Pentecost at Werden, which had been founded by God's

---

122 See 6.77.
123 The death of a *sanctimonialis* by this name is noted in *NMag.*, 16 March, fo. 4r.
124 Ps. 114: 9.
125 *NMer.*, 22 May, fo. 2v.

holy priest Liudger at his own expense.[126] The emperor's needs were fully accommodated by Abbot Heidenreich. On the following day, 10 June, Bishop Thiedegg of Prague, successor to Christ's martyr, Adalbert, faithfully went the way of all flesh. Thiedegg had been educated at Corvey and was especially skilled in the art of healing. When Boleslav the Elder was suffering from paralysis because of his disobedience to Christ's preacher, he summoned Thiedegg, with Abbot Thietmar's permission, and was much improved through his ministrations. Thus, when that burning lamp, Woyciech, was removed from the shadows of this world, as I have mentioned,[127] the duke's aid ensured that Otto III installed Thiedegg as his successor. After the death of Boleslav the Elder, his like-named son frequently expelled the bishop from his diocese, and just as often Margrave Ekkehard brought him back. He suffered many injuries. As St Gregory ordered, he not only invited guests to come to him, but even dragged them in.[128] His one major failing was that he drank immoderately, due to an undeserved illness. Indeed, the tremors in his hands prevented him from saying mass without the help of priest who stood next to him. He grew progressively weaker until the end, but, as I hope, cured his soul with good medicines.

CHAPTER FIFTY-SEVEN [1017]

Meanwhile, Moravian soldiers of Boleslav surrounded and killed a large but careless band of Bavarians. In no small measure, then, losses previously inflicted upon them by the Bavarians were now avenged.[129] As the emperor travelled towards the East, he ordered the empress to meet him at Paderborn. From there, the two of them moved on to Magdeburg where they were received, with honour, by Archbishop Gero. During the following night, 7 July, a Sunday, a horrible storm arose and caused widespread destruction of human beings, cattle, buildings, and the produce of the fields. In the forests, a huge number of trees and branches fell and blocked all of the roads. The next day, the emperor crossed the Elbe, along with his wife and the army, and proceeded to Lietzkau, an estate which formerly belonged to Bishop Wigo but was now the habitation of many wild animals. He set up

126 See 4.68.
127 4.28.
128 Greg., *Hom. Ev.* 2. 23. 1, col. 1182.
129 7.19.

camp and remained there for two nights, awaiting the arrival of more dilatory contingents. Subsequently, the empress and many others returned, while the emperor pressed on with his army. On that same day, Henry, formerly duke of the Bavarians, returned with a message from Boleslav which suggested that they negotiate a peace. After listening to this report, the emperor sent Henry back again, with a message of his own. When he could accomplish nothing, however, he was sent to join the emperor's wife, his sister.

CHAPTER FIFTY-EIGHT [1017]

Meanwhile, on the night of 21 July, a Sunday, something very sad occurred on the mount of St John the Baptist, which is located near Magdeburg and subject to it in every respect. An unusually large lamp in the dormitory caused a fire which began to spread and, since the sleeping brothers noticed it too late, eventually engulfed the entire building. Although everyone initially escaped the danger, one brother perished when he suddenly ran back to rescue some vestments. He confessed his sins amid the flames. His name was Hemiko. The next building to catch fire was the church. Abbot Siegfried had spent eight years decorating it, and everyone was brokenhearted at its destruction, whether they were actually present or arrived later. The spreading flames also consumed two chapels, the refectory, and other buildings which were attached to them. Through the love of God and the great devotion of those who rushed to help, all the relics of the saints were rescued from the fire's greedy jaws, along with the greater part of the treasure. In the morning, the inhabitants of Magdeburg arrived, along with the garrison which had been left there by the emperor. They surveyed the heavy damage with great sadness and lamentations. In the morning, as well, the brethren carefully collected the light ashes of the burned body and interred them among their predecessors.[130] A messenger was immediately sent to their abbot, who was then absent, to inform him of this unhappy event. As soon as the abbot heard the news, however, he recognized that the fire was the result of his own sins and treated the matter with all seriousness because it could not be changed.

---

130 A somewhat loose translation which, in my opinion, captures the sense of the passage.

CHAPTER FIFTY-NINE [1017]

While all of this was going on, Boleslav's son, Miesco, took ten war bands and invaded Bohemia. They encountered less resistance than they otherwise would have, due to the absence of the Bohemian duke, Ulrich. After pillaging the countryside for two days, Miesco returned, bringing many captives with him and much joy to his father. Accompanied by his army and a large contingent of Bohemians and Liutizi, the emperor anxiously made his way to the burg Glogau, wasting everything he encountered along the way. At Glogau, Boleslav awaited him with his army. Surrounded by archers, the enemy tried to provoke our forces to battle, but the emperor held them back. Instead, he selected twelve war bands from this already very strong army and sent them to the burg Nimptsch, so called because it was originally founded by us. These war bands were to prevent the inhabitants from receiving any aid from outside. They had barely set up camp, however, when news reached them that the enemy had arrived. Because of the exceedingly dark night and a heavy rain, there was little that our forces could do to them. They put some of them to flight, but reluctantly permitted others to enter the burg. The latter is situated in the region of Silesia, which was named long ago after a certain mountain of great height and width. While the detestable rites of the heathen were still practised here, this mountain was highly venerated by the populace, because of its unique character and size.

CHAPTER SIXTY [1017]

Three days later, the emperor arrived at Glogau with the rest of the army. He ordered that his camp be set up on all sides of the burg, in the hope that he might thereby prevent his enemy from entering. His wise plan and excellent intentions would have enjoyed great success, had his supporters shown greater enthusiasm when it came to the time to implement them. As it turned out, in the silence of night, a large body of troops managed to pass through all the guards and enter the burg. Our people were then ordered to construct various types of siege machinery. Immediately, our opponents began to do the same. I have never heard of an army which defended itself with greater endurance or more astutely. Against the pagans, they erected a holy cross, hoping to conquer them with its help. They never shouted for joy when something favourable to them occurred. Nor did they reveal their misfortunes by openly lamenting them.

CHAPTER SIXTY-ONE [1017]

Meanwhile, the Moravians invaded Bohemia where they seized a certain burg and returned, unharmed and with much booty. Margrave Henry had attempted to engage them with an army.[131] When he heard of their attack on the burg, however, he quickly set off in pursuit. As a result, more than one thousand of their men were killed and the rest were put to flight. The margrave also managed to free all of their captives and bring them home. Nor should I fail to mention that other *milites* of Boleslav attacked the burg Belgern on 15 August. In spite of a long siege, they had no success. Thanks be to God! Among those Liutizi who had remained at home, a large number attacked one of the duke's burgs. On this occasion, they lost more than one hundred warriors and their return was marked by great sadness. Later, they inflicted much devastation on Boleslav's lands.

CHAPTER SIXTY-TWO [1017]

Here, I should add an account of the deadly encounter between Duke Gottfried and Count Gerhard.[132] There had long been discord between them. At last, however, a day was set on which they and their supporters were to settle the matter through the unquestionable judgement of a judicial duel. On 27 August, they met at the agreed-upon location, the flattest area of a certain flowery meadow. There, the humility of Christ overcame Gerhard's pride and, as his companions suddenly took flight, no less than three hundred of them were killed. One of the casualties was called Walter Pulverel, because he was accustomed to reduce his opponents to dust. In terms of his clothing, he was a cleric. In fact, however, he was an exceptional bandit. Along with his followers, this particular leader fell into a pond. Now, lying there, he was satiated with battle even though his lust for blood had never previously been satisfied. People say that he only considered a day well spent if his spear was covered with human blood and he could see the house of the Lord, which other wicked men spared, in flames and collapsing. He came from Burgundy. On one occasion, he was captured by Count Gerhard who would not release him until he swore that he would stand by him for ever and faithfully

---

131 Margrave of the Bavarian eastern march.

132 Here, referring to. Duke Gottfried II of Lower Lotharingia and Count Gerhard I of Alsace (c.1000–20), the latter being the husband of Eva, daughter of Count Siegfried of Luxembourg and sister of Empress Cunegunde (*LMA*, vol. 4, p. 1310).

provide military support. So too, he was summoned and came to this deadly encounter, but God's mercy prevented him from returning and ensured that his customary outrages would not continue. From among Gerhard's followers, the number of those captured included the count's own son, Siegfried – he was also the empress's nephew – as well as Balderich, and many others.[133] Among the wounded was Conrad, who had illegally married his own cousin, the widow of Duke Ernst.[134] The duke lost only thirty *milites*, admittedly among his best.

CHAPTER SIXTY-THREE [1017]

In the meantime, the siege machinery had been completed, and now, after three weeks of silence, the emperor ordered an attack on the burg. As he looked on, however, all of this machinery went up flames, destroyed by fire thrown down from the ramparts. After this, Ulrich and his companions tried to scale the fortifications, but accomplished nothing. A similar attack by the Liutizi was also turned back. Finally, the emperor realized that his army, already weakened by disease, had no prospect of capturing the burg and decided to undertake the arduous march to Bohemia. There, he was honoured with suitable gifts by Ulrich, who illegally held the title of duke in that region. Meanwhile, 18 September marked the death, following a long illness, of Margrave Henry, my aunt's son and the glory of eastern Franconia.[135] Three bishops, Henry, Eberhard, and the venerable Rikulf, attended to his burial.[136] His grave was located on the north side of the monastery at Schweinfurt, outside of the church, and next to the door, as he himself had wished. The emperor, who learned of his death while residing in Meißen, was very sad.

CHAPTER SIXTY-FOUR [1017]

Boleslav anxiously awaited the outcome of events in his burg at Wroclaw. When he heard that the emperor had departed and that the burg at Glogau was unharmed, he rejoiced in the Lord and joyfully celebrated with his warriors. More then six hundred of his foot-

---

133 On Balderich see 7.47–49.

134 Conrad II, the future emperor, who married Gisela, widow of Duke Ernst I of Swabia and Bruno of Braunschweig.

135 Margrave Henry of Schweinfurt (*NMer.*, 19 September, fo. 5v, p. 12).

136 Henry of Würzburg, Eberhard of Bamberg, Rikulf of Triest.

soldiers secretly invaded Bohemia and, as usual, hoped to return with much booty. Except for a few, however, they were trapped by the very snare that they had wanted to lay for their enemies. The Liutizi returned to their homeland in an angry mood and complaining about the dishonour inflicted upon their goddess. One of Margrave Herman's retainers had thrown a rock at a banner which bore her image. When their servants sadly related this event to the emperor, he gave them twelve pounds as compensation. When they attempted to cross the swollen waters of the Mulde, near the burg Wurzen, they lost yet another image of their goddess and a most excellent band of fifty *milites.* The rest returned under this evil omen and, at the instigation of wicked men, tried to remove themselves from the emperor's service. Yet, afterwards, a general assembly was held at which their leading men convinced them otherwise. If an entry could barely be forced into the territories of Bohemia, it was even more difficult to exit from them. This expedition was undertaken in order to annihilate the enemy, but it also inflicted many wounds on us, the victors, because of our sins. What the enemy could not do to us then occurred to us later because of our misdeeds. May I also bemoan the outrage which Boleslav's followers committed, between the Elbe and the Mulde. On 19 September, at their lord's order, they quickly departed, taking with them more than one thousand prisoners and leaving much of the area in flames. With luck, they returned home safely.

CHAPTER SIXTY-FIVE [1017]

On 1 October, the emperor came to Merseburg, where he installed Ekkehard as bishop of Prague. As abbot, Ekkehard had presided over the monastery of Nienburg for twenty-three years and five months. With my permission, the emperor had him consecrated as bishop by Archbishop Erkanbald, on 4 November. On the same occasion, a messenger sent by Boleslav promised that Liudolf the Younger, long held in captivity, would be allowed to return.[137] In return for Liudolf's freedom, he sought the release of certain of Boleslav's *milites* who were being held in firm custody by us. Furthermore, the messenger carefully inquired whether Boleslav might send a representative to negotiate his return to the emperor's grace. Relying on the constant advice of his leading men, the emperor agreed to all of these propositions. Only afterwards did he learn that the king of the Russians

137 His capture is noted at 7.21.

had attacked Boleslav, as his messengers had promised, but had accomplished nothing in regard to the besieged burg.[138] Subsequently, Duke Boleslav invaded the Russian king's realm with his army. After placing his long-exiled brother-in-law, the Russian's brother, on the throne, he returned in high spirits.

CHAPTER SIXTY-SIX [1017]

At his departure, the emperor bestowed upon us three dorsals for the altar and a silver ewer. He then moved on to Allstedt, where he celebrated the feast of All Saints, with due solemnity [1 November]. On the same day, Harding was made Abbot of Nienburg by the emperor and consecrated by Archbishop Gero.[139] On the following Sunday, 3 November, he granted to our brothers serving Christ at Magdeburg a property called Röglitz. He had acquired this property through an agreeable exchange with the *miles* Hathold. He also gave the brothers the right to use a certain wood which he had purchased from Hathold's brother, Hager, for ten silver pounds. He also conceded to me three churches, located in Leipzig, Ölschütz, and Geusa,[140] Furthermore, in the spring of this year, he ordered the fabrication of a gold altar for the decoration of our church. I contributed six pounds of gold taken from the previous altar. After the emperor had resided at Allstedt for five weeks and four days, he visited his beloved Bamberg. There, on the night following the emperor's arrival, Gunzelin was released from his long captivity.[141] Indeed, God caused the chains to fall effortlessly from his feet, without falling apart. On a Sunday, Henry, the former duke of the Bavarians whose misdeeds had caused his deposition, eight years and as many months ago, was restored by the emperor to his original dignity.[142] All of this occurred just as Archbishop Poppo of Trier had previously promised him.

CHAPTER SIXTY-SEVEN

Before concluding my account of this year, I must add a few more observations. In the previous year, Thietmar, venerable bishop of the

138 7.72–74; 8.31–33.
139 Abbot Harding of Nienburg (1017–25).
140 D H II 374 (Geusa).
141 6.54.
142 6.41, 51; 7.54.

church of Osnabrück, servant of St Maurice at Magdeburg, and formerly the very accomplished provost of Mainz and Aachen, lost the use of his eyes which were now clouded by a kind of darkness. His inner vision shone all the more brightly, however, and he was able to contemplate Christ, the source of all light, with constant zeal. At King Henry's instigation, he succeeded Nonno, his predecessor, whose given name was Odilulf.[143] The following year was marked by the deaths of the illustrious bishops Amalrich, Fermund, Bezelin, and Altmann. The last of these had only occupied his see for a few weeks. He had been a monk of St John the Baptist, at Magdeburg, but also figured among Abbess Adelheid's dependants. At the Abbess's instigation, he was transferred to the household of Arnulf, the king's brother, who at the time was archbishop of the church of Ravenna. He was subsequently ordained as a priest by the archbishop, but his health was seriously damaged by his own people, who gave him a drink laced with poison.

CHAPTER SIXTY-EIGHT [1017]

In my neighbourhood, in a place called Sülfeld, a miracle occurred in the second week of December. A certain woman there had barred herself and her children in her house, because her husband was not at home. Behold, just before the rooster crowed, she heard a loud noise. Horrified by this intrusion, she cried out to her neighbours and indicated that she needed help. When the neighbours rushed to her aid, however, they were repeatedly thrown back by some force. Finally, breaking down the doors, they entered with drawn swords and diligently searched for whatever had attacked the mistress of house, and them as well. Because of its supernatural character, however, this enemy could not be discovered. The searchers went away, disheartened, while the woman anxiously awaited the break of day. In the morning, she fetched the closest priest who purified the entire house with the relics of saints and consecrated water. During the following night, she was assailed by the same terror, but to a much lesser extent. Thanks be to God, repeated visits by the priest freed her from it completely.

CHAPTER SIXTY-NINE [1017]

Whenever such things occur, they foretell a change of some kind. There is no reason for faithful Christians to fear them, however. If

---

143 Bishop Odilulf of Osnabrück (999/1002–23).

they honestly confess their sins and immediately fortify themselves with the sign of the cross, they can repel any hostile power. The enemy deludes only those who are careless and, in the end, fools all who believe in him in any way. Yet it is good for us to cling to God and place our hope in him. Let us approach his holy face with constant prayers so that, for us sinners, all may be fulfilled according to his merciful love, whether it be revealed to us or concealed. One should scarcely be surprised to find that such portents occur in our regions. For the inhabitants rarely come to church and show little concern at the visits of their pastors. They worship their household gods and sacrifice to them, hoping thereby to obtain their aid. I have heard of a certain staff which had, on its end, a hand holding an iron ring. The pastor of the village where the hand was preserved would carry it from household to household, and salute it as he entered, saying: 'Awake, Hennil, awake!' Hennil is what the rustics call the hand in their language. Then the fools enjoyed a lavish feast and believed that they were secure in the hand's protection. They knew nothing of David's words: 'The idols of the heathen are the works of men, and so on... Similar to those are all who make and put their trust in them.'[144]

CHAPTER SEVENTY

Because anything unusual is certain to attract astonishment and will often be considered a portent, I shall describe an incident of this sort which occurred in our day. This incident occurred during the reign of Henry, our most serene king, in the lifetime of my predecessor, Wigbert, and in the village of Rödlitz, which was given to our church by the venerable matron Ida, a daughter-in-law of Otto I.[145] It was truthfully recounted to me by Provost Gezo, who held the village as a benefice. One day, during the arduous time of the harvest, the tired labourers wished to refresh themselves. As soon as they cut their bread, however, they saw blood pouring out. Astonished, they showed the bread to their lord, and also to their neighbours. In my opinion, this was an omen relating to the conclusion of some future war in which much human blood would be shed.

144 Ps. 113: 12, 16 (RSV Ps. 15: 4, 8).
145 Wife of Liudolf (2.4).

CHAPTER SEVENTY-ONE

I shall also describe another incident, more laudable, but still miraculous and worthy of note. This incident occurred in the burg of Romulus which, for various reasons, is held to be the head of all cities. At a certain church, oil began to flow from a hole in the pavement, to the right of the altar, and continued for an entire day. Many witnessed and were astonished by this marvel. John, the son of Crescenzio, put some of the oil in a vase and sent it to his lord, Henry, who was then our king.[146] Sometimes, oil stands for mercy, according to the saying: 'Let oil not be absent from your head'.[147] Otherwise, it signifies flattery, as it is said: 'May the oil of the sinner never anoint my head.'[148] In my opinion, however, this sign was intended to reveal both the abundant mercy of our ruler and the hidden desires of this patrician. For in public, that destroyer of the Apostolic See was accustomed to honour the king, who had been constituted by God, with gifts and attractive promises. Nevertheless, he greatly feared the king's ascent to the height of the imperial dignity and, in secret, did everything he could to prevent it. Indeed, as the blessed Gregory asserts: 'Earthly majesty is confounded, when the majesty of heaven is revealed.'[149] Although our king was only a man, he was filled with zeal for God and used his strong arm to punish those who attacked and pillaged holy churches. Such a beneficent character could only have been granted to him by heaven. That patrician, in contrast, was worldly both in character and in deed. Into his filthy maw, as if so much plunder, he gathered the offerings that so many devout hands had heaped upon the altar of the Apostles, for the sake of their sins. Because he died, not long afterwards, I fear that he suffered a double punishment. For the lord pope, however, the result was greater security, and for our king, greater power.

CHAPTER SEVENTY-TWO

Now I shall continue my criticism and condemnation of the wicked deeds of the king of the Russians, Vladimir. He obtained a wife, named Helena, from the Greeks.[150] She had formerly been betrothed to Otto

146 John the Younger.
147 Eccles. 9: 8.
148 Ps. 140: 5 (RSV 141: 5).
149 Greg., *Hom. Ev.* 1. 10. 1, col. 1110.
150 In fact, Vladimir was married to Anna, a daughter of Emperor Romanos II (959–63).

III, but was then denied to him, through fraud and cunning. At her instigation, Vladimir accepted the holy Christian faith which, however, he did not adorn with righteous deeds. He was an unrestrained fornicator and cruelly assailed the feckless Greeks with acts of violence. He married one of his three sons to the daughter of Duke Boleslav, our persecutor.[151] Bishop Reinbern of Kolberg was sent with her. He had been born in Hassegau, educated by wise teachers in the liberal sciences, and was elevated to the episcopate, worthily, so I hope. My knowledge and faculties would not suffice to describe the effort he expended in fulfilling his assigned task. He destroyed the shrines of idols by burning them and purified a lake inhabited by demons, by throwing into it four rocks anointed with holy oil and sprinkling it with consecrated water. Thus he brought forth a new sprout on a tree which had hitherto borne no fruit for the omnipotent Lord, that is, through the propagation of holy preaching among an extremely ignorant people. He afflicted his body with continual vigils, fasts, and with silence, thereby transforming his heart into a mirror of divine contemplation. Meanwhile, King Vladimir heard that his son had secretly turned against him, at the urging of Duke Boleslav. He then seized not only his son and wife, but also Reinbern as well, placing each of them in solitary confinement. With tears and through the sacrifice of constant prayers offered from a contrite heart, Reinbern reconciled himself to the highest priest. Then, freed from the narrow prison of his body, he joyfully crossed over to the freedom of perpetual glory.

CHAPTER SEVENTY-THREE

King Vladimir's name is wrongly interpreted to mean 'power of peace'. Indeed, that which the impious hold among themselves or the occupants of this world possess is no true peace because it constantly changes. True peace is attained only by one who lays aside the soul's every passion and seeks the Kingdom of God with the aid of patience which conquers every obstacle.[152] Sitting in the security of heaven, Bishop Reinbern can laugh at the threats of that unjust man and, in his twofold chastity, contemplate that fornicator's fiery punishment since, according to our teacher Paul, God judges adulterers.[153] As

151 Sventipulk (4.58, 8.32).
152 My translation reflects emendations suggested by Fickermann 1957: 42.
153 Heb. 13: 4.

soon as Boleslav learned what had happened, he worked ceaselessly to get whatever revenge he could. Subsequently, King Vladimir died, in the fullness of his days,[154] and left his entire inheritance to his two sons. The third son remained in prison, but later escaped and fled to his father-in-law, leaving his wife behind.

CHAPTER SEVENTY-FOUR

King Vladimir wore a cloth around his loins as an aphrodisiac, thereby increasing his innate tendency to sin. When Christ, the master of our salvation, ordered us to bind up our loins, overflowing with dangerous desires, it was greater continence that he demanded, not further provocation.[155] Because the king heard from his preachers about the burning light, he tried to wash away the stain of his sins by constantly distributing alms. It is written, moreover: 'Give alms, and all will be clean for you.'[156] Vladimir died when he was already weak with age and had held his kingdom for a long time. He was buried next to his wife in the great city of Kiev, in the church of Christ's martyr, Pope Clement. Their sarcophagi are displayed openly, in the middle of the church. The king's power was divided among his sons, thereby completely affirming the words of Christ. For I fear that we will witness the fulfilment of that which the voice of truth predicted with the words: 'Every kingdom divided within itself will be wasted', and so on.[157] All Christendom should pray that, in regard to these lands, God may change his judgement.

CHAPTER SEVENTY-FIVE [1017]

Because I have digressed somewhat from my theme, I shall now return to it. I must briefly relate certain incidents that occurred in this year, but were not discussed above. In a series of accidents, fires destroyed the greater part of the imperial estate at Pöhlde, the cathedral at Utrecht, with all the construction undertaken by Bishop Adalbold, and the Eilenburg of Count Dietrich. The emperor departed from Bamberg, proceeded to Würzburg, and then moved on to Frankfurt where he celebrated the birth of the Lord with festivity and

154 Gen. 25: 8.
155 Luke 12: 35.
156 Luke 11: 41.
157 Luke 11: 17.

joy. That the origin of the name Frankfurt might not remain hidden from you, O reader, I will explain it to you, just as I myself heard it from a certain trustworthy man. During the reign of the emperor Charlemagne, the son of King Pippin, there was a war between his people and our ancestors. In this battle, the Franks were defeated. When they subsequently wished to cross the river Main, they were uncertain as to the location of the ford. Through divine mercy, however, a doe preceded them, as if showing them the way. They followed her. and so reached the safety of the other shore in high spirits. Henceforth this place was called the 'Franks' ford'. In the midst of this campaign, the emperor, realizing that the enemy had defeated him, turned back, with the following explanation: 'I would prefer that my people reproach me and say that I fled, rather than die here. Indeed, as long as I still live, I may hope to avenge the heavy loss that has just been inflicted upon me.' In the year of the Lord's Incarnation, 8 [lacuna], in a Saxony now subject to Christ, the emperor gilded his reputation for virtue and good works by founding eight bishoprics in a single day, and by establishing a diocese for each.

CHAPTER SEVENTY-SIX [1017]

In this year, four large Venetian ships, filled with different kinds of spices, were lost in shipwrecks. As I have previously mentioned, the western regions which had rarely known peace in the past were now completely pacified.[158] Thanks be to God! Ekkehard, a monk of St John the Baptist at Magdeburg, who was also one of my brethren, lost his speech due to a paralysing illness. In the lands of the Bavarians and Moravians, a certain pilgrim, named Koloman, was seized by the inhabitants and accused of being a spy. Compelled by their harsh treatment, he confessed his guilt although it was not merited. He made every effort to justify himself and explained that he was wandering, in this way, because he was one of the poor men of Christ. Nevertheless, they hanged this innocent man from a tree which had long ceased to bear fruit. Later, when his skin was slightly cut, blood poured forth. His nails and hair continued to grow. The tree itself began to bloom, moreover, thereby proving that Koloman was a martyr for Christ. As soon as Margrave Henry learned of these events, he had the body buried at Melk.[159]

158 7.54.
159 Died 1012; feast day 13 October.

BOOK EIGHT: THE BEGINNING OF BOOK II OF EMPEROR HENRY II

CHAPTER ONE [1018]

In the year 1018 of the Incarnation, in the second indiction, in the sixteenth year of Lord Henry's reign, and his fourth as emperor, the same Henry celebrated the Circumcision and Epiphany of the Lord in Frankfurt, with great solemnity (1, 6 January).[1] On 25 January, Ezzelin the Lombard was granted his liberty. He had been held in custody for four years.[2] Afterwards, on 30 January, Bishops Gero and Arnulf, the counts Herman and Dietrich, and the emperor's chancellor Frederick agreed to a sworn peace at the burg Bautzen.[3] The agreement was made at the emperor's order and in response to Boleslav's constant supplications. This was not as it should have been, however. Rather, it was the best that could be accomplished under the circumstances. In the company of a select group of hostages, the aforesaid lords returned. After four days, Oda, Margrave Ekkehard's daughter, whom Boleslav had long desired, was escorted to Zützen by Otto, the duke's son.[4] When they arrived, they were greeted by a large crowd of men and women, and by many burning lamps, since it was night-time. Contrary to the authority of the canons, Oda married the duke after Septuagesima.[5] Until now, she has lived outside the law of matrimony and thus in a manner worthy only of a marriage such as this one.

CHAPTER TWO

In her husband's kingdom, the customs are many and varied. They are also harsh, but occasionally quite praiseworthy. The populace

---

1 The monarch had been in the city since Christmas (7.25).

2 See 7.1.

3 Aside from Henry's chancellor, the other identifiable members of the embassy are: Archbishop Gero of Magdeburg, Bishop Arnulf of Halberstadt, Margrave Herman of Meißen (BG 1920b).

4 Oda, a sister of Margrave Herman, was Boleslav's fourth wife (4.58).

5 I.e. after 2 February 1018, the beginning of the period of strict fasting that preceded the celebration of Easter.

must be fed like cattle and punished as one would a stubborn ass. Without severe punishment, the prince cannot put them to any useful purpose. If anyone in this land should presume to abuse a foreign matron and thereby commit fornication, the act is immediately avenged through the following punishment. The guilty party is led on to the market bridge, and his scrotum is affixed to it with a nail. Then, after a sharp knife has been placed next to him, he is given the harsh choice between death or castration. Furthermore, anyone found to have eaten meat after Septuagesima is severely punished, by having his teeth knocked out. The law of God, newly introduced in these regions, gains more strength from such acts of force than from any fast imposed by the bishops. There are also other customs, by far inferior to these, which please neither God nor the inhabitants, and are useful only as a means to inspire terror. To some extent, I have alluded to these above. I think that it is unnecessary for me to say any more about this man whose name and manner of life, if it please Almighty God, might better have remained concealed from us. That his father and he were joined to us, through marriage and great familiarity, has produced results so damaging that any good preceding them is far outweighed, and so it will remain in the future. During false periods of peace, Boleslav may temporarily regard us with affection. Nevertheless, through all kinds of secret plots, he constantly attempts to sow dissension, diminish our inborn freedom, and, if time and place permit, rise up and destroy us.

CHAPTER THREE

In the days of his father, when he still embraced heathenism, every woman followed her husband on to the funeral pyre, after first being decapitated.[6] If a woman was found to be a prostitute, moreover, she suffered a particularly wretched and shameful penalty. The skin around her genitals was cut off and this 'foreskin', if we may call it that, was hung on the door so that anyone who entered would see it and be more concerned and prudent in the future. The law of the Lord declares that such a woman should be stoned, and the rules of our

---

6 Miesco converted to Christianity in 966/67 (4.56). Cf. the comments of St Boniface regarding the marital practices of the Wends who 'observed the mutual love of matrimony with such great zeal that a woman would refuse to live after her husband had died. Among them, moreover, a woman was judged praiseworthy if she chose to die by her own hand and burned together with her husband on a single pyre' (Bon., *Ep.* 73, p. 150).

ancestors would require her beheading.[7] Nowadays, the freedom to
sin dominates everywhere and to a degree that is not right or normal.
And so it is not just a large number of frustrated girls who engage in
adultery, having been driven by the desire of the flesh to harmful lust,
but even some married women and, indeed, with their husbands still
living. As if this were not enough, such women then have their
husbands murdered by the adulterer, inspiring the deed through
furtive hints. After this, having given a wicked example to others,
they receive their lovers quite openly and sin at will. They repudiate
their legal lord in a most horrible fashion and prefer his retainer, as if
the latter were sweet Abro or mild Jason.[8] Nowadays, because a harsh
penalty is not imposed, I fear that many will find this new custom
more and more acceptable. O you priests of the Lord, forcefully rise
up and let nothing stop you! Take a sharp ploughshare and extirpate
this newly sprouted weed, down to the roots! You also, lay people, do
not give aid to such as these! May those joined in Christ live innocently
and, after these supplanters have been rooted out, forever groan in
shame. Unless these sinners return to their senses, may our helper,
Christ, destroy them with a powerful breath from his holy mouth and
scatter them with the great splendour of his second coming.[9]

CHAPTER FOUR

Now, I have said enough regarding that matter, since I must still
relate certain things regarding Duke Boleslav's misfortune. The
latter's territory included a certain burg, located near the border with
the Hungarians.[10] Its guardian was lord Prokui, an uncle of the
Hungarian king.[11] Both in the past and more recently, Prokui had
been driven from his lands by the king and his wife had been taken
captive.[12] When he was unable to free her, his nephew arranged for
her unconditional release, even though he was Prokui's enemy. I have

7 Cf. John 8: 5.
8 Abro = Habron; typifies 'high living' (*PW* 7. 2155. 2).
9 See 2 Thess. 2: 8.
10 I.e. 'urbem in confinio regni suimet'. We have already noted the many possible
   meanings of the latin term 'regnum' at 1, prologue, n. 2. In this passage, because of
   the still-raging controversy regarding Boleslav's status (was he a king or not?), I
   have chosen to avoid the more obvious English equivalents (kingdom, realm) in
   favour of the more neutral, but equally justifiable 'territory'.
11 I.e. of King Waik/Stephan (4.59).
12 *AH* an. 1003, p. 29.

never heard of anyone who showed such restraint towards a defeated foe. Because of this, God repeatedly granted him victory, not only in the burg mentioned above, but in others as well. His father, Deuvix, was very cruel and killed many people because of his quick temper. When he became a Christian, however, he turned his rage against his reluctant subjects, in order to strengthen this faith. Thus, glowing with zeal for God, he washed away his old crimes. He sacrificed both to the omnipotent God and to various false gods. When reproached by his priest for doing so, however, he maintained that the practice had brought him both wealth and great power. His wife, Beleknegini – the name means beautiful lady in Slavonic – drank immoderately and rode a horse like a warrior. Once, in a fit of anger, she killed a man. These polluted hands would have been better employed at the spindle, and her frenzied spirit should have been restrained by patience.

CHAPTER FIVE [1018]

The Liutizi were always united in evil. Now, they attacked lord Mistislav who had not supported them with troops during the emperor's expedition, the latter having taken place in the previous year.[13] They devastated much of Mistislav's territory, forcing his wife and daughter-in-law to flee, and compelling him to seek protection within the burg Schwerin. He was joined there by his best *milites*. Then, the evil cunning of the populace, rebellious against both Christ and their own lord, forced him to abandon his paternal inheritance. He barely managed to get away. This detestable presumption occurred in the month of February which the heathen venerate with rites of purification and obligatory offerings. The month takes its name from the god of hell, Pluto, who is also called Februus. Then, all of the churches, dedicated to the honour and service of Christ, were wasted by fire and other forms of destruction. Even worse, the image of the crucified Christ was mutilated and the worship of idols was preferred to that of God. The minds of this folk, called the Abodrites and Wagrii, hardened like the heart of Pharoah.[14] They seized for themselves the kind of liberty possessed by the Liutizi and, following the model of that famous deception, removed their neck from the sweet yoke of Christ even as they willingly submitted to the burdensome

13 Prince of the Abodrites. See also 7.59–61.
14 Exod. 7: 13. The Wagrii occupied the eastern part of Holstein.

weight of the Devil's rule.[15] They did this even though they had previously had a much better father and nobler lord. The members of Christ should lament this weakness of theirs and complain about it to their head, constantly asking, with the voice of their hearts, that this might be changed for the better. They themselves should not allow this situation to continue, to the extent that this is possible.

CHAPTER SIX [1018]

As soon as he learned of these events, Bernhard, one of my brethren at Magdeburg and formerly bishop of those apostates, did not hesitate to bring the issue to the emperor's attention. It was not from concern over his secular losses that he did this, but rather from a deep spiritual sadness. After receiving the news, the emperor gave a heavy sigh. Nevertheless, he decided to delay his response until Easter, so that, with more prudent advice, what had been engendered through an unfortunate conspiracy might be utterly destroyed. May omnipotent God support both his vow and his salutary plan. Let no faithful heart despair because of this misfortune, or believe that the Day of Judgement is fast approaching since, according to Paul's truthful admonition, one should not speak of such things prior to the discord and cursed arrival of Antichrist.[16] Nor should there be any sudden unrest among Christians, since their unanimity and stability ought to be of the highest. May all sorts of mortal beings, with their diversity of customs, change as they will. All mortals, like the flowers of the field, must first be reborn into the innocence of Christ the Saviour, through mother church.[17] And then one must still fear unexpected misfortune, even if peace and tranquillity are spoken of everywhere. Let this be a warning to us, that we may always be careful and vigilant, since we have no certainty regarding the future and our very weakness denies us any permanence. Moreover, one should neither doubt the coming of the last day nor hope that it is close by, since it is fearful even for the righteous, and much worse for anyone worthy of punishment.

15 Matt. 11: 30.
16 2. Thess. 2: 1–3.
17 Ps. 102: 15 (RSV Ps. 103: 15).

CHAPTER SEVEN [1018]

Now I will leave this topic and speak of our emperor's most recent success. For his uncle, King Rudolf of Burgundy, conceded his crown and sceptre to him, in the presence of his wife, stepson, and all of his leading men. By way of confirmation, he also repeated his oath. This took place at Mainz, in February. On 17 February, a marvel occurred at Eisdorf. It was the same month in which a great synod took place in Nijmegen, on 16 March. My cousin Otto, and his wife, Irmgard, long married in spite of their consanguinity, were excommunicated for having disobeyed repeated summonses to appear.[18] Others who shared their guilt were, however, summoned by their bishops and required to render satisfaction. There too, after an ancient formula was read out, it was decreed that the body of the Lord should be placed *on the left* side of the altar and the chalice on the right side. At that time, the archbishop of Milan died and the provost of the same church, Aribert, succeeded him.[19] The king of the Angles, one of King Sven's sons, massacred the occupants of thirty pirate ships – thanks be to God![20] Thus, like the basilisk in the deserted wastes of Libya, a man who had previously joined his father in invading and thoroughly wasting the land of the Angles was now its sole defender.[21] During this Lenten period, and in my bishopric, a certain man killed his brother – alas! The emperor, moreover, celebrated Palm Sunday and Easter in Nijmegen (30 March; 6 April). In the matter of Count Wichman's death, he learned that Balderich had not freed himself from guilt and was still holding out, along with his fellow conspirators. Abbot Folkmar of Fulda and Lorsch died.[22] In those days, at dusk, some people saw only half a sun. This was judged to be an omen.

18 Count Otto of Hammerstein was a cousin of Thietmar's mother and son of Count Herbert (5.24). The precise relationship between Otto and Irmgard is far from clear, but whatever it was, it fell within the prohibited degrees. That the couple attracted attention in part reflects the climate of the times, illicit marriages and especially incestuous ones being a prime concern of the Ottonian clergy (Corbet 1990: 187–88, 199). It has also been suggested that the prime motivation was political, namely Henry II's desire to crush the Conradines whose members included his erstwhile rival for power, Duke Herman II of Swabia. In any case, despite Otto's temporary submission (8.18), the issue sputtered on until a new monarch, Conrad II, tacitly allowed it to die (in general see Reicke 1974; also Fichtenau 1991: 95). The synod noted at 8.7. was also the occasion on which Count Berthold of Walbeck, one of Count Balderich's supporters, made his submission to the emperor (8.18).

19 Archbishop Arnulf (d. 25 February 1018); Archbishop Aribert (1018–45).

20 King Cnut of England (since 1016) and Denmark (1018–35).

21 Lucan, *Bellum civile* 9.726.

22 Folkmar or Poppo (d. 7 April).

CHAPTER EIGHT

Meanwhile, until the arrival of fresh news gives me something else to write, I would be most eager to say something regarding the lives of pious mortals, especially since my own failings and forgetfulness previously caused me to neglect this topic. In the days of King Henry II, a certain anchoress, named Sisu, dwelt in a place called Drübeck. She was a woman of immense piety and therefore most dear to me. She reached adulthood in the time of the greatest of the Ottos and had been betrothed to a certain man, but quickly fled to Christ whom she had fixed in her heart, above all others, as a sign of her special faith. In the seclusion of the aforesaid burg, for sixty-four years, this chaste virgin devoted herself to her celestial spouse and, far more than human weakness permits, made every effort to remain free from the stain of sin. Never, in all those years, did she relieve the harsh cold with a fire. At most, she would warm herself a little by using a hot stone to revive her almost frozen feet and hands. The interior of her cell was decorated with her constant prayers and weeping. She distinguished the exterior by helping the crowds of people who passed by, offering them advice and consolation in their time of need. Like Symeon the monk, who stood for so long on his column, she did not reject the vermin which fed upon her, but rather put them back whenever they fell off. From the gifts that were constantly bestowed upon her, she took nothing for herself. Instead, by sharing them with the poor of Christ, she sought to redeem the sins of the donor. This woman was dear to my mother and had firmly promised that she would be remembered in the prayers of future generations. While contending in the contest of this uncertain world, she abstained from anything illicit, doing so that she might obtain her flowery crown in heaven, and not for the sake of temporal glory. On 17 February, God judged that she was worthy to receive that crown.

CHAPTER NINE

On the night in which Christ placed this beloved light among the stars of heaven, I, a sinner, was sleeping in the dormitory at Magdeburg. May God be my witness that I am not lying! Right before matins, I dreamed that I saw two boys coming out of the old treasury, which was still standing at that time. The boys were singing this antiphon: 'Happy Martin is received in the bosom of Abraham, and so on, in his piety, spiritual poverty, and humility.'[23] All of this, and the

23 Roman Breviary, 11 November, resp. following reading 8.

following, came true. The boys declared both Sisu's twofold innocence
and her reward. I then announced this to my brethren, saying: 'You
should know, for certain, that a soul dear to God has just departed
from this light.' Six days later, I was told that the true servant of
Christ had abandoned this mortal prison, just as I had foreseen (23
February).

CHAPTER TEN

Now I shall turn to the remembrance of one of my brethren, Berner,
who earned my heartfelt love through the great affection he showed
for me. If it may be of any use to him, he is worthy of my careful
attention. Berner was closely related to me and, even more important,
joined to me by friendship. Otto III valued him highly because he had
rendered loyal service both to him and to his aunt, the venerable
Abbess Mathilda.[24] From them, he obtained full possession of property,
at Salbke, which he had previously held as a benefice. He served Archbishop Adalbert and his successors, up to lord Gero, and was suitably
rewarded for his efforts. At last, after becoming gravely ill, he
dedicated himself to that omnipotent God whom he had always loved
above all. From the love of God, and to venerate and honour him, he
constructed a church on that property which we have just mentioned.
He asked me to consecrate it though I was most unworthy of this.
Prior to the consecration, he showed me a long letter in which all of
his misdeeds were described. It had previously been shown to his other
confessors. Now, with profound sadness, he read it aloud and humbly
asked me for absolution. I took Berner's letter and, in the name of
God, granted him forgiveness for his sins. The consecration was to be
performed on 17 March, the anniversary of his father's death. On the
same day, I placed this written confession on a box filled with relics of
the saints, in the hope that, through their constant intervention, he
who had so tearfully revealed the truth might obtain his long-desired
redemption. I have never seen this done by anyone else, nor have I
ever heard of it. Rather, I resorted to those holy intercessors because
I feared that my own sinfulness would prevent me from helping him.
This venerable father lived for another thirteen weeks and found the
release he desired on 17 May.[25]

24 Abbess of Quedlinburg.

25 The necrology at Merseburg notes the death of 'Bernharius the Priest' on 18 June
(*NMer.*, fo. 3r, p. 7).

CHAPTER ELEVEN

As an exemplary model, I will also describe the excellent deeds of that pious abbot, Alfger.²⁶ Aside from his other virtues, he was in the habit of writing his name on each altar. While he was singing the mass, moreover, his tears were so profuse and constant that a good part of the *corporale* became wet. It is written that, through heartfelt tears, shed for our sins, the favour of God can not only be sought, but also obtained.²⁷ That he might more freely implore the forgiveness of heaven on his own behalf, he was merciful to all his debtors. Woe is me! Unworthy priest! I have never reconciled with any of the brethren mentioned above. I have encountered examples of many good men in my reading, and have often seen them as well, but I have never taken them to heart. Rather than forcefully reject the various temptations which one ought to resist, I have willingly succumbed to them. Those whom I ought to have helped, I have been more likely to harm. And I have always concealed my sin as if it were a costly and secret treasure.

CHAPTER TWELVE

It is unnecessary for you, my reader, or you, my dear successor, to follow the unreliable crowd in praising my success. Rather, in recognition of my long-standing wickedness, come to my aid with the medicine of constant prayer and alms-giving; and prevent me from being torn to pieces in the jaws of voracious wolves. Being well aware of my own character, I can give you a more credible report than anyone else. There are people whom I treated mildly, without good reason. When you justly rebuke them, do not be surprised if they say something false about me. You should take the middle road, between my detractors and unreliable admirers, and constantly intercede with God on my behalf. Clearly, much that I have done will displease you – it is always this way. If there is change for the better, may it please both God and humankind. Whatever I have acquired or accomplished, in the time permitted to me, has been set down in writing.²⁸ Do not be overly proud of your high office, as it will weigh that much more heavily upon you. As a careful administrator, may you always tend to the welfare of the flock committed to your care; and may you always

26 Abbot of Berge (d. 1009).
27 Judith 8: 14.
28 In the chronicle and in the martyrology mentioned in 8.13.

strive to place divine concerns above merely temporal ones. Increase whatever I have bestowed upon my spiritual brethren, to the best of your ability, and by no means diminish it. I ask you this in the name of Christ. These brethren share the tasks of your sacred order and will support you in your hopes for the future. You should also be solicitous in regard to the laity, who can wander and move here and there as they wish, but do so only to the extent that the clergy are not harmed. If you carefully guard your flock, both God and pious mortals will support you. Otherwise, you will destroy all those who are subject to you and have to endure much opposition, both now and in the future.

CHAPTER THIRTEEN

Hear me, your most unlearned teacher and unexemplary model! Willingly accept poverty for yourself so that, through you, your flock may be made wealthy. Thus did Christ act on our behalf, so that we might become his sheep. In this regard, you should express no shame in the presence of the people, so that you may stand more confidently before God. I was generous enough towards this world, but most often on behalf of my relatives.[29] Toward foreigners I appeared contemptuous. If anyone strives to rise above himself, he will fall that much deeper, through a shameful end and regret too long postponed. Treat the wealthy among your flock with respect, the poor with kindness and affection. An ancient proverb affirms that they always arrive in great numbers. *Guard well that impoverished household, committed to you by God, and barely held together by me. Nor should you lend a trusting ear to anyone murmuring evil things about it, or offering bad advice. Your resources are limited and must never be treated as though they were greater. Indeed, it is much wiser to increase by growing gradually, from day to day, than to risk losing everything, to the detriment of so many. These times, far inferior to all previous ones, take more away than they give to anyone.* Whether innate or bestowed, all honour is diminished by the burden of guilt and by harsh poverty. I beg you, do not be stingy, for that is shameful. But this I repeat, do not be too generous, for that is neither wise nor proper. You should care for the soul of the pilgrim, Godebert, a man most useful to our church, and for many others as well.[30] You

---

29 By the term *meos* Thietmar may well refer not just to blood relations, but also all those to whom he was tied by bonds of dependence, patronage, or friendship.

30 Perhaps the same Godebert noted at *NMer.*, 23 October, fo. 6v, p. 14.

have enough books. Our predecessors collected some, which I found here, and I have added more. In these books, you will discover many salutary teachings. Hear them, and you will be saved. I have acquired relics of the saints and beautiful containers for them. In terms of land and the number our dependants, I have made many beneficial acquisitions. To prevent any of these possessions from escaping your notice, I have listed them in my martyrology.

CHAPTER FOURTEEN

As a pious man, you should know of the various good deeds performed by Henry, our king and emperor, on behalf of our church. I have mentioned some of them above, but have not discussed the majority. Now, I think it best to describe them for you. See that you are always on his mind, and that he continues to renew and aid our church. It will be a most unfortunate time, when neither the poor nor the church of Merseburg can look to him for help! Now we must chiefly pray for him. Then we will have to grieve over him as well. Our church has received the following items from him. Indeed, while he lives, his unselfish generosity will ensure still more growth. Now he considers in his deepest thoughts what gifts he will employ to raise it up.[31] Now I will speak of the past. The future I humbly commit to omnipotent God, for whom everything is in the present. I do not plan to describe, individually, anything that you can find confirmed in the emperor's documents. Rather, I will refer only to those matters which lack such authority and, so I fear, may well be lost in the future. With a generous hand, the emperor gave to our church a piece of the holy and victorious cross, along with other relics of the saints, a gold altar beautifully decorated with gems, a gold reliquary adorned with precious stones, a collectar decorated at our mutual expense, two censers, and a silver beaker. We should not only preserve these possessions, but rather add to them. Because I can never say enough about his sweet kindness, instead, I shall devote my efforts to an orderly description of his life.

CHAPTER FIFTEEN [1018]

The year in which I dedicated this book was the forty-first since my birth, or a little more; 27 April marked the beginning of the tenth

31 Virgil, *Aeneid* 1.26.

year since my ordination (1018). On the day before, in a suburb of
Gniezno, the church of the archbishops burned down, together with
other buildings. Indeed, because the affairs of humankind are always
so doubtful, I shall now bring up that dangerous remedy which I, a
wretch, previously ingested. I sense that it has subsequently done me
much harm. One night, when I was resting at an estate of mine, called
Heeslingen, I dreamed that I saw a large crowd of people standing
near by. They were urging me to ingest something from a crock which
had been placed next to me. I initially refused, realizing that they were
hostile. Finally, I replied that I would take it, but only in the name of
God the Father. They were most displeased with this. When they saw
that otherwise it would not be done, however, this hateful gathering
agreed, though with much grumbling. It had been decided that I
would be completely destroyed. If I had not then invoked the name of
the Lord, any chance of eternal salvation would have been lost to me.
From this drink, which seemed to be a mixture of different types of
herbs, I began to conceive various evil thoughts. They especially
disturb me during celebrations of the liturgy, but with the help of
God, which I always invoke, they have rarely or never led me to evil
deeds. Nevertheless, it satisfied the evil will of these people, if they
believed themselves to possess some part of me. On another occasion,
they surrounded me again, although at a distance, and said: 'Are you
guarding yourself well?' I responded that I hoped so. They continued,
saying: 'But it will not be so at the end!' I neither fear their threats,
nor believe their flattery, since both are as empty as their authors. It
is only in respect to my own misdeeds that I feel any great concern.

CHAPTER SIXTEEN

In truth, I know that such apparitions may not harm us on their own
account, however corporeal they may appear. But when our sinning
causes God to avert his face from us, we wretched mortals fall into
their frenzied and merciless hands. We are immediately freed from
them, however, if we mend our ways or if we benefit from the
constant intercession of God's chosen ones. Anyone who exhibits self-
control and thinks on God's law will not be sought out by them, but
rather feared. Indeed, this fear is not inspired by such mortals
themselves, but rather by the holy power of the one they love. God is
the protector of all who love him with constancy and with all their
heart. If I, a sinner well aware of my weakness in all things, do not
build on such a secure foundation, is it any surprise that I am shaken

by those vile beings? Dear reader, similar to me in your mortality and innate humanity, I have said these things that you may know how grievously I sinned by agreeing to their demand, and support me with unfailing aid. Woe is me, this miserable wretch who ought to render spiritual aid to so many of his fellow mortals, but can protect neither them nor himself! I shall now entrust to your faithful ears the source of the aforesaid temptation. I have tried to support many persons suffering from the persecution of the enemies mentioned above. By doing so, I have incited them to attack me even more, though, to be sure, they are always prone to evil. I hope that omnipotent God will not permit me to be consumed by them, but rather, following a dreadful purgation, mercifully rescue me.

CHAPTER SEVENTEEN [1018]

On 14 April, Archbishop Gero and Margrave Bernhard were reconciled at Wanzleben. The priest Liuthard died.[32] Also, Duke Gottfried and Count Gerhard were forced to make peace, by the power of the emperor.[33] Along with his supporters, Berthold, the conqueror of the burg Monreberg, voluntarily surrendered to the power of the emperor and, as a punishment for many, the burg itself was burned down.[34] May God, the King of Peace, grant that it is never again raised up. How good it would be if the inhabitants of this region could find no protection at all when it came to implementing that wickedness in which they seem always so united! Now, alas, such places continue to stand, as the populace demands.

CHAPTER EIGHTEEN

After a long stay, the emperor departed from Nijmegen and zealously celebrated the Rogation days at Aachen.[35] Afterwards, on 16 May, Bishop Lambert of Constance died. The emperor heard the news at Ingelheim, where he had celebrated Pentecost with great solemnity.[36] He installed his chaplain, Rothard, as Lambert's successor.[37] When

32 NMer., fo. 1v, p. 4.
33 7.62.
34 7.53, 8, 7.
35 On 12–14 May.
36 On 25 May.
37 Bishop Rothard 1018–22.

these matters had been resolved, a great meeting of the leading men was held at Bürgel so that, by their judgement, they might correct the damage caused by the long-standing negligence and audacity of its populace. After this, Count Otto, whom we have already mentioned, offered his humble supplication before the emperor and Archbishop Erkanbald; and after swearing a threefold oath, separated from his unlawful wife.[38] Balderich was reconciled and the divine promise forgotten. After a few days, on 24 June, Henry died. He had held the march between the Hungarians and the Bavarians; and was formidable in arms. Meanwhile, the emperor came to the city of Basel and, after collecting an army, proceeded to Burgundy. The empress, moreover, came to her beloved Kaufungen where she established a community of nuns.[39] From thence, she proceeded through eastern Franconia and on to Bavaria, where she enthroned her brother Henry as duke of Bavaria. In the month of June, changeable weather caused severe damage to many people and their property.

CHAPTER NINETEEN

At the same time, the church, committed to me in spite of my unworthiness sustained much damage because of my guilt. For our patient and merciful God was no longer willing to leave unavenged that which his constant warnings had failed to prevent. He had previously treated our church with mildness and withheld his deservedly angry punishment. Now our church lost many useful servants and daily had cause to lament my misdeed. In the month of June, a great outrage was inflicted upon it – and me – by the bastard Adalbert, who dared to attack and destroy one of my estates with a servile mob.

CHAPTER TWENTY

Now, I shall truthfully explain what provoked them to do this. In the times of Bishop Giselher and Margrave Gunther, the generous beneficence of Otto II, smiling broadly upon everyone, granted to our

38 Otto of Hammerstein. See 7.7.

39 In response to her vow, 7.54. The foundation at Kaufungen reflected a variety of interests and intentions. From the queen's perspective, perhaps most important, it would provide a place of refuge and a suitable income should she outlive Henry. Indeed, this was the case and it was to the convent that Cunegunde retired. As a repository of royal property and incomes, clearly, it was also foreseen that the community would fulfil a number of political tasks (Bernhardt 1993: 222–34).

church a certain forest.[40] It was situated between the rivers Saale and Mulde, and between the districts of Siusuli and Plisne. After the sad destruction of our diocese, during the reign of Otto III, Margrave Ekkehard [I] acquired another forest, in a place called Sömmering, and traded it for the one belonging to us.[41] Afterwards, along with most of our property, this forest was returned to us by King Henry, the restorer of our office. This restitution was confirmed through a legal judgement, in the presence of all the king's leading men, and with the brothers Herman and Ekkehard II unable to support their claim. This forest had been in our church's possession for more than twelve years. And Margrave Herman had in no way succeeded in reacquiring it by offering me sixty manses of land. Nevertheless, he thought that he and his brother might still claim it by means of imperial diplomata relating to the possession of two burgwards, Rochlitz and Teitzig. He hoped that the old document which confirmed our rights had long been lost. When he showed me his documents, he realized that they would do him no good. For at Magdeburg, when our respective diplomata were presented before the emperor, it was clear that our church's claims took precedence, in every way. At last, in his brother's presence and hearing, the aforesaid margrave declared: 'Until now, whatever we have done regarding this matter has been undertaken because we hoped to have justice, and not out of recklessness. Now let us give it all up.'[42]

CHAPTER TWENTY-ONE [1018]

Ekkehard was a young man and therefore immature. Shortly afterwards, at the instigation of his *miles* Budislav, he began to erect tall enclosures in his burgward, Rochlitz, for the purpose of capturing wild game. When subsequently informed of his actions, I accepted the news peacefully. Nevertheless, through my intermediary – namely his brother – I asked that he desist.[43] Also, I immediately complained to his brother. In each case, I was completely unsuccessful, and so things stood until Easter had passed. Then, because both the weather and the condition of the roads were favourable, and because I had never

40 3.1.

41 Margrave Ekkehard obtained the forest through an exchange with Archbishop Giselher of Magdeburg (D O III 252).

42 I.e. the two men had not renounced their claim, but rather signalled their intent to pursue it by feud (Reuter 1993: 192).

43 Chancellor Gunther (7.22).

visited that part of my diocese, I decided to go there and carefully investigate the situation, as yet unfamiliar to me. On 2 May, a Friday, I went to Kohren and confirmed the people who gathered there. Continuing my trip, I encountered the area, mentioned above, which had been fitted out with ropes and great nets. I was astonished and wondered what I should do. Finally, because I could not take the apparatus with me, I immediately ordered that part of it to be cut down. Afterwards, I went directly to Rochlitz. There I confirmed a few people and, under threat of the ban, forbade the withholding of my rightful tithes and use of the forest. I declared all of this to be property of our church, and made peace.

CHAPTER TWENTY-TWO [1018]

Then I returned to my estate at Kohren where, after seven days, I heard that Ekkehard's *milites* were threatening my people. At that time, the chancellor happened to be spending the night with me.[44] When I explained the situation to him, he responded favourably. On numerous occasions, those same warriors gathered together and tried to attack me, but our guards stopped them, in timely fashion.[45] Meanwhile, I sent my representative to the emperor, at Mainz, and humbly sought his mediation. Now, on his own behalf, Ekkehard agreed to a truce; and his brother, whom I had long awaited, returned from Poland and offered his own hand in peace.[46] Neither kept his word very well, however. Six flogged and shaved men, and as many devastated houses, prove how others must defend themselves against such lords. In their accustomed manner, their dependants not only raged against me, but also harmed other, better men. They attacked Archbishop Gero in Werben and Count Siegfried at Nischwitz, and took whatever they wished.[47]

CHAPTER TWENTY-THREE [1018]

The pride of the lords incited the fury of their retainers and, because this was enough for the latter, they refused to accept any of their landsmen as their equals. If a neighbour offended them, even if

44 Above n. 43.
45 Warriors = satellites.
46 Margrave Herman.
47 Son of Margrave Hodo (4.60).

unintentionally or by accident, no appropriate compensation was
acceptable to them and later they would demand most unreasonable
compensation. Their neighbours were so severely beaten down by
this whip that they would not dare to rise up against them, whether
they had right on their side or not. The bishops of this region were
greatly oppressed by their power. We, their stewards, could only
demand respect and service if we turned against God and his justice,
and satisfied their will in every way. Otherwise, we were held in
contempt and plundered, as no lord either ruled or commanded on our
behalf. So, a newborn, butting with its horns, breaks both ancient law
and the good, hitherto flourishing customs, and forcefully shows that
it is exalted above all others. If heaven does not quickly suppress him,
his intolerable insolence will become permanent. He knows not the
Davidic judgement which so sweetly admonishes him: 'Do not lift up
your horn on high, etc.'⁴⁸ The holy psalmist prays for such people:
'Lord, take away their breath that they may die and return to their
dust. When you send out your spirit, they are created, etc.'⁴⁹ Anyone
who does not know himself requires forceful admonition, since even
those who meditate constantly on their existence can do nothing without a good word. May sinners come to their senses, therefore, and make
every effort both to guard themselves and show mercy to the poor.

CHAPTER TWENTY-FOUR

In regard to my misdeeds, I am a wretch. In terms of my abilities, I
am a pauper. In either case, however, I am far worse than all men of
my order. Nevertheless, I have not been the only one to suffer the
outrages noted above. To these examples I will add nothing about
other bishops, in different parts of the world, who have suffered
unspeakable harm. I grieve that they are utterly without honour,
except in regard to their consecration. At most, I have time to speak
of those who, from our own landsmen, have recently experienced
similar or − alas! − worse punishment. Bernward, venerable pastor of
the holy church of Hildesheim, was profoundly hated by Count
Bruno.⁵⁰ As a result, the bishop saw his *miles* Rim deprived of hair and

48 Ps. 74: 6 (RSV 75: 6).
49 Ps. 103: 29 (RSV 104: 29).
50 Count Bruno of Braunschweig (d. 1016). Bernward's biographer (*Thangmar*, c. 38,
   p. 775) associates this antagonism with the bishop's unwavering loyalty to Duke
   Henry of Bavaria (i.e. Emperor Henry II) during the interregnum of 1002
   although, if we follow Thietmar (cf. 4.4), he originally numbered among Ekkehard

skin, and then killed, by Altman the Younger. This occurred as Rim and Bernward were travelling together. A certain high-born warrior attacked Swidger, illustrious bishop of the high church of Münster, on the latter's own estate. The bishop was stained by the blood of his steward, who was murdered in front of him. Did these men deserve such treatment? Although both were pious priests, they still had to endure this unmerited outrage.

CHAPTER TWENTY-FIVE

Impeded by that pest, lethargy, I have hitherto said nothing in regard to Bishop Swidger. Now it would be appropriate for me to emend this fault. Swidger was born in Saxony and educated, from boyhood, at Halberstadt and Magdeburg. Otto III installed him as bishop of Münster. He presided over his see with all diligence and, strengthened with divine gifts, manifested his virtues in various ways. Of the latter, I will offer only two instances, both having been confirmed for me by reliable witnesses.

Once, Swidger's chamberlain wanted to conceal a certain hat which he had secretly stolen. After careful questioning by his pious lord, he revealed nothing. But when forced to pick up a knife which had been blessed and placed on the table, he immediately dropped it, as if it were on fire, thereby revealing his guilt. On another occasion, a man who had been possessed by an evil spirit was forcibly captured and led before the aforesaid priest. Immediately Swidger ordered the spirit to depart, expelling the angry invader with his staff alone. After making the sign of the cross over the man, now at peace, he allowed him to depart.

CHAPTER TWENTY-SIX

Swidger did not take credit for such deeds himself, but rather ascribed them to the one who did so many things through him. The days conceded to him, in this earthly existence, he spent in Christ, zealously ministering to him as a faithful servant. He presided over his diocese for sixteen years, suffering all the while from a severe illness, which is the source of all virtue. He died in Christ, for whom

---

of Meißen's supporters. In any case, it has been argued that Bruno may actually have viewed the bishop as an obstacle to his own (i.e. the count's) claims to the throne, which were based on descent from an older branch of the Liudolfing/ Ottonian house (Wolf 1995: 90–101).

he had lived, on 19 November, in the tenth year of the reign of our Emperor Henry.[51] As I have mentioned, Swidger's successor, Dietrich, the son of my mother's sister, had endured many outrages at the hands of Henry, the son of Count Herman.[52] This dispute had been quieted for a while, but now it rose up once again. For some time, the same count also inflicted much suffering on Archbishop Heribert of Cologne, and no wonder, since the latter had long held the count's mother in custody.[53] Furthermore, Bishop Meinwerk was despoiled by my cousin Thietmar, Duke Bernhard's brother.[54]

CHAPTER TWENTY-SEVEN [1018]

But why am I explaining all of this? None of these events seem to offer me a good example or any kind of comfort. It would be wiser to

51 *NMer.*, 16 November, fo. 7r, p. 15. Holtzmann (1935: 523, n. 4), interprets the phrase 'et tunc obiit, in quo deguit' to mean, 'he died in his episcopal city'. I have followed Fickermann (1957: 76) in my translation.

52 See perhaps 7.49.

53 Herman's mother, Gerberga.

54 The dispute between Thietmar Billung (d. 1048), brother of Bernhard II, and Bishop Meinwerk of Paderborn revolved around the royal abbey of Helmarshausen. Although its founders had supported the community's transformation into a royal monastery, other members of their lineage seem to have objected. Their continuing hostility ensured that the monastery failed to thrive, remaining poor, threatened, and presumably unable to fulfil its obligations to the king. On 11 July 1017, Henry II granted possession of the community to Bishop Meinwerk, at once providing it with a powerful protector and source of patronage (D H II 371; Hucke 1956: 78; Bernhardt 1993: 212–16). An attempt by Thietmar to take over and exploit the wealth of the convent of Herford led to another unsuccessful encounter with Bishop Meinwerk (Bernhardt 1993: 206; Reuter 1995: 179, 184): 'Lord Thietmar, brother of Duke Bernhard [II] of Saxony, was a man most worthy in worldly matters, but was even more full with the things of corruption; puffed up with arrogance and burning to acquire possessions through acts of greed. At that time, in violation of both divine and human law, he everywhere attacked and pillaged the property of the faithful. On one occasion, among his various works of tyranny, he directed his journey to the monastery of Herford. There, having made a great fortress, he plundered the treasure of the resident saints, of his sister Abbess Godesti, and of the congregation of St Mary. From thence, indeed, he extracted more riches than was just. Afterwards, having been summoned before a synod constituted by Bishop Meinwerk, in accordance with the canons, he was admnished to correct what he had done. After his actions had been suitably compounded and usefully coreccted, it was decided that he should give the bishop thirty solidi. Thietmar did not possess such a great sum, however. Hence, with the consent and will of his heir and brother, Duke Bernhard [II], he paid the fine by conveying all of his lands and possessions at Bründorf into the dominion and full possession of the church of Paderborn. The bishop reinforced this gift with the protection of his ban, and with the support of Counts Udo, Herman, Bernhard, Liuder, and many others' (*V.M.*, c. 100, pp. 54–55).

restrict myself to the subject matter with which I began. While considering this, I am struck by that vision of St John: *The first woe is past, behold, two woes are still to come!*[55] In the above passages, I have related many exceedingly unfortunate incidents. Nevertheless, in the days of our ruler and unconquered defender, Henry, no other misfortune can compare with the one that our misdeeds now produced. On 29 July, a Tuesday, Mars raged among us in a fashion that mother church would forever lament. In the company of Duke Gottfried, and with the support of his companions and allies, Bishop Adalbold of Utrecht moved to attack Dietrich, the empress's nephew.[56] The latter had previously murdered the bishop's retainers, thereby causing him much harm. Their warriors gathered on a certain island and quickly prepared for battle. But alas, the death with which they had threatened the enemy came to them instead. For they were attacked on all sides by the Frisians, who rushed out from their places of concealment. Without warning, the young man's retainers were surrounded and, terrible to say, lost their lives by the sword or in the water. They were unable to cause any harm to their opponents. The bishop escaped in a boat, and the duke was also rescued from the enemy. According to reliable testimony, the number of the dead exceeded three legions.[57] Now, the entire region lacks a strong defender and, in its misery, must daily fear the arrival of pirates. Count Gottfried was killed. John, the best of *milites*, lay dead – our homeland will always mourn his loss! Their noble and illustrious companions, hitherto fighting with a victorious hand, now rested in their misfortune. Their bodies endured the punishment earned by our sins. Yet I hope that their souls will rejoice, since they have been purified by such great suffering.

CHAPTER TWENTY-EIGHT [1018]

O reader, do not be astonished at this incident, but rather consider the cause. That cursed Dietrich was a retainer of the aforesaid bishop. He also held a large property in the forest of Merwede.[58] At Nijmegen, however, in the emperor's presence, the occupants of that place

---

55 Apocal./Rev. 9: 12.

56 Count Dietrich III of Holland (993–1039), son of Count Arnulf and Liudgard, niece of Empress Cunegunde. The various accounts of this much noted battle are listed in BG 1935a.

57 The necrology at Merseburg notes the high death toll (*NMer.*, 30 July, fo. 4r).

58 6.10.

complained that it had been taken from them illegally.[59] On the advice of his leading men, the emperor then ordered the bishop of Utrecht to burn down the count's residence and return the property to the plaintiffs. When the wicked youth could not stop his lord from attempting to carry out this order, he asked permission to leave, promising that he would himself prevent it. Without delay, it came to pass, as I have already noted. This was more the result of our misdeeds than the just reward of victory. Long before, a flock of birds had descended on the spot from everywhere and eaten with their claws, thereby predicting this unspeakable and yet unforgettable sorrow, and marking the place at which so many were later to die. In regard to this island, though I am unworthy, I will always repeat holy David's prayer for Mount Gilboa.[60] On the same day, Bishop Balderich of Liège died at Tiel.[61]

CHAPTER TWENTY-NINE [1018]

In those days, seven serfs of my diocese ate poisoned mushrooms and quickly died from a burning fever. In the month of August, a new star appeared next to the Plough and terrified all who saw it, with its distant rays.[62] As far as we can remember, nothing like this has ever been seen, and therefore everyone was astonished at it. The majority feared that it was some kind of omen, but faithful Christians, a much smaller number, hoped for a merciful outcome. Concerning a similar event, Jeremiah, speaking truthfully, said: *He who knows all things, knows her; and he found her by his understanding.*[63] This shining star was visible for more than fourteen days. In the region of northern Thuringia, three wolves, which always travelled together, something never before seen by the inhabitants, did immeasurable damage to many mortals and to cattle as well. This also terrified the entire population, and raised the fear that greater misfortunes would follow. For the blessed Gregory has said: *Much wickedness must first occur in*

---

59 Bishop Adalbold and the merchants of Tiel complained that Dietrich had seized possession of the island of Merwede, where a number of religious communities had rights, and was exacting tolls from the commercial traffic that passed by. Aside from the bishop and Duke Gottfried, the number of those participating in the campaign included the bishops of Liège and Cambrai (BG 1923c).

60 2 Reg. 1: 21 (RSV 2 Sam. 1: 21).

61 Bishop Balderich II of Liège (1008–18).

62 Next to the Plough.

63 Baruch 3. 32.

order to announce the arrival of eternity.[64] In everything that we have
mentioned above, the anger of heaven is revealed to us, but human
weakness does not attend this with a watchful eye.

CHAPTER THIRTY [1018]

That year might truthfully be called by a different name: either that of
the earthquake or of the great sorrow. Unspeakable tribulation
descended upon this inconstant world, and everywhere disturbed its
inhabitants. In part, I have already discussed this. That which I
omitted, I will now explain although with profound sadness. Almost
all the retainers of Bishop Balderich, and of the bishop of Cambrai,
were killed on that island, of which we have already spoken.[65] In
neighbouring districts, there was not a single household which had
not lost at least one of its inhabitants. According to tradition, such
slaughter has not occurred in those lands, on any day, or in any year,
since the time of Charles [the Great, Charlemagne]. How could so
many men die, without their enemy also suffering losses? Indeed,
anyone who meditates rightly on this matter will not be surprised at
the answer; no one can fight if, because of his burdensome guilt, he is
brought down by the punishment of God. Later, this insurmountable
misfortune was quickly forgotten, and, with the aid of Duke Gottfried,
Bishop Adalbold was reconciled with his enemy, Dietrich. He did not
agree to this voluntarily, but rather from the highest necessity. For,
in the event that a stronger enemy should arise, that region would
have lacked any powerful defender. If this misfortune occurred
through the will of God, who may demand vengeance? If otherwise,
who can exact a more effective revenge than he can? Now, as St
Columba did, following the death of the great Emperor Charles, let us
dry our tears and instead pour out salutary prayers.[66]

CHAPTER THIRTY-ONE [1018]

We may not keep silent regarding the sad and harmful events that
occurred in Russia. For, on our advice, Boleslav attacked it with a

---

64 Greg., *Hom. Ev.* 35. 1. 1259–60.

65 Bishop Gerhard of Cambrai (1012–51).

66 Columbanus (d. 615), founder of the Italian monastery of Bobbio which had richly
benefited from Charlemagne's patronage. Here, perhaps alluding to verses from an
anonymous lament on the emperor's death: 'O Columbanus, hold back your tears, pour
forth prayers on his behalf to the Lord' (ed. and trans. Godman 1985: 211, verse 17).

large army and caused much destruction. On 22 July, the duke came to a certain river, where he ordered his army to set up camp and prepare the necessary bridges.[67] Also camped near the river, along with his army, was the king of the Russians.[68] He was anxiously awaiting the outcome of the upcoming battle, for which both rulers had called. Meanwhile, the Poles provoked the enemy into fighting and, with unexpected success, drove them from the river bank which they were supposed to defend. Elated by this news, Boleslav hastily notified his companions and quickly crossed the river although not without effort. In contrast, the hostile army, drawn up in battle formation, vainly attempted to defend its homeland. It collapsed at the first attack, however, and failed to mount any effective resistance. Among those who fled, many were killed, but only a few of the victors were lost. On our side, the dead included Erich, an illustrious *miles* whom our emperor had long held in chains.[69] From that day on, with every success, Boleslav drove his scattered enemies before him; and the whole populace received and honoured him with many gifts.

CHAPTER THIRTY-TWO [1018]

Meanwhile, Jaroslav captured a city which had been subject to his brother,[70] and abducted the inhabitants. At Boleslav's instigation, the very strong city of Kiev was disturbed by the constant attacks of hostile Petchenegs and severely weaked by fire. It was defended by its inhabitants, but quickly surrendered to the foreign warriors, after its king fled and abandoned it. On 14 August, the city received Boleslav and Sventipolk, its long-absent lord. Thereafter, through his favour, and from fear of us, the whole region was brought into submission. When they arrived, the archbishop of that city received them, at the church of St Sophia, with relics of the saints and other kinds of ceremonial apparatus.[71] In the previous year, this church had been severely, but unintentionally damaged by fire. Here were found the king's stepmother, wife, and nine sisters, one of whom had previously been desired by Boleslav, that old fornicator. Unmindful of her husband,

67 The river Bug.
68 Jaroslav (7.65).
69 7.16.
70 Sventopolk.
71 Archbishop John of Kiev (1008–33).

the duke unlawfully took her away.[72] There, too, he was shown an unspeakable amount of treasure, most of which he distributed among his friends and supporters. He sent some of it back to his homeland, however. Among those rendering assistance to the aforesaid duke were three hundred of our warriors, five hundred Hungarians, and one thousand Petchenegs. All of these were now sent home, since, as Sventipolk was happy to see, the populace flocked to him and appeared loyal. In this great city, the centre of that kingdom, there are more than four hundred churches, eight markets, and an unknown number of inhabitants. As in this entire land, the city gains its strength from fugitive serfs who converge on this place from everywhere, but especially from areas overrun by the fast-moving Danes. Until now, it successfully resisted the attacks of the Petchenegs and was also victorious over other enemies.

CHAPTER THIRTY-THREE [1018]

Elated by this success, Boleslav sent the bishop of this city to Jaroslav, to ask that his daughter be sent back to him. In return, he promised to send back Jaroslav's wife, stepmother, and sisters. Afterwards, he sent his beloved Abbot Tuni to our emperor, with splendid gifts that he might more firmly secure his favour and aid.[73] He also indicated that he would follow the emperor's wishes in all matters. He also sent messengers to nearby Greece, who promised good things to the emperor there, if he would consider him as his faithful friend.[74] Otherwise, they intimated, he would be a most obdurate and invincible enemy. Among all of these, omnipotent God stands firm, mercifully revealing what pleases him and profits us. In those days, my cousin Count Udo, took Herman prisoner.[75] This was a man equal to him in nobility and power; and he led him to his burg against his will. I fear that another dangerous weed will sprout from this, and be exceedingly difficult or impossible to eradicate.

---

72 Predizlava.

73 The Quedlinburg annalist notes that Boleslav made peace with the emperor through emissaries and was restored to favour (*AQ* an. 1016, p. 84).

74 To Emperor Basil II, 'The Bulgar-Slayer' (976–1025).

75 Holtzmann (1935: 532, n. 2) suggests that Thietmar is refering to Liudolf, the son of Count Siegfried of Stade whose nickname was Udo, and to Count Herman of Werl.

CHAPTER THIRTY-FOUR [1018]

Now, I will speak once again of our emperor who, returning from his
unfortunate campaign, received nothing that had been promised to
him, and also had not done much harm to his opponents.[76] His
excellent and loyal *miles* Dietrich had separated from him, and was
making his way home, when he was ambushed by a certain lord
Stephen who apparently was hostile both to him and to the emperor.[77]
Although he emerged victorious, he was attacked again, as his
warriors fell on the plunder. Alas! They were overcome although he
himself escaped with a few others. For him, this was the second
misfortune of this type.[78] May God grant that he does not fall into
danger a third time. When our emperor learned of all this, he held a
meeting in Swabia to discuss the state of the realm. Then, full of
anxiety, he travelled down the Rhine. Alas! Most of his helpers, the
columns of the realm, had died. In private, moreover, he was deeply
troubled by men who pretended to be loyal, but secretly plotted
resistance with the help of foreigners. He could not rule with the
liberty appropriate to his office and in no way could he diminish their
arrogance in regard to the law.

76 I.e. returning from his expedition to Burgundy (8.18).
77 Duke Dietrich of Upper Lotharingia.
78 6.52.

BIBLIOGRAPHY

Abulafia, A. S. 1981. 'An Eleventh-Century Exchange of Letters between a Christian and a Jew', *JMH*, vol. 7, pp. 153–74.

Abulafia, D. et al. (eds) 1992. *Church and City, 1000–1500: Essays in Honour of Christopher Brooke*, Cambridge.

Adiaen, M. (ed.) 1971. *Homiliae in Hiezechihelem prophetam sancti Gregorii magni*, CCL, vol. 142. Turnhout.

Altenburg, D. et al. 1991. *Feste und Feiern im Mittelalter*. Sigmaringen.

Althoff, G. 1982. 'Das Bett des Königs in Magdeburg. Zu Thietmar II, 28', in Maurer, H. and Patze, H. (eds) 1982, pp. 141–53.

Althoff, G. 1988. 'Causa scribendi und Darstellungsabsicht: Die Lebensbeschreibungen der Königin Mathilde und andere Beispiele', in Borgolte, M. and Spilling, H. (eds) 1988, pp. 117–33.

Althoff, G. 1988a. '*Gloria et nomen perpetuum*. Wodurch wurde man im Mittelalter berühmt?', in Althoff, G. et al. (eds) 1988, pp. 297–313.

Althoff, G. 1989. 'Königsherrschaft und Konfliktbewältigung im 10. und 11. Jahrhundert', *FMSt*, vol. 23, pp. 265–90.

Althoff, G. 1991. 'Gandersheim und Quedlinburg. Ottonischer Frauenklöster als Herrschafts- und Überlieferungszentren', *FMSt*, vol. 25, pp. 123–44.

Althoff, G. 1991a. 'Die Billunger in der Salierzeit', in Weinfurter, S. (ed.) 1991, vol. 1, pp. 309–29.

Althoff, G. 1994. 'Verformungen durch mündliche Tradition. Geschichten über Erzbischof Hatto von Mainz', in Keller, H. and Staubach, N. (eds) 1994, pp. 438–60.

Althoff, G. 1996. *Otto III, Gestalten des Mittelalters*. Darmstadt.

Althoff, G. 1997. *Spielregeln in der Politik im Mittelalter. Kommunikation in Frieden und Fehde*. Darmstadt.

Althoff, G. 1998. 'Magdeburg–Halberstadt–Merseburg. Bischöfliche Repräsentation und Interessenvertretung im ottonischen Sachsen', in Althoff and Schubert (eds) 1998, pp. 267–93.

Althoff, G. 1998a. 'Ira Regis: Prolegomena to a History of Royal Anger', in Rosenwein, B. (ed.) 1998, pp. 59–74.

Althoff, G. and Schubert, E. (eds) 1998. *Herrschaftsrepräsentation im ottonischen Sachsen*, VF, vol. 46, Sigmaringen.

Althoff, G. and Wollasch, J. (eds) 1983. *Die Totenbücher von Merseburg, Magdeburg und Lüneburg*, MGH, Libri Memoriales et Necrologia, n. s. 2. Hanover.

Althoff, G. et al. (eds) 1988. *Person und Gemeinschaft im Mittelalter. Karl Schmid zum fünzigsten Geburtstag*. Sigmaringen.

Alvermann, D. 1995. 'La battaglia di Ottone II contro i Sarraceni nel 982', *Archivio Storico per la Calabria e la Lucana*, vol. 62, pp. 115–30.

Amiet, A. 1976. 'Die liturgische Gesetzgebung der deutschen Reichskirche in der Zeit der sächischen Kaiser 922–1023, pt.1', *ZSKg*, vol. 70, pp. 1–167.

Arnold, B. 1989. 'German Bishops and their Military Retinues in the Medieval Empire', *German History*, vol. 7, pp. 161–83.

Arnold, B. 1997. *Medieval Germany 500–1300: A Political Interpretation*. Toronto and Buffalo.

Bannasch, H. 1972. *Das Bistum Paderborn unter den Bischöfen Rethar und Meinwerk (983–1036)*, Studien und Quellen zur Westfälischen Geschichte, vol. 12. Paderborn.

Bardach, J. 1982. 'La formation et les structures de l'état polonais du Xe justqu'au XIIIe siècle', Centro Italiano di Studi (ed.) 1982, pp. 201–45.

Becher, M. 1996. *Rex, Dux und Gens. Untersuchungen zur Entstehung des sächsischen Herzogtums im 9. und 10. Jahrhundert*, Historische Studien, vol. 444. Husum.

Becker, J. (ed.) 1915. *Die Werke Liudprands von Cremona*, 3rd edn, MGH, SrG, vol. 41, Hanover.

Becksmann, R. et al. (eds) 1975. *Beiträge zur Kunst des Mittelalters. Festschrift für Hans Wentzel zur 60. Geburtstag*. Berlin.

Benson, R. L. 1968. *The Bishop Elect: A Study in Medieval Ecclesiastical Office*. Princeton.

Benz, K. J. 1975. *Untersuchungen zur politischen Bedeutung der Kirchweihe unter Teilnahme der deutschen Herrschen im hohen Mittelalter*, Regensburgen historische Forschungen, vol. 4. Kallmünz.

Berg, D. and Goetz, H.-W. (eds) 1988. *Historiographia Mediaevalis. Studien zur Geschichtsschreibung und Quellenkunde des Mittelalters. FS. für Franz-Josef Schmale zum 65. Geburtstag*. Darmstadt.

Bernhardt, J. W. 1987. 'Servitium regis and Monastic Property in Early Medieval Germany', *Viator*, vol. 18, pp. 53–87.

Bernhardt, J. W. 1993. *Itinerant Kingship and Royal Monasteries in Early Medieval Germany c.936–1075*. Cambridge.

Bethmann, L. C. and Wattenback, W. (eds) 1848. *Gesta archiepiscoporum Mediolanensium*, MGH, ss, vol. 8. Hanover.

Beumann, H. (ed.) 1984. *Kaisergestalten des Mittelalters*. Munich.

Beumann, H. 1984a. 'Otto I', in Beumann, H. (ed.) 1984, pp. 50–72.

Beumann, H. 1984b. 'Otto III', in Beumann, H. (ed.) 1984, pp. 73–97.

Beumann, H. 1991. *Die Ottonen*, 2nd edn. Stuttgart, Berlin, and Cologne.

Beumann, H. 1991a. 'Entschädigungen von Halberstadt und Mainz bei Gründung des Erzbistums Magdeburg', in Herbers, K. et al. (eds) 1991, pp. 383–98.

Beyreuter, G. 1991. 'Die Osterfeier als Akt königlicher Repräsentanz und Herrschaftsausübung unter Heinrich II (1002–1024)', in Altenburg, D. et al. (eds) 1991, pp. 245–53.

Bisson, T. N. 1994. 'The Feudal Revolution', *P&P*, vol. 142, pp. 6–42.

Bisson, T. N. 1998. 'On Not Eating Polish Bread in Vain: Resonance and Conjuncture in the Deeds of the Princes of Poland (1109–1113)', *Viator*, vol. 29, pp. 275–88.

Blumenkranz, B. 1960. *Juifs et Chrétiens dans le monde occidental, 430–1096* Études Juives, vol. 2. Paris.

Böhmer, J. F. 1950. *Regesta imperii 2. (Sächsisches Haus 919–1024) 2: Die Regesten des Kaiserreiches unter Otto II 955 (973)–983*, new edn by H. L. Mikoletsky. Graz.

Böhmer, J. F. 1956. *Regesta imperii 2. (Sächsisches Haus 919–1024) 2: Die Regesten des Kaiserreiches unter Otto III 980 (983)–1002*, new edn by M. Uhlirz. Cologne and Graz.

Böhmer, J. F. 1967. *Regesta Imperii 2 (Sächsisches Haus 919–1024) 2: Die Regesten des Kaiserreiches unter Heinrich I. und Otto I. 919–973*, new edn by E. Ottenthal, with additions by H. H. Kaminsky. Hildesheim.

Böhmer, J. F. 1971. *Regesta Imperii 2 (Sächsiches Haus 919–1024) 4: Die Regesten des Kaiserreiches unter Heinrich II. 1002–1024*, new edn by T. Graff. Vienna, Cologne and Graz.

Borgolte, M. 1993. 'Die Stiftungsurkunden Heinrichs II. Eine Studie zum Handlungsspielraum des letzten Liudolfingers', in Schnith, K. R. and Pauler, R. (eds) 1993, pp. 231–50.

Borgolte, M. and Spilling, H. (eds) 1988. *Litterae medii aevi. Festschrift für Johanne Autenrieth zu ihrem 65. Geburtstag*. Sigmaringen.

Borst, A. 1976. *Das Rittertum im Mittelalter*, Wege der Forschung, vol. 349. Darmstadt.

Bouchard, C. 1981. 'Consanguinity and Noble Marriages in the Tenth and Eleventh Centuries', *Speculum*, vol. 56, pp. 268–87.

Bowlus, C. R. 1995/96. 'Die Reitervölk des frühen Mittelalters im Osten des Abendlands. Ökologische und militärische Gründe für ihr Versagen', *Ungarn-Jahrbuch*, vol. 22, pp. 1–25.

Boyd, K. (ed.) 1999. *Encyclopedia of Historians and Historical Writing*, 2 vols. London and Chicago.

Brandt, M. et al. (eds) 1993. *Bernward von Hildesheim und das Zeitalter der Ottonen*, 2 vols. Hildesheim.

Bresslau, H. (ed.) 1915. *Wiponis opera/ Die Werke Wipos*, 3rd edn, MGH, SrG, vol. 61. Hanover and Leipzig.

Bresslau, H. et al. (eds) 1957. *MGH Diplomata regum et imperatorum Germaniae 3: Heinrici II. et Arduini Diplomata*. Berlin.

Brundage, J. 1987. *Law, Sex and Christian Society in Medieval Europe*. Chicago.

Brüske, W. 1955. *Untersuchungen zur Geschichte des Lutizenbundes. Deutsch–wendische Beziehungen des 10.-12. Jahrhunderts*, MdF, vol. 3. Cologne.

Bührer-Thierry, G. 1997. *Évêques et pouvoir dans le royaume de Germanie: les églises de Bavière et de Suabe, 876–973*. Paris.

Bührer-Thierry, G. 1998. '"Just Anger" or "Vengeful Anger"? The Punishment of Blinding in the Early Medieval West', in Rosenwein, B. (ed.) 1998, pp. 75–91.

Burleigh, M. 1988. 'Albert Brackmann (1871–1952) Ostforscher. The Years of Retirement', *Journal of Contemporary History*, vol. 23, pp. 573–88.

Burleigh, M. 1988a. *Germany Turns Eastwards. A Study of Ostforschung in the Third Reich*. Cambridge.

Burns, J. H. (ed.) 1988. *The Cambridge History of Medieval Political Thought c.350–c.1450*. Cambridge.

Centro di Studio del Centro Italiano di Studi sull' alto Medioevo (ed.) 1982. *Gli Slavi occidentali e meridionali nell'alto medioevo*, vol. 30, 1–2. Spoleto.

Centro di Studio del Centro Italiano di Studi sull' alto Medioevo (ed.) 1986. *Angli e Sassoni al di qua e al di là del mare*, Settimane, vol. 32, pts 1–2. Spoleto.

Centro di Studio del Centro Italiano di Studi sull' alto Medioevo (ed.) 1991. *Il secolo di ferro: mito e realtà del secolo X*, Settimane, vol. 38, pts 1–2. Spoleto.

Claessen, H. and Oosten, J. (eds) 1996. *Ideology and the Formation of Early States*. Studies in Human Society, vol. 2. Leiden.

Claude, D. 1972. *Geschichte des Erzbistums Magdeburg bis in das 12. Jahrhundert*, pt. 1. Mitteldeutsche Forschungen, vol. 67.1. Cologne and Vienna.

Claude, D. 1975. *Geschichte des Erzbistums Magdeburg bis in das 12. Jahrhundert*, pt. 2. Mitteldeutsche Forschungen, vol. 67.2. Cologne and Vienna.

Corbet, D. 1993. 'Pro anima senioris. La pastorale Ottonienne du veuvage', in Parisse, M. (ed.) 1993, pp. 233–52.

Corbet, P. 1986. *Les Saints Ottoniens. Sainteté dynastique, sainteté royale et sainteté féminine autour de l'an Mil*, Beihefte der Francia, vol. 15. Sigmaringen.

Corbet, P. 1990. 'Le marriage ein Germanie Ottonienne d'après Thietmar de Mersebourg', in Rouche, M. and Heuclin, J. (eds) 1990, pp. 187–214.

Cross, S. H. and Sherbowitz-Wetzor, O. P. (ed. and trans.) 1953. *The Russian Primary Chronicle: Laurentian Text* Cambridge, MA.

Crusius, I. (ed.) 1989. *Beiträge zu Geschichte und Struktur der mittelalterlichen Germania Sacra*, Veröffentlichungen des Max-Planck-Instituts für Geschichte, vol. 93. Studien zur Germania Sacra, vol. 17. Göttingen.

Dameron, G. 1987. 'The Cult of St. Minias and the Struggle for Power in the Diocese of Florence, 1011–1018', *JMH*, vol. 13, pp. 125–41.

Davies, W. and Fouracre, Paul (eds) 1995. *Property and Power in the Early Middle Ages*. Cambridge.

Demidoff, L. 1973. 'The Poppo Legend', *Medieval Scandinavia*, vol. 6, pp. 39–67.

Dombart, B. and Kalb, A. (eds) 1955. *[Augustine] De civitate Dei libri I–X*, CCL, vol. 47, pt 1. Turnhout.

Dormeier, H. 1997. *Die ottonischen Kaiser und die Bischöfe im Regnum Italiae*, Antrittsvorlesung, Kiel, 1997. Kiel.

Dubois, J. and Renaud, G. (ed.) 1984. *Le Martyrologe d'Adon: ses deux families ses trois recensions. Texte et Commentaire*. Paris.

Duggan, A. 1993. *Kings and Kingship in Medieval Europe*, King's College Medieval Studies, vol. 10. London.

Ehlers, C. 1997. 'Die Anfänge Goslars und das Reich im elften Jahrhundert', *DA*, vol. 53, pp. 45–80.

Ehlers, J. 1998. 'Heinrich I. in Quedlinburg', in Altfhoff and Schubert (eds) 1998, pp. 235–66.

Eichmann, E. 1942. *Die Kaiserkrönung im Abendland. Ein Beitrag zur Geistesgeschichte des Mittelalters*, 2 vols. Würzburg.

Elze, R. 1978. '*Sic transit gloria mundi*. Zum Tode des Papstes im Mittelalter', *DA*. vol. 34, pp. 1–18.

Endres, R. 1972. 'Die Rolle des Grafen von Schweinfurt in der Besiedlung Nordostbayerns', *Jahrbuch für Fränkischer Geschichtsforschung*, vol. 32, pp. 1–44.

Engelbert, K. 1954. 'Die deutschen Frauen der Piasten von Mieszko I (×992) bis Heinrich I (×1238)', *Archiv für schlesische Kirchengeschichte*, vol. 12, pp. 1–51.

Ennen, E. 1987. *Die europäische Stadt des Mittelalters*, 4th edn. Göttingen.

Erdmann, C. 1977. *The Origin of the Idea of the Crusade*, trans. M. W. Baldwin and W. Goffert. Princeton.

Erkens, F.-R. 1991. 'Die Frau als Herrscherin in ottonisch-frühsalischer Zeit', in Euw, A. von and Schreiner, P. (eds) 1991b, pp. 245–59.

Erkens, F -R. 1993. '... *more Grecorum conregnantem instituere vultis?* Zur Legitimation der Regentschaft Heinrichs des Zänkers im Thronstreit von 984', FMSt, vol. 27, pp. 273–89.

Euw, A. von and Schreiner, P. (eds) 1991b. *Kaiserin Theophanu. Begegnung des Ostens und Westens um die Wende des erstens Jahrtausends*, vol. 2. Cologne.

Farmer, S. 1986. 'Persuasive Voices: Clerical Images of Medieval Wives', *Speculum*, vol. 61, pp. 517–43.

Fasoli, G. 1979. 'Il dominio territoriale degli archivescovi di Ravenna fra l'VIII e l'XI secolo', in Mor, C. G. and Schmidinger, H. (eds) 1989, pp. 87–140.

Faußner, H.-C. 1991. 'Die Thronerhebung des deutschen Königs im Hochmittelalter und die Enstehung des Kurfürstenkollegiums', *ZRG, GA*, vol. 108, pp. 1–66.

Fenske, L. et al. (eds) 1984. *Institutionen, Kultur und Gesellschaft im Mittelalter. Festschrift für Josef Fleckenstein zu seinem 65. Geburtstag*. Sigmaringen.

Fichtenau, H. 1991. *Living in the Tenth Century: Mentalities and Social Order*, trans. P. Geary. Chicago and London.

Fickermann, N. 1957. 'Thietmar von Merseburg in der lateinischen Sprachtradition. Für eine sprachgerechtere Edition seiner Chronik', *Jahrbuch für Geschichte Mittel- und Ostdeutschlands*, vol. 5, pp. 21–76.

Finckenstein, A. von 1989. *Bischof und Reich. Untersuchungen zum Integrationsprozess des ottonisch-frühsalischen Reiches (919–1056)*. Sigmaringen.

Fleckenstein, J. 1956. 'Königshof und Bischofsschule unter Otto dem Großen', *AfKg*, vol. 38, pp. 38–62.

Fleckenstein, J. 1987. *Über die Anfänge der deutschen Geschichte*, Gerda Henkel Vorlesung. Opladen.

Fleckenstein, J. 1991. 'Zum Aufstieg der Wettiner. Bemerkungen über den Zusammenhang und die Bedeutung von Geschlecht, Burg und Herrschaft in der mittelalterlichen Adels- und Reichsgeschichte', in Kintzinger, M. et al. (eds) 1991, pp. 83–99.

Fornasari, M. 1964. 'Enrico II e Benedetto VIII e i canoni del presunto consilio di Ravenna del 1014', *Rivista di storia della chiesa in Italia*, vol. 18, pp. 46–55.

Fried, J. 1989. *Otto III und Boleslaw Chrobry. Das Widmungsbild des Aachener Evangeliars, der 'Akt von Gnesen' und das frühe polnische und ungarische Königtum. Eine Bildanalyse und ihre historischen Folgen*. Stuttgart.

Fried, J. (ed.) 1991. *Die Abendländische Freiheit vom 10. zum 14. Jahrhundert. Der Wirkungszusammenhang von Idee und Wirklichkeit im europäischen Vergleich*, VF, vol. 39. Sigmaringen.

Fuhrmann, H. 1991. 'Vom einstigen Glanze Quedlinburg', in Mutherich, F. and Dachs, K. (eds) 1991, pp. 13–22.

Fußbroich, H. 1991. 'Metamorphosen eines Grabes. Grabstätten der Theophanu in der Kirche der ehemaligen Benediktinerabtei Sankt Pantaleon', in Euw, A. and Schreinger, P. (eds) 1991b, pp. 231–41.

Geary, P. J. 1990. *Furta Sacra: Thefts of Relics in the Middle Ages*, 2nd edn. Princeton.

Geary, P. J. 1994. *Phantoms of Remembrance: Memory and Oblivion at the End of the First Millenium*. Princeton.

Geary, P. J. 1994a. *Living with the Dead in the Middle Ages*. Ithaca, NY.

Geary, P. J. 1994b. 'Living with Conflicts in Stateless France: A Typology of Conflict Magacement Mechanisms, 1050–1200', in Geary 1994a, pp. 125–60.

Giese, W. 1993. 'Venedig-Politik und Imperiums-Idee bei den Ottonen', in Jenal, G. and Haarländer, S. (eds), pp. 219–43.

Ginzburg, C. et al. 1991. 'Ritual Pillages: A Preface to Research in Progress', in Muir, E. and Ruggiero, G. (eds) 1991, pp. 20–41.

Glocker, W. 1989. *Die Verwandten der Ottonen und ihre Bedeutung in der Politik. Studien zur Familienpolitik und zur Genealogie des sächsischen Kaiserhauses*, Dissertationen zur Mittelalterlichen Geschichte, vol. 5. Cologne and Vienna.

Gluckman, M. 1956. *Custom and Conflict in Africa*. Oxford.

Godman, P. (ed.) 1985. *Poetry of the Carolingian Renaissance*. Norman, OK.

Görich, K. 1993. *Otto III. Romanus Saxonicus et Italicus. Kaiserliche Rompolitik und sächsische Historiographie*, Historische Forschungen, vol. 18. Sigmaringen.

Görich, K. 1994. 'Die de Imiza–Versuch über eine römische Adelsfamilie zur Zeit Ottos III.', *QFIAB*, vol. 74, pp. 1–41.

Görich, K. 1997. 'Eine Wende im Osten: Heinrich II und Boleslaw Chrobry', in Schneidmüller, B. and Weinfurter, S. (eds) 1998, pp. 95–167.

Görich, K. 1998. 'Otto III. Öffnet das Karlsgrab in Aachen. Überlegungen zu Heiligen Verehrung, Heiligsprechung und Traditionsbildung', in Althoff and Schubert 1998, pp. 381–430.

Goetting, H. 1973. *Das Reichsunmittelbare Kanonissenstift Gandersheim*, Das Bistum Hildesheim, vol. 1. Germania Sacra, n. s. vol. 7. Berlin and New York.

Goetting, H. 1984. *Die Hildesheimer Bischöfe von 815 bis 1221 (1227)*, Das Bistum Hildesheim, vol. 3. Germania Sacra, n. s. vol. 20. Berlin and New York.

Götz, W. 1966. 'Der Magdeburger Domchor. Zur Bedeutung seiner monumentalen Ausstattung', *Zeitschrift des deutschen Vereins für Kunstwissenschaft*, vol. 20, pp. 97–120.

Goez, H.-W. 1987. 'Regnum. Zum politischen Denken der Karolingerzeit', *ZRG, GA*, vol. 104, pp. 110–89.

Goez, W. 1983. *Gestalten des Hochmittelalters. Persongeschichtliche Essays im allgemeinhistorischen Kontext*. Darmstadt.

Goez, W. 1990. 'Leben und Werk des heiligen Willigis', in Hinkel, H. (ed.) 1990, pp. 15–32.

Goldbacher, A. (ed.) 1904. *S. Aureli Augustini Hipponensis episcopi epistulae*. CSEL, vol. 44, pt 3 (Epp. 124–84a). London and Leipzig.

Graus, F. 1967. 'Social Utopias in the Middle Ages', *P&P*, vol. 38, pp. 3–19.

Graus, F. 1980. 'St. Adalbert und St. Wenzel. Zur Function der mittelalterlichen Heiligenverehrung in Böhmen', in Grothusen, K.-D. and Zernack, K. (eds) 1980, pp. 205–31.

Grothusen, K.-D. and Zernack, K. (eds) 1980. *Europa Slavica–Europa Orientalis. Festschrift für Herbert Ludat zum 70. Geburtstag*. Osteuropastudien in der Hochschulen des Landes Hessen, ser. 1, Giessener Abhandlungen zur Agrar- und Wirtschaftsforschung des europäischen Ostens, vol. 100. Berlin.

Guth, K. 1988. 'Kulturkontakte zwischen Deutschen und Slawen nach Thietmar von Merseburg', in Berg and Goetz (eds) 1988, pp. 88–102.

Hallam, E. 1980. *Capetian France, 987–1328*. London and New York.

Hauck, K. and Mordek, H. (eds) 1978. *Geschichtsschreibung und geistiges Leben im Mittelalter. Festschrift für Heinz Löwe zum 65. Geburtstag*. Cologne and Vienna.

Head, T. 1987. 'Art and Artifice in Ottonian Trier', *Gesta*, vol. 86, pp. 65–82.

Head, T. 2000 (ed.) *Medieval Hagiography: An Anthology*. New York and London.

Head, T. and Landes, R. (eds) 1992. *The Peace of God: Social Violence and Religious Response in France around the year 1000*. Ithaca, NY and London.

Hehl, E.-D. 1997. 'Merseburg – eine Bistumsgründungen unter Vorbehalt. Gelöbde, Kirchenrecht und politischer Spielraum im 10. Jahrhundert', *FMSt*, vol. 31, pp. 96–119.

Hehl, E.-D. 1998. 'Der widerspenstige Bischof. Bischöfliche Zustimmung und bischöflicher Protest in der ottonischen Reichskirche', in Althoff, G. and Schubert, E. (eds) 1998, pp. 295–344.

Heidenreich, R. 1967. 'Die Marmorplatte auf dem Sarkophag Ottos I. im Dom zu Magdeburg', in Hütter, E. (ed.) 1967, pp. 265–68.

Heinemeyer, W. 1976. 'Erzbischof Willigis von Mainz', *Blätter für deutsche Landesgeschichte*, vol. 112, pp. 41–57.

Herbers, K. et al. (eds) 1991. *Ex ipsis rerum documentis. Beiträge zur Mediaevistik. Festschrift für Harald Zimmermann zum 65. Geburtstag*. Sigmaringen.

Herzog, E. 1964. *Die ottonische Stadt. Die Anfänge der mittelalterlichen Stadtbaukunst in Deutschland*, Frankfurter Forschungen zur Architekturgeschichte, vol. 2. Berlin.

Hinkel, H. (ed.) 1990. *1000 Jahre St. Stephan in Mainz*, Quellen und Abhandlungen zur mittelrheinischen Kirchengeschichte, vol. 63. Mainz.

Historischer Seminar der Universität Hannover (eds) 1983. *Staat und Gesellschaft in Mittelalter und Früher Neuzeit. Gedenkschrift für Joachim Leuschner*. Göttingen.

Hlawitschka, E. 1976. 'Die Verwandtschaftlichen Verbindungen zwischen dem hochburgundischen und dem niederburgundischen Königshaus. Zugleich ein Beitrag zur Geschichte Burgunds in der 1. Hälfte des 10. Jahrhunderts', in Schlogl, W. and Herde, P. (eds) 1976, pp. 28–57.

Hlawitschka, E. 1978. 'Merkst du nicht, dass dir das vierte Rad am Wagen fehlt? Zur Thronkandidatur Ekkehards von Meißen (1002) nach Thietmar, Chronicon iv. c.52', in Hauck, K. and Mordek, H. (eds) 1978, pp. 281–311.

Hlawitschka, E. 1986. *Von Frankenreich zur Formierung der europäischen Staaten- und Völkergemeinschaft 840–1046: Ein Studienbuch zur Zeit der späten Karolinger, der Ottonen und der frühen Salier in der Geschichte Mitteleuropas*. Darmstadt.

Hlawitschka, E. 1987. *Untersuchungen zu den Thronwechseln der ersten Hälfte des 11. Jahrhunderts und zur Adelgeschichte Süddeutschlands. Zugleich klärende Forschungen um Kuno von Öhnungen*, VF, Sonderband 35. Sigmaringen.

Hlawitschka, E. 1993. 'Der Thronwechsel des Jahres 1002 und die Konradiner. Eine Auseinandersetzung mit zwei Arbeiten von Armin Wolf und Donald Jackman', *ZRG, GA*, vol. 110, pp. 149–248.

Hörtel, R. (ed.) 1987. *Geschichte und ihre Quellen. Festschrift für Friedrich Hausmann zum 70. Geburtstag*. Graz.

Hoffmann. H. (ed.) 1980 [*Leo of Ostia*] *Chronica monasterii Casinensis*, MGH, ss, vol. 34. Hanover.

Hofmann, H. 1991. 'Profil der lateinischen Historiographie im zehnten Jahrhundert', in Centro di Studio del Centro Italiano di Studi sull'Alto Medioevo (ed.) 1991, vol. 2, pp. 837–905.

Hoffmann, H. 1993. *Mönchskönig und rex idiota. Studien zur Kirchenpolitik Heinrichs II. Und Konrads II*, MGH, Studien und Texte, 8. Hanover.

Hollister, W. and Baldwin, J. 1978. 'The Rise of Administrative Kingship: Henry I and Philip Augustus', *American Historical Review*, vol. 83, pp. 867–905.

Holtzmann, R. 1925. 'Die Quedlinburger Annalen', *Sachsen und Anhalt*, vol. 1, pp. 64–125; also in idem, 1962, with double pagination.

Holtzmann, R. 1926. 'Die Aufhebung und Wiederherstellung des Bistums Merseburg', Sachsen und Anhalt, vol. 2, pp. 35–75; also in idem, 1962, with double pagination.

Holtzmann, R. 1962. *Aufätze zur deutschen Geshichte in Mittelelberaum*, A. Timm (ed.). Darmstadt.

Holtzmann, R. (ed.) 1935. *Thietmari Merseburgensis episcopi chronicon/ Die Chronik des Bischofs Thietmar von Merseburg und ihre Korveier Überarbeitung*, MGH, SrG. n. s. vol. 9. Berlin.

Houben, H. 1989. *Tra Roma e Palermo: aspetti e momenti del Mezzogiorno medioevale*, Saggi e Ricerche, vol. 7. Lecce.

Houts, E. van 1992. 'Women and the Writing of History in the Early Middle Ages: The Case of Abbess Mathilda of Essen and Aethelweard', *EME*, vol. 1, pp. 53–68.

Hucke, R. 1956. *Die Grafen von Stade 900–1144. Geneologie, politische Stellung, Comitat und allodial Besitz der sächsischen Uddonen*. Stade.

Hütter, E. (ed.). 1967. *Kunst des Mittelalters in Sachsen. FS Wolf Schubert*. Weimar.

Israäl, F. and Müllenberg, W. (eds) 1937. *Urkundenbuch des Erzstifts Magdeburg Geschichtsquellen der Provinz Sachsen und des Freistaates Anhalt*, n. s., vol. 18. Magdeburg.

Istituto Storico Italiano per il Medioevo 1988. *Formazione e strutture dei ceti dominante nel regno Italico (sec. IX–XII) nuovi studi storici*, vol. 1. Rome.

Jacobsen, W. et al. (eds) 1991. *Vorromanische Kirchenbauten. Katalog der Denkmäler bis zum Ausgang der Ottonen*. Nachtragsband, Munich, 1991.

Jaeger, C. S. 1985. *The Origins of Courtliness: Civilizing Trends and the Formation of Courtly Ideals, 939–1210*. Philadelphia.

Jaeger, C. S. 1994. *The Envy of Angels: Cathedral Schools and Social Ideals in Medieval Europe, 950–1200*. Philadelphia.

Jank, D. 1979. 'Die Darstellung Ottos des Großen in der spätmittelalterlichen Historiographie', *AgKg*, vol. 61, pp. 69–101.

Jenal, G. and Haarländer, S. (eds) 1993. *Herrschaft, Kirche, Kultur. Beiträge zur Geschichte des Mittelalters. FS. für Friedrich Prinz zu seinem 65. Geburtstag*, Monographien zur Geschichte des Mittelalters, vol. 37. Stuttgart.

Johrendt, J. 1976. '"Milites" und "Militia" im 11. Jahrhundert in Deutschland', in Borst, A. (ed.) 1976, pp. 419–36.

Kahl, H. D. 1955. 'Compellere intrare. Die Wenden politik Bruns von Querfurt im Lichte hochmittelalterlichen Missions und Völkerrechts', *Zeitschrift für Ostforschung*, vol. 4, pt. 1, pp. 161–93, pt. 2, pp. 360–401.

Karpf, E. 1986. 'Von Widukinds *Sachsengeschichte* bis zu Thietmars *Chronicon*. Zu den literarischen Folgen des politischen Aufschwungs im ottonischen Sachsen', in Centro di Studio (ed.) 1986, pp. 547–80.

Karwasin'ska, J. (ed.) 1969. *[Brun of Querfurt] Epistola ad Heinricum regem*, MPH, n. s. vol. 4, pt 2, pp. 97–106. Warsaw.

Karwasin'ska, J. (ed.) 1973. *[Brun of Querfurt], Sancti Adalberti episcopi Pragensis et martyris. redactio longior*, MPH, n. s. vol. 4, pt 3, pp. 3–41. Warsaw.

Kaufmann, V. R. 1989. 'Magdeburger Rider Group: State of Research and Preliminary Suggestions for Further Work', in Ullmann, E. 1989, pp. 205–30.

Keller, H. 1975. 'Reliquien in Architekturteilen beigesetzt', in Becksmann, R. et al. (eds) 1975, pp. 105–14.

Keller, H. and Staubach, N. (eds) 1994. *Iconologia Sacra. Mythos, Bildkunst und Dichtung in der Religions- und Sozialgeschichte Alteuropas. FS. Karl Hauck zum 75. Geburtstag*, Arbeiten zur Frühmittelalterforschung, vol. 23. Berlin and New York.

Kintzinger, M. et al. (eds) 1991. *Das Andere Wahrnehmen. Beiträge zur europäischen Geschichte. August Nitschke zum 65. Gebrutstag gewidmet* Cologne, Weimar and Vienna.

Klapisch-Zuber, C. (ed.) 1992. *A History of Women in the West*, vol. 2, *Silences of the Middle Ages*. Cambridge and London.

Klewitz, H.-W. 1944. 'Namengebung und Sippenbewusstsein in den deutschen Königsfamilien des 10. bis 12. Jahrhunderts. Grundfragen historischer Genealogie', *AUF*, vol. 18, pp. 23–37.

Kreutz, B. M. 1991. *Before the Normans: Southern Italy in the Ninth and Tenth Centuries.* Philadelphia.

Kurze, F. (ed.) 1890. [*Regino of Prüm*] *Chronicon cum continuatione Treverense*, MGH, SrG, vol. 50. Hanover.

Ladner, G. 1960. 'The Holy Roman Empire of the Tenth Century and East Central Europe', *The Polish Review*, vol. 5, pp. 3–14 [cited from Ladner, G. 1983, vol. 2, pp. 457–70].

Ladner, G. 1983. *Images and Ideas in the Middle Ages: Selected Studies in History and Art*, 2 vols. Rome.

Lang, G. 1942. 'Gunther, der Eremit, in Geschichte, Sage und Kult', *SMGBZ*, vol. 59, pp. 3–85.

Latouche, R. (ed. and trans.) 1930/1937. *Richer of Reims. Histoire de France*, Les Classiques de l'histoire de France au Moyen Age, vol. 17, pts 1–2. Paris.

Laudage, J. 1992. 'Hausrecht und Thronfolge. Überlegungen zur Königserhebung Ottos des Großen und zu den Aufständischen Thankmars, Heinrichs, und Liudolf', *HJb*, vol. 112, pp. 23–71.

Leopold, G. and Schubert, Ernst. 1991 'Otto III. und Sachsen. Die ottonischen Kirche in Memleben. Geschichte und Gestalt', in Euw, A. and Schreiner, P. (eds) 1991b, pp. 371–82.

Levillain, P. (ed.) 1994. *Dictionnaire historique de la papauté*. Paris.

Lewald, U. 1979. 'Die Ezzonen. Das Schicksal eines rheinischen Fürstengeschlechts', *RVjB*, vol. 43, pp. 120–68.

Lewis, A. 1992. 'Successions ottoniennes et robertiennes: un essai de comparison', in Parisse, M. and Barral i Allet, X. (eds) 1992, pp. 47–53.

Leyser, K. J. 1965. 'The Battle at the Lech', *History*, vol. 50, pp. 1–25 [cited from Leyser, K. J. 1982, pp. 43–68].

Leyser, K. J. 1968. 'The German Aristocracy from the Ninth to the Early Twelfth Century: A Historical and Cultural Sketch', *P&P*, vol. 41, pp. 25–53 [cited from Leyser, K. J. 1982, pp. 161–89].

Leyser, K. J. 1968a. 'Henry I and the Beginnings of the Saxon Empire', *EHR*, vol. 83, pp. 1–32.

Leyser, K. J. 1979. *Rule and Conflict in an Early Medieval Society: Ottonian Saxony.* London.

Leyser, K. J. 1981. 'Ottonian Government', *EHR*, vol. 96, pp. 721–53 [cited from Leyser, K. J. 1982, pp. 69–102].

Leyser, K. J. 1982. *Medieval Germany and its Neighbours, 900–1250.* London.

Leyser, K. J. 1982a. 'The Tenth-Century Condition', in Leyser, K. J. 1982, pp. 1–10.

Leyser, K. J. 1983. 'The Crisis of Medieval German', *Proceedings of the British Academy*, vol. 69, pp. 409–43 [cited from Leyser, K. J. 1994a, pp. 21–49].

Leyser, K. J. 1984. 'Early Medieval Canon Law and the Beginnings of Knighthood', in
    Fenske, L. et al. (eds) 1984, pp. 549–66.

Leyser, K. J. 1986. *The Ascent of Latin Europe*. Oxford.

Leyser, K. J. 1994. *Communications and Power in Medieval Europe: The Gregorian
    Revolution and Beyond*, T. Reuter (ed.). London.

Leyser, K. J. 1994a. *Communications and Power in Medieval Europe: The Carolingian and
    Ottonian Centuries*. London.

Leyser, K. J. 1994b. 'From Saxon Freedoms to the Freedom of Saxony: The Crisis of
    the Eleventh Century', in Leyser, K. J. 1994, pp. 51–67.

Leyser, K. J. 1994c. 'The Ottonians and Wessex', in Leyser, K. J. 1994a, pp. 73–104.

Leyser, K. J. 1994d. 'Ritual, Ceremony and Gesture: Ottonian Germany', in Leyser,
    K. J. 1994a, pp. 189–213.

Leyser, K. J. 1994e. 'Medieval Warfare', in Leyser, K. J. 1994a, pp. 29–50

Leyser, K. J. 1994f. 'Three Historians', in Leyser, K. J. 1994a, pp. 19–28.

Lippelt, H. 1973. *Thietmar von Merseburg. Reichsbischof und Chronist*, Mitteldeutsche
    Forschungen, vol. 72. Cologne and Vienna.

Lohmann H.-E and Hirsch, P. (eds) 1935. *Widukindi monachi Corbeiensis Rerum Gestarum
    Saxonicarum libri tres*, 5th edn, MGH, SrG. Hanover.

Lotter, F. 1973. 'Designation und angeliches Kooptationsrecht bei Bischofserhebungen.
    Zu Ausbildung und Anwendung des Prinzips der kanonischen Wahl bis zu den
    Anfängen der fränkischen Zeit', *ZRG, KA*, vol. 59, pp. 112–50.

Lotter, F. 1993. 'Die Juden zwischen Rhein und Elbe im Zeitalter Bernwards von
    Hildesheim', in Brandt, B. et al. (eds) 1993, vol. 1, pp. 225–30.

McGuire, P. (ed.) 1996. *The Birth of Identitities: Denmark and Europe in the Middle Ages*.
    Copenhagen.

McKitterick, R. 1983. *The Frankish Kingdoms under the Carolingians*. London.

McKitterick, R. 1990. 'Women in the Ottonian Church: An Iconographic Perspective',
    in Wood, D. (ed.) 1990, pp. 79–100 [also in McKitterick, M. 1995 with original
    pagination].

McKitterick, R. 1993. 'Ottonian Intellectual Culture in the Tenth Century and the Role
    of Theophanu', *EME*, vol. 2, pp. 53–74.

McKitterick, R. 1995. *The Frankish Kings and Culture in the Early Middle Ages*. Aldershot.

Maleczynski, C. (ed.) 1952. *Galli anonymi cronicae et gesta ducum sive principum
    Polonorum*, MPH, n. s. vol. 2. Krakow.

Manaresi, C. (ed.) 1958, *I Placiti del Regnum Italiae*, 3 vols. in 5. Rome.

Martin, J. 1995. *Medieval Russia, 980–1584*. Cambridge and New York.

Matzenbecher, A. (ed.) 1975. *[St Augustine] De diversis quaestionibus*, CCL, vol. 44a.
    Turnholt.

Maurer, H. 1978. *Der Herzog von Schwaben. Grundlagen, Wirkungen, und Wesen seiner
    Herrschaft in ottonischer, salischer und staufischer Zeit*. Sigmaringen.

Maurer, H. and Patze, H. (eds) 1982. *Festschrift für Berent Schwineköper zu seinem
    siebzigsten Geburtstag*. Sigmaringen.

Mayer-Harting, H. 1992. 'The Church of Magdeburg: Its Trade and its Town in the
    Tenth and Early Eleventh Centuries', in Abulafia, D. et al. (eds) 1992, pp. 129–50.

Mellinkoff, R. 1973. 'Riding Backwards, Theme of Humiliation and Symbol of Evil', *Viator*, vol. 4, pp. 153–76.

Michalowski, R. 1992. 'Aix-la-Chapelle et Cracovie au XIe siècle', *Bulletino dell' Istituto Storico Italiano per il Medio Evo e Archivio Muratorano*, vol. 95, pp. 45–69.

Mitchell, L. E. (ed.) 1999. *Women in Medieval Western Europe*. New York and London.

Mitterauer, M. 1988. '"Senioris sui nomine". Zur Verbreitung von Fürstennamen durch das Lehenswesen', *MIÖG*, vol. 97, pp. 275–330.

Mommsen, T. E. and Morrison, K. F. (trans.) 1962. *Imperial Lives and Letters of the Eleventh Century*. New York.

Monticolo, G. (ed.) 1890. *Cronaca veneziana*, FSI, vol. 9, pp. 57–171. Rome.

Mor, C. G. and Schmidinger, H. (eds) 1979. *I poteri temorali dei vescovi in Italia e in Germania nel Medioevo*, Annali dell' Istituto storico italo-germanico, vol. 3. Bologna.

Moriccca, U. (ed.) 1924. *Gregorii magni dialogi libri IV Fonti per la storia d'Italia*, vol. 1. Rome.

Muir, E. and Ruggiero, G. (eds) 1991. *Microhistory and the Lost Peoples of Europe*. Baltimore and London.

Muldoon, J. 1997. 'The Conversion of Europe', in Muldoon, J. (ed.) 1997a, pp. 1–10.

Muldoon, J. (ed.) 1997a. *Varieties of Religious Conversion in the Middle Ages*. Gainsville, FL.

Mutherich, F. and Dachs, K. (eds) 1991. *Das Quedlinburger Evangeliar. Das Samuhel-Evangeliar aus dem Quedlinburger Dom*. Munich.

Nelson, J. 1988. 'Kingship and Empire', in Burns, J. H. (ed.) 1988, pp. 211–52.

Nelson, J. 1999. 'Medieval Queenship', in Mitchell, L. (ed.) 1999, pp. 179–207.

Nightingale, J. 1992. 'Bishop Gerard of Toul (963–94) and Attitudes to Episcopal Office', in Reuter, T. 1992, pp. 41–62.

Nitschke, A. 1983. 'Der mißhandelte Papst. Folgen ottonischer Italienpolitik', in Historischer Seminar (eds), pp. 40–53.

Oswald, F. et al. (eds) 1966. *Vorromanische Kirchenbauten. Katalog der Denkmäler bis zum Ausgang der Ottonen*. Munich.

Ott, I. (ed.) 1951. [*Ruotger*] *Vita Brunonis archiepiscopi Coloniensis*, MGH, SrG, n. s. 10. Weimar.

Parisse, M. 1991. 'Princes, laïques et/ou moines, les évêques du Xe siècle', in Centro di Studio (ed.) 1991, vol. 1, pp. 449–513.

Parisse, M. (ed.) 1993. *Veuves et vervage dans le Haut Moyen Age*. Paris.

Parisse, M. and Barral i Allet, X. (eds) 1992. *Le Roi de France et son royaume autour de l'an mil*. Paris.

Patchovsky, A. 1998. 'The Holy Emperor Henry "the First" as One of the Dragon's Heads of the Apocalypse: On the Image of the Roman Empire under German Rule in the Tradition of Joachim of Fiore', *Viator*, vol. 29, pp. 291–322.

Patze, H. 1962. *Die Entstehung der Landesherrschaft in Thüringen*, Mitteldeutsche Forschungen, vol. 22, no. 1. Cologne and Graz.

Pauler, R. 1982. *Das Regnum Italiae in ottonischer Zeit. Markgrafen, Grafen, und Bischöfe als politische Kräfte*. Tübingen.

Paulhart, H. (ed.). 1962. *Die Lebensbeschreibung der Kaiserin Adelheid von Abt Odilo von Cluny*, MIÖG, Ergänzungsband 20, pt. 2. Graz and Cologne.

Pertz, G. (ed.) 1839. *Annales Quedlinburgensis*, MGH, ss, vol. 3, pp. 22–90. Hanover.

Pertz, G. (ed.) 1839a. *Annales Einsidlenses*, MGH, ss, vol. 3, pp. 145–49. Hanover.

Pertz, G. (ed.) 1841. [*Thangmar*] *Vita Bernwardi episcopi Hildesheimensis*, MGH, ss, vol. 4, pp. 764–82. Hanover.

Perz, G. (ed.) 1841a. [Alpert of Metz] *De diversitate temporum libri II*, MGH, ss, vol. 3, pp. 700–23. Hanover.

Pertz, G. (ed.) 1854. *Vita Godehardi episcopi prior*, MGH, ss, vol. 11, pp. 167–96. Hanover.

Platelle, H. 1990. 'L'epouse "gardienne aimante de la vie et de l'âme de son mari"', in Rouche, M. and Heuclin, J. 1990, pp. 171–84.

Pötzl, W. 1973. 'Die Anfänge der Ulrichsverehrung im Bistum Augsburg und im Reich', *Jahrbuch des Vereins für Augsburger Bistumsgeschichte*, vol. 7, pp. 82–115.

Rader, O. B. 1995. 'Adalbert, Erzbischof von Magdeburg (968–981)', in Hotz, E. and Huschner, W. (eds) 1995, pp. 77–86.

Rädlinger-Prömper, C. 1987. *Sankt Emmeram in Regensburg. Struktur- und Funktionswandel eines bayerischen Klosters im früheren Mittelalter*, Thurn und Taxis-Studien, vol. 16. Kallmünz.

Reicke, S. 1974. 'Der Hammersteinsche Ehehandel im Lichte der mittelalterlichen Herrschaftsordnung', *Rheinische Vierteljahrsblätter*, vol. 38, pp. 203–24.

Reuter, T. 1991. *Germany in the Early Middle Ages, 800–1056*. London and New York.

Reuter, T. 1991a. 'Otto III and the Historians', *History Today*, vol. 41, pp. 21–27.

Reuter, T. (ed.) 1992. *Warriors and Churchmen in the High Middle Ages: Essays Presented to Karl Leyser*. London and Rio Grande, 1992.

Reuter, T. 1993. 'The Medieval German Sonderweg? The Empire and its Rulers in the High Middle Ages', in Duggan, A. J. (ed.) 1993, pp. 179–211.

Reuter, T. 1995. 'Property Transactions and Social Relations between Rulers, Bishops, and Nobles in early Eleventh-Century Saxony: The Evidence of the *Vita Meinwerci*', in Davies, W. and Fouracre, P. 1995, pp. 165–99.

Rosenwein, B. (ed.) 1998. *Anger's Past: The Social Uses of an Emotion in the Middle Ages*, Ithaca, NY and London.

Rouche, M. and Heuclin, J. (eds) 1990. *La Femme au moyen-âge*. Maubeuge.

Sawyer, B. and Sawyer, P. 1993. *Medieval Scandinavia: From Conversion to Reformation, circa 800–1500*. Minneapolis and London.

Schaller, H.-M. 1974. 'Der heilige Tag als Termin mittelalterlicher Staatsakte', *DA*, vol. 30, pp. 1–24.

Schauerte, H. 1964. 'Sankt Cyriacus im westfälischen Raum', *Rheinisch-westfälische Zeitschrift für Volkskunde*, vol. 11, pp. 64–73.

Schieffer, R. 1989. 'Der ottonische Reichsepiskopat zwischen Königtum und Adel', *FMSt*, vol. 23. pp. 291–301.

Schieffer, R. 1991. 'Freiheit der Kirche: vom 9. zum 11. Jahrhundert', in Fried (ed.) 1991, pp. 49–66.

Schlogl, W. and Herde, P. (eds) 1976. *Grundwissenschaften und Geschichte. Festschrift für Petter Acht*, Münchener Historische Studien, Abteilung geschichtliche Hilfswissenschaften, vol. 15. Kallmunz.

Schmeidler, B. 1917. *Magistri Adam Bremensis gesta Hammaburgensis ecclesiae pontificum*, 3rd edn. MGH, SrG in usum scholarum. Hanover and Leipzig.

Schmid, K. 1964. 'Die Nachfahren Widukinds', *DA*, vol. 20, pp. 1–47.

Schmidt-Wiegand, R. 1982. 'Gebärdensprache im mittelalterlichen Recht', *FMSt*, vol. 16, pp. 363–79.

398   BIBLIOGRAPHY

Schneider, A. 1962. 'Thietmar von Merseburg über kirchliche, politische und ständische Fragen seiner Zeit', *AfKg*, vol. 44, pp. 34–71.

Schneidmüller, B. and Weinfurter, S. (eds) 1997. *Otto III.–Heinrich II. Eine Wende?* Mittelalter-Forschungen, vol. 1. Sigmaringen.

Schnith, K. R. and Paulen, R. (eds) 1993. *Festschrift für Eduard Hlawischka zum 65. Geburtstag*, Müchener Historische Studien, Abteilung Mittelalterliche Geschichte, vol. 5, Kallmünz.

Schramm, P. E. 1929. *Kaiser Rom und Renovatio. Studien zur Geschichte des römischen Erneuerungsgedankens vom Ende des karolingischen Reiches bis zum Investiturstreit*, 2 vols. Berlin and Leipzig.

Schreiner, K. 1989. '"Consanguinitas" "Verwandtschaft" ab Strukturprinzip religiöser Gemeinschafts- und Verfassungsbildung in Kirche und Mönchtum des Mittelalters', in Crusius, I. (ed.) 1989, pp. 176–305.

Schubert, E. 1998. 'Imperiale Spolien im Magdeburger Dom', in Althoff and Schubert (eds) 1998, pp. 9–32.

Schütte, B. 1994. *Untersuchungen zu den Lebensbeschreibungen der Königin Mathilde*, MGH, Studien und Texte, vol. 9. Hanover.

Schütte, B. (ed.) 1994a. *Die Lebensbeschreibungen der Königin Mathilde*, MGH, SrG, vol. 66. Hanover.

Schulze, H. K. et al. 1965. *Das Stift Gernrode*, Mitteldeutsche Forschungen, vol. 38. Cologne and Graz.

Schwaiger, G. (ed.) 1989. *Lebensbilder aus der Geschichte des Bistums Regensburg*, Beiträge zur Geschichte des Bistums Regensburg, vols 23/24. Regensburg.

Schwaiger, G. 1989a. 'Der heilige Wolfgang', in Schwaiger, G. (ed.) 1989, pp. 93–107.

Sergi, G. 1988. 'Anscarici, Arduinici, Aleramici: elementi per una comparazione fra dinastie marchionali', in Istituto Storico Italiano per il Medio Evo, pp. 11–28.

Sergi, G. 1991. 'Istituzioni politiche e società nel regno di Borgogna', in Centro di Studio (ed.) 1991, vol. 1, pp. 205–36.

Settia, A. 1989. 'Le frontiere del regno Italico nei secolo VI–XI: l'organizzazione della difesa', *Studi Storici*, vol. 30, pp. 159–69.

Sickel, T. (ed.) 1879–84. *MGH Diplomata regum et imperatorum Germaniae 1: Conradii I, Heinrici I, et Ottonis I diplomata*. Hanover.

Sickel, T. (ed.). 1888. *MGH Diplomata regum et imperatorum Germaniae, 2.1: Ottonis II diplomata*. Hanover.

Sickel, T. (ed.) 1926–31. *MGH Diplomata regum et imperatorum Germaniae 2.2: Ottonis III diplomata*. Hanover.

Skibinski, E. 1996. 'Identity and Difference. Polish Identity in the Historiography of the Twelfth and Thirteenth Centuries', in McGuire, P. (ed.) 1996, pp. 93–106.

Sonnleitner, K. 1987. 'Selbstbewußtsein und Selbstverständnis der Ottonen Frauen im Spiegel der Historiographie des 10. Jahrhunderts', in Hörtel (ed.) 1987, pp. 111–19.

Sonnleitner, K. 1988. 'Die Annalistik der Ottonenzeit als Quelle für die Frauengeschichte', *Schriftenreihe des Instituts für Geschichte: Darstellungen*, pp. 233–49. Graz.

Spiegel, G. 1997. *The Past as Text: The Theory and Practice of Medieval Historiography*. Baltimore and London.

Spiegel, G. 1997a. 'In the Mirror's Eye: The Writing of Medieval History in North America', in Spiegel 1997, pp. 57–80.

Stach, W. 1952. 'Wort und Bedeutung im mittelalterlichen Latein', *DA*, vol. 9, pp. 332–52.

Störmer, W. 1997. 'Kaiser Heinrich II., Kaiserin Kunigunde und das Herzogtum Bayern', *ZBL*, vol. 60, pp. 437–63.

Strecker, K. 1926. *Carmina Cantabrigiensia*, MGH, SrG in usum scholarum, vol. 40. Berlin.

Tangl, M. (ed.) 1955. S. *Bonifatii et Lulii epistolae: Die Briefe des Heiligen Bonifatius und Lullus*, MGH, Epistolae Selectae, vol. 1. Berlin.

Tellenbach, G. 1973. 'Die Stadt Rom in der Sicht ausländischer Zeitgenossen (800–1200)', *Saeculum*, vol. 24, pp. 1–40.

Tellenbach, G. 1993. *The Church in Western Europe from the Tenth to the Early Twelfth Century*, trans. T. Reuter. Cambridge.

Tenckhoff, F. (ed.). 1921. *Vita Meinwerci episcopi Patherbrunnensis (Das Leben des Bischofs Meinwerk von Paderborn)*, MGH, SrG in usum scholarum, vol. 59. Hanover.

Thiele, E. 1995. 'Klosterimmunität, Wahlbestimmungen und Stiftervogteien im Umkreis des ottonischen Königtums', *BdLg*, vol. 131, pp. 1–50.

Trillitzach, W. (ed. and trans.) 1964. *Ecbasis ciusdam captivi per tropologiam: Die Flucht eines Gefangenen (tropologisch)*. Leipzig.

Trillmich, W. (ed. and trans.) 1974. *Thietmar von Merseburg. Chronik*, Ausgewählte Quellen zur deutschen Geschichte des Mittelalters, Freiherr vom Stein-Gedächtnisausgabe, vol. 9. Darmstadt.

Tschan, F. J. (trans.) 1959. *Adam of Bremen: History of the archbishops of Hamburg–Bremen*. New York.

Turano, C. 1997. 'Reggio bizantina dal IX secolo all'arrivo dei Normanni', pt. 2, *Historica*, vol. 50, pp. 55–71.

Tymowski, M. 1996. 'Oral Tradition, Dynastic Legend and Legitimation of Ducal Power in the Process of the Formation of the Polish State', in Claessen, H. and Oosten, J. (eds) 1996, pp. 242–55.

Ullmann, E. (ed.) 1989. *Der Magdeburger Dom ottonische Gründung und staufischer. Neubau*. Leipzig.

Van Deusen, N. (ed.) 2000. *Medieval Germany: Associations and Delineations*, Claremont Cultural Studies, vol. 5. Ottawa.

Waitz, G. (ed.) 1841. *Vita S. Oudalrici episcopi*, MGH, ss, vol. 4, pp. 377–428. Hanover.

Waitz, G. (ed.) 1841a. *Ex vita sancti Nili*, MGH, ss, vol. 4, pp. 616–18. Hanover

Waitz, G. (ed.) 1841b. *[Adalbold] Vita Heinrici II imperatoris*, MGH, ss, vol. 4, pp. 679–95. Hanover.

Waitz, G. (ed.) 1841c. *Vita Burchardi episcopi Wormatensis*, MGH, ss, vol. 4, pp. 829–46. Hanover.

Waitz, G. (ed.) 1844. *Annalista Saxo*, MGH, ss, vol. 6, pp. 542–777. Hanover

Waitz, G. (ed.) 1878. *Annales Hildesheimenses*, MGH, SrG in usum scholarum. Hanover.

Waitz, G. (ed.) 1883. *Brunwilarensis monasterii fundatorum actus*, MGH, ss, vol. 14, pp. 121–44. Hanover.

Warner, D. A. 1994. 'Henry II at Magdeburg: Kingship, Ritual and the Cult of Saints', *EME*, vol. 4, pp. 135–66.

Warner, D. A. 1995. 'Thietmar of Merseburg on Rituals of Kingship', *Viator*, vol. 26, pp. 53–76.

Warner, D. A. 1999. 'Ideals and Action in the Reign of Otto III', *JMH*, vol. 25, pp. 1–18.

Warner, D. A. 2000. 'Saints and Politics in Ottonian Germany', in Van Deusen, N. (ed.) 2000, pp. 7–28.

Warner, D. A. (trans.) 2000. 'Odilo of Cluny, Epitaph of the August Lady, Adelheid', in Head, T. (ed.) 2000, pp. 255–71.

Weiland, L. (ed.) 1874. Gesta episcoporum Halberstadensium, MGH, ss, vol. 23, pp. 73–123. Hanover.

Weiland, L. (ed.) 1893. Constitutiones et acta public imperatorum et regum (911–1197), MGH. Hanover.

Weinrich, L. 1972. 'Laurentius-Verehrung in ottonischer Zeit', JGMO, vol. 21, pp. 45–66.

Weinrich, L. 1988. 'Der Slawenaufstand von 983 in der Darstellung des Bischofs Thietmar von Merseburg', in Berg and Goetz (eds) 1988, pp. 77–87.

Weinfurter, S. 1986. 'Die Zentralisierung der Herrschaftsgewalt im Reich durch Kaiser Heinrich II', HJb, vol. 106, pp. 241–97.

Weinfurter, S. (ed.) 1991. Die Salier und das Reich, 3 vols. Sigmaringen.

Wemple, S. F. 1992. 'Women from the Fifth to the Tenth Century', in Klapisch-Zuber (ed.) 1992, pp. 169–201.

Whitelock, D. (ed.) 1955. English Historical Documents, c.500–1042, London.

Wollasch, J. 1968. 'Das Grabkloster der Kaiserin Adelheid in Selz am Rhein', FMST, vol. 2, pp. 135–44.

Wollasch, J. 1980. 'Geschichtliche Hintergründe der Dortmunder Versammlung des Jahres 1005', Westfälen, vol. 58, pp. 55–69.

Wolf, A. 1991. 'Königskandidaten und Königsverwandtschaft', DA, vol. 47, pp. 45–117.

Wolf, A. 1995. 'Quasi hereditatem inter filios. Zur Kontroverse über das Königswahlrecht im Jahre 1002 und die Genealogie der Konradiner', ZRG, GA, vol. 112, pp. 64–157.

Wolf, G. 1990. 'Königinnen-Krönungen des frühen Mittelalters, bis zum Begin des Investiturstreits', ZRG, KA, vol. 76, pp. 62–88.

Wolf, G. 1992. 'König Heinrichs I. Romzugsplan 935/36', ZKg, vol. 103, pp. 33–45.

Wolf, G. 1993. 'Der sogenannte "Gegenkönig" Arduin von Ivrea (c.955–1015)', AfD, vol. 39, pp. 19–34.

Wolf, G. 1994. 'Die Kanonisationsbulle von 993 für den Hl. Oudalrich von Augsburg und Vergleichbares', AfD, vol. 40, pp. 85–104.

Wolf, G. 1994a. 'Nochmals zur benedictio Ottonis in regem. 927 oder 929?' AfD, vol. 40, pp. 79–84.

Wright, F. A. (trans.) 1930. Liudprand of Cremona: The Embassy to Constantinople and other Writings. London.

Wright, F. A. (trans.) 1933. Select Letters of St Jerome, Loeb Classical Library. New York and London.

Zimmermann, H. 1968. Papstabsetzungen des Mittelalters, Graz, Vienna and Cologne.

Zoepfe, F. 1955. Das Bistum Augsburg und seine Bischöfe im Mittelalter, vol. 1. Augsburg.

Zotz, T. 1993. 'Carolingian Tradition and Ottonian-Salian Innovation: Comparative Observations on Palatine Policy in the Empire', in Duggan, A. 1993, pp. 69–100.

Zuchetti, G. (ed.) 1820. Il chronicon di Benedetto monaco di S. Andrea del Soratte e il libellus de imperatoria potestate in urbe Roma, Istituto Storico Italiano, Fonti per la storia italiano, vol. 55. Rome.

INDEX